idle days

idle days

THOMAS DESAULNIERS-BROUSSEAU

ART BY
SIMON LECLERC

:01
First Second
NEW YORK

À MES GRANDS-PÈRES.

—T.D.-B.

À MES PARENTS.

—S.L.

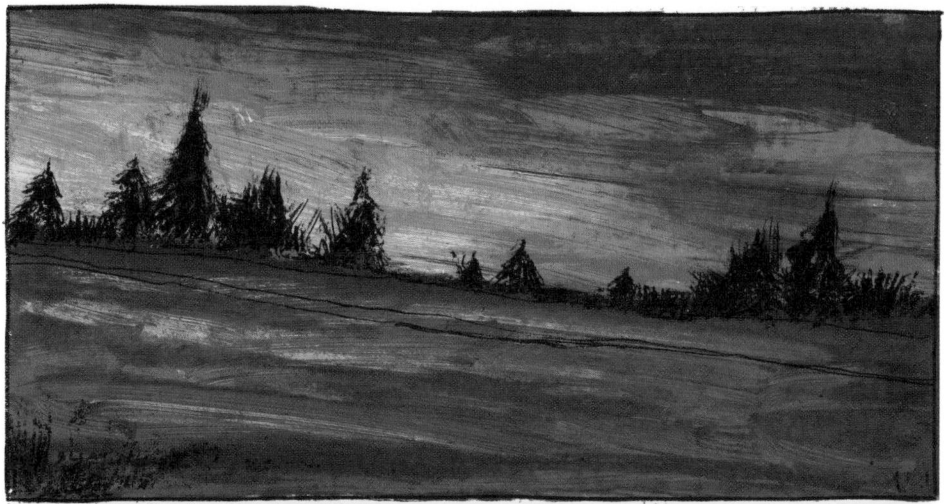

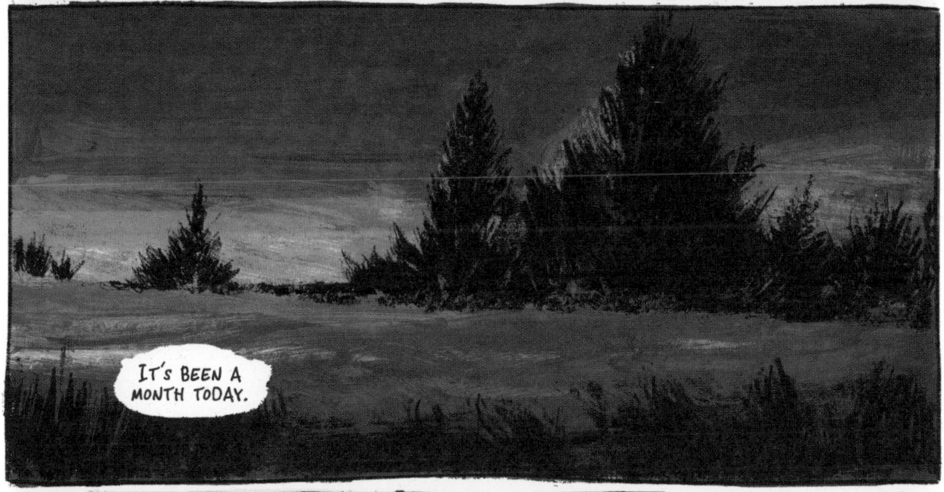
It's been a month today.

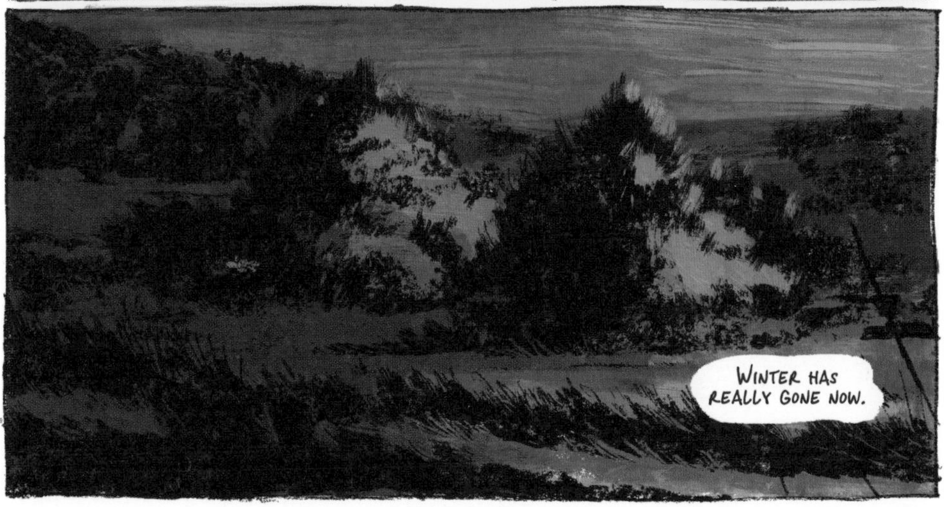
Winter has really gone now.

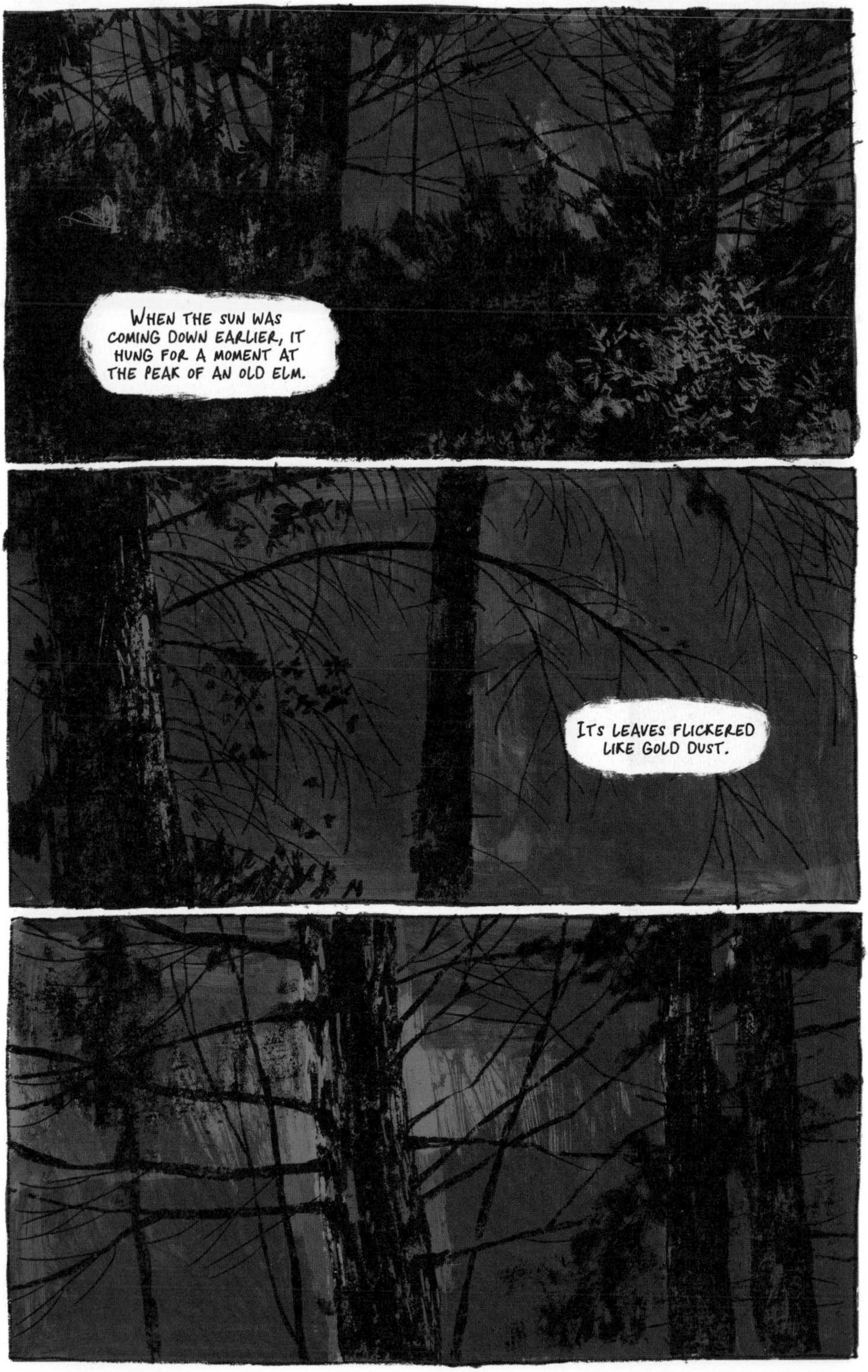
WHEN THE SUN WAS COMING DOWN EARLIER, IT HUNG FOR A MOMENT AT THE PEAK OF AN OLD ELM.
ITS LEAVES FLICKERED LIKE GOLD DUST.

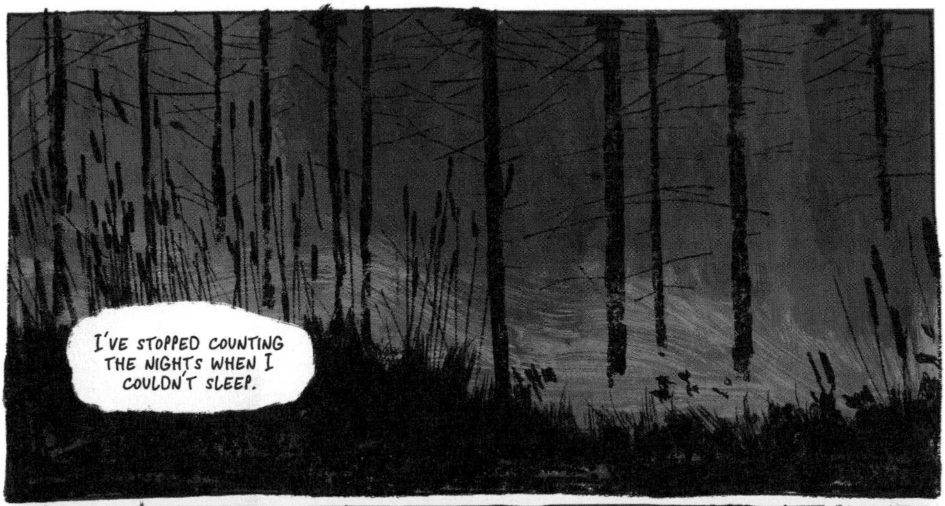
I'VE STOPPED COUNTING THE NIGHTS WHEN I COULDN'T SLEEP.

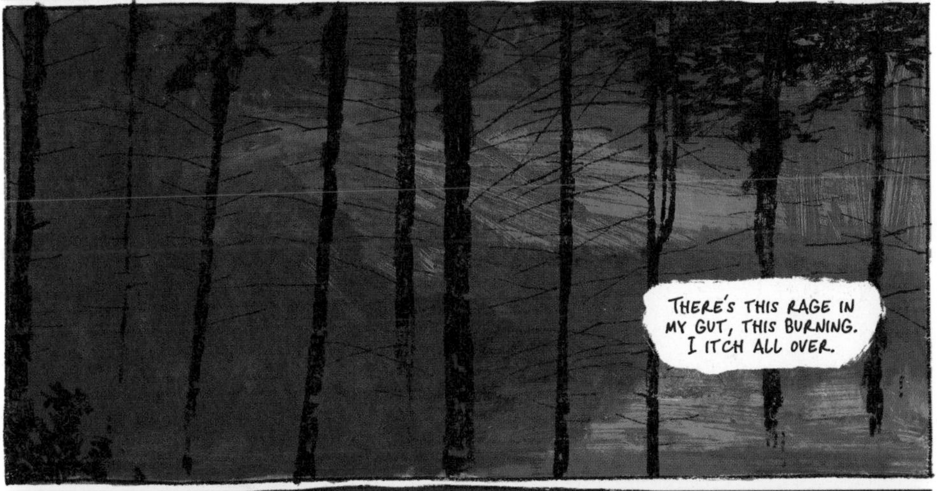
THERE'S THIS RAGE IN MY GUT, THIS BURNING. I ITCH ALL OVER.

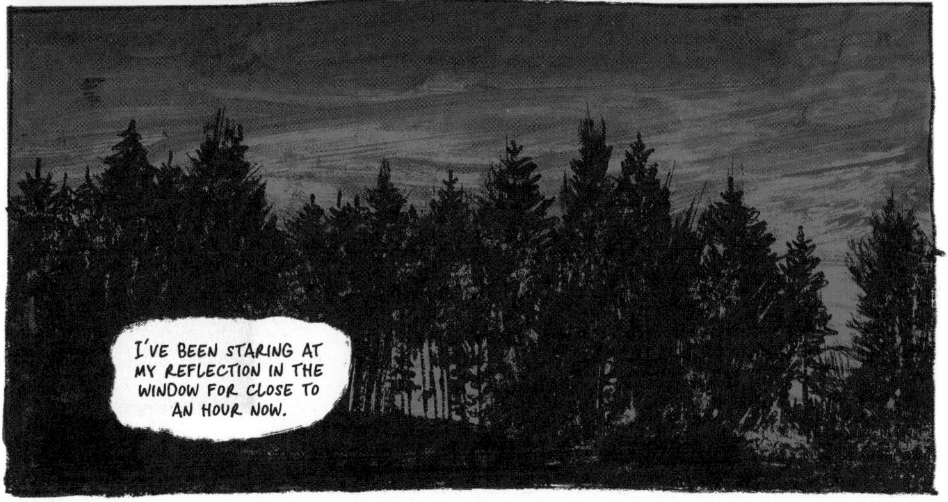
I'VE BEEN STARING AT MY REFLECTION IN THE WINDOW FOR CLOSE TO AN HOUR NOW.

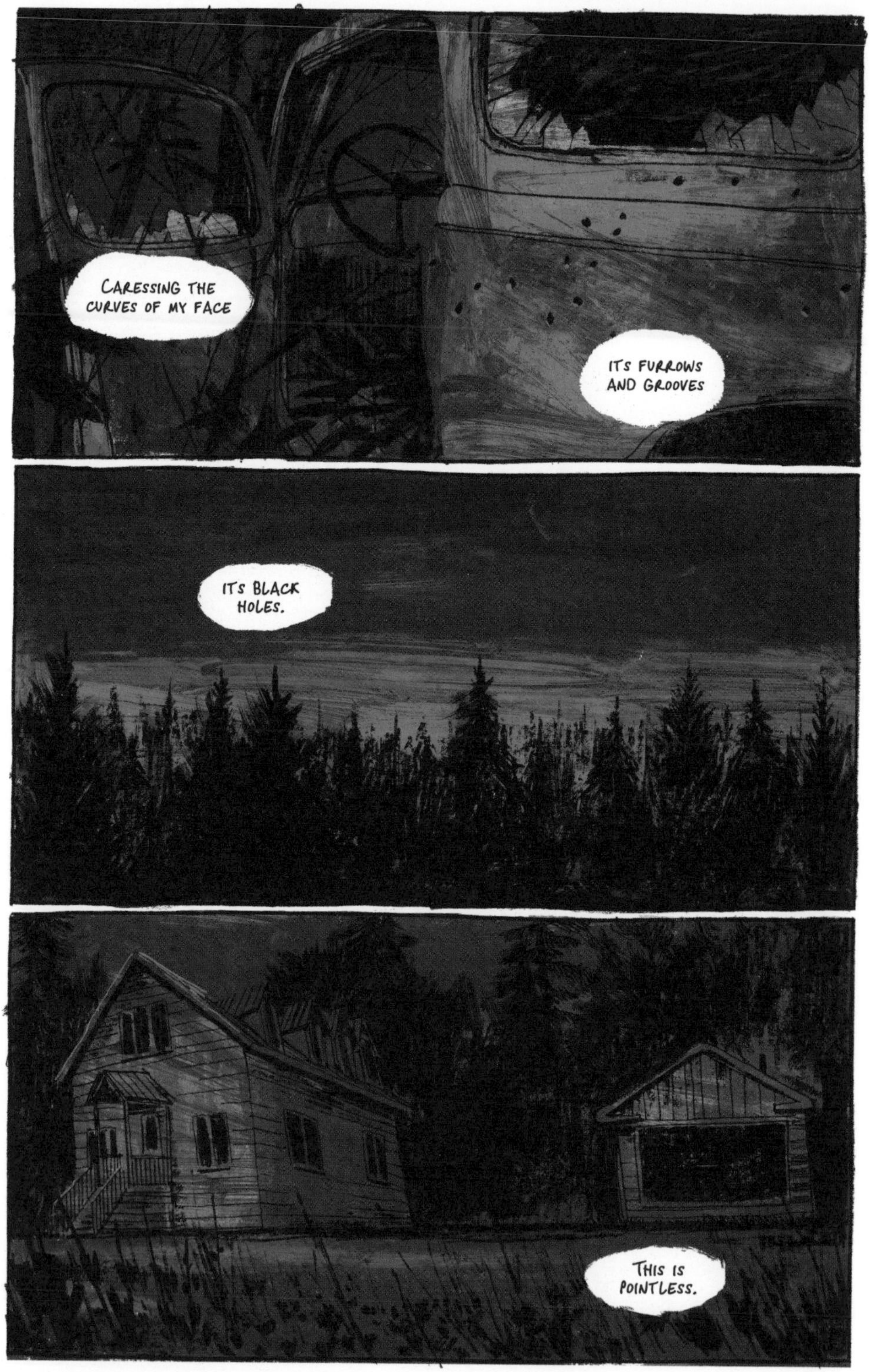
CARESSING THE CURVES OF MY FACE
ITS FURROWS AND GROOVES
ITS BLACK HOLES.
THIS IS POINTLESS.

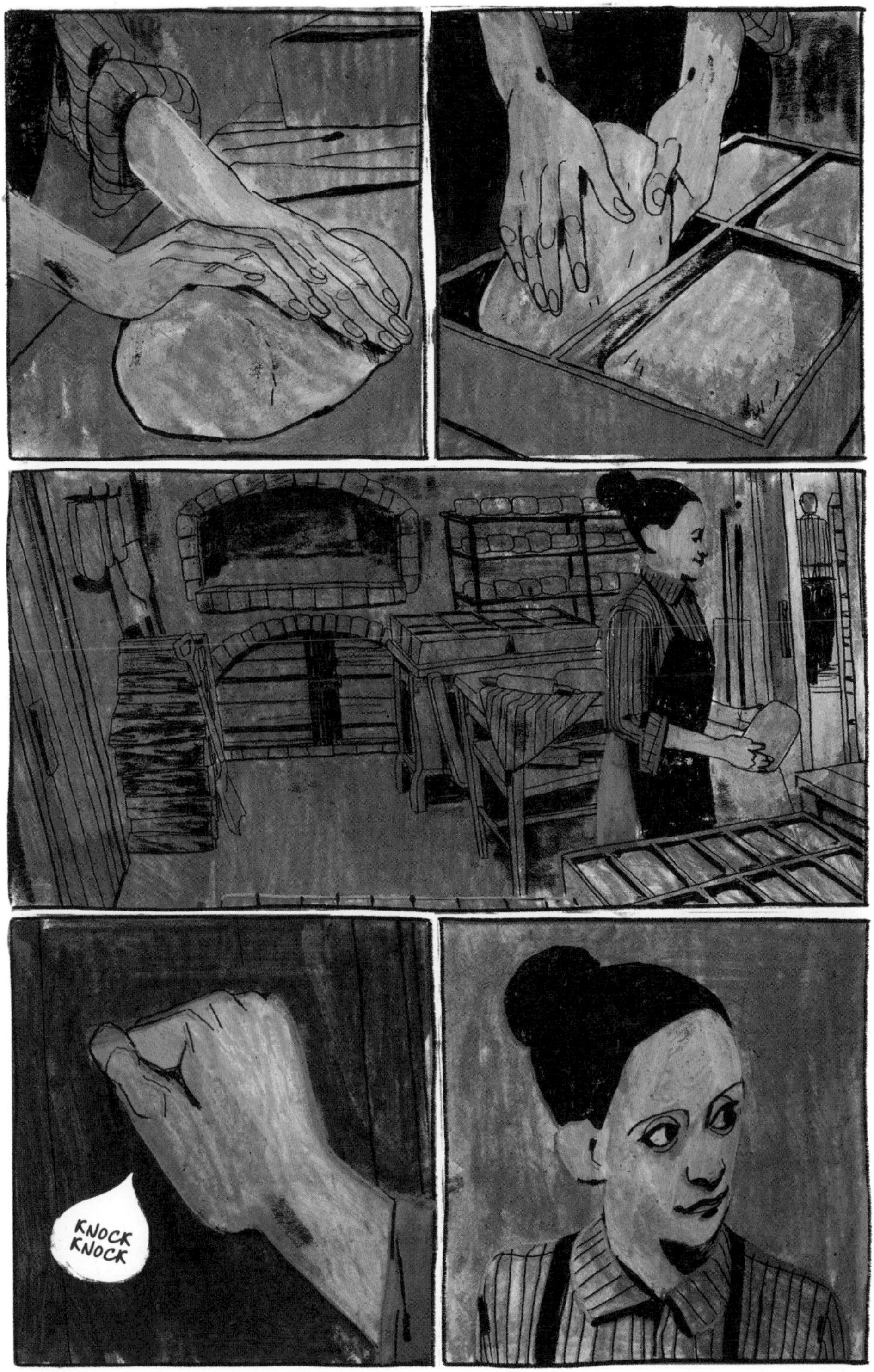
KNOCK
KNOCK

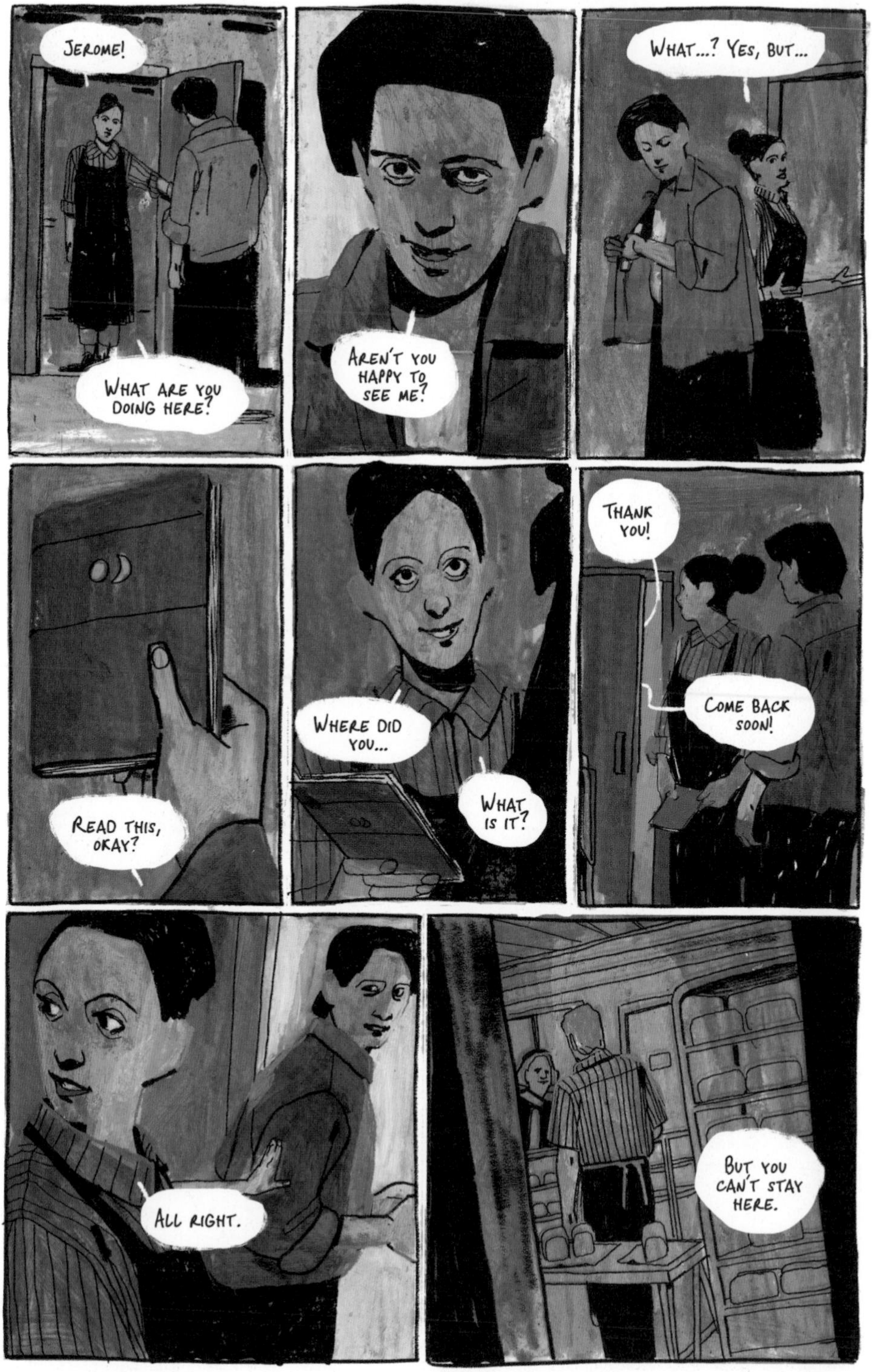

Jerome!
What are you doing here?
Aren't you happy to see me?
What...? Yes, but...
Read this, okay?
Where did you...
What is it?
Thank you!
Come back soon!
All right.
But you can't stay here.

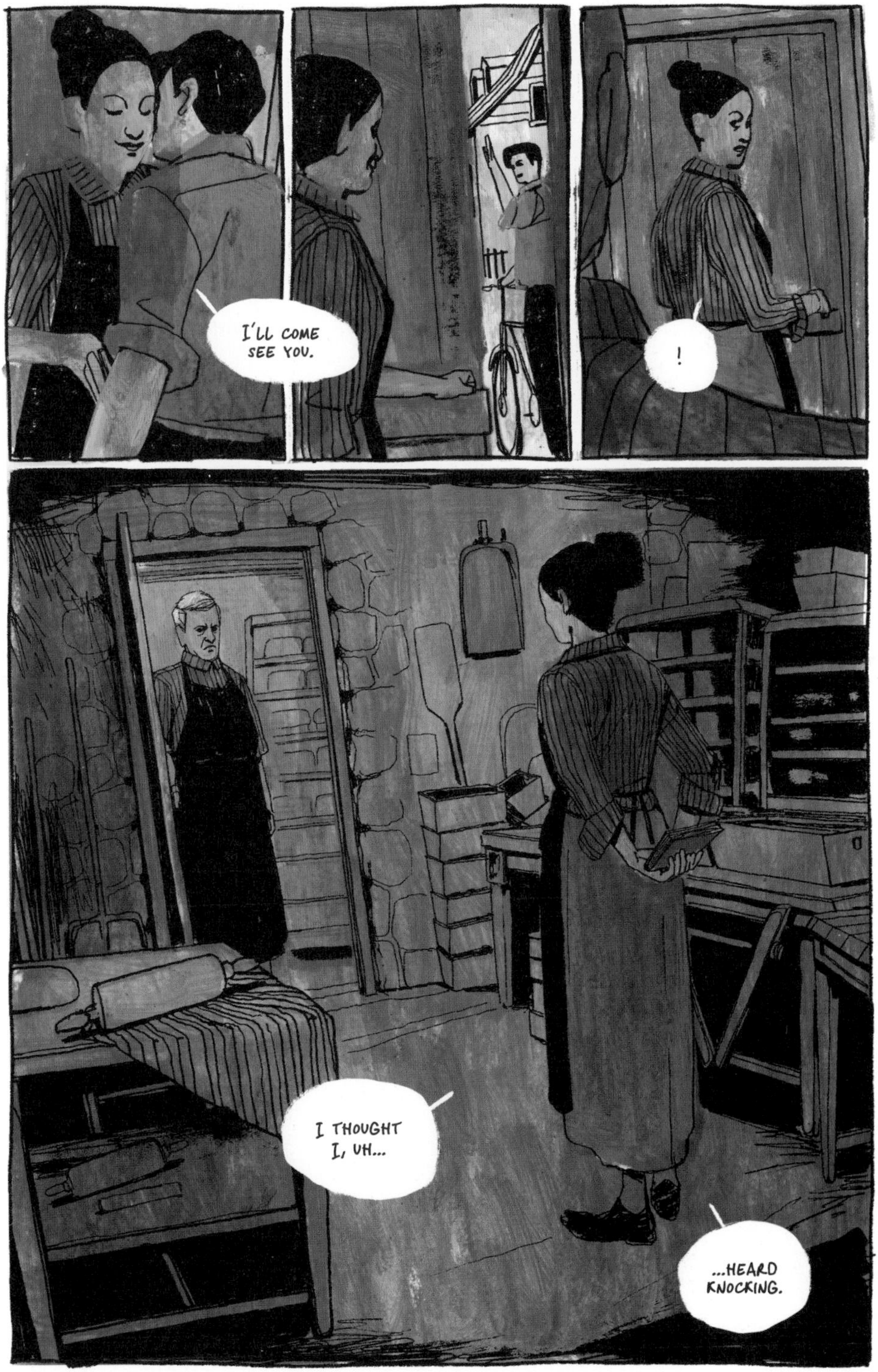
I'LL COME SEE YOU.
!
I THOUGHT I, UH...
...HEARD KNOCKING.

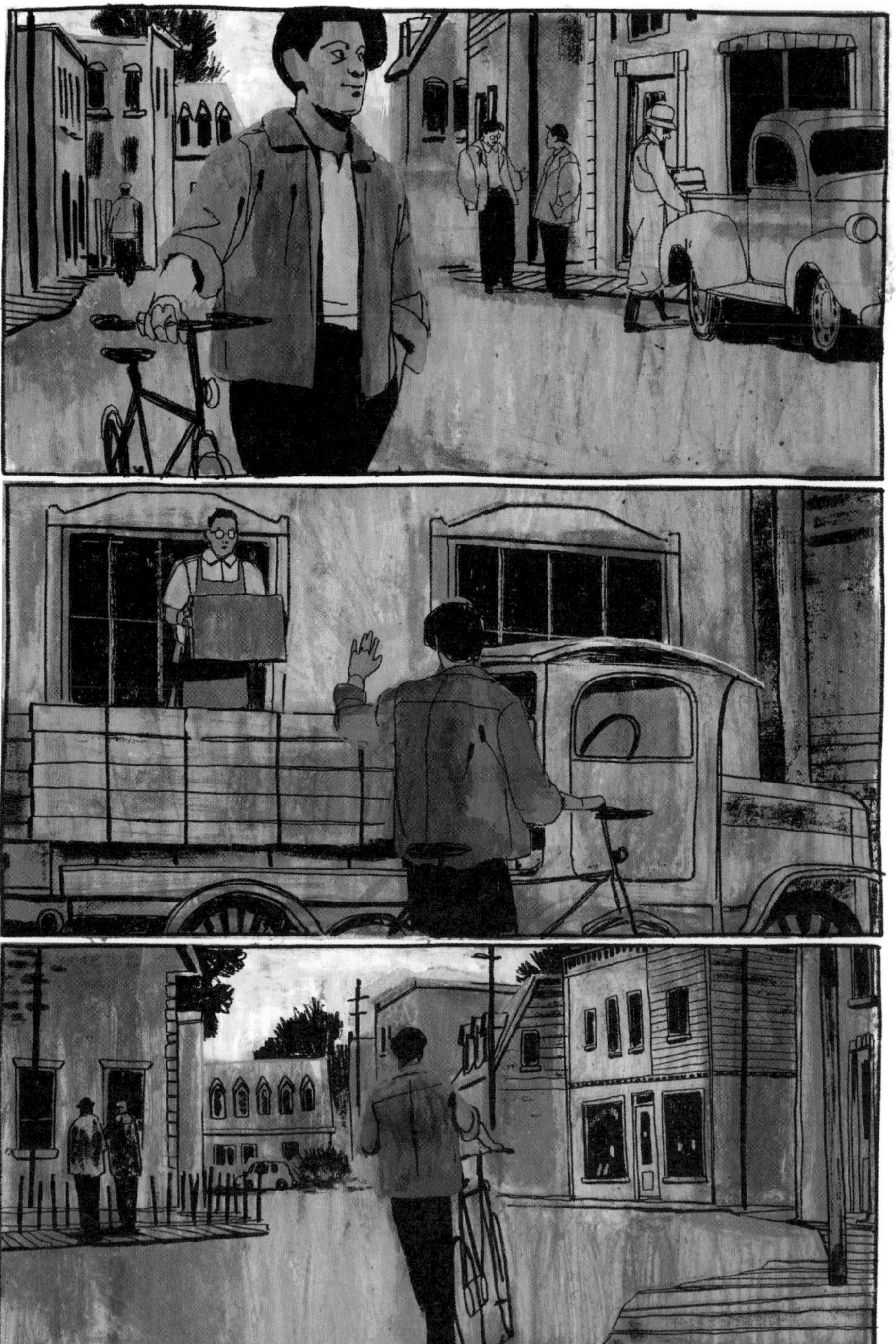

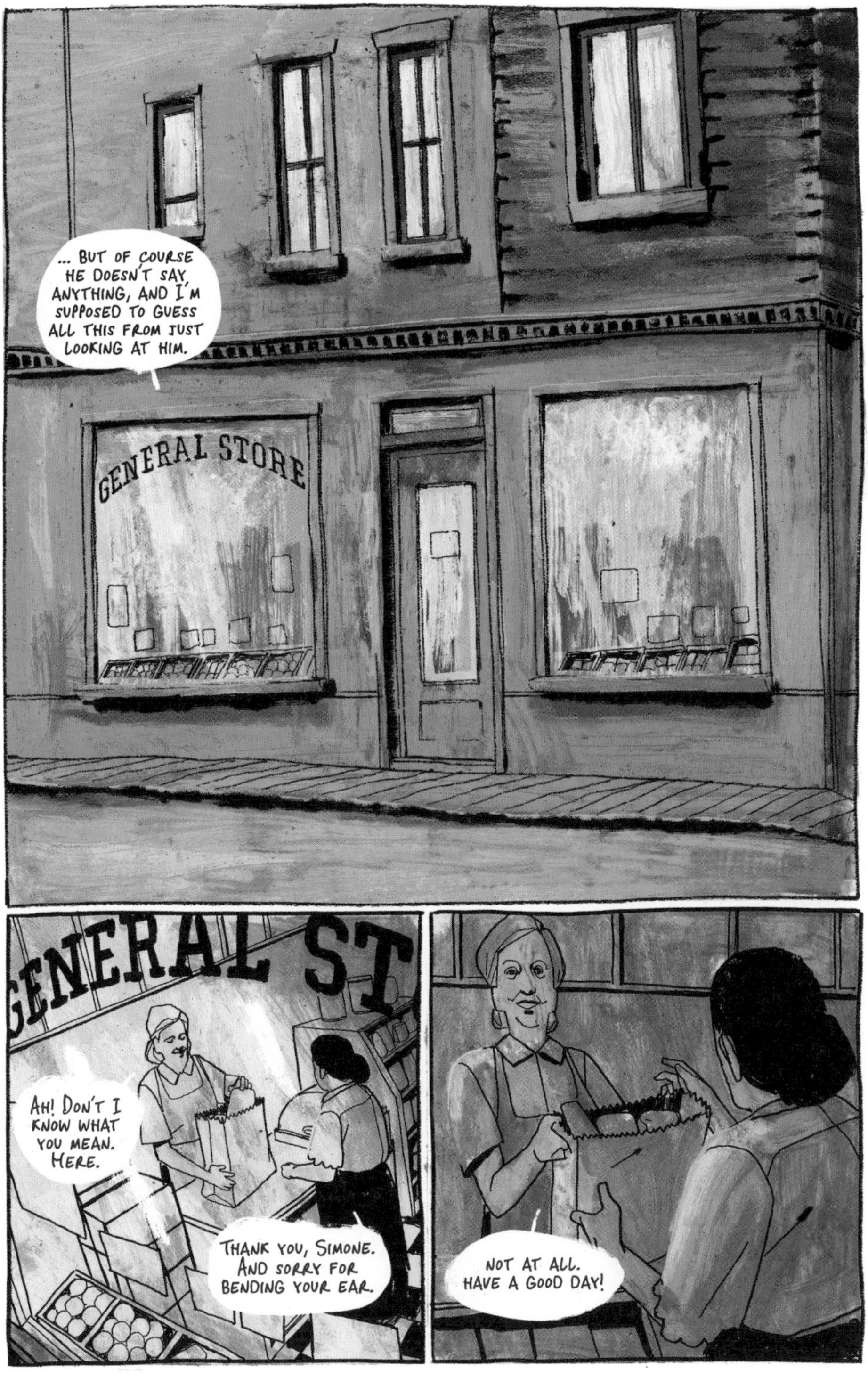
GENERAL STORE
... BUT OF COURSE HE DOESN'T SAY ANYTHING, AND I'M SUPPOSED TO GUESS ALL THIS FROM JUST LOOKING AT HIM.
GENERAL ST
AH! DON'T I KNOW WHAT YOU MEAN. HERE.
THANK YOU, SIMONE. AND SORRY FOR BENDING YOUR EAR.
NOT AT ALL. HAVE A GOOD DAY!

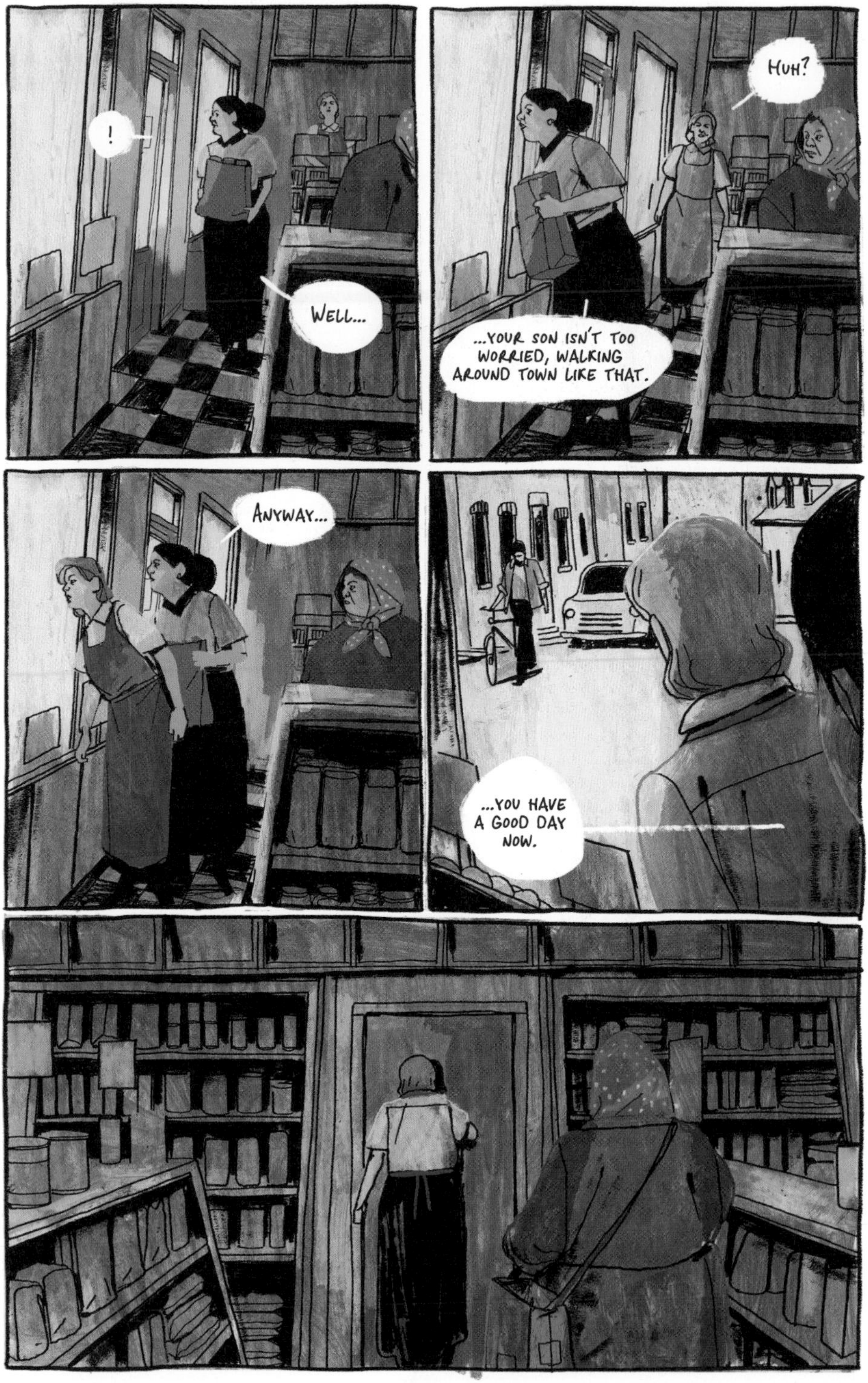
!
Well...
Huh?
...your son isn't too worried, walking around town like that.
Anyway...
...you have a good day now.

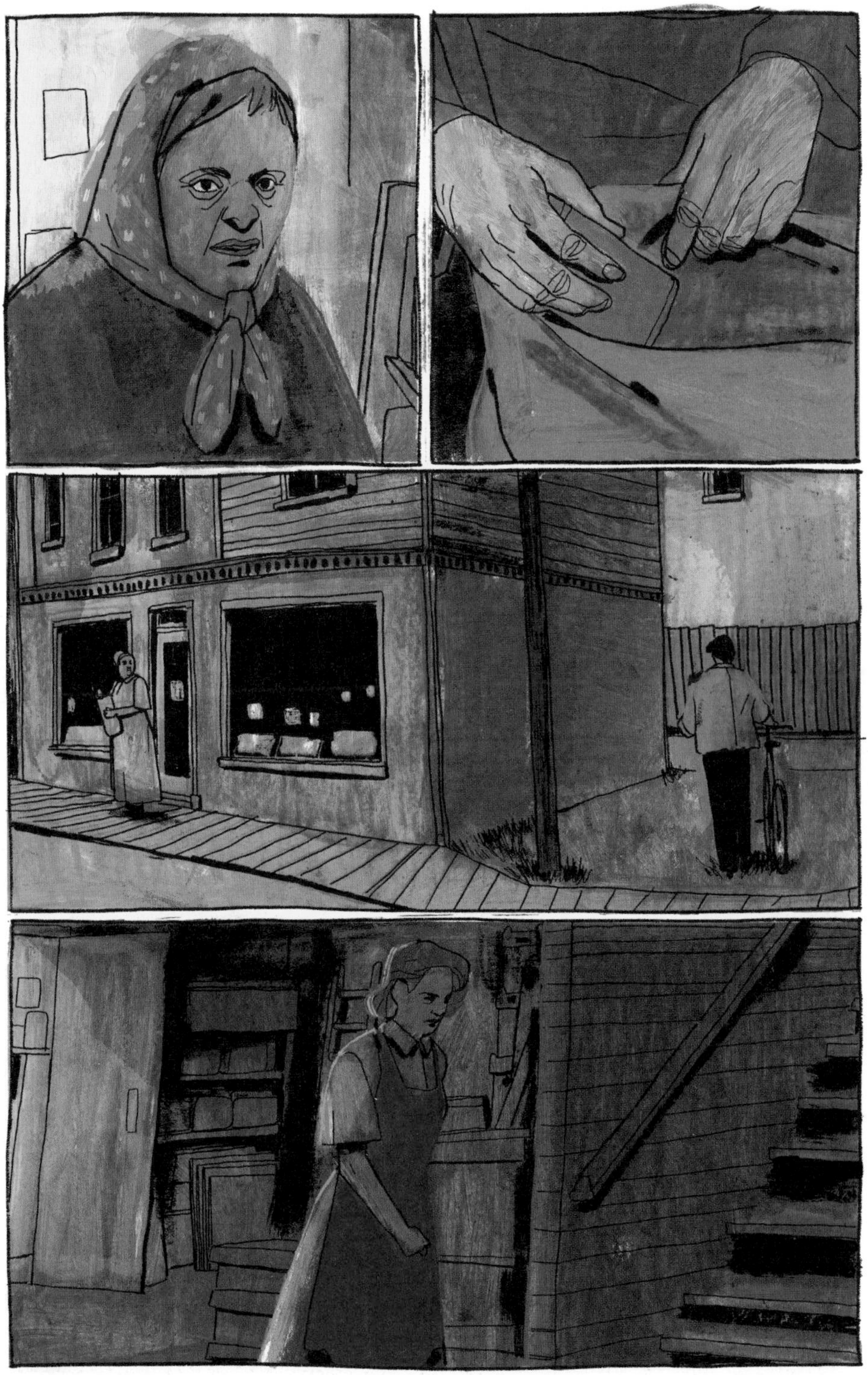

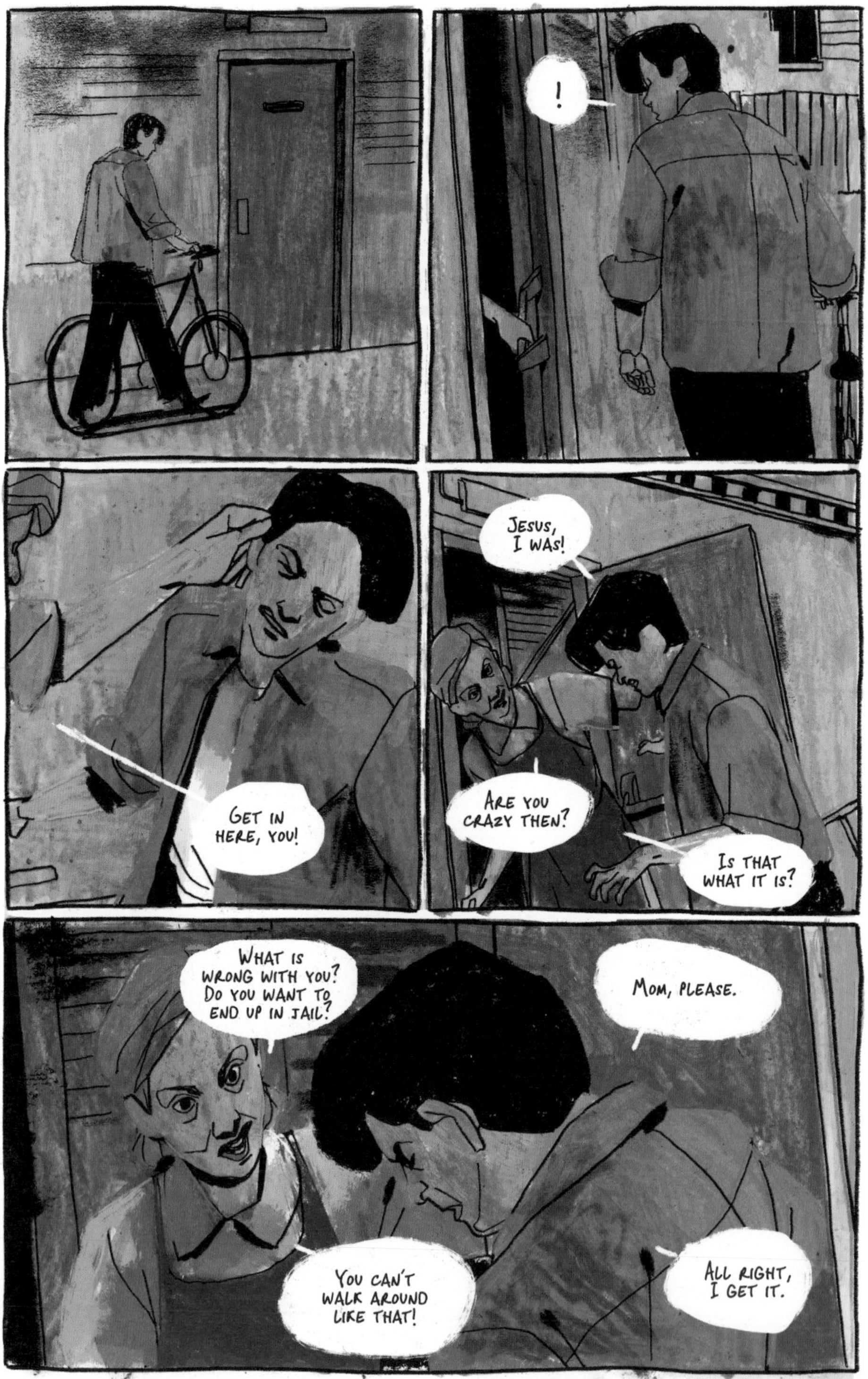
!
Get in here, you!
Jesus, I was!
Are you crazy then?
Is that what it is?
What is wrong with you? Do you want to end up in jail?
Mom, please.
You can't walk around like that!
All right, I get it.

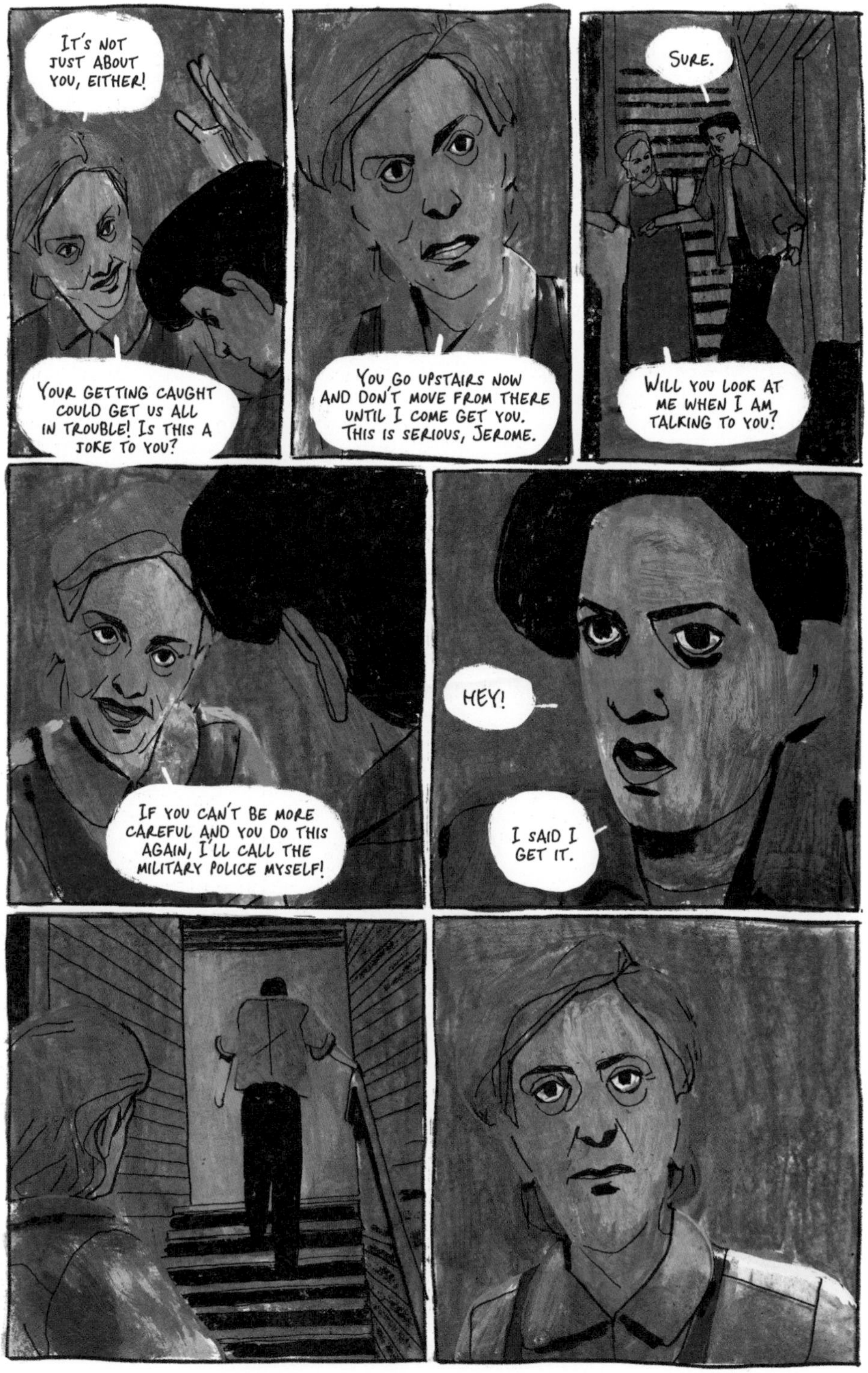
It's not just about you, either!
Your getting caught could get us all in trouble! Is this a joke to you?
You go upstairs now and don't move from there until I come get you. This is serious, Jerome.
Sure.
Will you look at me when I am talking to you?
If you can't be more careful and you do this again, I'll call the military police myself!
Hey!
I said I get it.

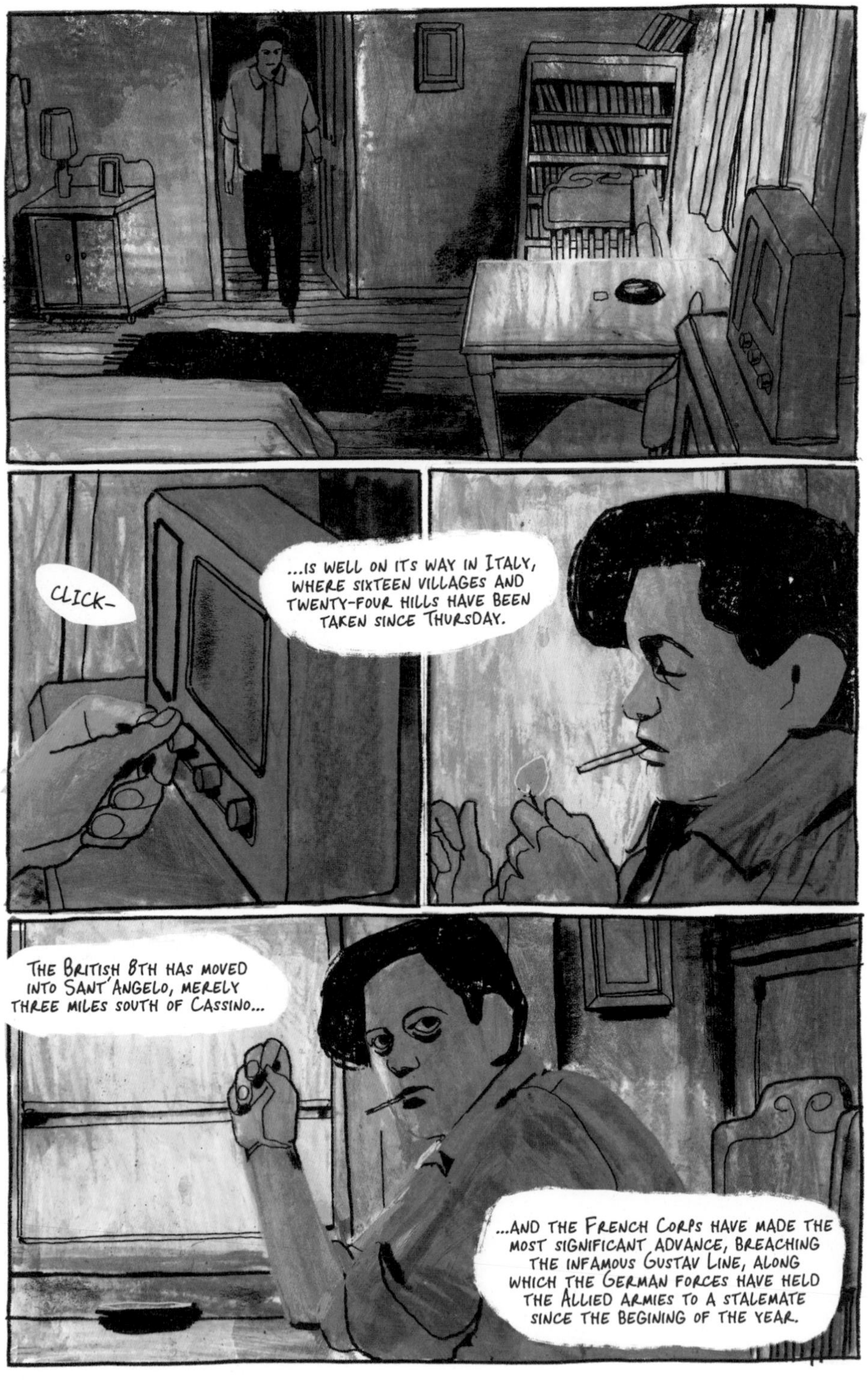
CLICK-
...IS WELL ON ITS WAY IN ITALY, WHERE SIXTEEN VILLAGES AND TWENTY-FOUR HILLS HAVE BEEN TAKEN SINCE THURSDAY.
THE BRITISH 8TH HAS MOVED INTO SANT'ANGELO, MERELY THREE MILES SOUTH OF CASSINO...
...AND THE FRENCH CORPS HAVE MADE THE MOST SIGNIFICANT ADVANCE, BREACHING THE INFAMOUS GUSTAV LINE, ALONG WHICH THE GERMAN FORCES HAVE HELD THE ALLIED ARMIES TO A STALEMATE SINCE THE BEGINING OF THE YEAR.

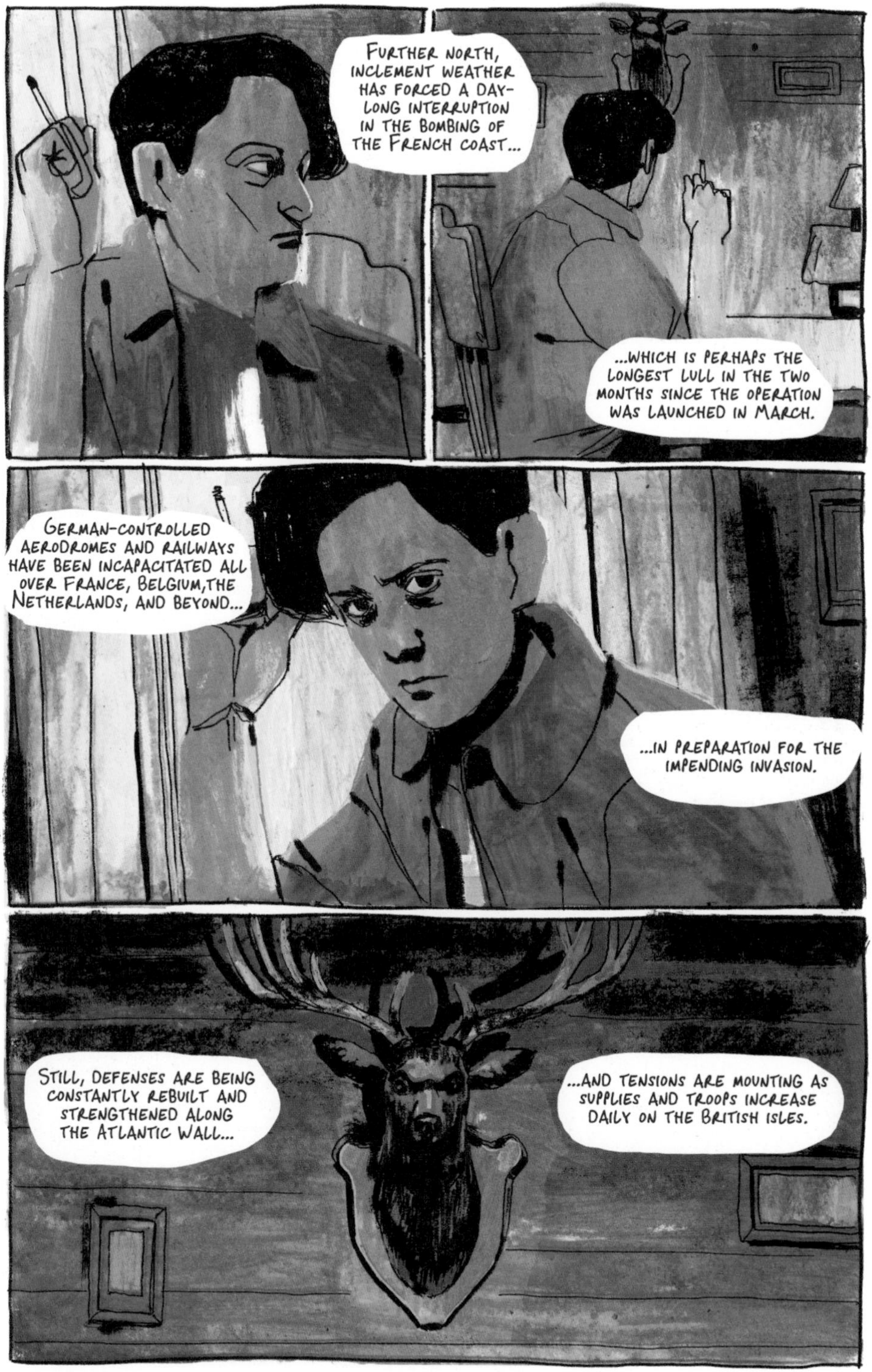

Further north, inclement weather has forced a day-long interruption in the bombing of the French coast...
...which is perhaps the longest lull in the two months since the operation was launched in March.
German-controlled aerodromes and railways have been incapacitated all over France, Belgium, the Netherlands, and beyond...
...in preparation for the impending invasion.
Still, defenses are being constantly rebuilt and strengthened along the Atlantic Wall...
...and tensions are mounting as supplies and troops increase daily on the British Isles.

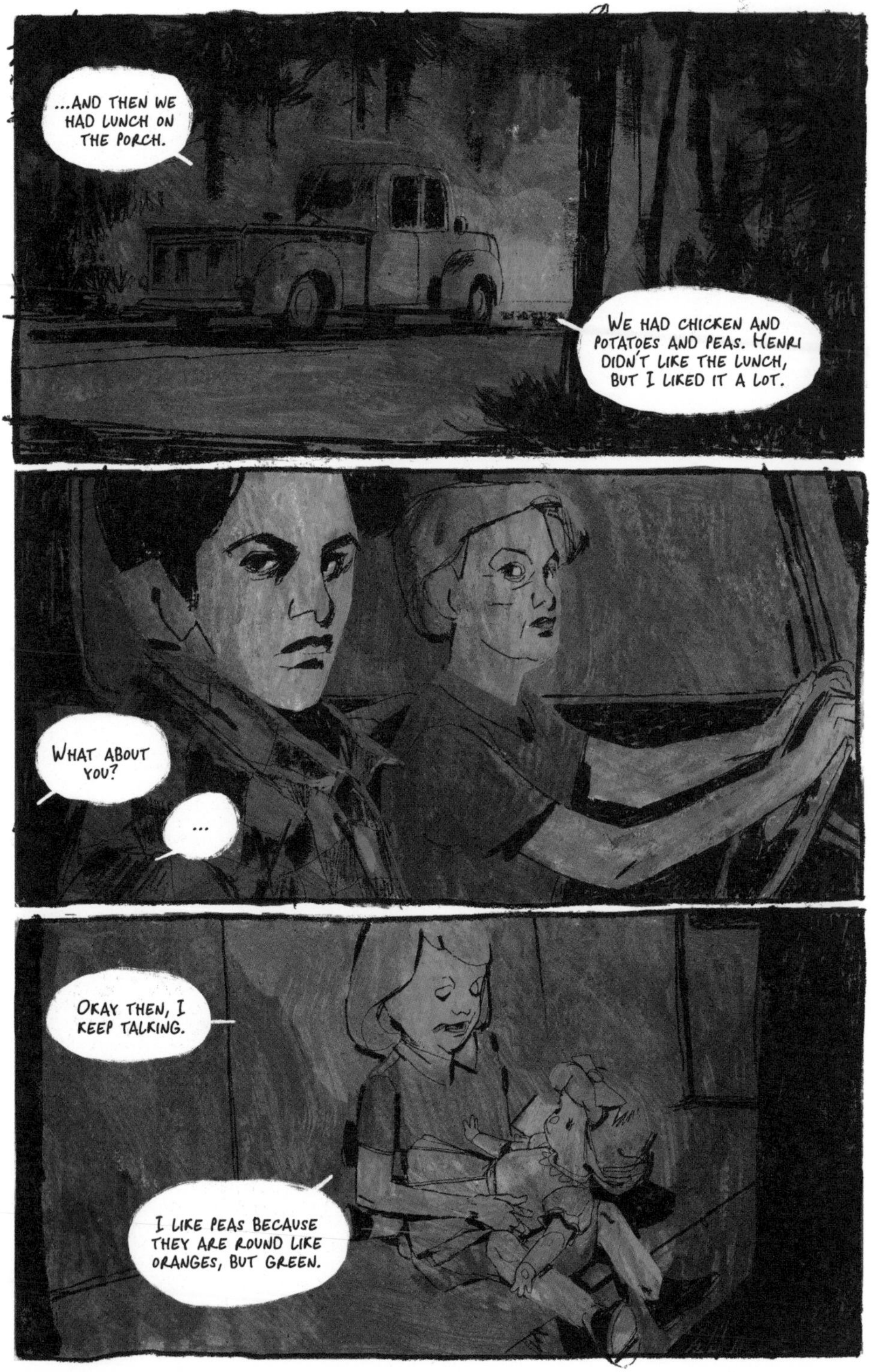
...AND THEN WE HAD LUNCH ON THE PORCH.
WE HAD CHICKEN AND POTATOES AND PEAS. HENRI DIDN'T LIKE THE LUNCH, BUT I LIKED IT A LOT.
WHAT ABOUT YOU?
...
OKAY THEN, I KEEP TALKING.
I LIKE PEAS BECAUSE THEY ARE ROUND LIKE ORANGES, BUT GREEN.

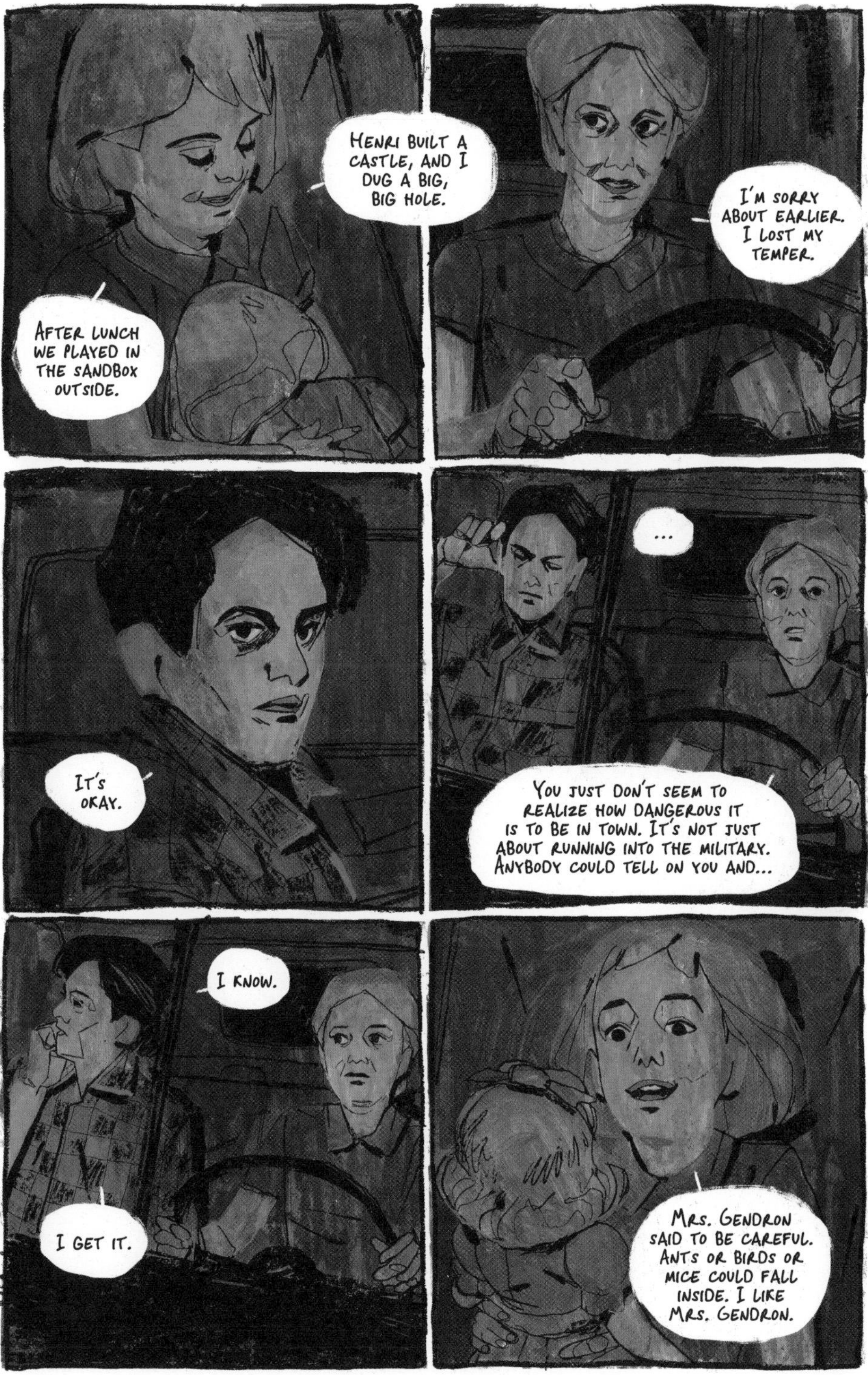
Henri built a castle, and I dug a big, big hole.
After lunch we played in the sandbox outside.
I'm sorry about earlier. I lost my temper.
It's okay.
...
You just don't seem to realize how dangerous it is to be in town. It's not just about running into the military. Anybody could tell on you and...
I know.
I get it.
Mrs. Gendron said to be careful. Ants or birds or mice could fall inside. I like Mrs. Gendron.

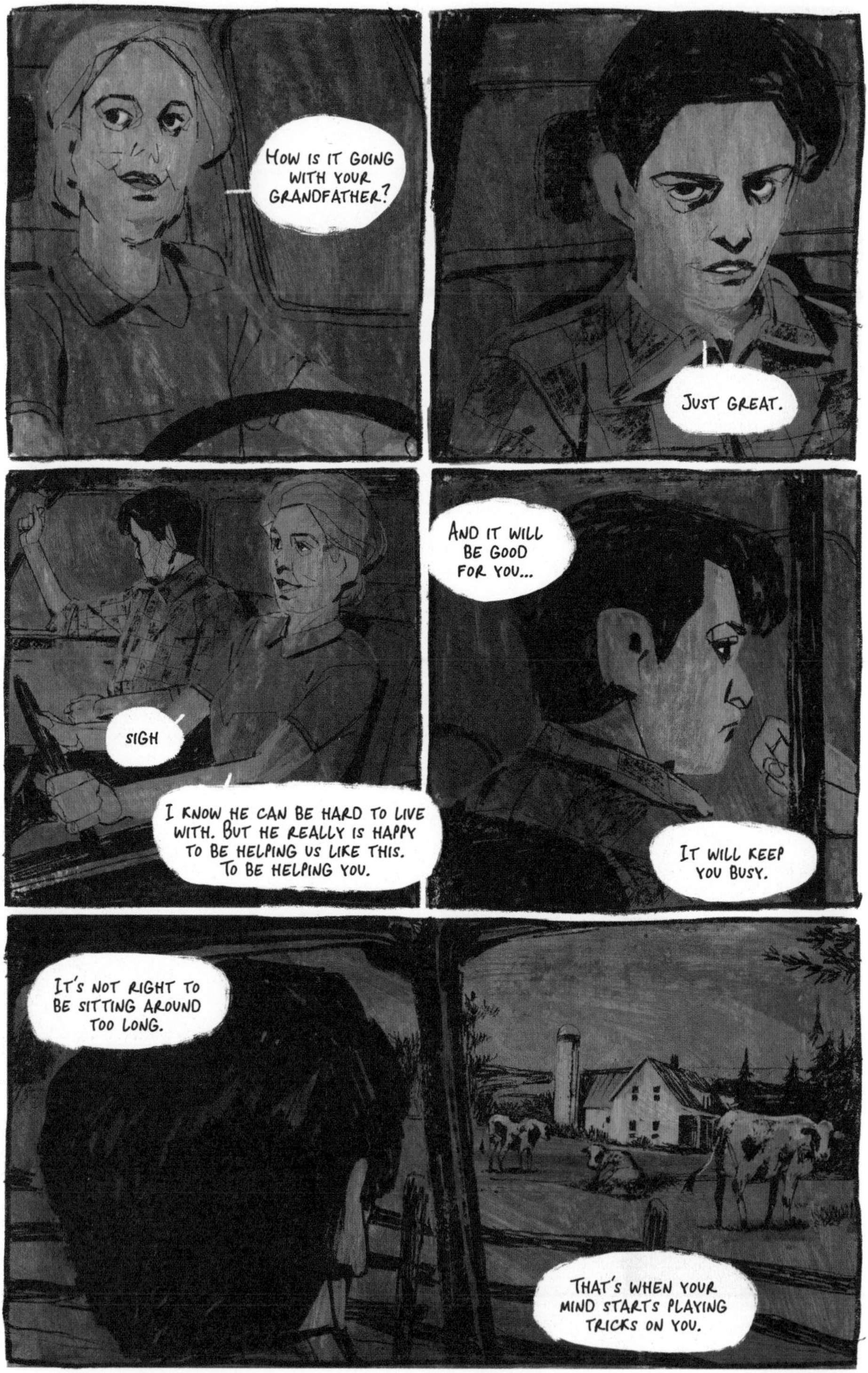
How is it going with your grandfather?
Just great.
Sigh
I know he can be hard to live with. But he really is happy to be helping us like this. To be helping you.
And it will be good for you...
It will keep you busy.
It's not right to be sitting around too long.
That's when your mind starts playing tricks on you.

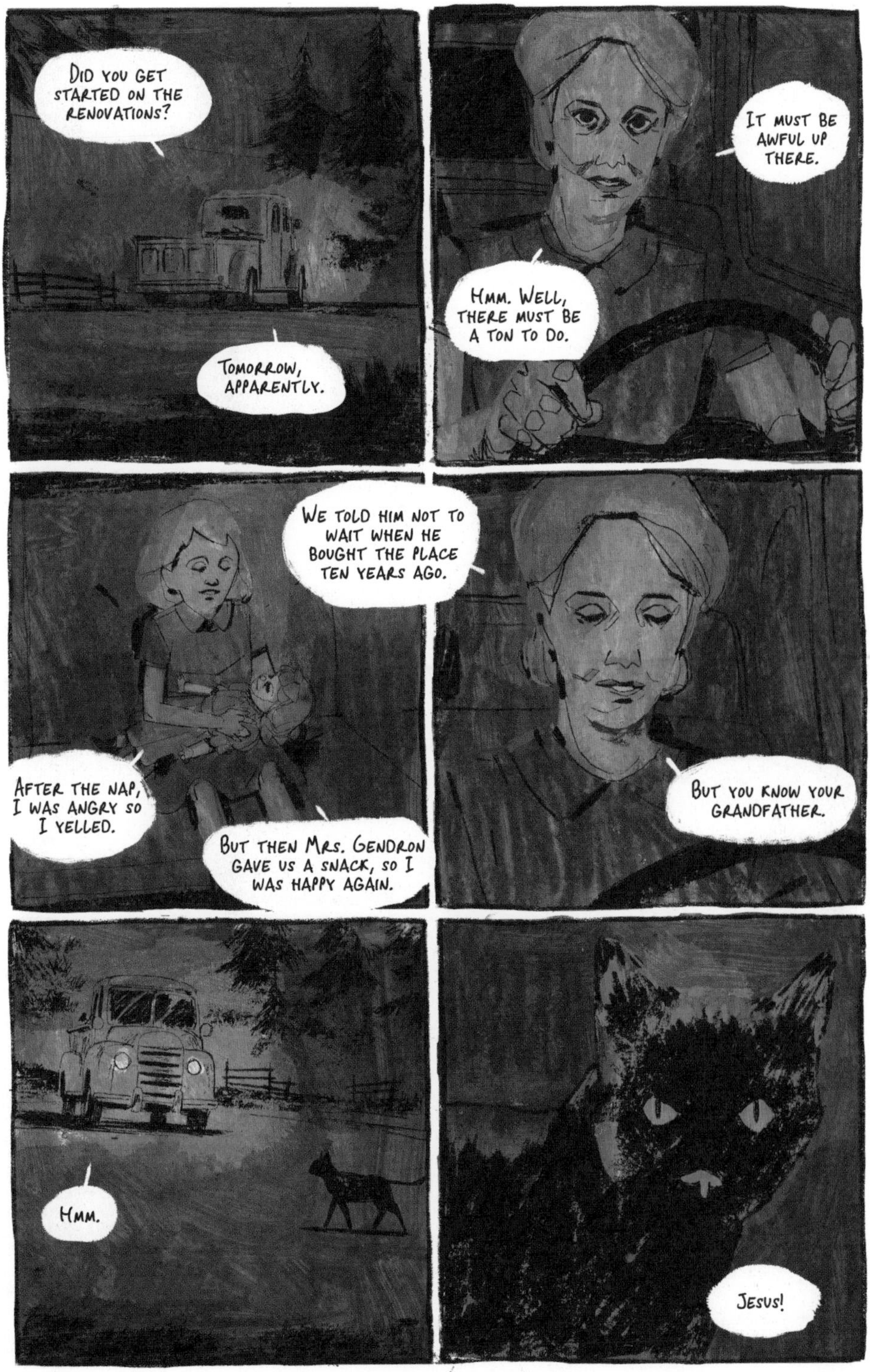
Did you get started on the renovations?
Tomorrow, apparently.
It must be awful up there.
Hmm. Well, there must be a ton to do.
We told him not to wait when he bought the place ten years ago.
After the nap, I was angry so I yelled.
But then Mrs. Gendron gave us a snack, so I was happy again.
But you know your grandfather.
Hmm.
Jesus!

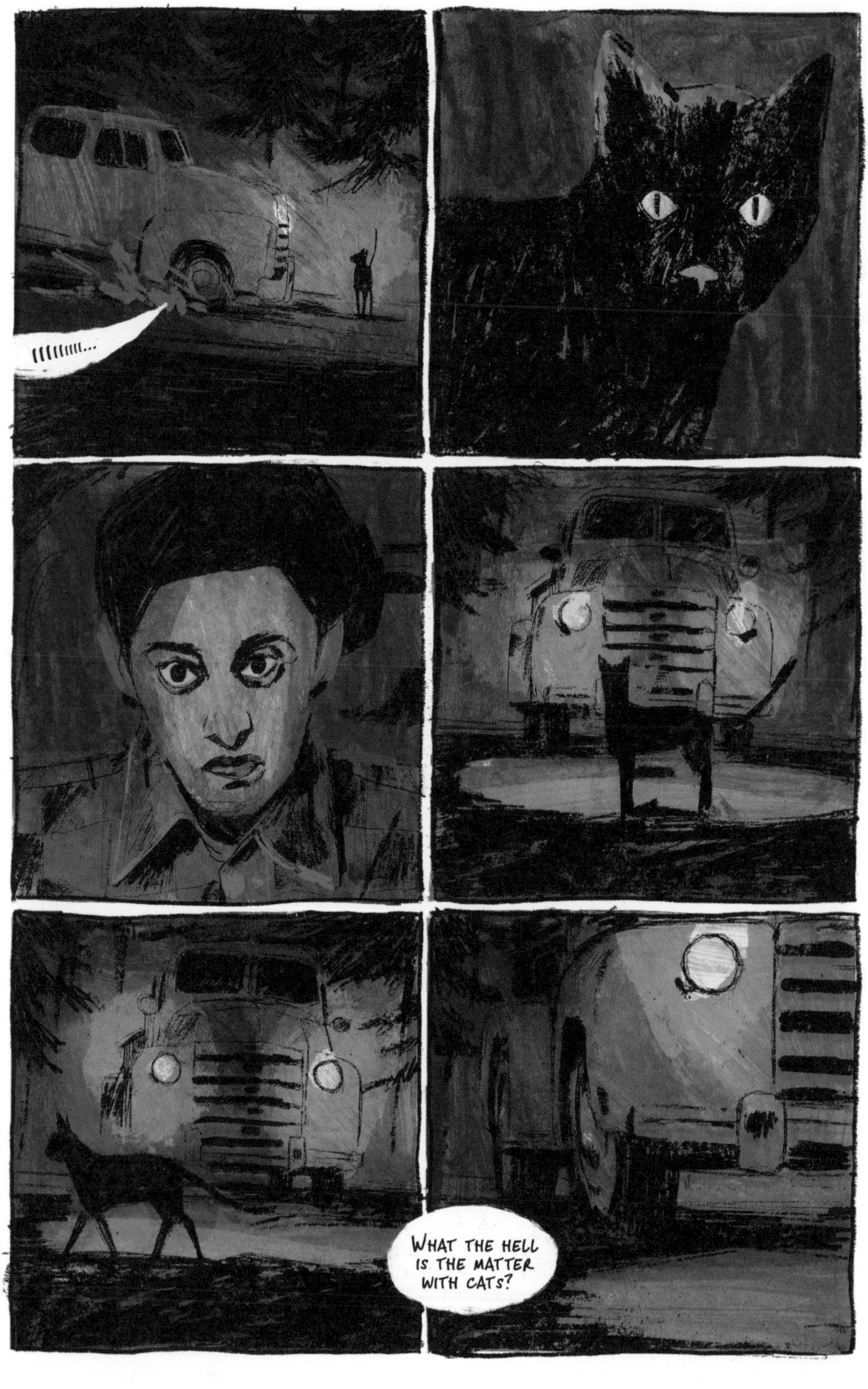

Mmmm...
WHAT THE HELL IS THE MATTER WITH CATS?

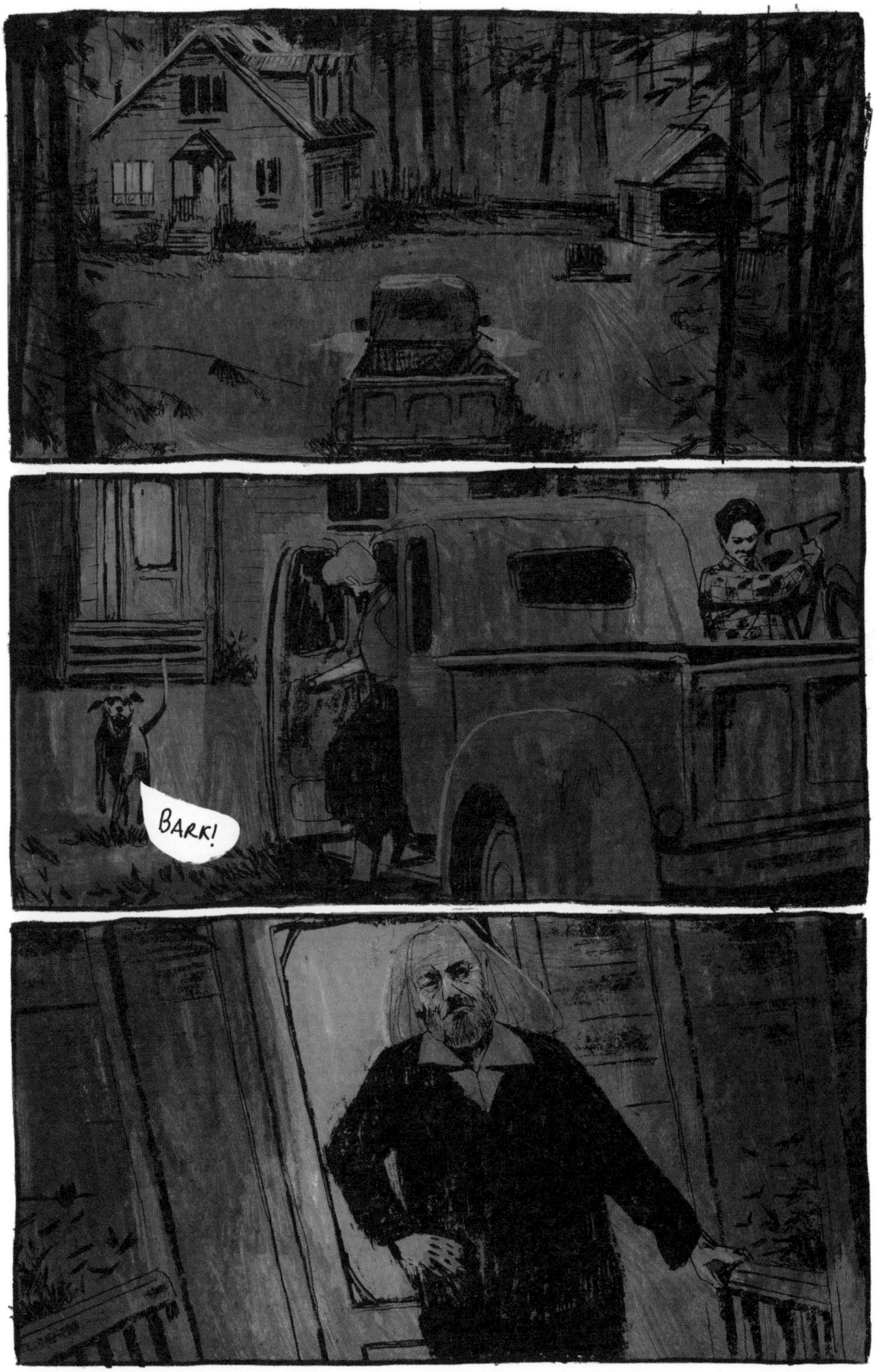
BARK!

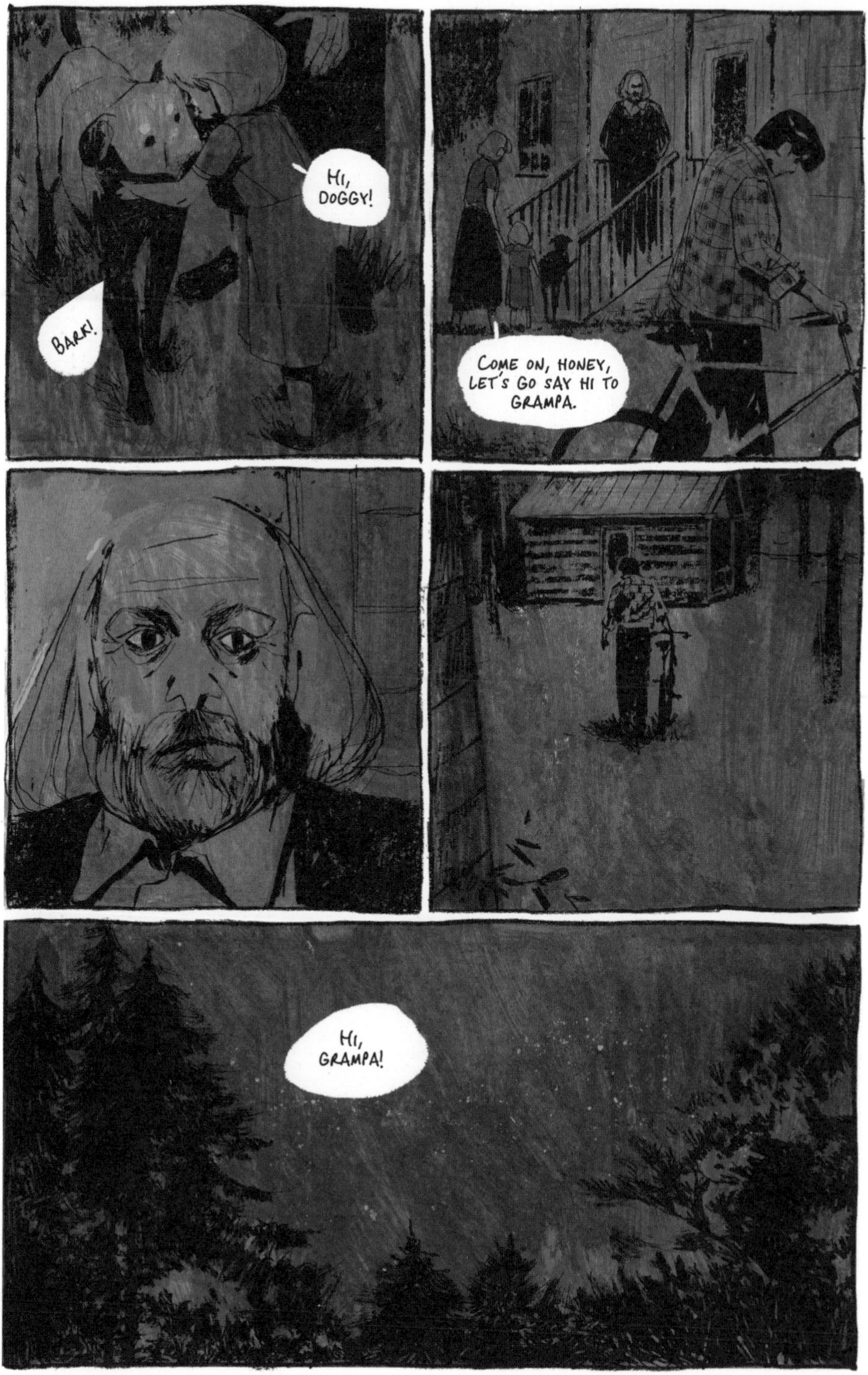
Hi, doggy!
Bark!
Come on, honey, let's go say hi to Grampa.
Hi, Grampa!

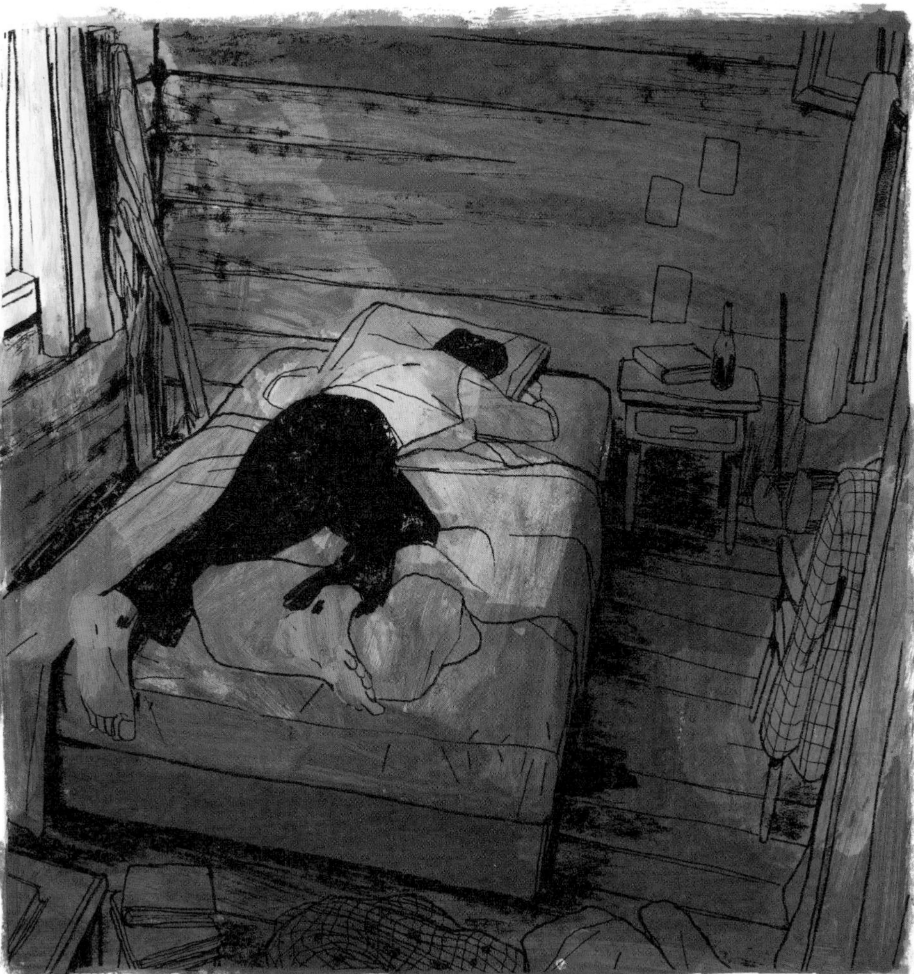

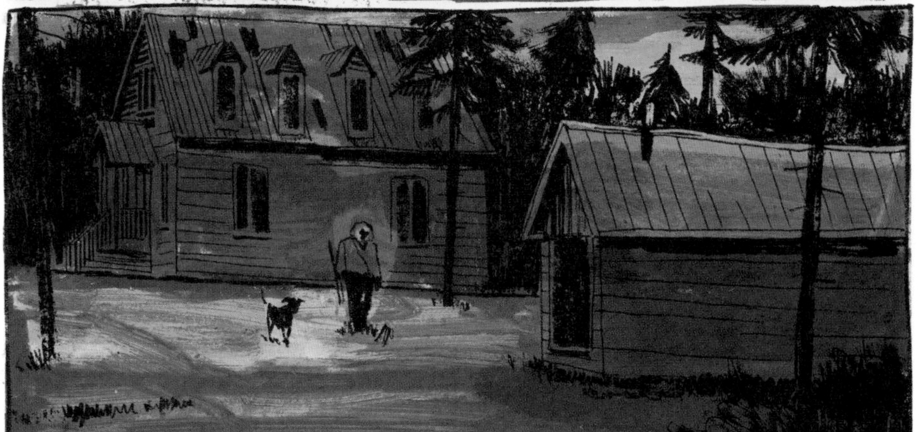

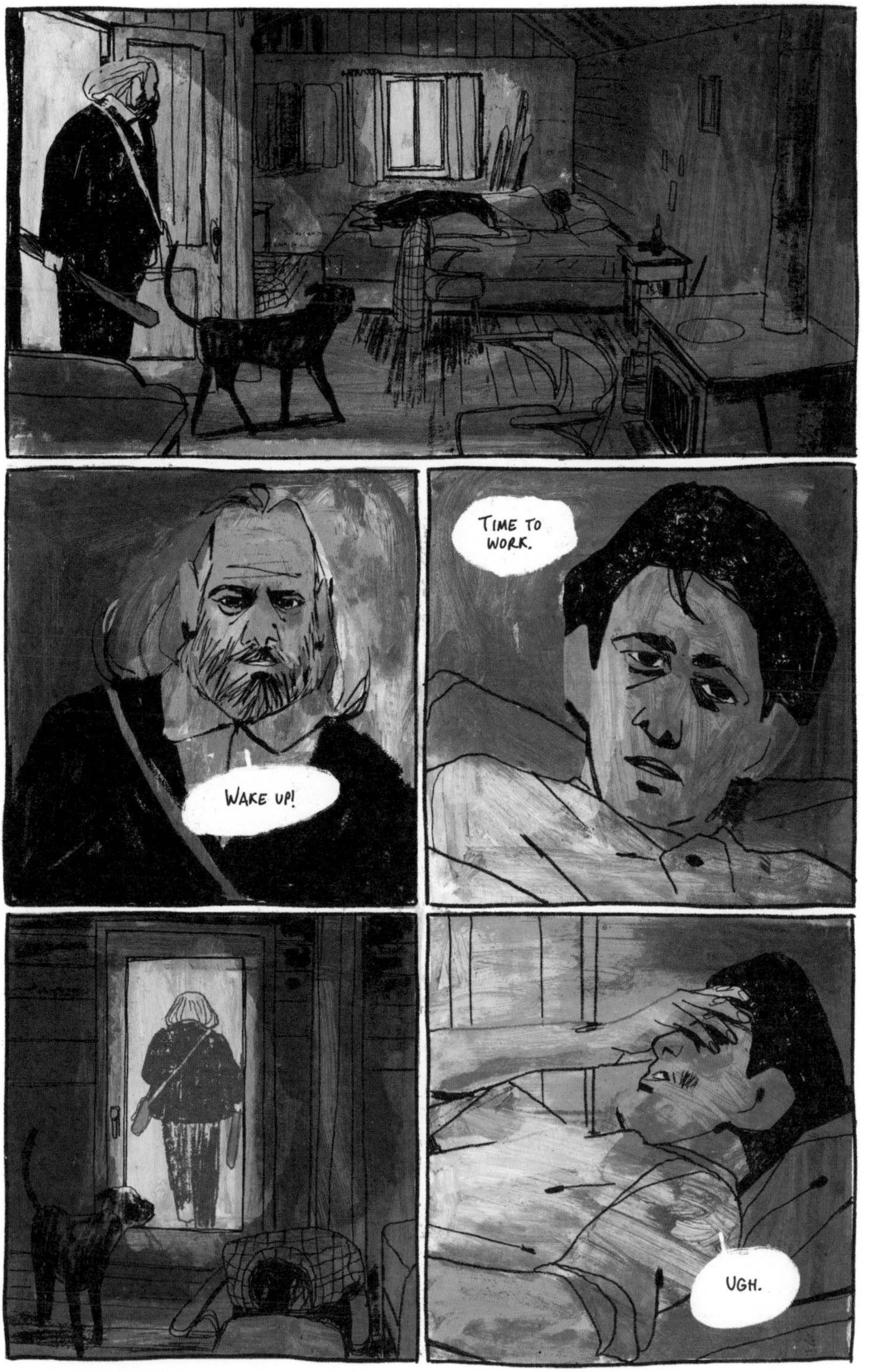
WAKE UP!
TIME TO WORK.
UGH.

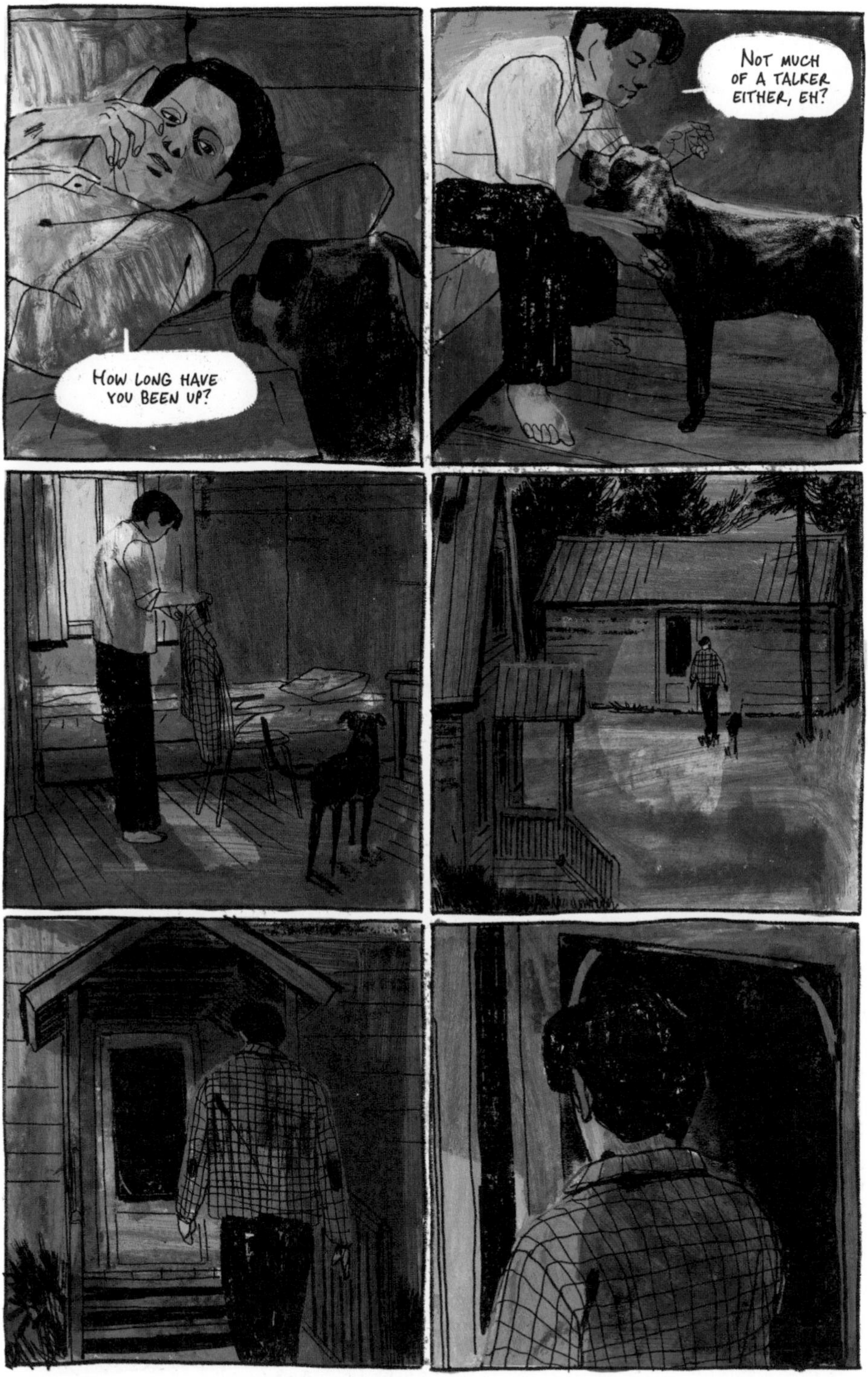
How long have you been up?
Not much of a talker either, eh?

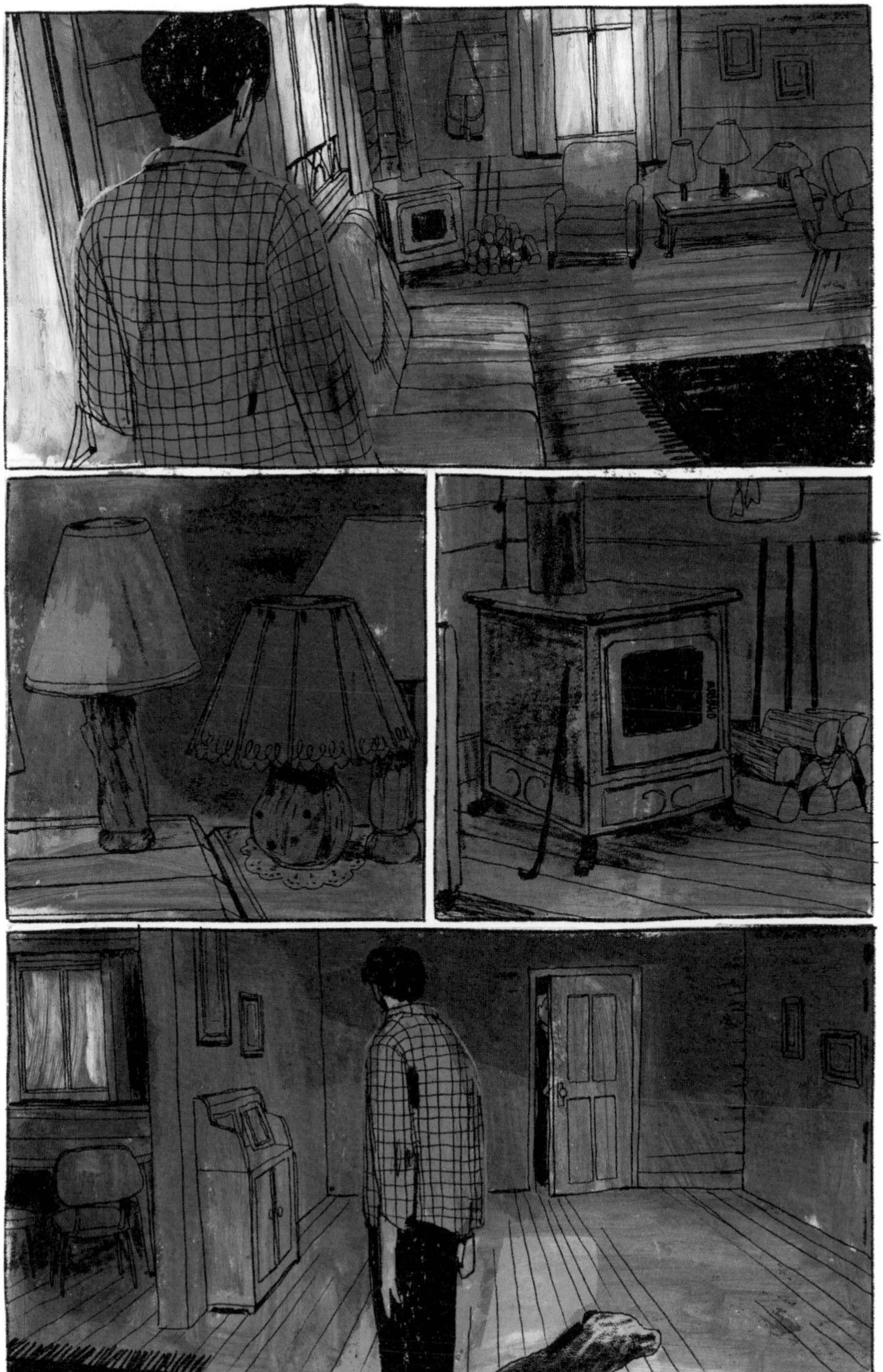

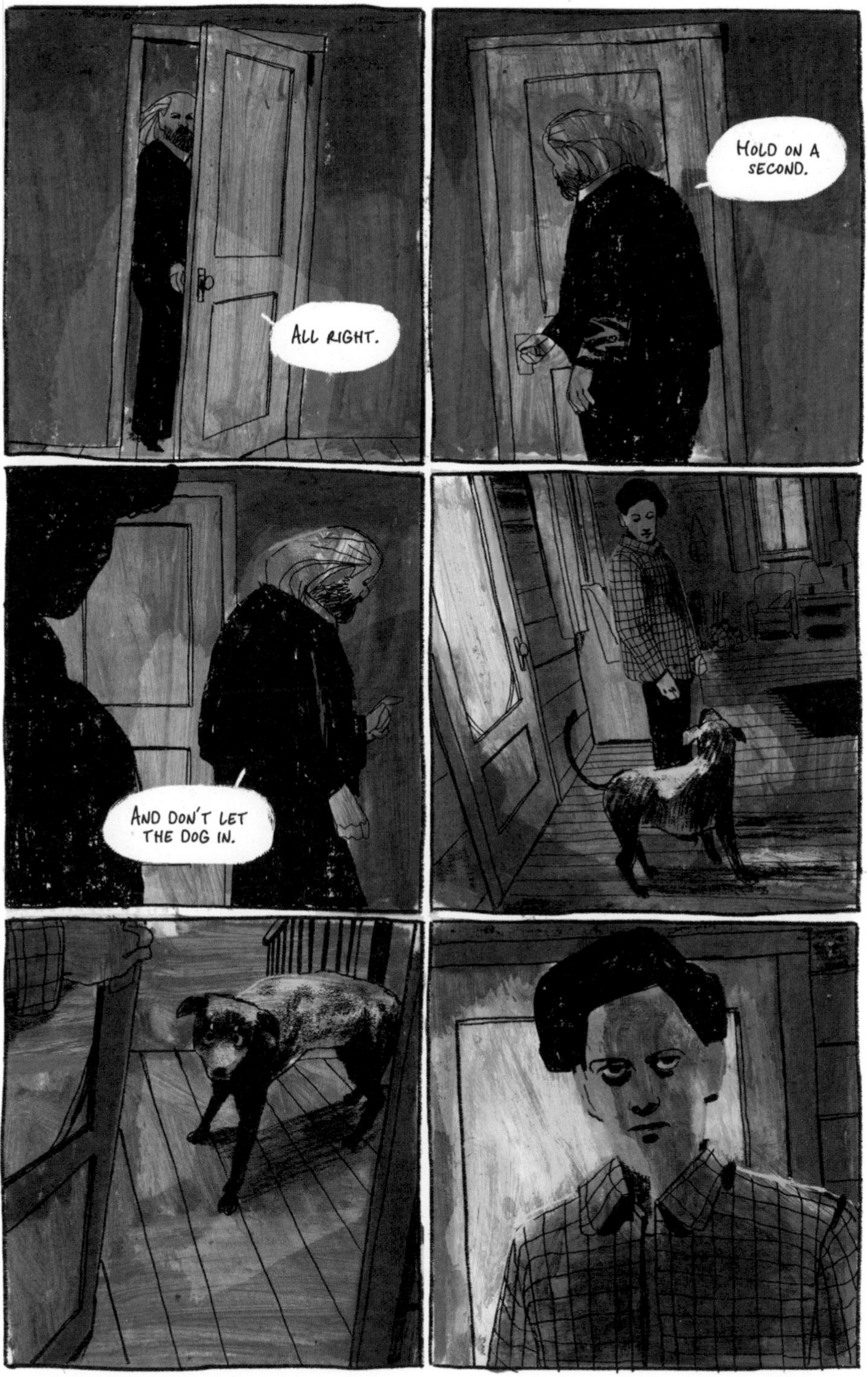
All right.
Hold on a second.
And don't let the dog in.

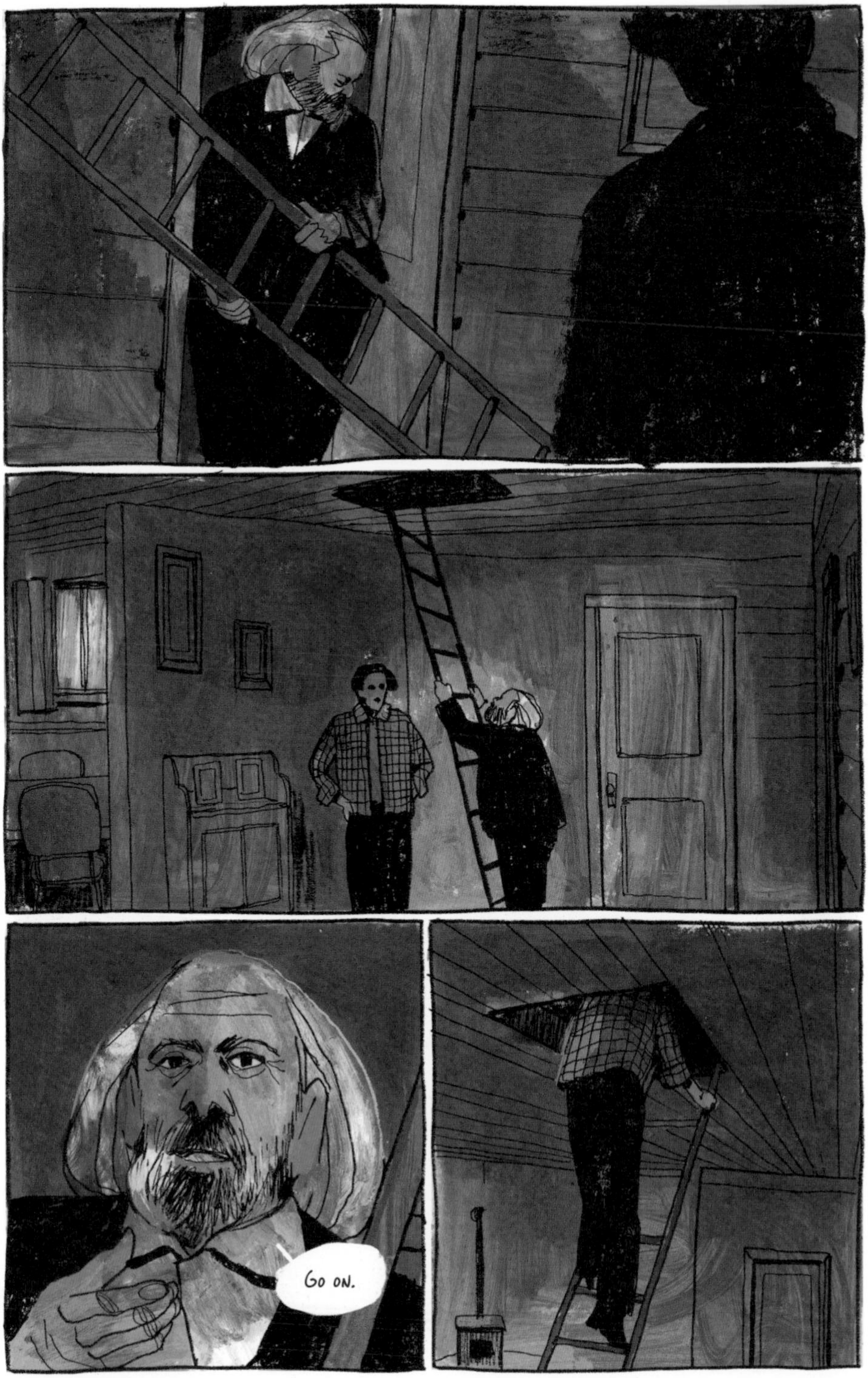
Go on.

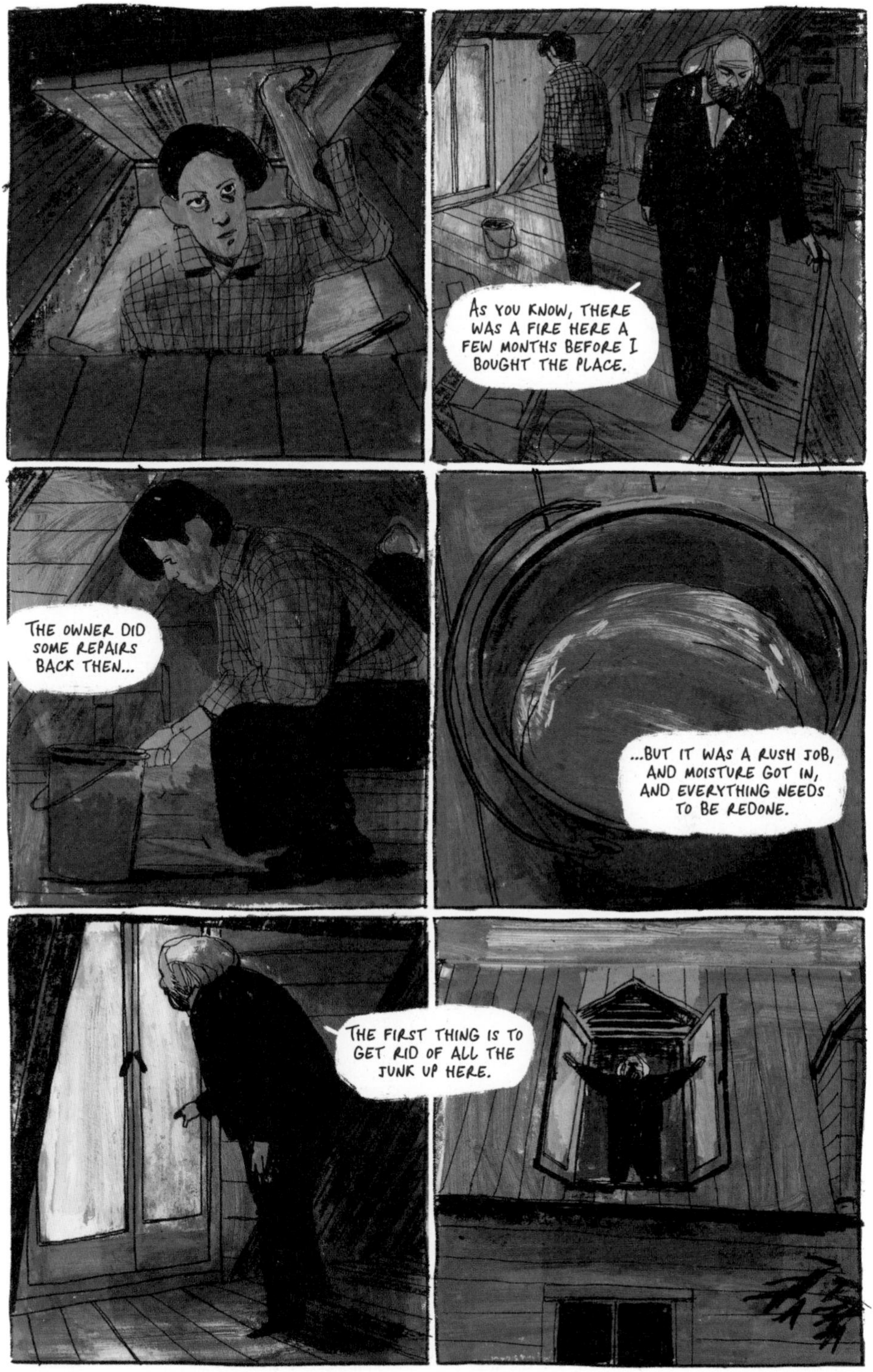
As you know, there was a fire here a few months before I bought the place.
The owner did some repairs back then...
...but it was a rush job, and moisture got in, and everything needs to be redone.
The first thing is to get rid of all the junk up here.

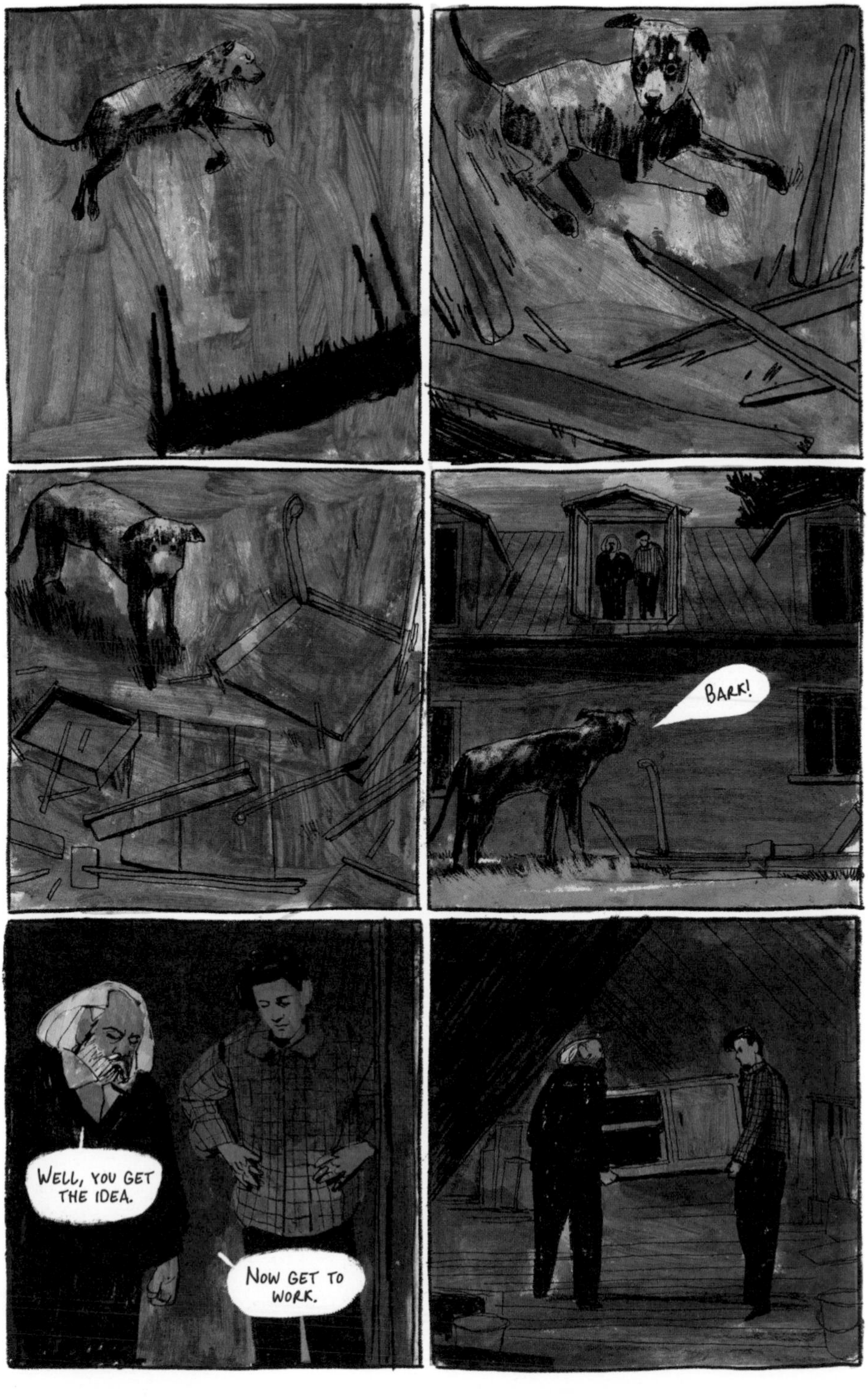
BARK!
WELL, YOU GET THE IDEA.
NOW GET TO WORK.

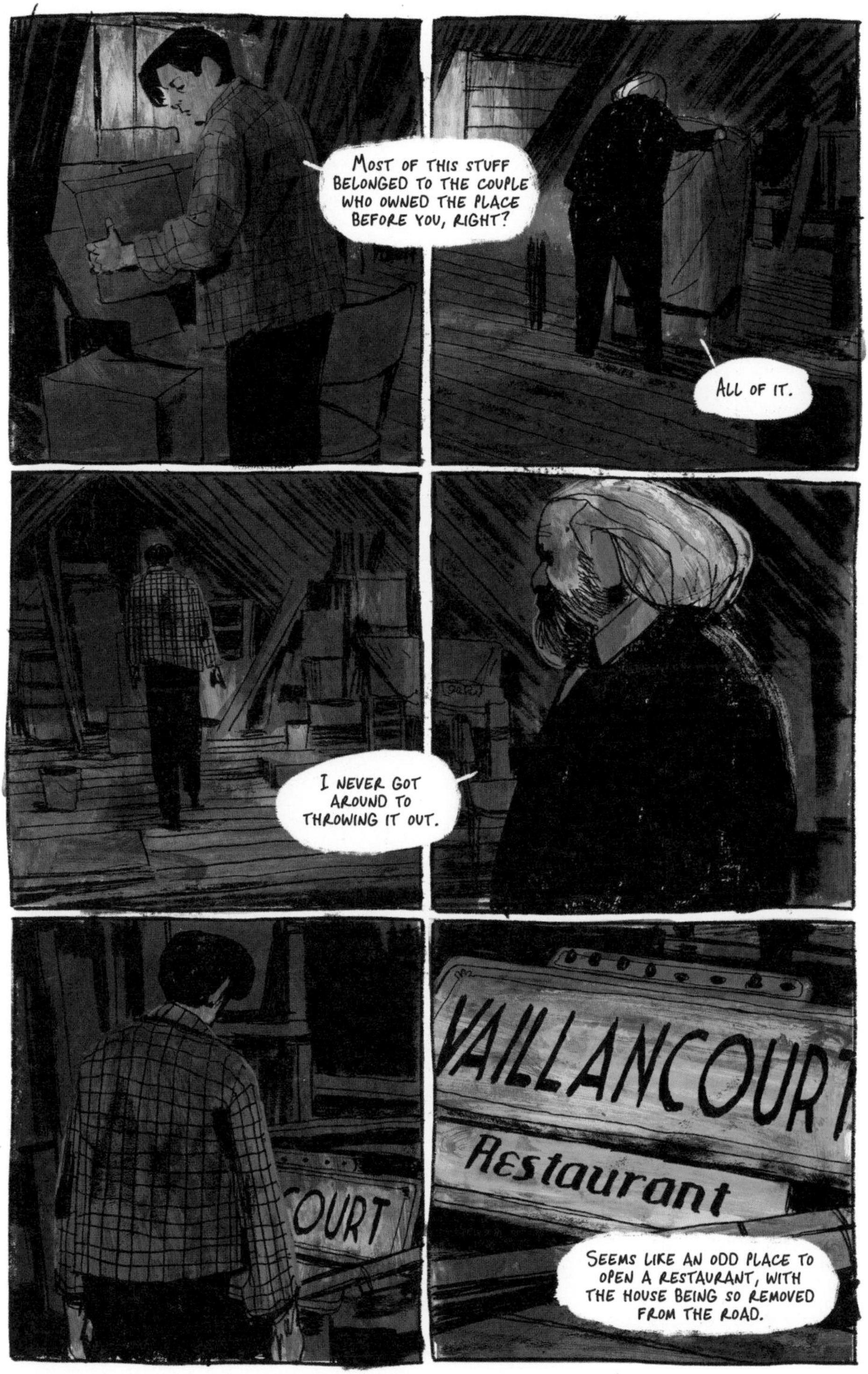
MOST OF THIS STUFF BELONGED TO THE COUPLE WHO OWNED THE PLACE BEFORE YOU, RIGHT?
ALL OF IT.
I NEVER GOT AROUND TO THROWING IT OUT.
OURT
VAILLANCOURT
Restaurant
SEEMS LIKE AN ODD PLACE TO OPEN A RESTAURANT, WITH THE HOUSE BEING SO REMOVED FROM THE ROAD.

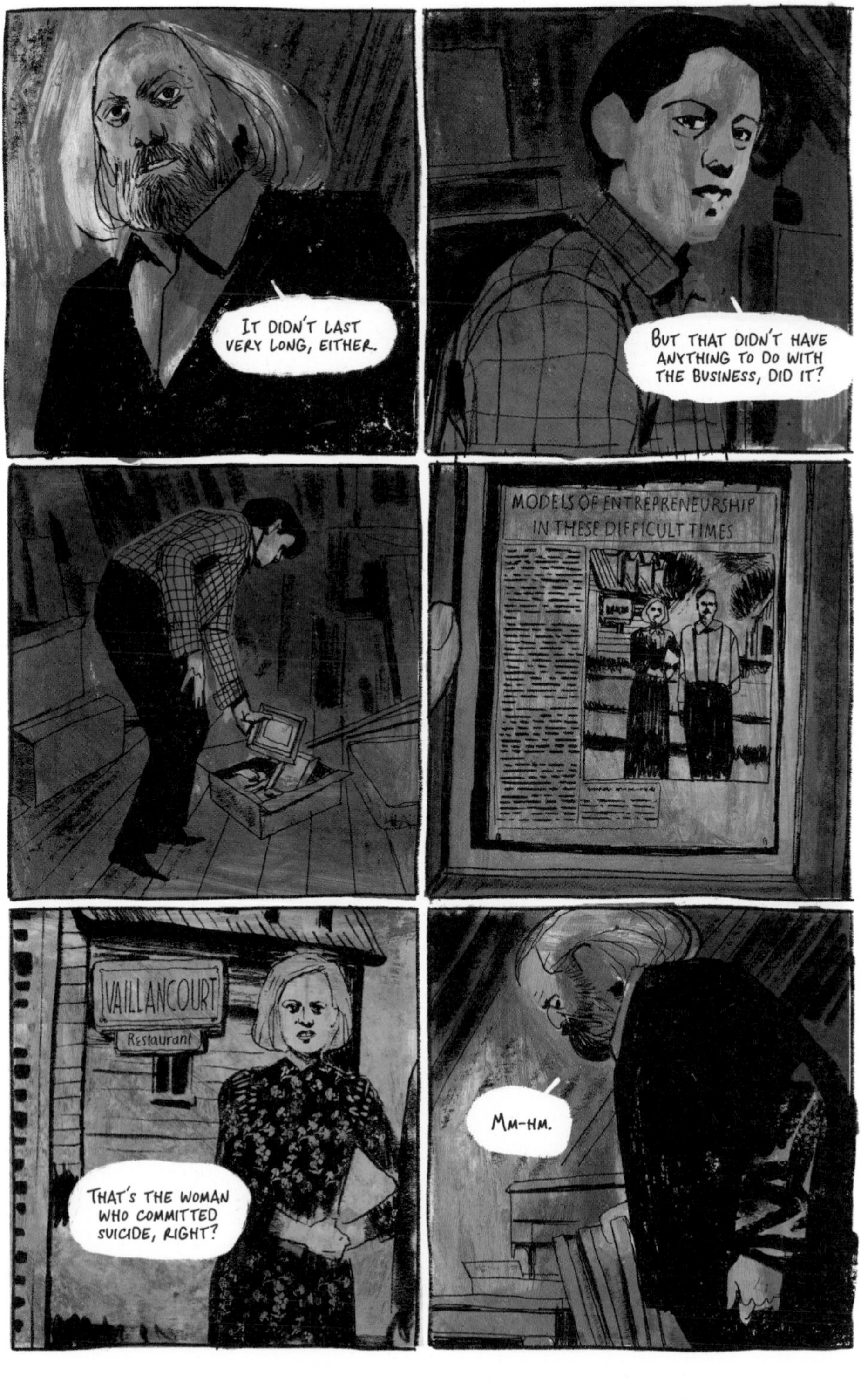
IT DIDN'T LAST VERY LONG, EITHER.
BUT THAT DIDN'T HAVE ANYTHING TO DO WITH THE BUSINESS, DID IT?
MODELS OF ENTREPRENEURSHIP IN THESE DIFFICULT TIMES
VAILLANCOURT
Restaurant
THAT'S THE WOMAN WHO COMMITTED SUICIDE, RIGHT?
MM-HM.

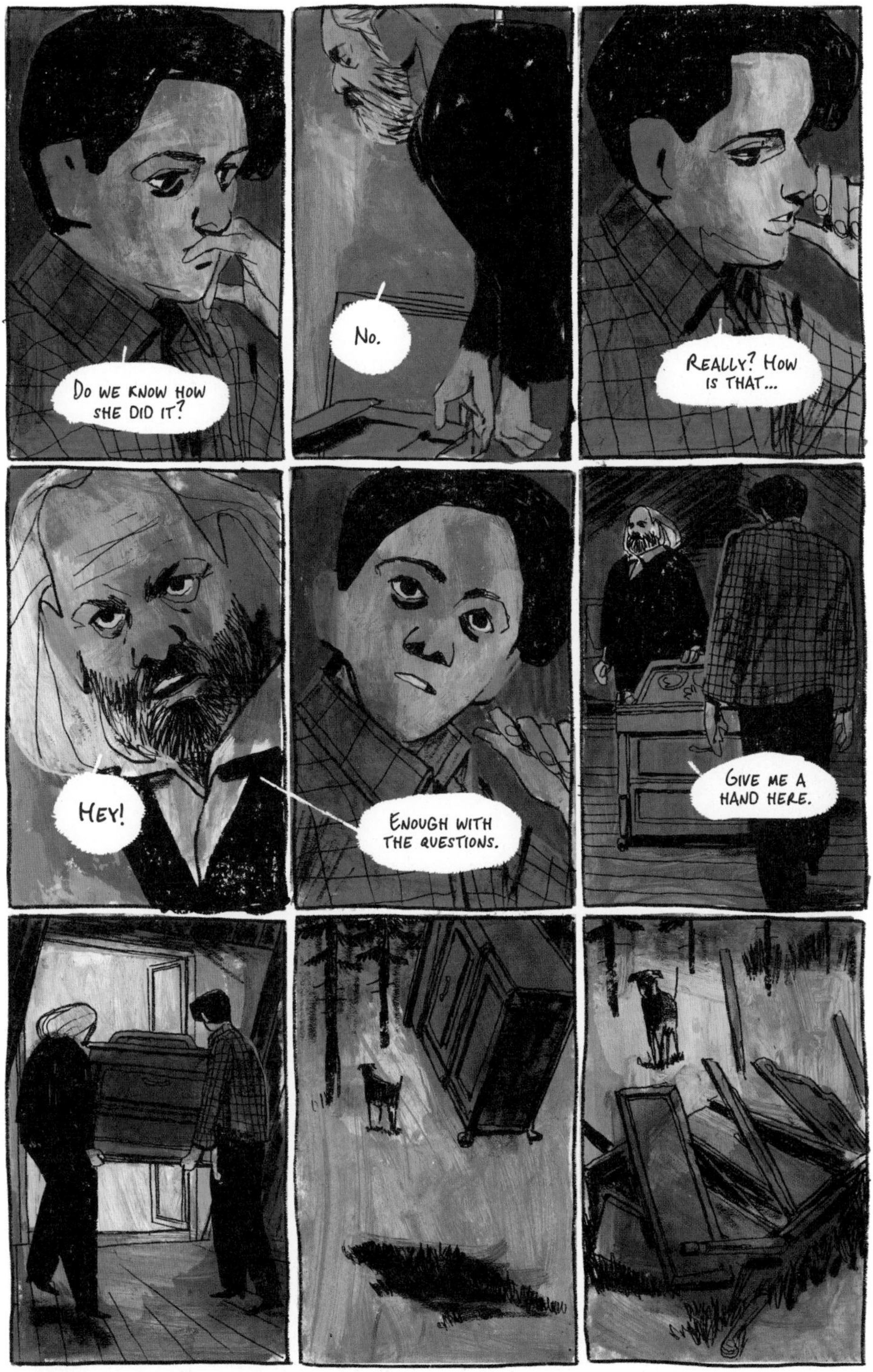
Do we know how she did it?
No.
Really? How is that...
Hey!
Enough with the questions.
Give me a hand here.

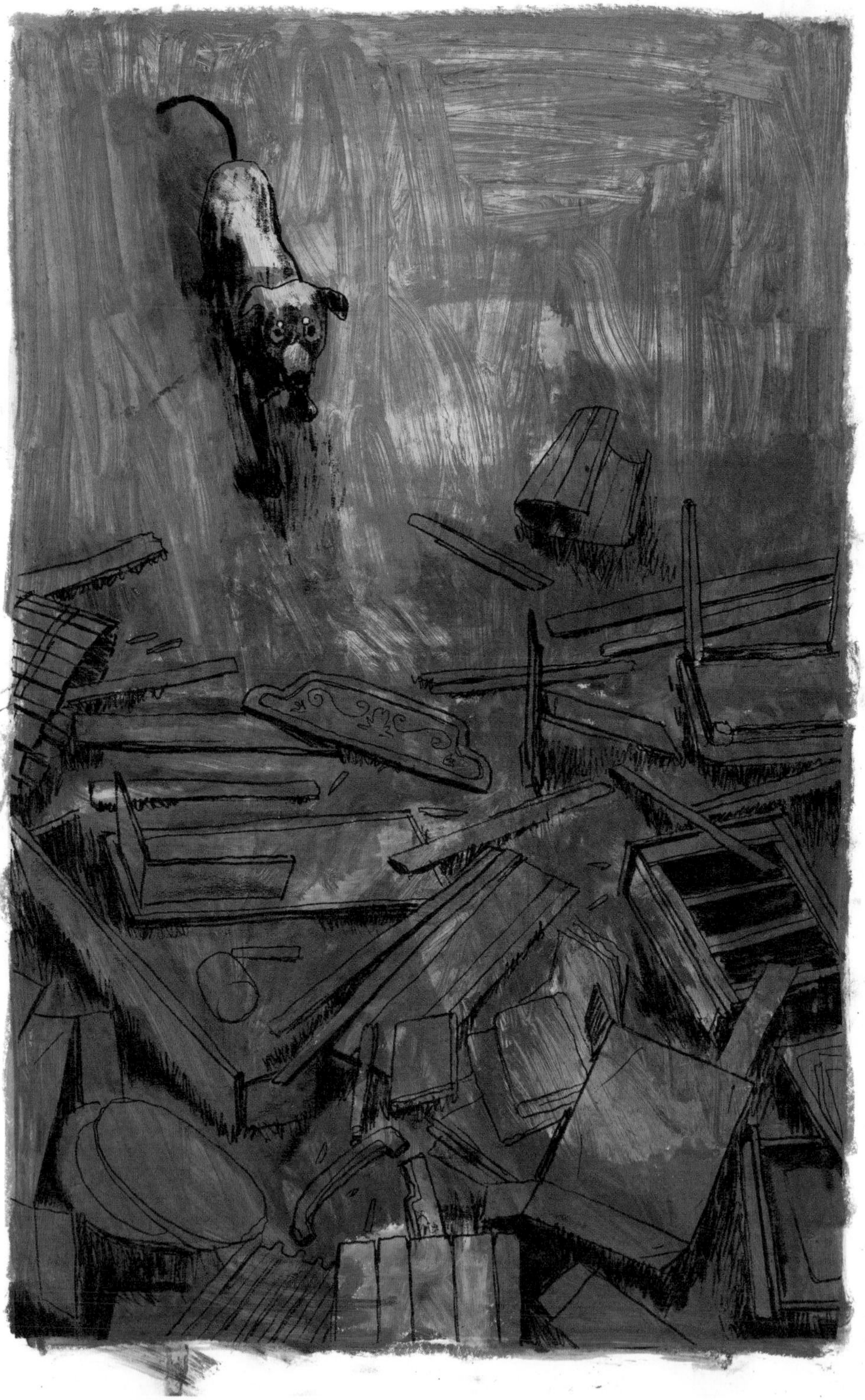

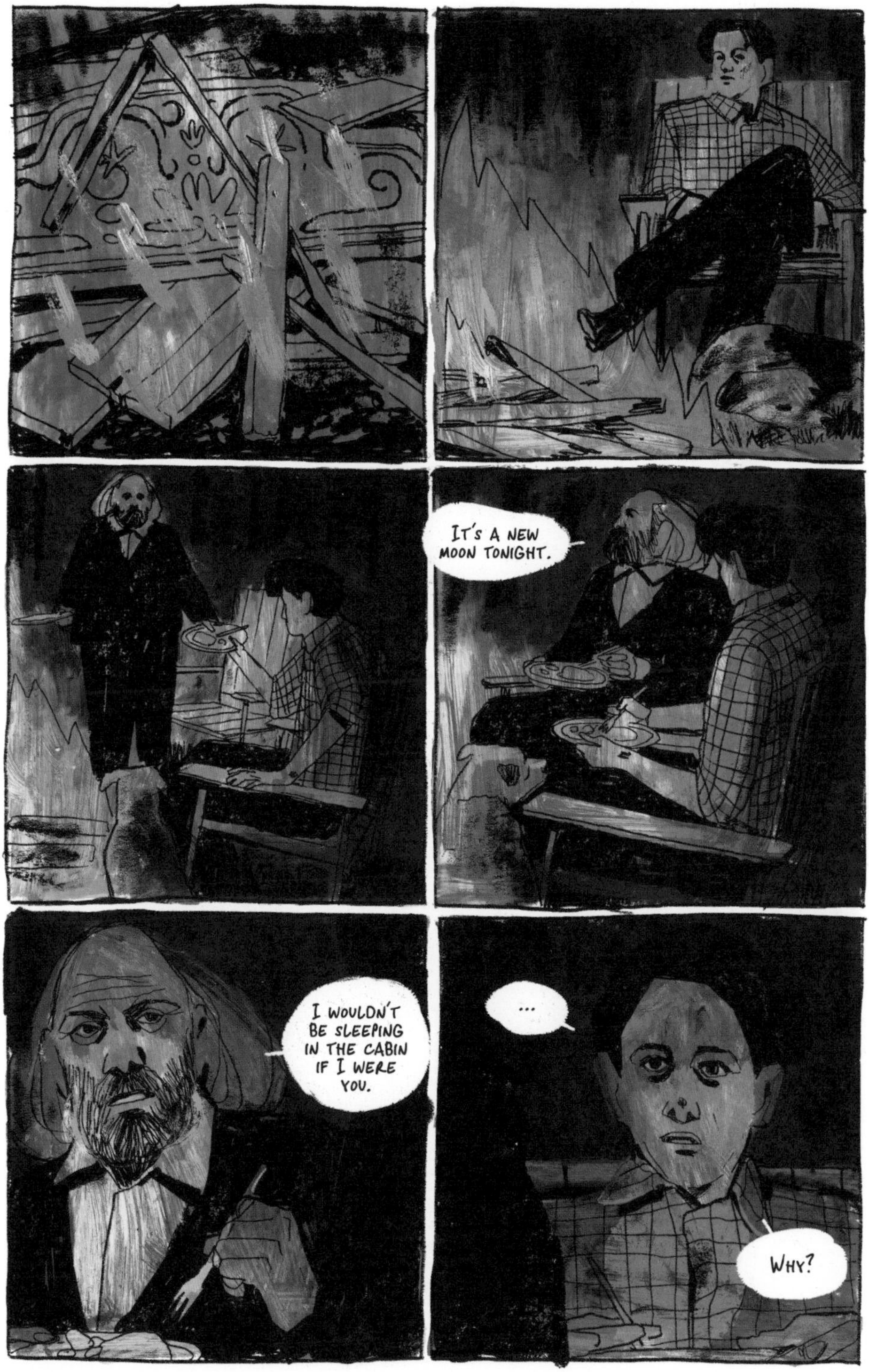
It's a new moon tonight.
I wouldn't be sleeping in the cabin if I were you.
...
Why?

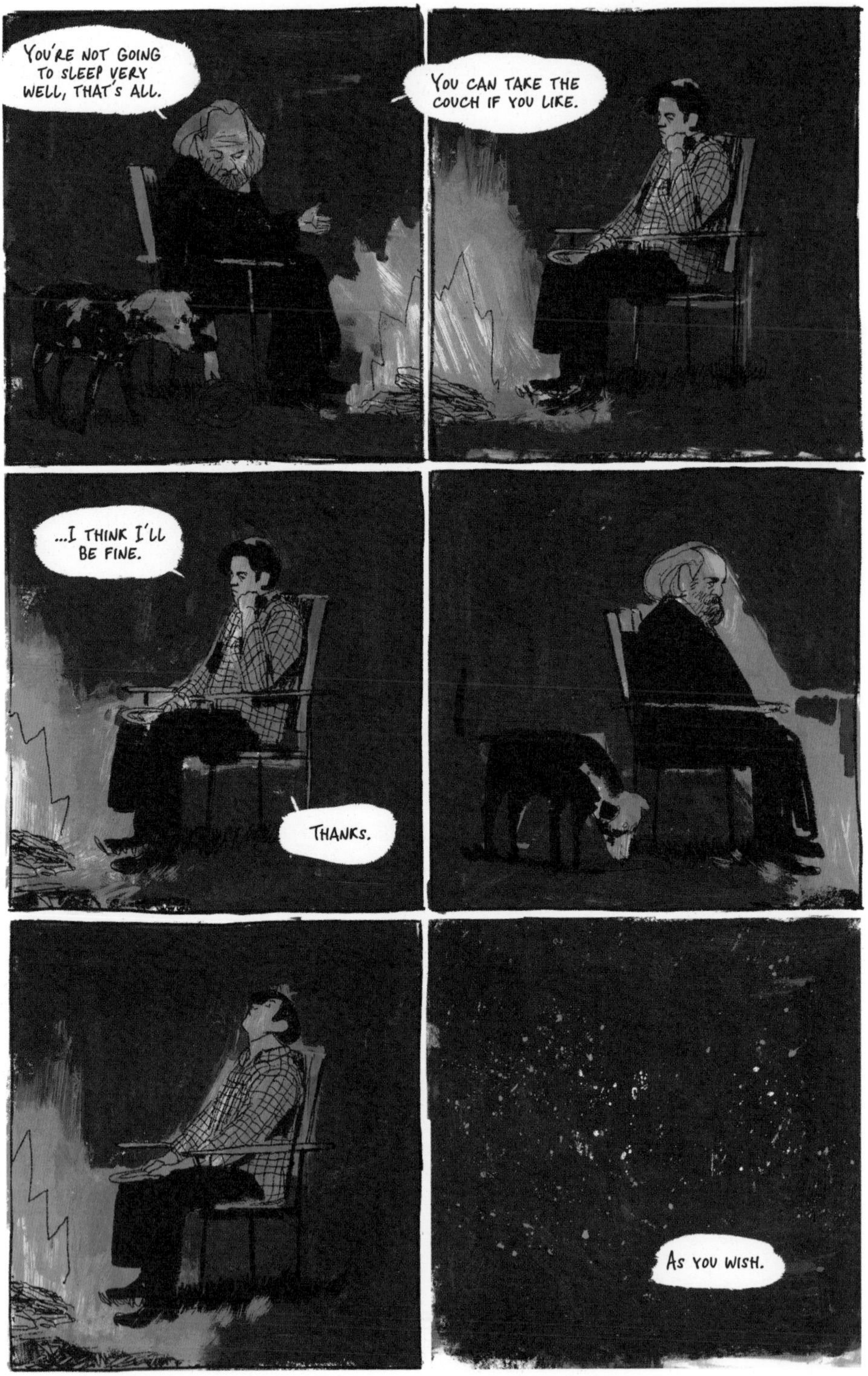

You're not going to sleep very well, that's all.
You can take the couch if you like.
...I think I'll be fine.
Thanks.
As you wish.

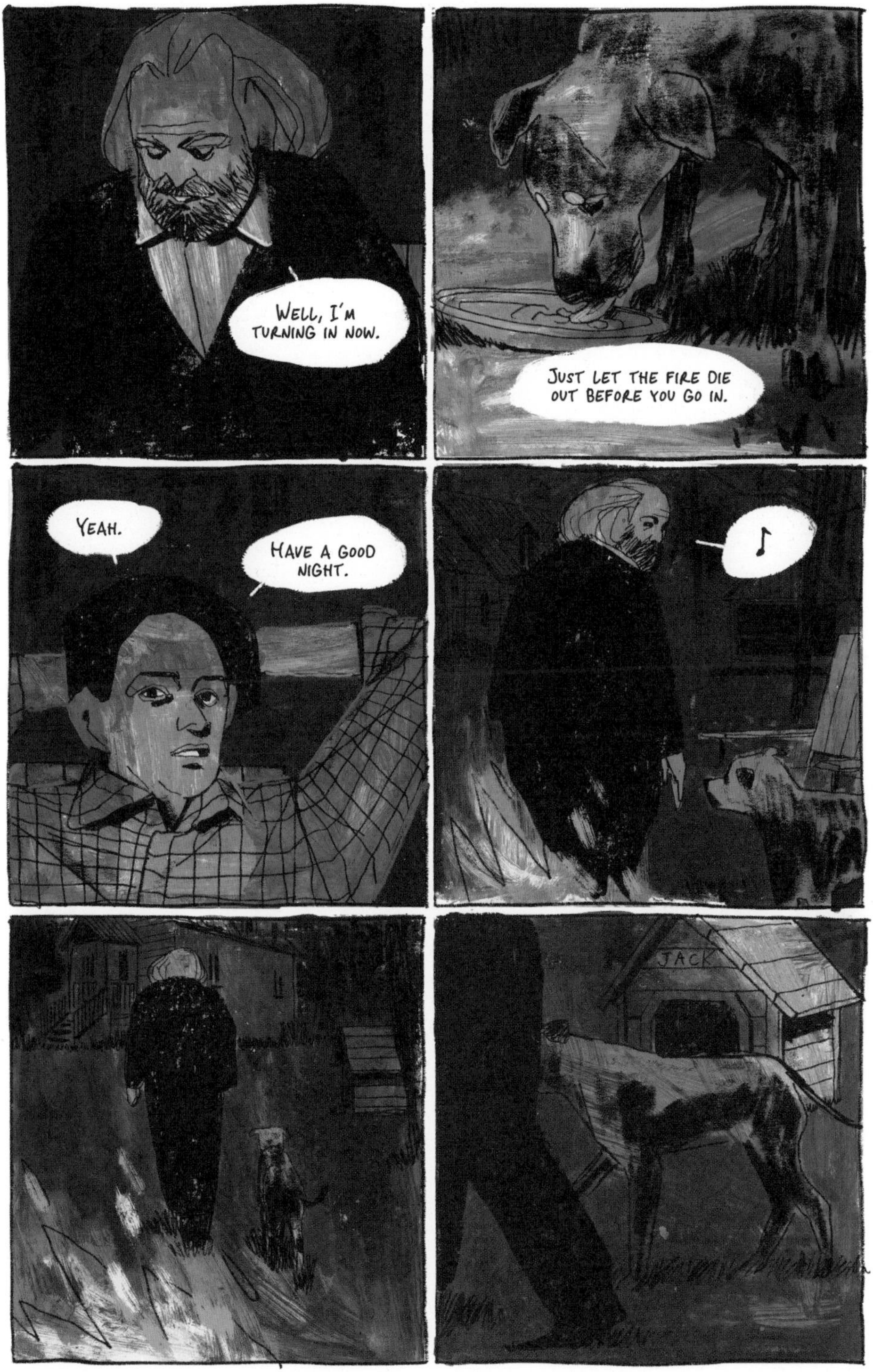
WELL, I'M TURNING IN NOW.
JUST LET THE FIRE DIE OUT BEFORE YOU GO IN.
YEAH.
HAVE A GOOD NIGHT.
♪
JACK

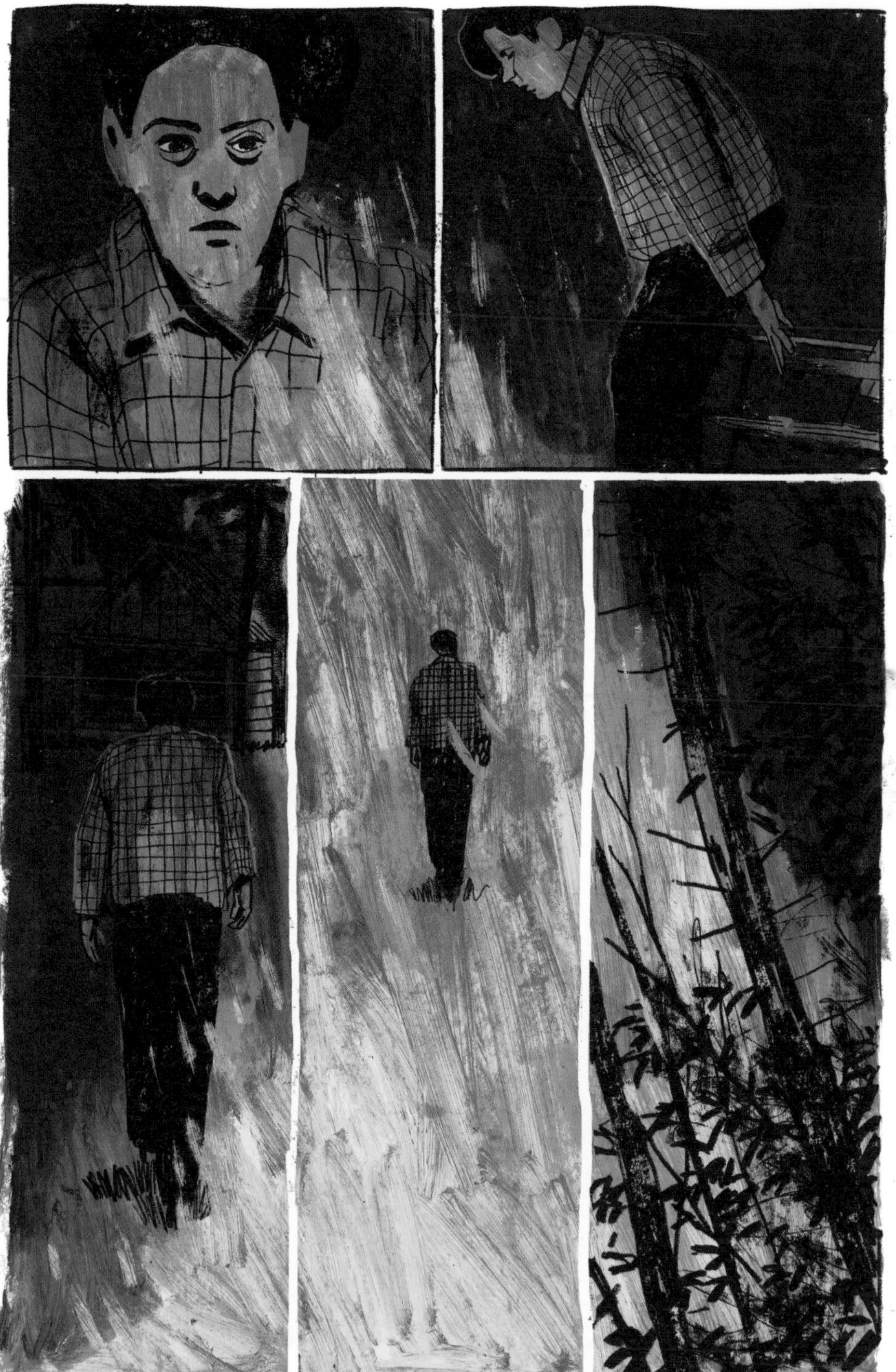

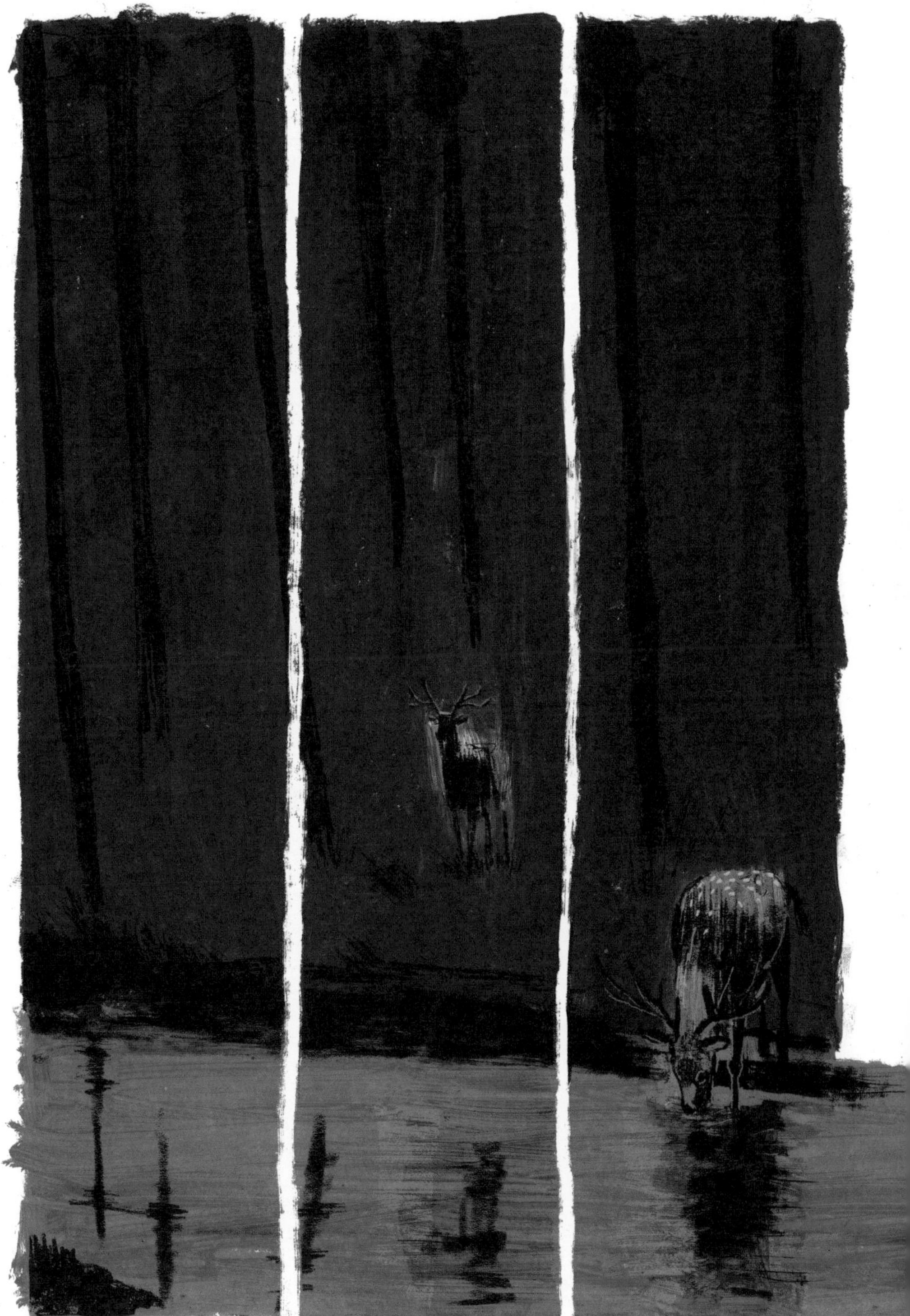

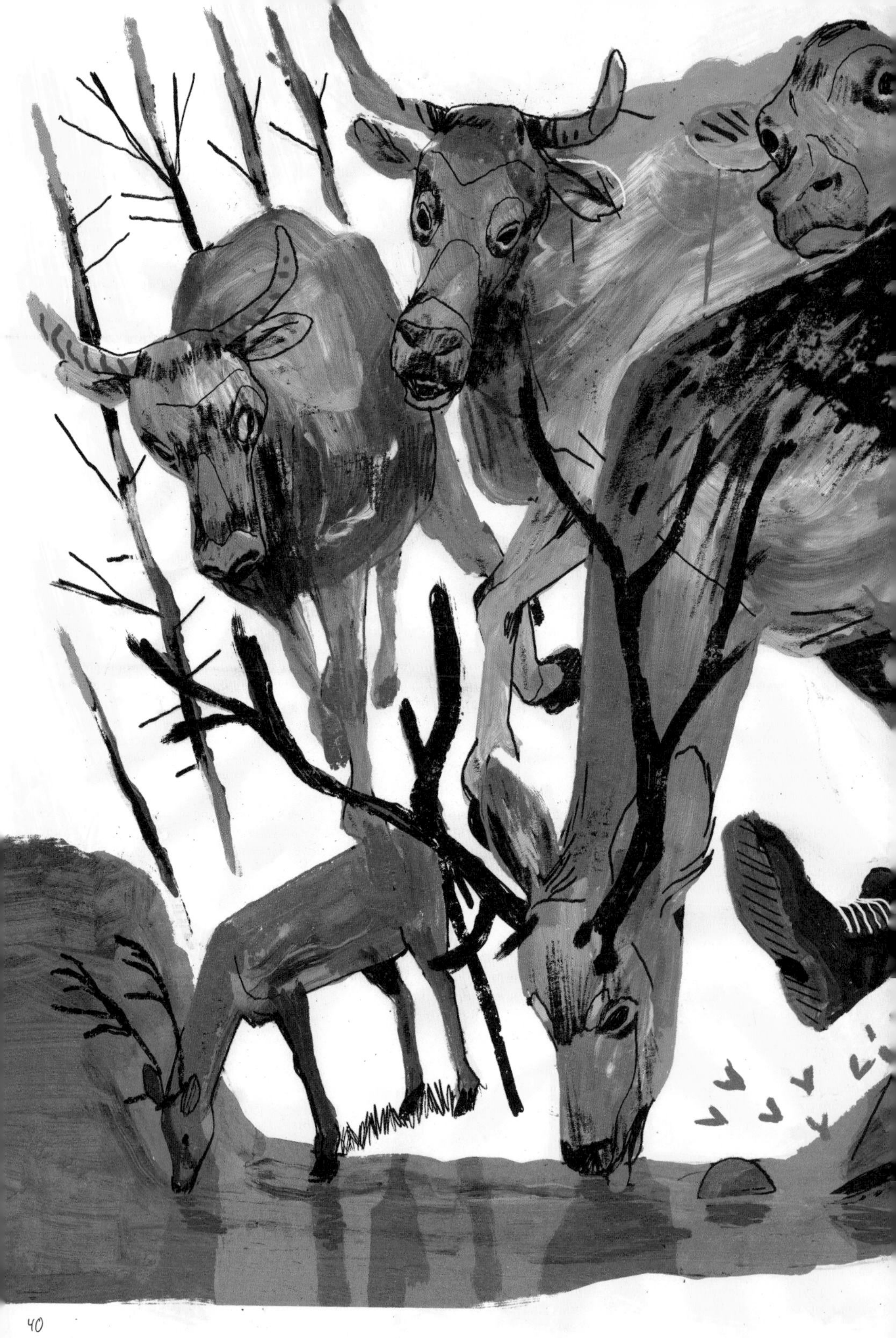

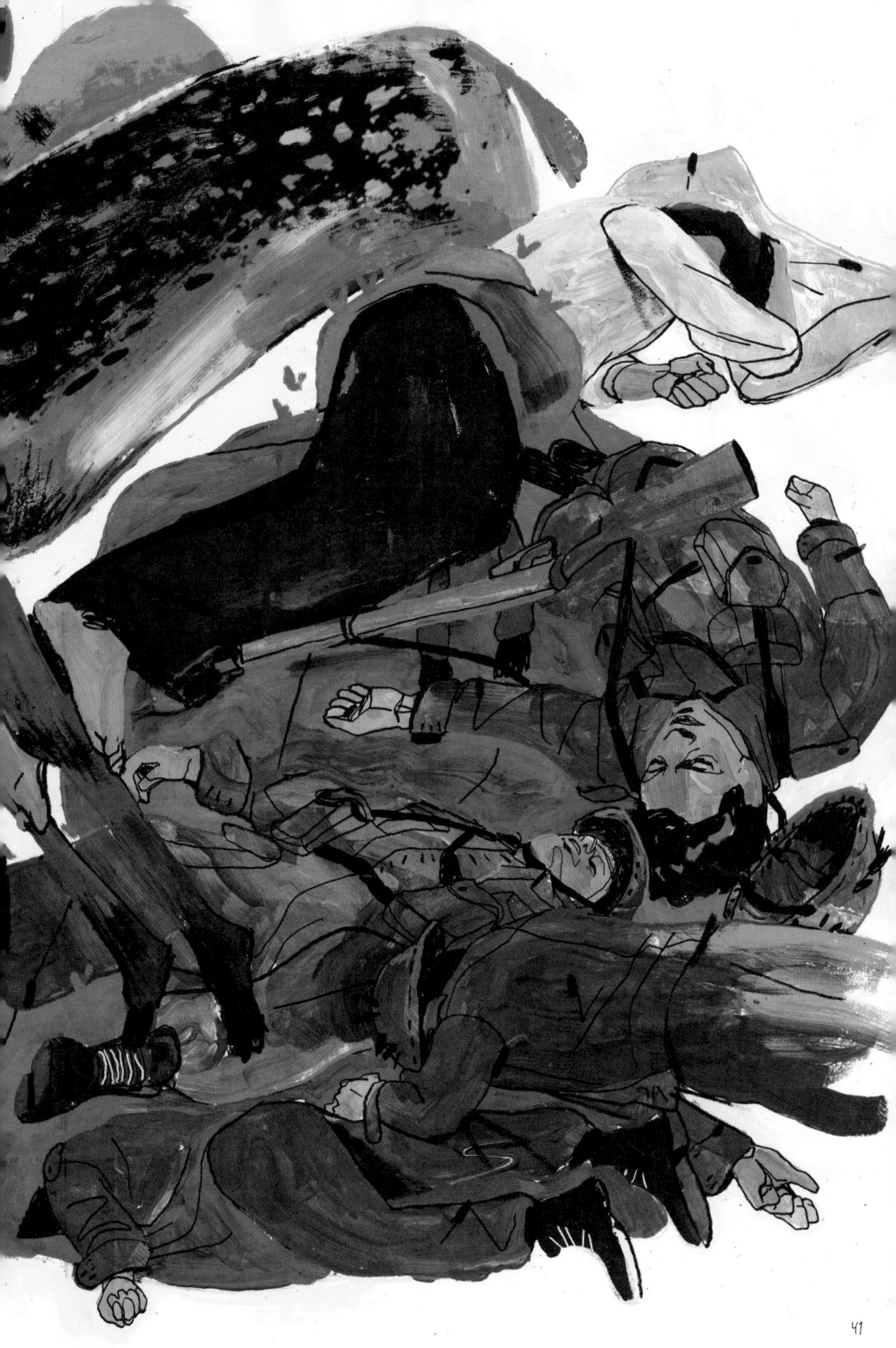

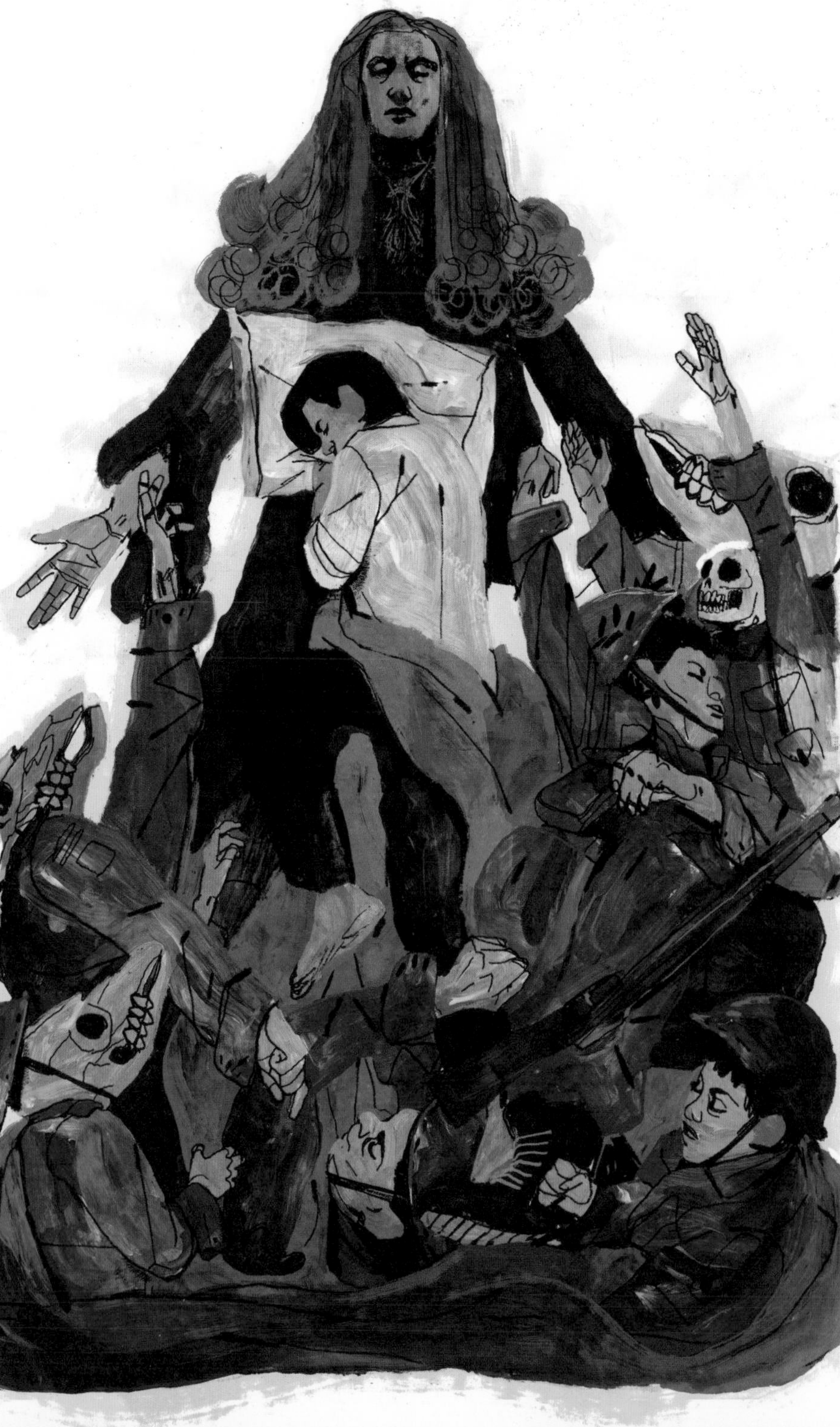

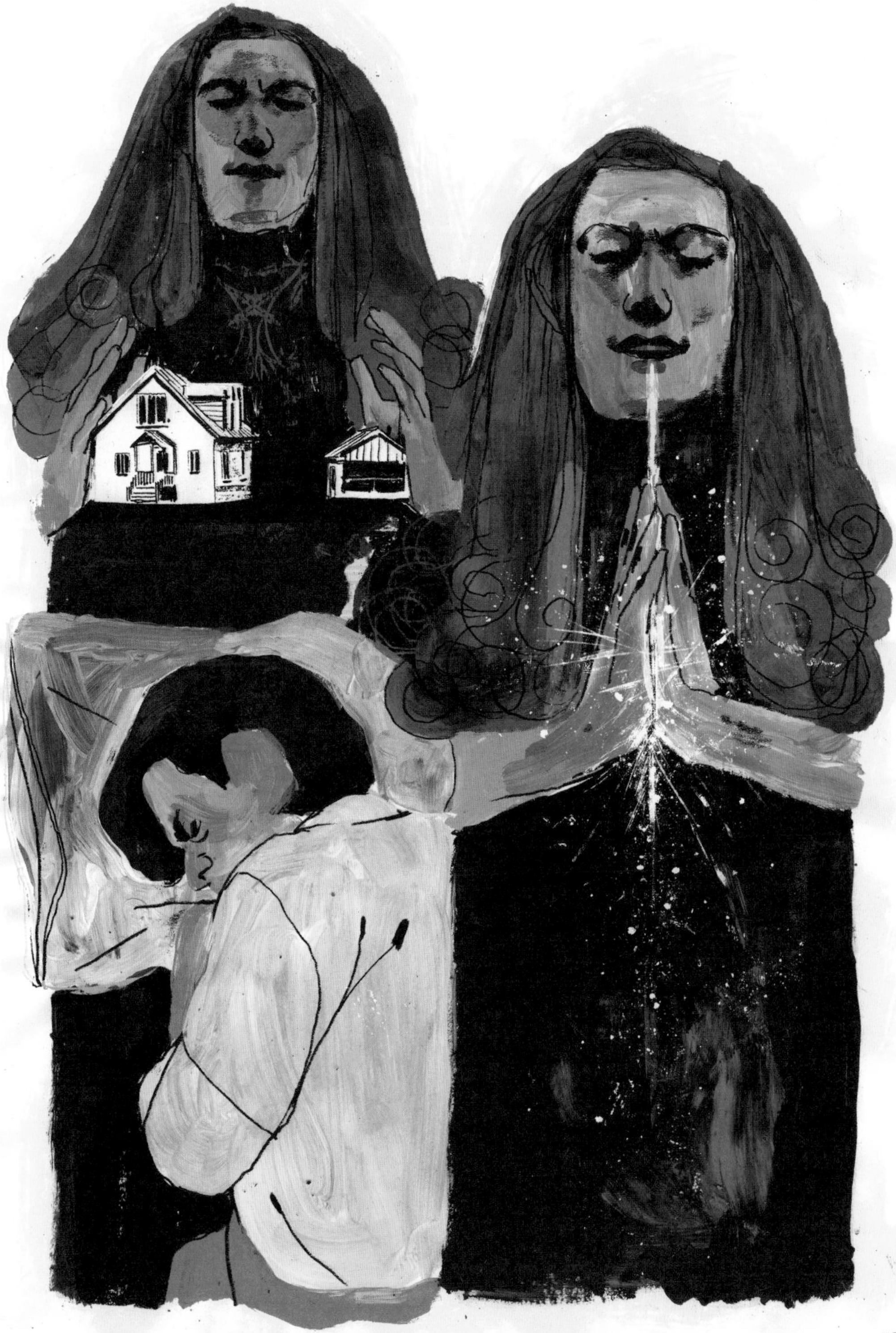

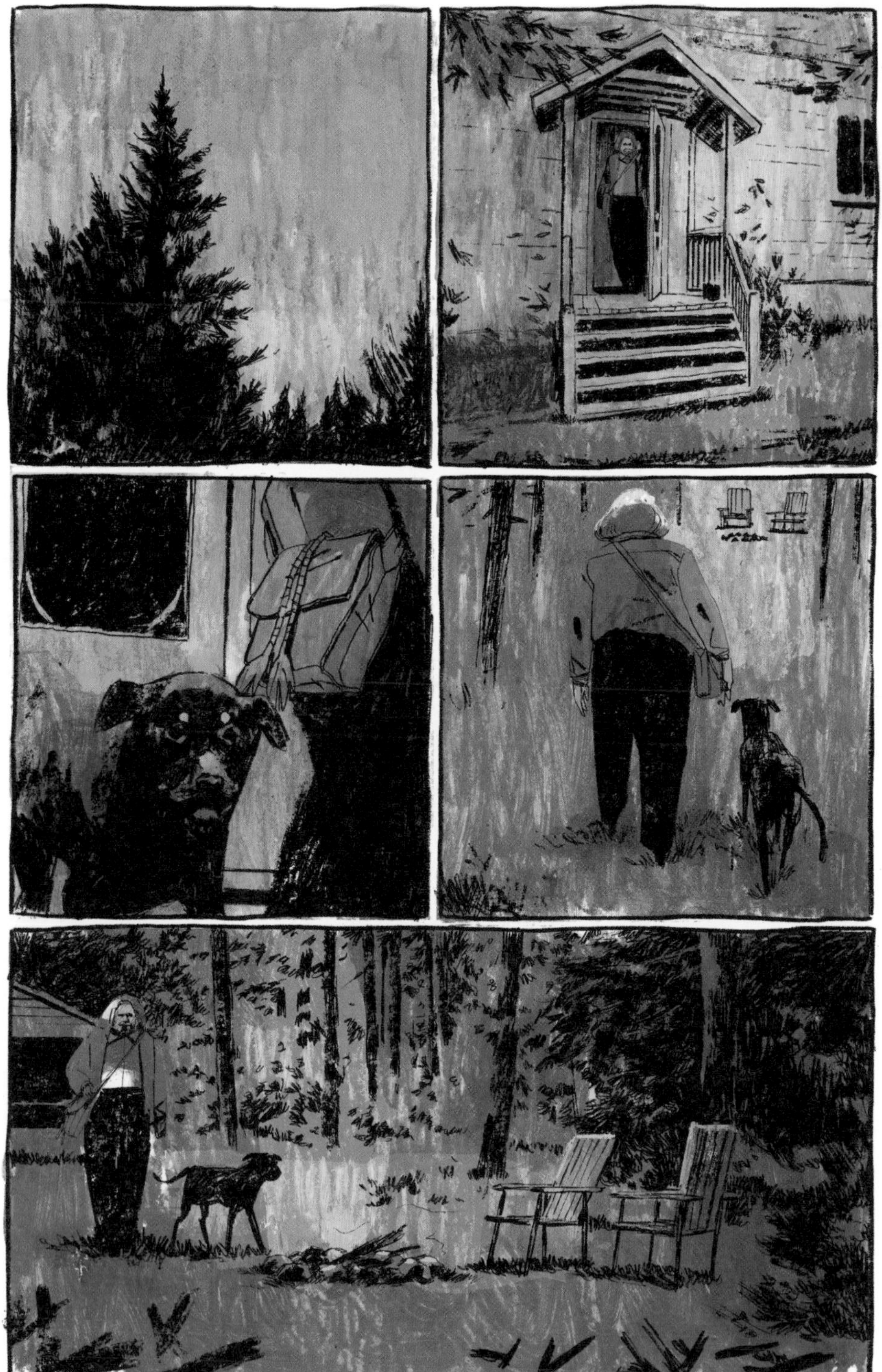

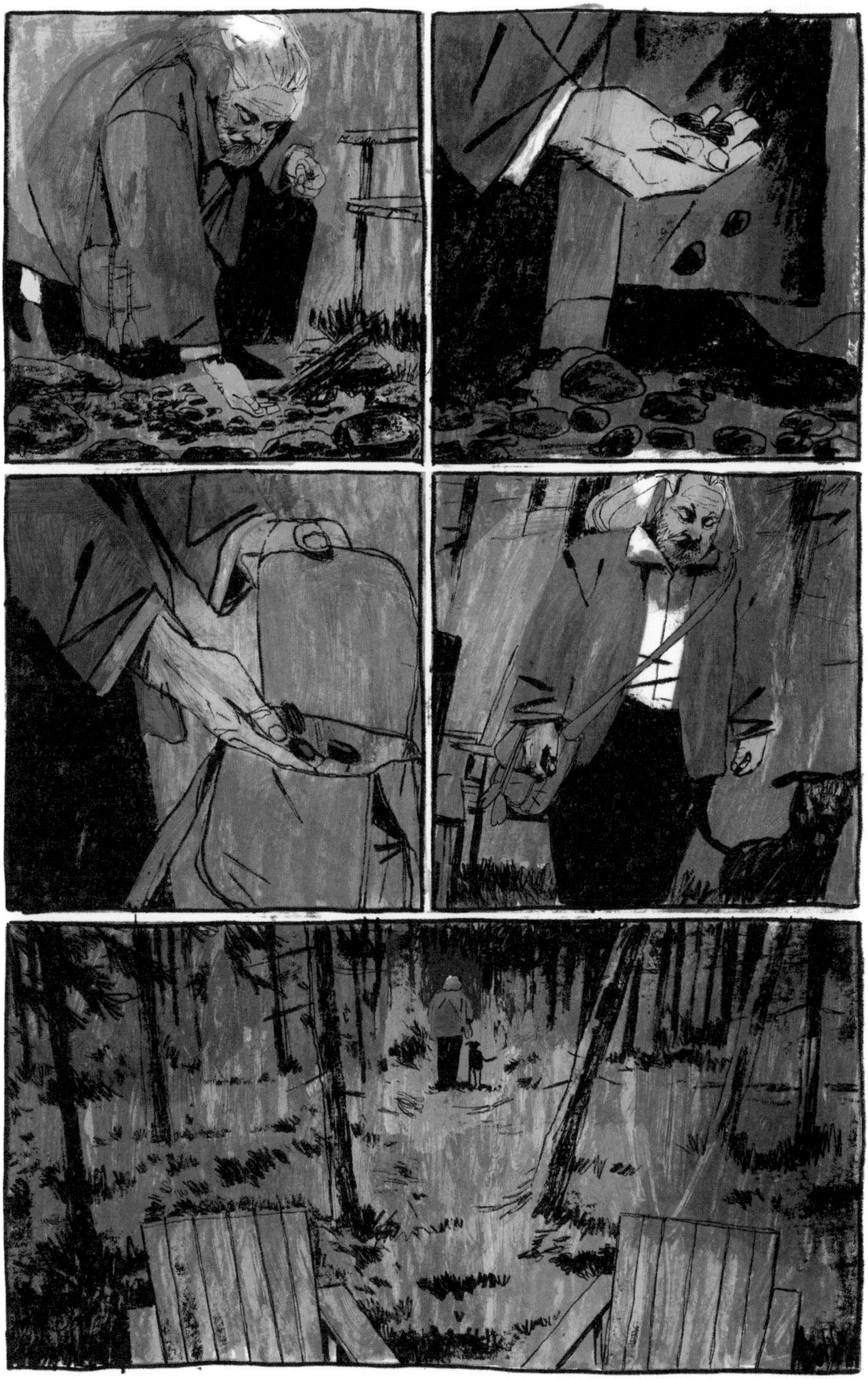

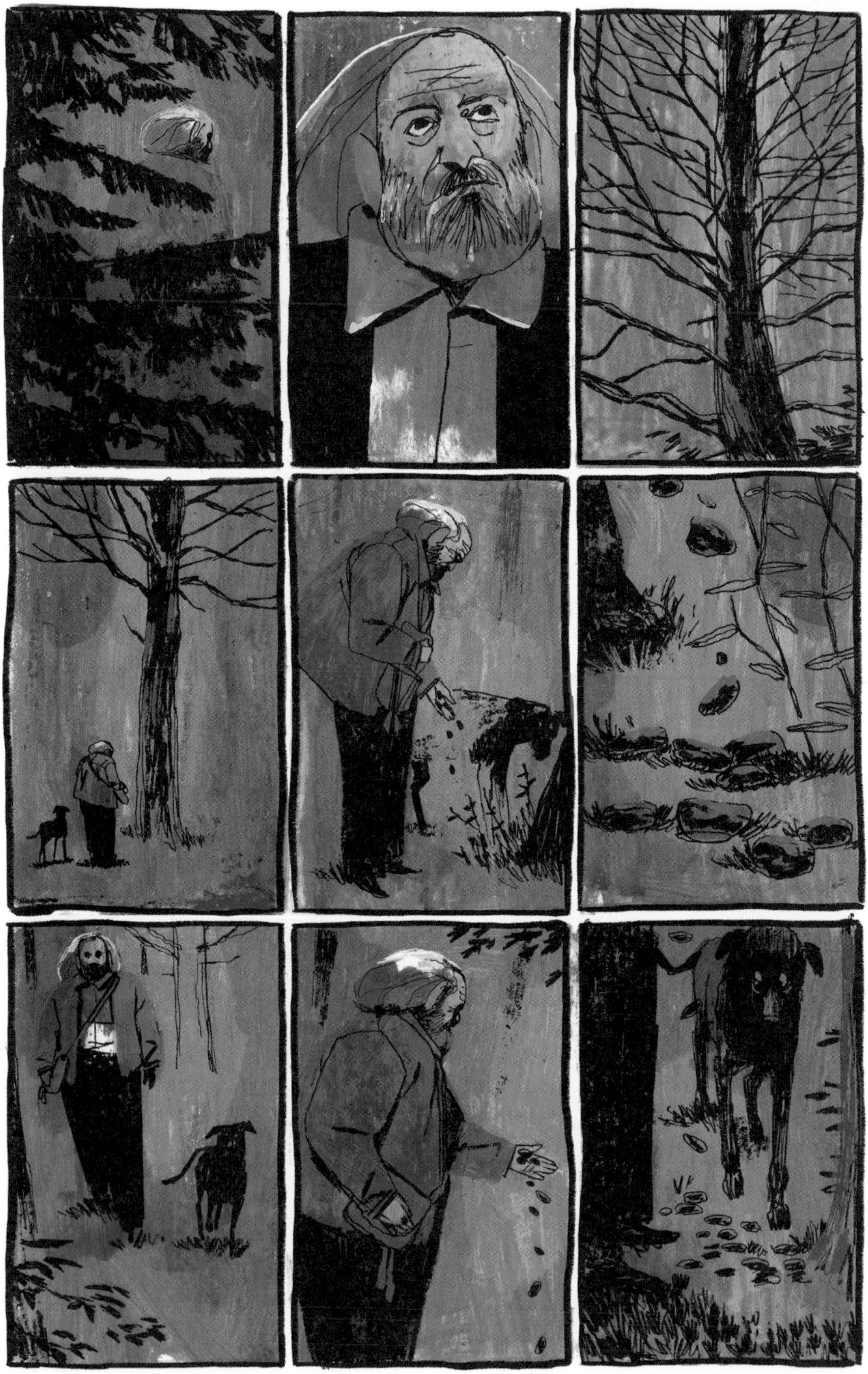

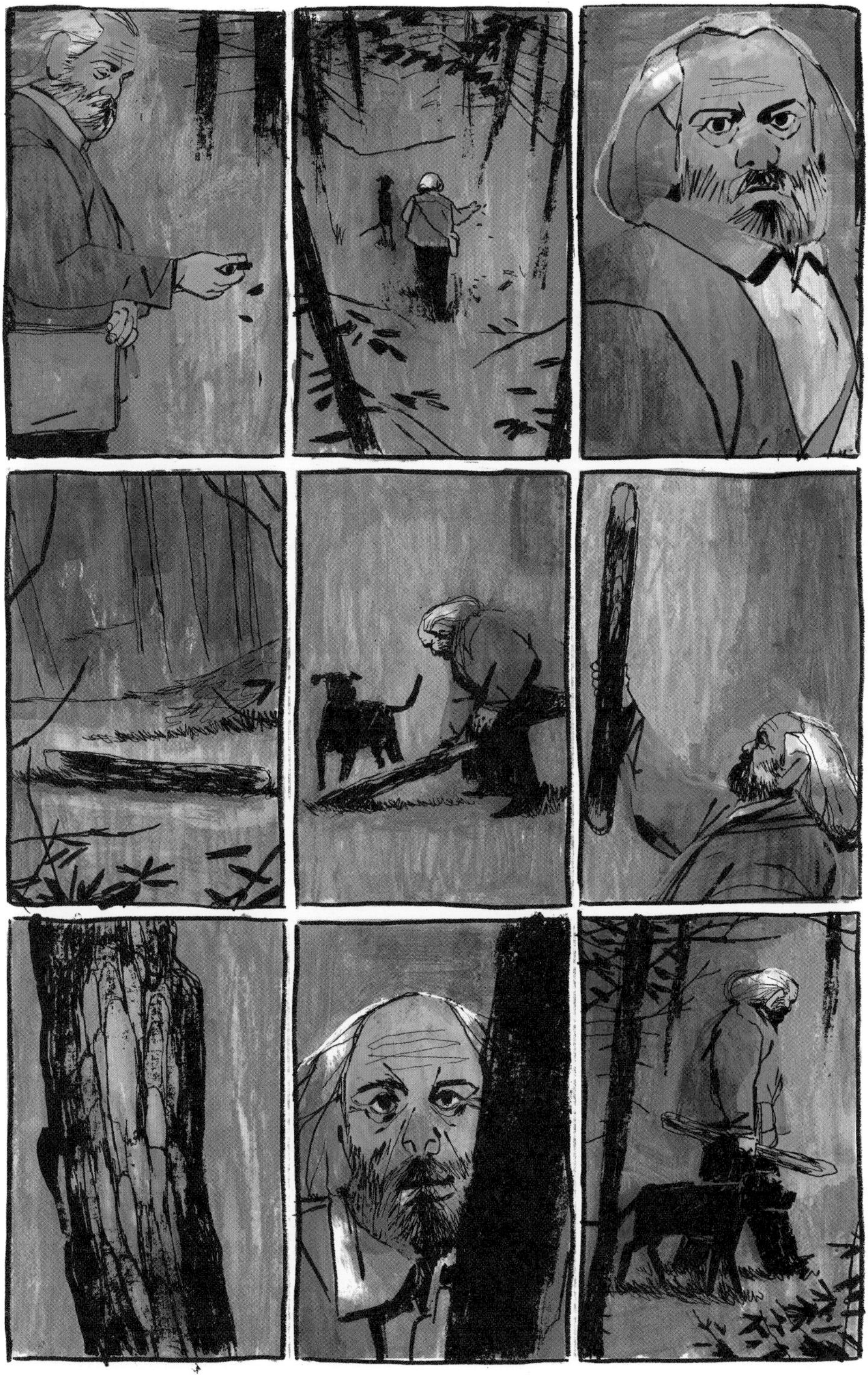

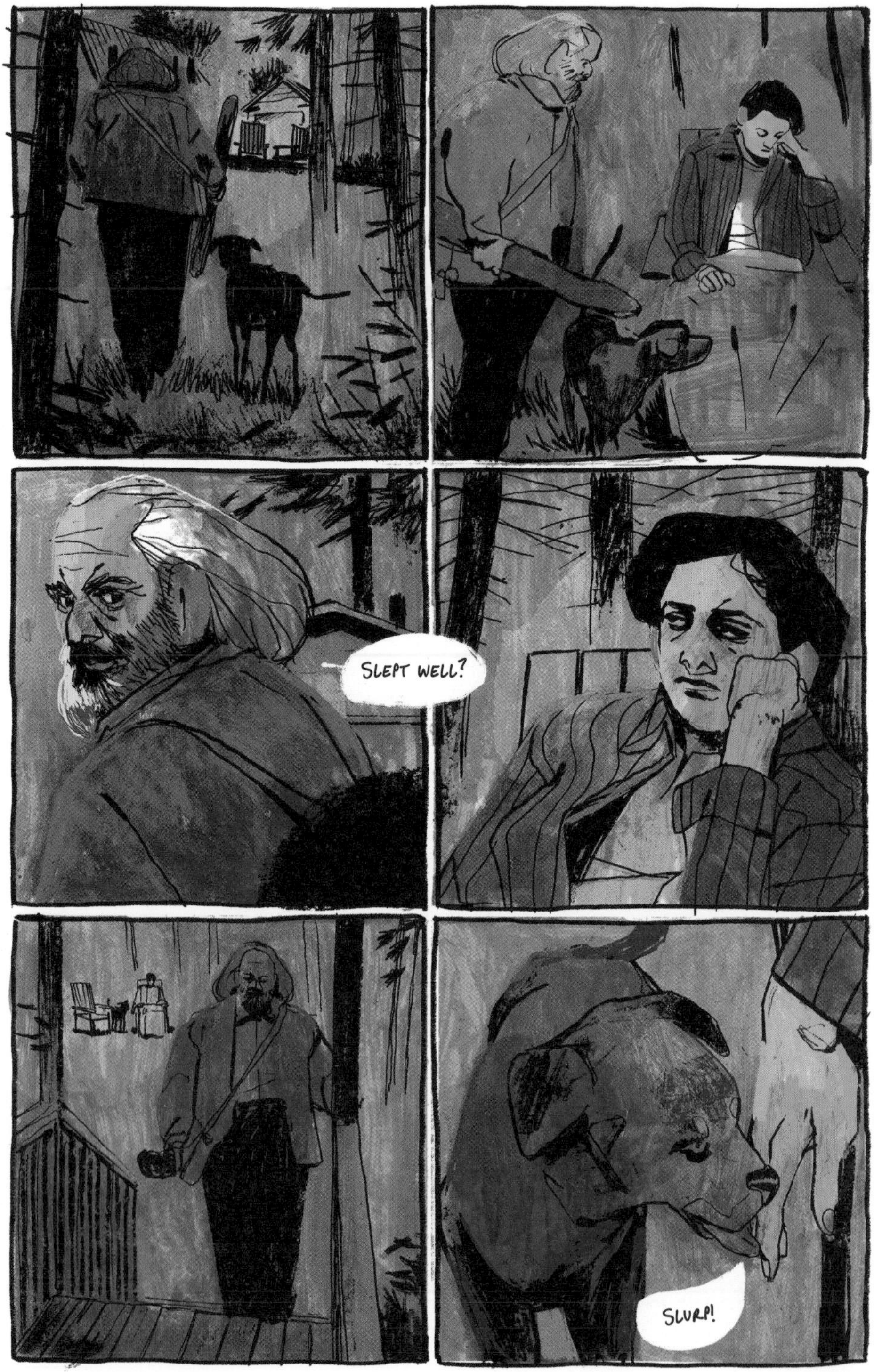
SLEPT WELL?
SLURP!

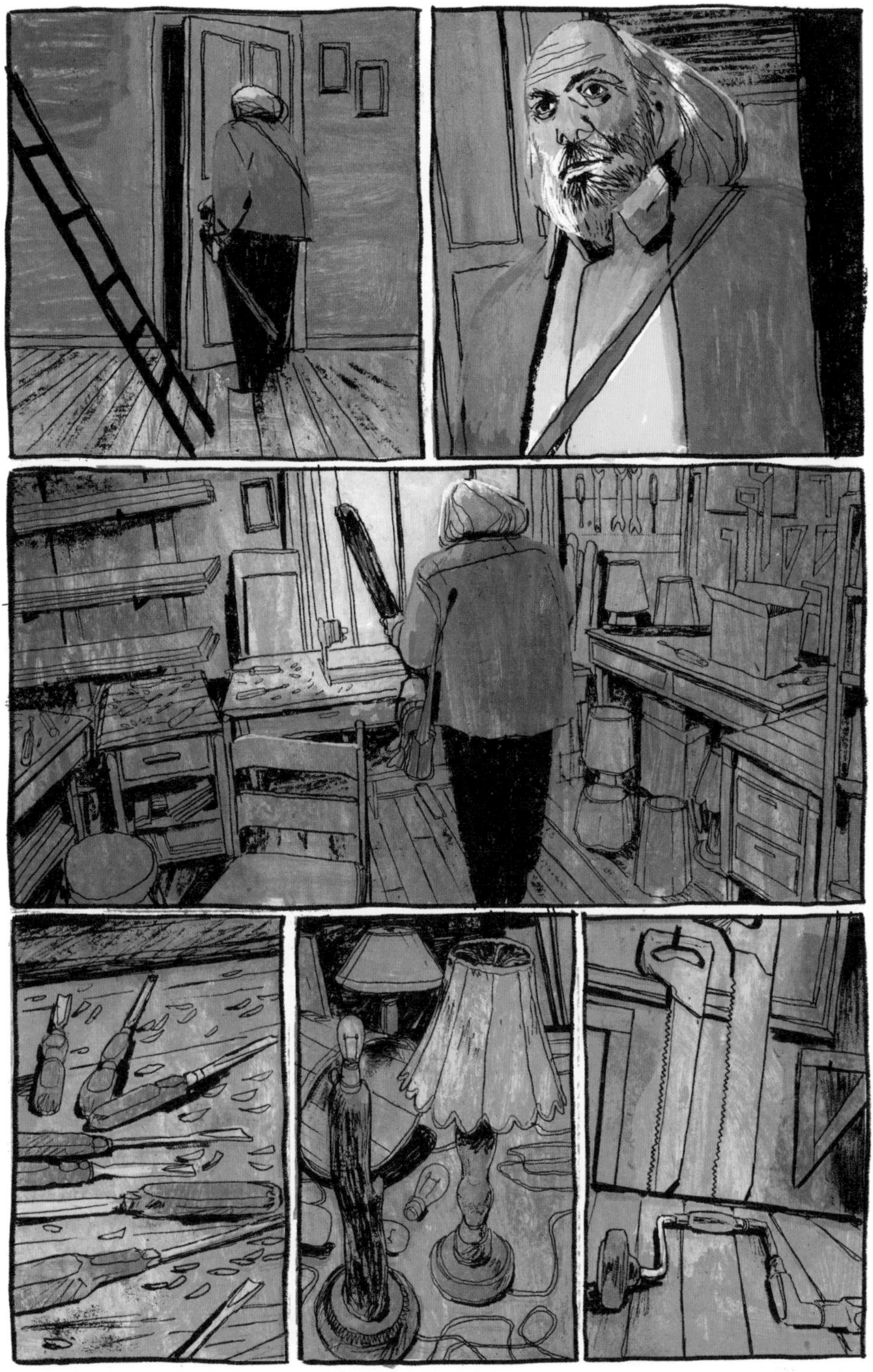

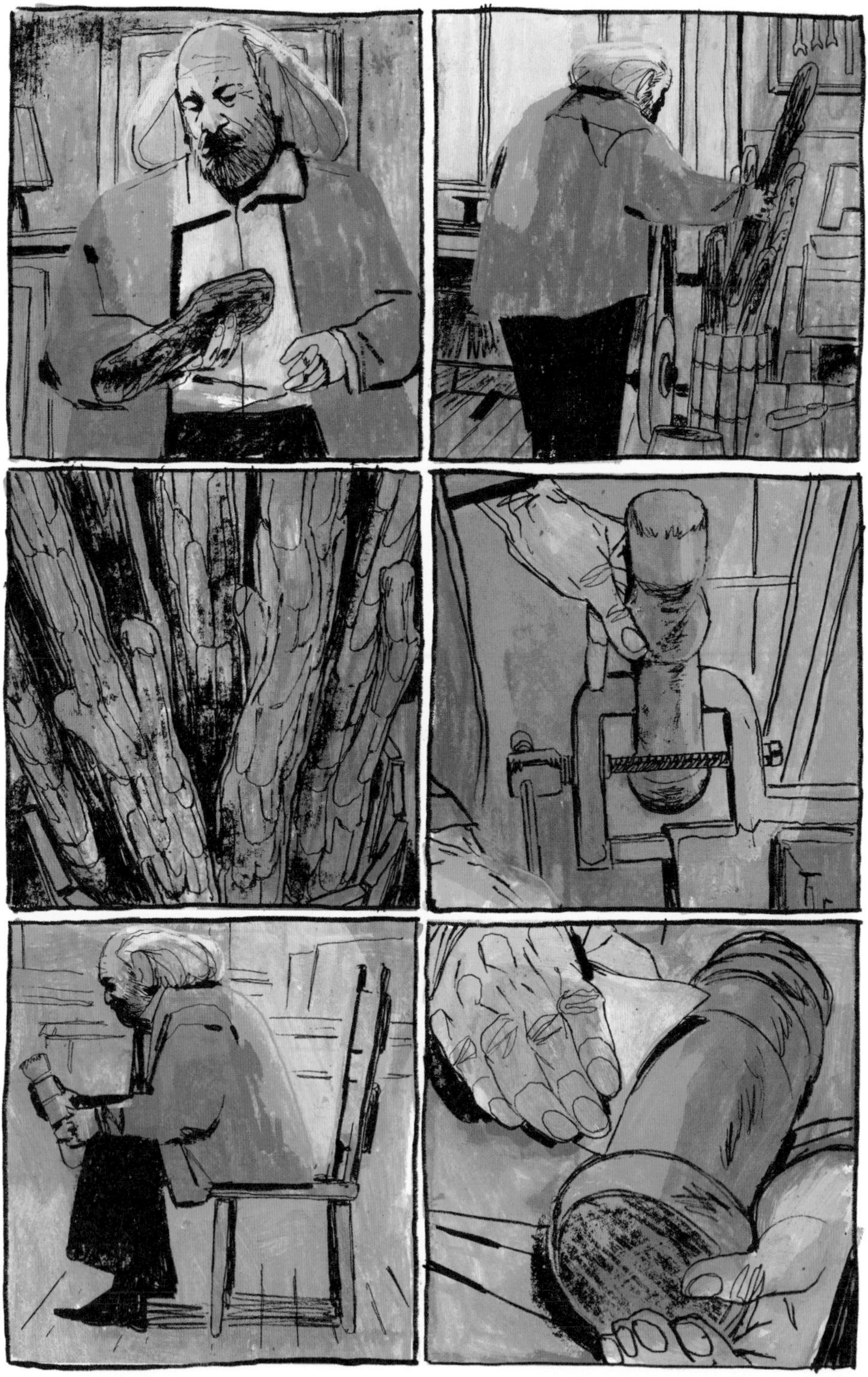

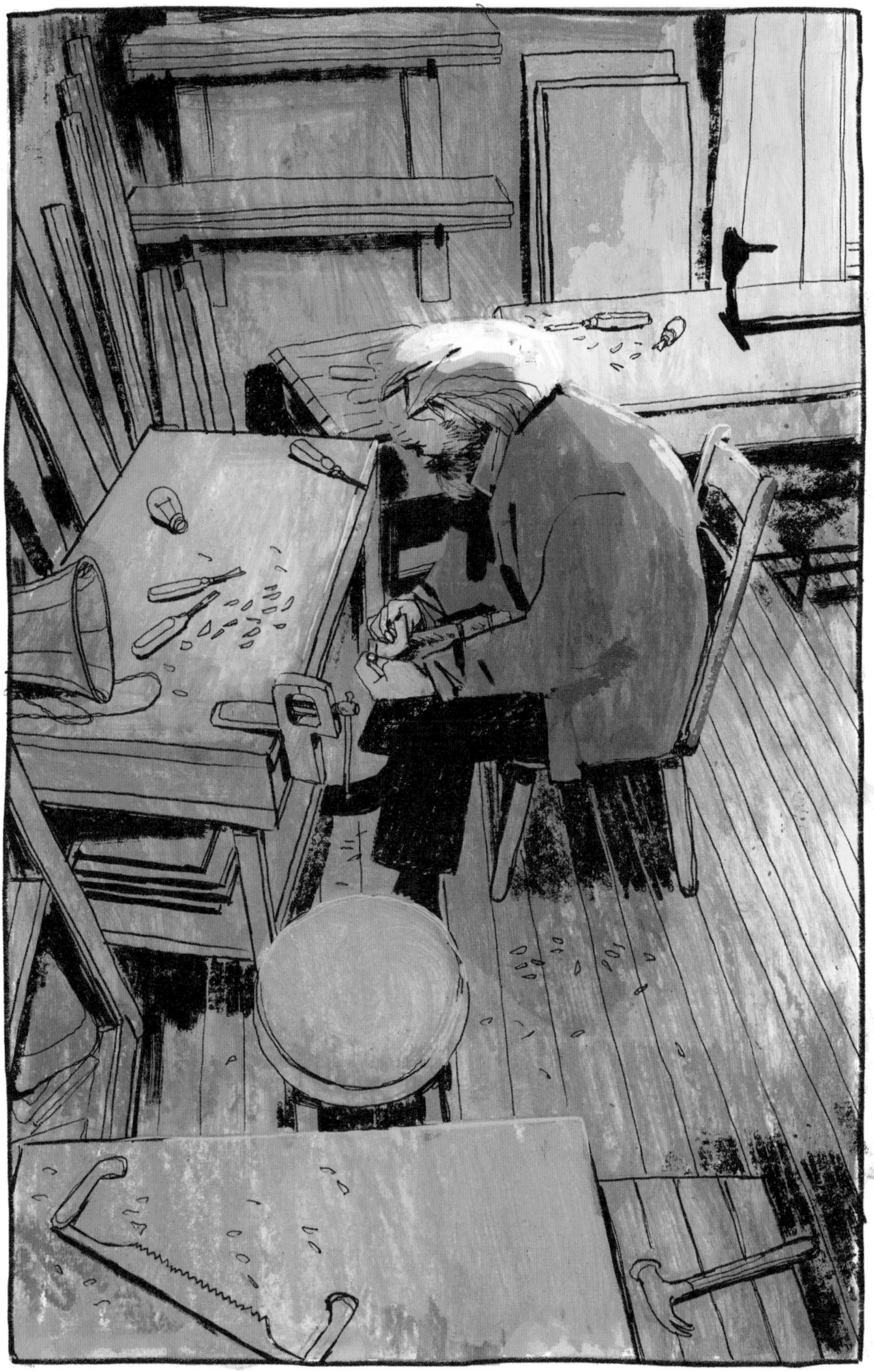

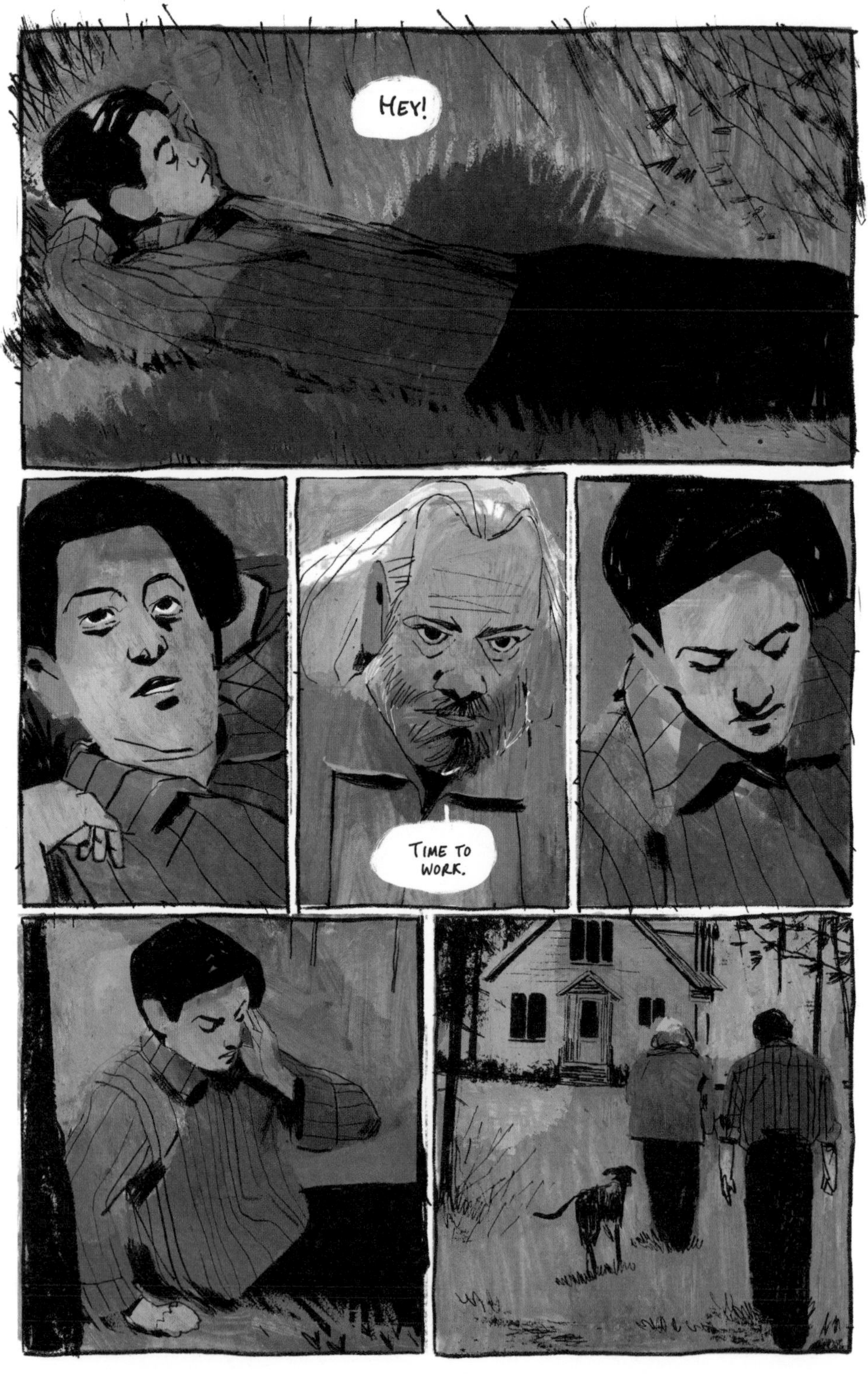
HEY!
TIME TO WORK.

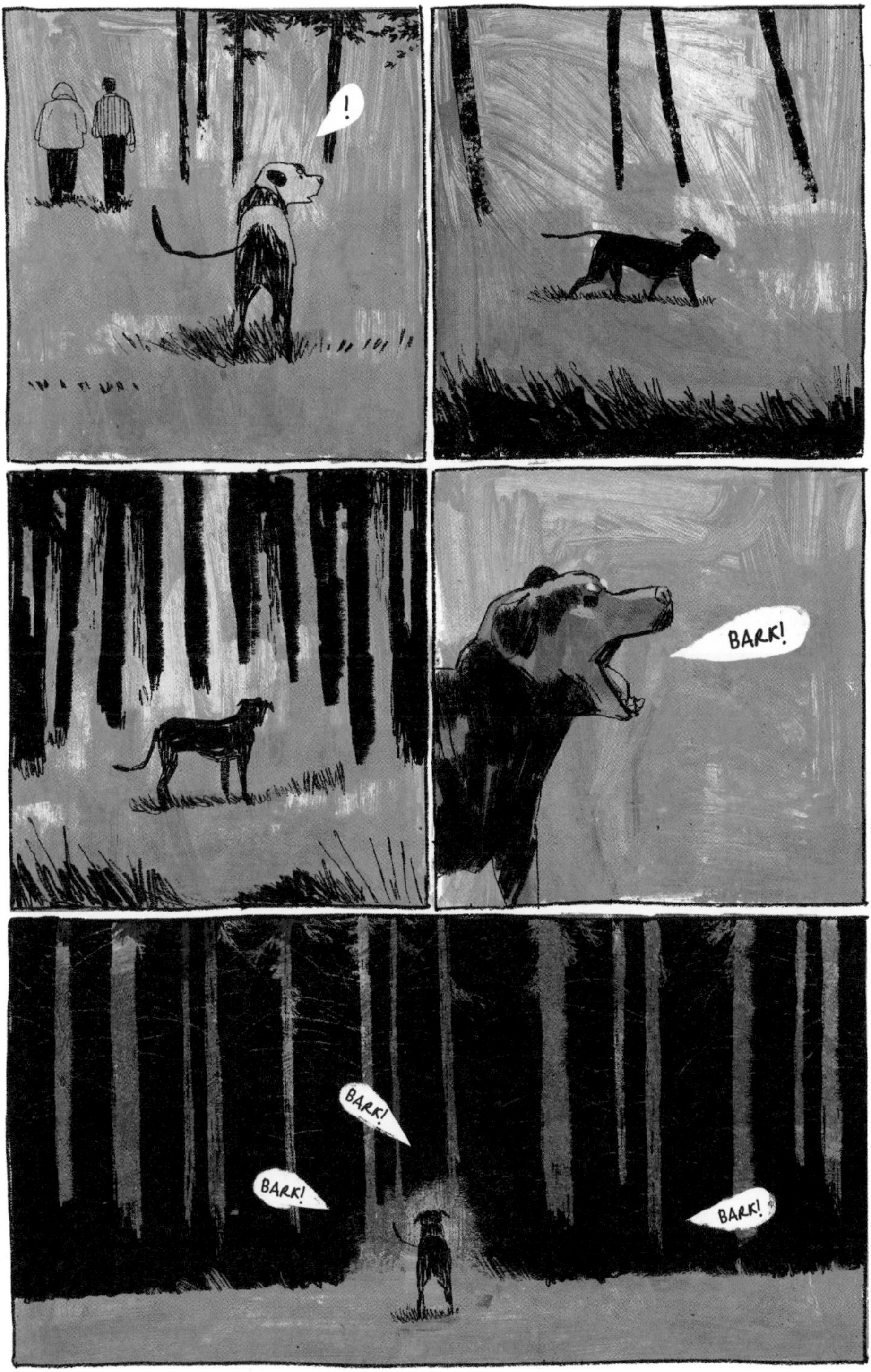
!
BARK!
BARK!
BARK!
BARK!

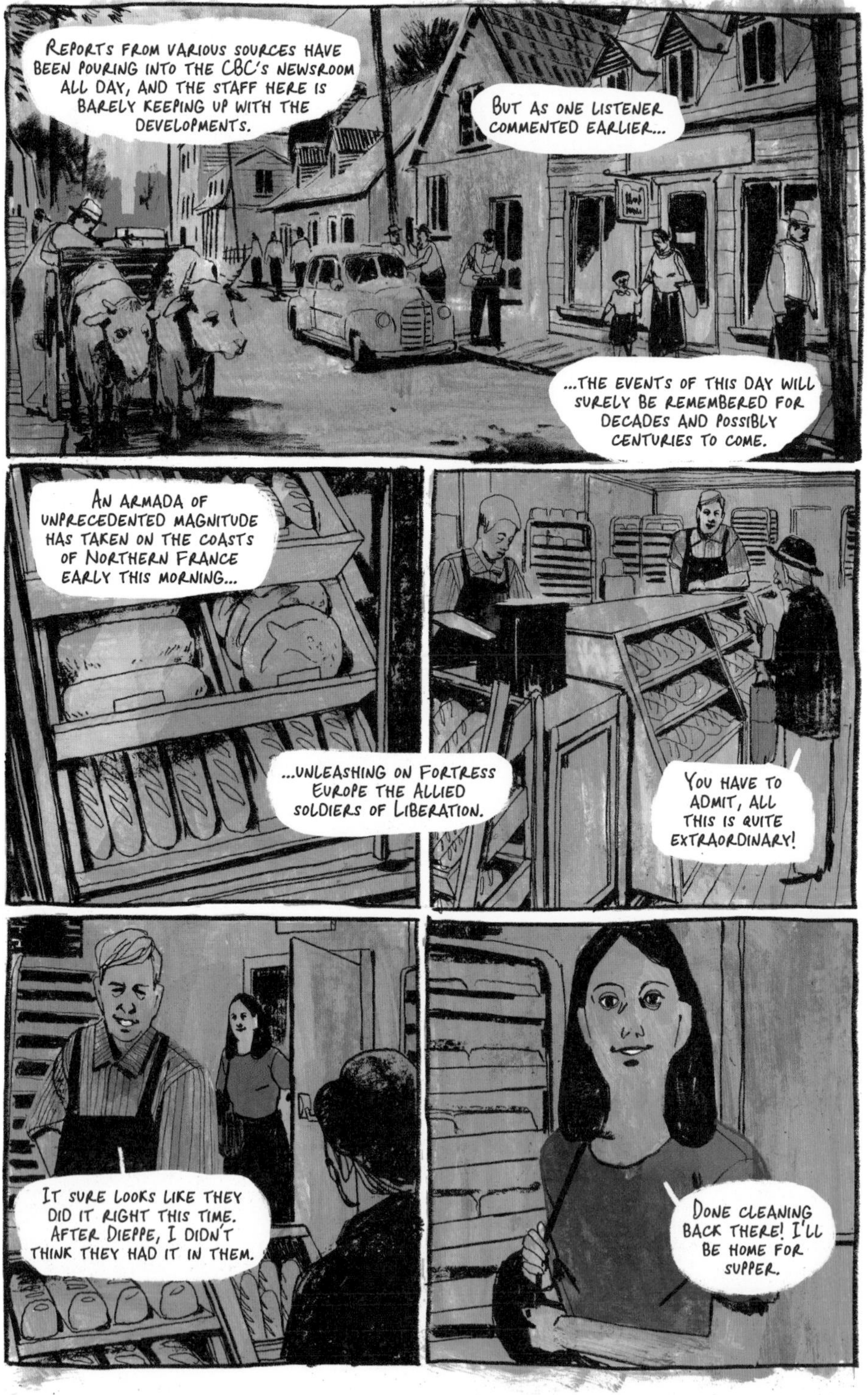
Reports from various sources have been pouring into the CBC's newsroom all day, and the staff here is barely keeping up with the developments.
But as one listener commented earlier...
...the events of this day will surely be remembered for decades and possibly centuries to come.
An armada of unprecedented magnitude has taken on the coasts of Northern France early this morning...
...unleashing on Fortress Europe the Allied soldiers of Liberation.
You have to admit, all this is quite extraordinary!
It sure looks like they did it right this time. After Dieppe, I didn't think they had it in them.
Done cleaning back there! I'll be home for supper.

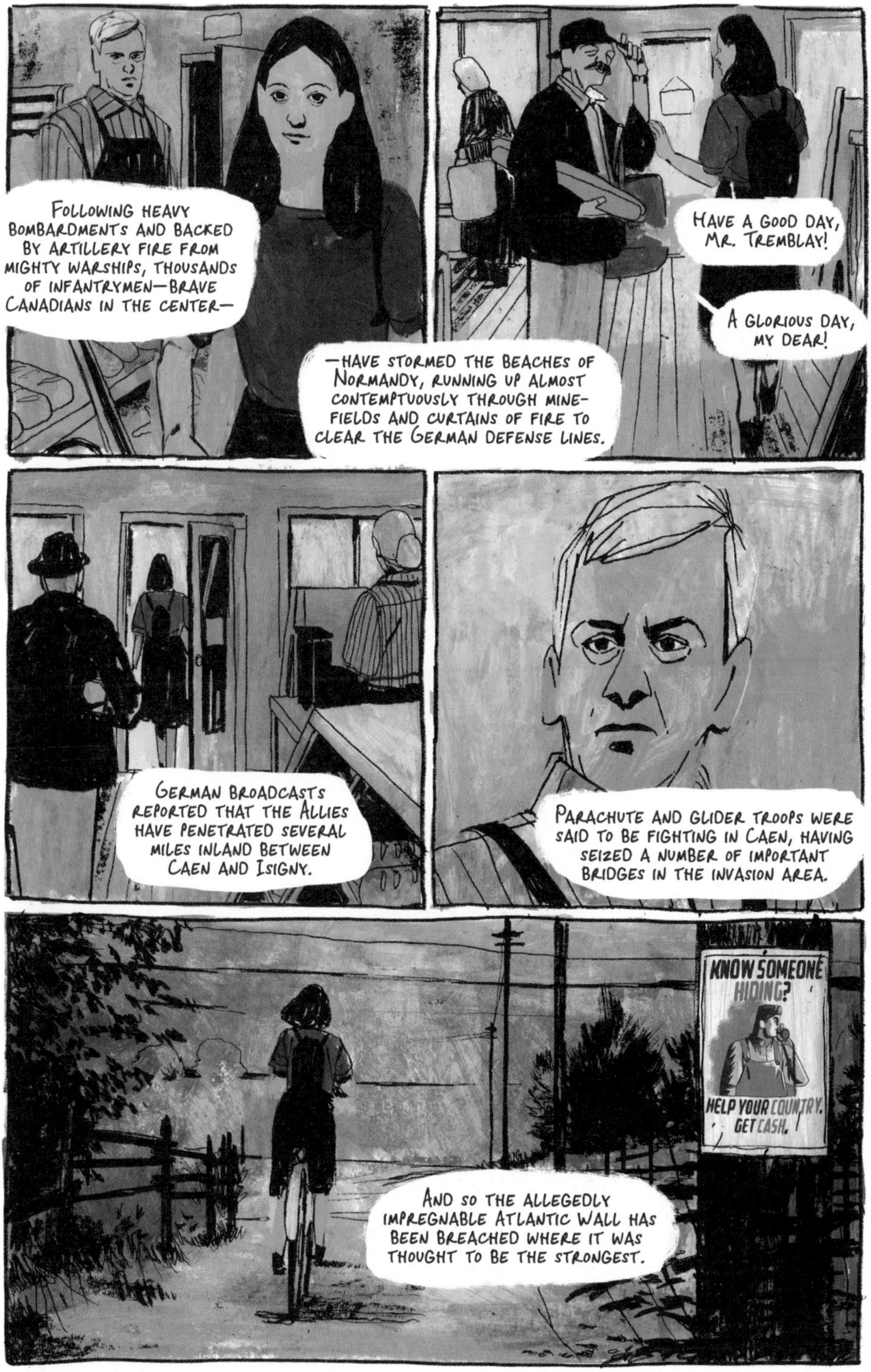
Following heavy bombardments and backed by artillery fire from mighty warships, thousands of infantrymen—brave Canadians in the center—
Have a good day, Mr. Tremblay!
A glorious day, my dear!
—have stormed the beaches of Normandy, running up almost contemptuously through mine-fields and curtains of fire to clear the German defense lines.
German broadcasts reported that the Allies have penetrated several miles inland between Caen and Isigny.
Parachute and glider troops were said to be fighting in Caen, having seized a number of important bridges in the invasion area.
KNOW SOMEONE HIDING?
HELP YOUR COUNTRY. GET CASH.
And so the allegedly impregnable Atlantic Wall has been breached where it was thought to be the strongest.

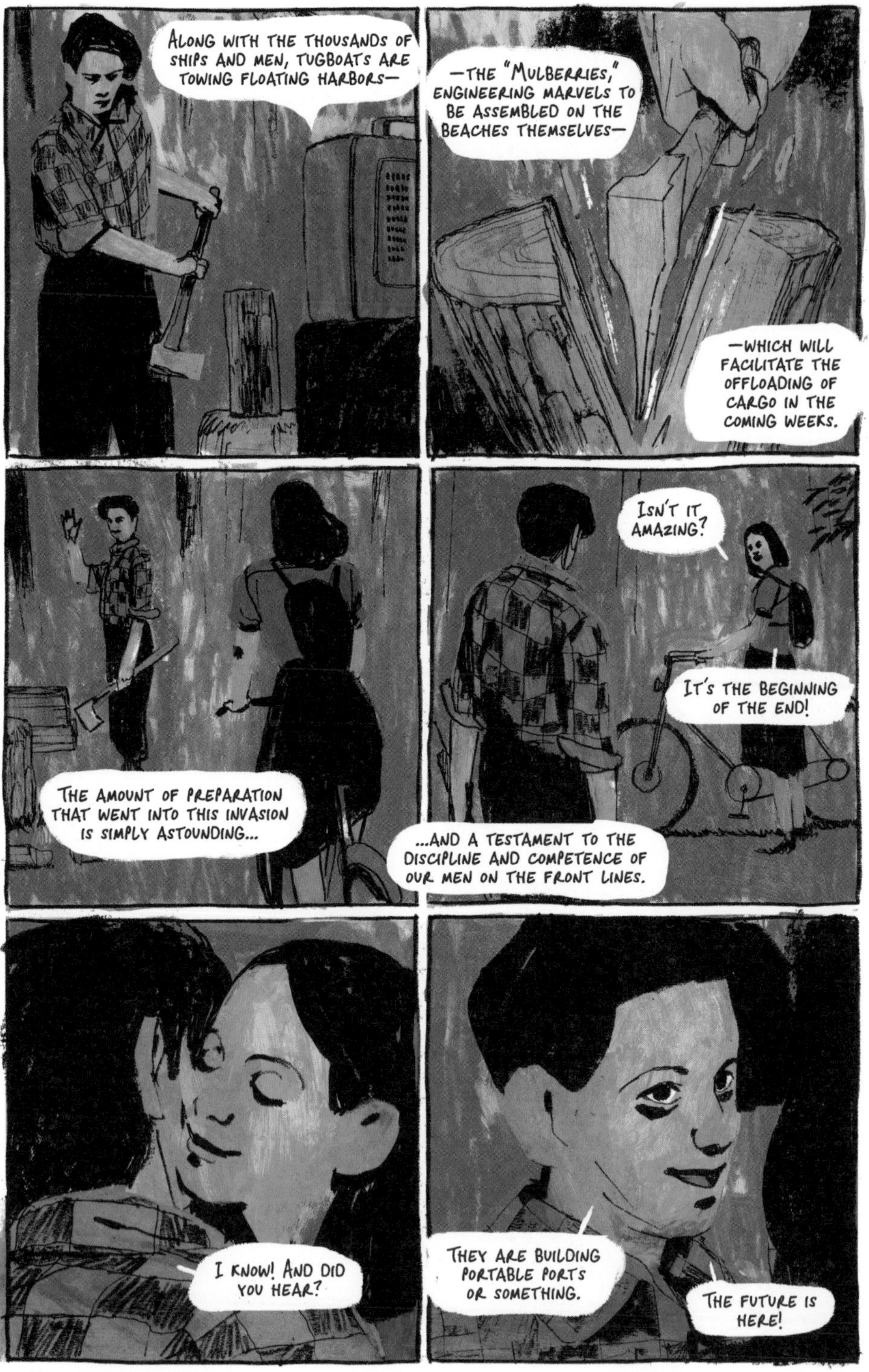
ALONG WITH THE THOUSANDS OF SHIPS AND MEN, TUGBOATS ARE TOWING FLOATING HARBORS—
—THE "MULBERRIES," ENGINEERING MARVELS TO BE ASSEMBLED ON THE BEACHES THEMSELVES—
—WHICH WILL FACILITATE THE OFFLOADING OF CARGO IN THE COMING WEEKS.
THE AMOUNT OF PREPARATION THAT WENT INTO THIS INVASION IS SIMPLY ASTOUNDING...
ISN'T IT AMAZING?
IT'S THE BEGINNING OF THE END!
...AND A TESTAMENT TO THE DISCIPLINE AND COMPETENCE OF OUR MEN ON THE FRONT LINES.
I KNOW! AND DID YOU HEAR?
THEY ARE BUILDING PORTABLE PORTS OR SOMETHING.
THE FUTURE IS HERE!

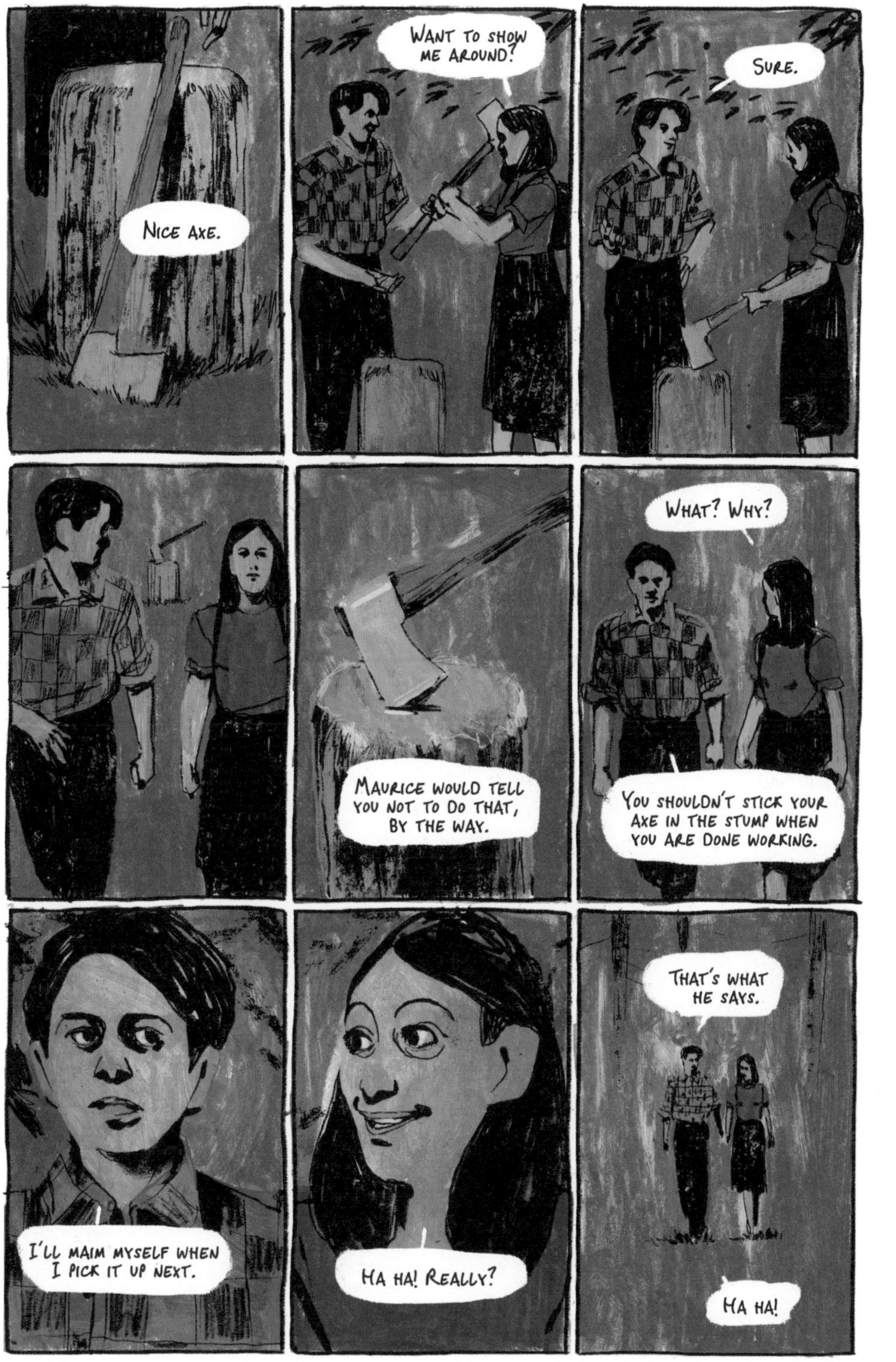
Nice axe.
Want to show me around?
Sure.
Maurice would tell you not to do that, by the way.
What? Why?
You shouldn't stick your axe in the stump when you are done working.
I'll maim myself when I pick it up next.
Ha ha! Really?
That's what he says.
Ha ha!

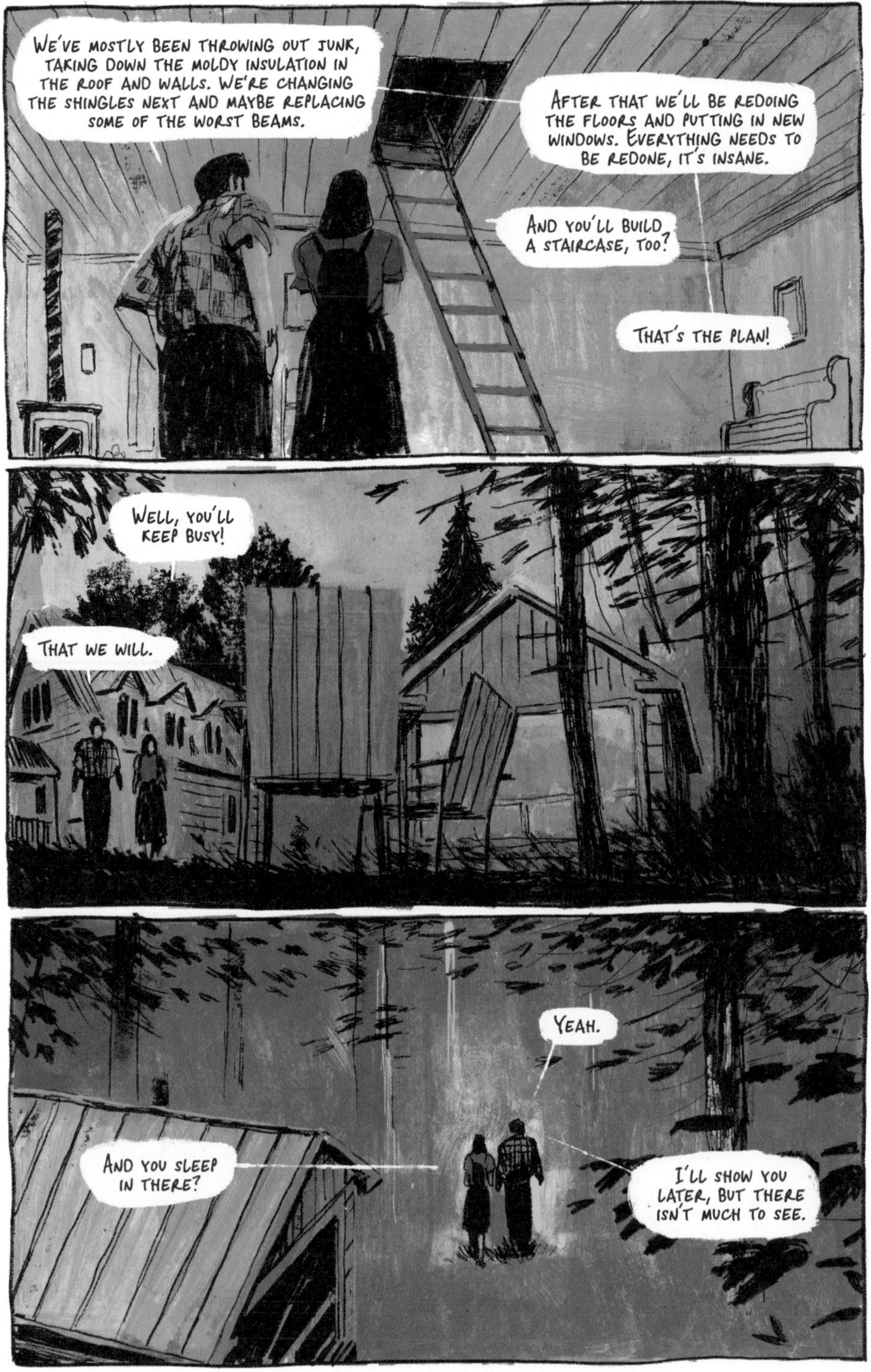
We've mostly been throwing out junk, taking down the moldy insulation in the roof and walls. We're changing the shingles next and maybe replacing some of the worst beams.
After that we'll be redoing the floors and putting in new windows. Everything needs to be redone, it's insane.
And you'll build a staircase, too?
That's the plan!
Well, you'll keep busy!
That we will.
Yeah.
And you sleep in there?
I'll show you later, but there isn't much to see.

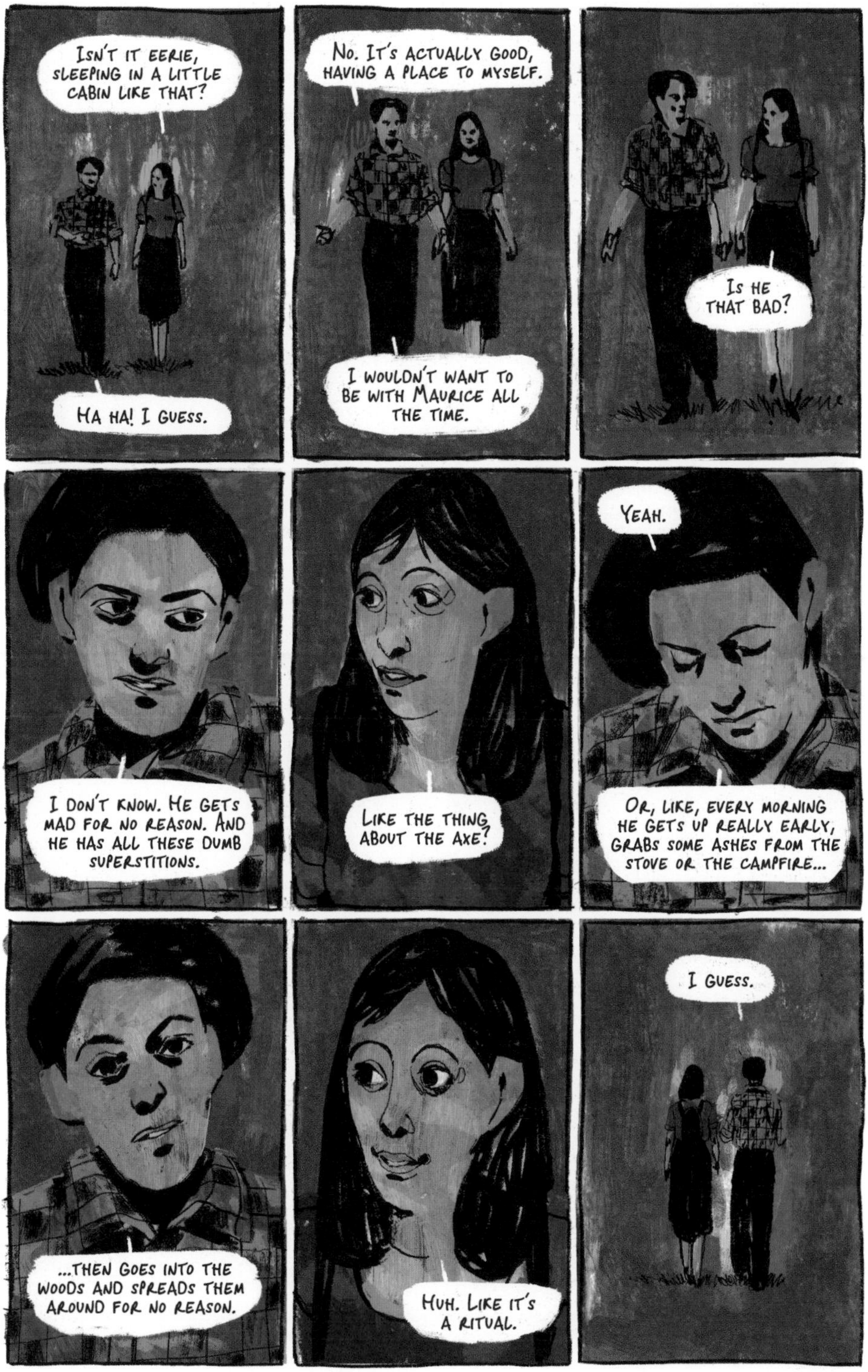
Isn't it eerie, sleeping in a little cabin like that?
Ha ha! I guess.
No. It's actually good, having a place to myself.
I wouldn't want to be with Maurice all the time.
Is he that bad?
I don't know. He gets mad for no reason. And he has all these dumb superstitions.
Like the thing about the axe?
Yeah.
Or, like, every morning he gets up really early, grabs some ashes from the stove or the campfire...
...then goes into the woods and spreads them around for no reason.
Huh. Like it's a ritual.
I guess.

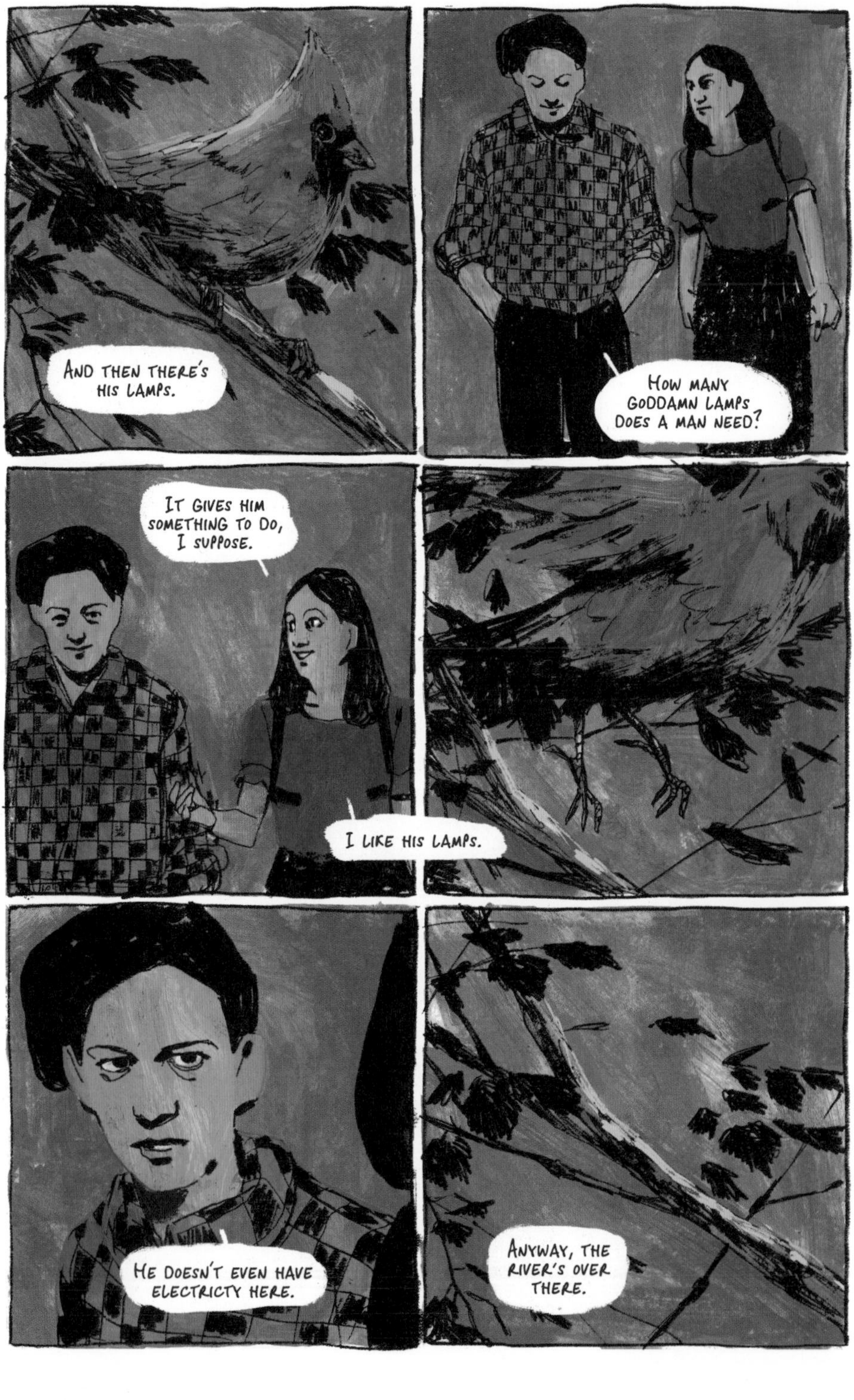
AND THEN THERE'S HIS LAMPS.
HOW MANY GODDAMN LAMPS DOES A MAN NEED?
IT GIVES HIM SOMETHING TO DO, I SUPPOSE.
I LIKE HIS LAMPS.
HE DOESN'T EVEN HAVE ELECTRICTY HERE.
ANYWAY, THE RIVER'S OVER THERE.

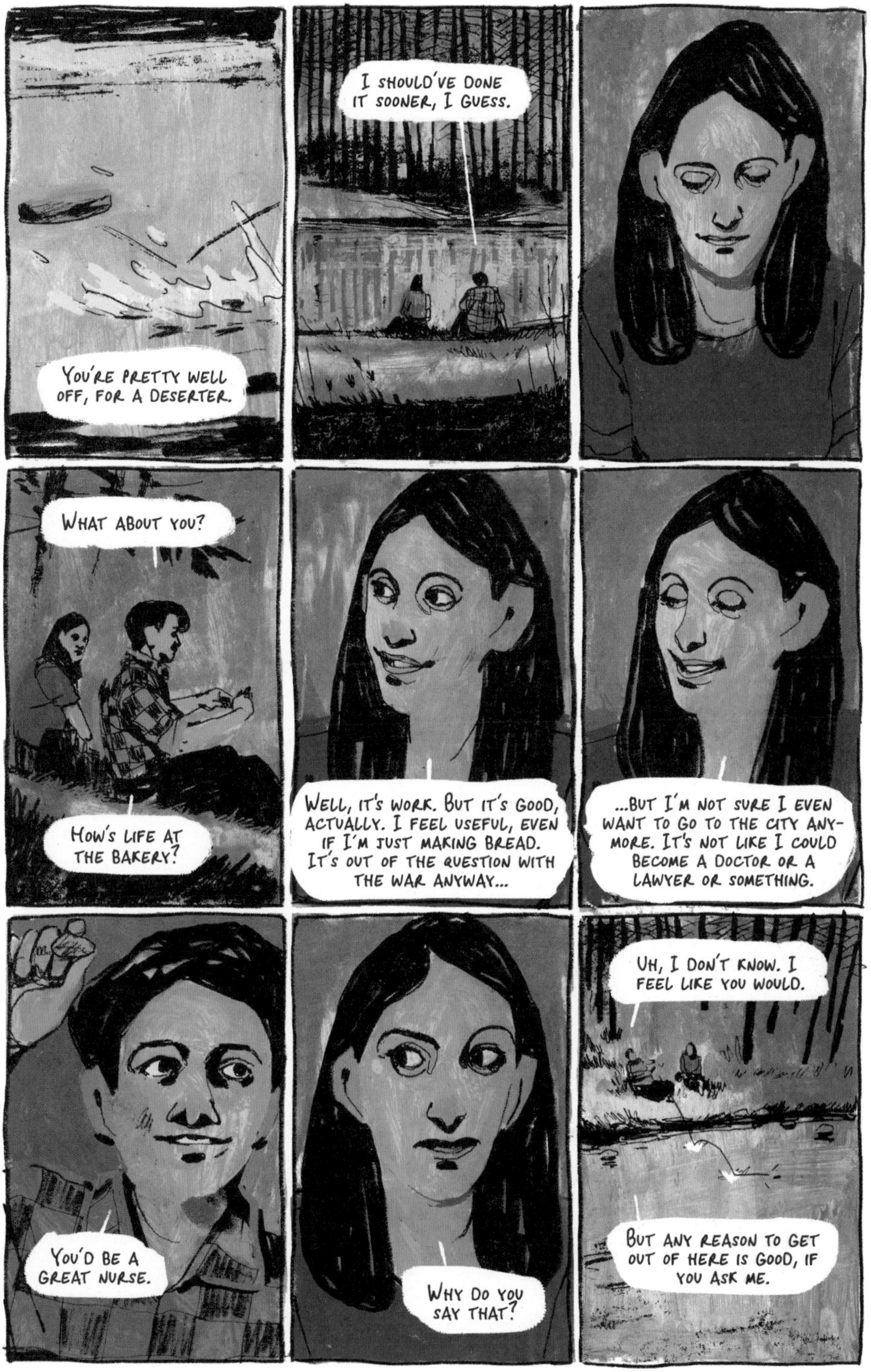

You're pretty well off, for a deserter.
I should've done it sooner, I guess.
What about you?
How's life at the bakery?
Well, it's work. But it's good, actually. I feel useful, even if I'm just making bread. It's out of the question with the war anyway...
...But I'm not sure I even want to go to the city anymore. It's not like I could become a doctor or a lawyer or something.
You'd be a great nurse.
Why do you say that?
Uh, I don't know. I feel like you would.
But any reason to get out of here is good, if you ask me.

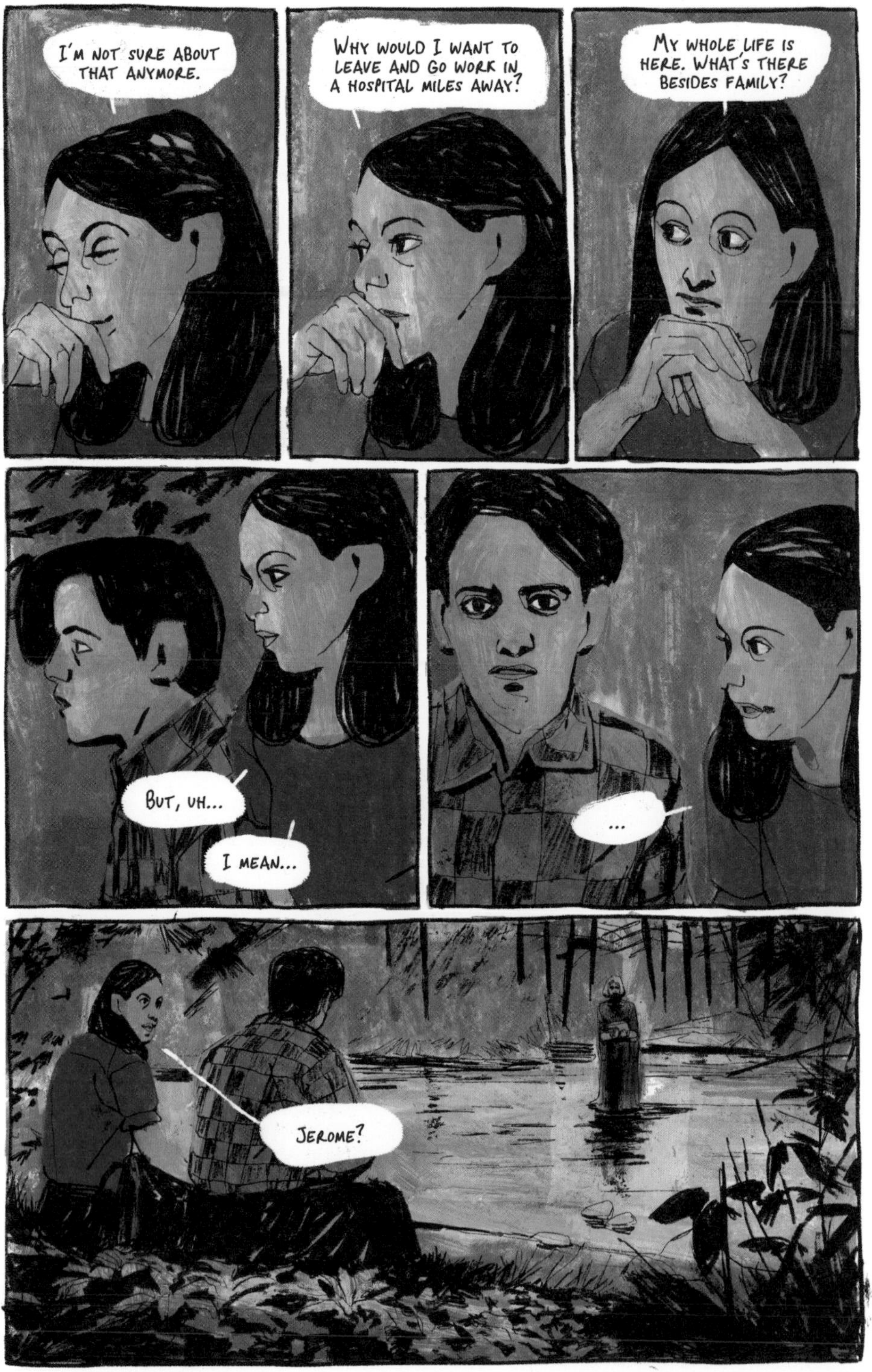
I'M NOT SURE ABOUT THAT ANYMORE.
WHY WOULD I WANT TO LEAVE AND GO WORK IN A HOSPITAL MILES AWAY?
MY WHOLE LIFE IS HERE. WHAT'S THERE BESIDES FAMILY?
BUT, UH...
I MEAN...
...
JEROME?

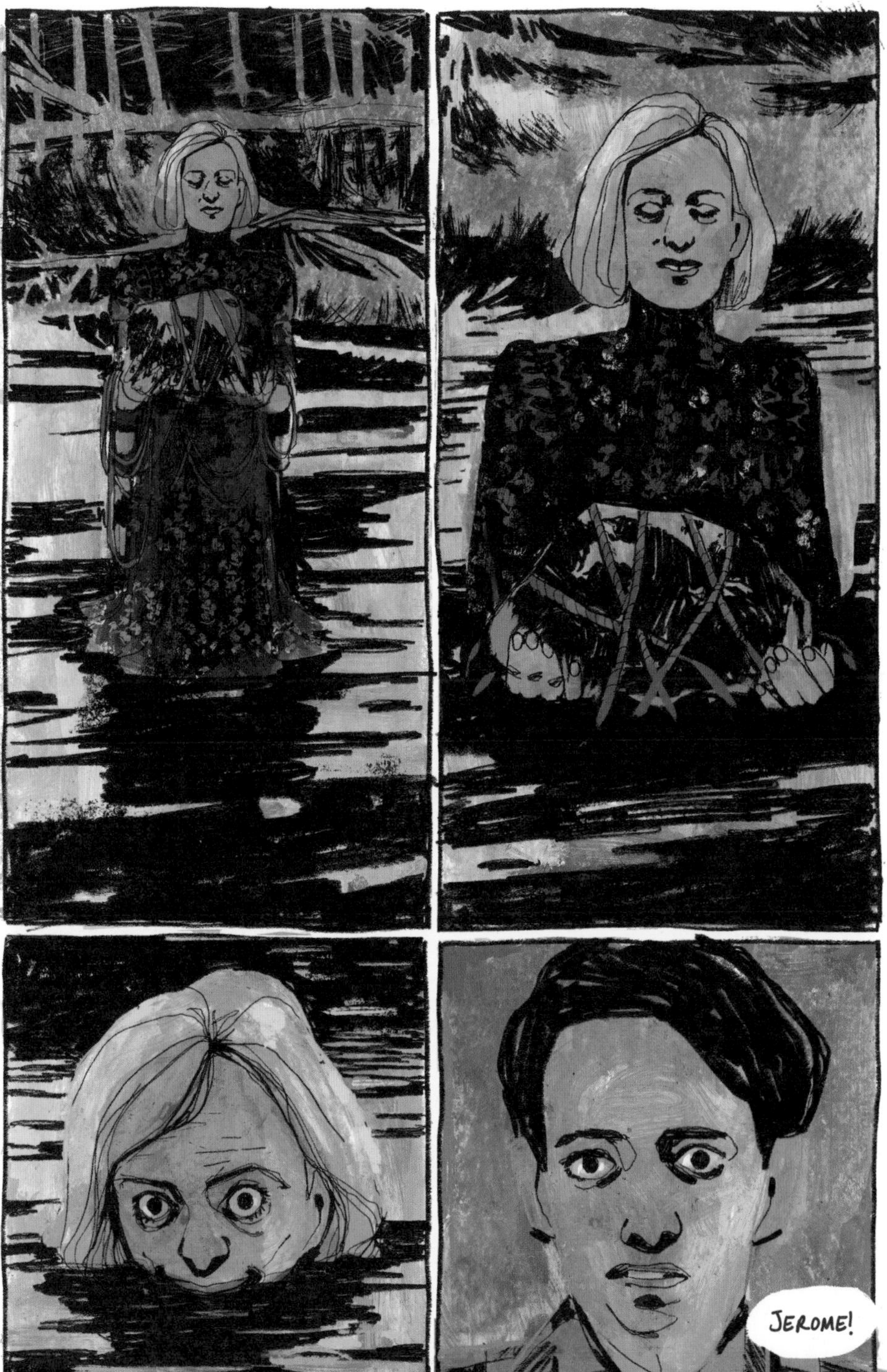
JEROME!

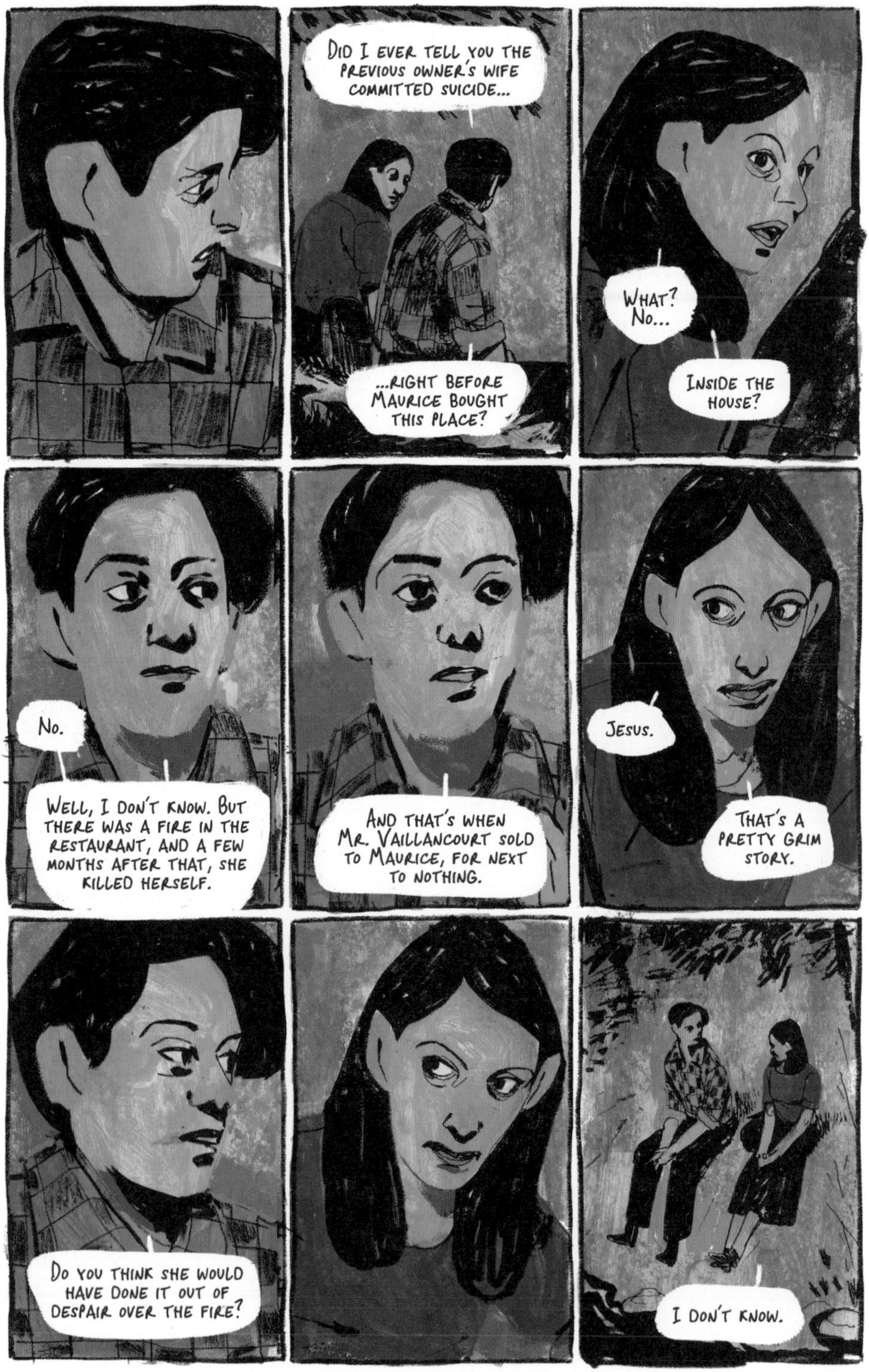
Did I ever tell you the previous owner's wife committed suicide...
...right before Maurice bought this place?
What? No...
Inside the house?
No.
Well, I don't know. But there was a fire in the restaurant, and a few months after that, she killed herself.
And that's when Mr. Vaillancourt sold to Maurice, for next to nothing.
Jesus.
That's a pretty grim story.
Do you think she would have done it out of despair over the fire?
I don't know.

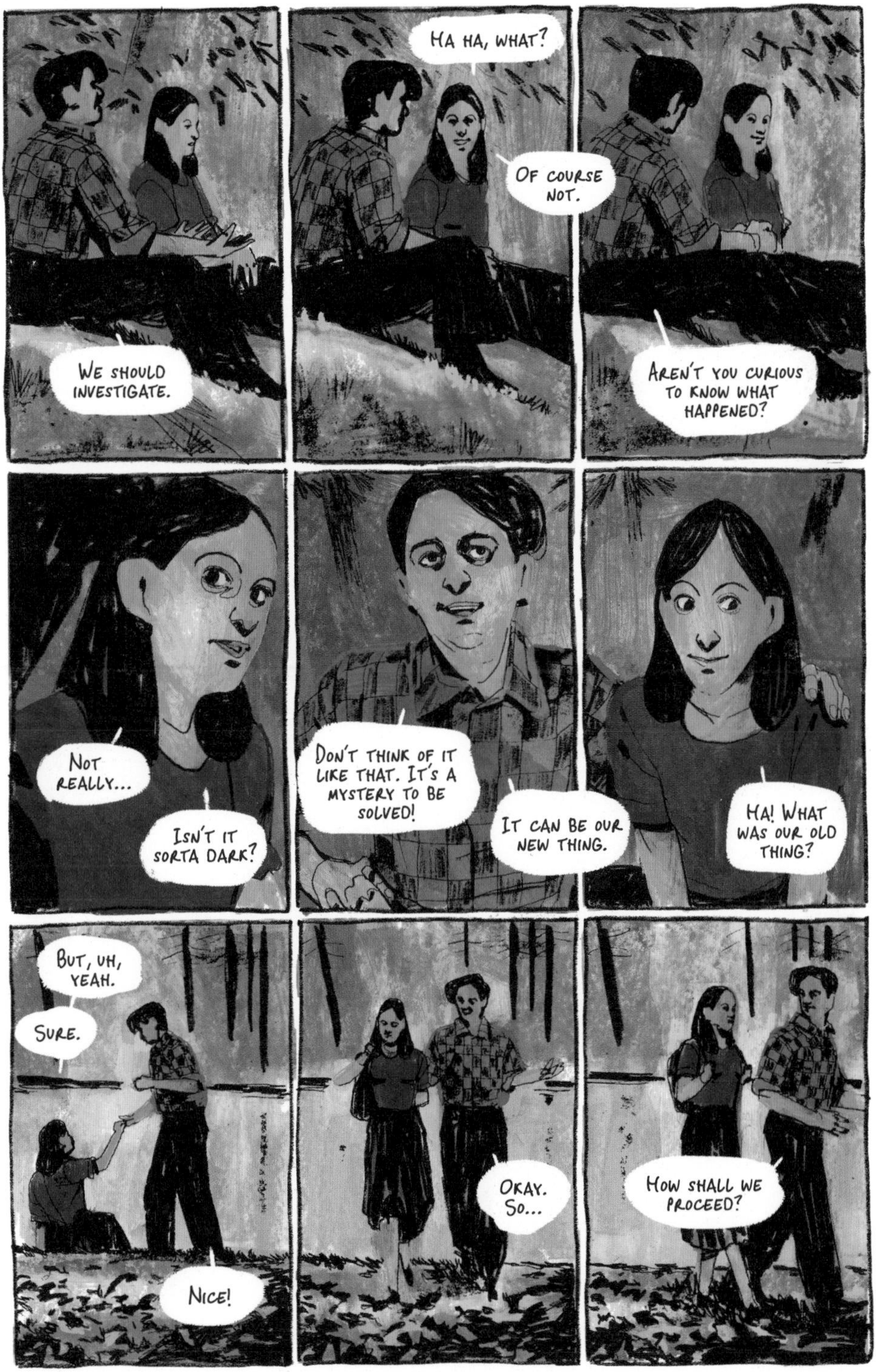
We should investigate.
Ha ha, what?
Of course not.
Aren't you curious to know what happened?
Not really...
Isn't it sorta dark?
Don't think of it like that. It's a mystery to be solved!
It can be our new thing.
Ha! What was our old thing?
But, uh, yeah.
Sure.
Nice!
Okay. So...
How shall we proceed?

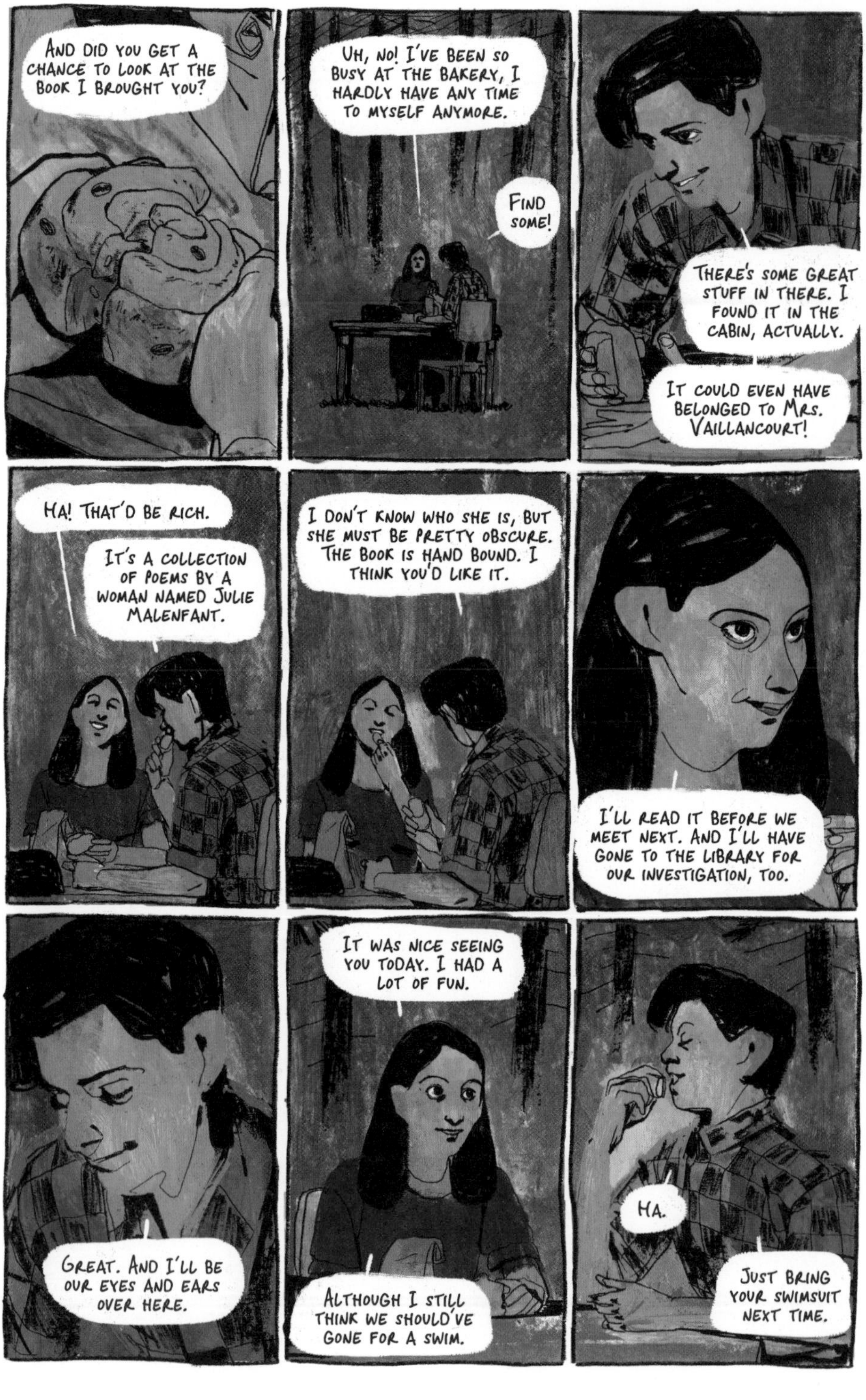
AND DID YOU GET A CHANCE TO LOOK AT THE BOOK I BROUGHT YOU?
UH, NO! I'VE BEEN SO BUSY AT THE BAKERY, I HARDLY HAVE ANY TIME TO MYSELF ANYMORE.
FIND SOME!
THERE'S SOME GREAT STUFF IN THERE. I FOUND IT IN THE CABIN, ACTUALLY.
IT COULD EVEN HAVE BELONGED TO MRS. VAILLANCOURT!
HA! THAT'D BE RICH.
IT'S A COLLECTION OF POEMS BY A WOMAN NAMED JULIE MALENFANT.
I DON'T KNOW WHO SHE IS, BUT SHE MUST BE PRETTY OBSCURE. THE BOOK IS HAND BOUND. I THINK YOU'D LIKE IT.
I'LL READ IT BEFORE WE MEET NEXT. AND I'LL HAVE GONE TO THE LIBRARY FOR OUR INVESTIGATION, TOO.
GREAT. AND I'LL BE OUR EYES AND EARS OVER HERE.
IT WAS NICE SEEING YOU TODAY. I HAD A LOT OF FUN.
ALTHOUGH I STILL THINK WE SHOULD'VE GONE FOR A SWIM.
HA.
JUST BRING YOUR SWIMSUIT NEXT TIME.

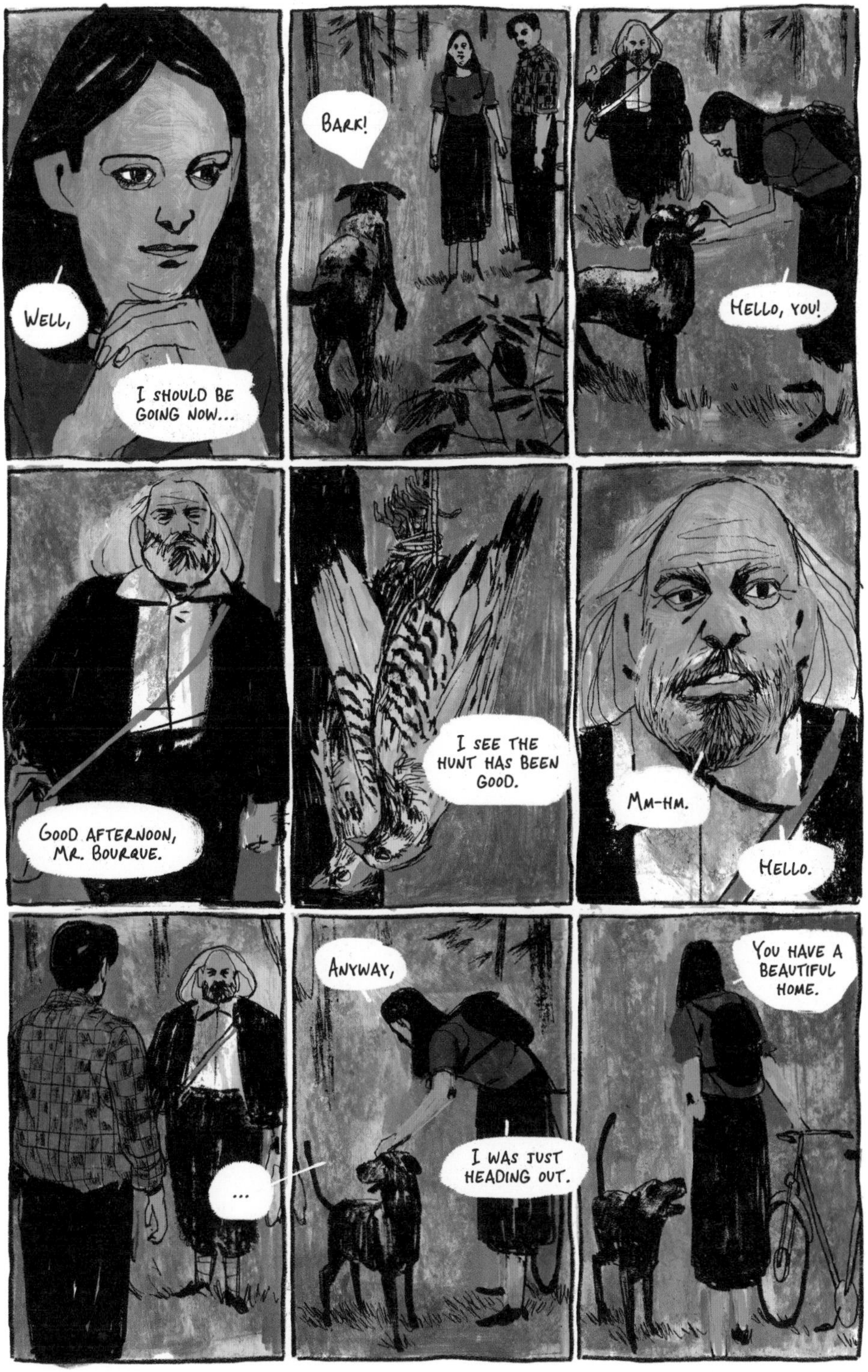
Well,
I should be going now...
Bark!
Hello, you!
Good afternoon, Mr. Bourque.
I see the hunt has been good.
Mm-hm.
Hello.
...
Anyway,
I was just heading out.
You have a beautiful home.

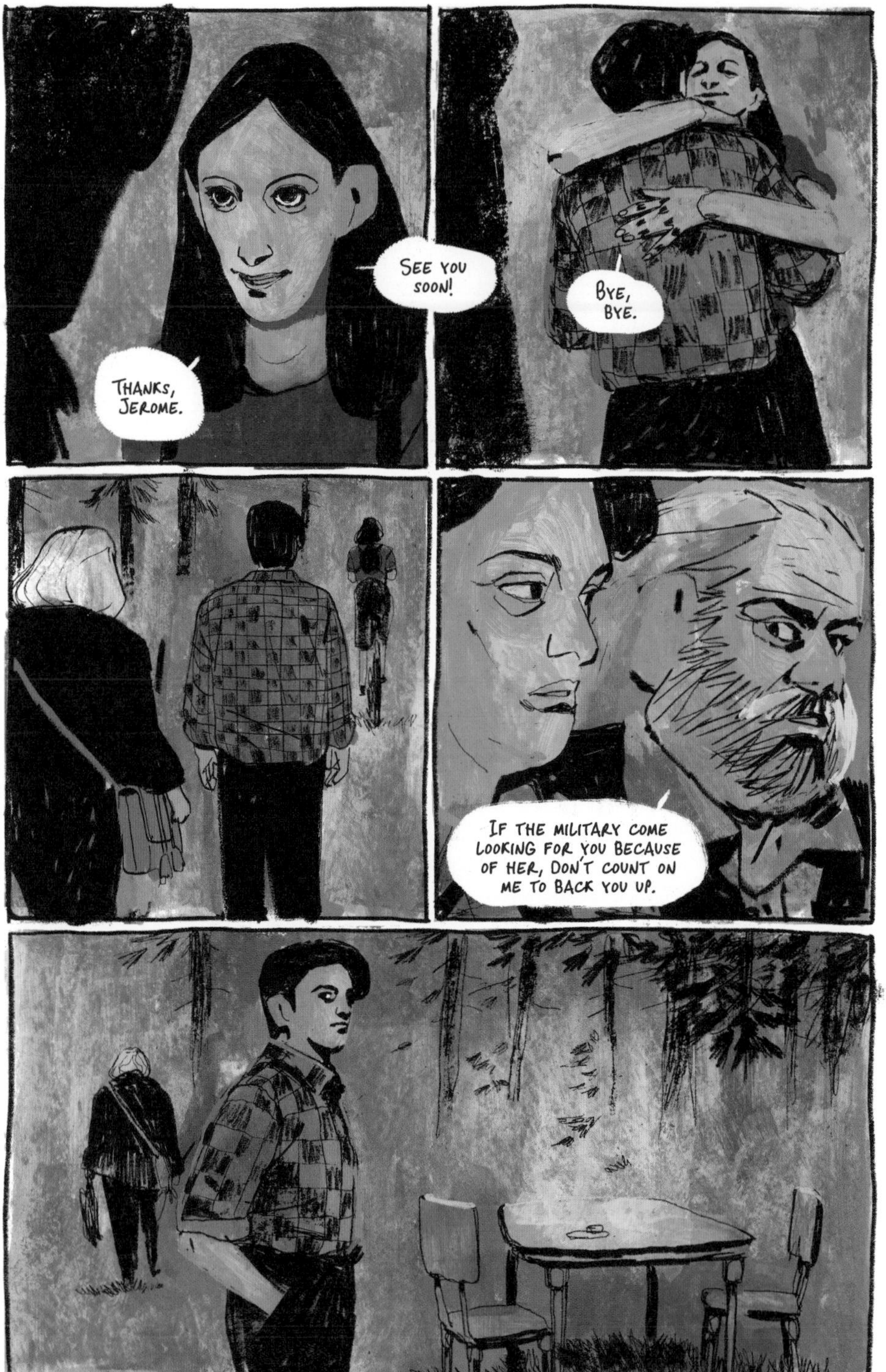
See you soon!
Thanks, Jerome.
Bye, bye.
If the military come looking for you because of her, don't count on me to back you up.

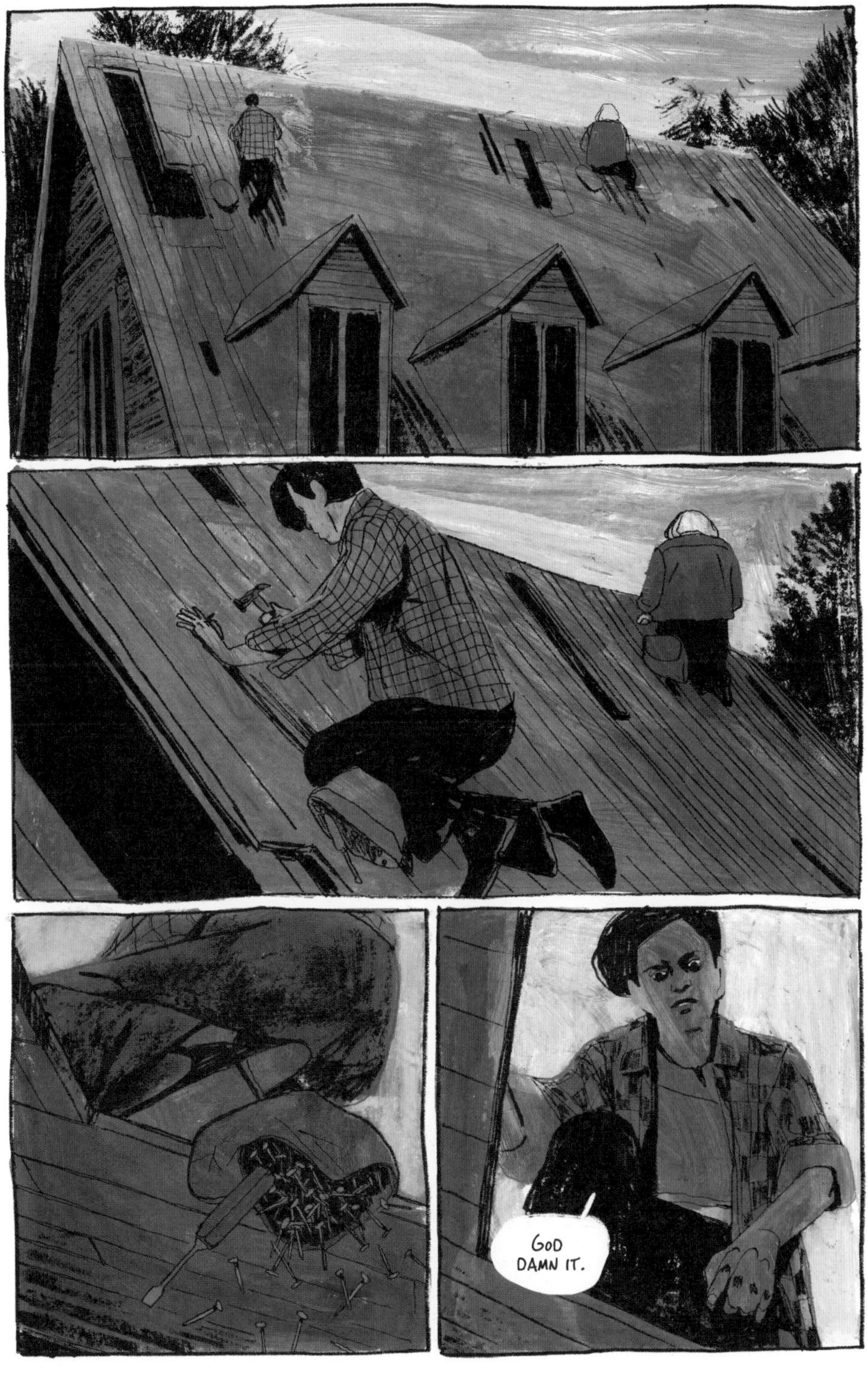
GOD
DAMN IT.

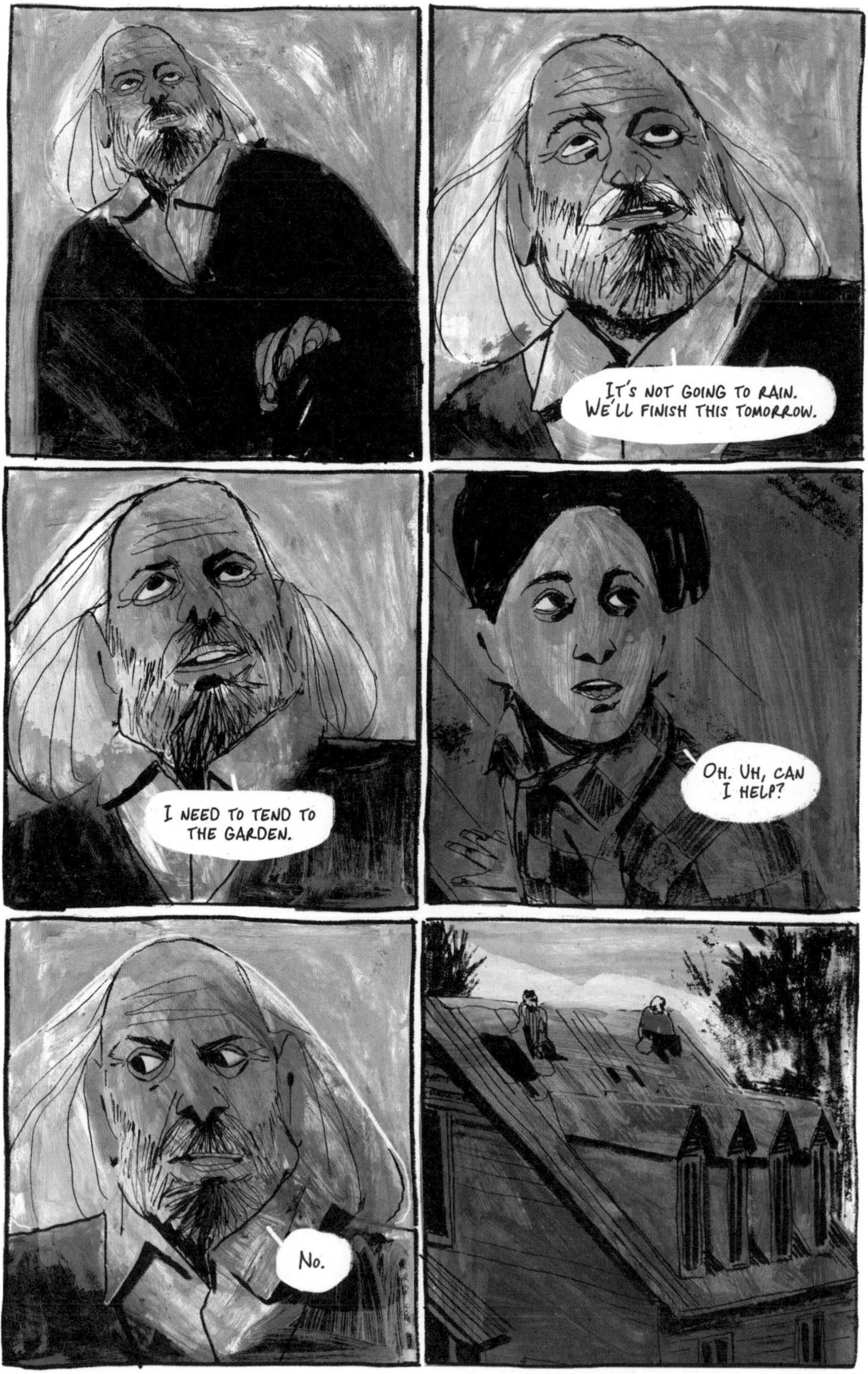
It's not going to rain. We'll finish this tomorrow.
I need to tend to the garden.
Oh. Uh, can I help?
No.

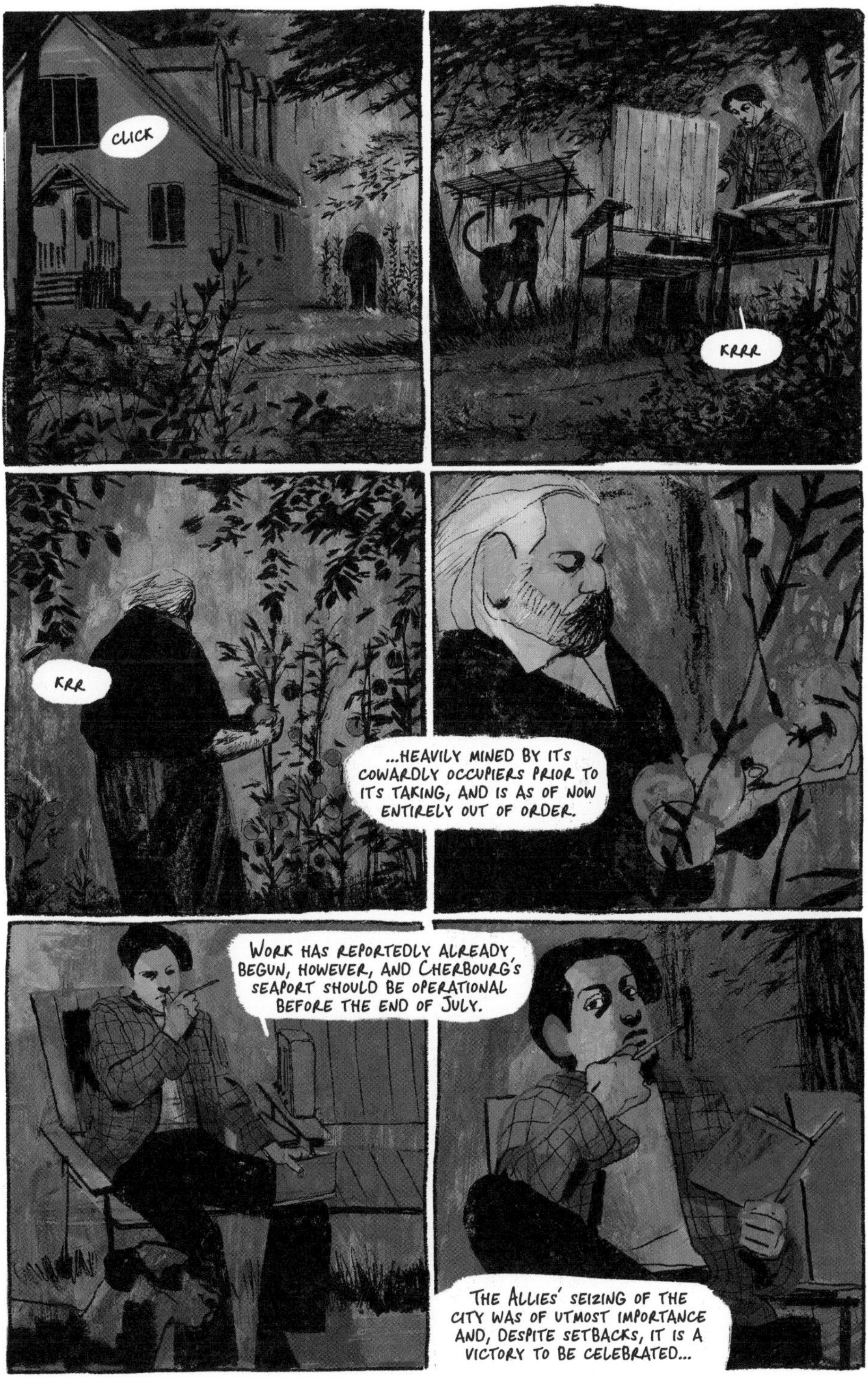
CLICK
KRRR
KRR
...HEAVILY MINED BY ITS COWARDLY OCCUPIERS PRIOR TO ITS TAKING, AND IS AS OF NOW ENTIRELY OUT OF ORDER.
WORK HAS REPORTEDLY ALREADY BEGUN, HOWEVER, AND CHERBOURG'S SEAPORT SHOULD BE OPERATIONAL BEFORE THE END OF JULY.
THE ALLIES' SEIZING OF THE CITY WAS OF UTMOST IMPORTANCE AND, DESPITE SETBACKS, IT IS A VICTORY TO BE CELEBRATED...

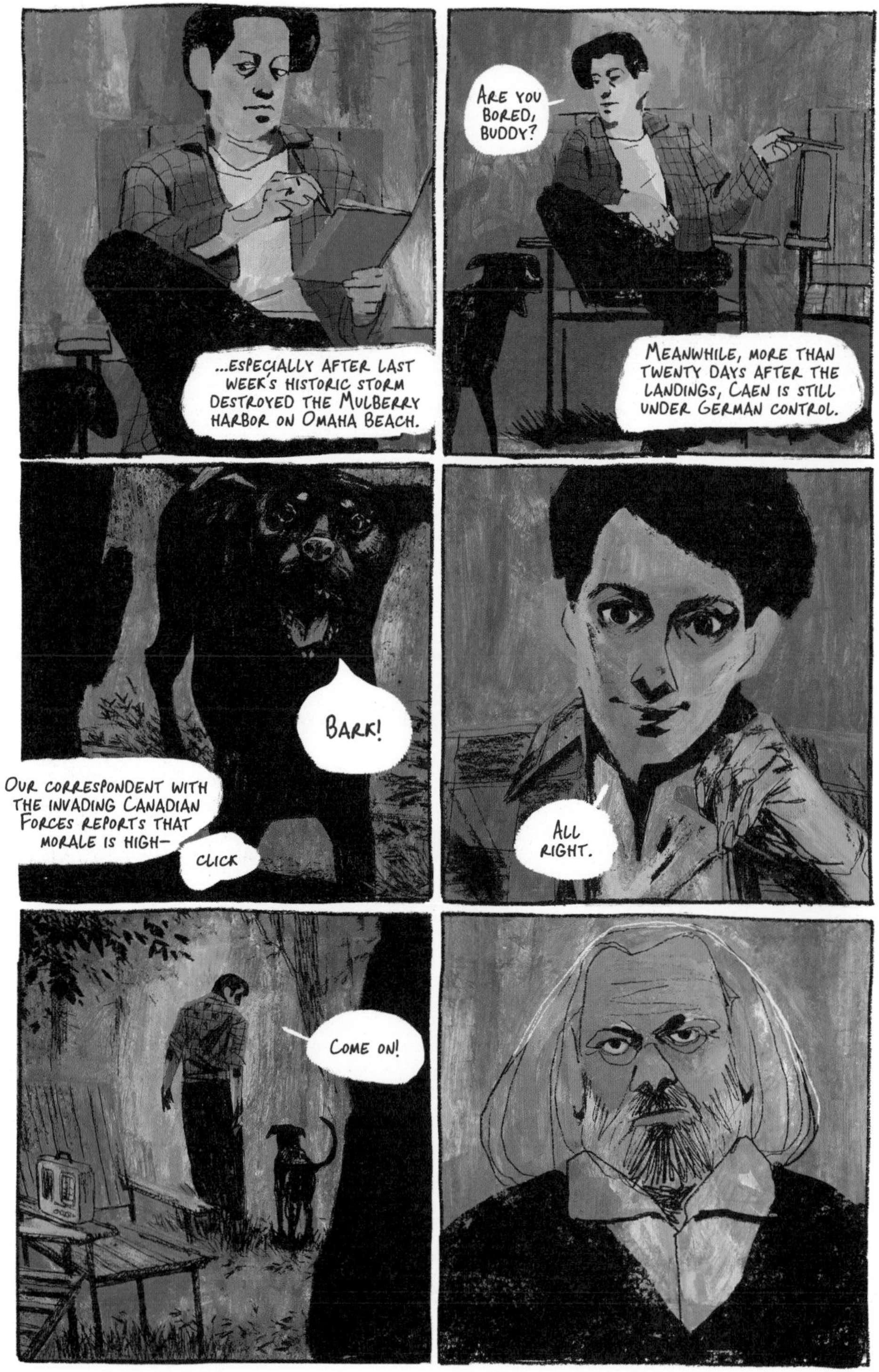
...ESPECIALLY AFTER LAST WEEK'S HISTORIC STORM DESTROYED THE MULBERRY HARBOR ON OMAHA BEACH.
ARE YOU BORED, BUDDY?
MEANWHILE, MORE THAN TWENTY DAYS AFTER THE LANDINGS, CAEN IS STILL UNDER GERMAN CONTROL.
BARK!
OUR CORRESPONDENT WITH THE INVADING CANADIAN FORCES REPORTS THAT MORALE IS HIGH—
CLICK
ALL RIGHT.
COME ON!

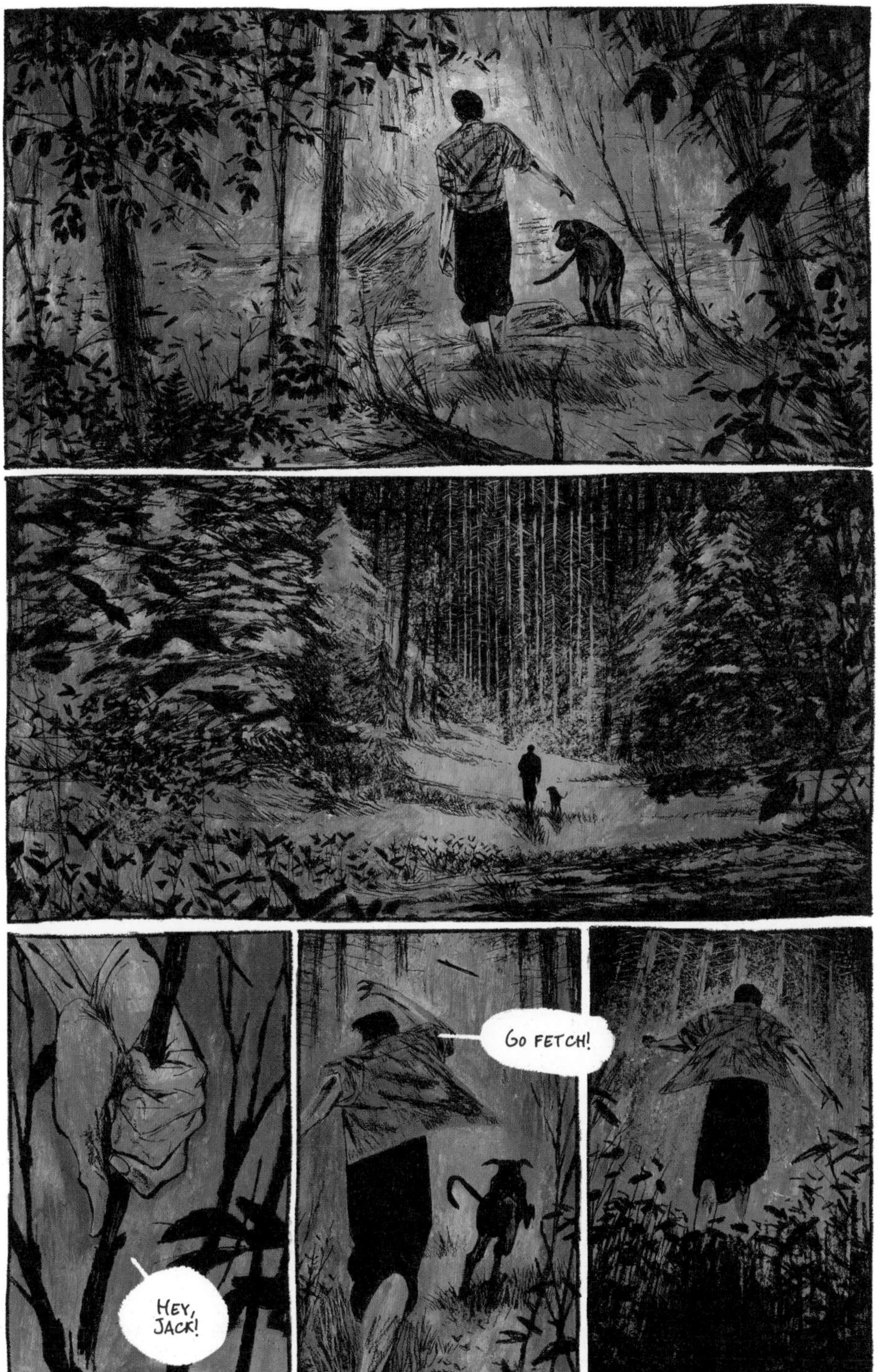
Hey, Jack!
Go fetch!

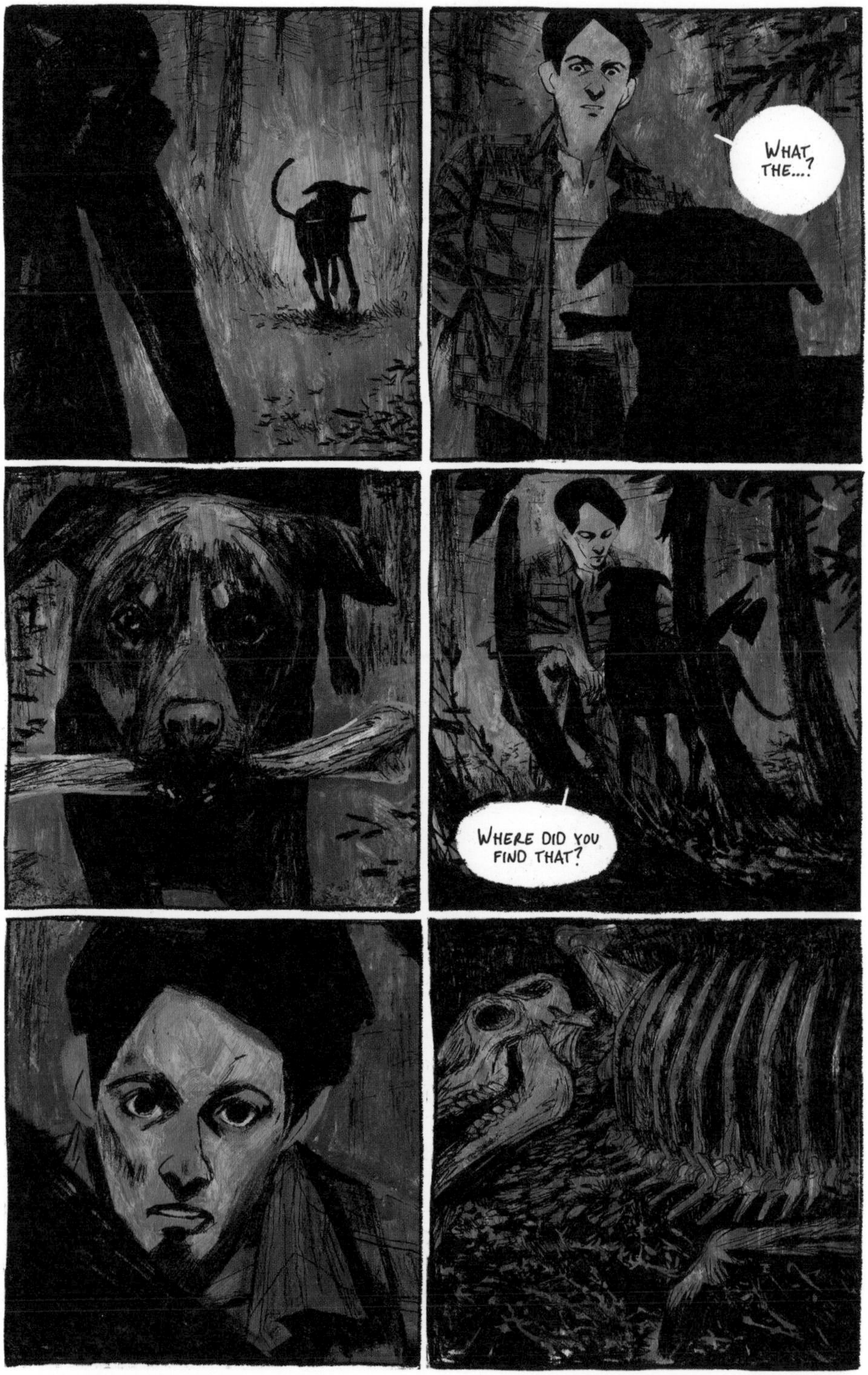
WHAT THE...?
WHERE DID YOU FIND THAT?

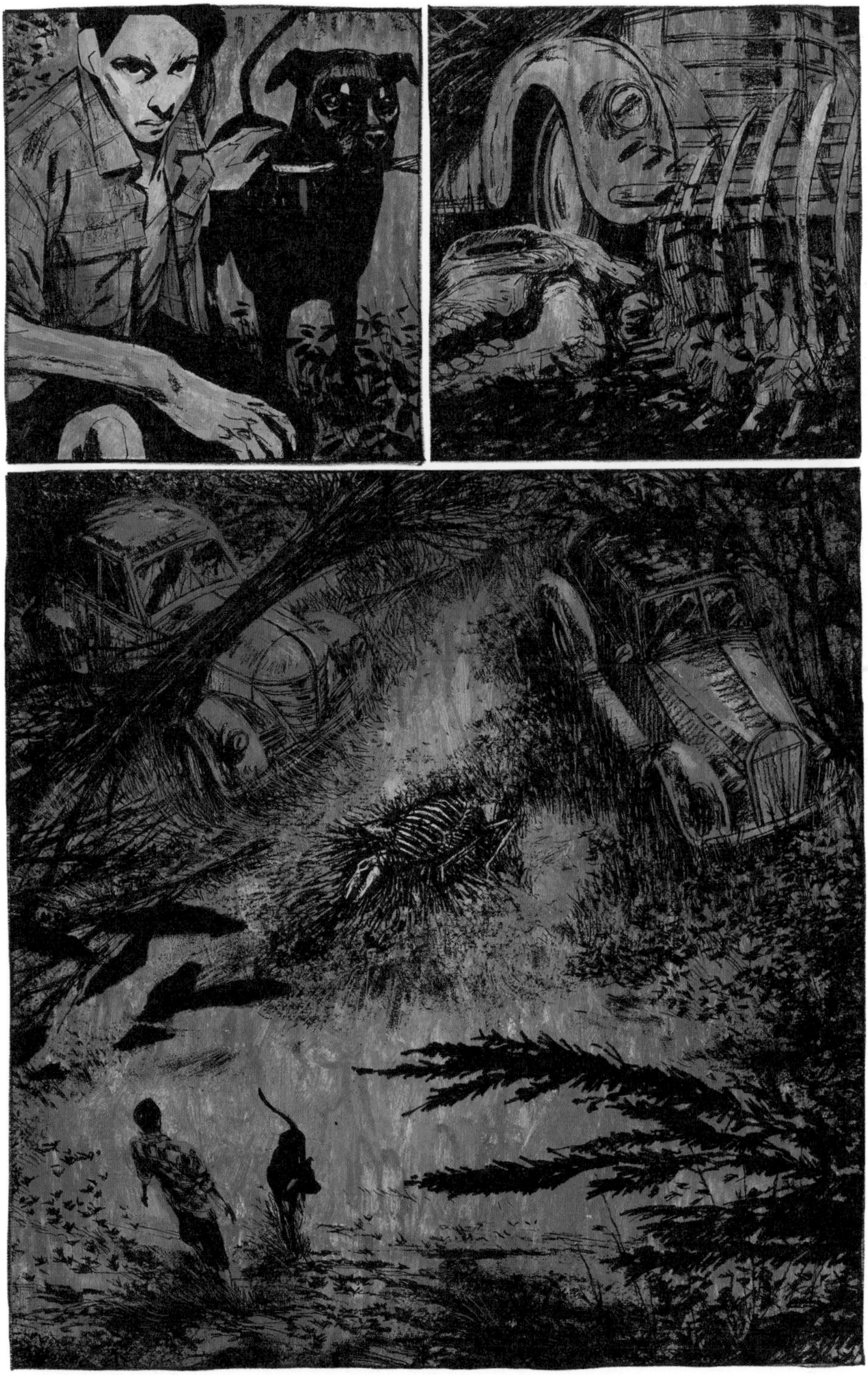

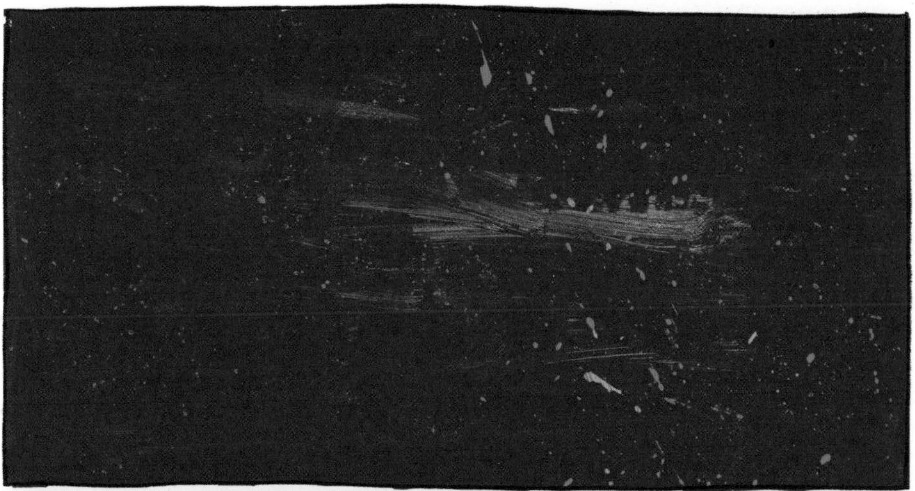
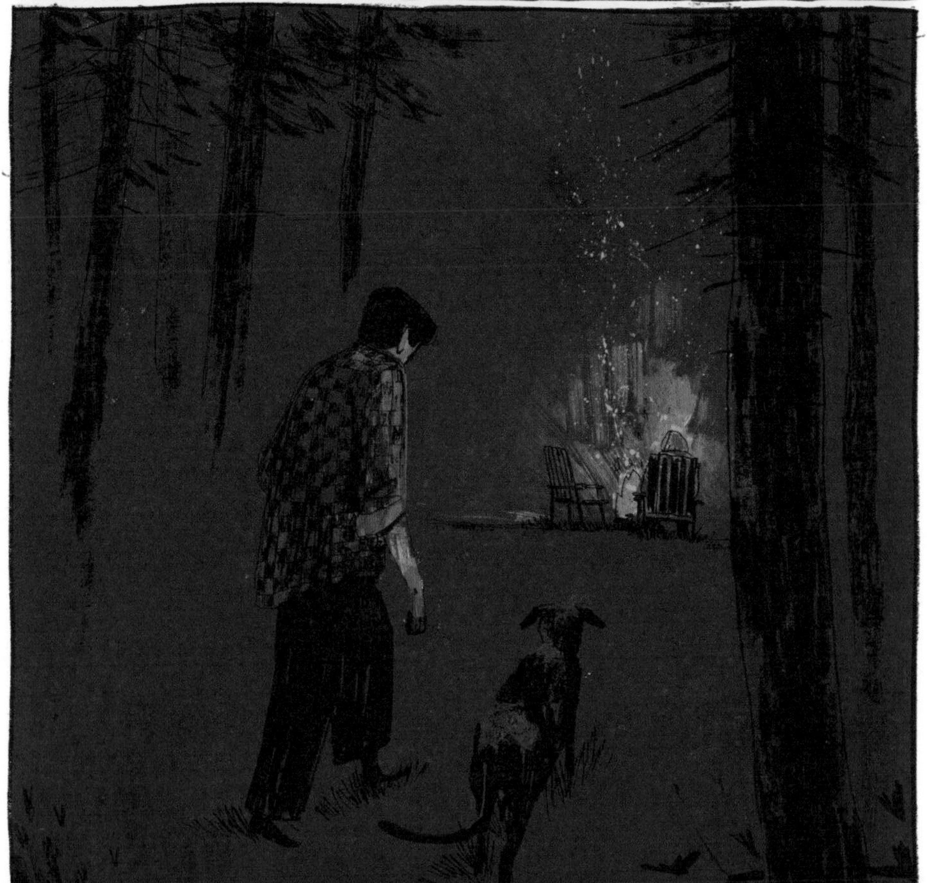

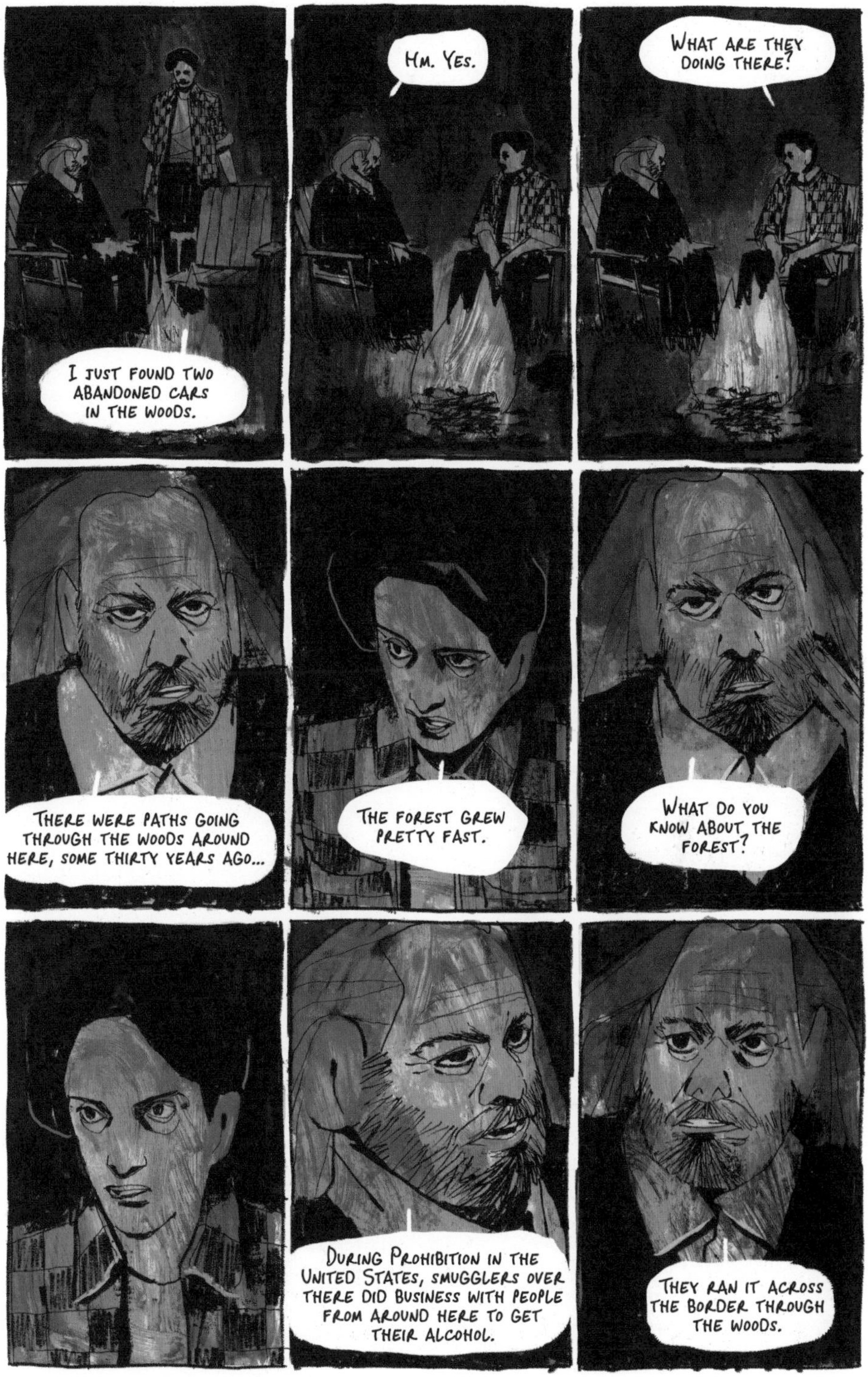
I JUST FOUND TWO ABANDONED CARS IN THE WOODS.
HM. YES.
WHAT ARE THEY DOING THERE?
THERE WERE PATHS GOING THROUGH THE WOODS AROUND HERE, SOME THIRTY YEARS AGO...
THE FOREST GREW PRETTY FAST.
WHAT DO YOU KNOW ABOUT THE FOREST?
DURING PROHIBITION IN THE UNITED STATES, SMUGGLERS OVER THERE DID BUSINESS WITH PEOPLE FROM AROUND HERE TO GET THEIR ALCOHOL.
THEY RAN IT ACROSS THE BORDER THROUGH THE WOODS.

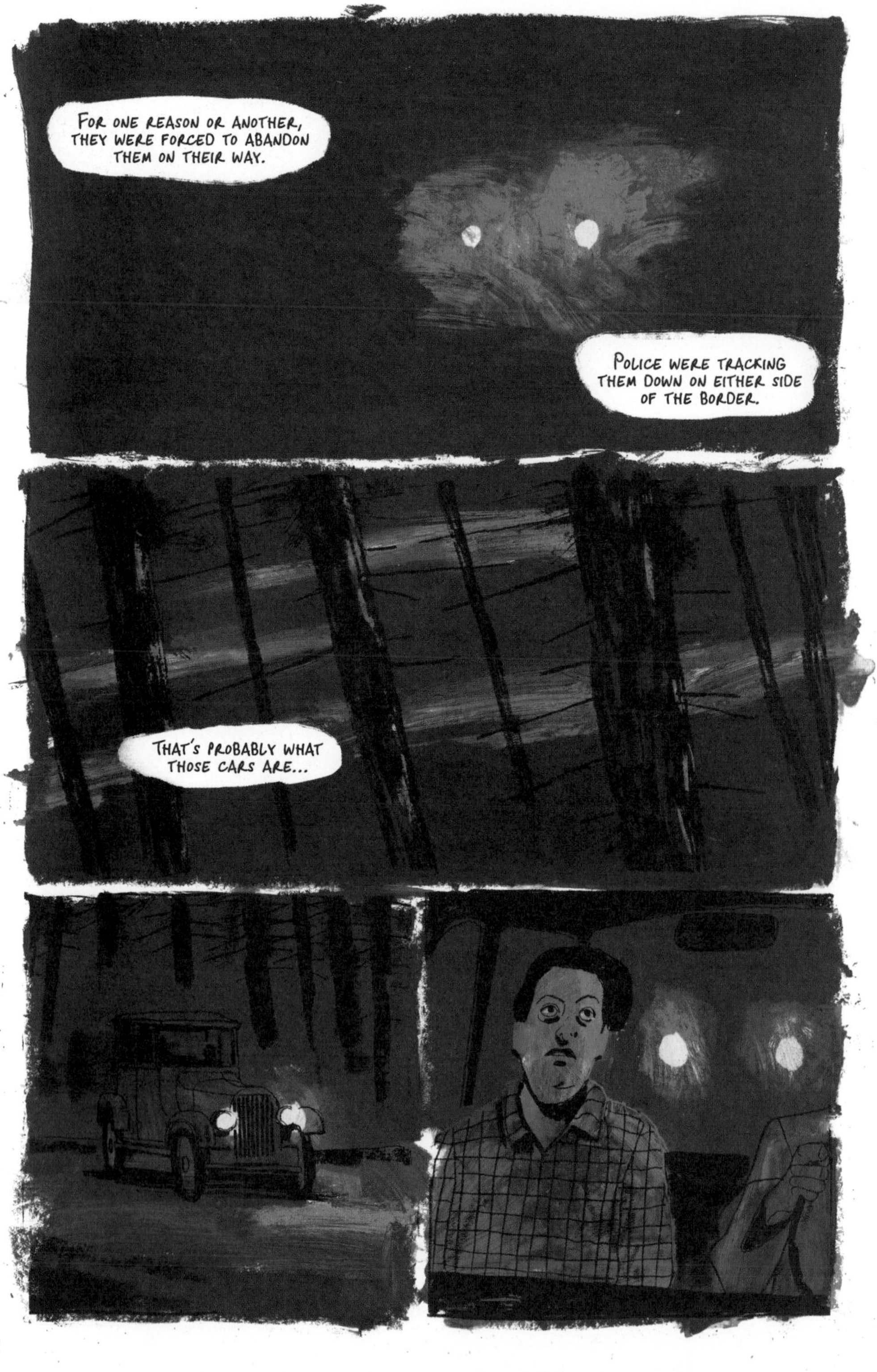
For one reason or another, they were forced to abandon them on their way.
Police were tracking them down on either side of the border.
That's probably what those cars are...

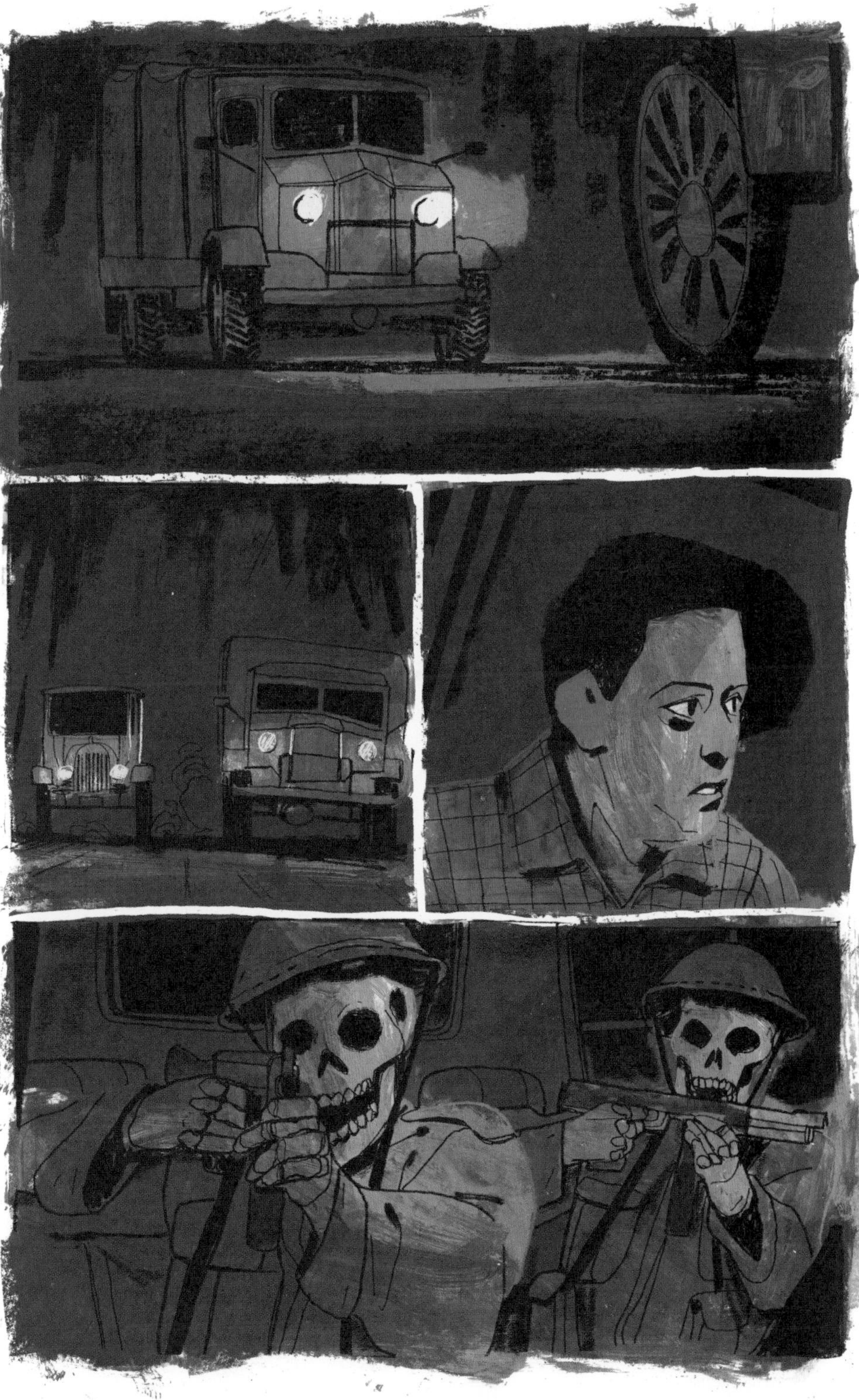

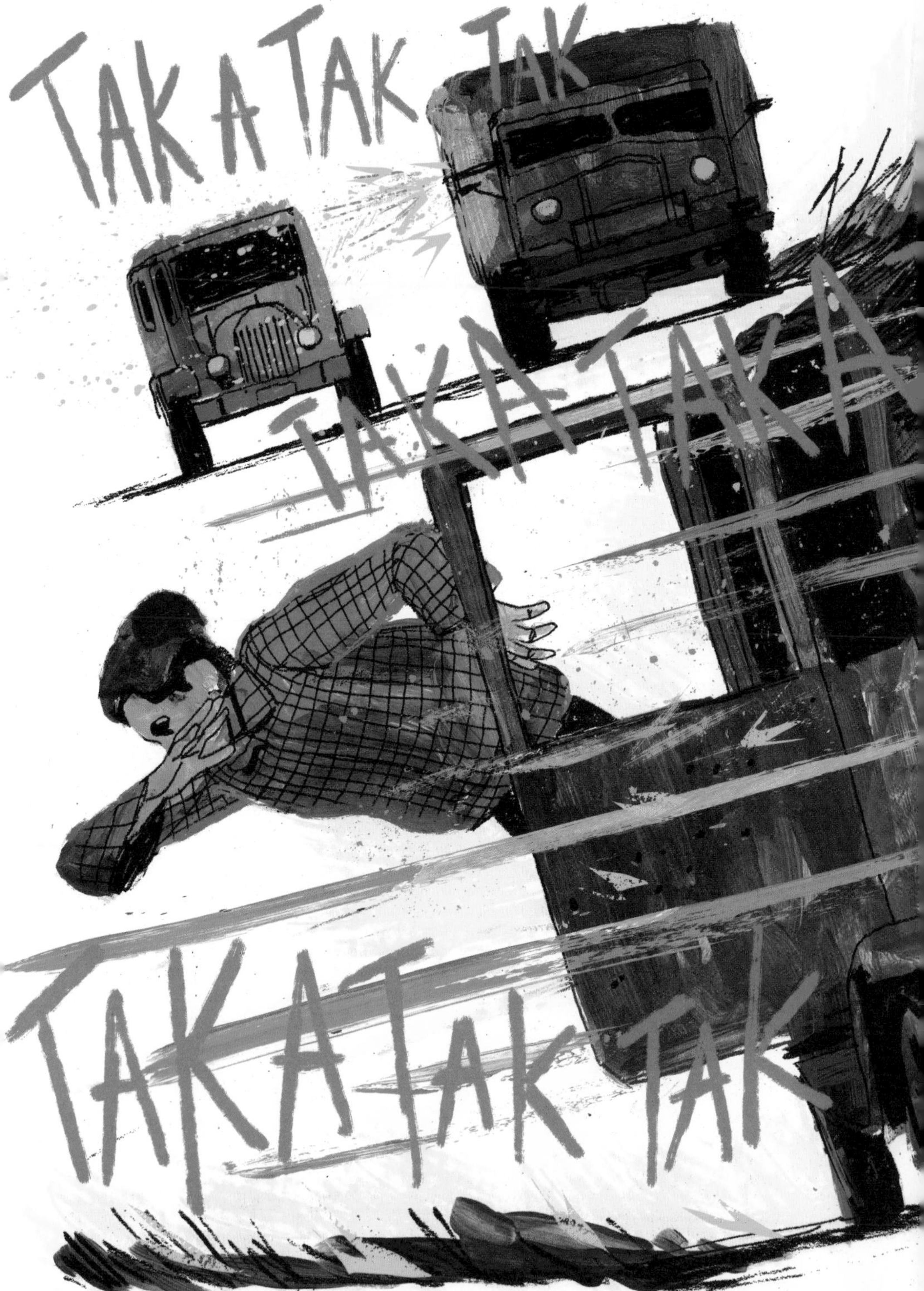
TAKATAK TAK
TAKATAKA
TAKATAK TAK

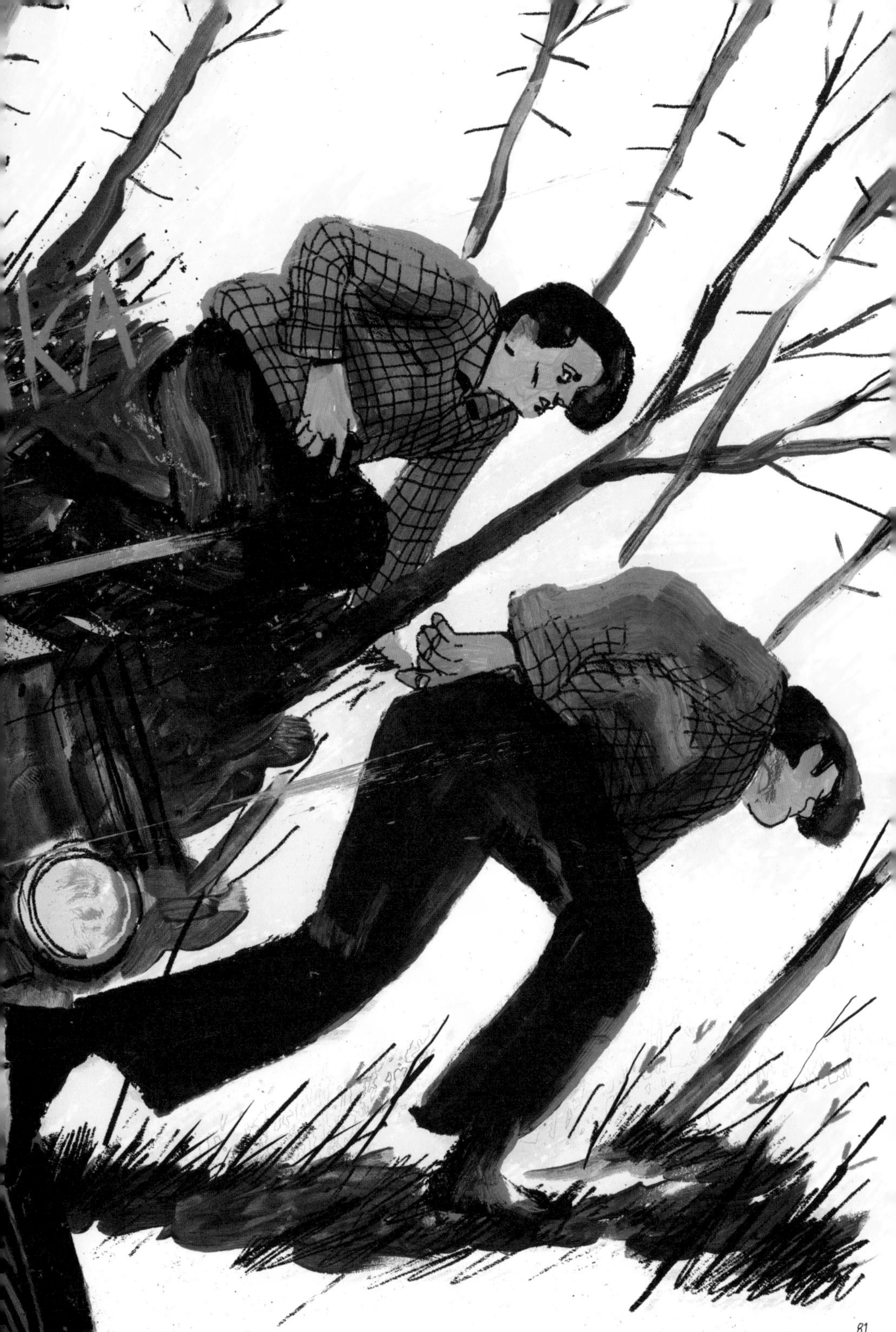
KA

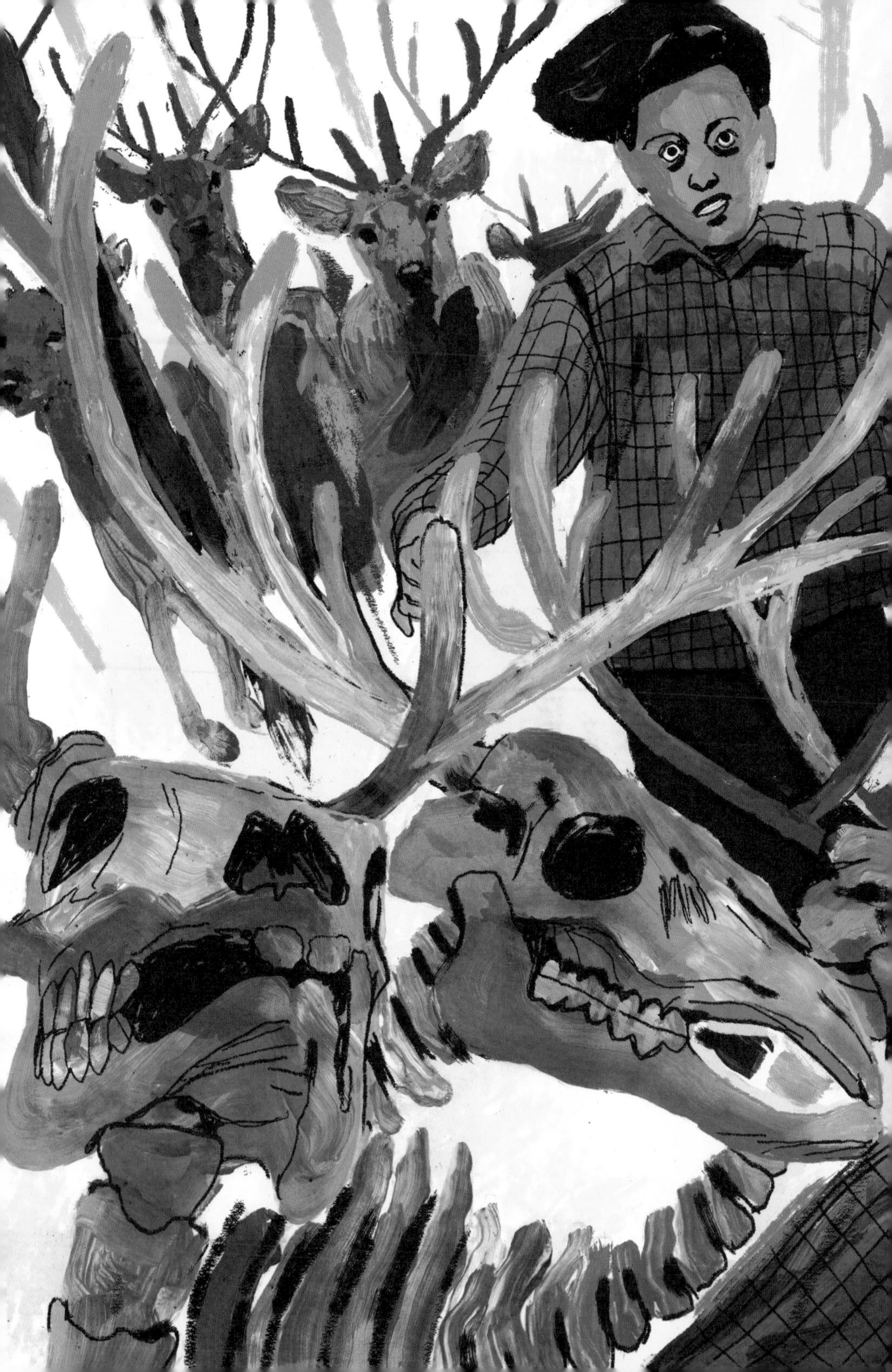

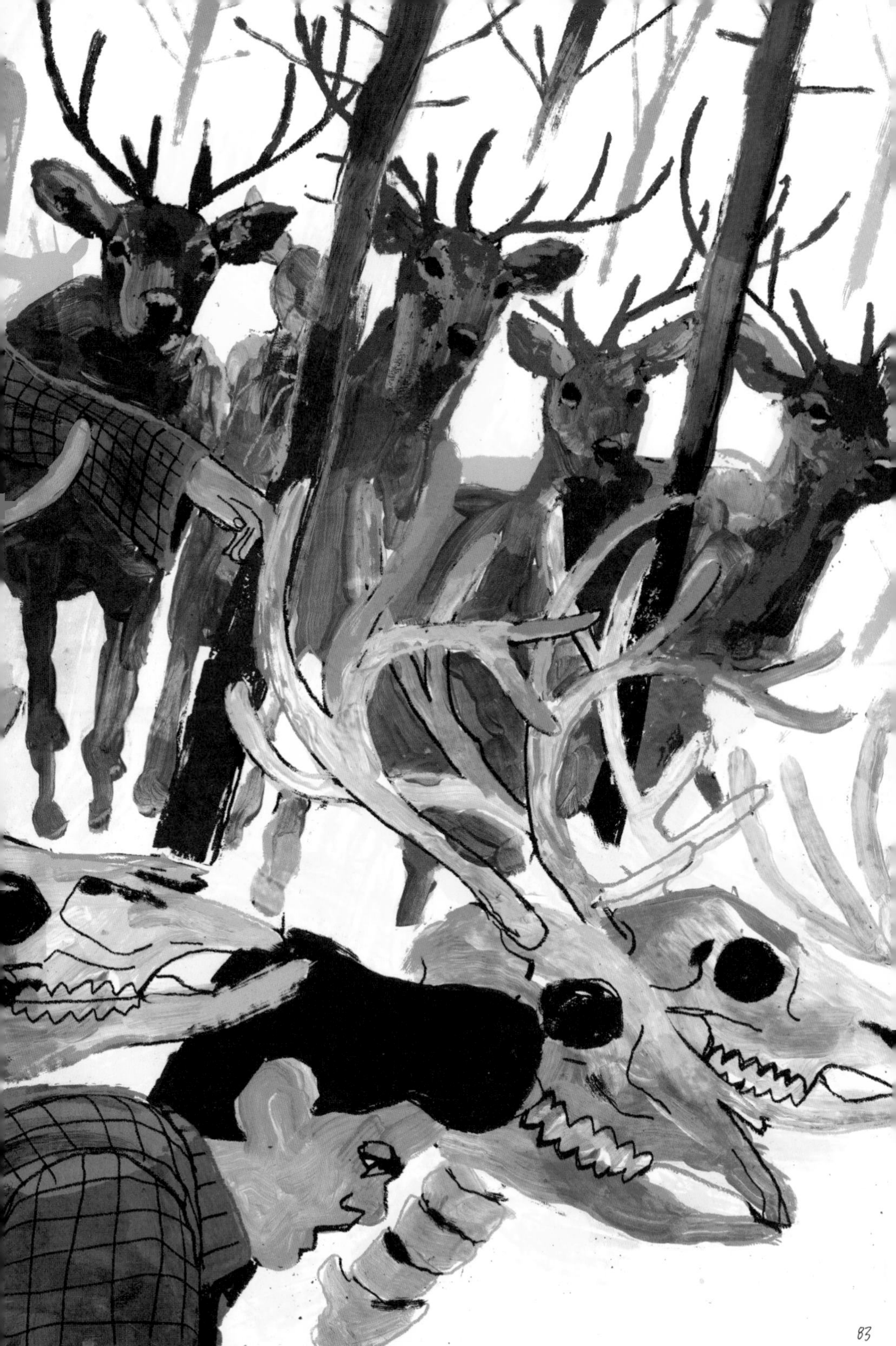

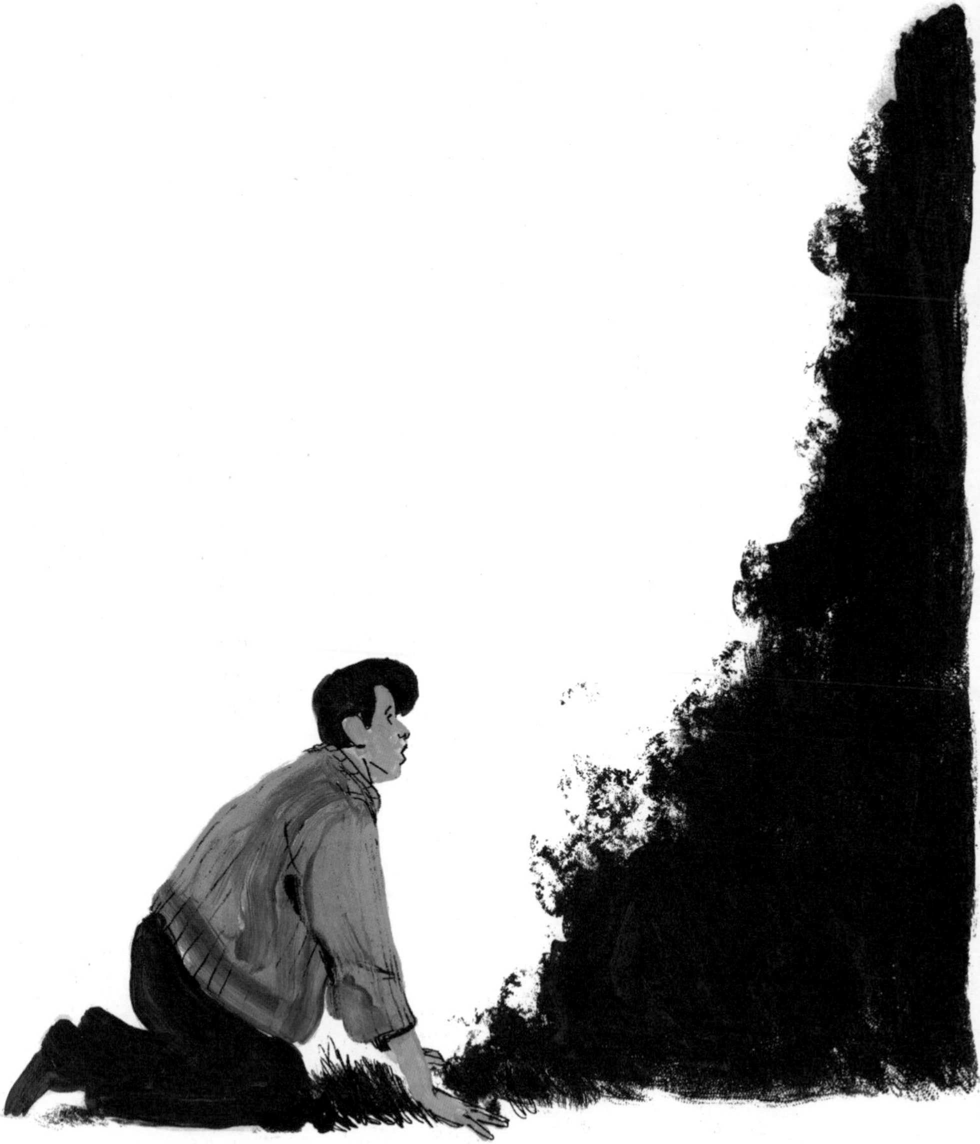

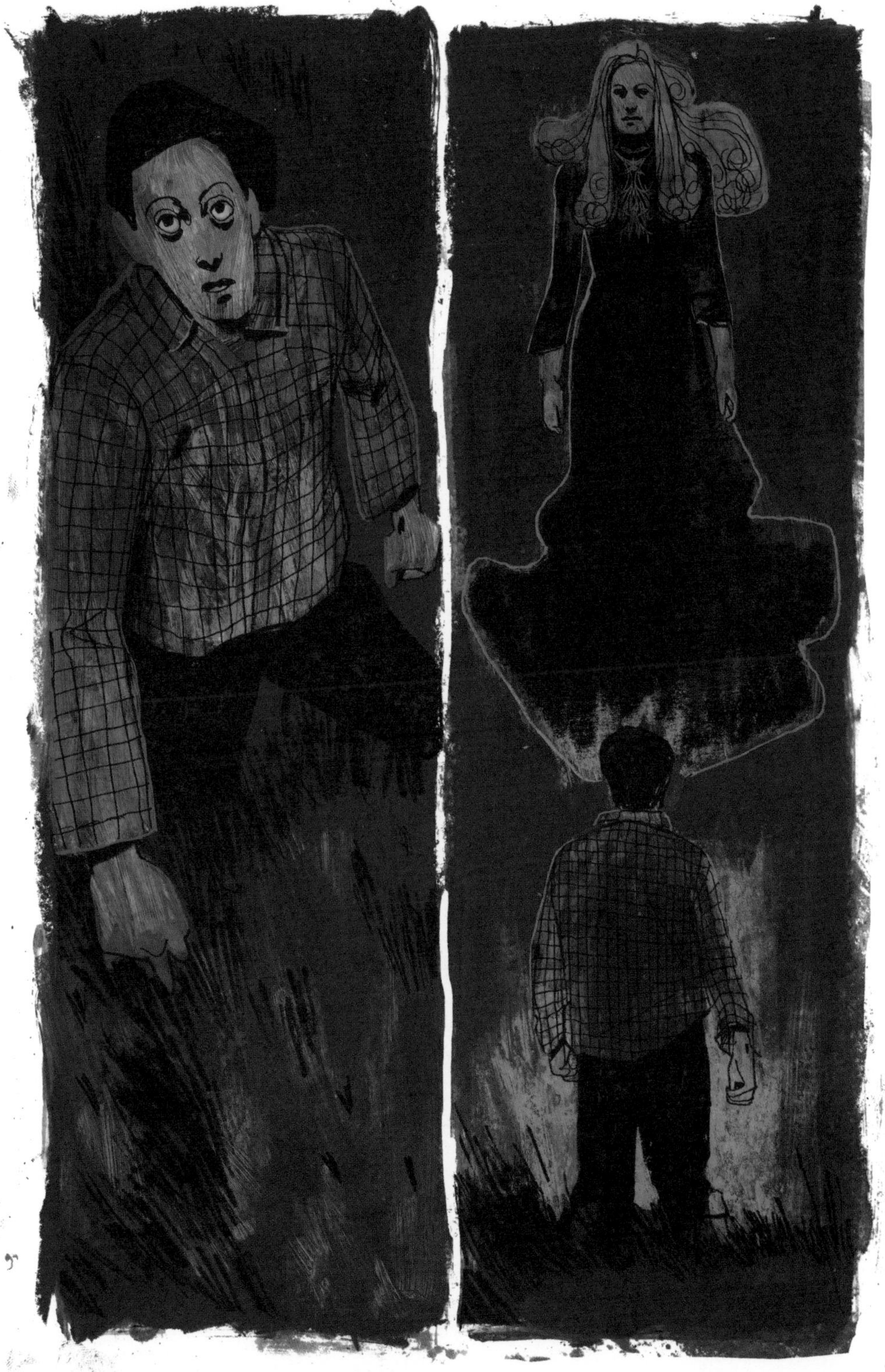

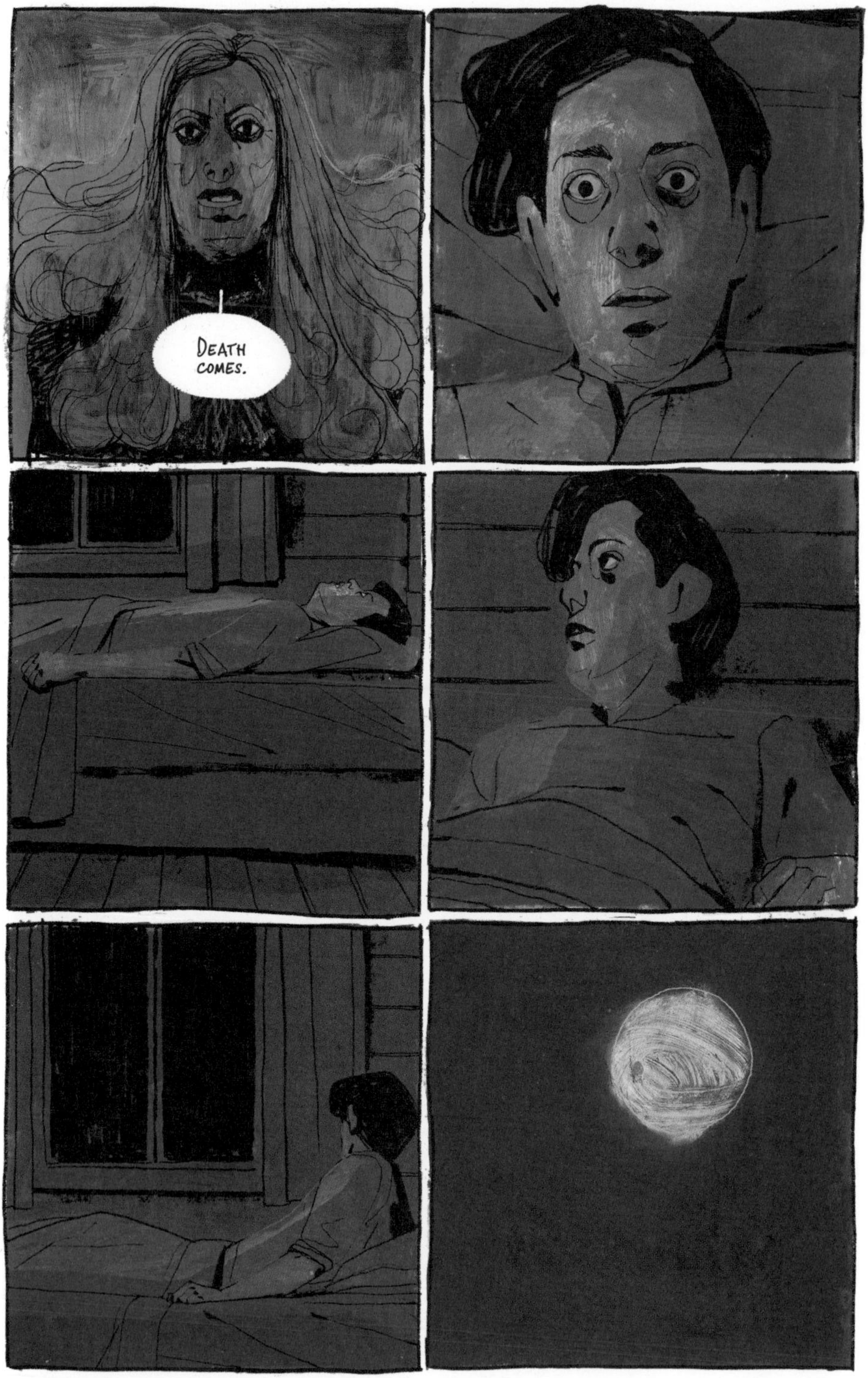
DEATH COMES.

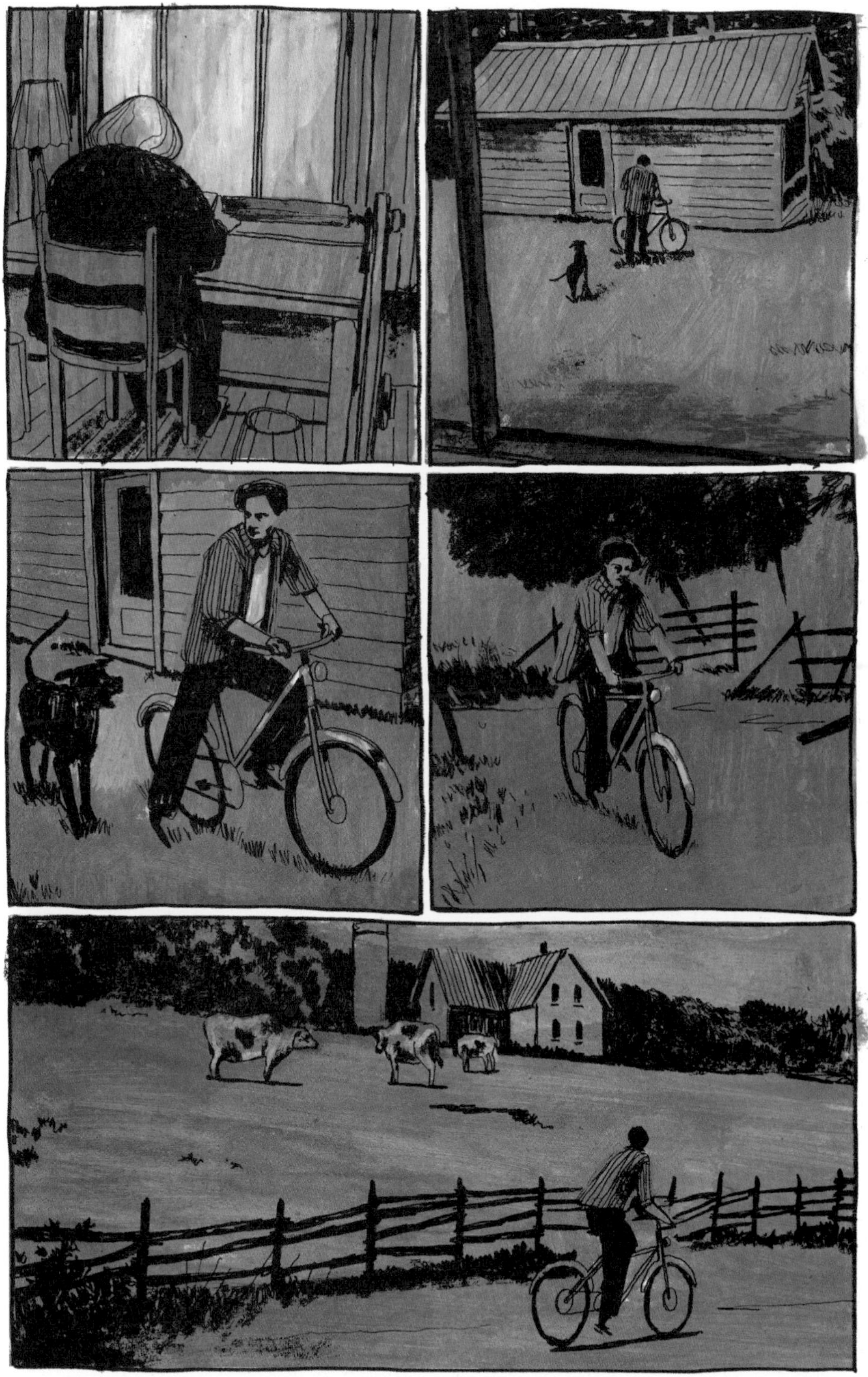

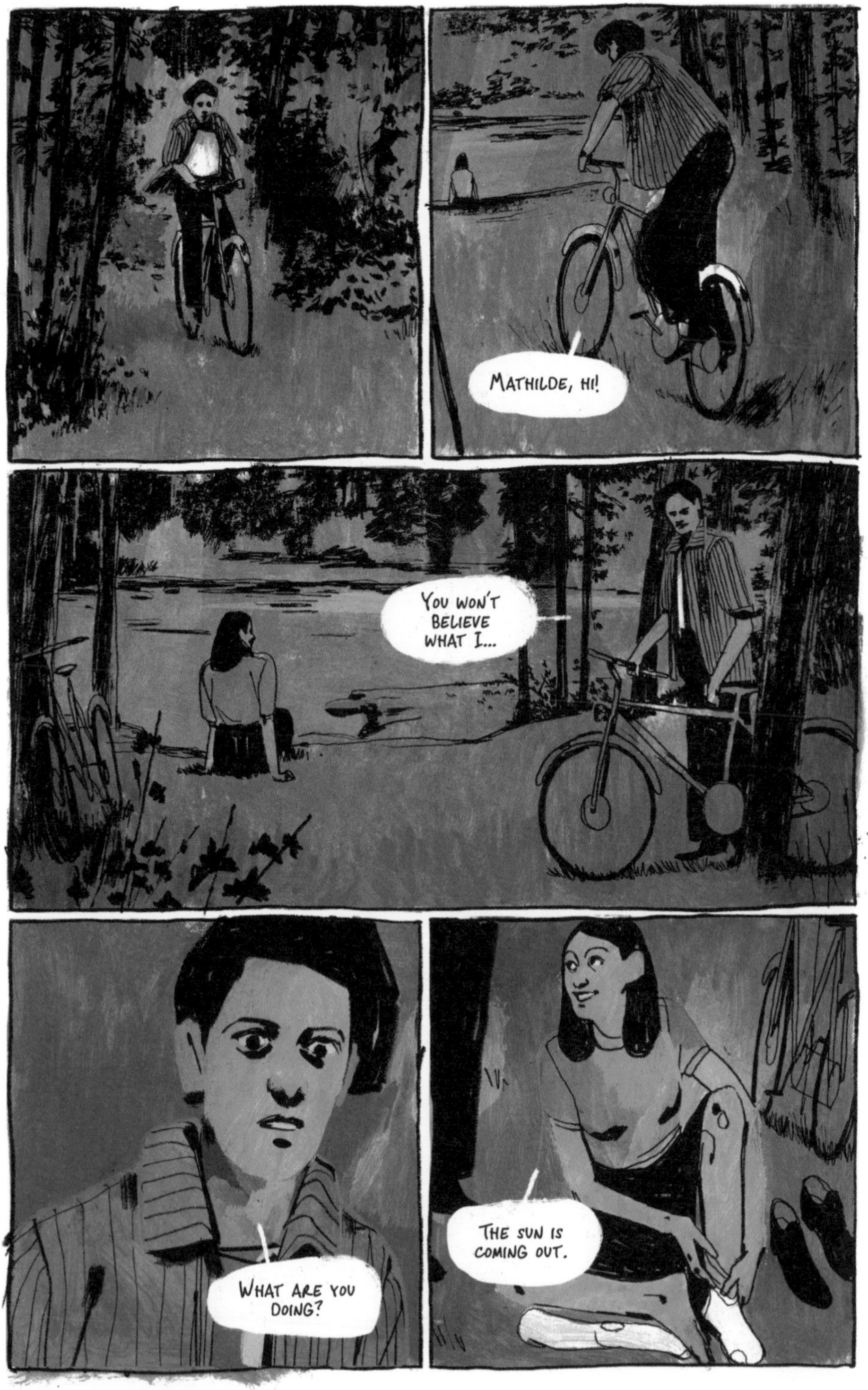
Mathilde, hi!
You won't believe what I...
What are you doing?
The sun is coming out.

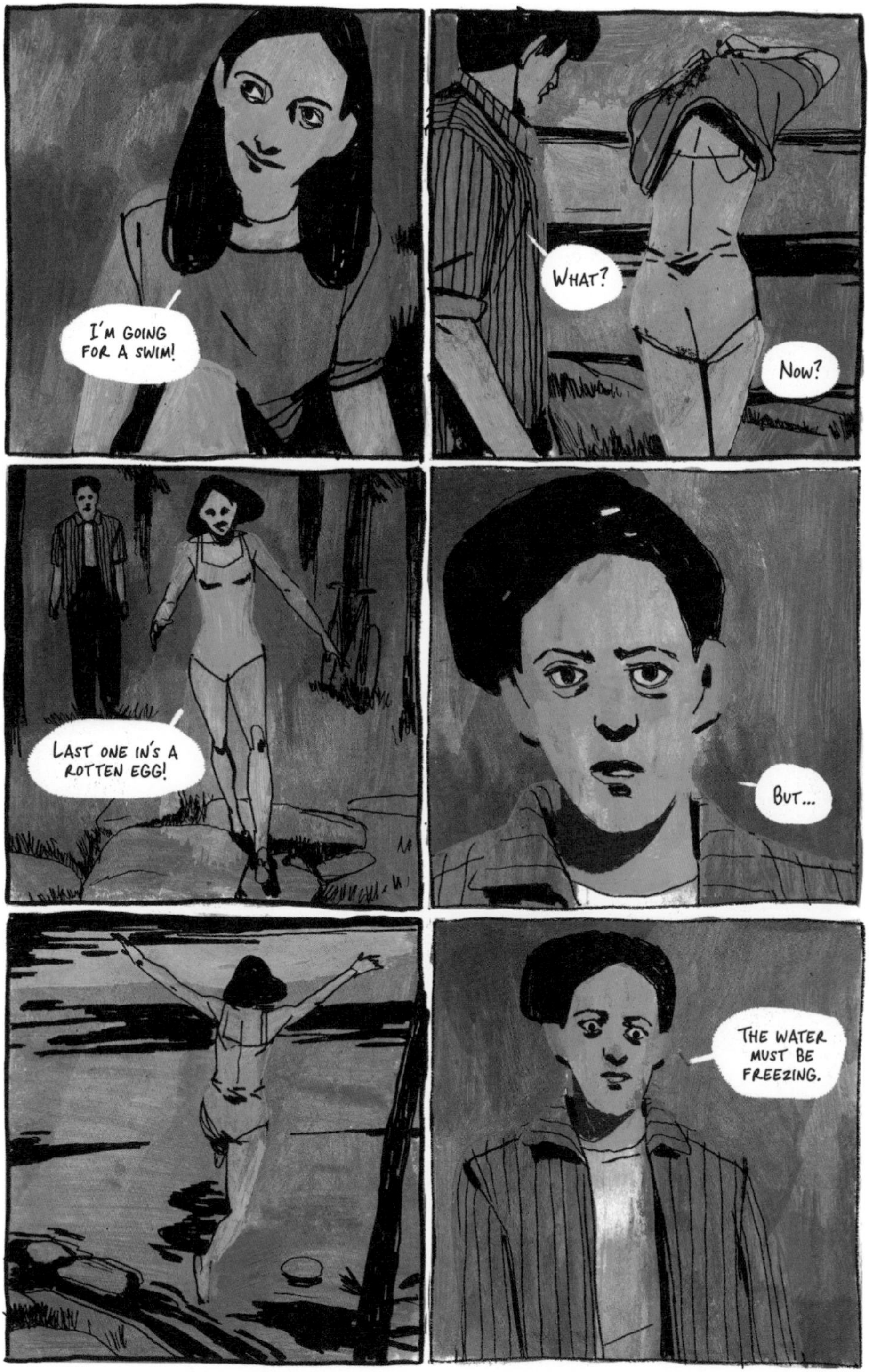
I'M GOING FOR A SWIM!
WHAT?
NOW?
LAST ONE IN'S A ROTTEN EGG!
BUT...
THE WATER MUST BE FREEZING.

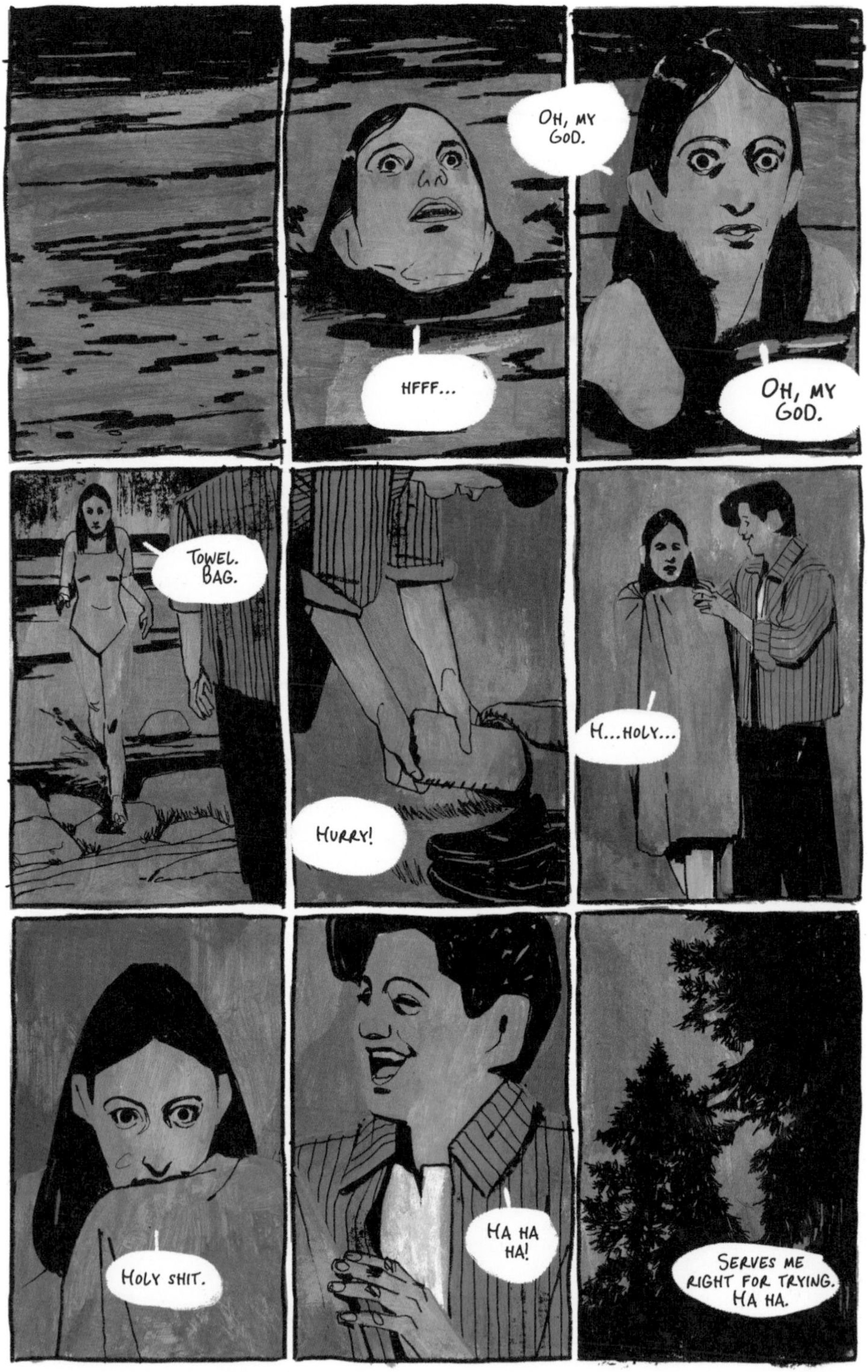
HFFF...
OH, MY GOD.
OH, MY GOD.
TOWEL. BAG.
HURRY!
H...HOLY...
HOLY SHIT.
HA HA HA!
SERVES ME RIGHT FOR TRYING. HA HA.

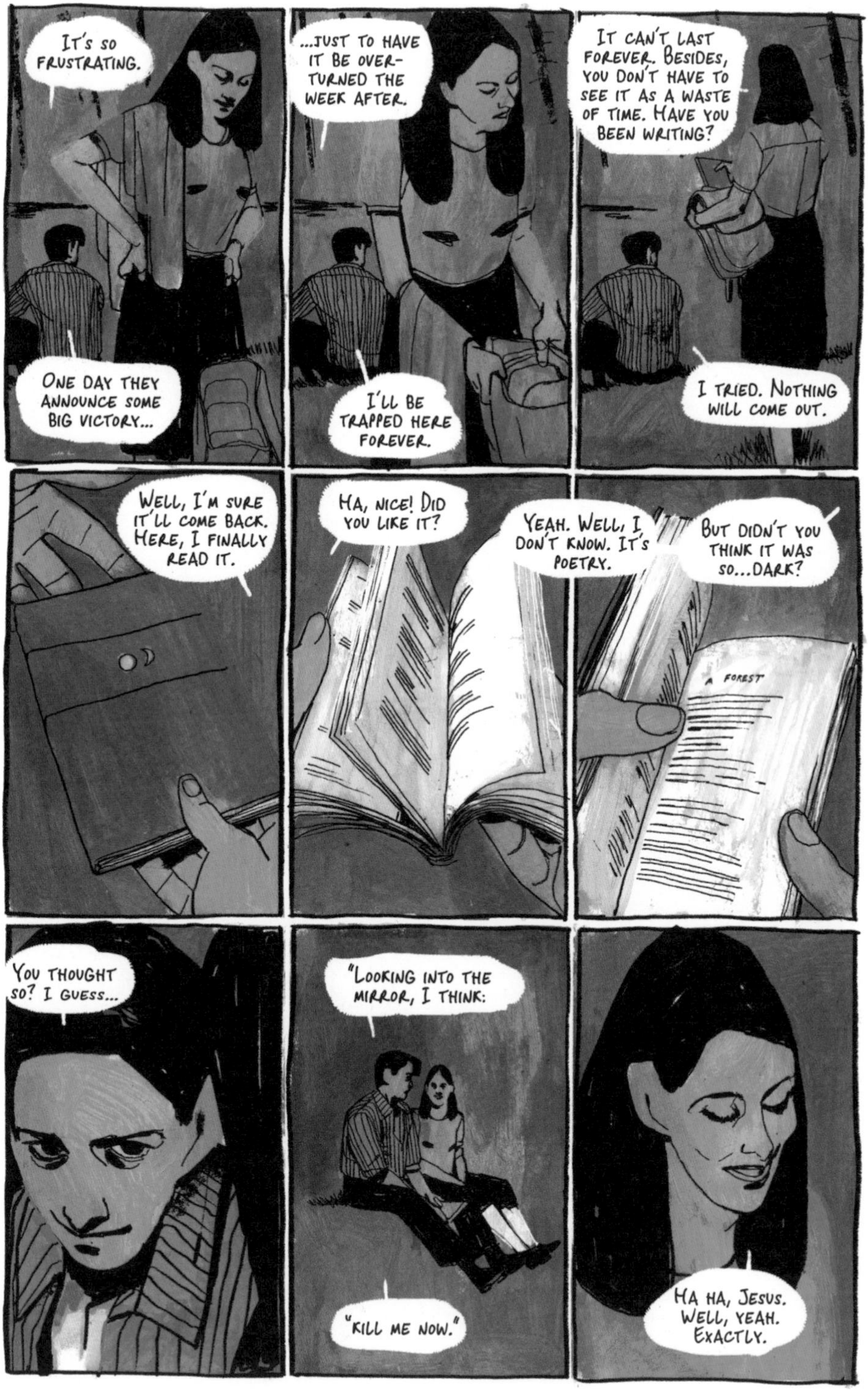
IT'S SO FRUSTRATING.
ONE DAY THEY ANNOUNCE SOME BIG VICTORY...
...JUST TO HAVE IT BE OVER-TURNED THE WEEK AFTER.
I'LL BE TRAPPED HERE FOREVER.
IT CAN'T LAST FOREVER. BESIDES, YOU DON'T HAVE TO SEE IT AS A WASTE OF TIME. HAVE YOU BEEN WRITING?
I TRIED. NOTHING WILL COME OUT.
WELL, I'M SURE IT'LL COME BACK. HERE, I FINALLY READ IT.
HA, NICE! DID YOU LIKE IT?
YEAH. WELL, I DON'T KNOW. IT'S POETRY.
BUT DIDN'T YOU THINK IT WAS SO...DARK?
A FOREST
YOU THOUGHT SO? I GUESS...
"LOOKING INTO THE MIRROR, I THINK:
"KILL ME NOW."
HA HA, JESUS. WELL, YEAH. EXACTLY.

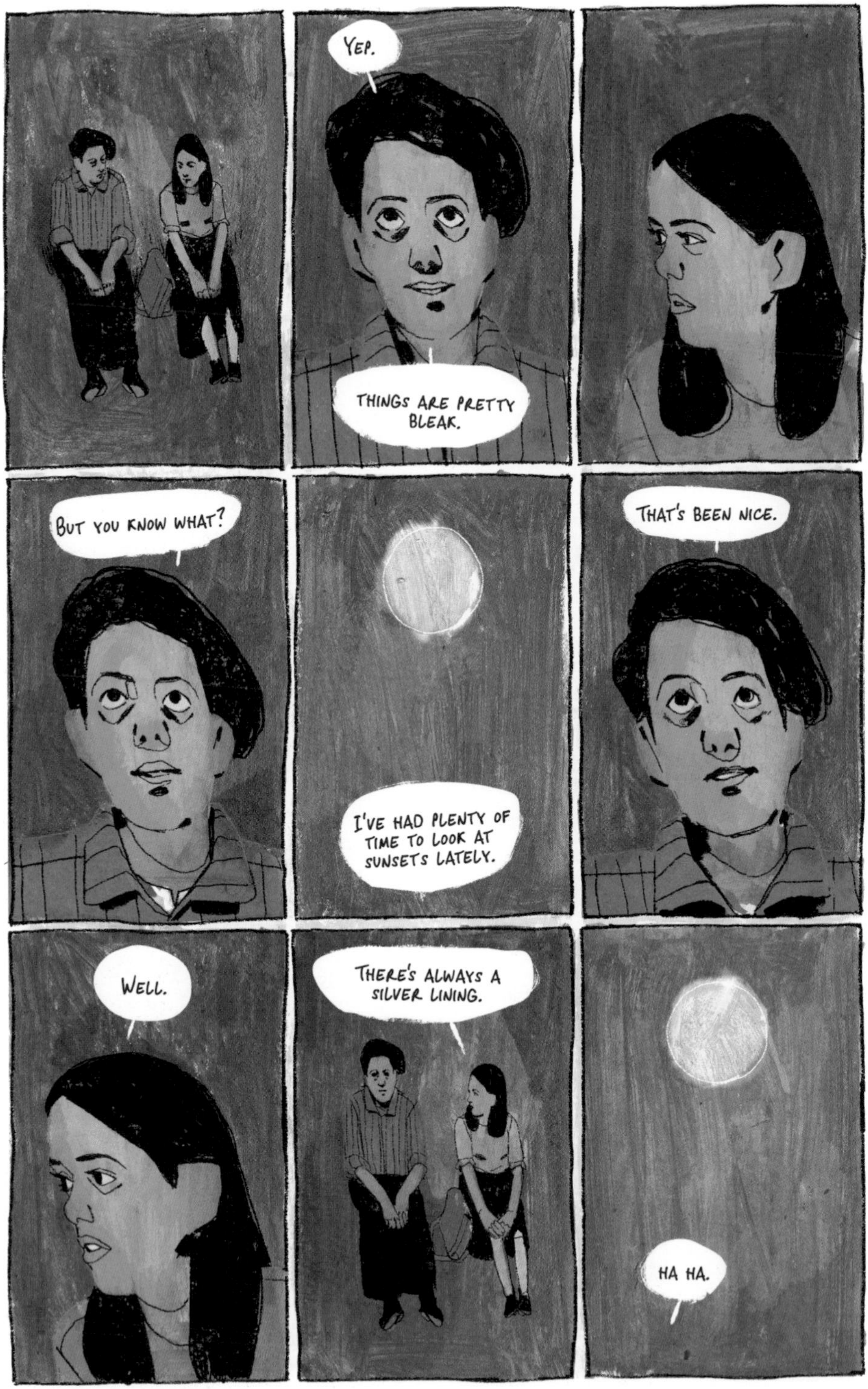
YEP.
THINGS ARE PRETTY BLEAK.
BUT YOU KNOW WHAT?
I'VE HAD PLENTY OF TIME TO LOOK AT SUNSETS LATELY.
THAT'S BEEN NICE.
WELL.
THERE'S ALWAYS A SILVER LINING.
HA HA.

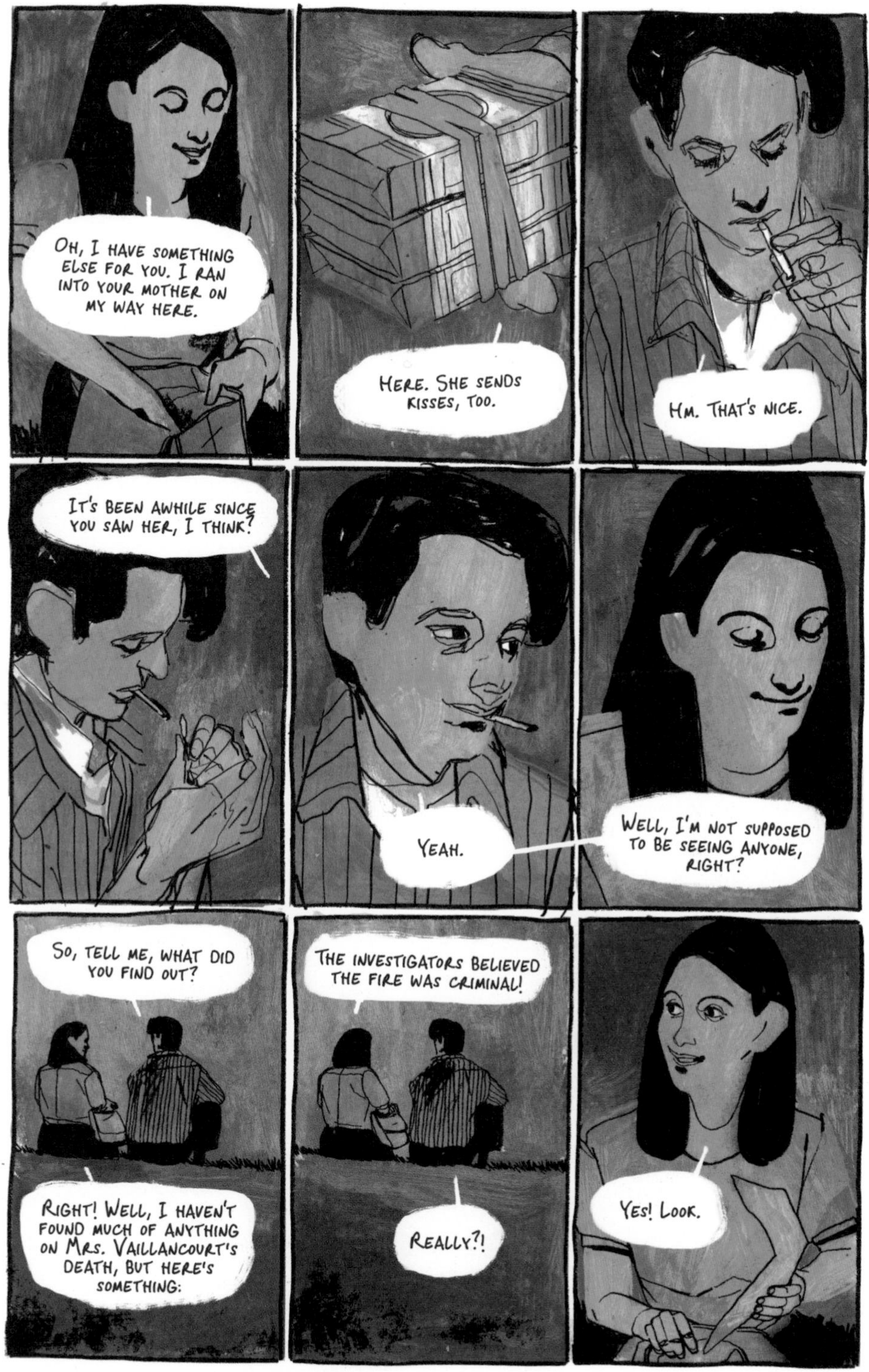

Oh, I have something else for you. I ran into your mother on my way here.
Here. She sends kisses, too.
Hm. That's nice.
It's been awhile since you saw her, I think?
Yeah.
Well, I'm not supposed to be seeing anyone, right?
So, tell me, what did you find out?
Right! Well, I haven't found much of anything on Mrs. Vaillancourt's death, but here's something:
The investigators believed the fire was criminal!
Really?!
Yes! Look.

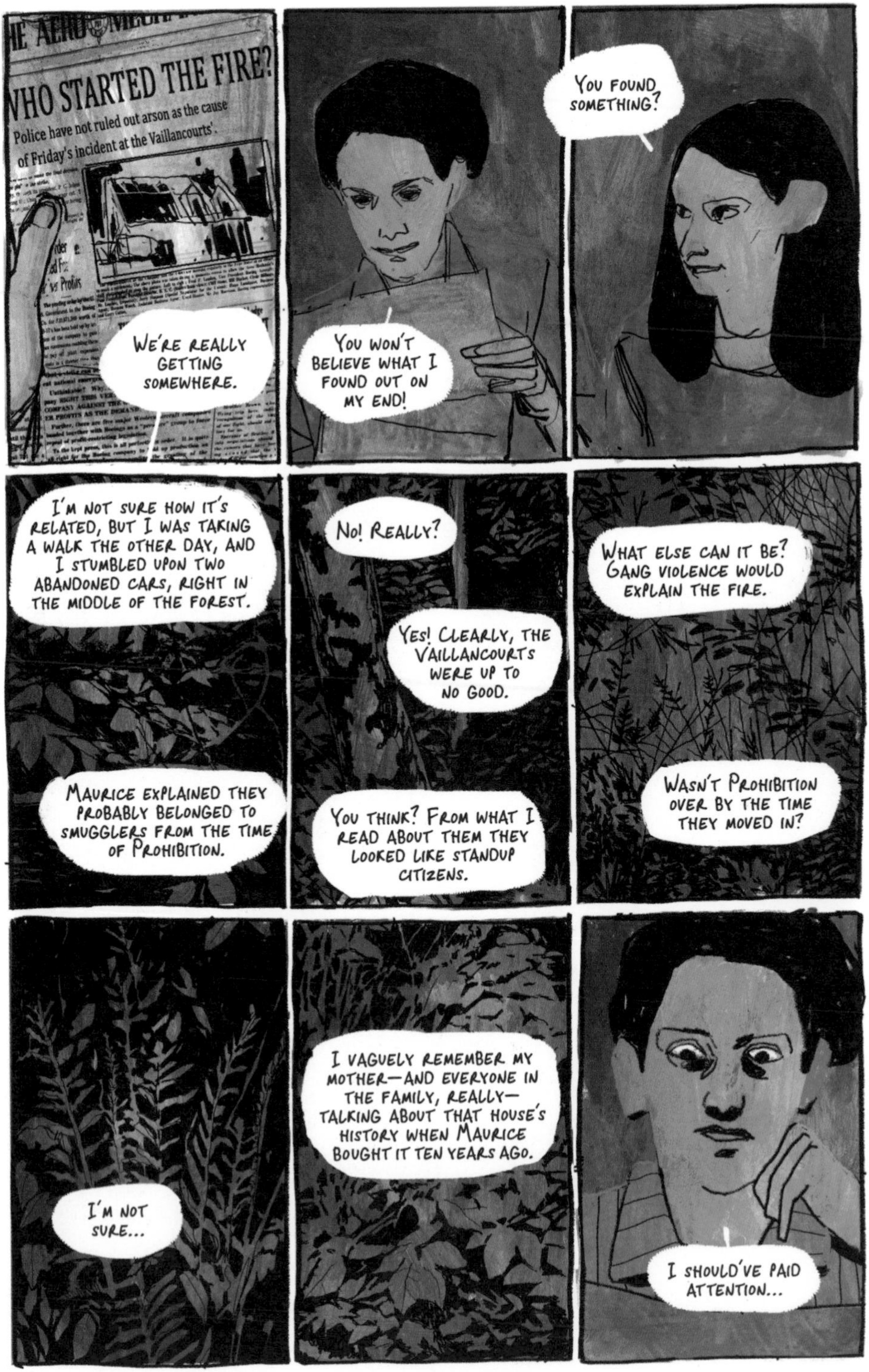
WHO STARTED THE FIRE?
Police have not ruled out arson as the cause of Friday's incident at the Vaillancourts'.
WE'RE REALLY GETTING SOMEWHERE.
YOU WON'T BELIEVE WHAT I FOUND OUT ON MY END!
YOU FOUND SOMETHING?
I'M NOT SURE HOW IT'S RELATED, BUT I WAS TAKING A WALK THE OTHER DAY, AND I STUMBLED UPON TWO ABANDONED CARS, RIGHT IN THE MIDDLE OF THE FOREST.
MAURICE EXPLAINED THEY PROBABLY BELONGED TO SMUGGLERS FROM THE TIME OF PROHIBITION.
NO! REALLY?
YES! CLEARLY, THE VAILLANCOURTS WERE UP TO NO GOOD.
YOU THINK? FROM WHAT I READ ABOUT THEM THEY LOOKED LIKE STANDUP CITIZENS.
WHAT ELSE CAN IT BE? GANG VIOLENCE WOULD EXPLAIN THE FIRE.
WASN'T PROHIBITION OVER BY THE TIME THEY MOVED IN?
I'M NOT SURE...
I VAGUELY REMEMBER MY MOTHER—AND EVERYONE IN THE FAMILY, REALLY—TALKING ABOUT THAT HOUSE'S HISTORY WHEN MAURICE BOUGHT IT TEN YEARS AGO.
I SHOULD'VE PAID ATTENTION...

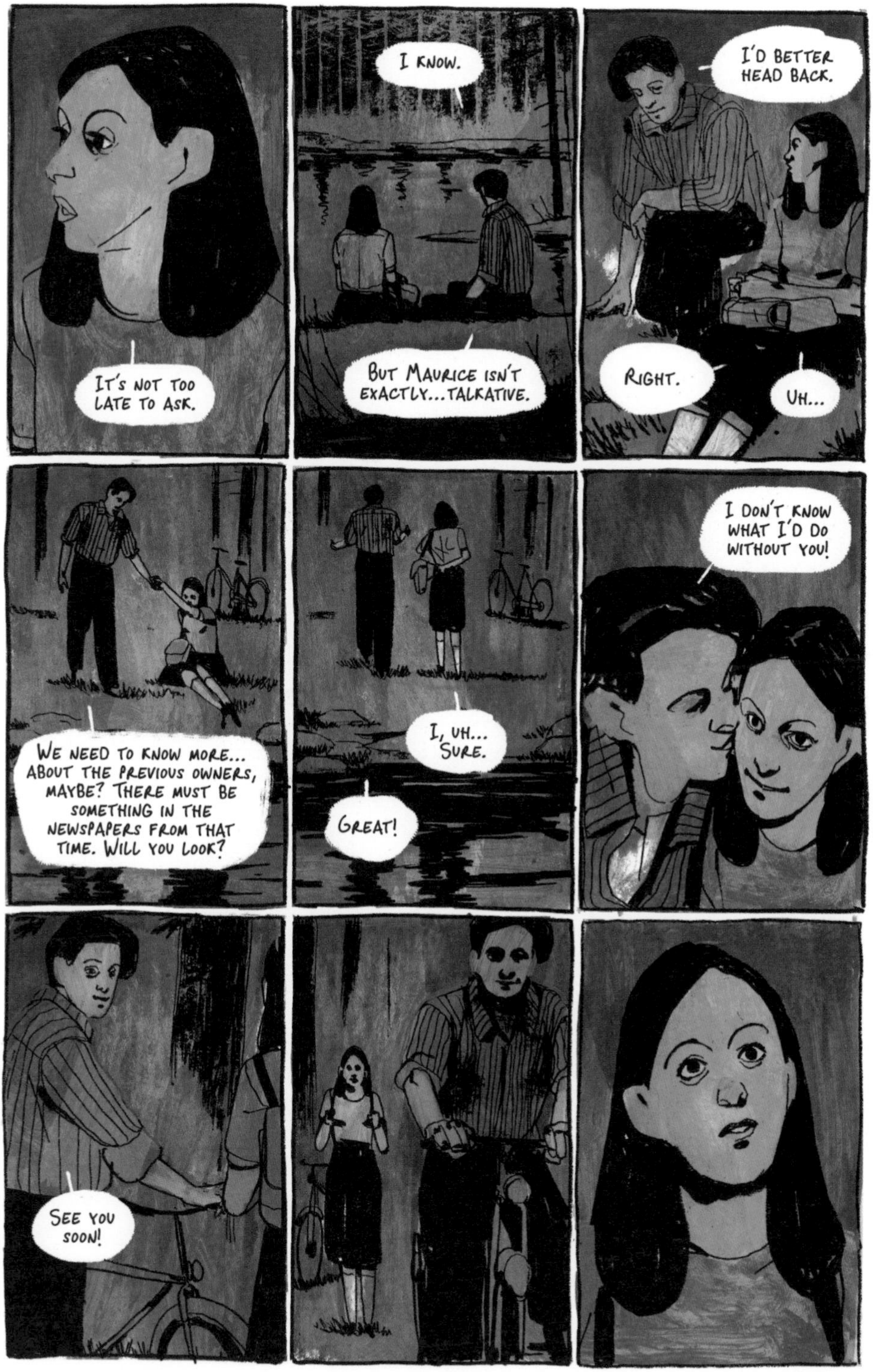
It's not too late to ask.
I know.
But Maurice isn't exactly...talkative.
I'd better head back.
Right.
Uh...
We need to know more... about the previous owners, maybe? There must be something in the newspapers from that time. Will you look?
I, uh... sure.
Great!
I don't know what I'd do without you!
See you soon!

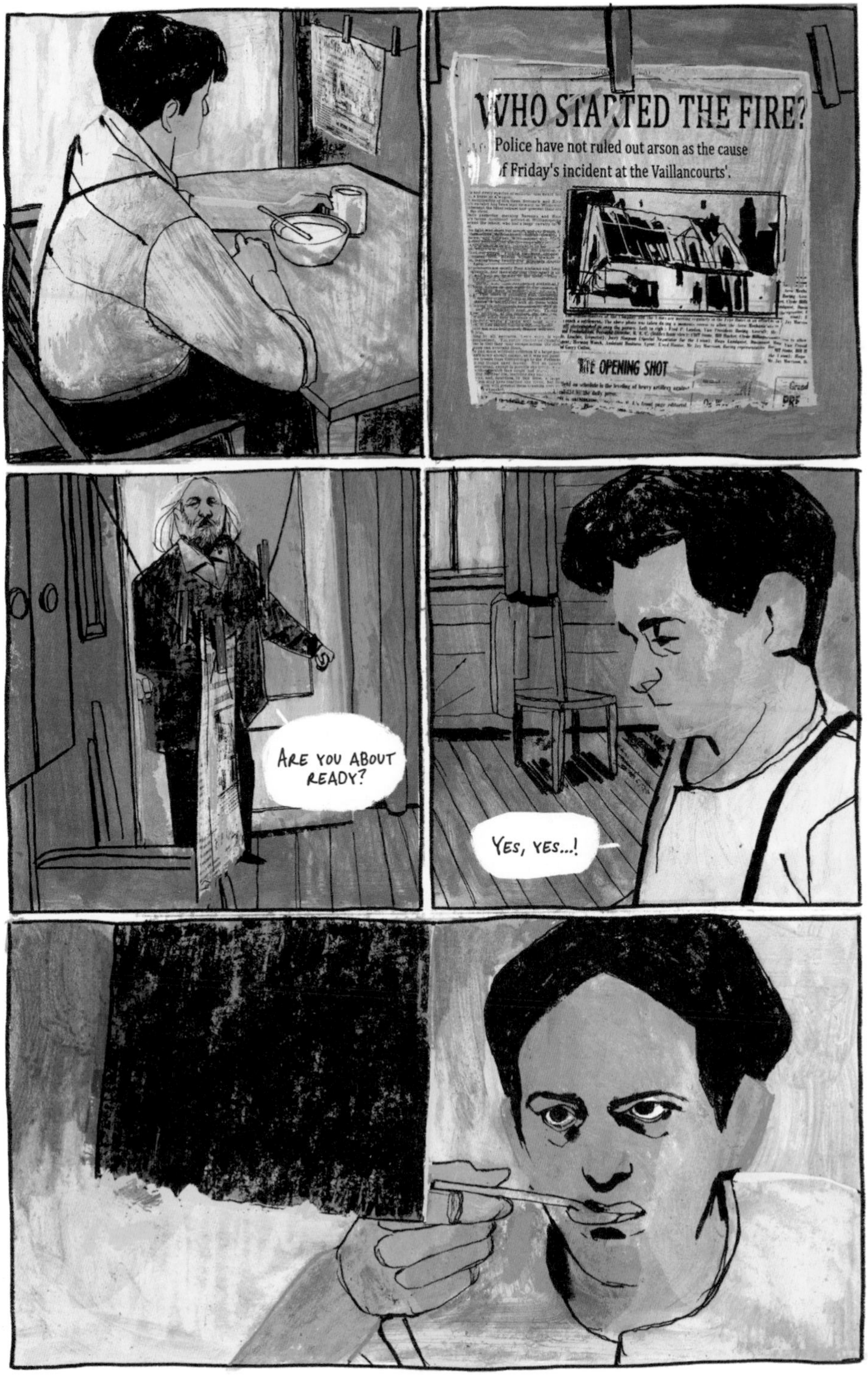
WHO STARTED THE FIRE?
Police have not ruled out arson as the cause
of Friday's incident at the Vaillancourts'.
THE OPENING SHOT
ARE YOU ABOUT READY?
YES, YES...!

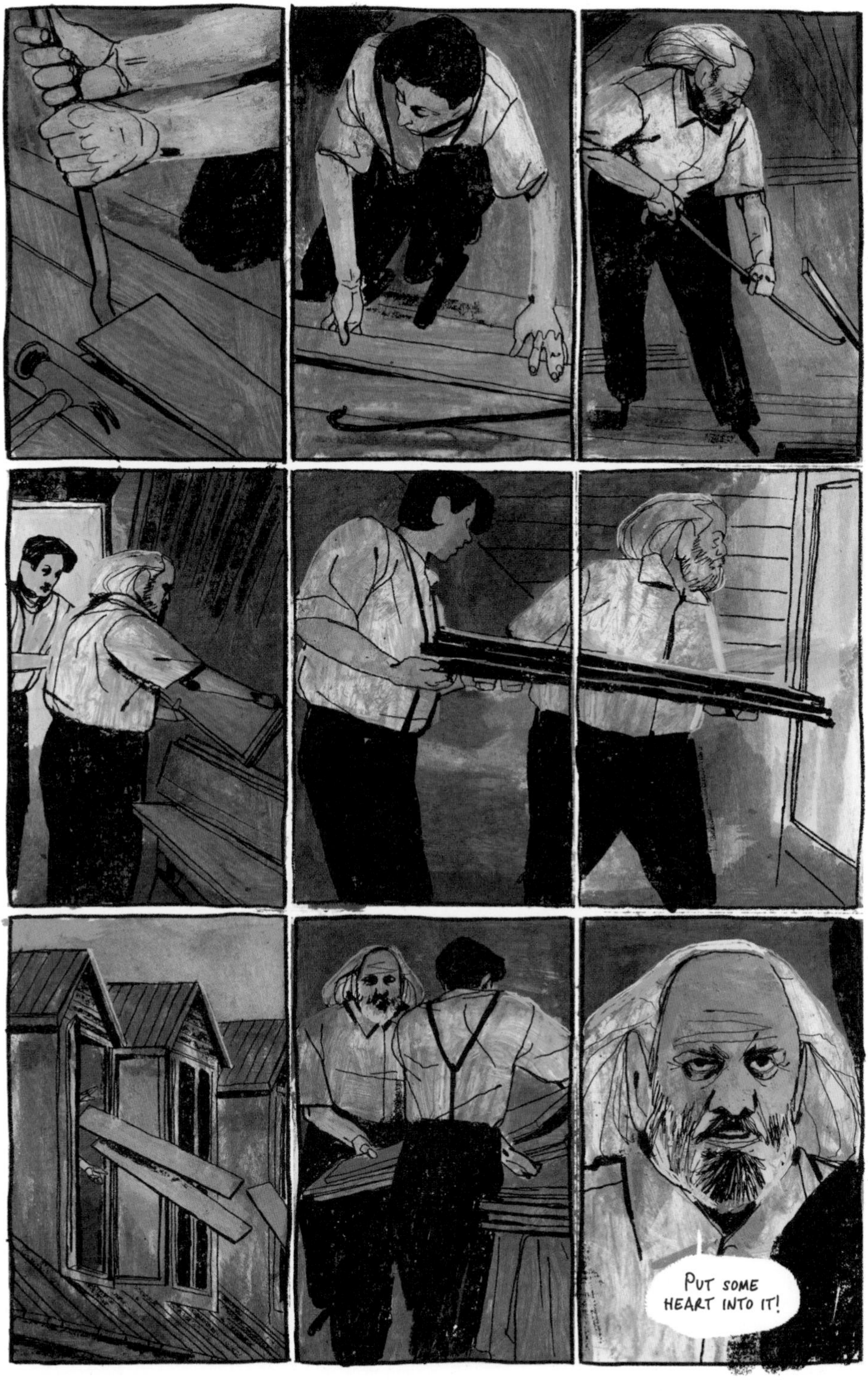
PUT SOME
HEART INTO IT!

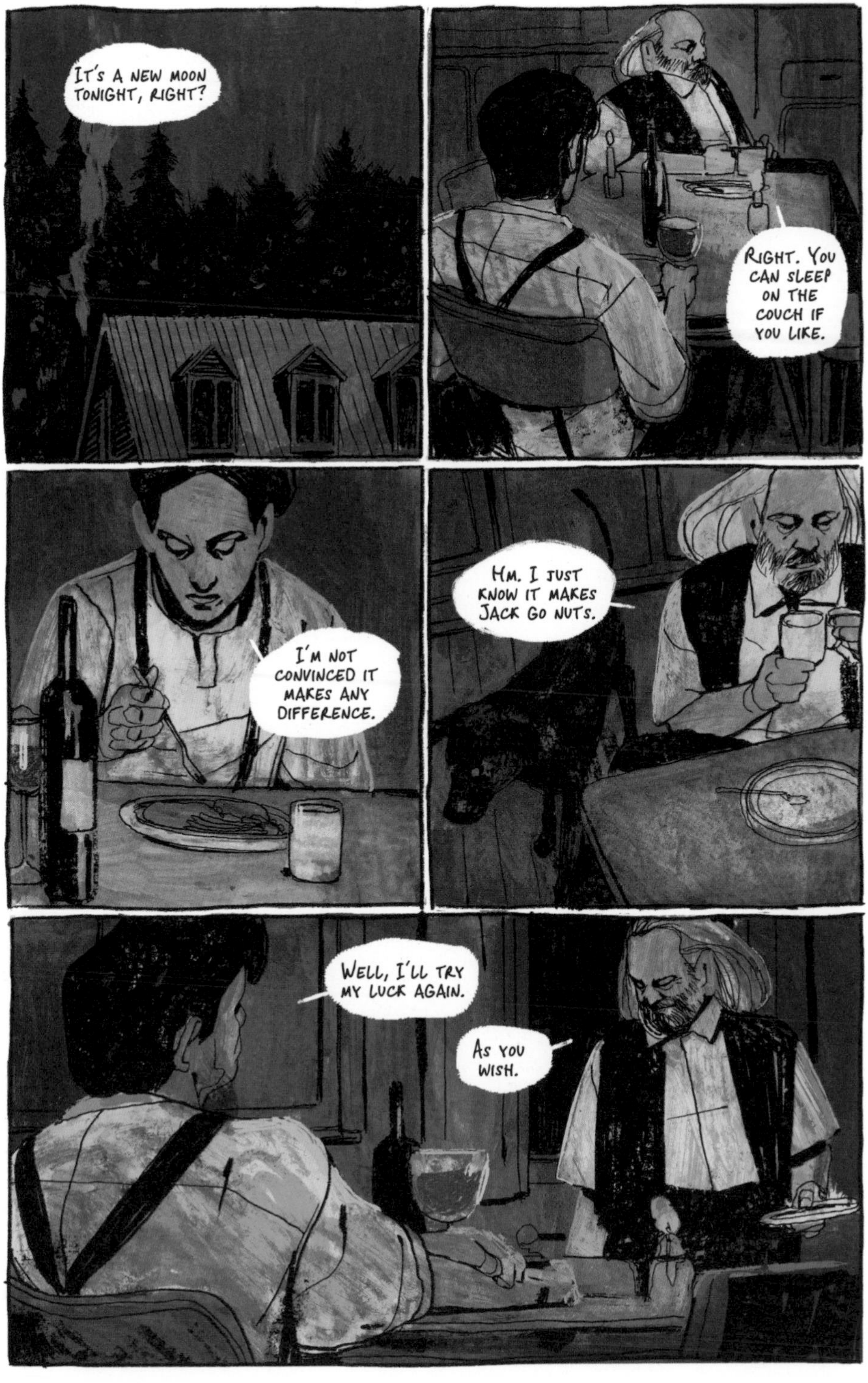
It's a new moon tonight, right?
Right. You can sleep on the couch if you like.
I'm not convinced it makes any difference.
Hm. I just know it makes Jack go nuts.
Well, I'll try my luck again.
As you wish.

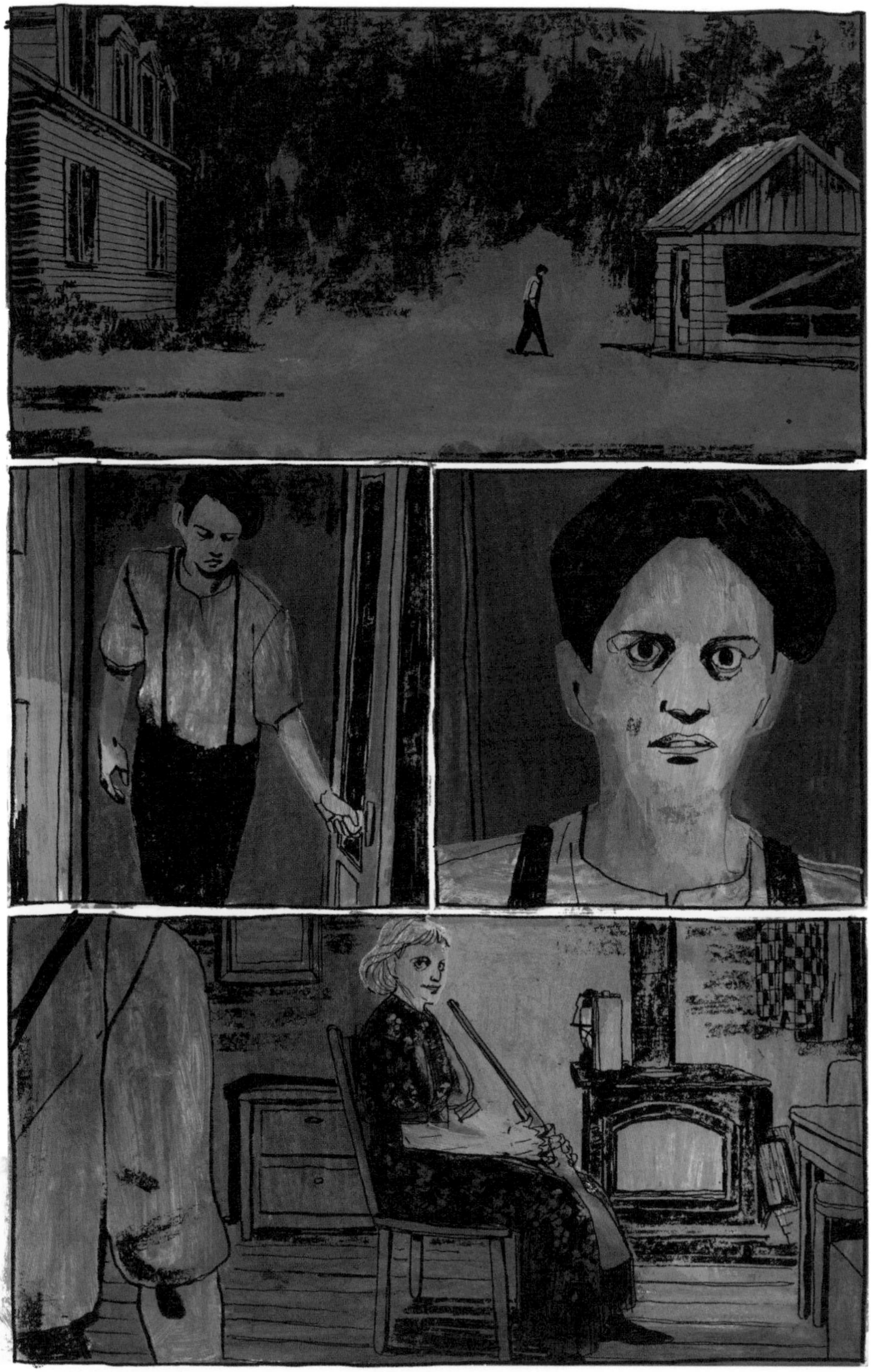

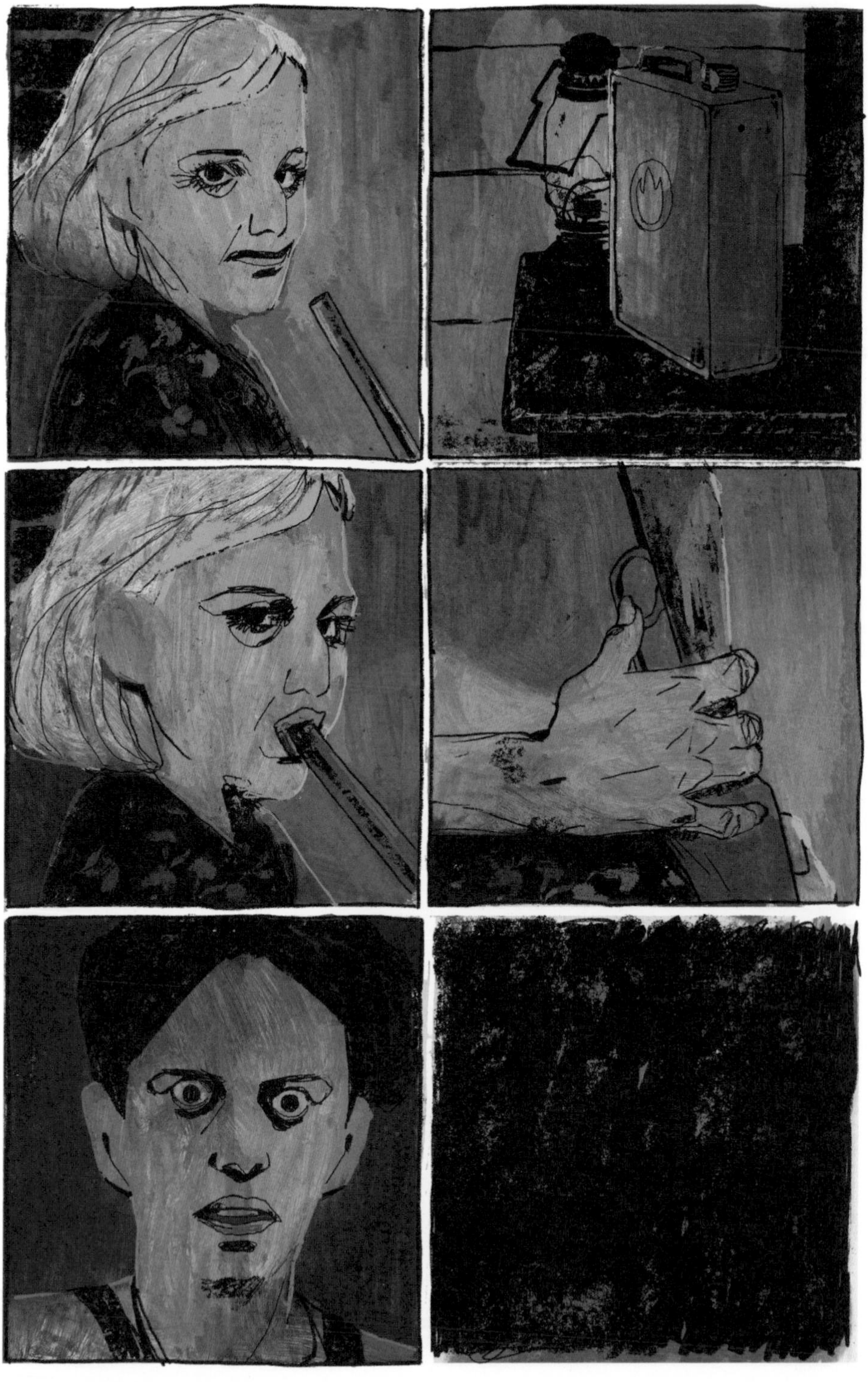

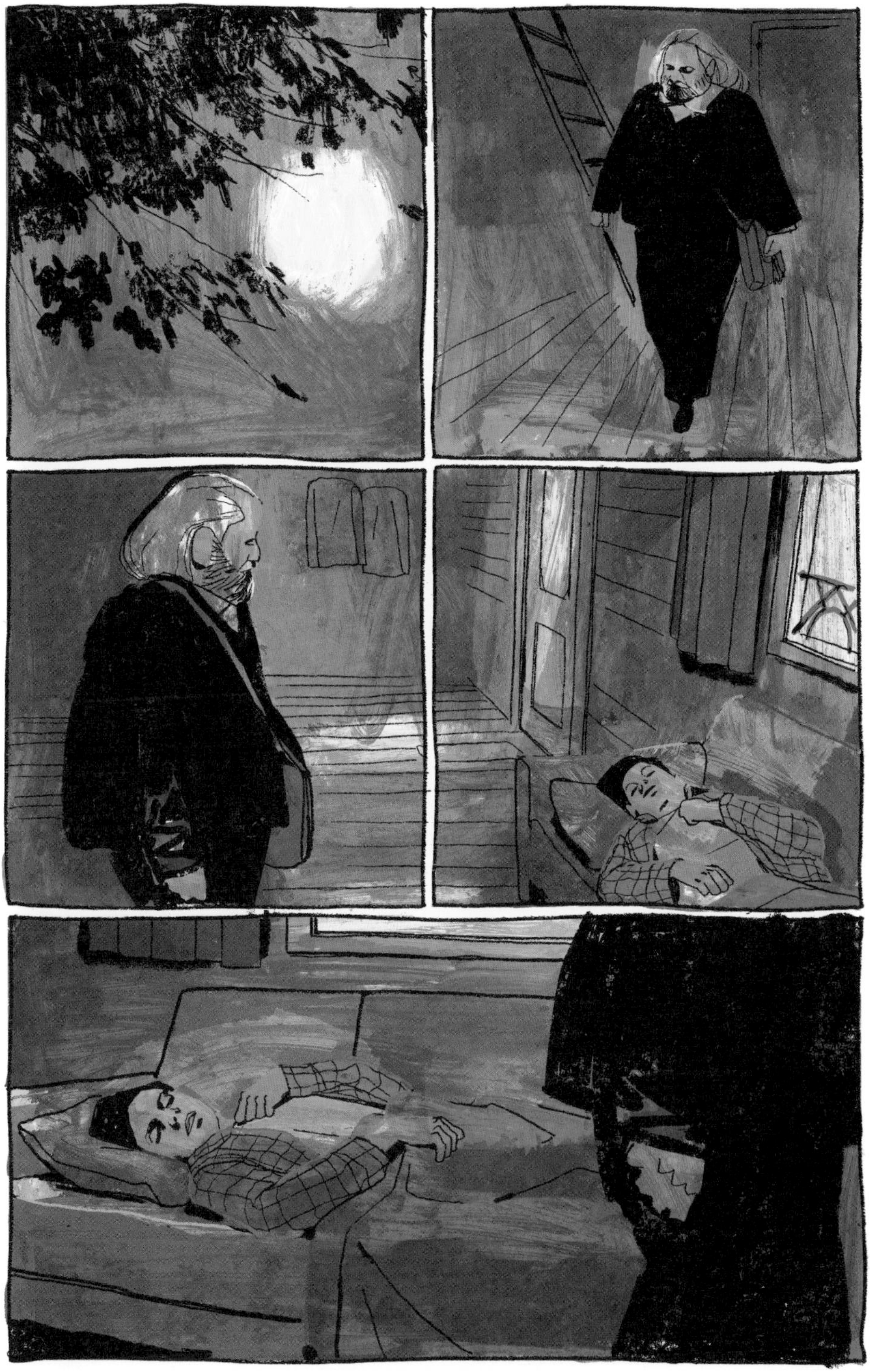

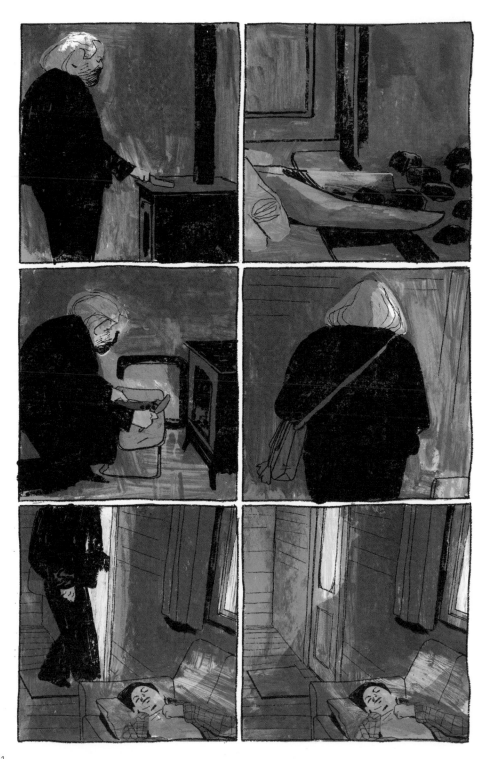

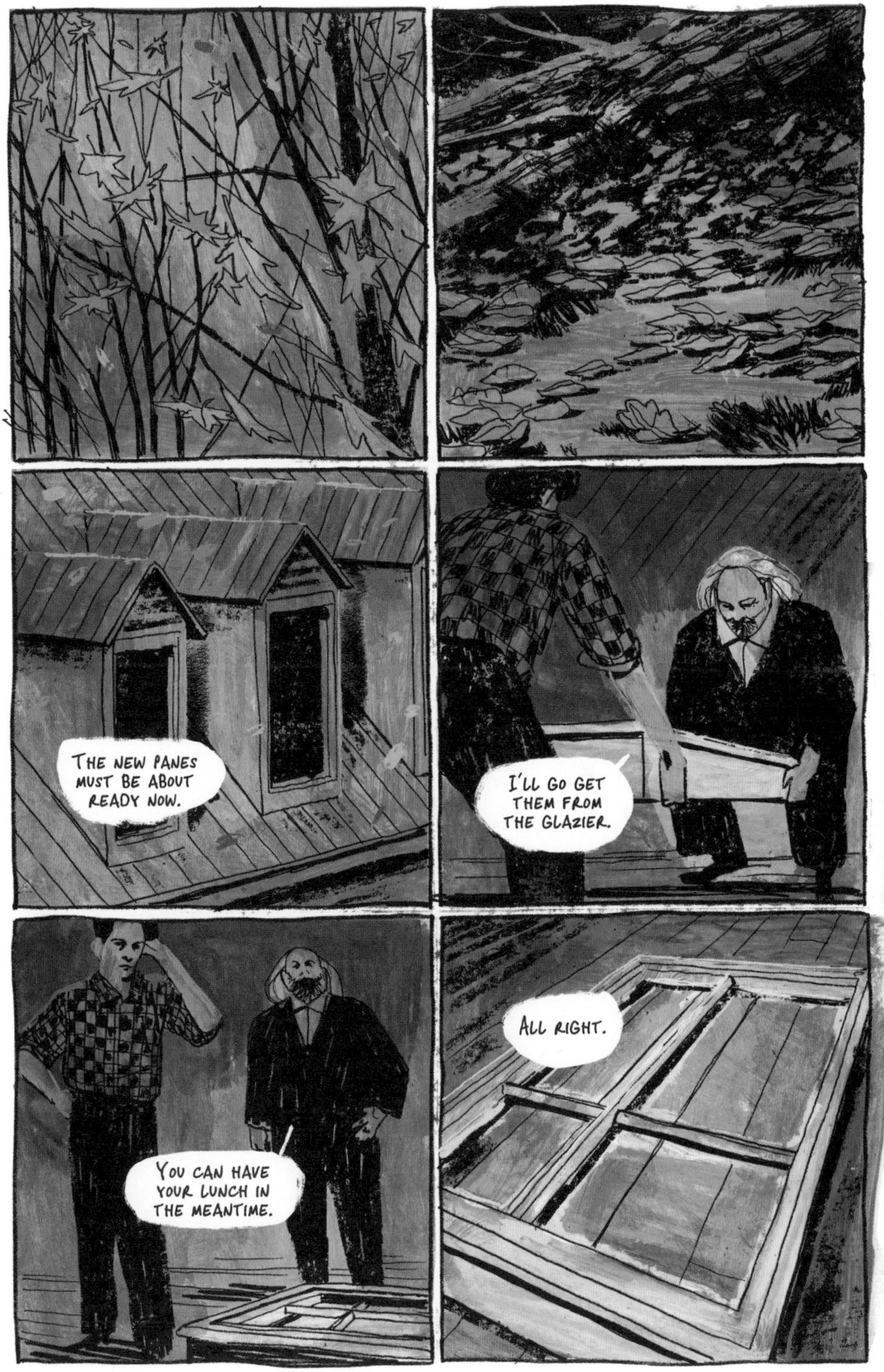
THE NEW PANES MUST BE ABOUT READY NOW.
I'LL GO GET THEM FROM THE GLAZIER.
YOU CAN HAVE YOUR LUNCH IN THE MEANTIME.
ALL RIGHT.

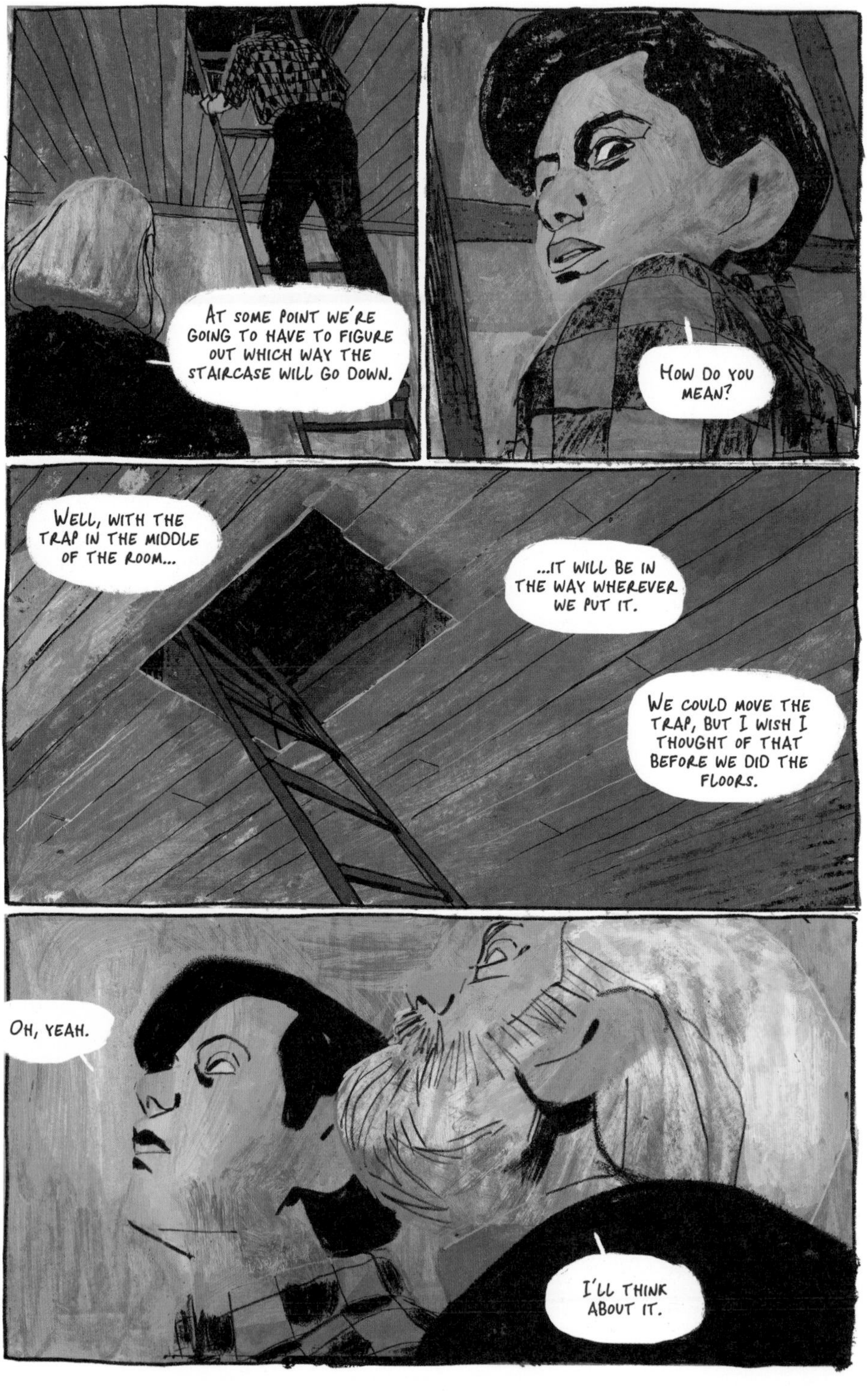

At some point we're going to have to figure out which way the staircase will go down.
How do you mean?
Well, with the trap in the middle of the room...
...it will be in the way wherever we put it.
We could move the trap, but I wish I thought of that before we did the floors.
Oh, yeah.
I'll think about it.

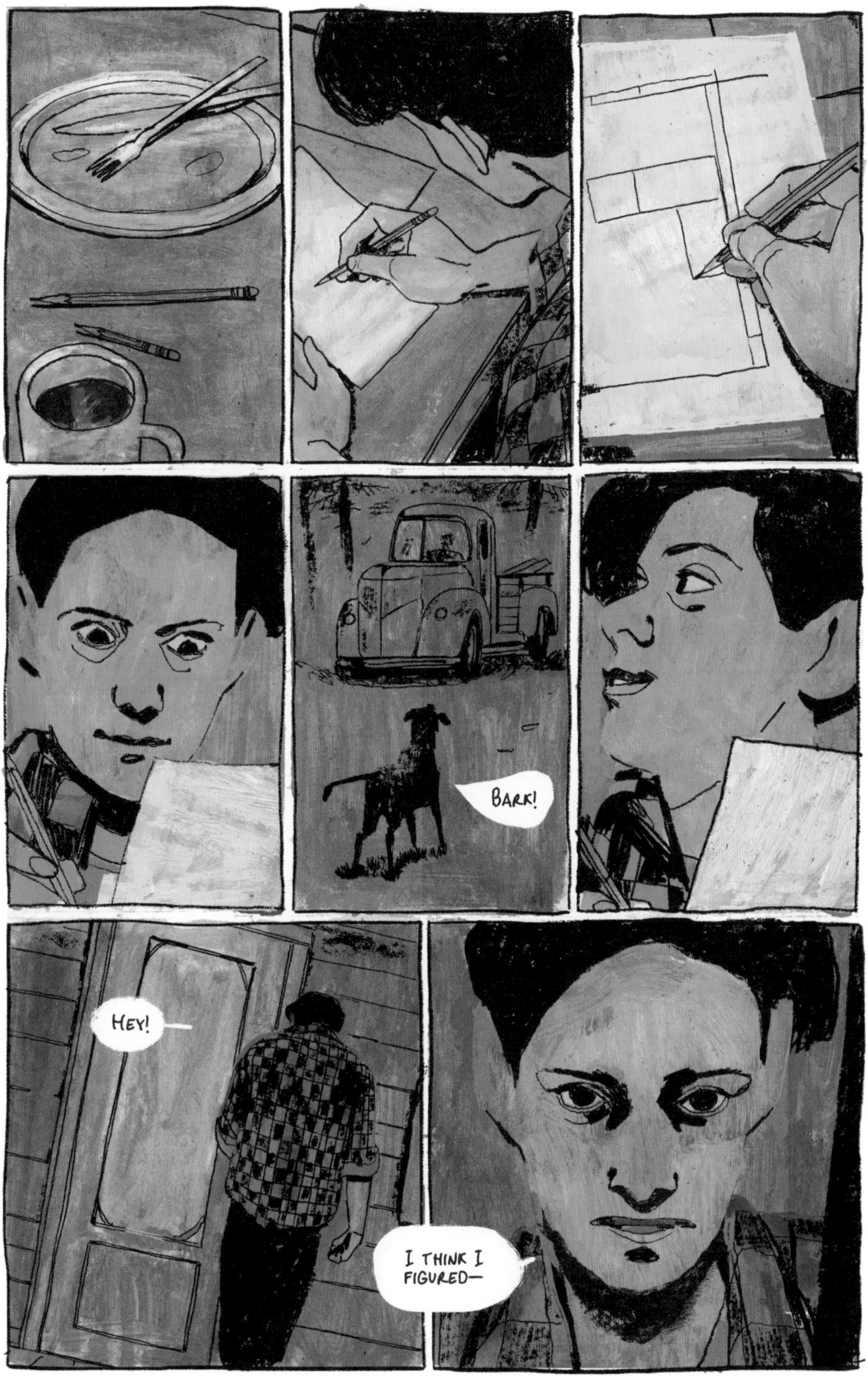
BARK!
HEY!
I THINK I FIGURED—

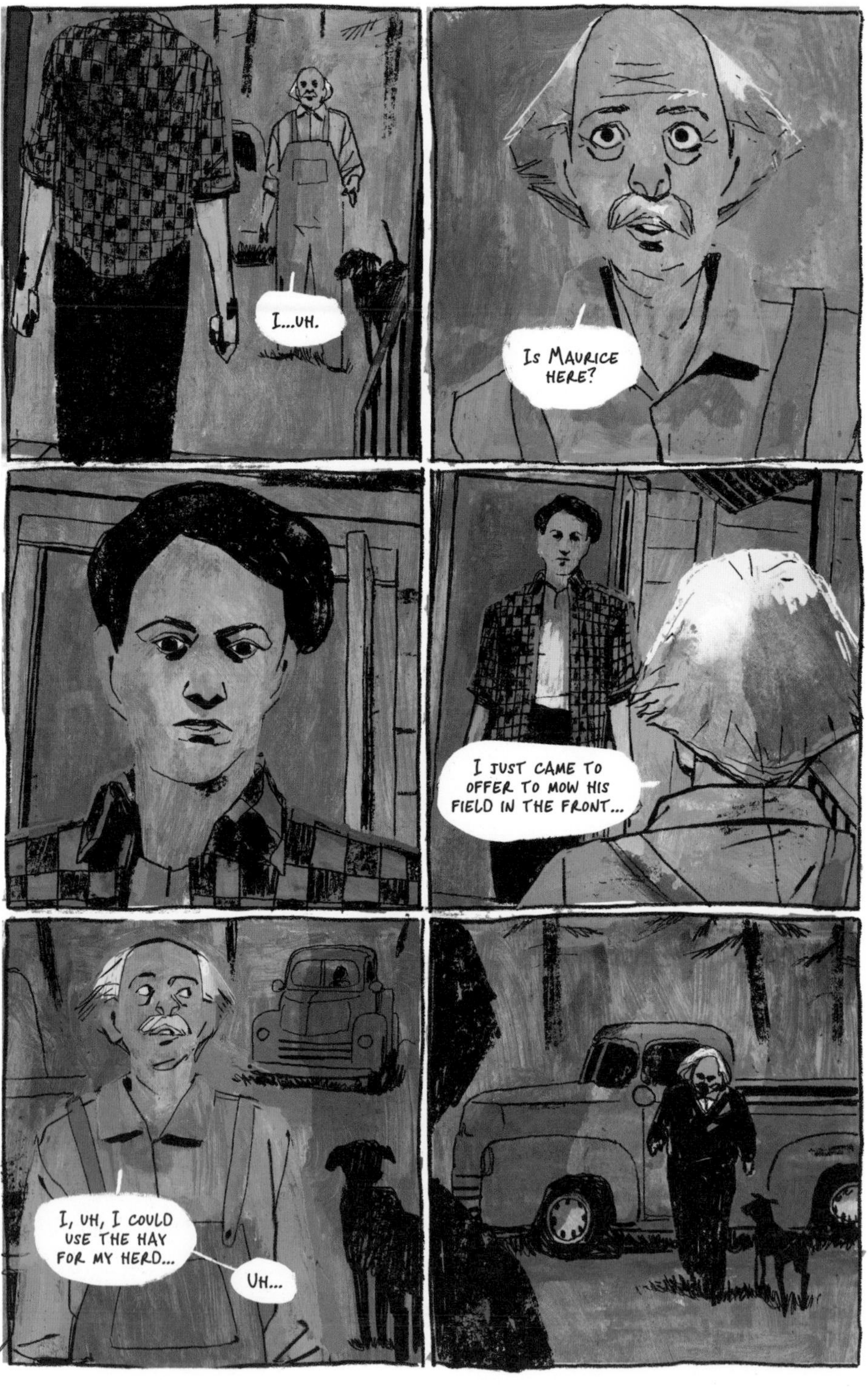
I...UH.
IS MAURICE HERE?
I JUST CAME TO OFFER TO MOW HIS FIELD IN THE FRONT...
I, UH, I COULD USE THE HAY FOR MY HERD...
UH...

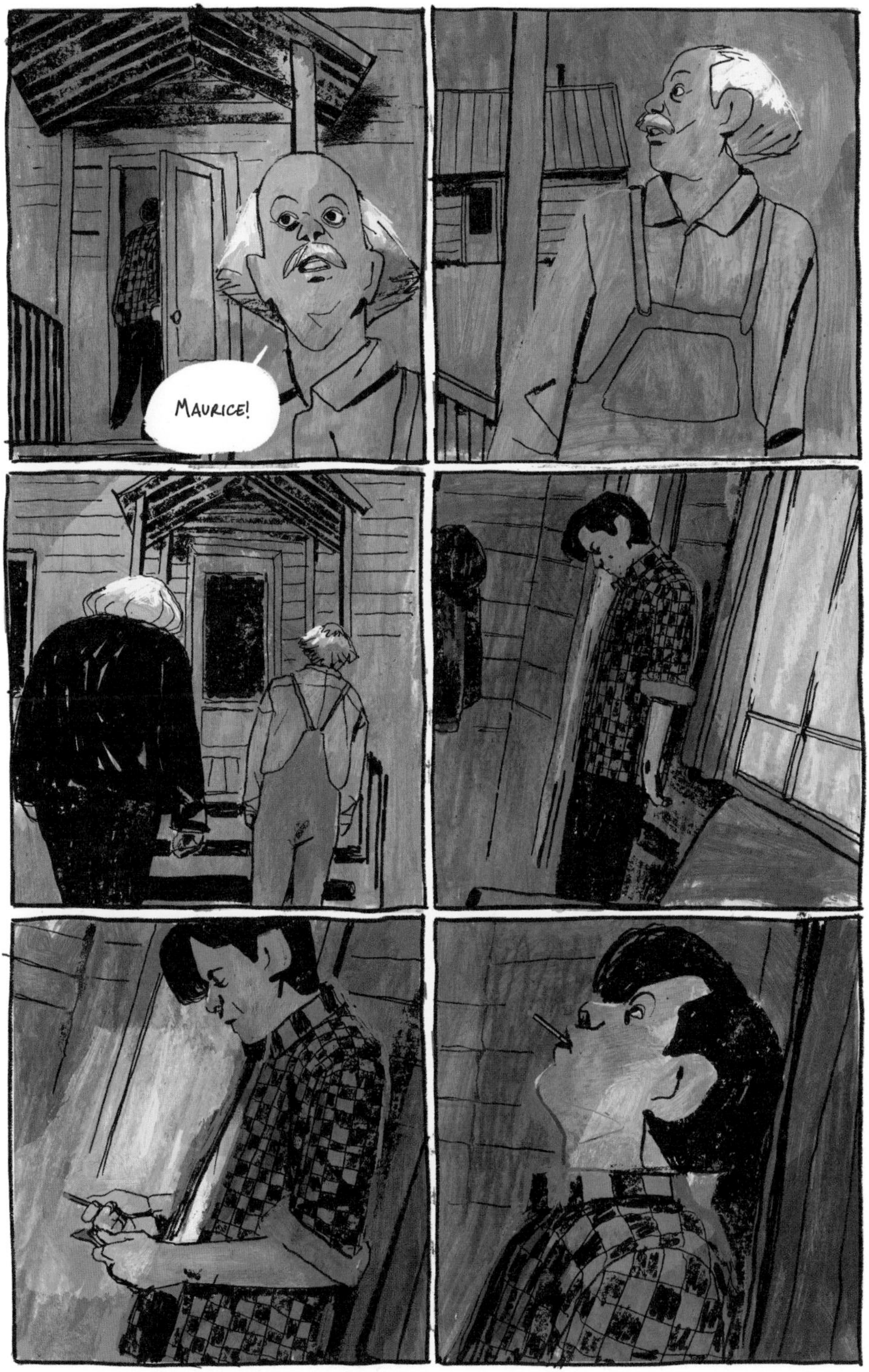
MAURICE!

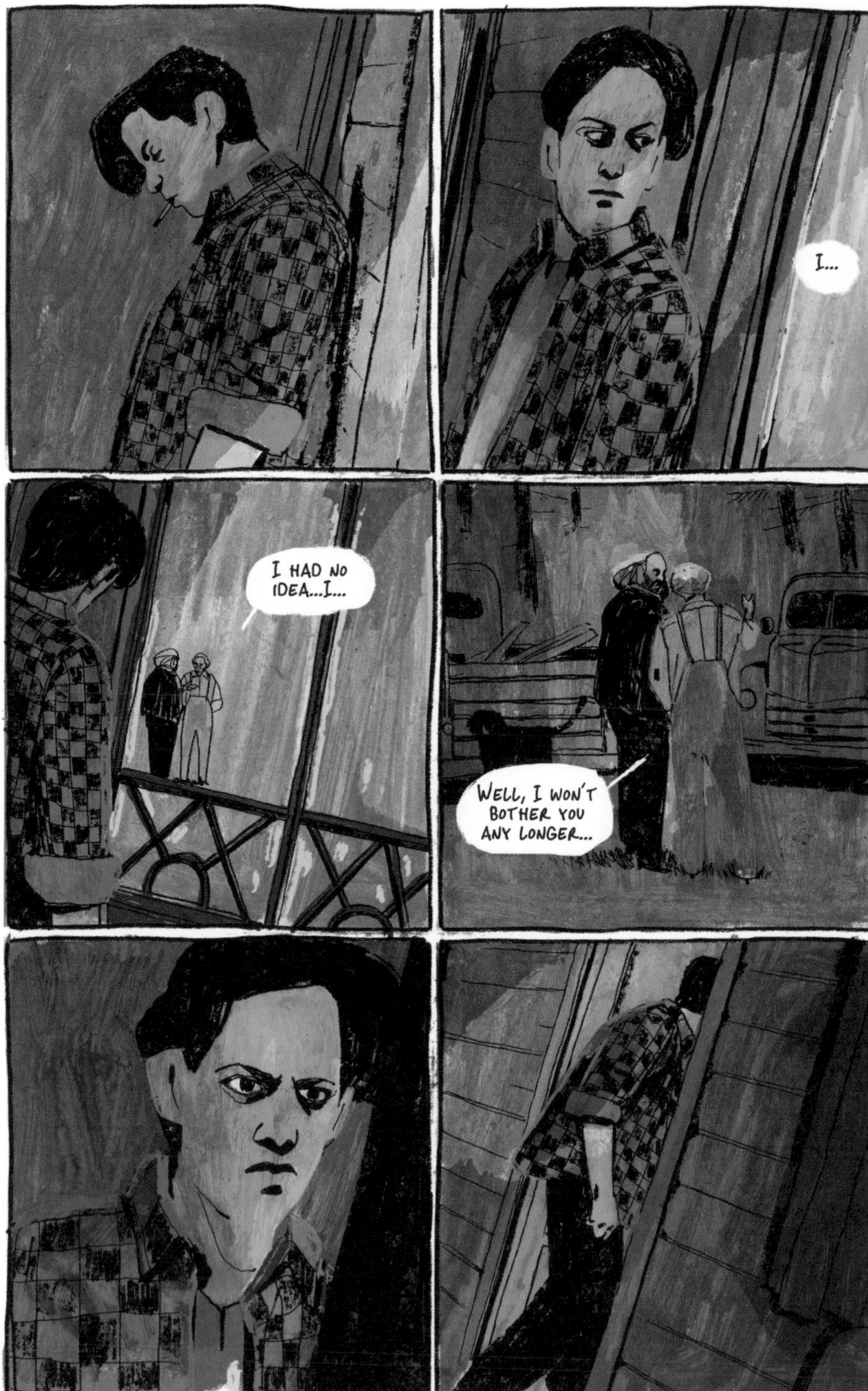
I...
I HAD NO IDEA...I...
WELL, I WON'T BOTHER YOU ANY LONGER...

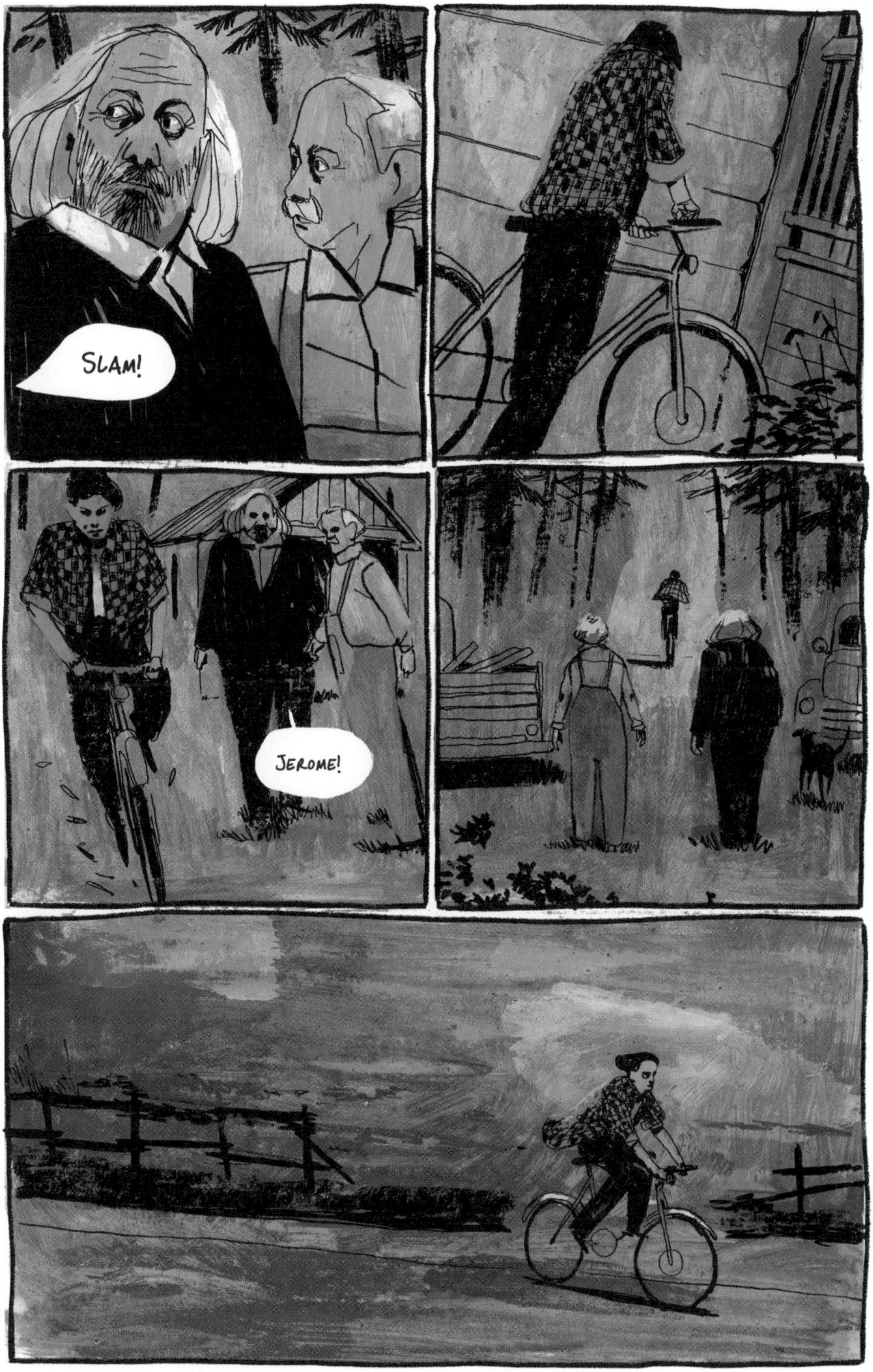
SLAM!
JEROME!

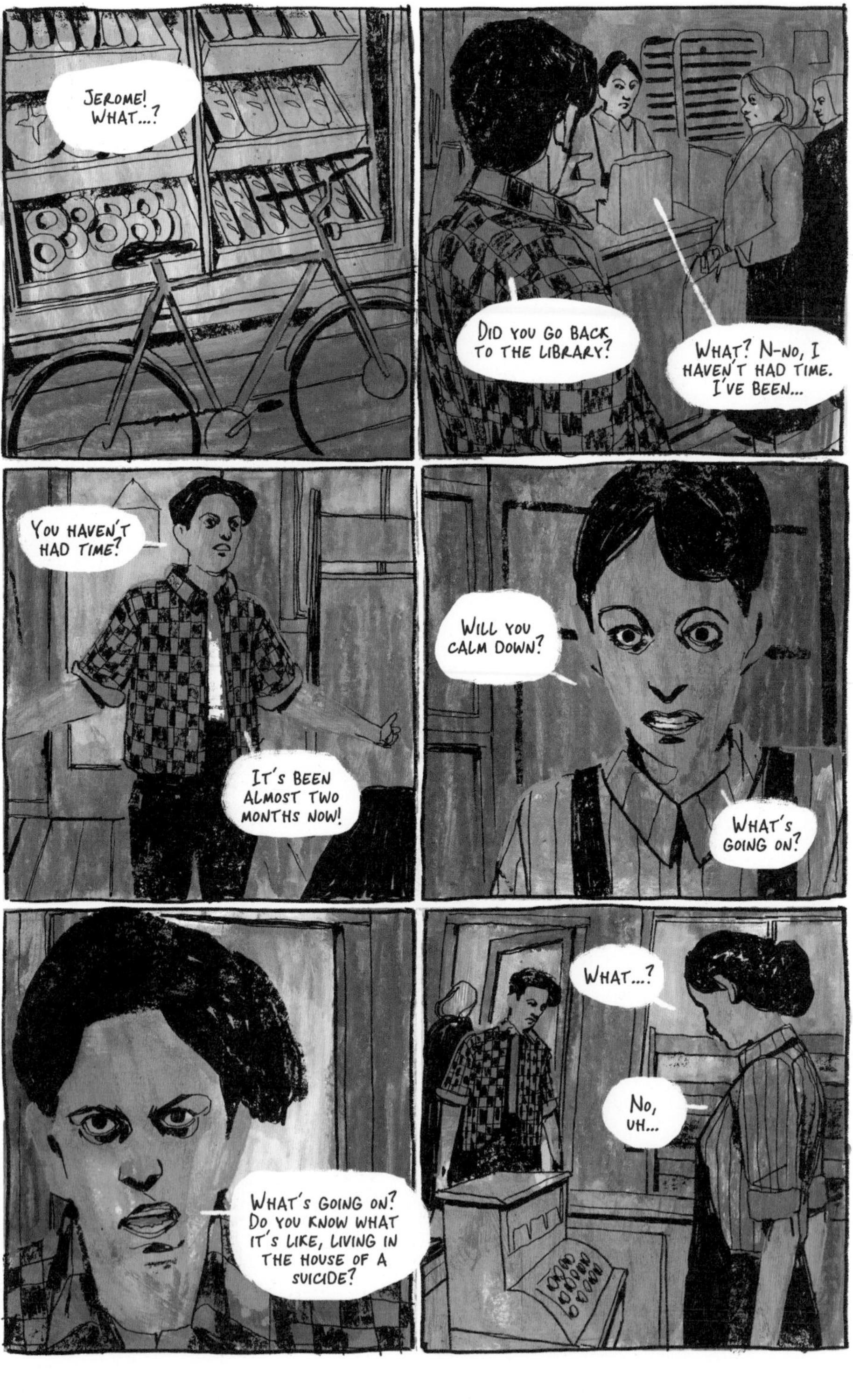
JEROME! WHAT...?
DID YOU GO BACK TO THE LIBRARY?
WHAT? N-NO, I HAVEN'T HAD TIME. I'VE BEEN...
YOU HAVEN'T HAD TIME?
IT'S BEEN ALMOST TWO MONTHS NOW!
WILL YOU CALM DOWN?
WHAT'S GOING ON?
WHAT'S GOING ON? DO YOU KNOW WHAT IT'S LIKE, LIVING IN THE HOUSE OF A SUICIDE?
WHAT...?
NO, UH...

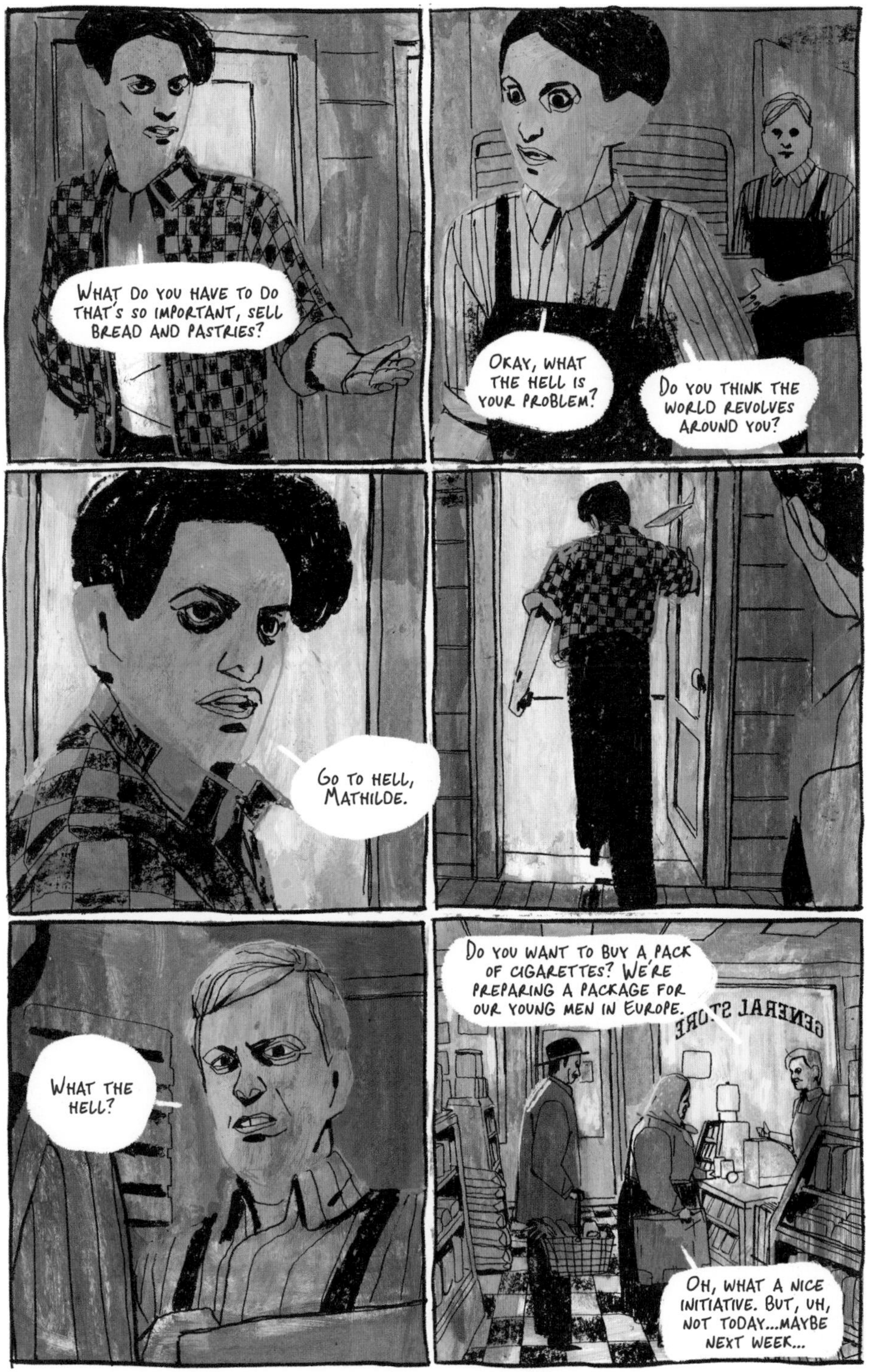
WHAT DO YOU HAVE TO DO THAT'S SO IMPORTANT, SELL BREAD AND PASTRIES?
OKAY, WHAT THE HELL IS YOUR PROBLEM?
DO YOU THINK THE WORLD REVOLVES AROUND YOU?
GO TO HELL, MATHILDE.
WHAT THE HELL?
DO YOU WANT TO BUY A PACK OF CIGARETTES? WE'RE PREPARING A PACKAGE FOR OUR YOUNG MEN IN EUROPE.
GENERAL STORE
OH, WHAT A NICE INITIATIVE. BUT, UH, NOT TODAY...MAYBE NEXT WEEK...

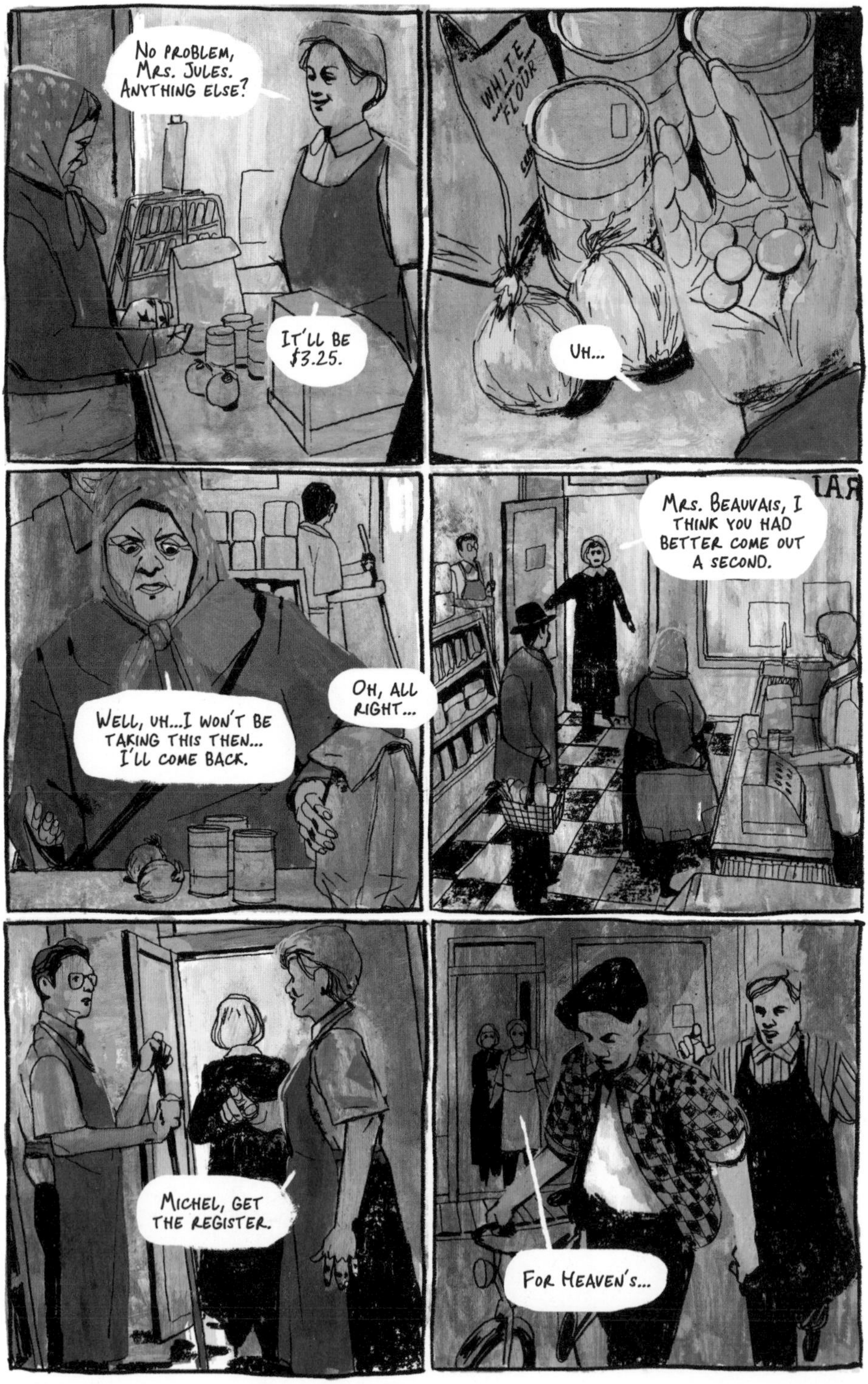

No problem, Mrs. Jules. Anything else?
It'll be $3.25.
Uh...
Well, uh...I won't be taking this then... I'll come back.
Oh, all right...
Mrs. Beauvais, I think you had better come out a second.
Michel, get the register.
For Heaven's...

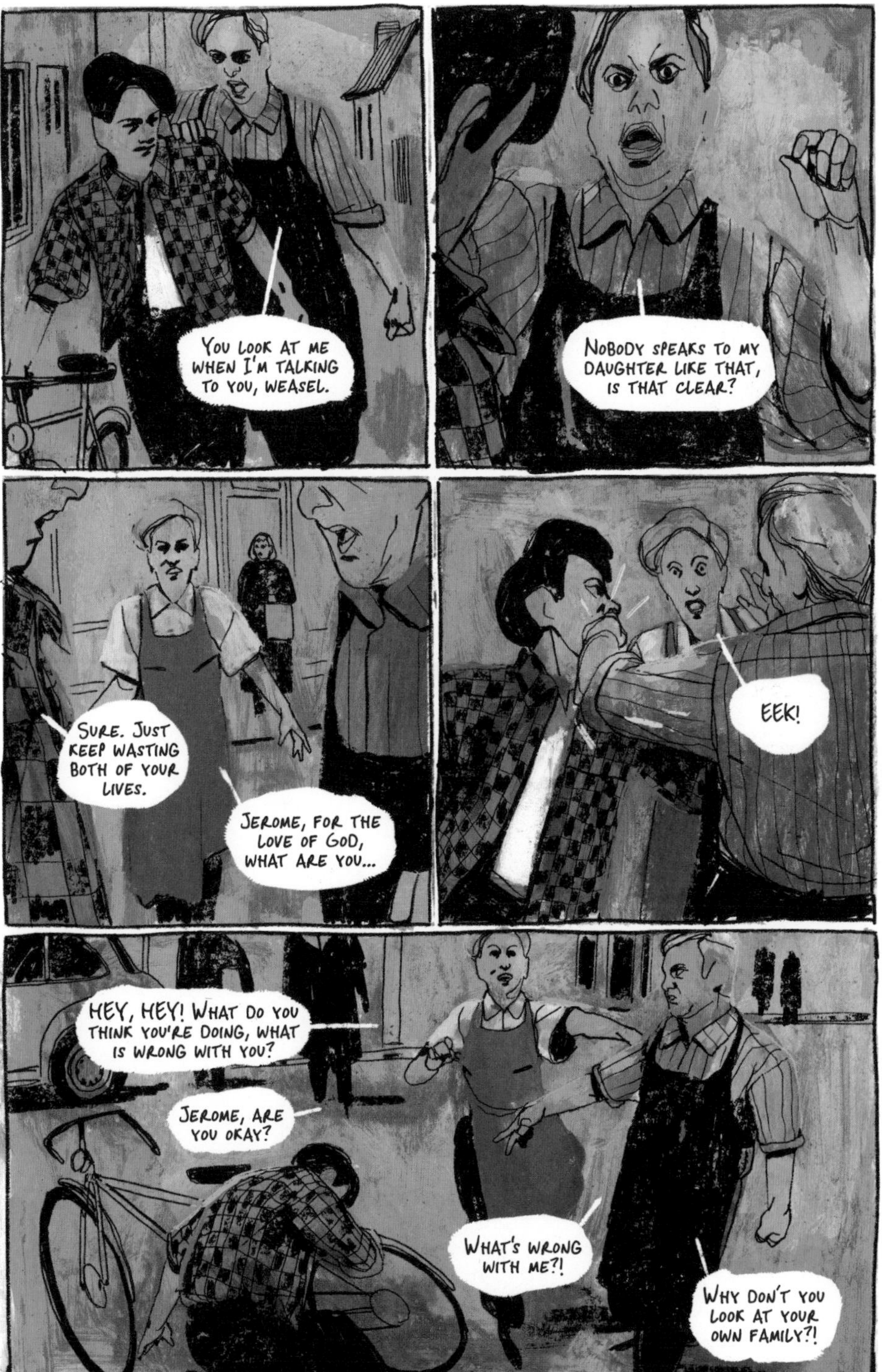

You look at me when I'm talking to you, weasel.
Nobody speaks to my daughter like that, is that clear?
Sure. Just keep wasting both of your lives.
Jerome, for the love of God, what are you...
EEK!
Hey, hey! What do you think you're doing, what is wrong with you?
Jerome, are you okay?
What's wrong with me?!
Why don't you look at your own family?!

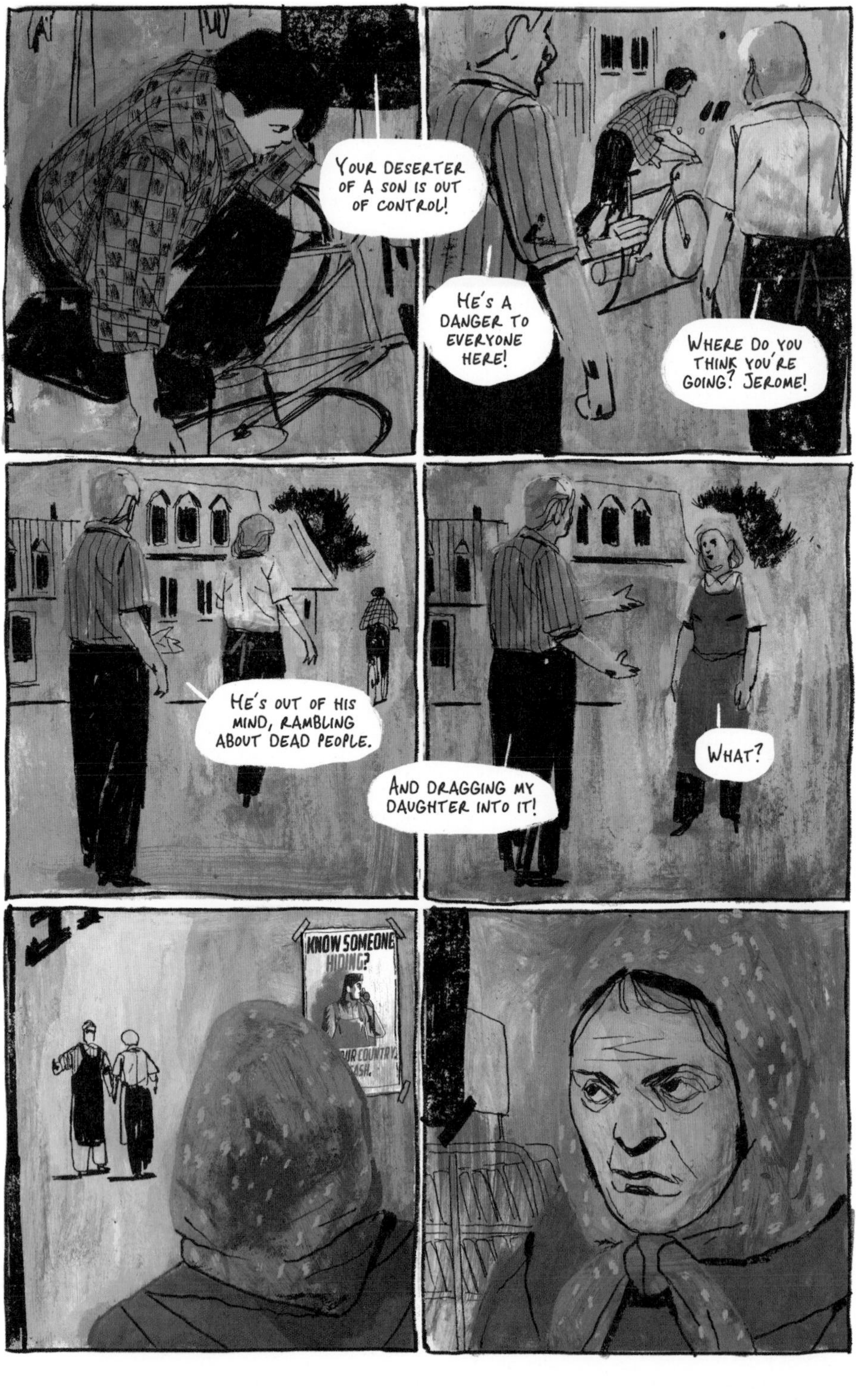
YOUR DESERTER OF A SON IS OUT OF CONTROL!
HE'S A DANGER TO EVERYONE HERE!
WHERE DO YOU THINK YOU'RE GOING? JEROME!
HE'S OUT OF HIS MIND, RAMBLING ABOUT DEAD PEOPLE.
AND DRAGGING MY DAUGHTER INTO IT!
WHAT?
KNOW SOMEONE HIDING?

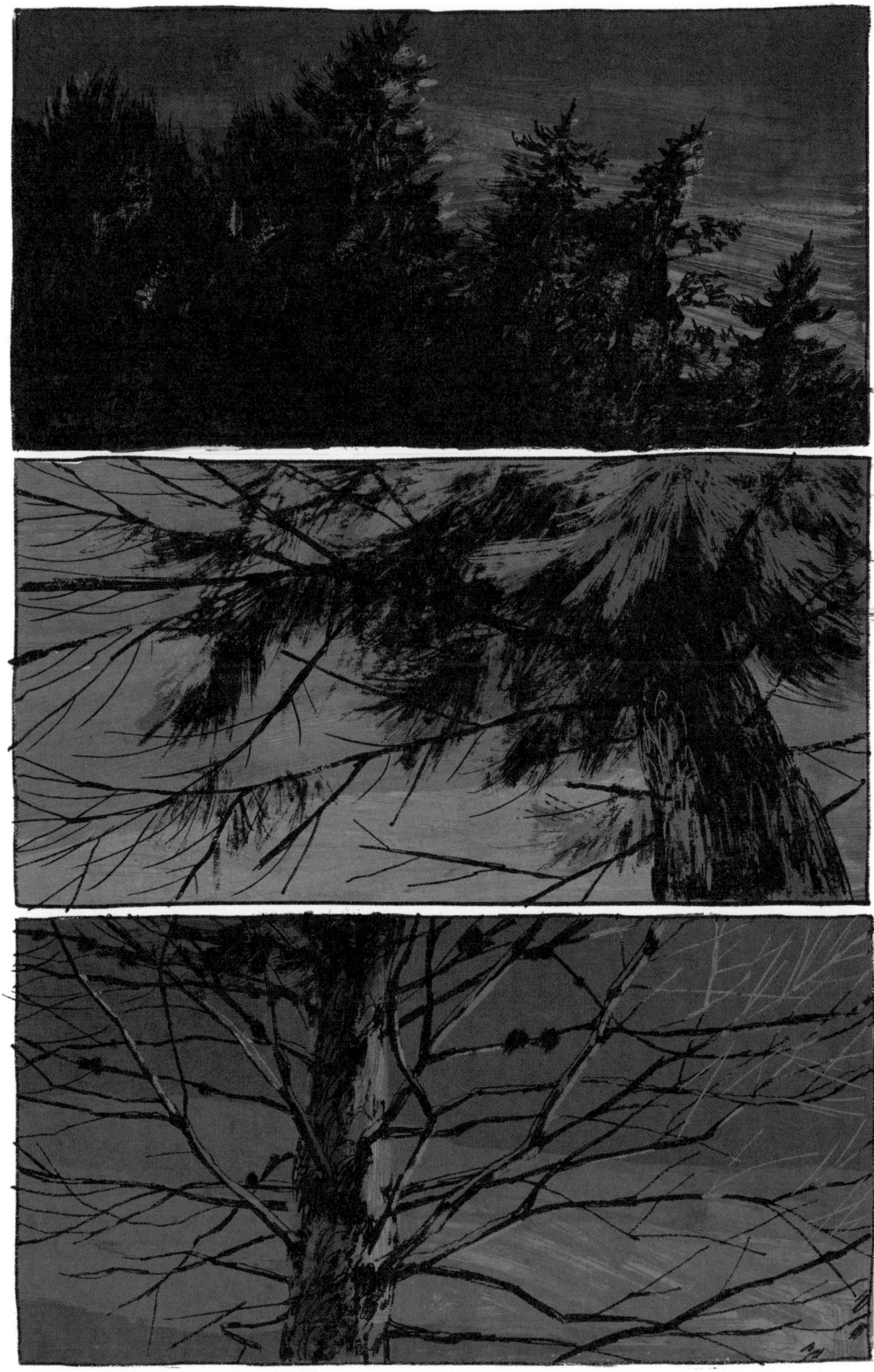

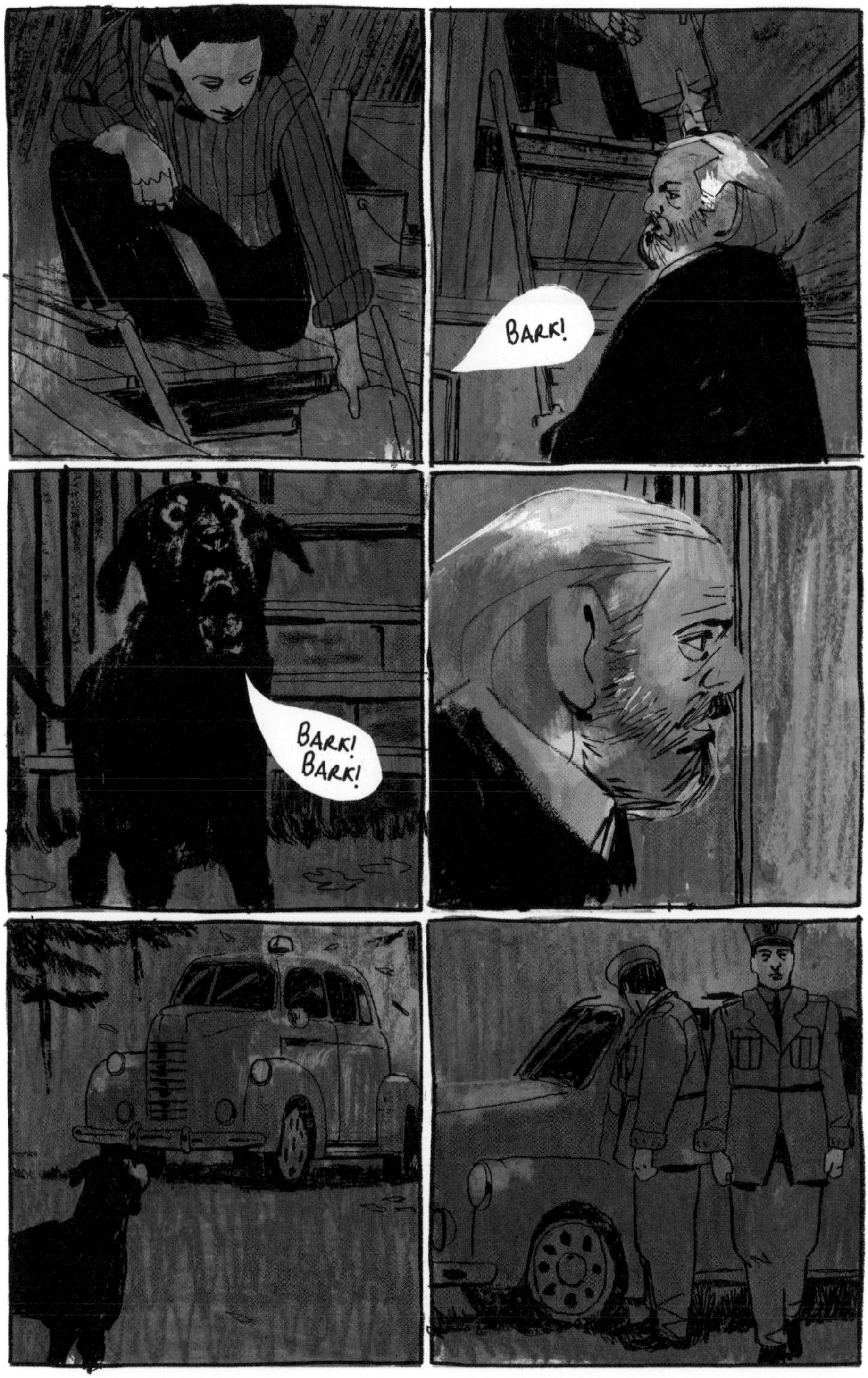
BARK!
BARK! BARK!

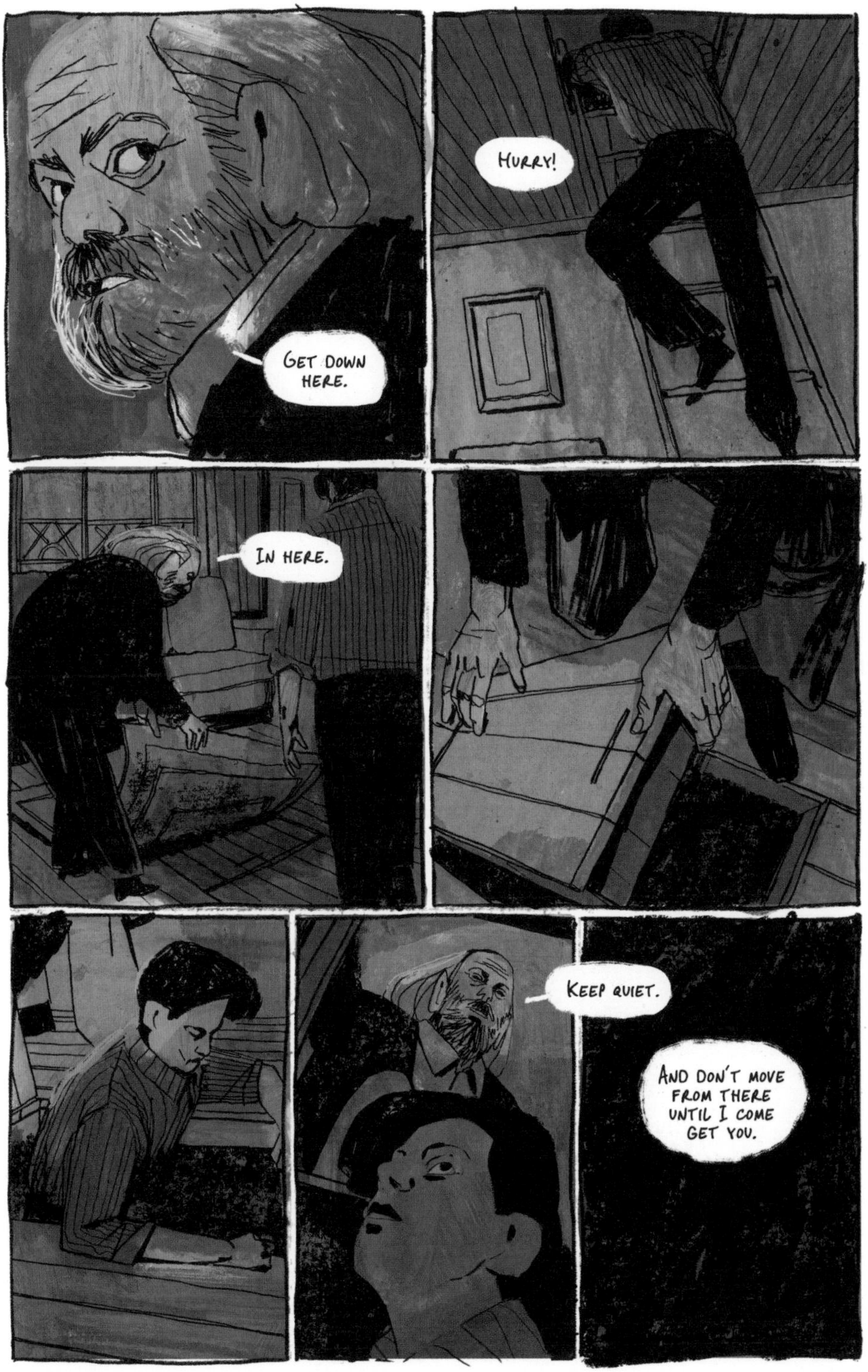
GET DOWN HERE.
HURRY!
IN HERE.
KEEP QUIET.
AND DON'T MOVE FROM THERE UNTIL I COME GET YOU.

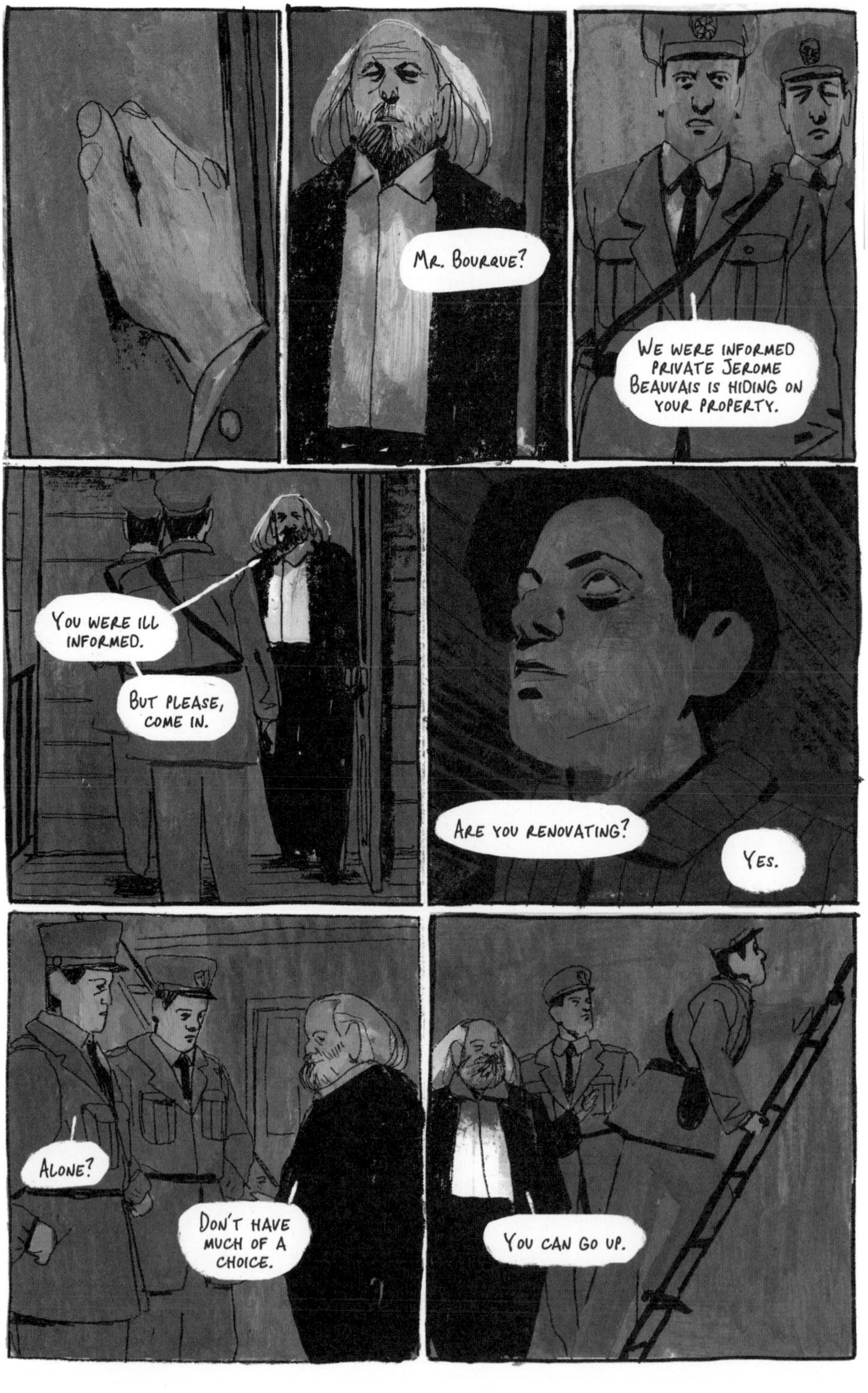
Mr. Bourque?
We were informed private Jerome Beauvais is hiding on your property.
You were ill informed.
But please, come in.
Are you renovating?
Yes.
Alone?
Don't have much of a choice.
You can go up.

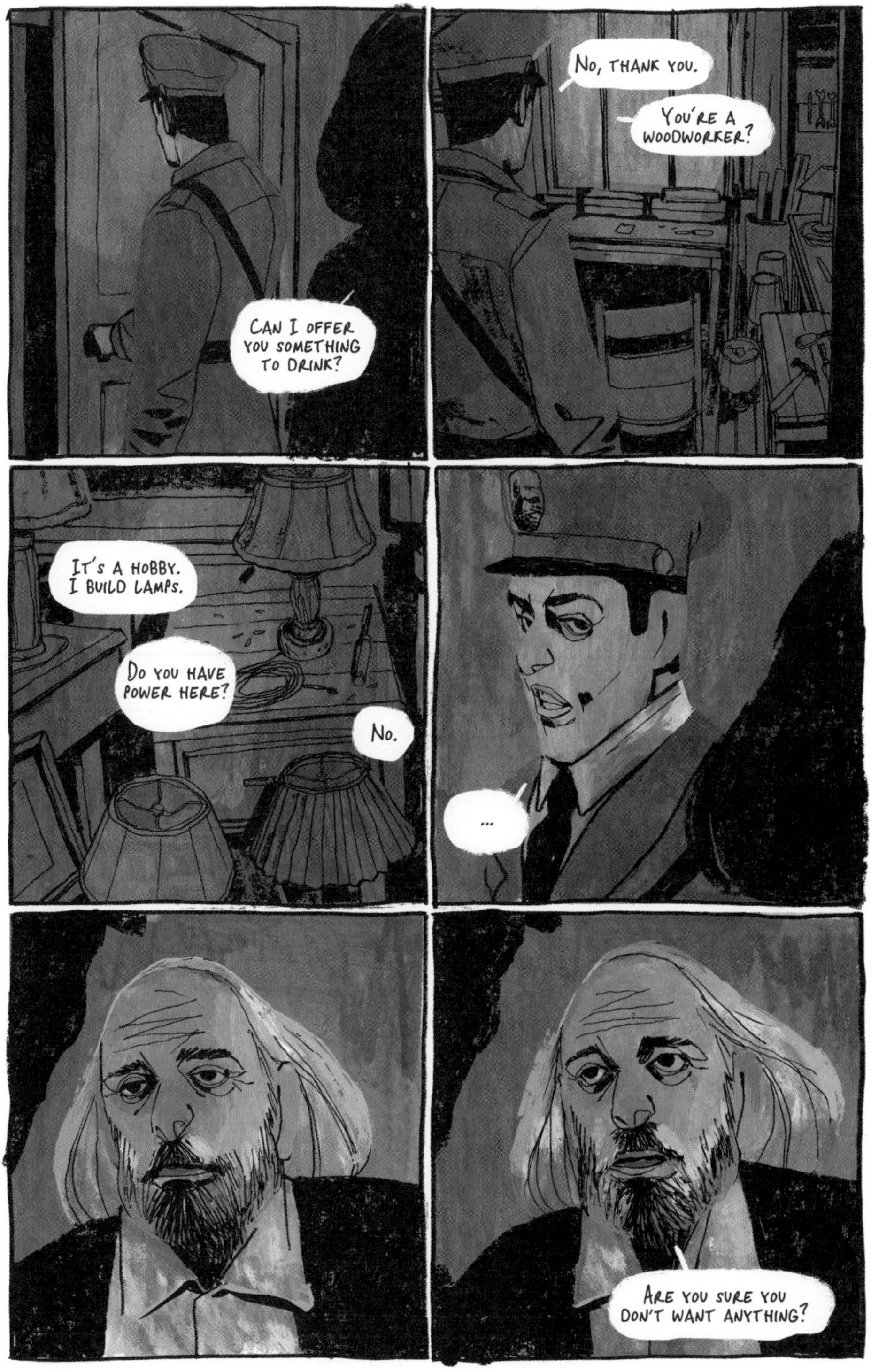

Can I offer you something to drink?
No, thank you.
You're a woodworker?
It's a hobby. I build lamps.
Do you have power here?
No.
...
Are you sure you don't want anything?

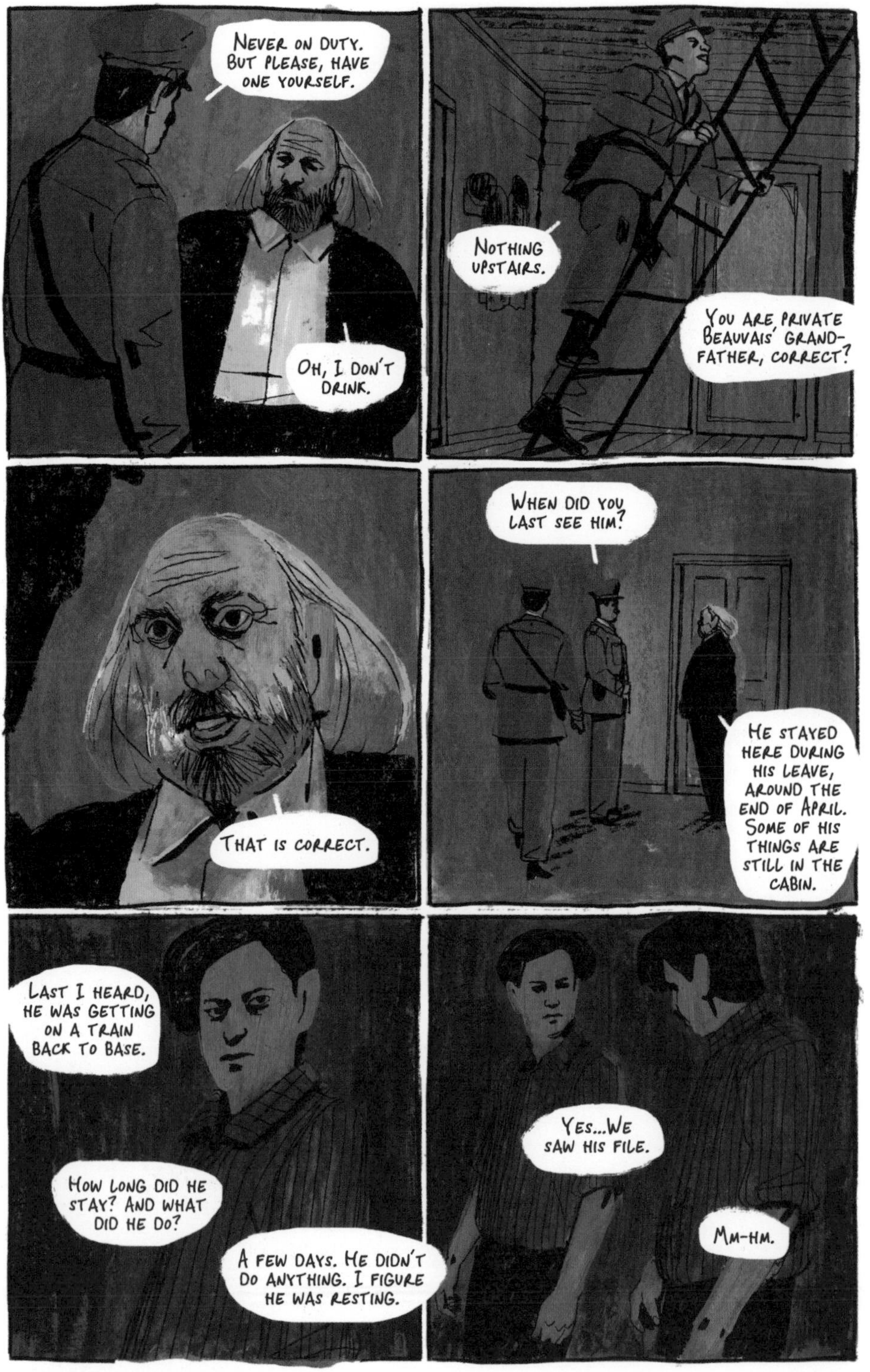
NEVER ON DUTY. BUT PLEASE, HAVE ONE YOURSELF.
OH, I DON'T DRINK.
NOTHING UPSTAIRS.
YOU ARE PRIVATE BEAUVAIS' GRANDFATHER, CORRECT?
THAT IS CORRECT.
WHEN DID YOU LAST SEE HIM?
HE STAYED HERE DURING HIS LEAVE, AROUND THE END OF APRIL. SOME OF HIS THINGS ARE STILL IN THE CABIN.
LAST I HEARD, HE WAS GETTING ON A TRAIN BACK TO BASE.
HOW LONG DID HE STAY? AND WHAT DID HE DO?
A FEW DAYS. HE DIDN'T DO ANYTHING. I FIGURE HE WAS RESTING.
YES...WE SAW HIS FILE.
MM-HM.

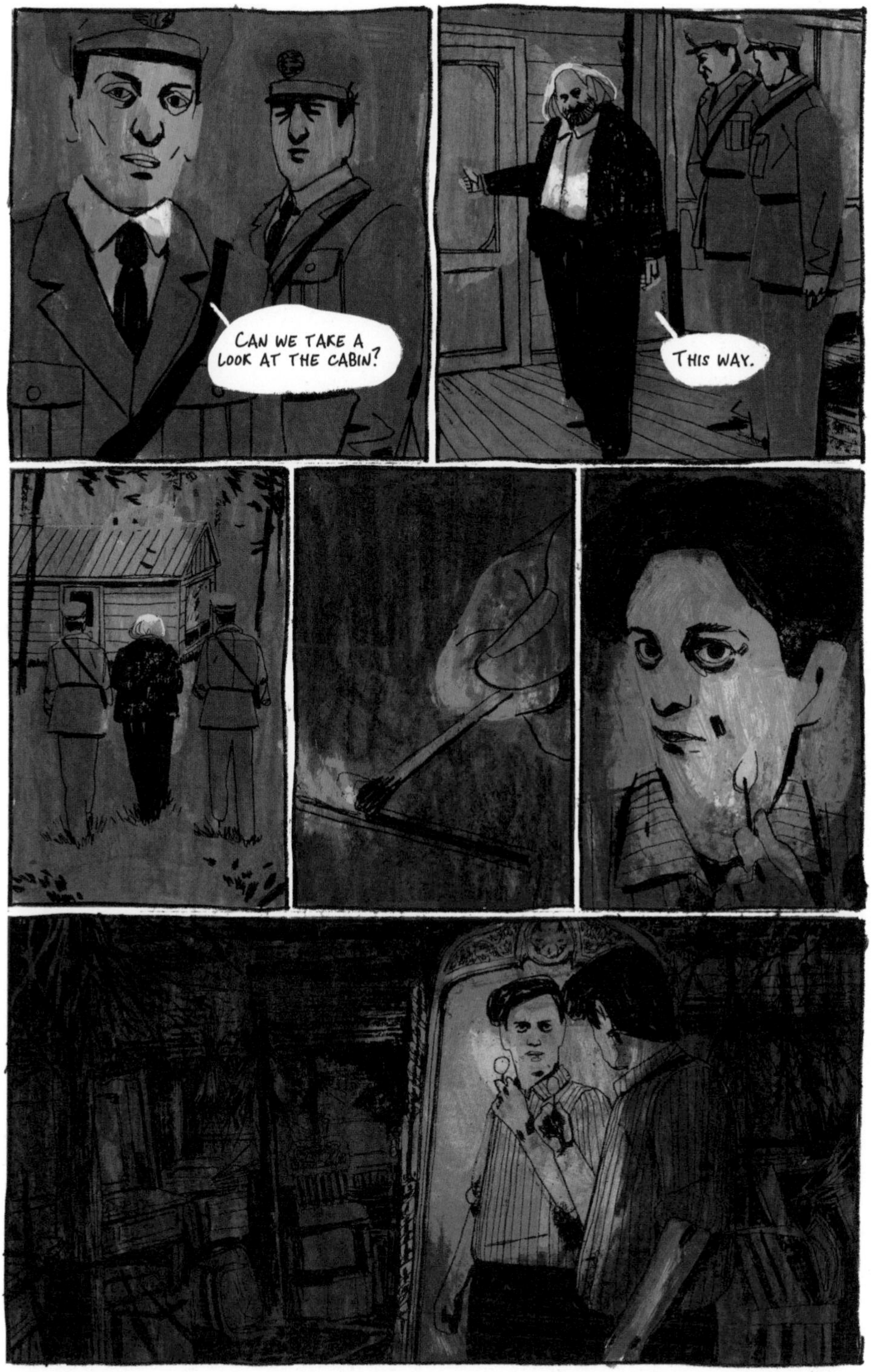
CAN WE TAKE A LOOK AT THE CABIN?
THIS WAY.

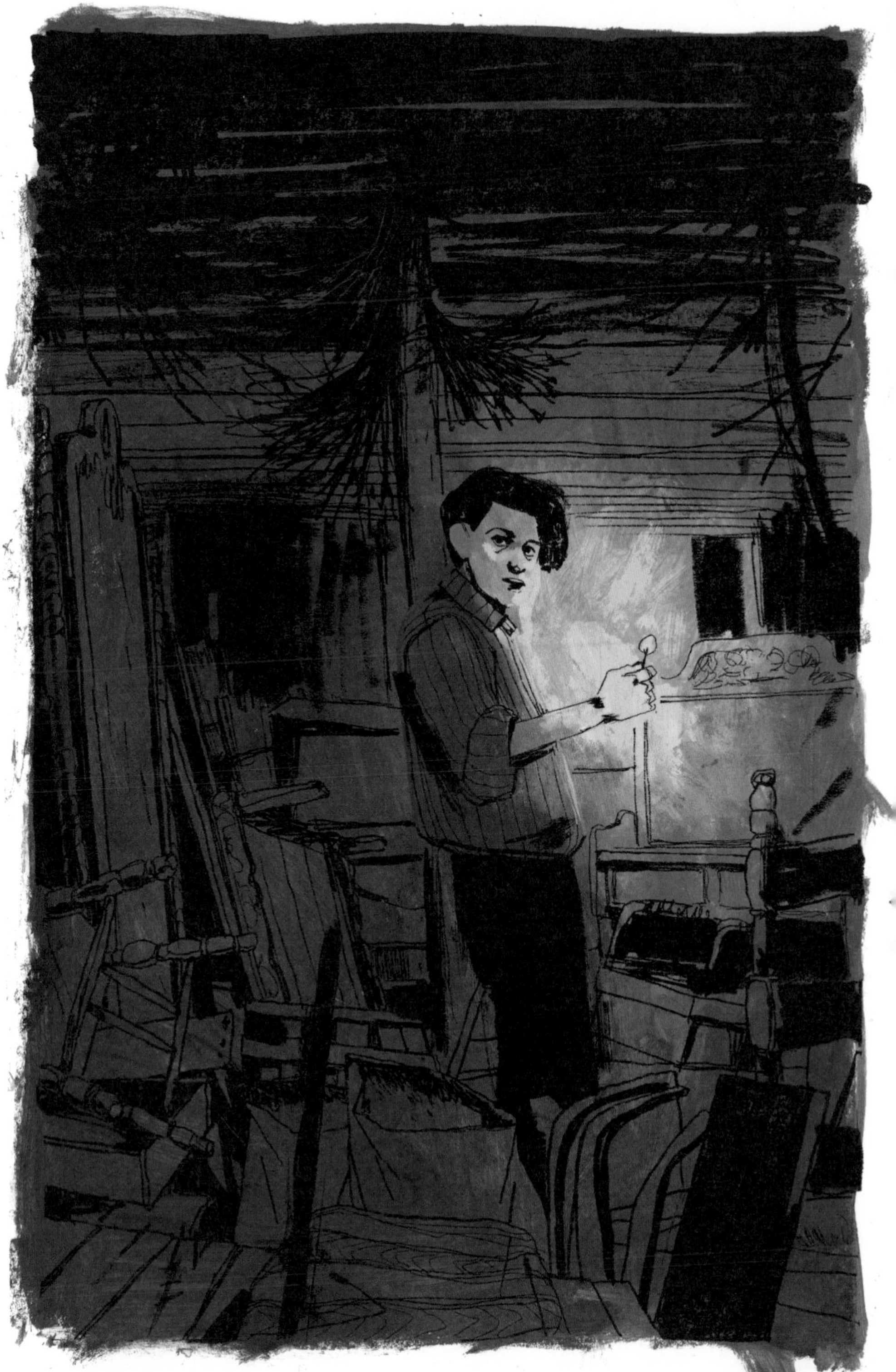

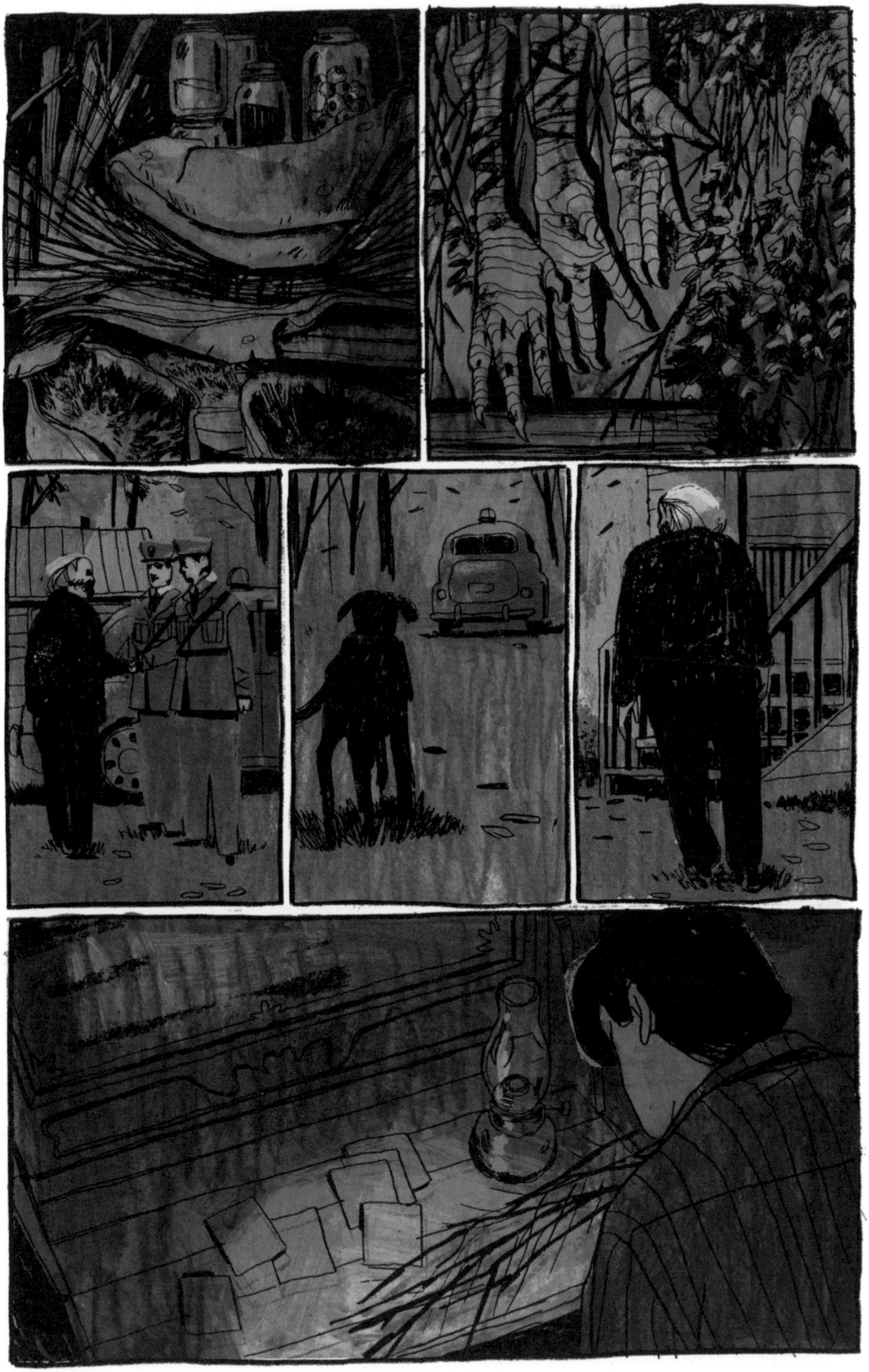

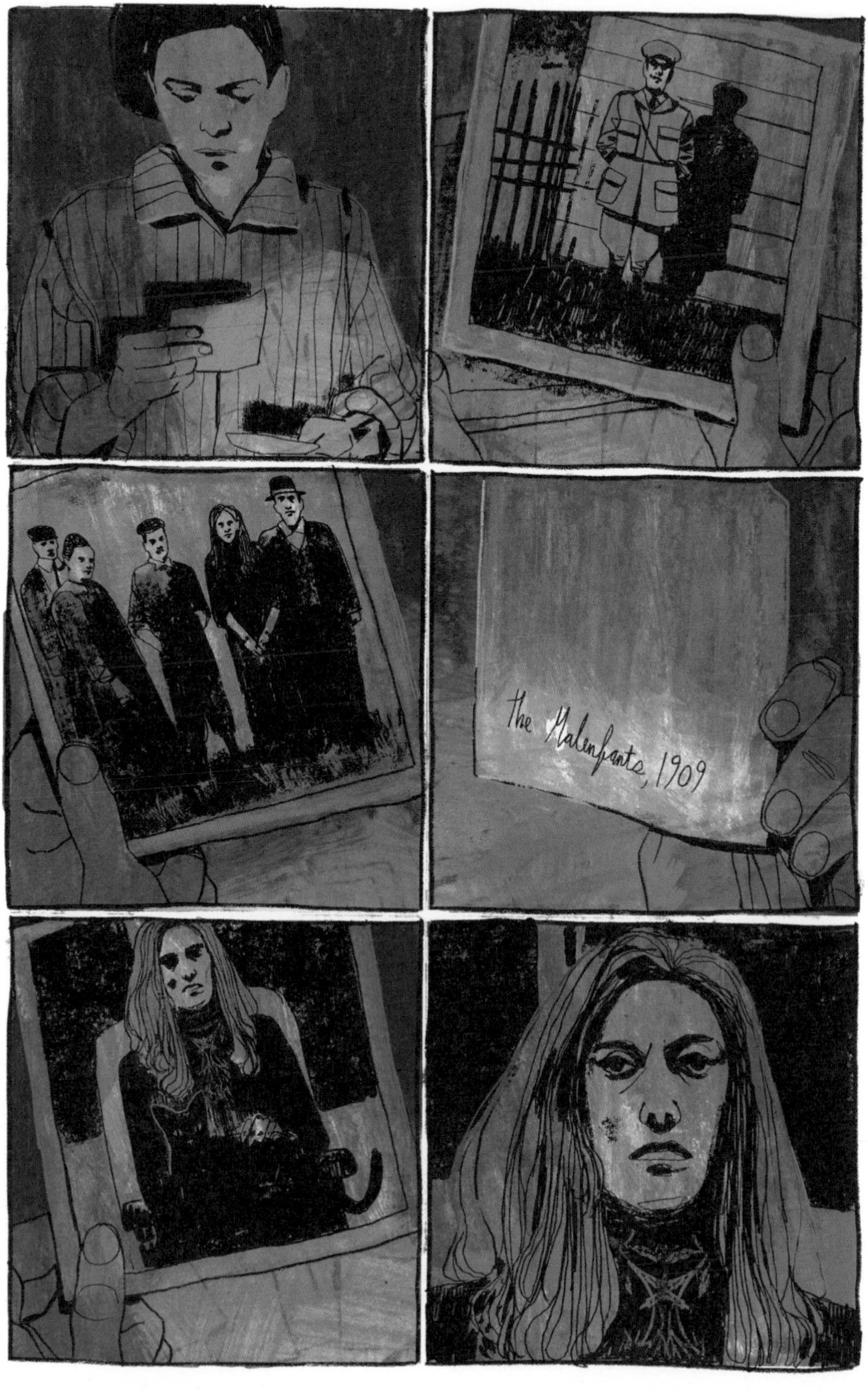
The Malenfants, 1909

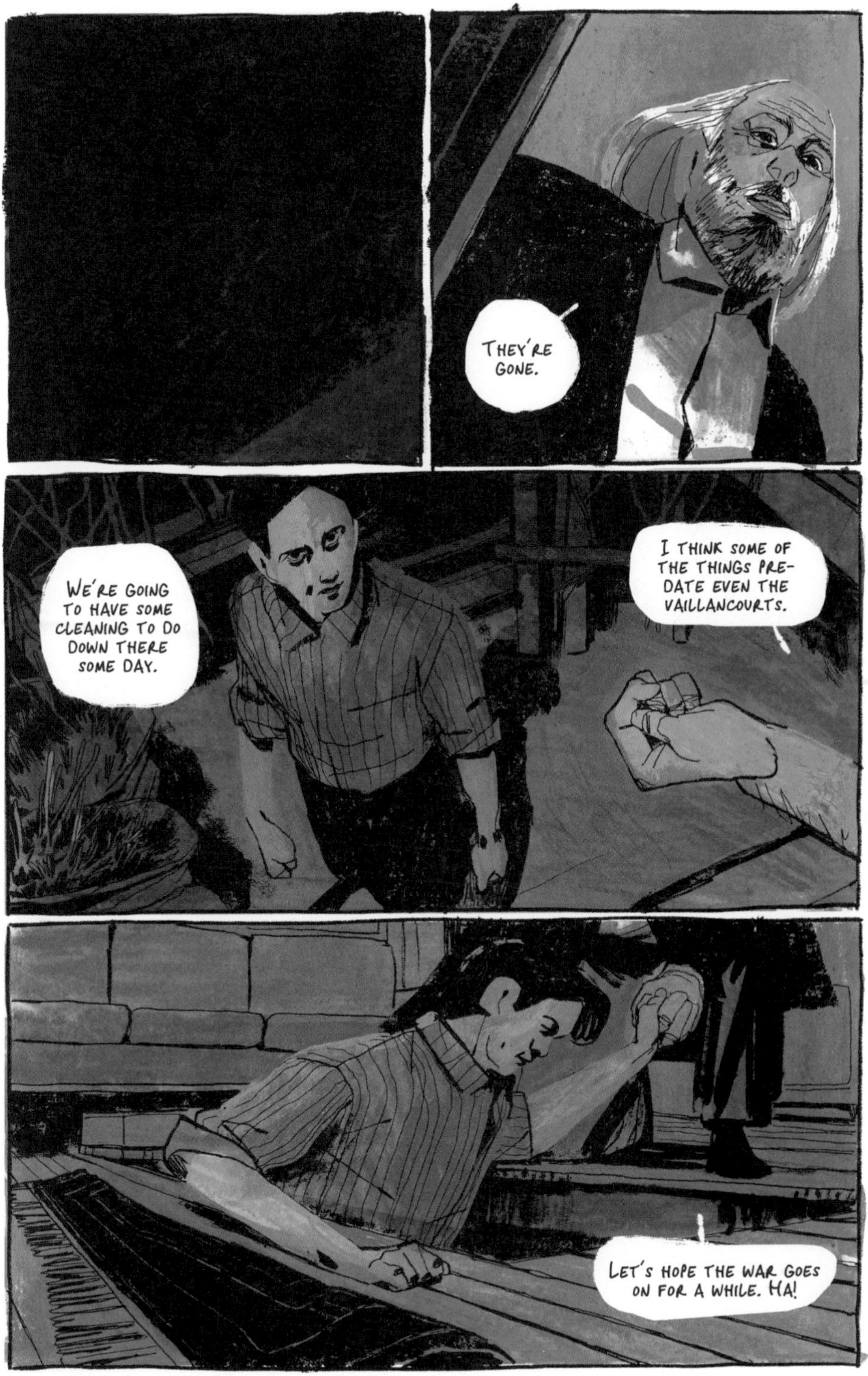
They're gone.
We're going to have some cleaning to do down there some day.
I think some of the things pre-date even the Vaillancourts.
Let's hope the war goes on for a while. Ha!

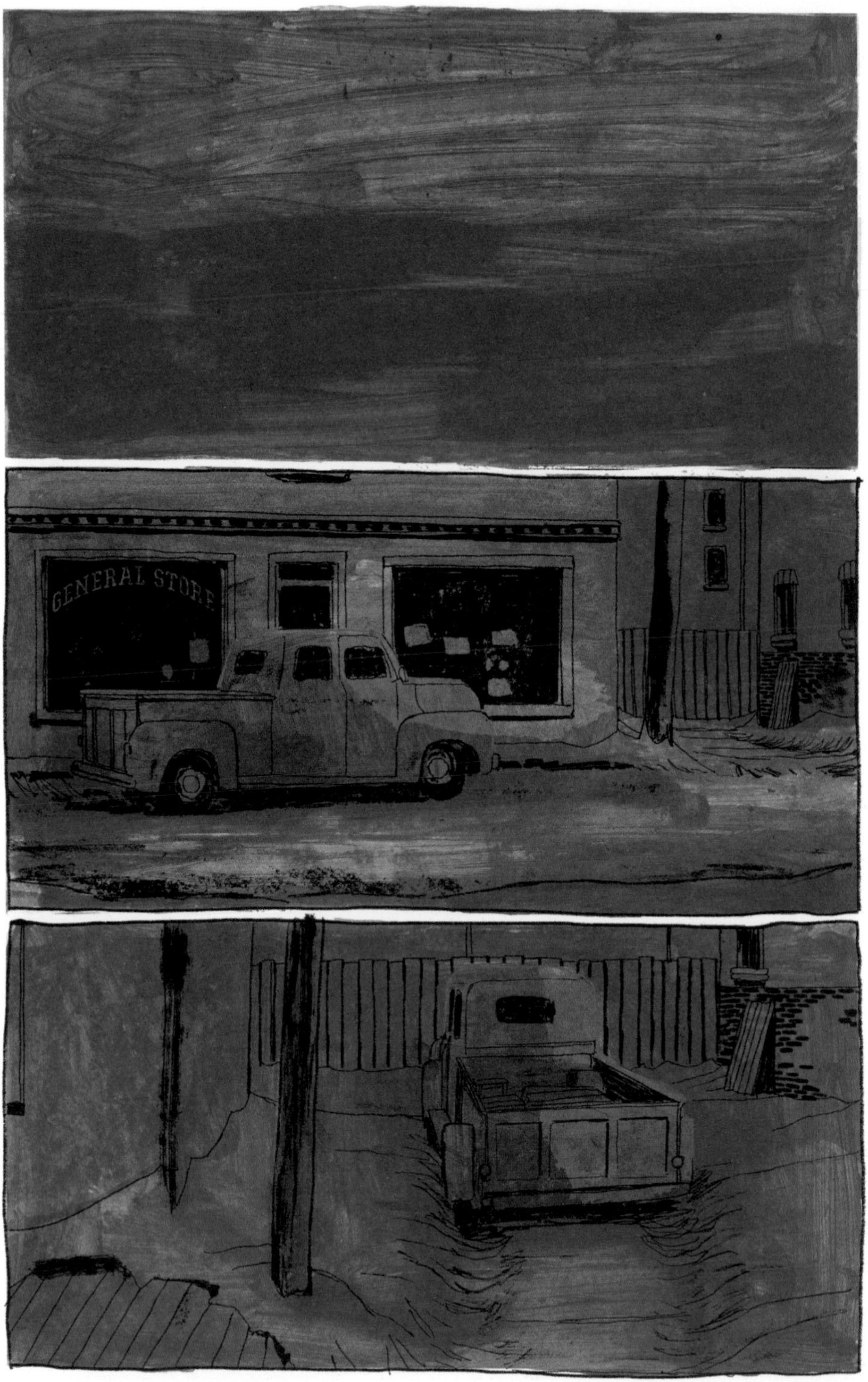
GENERAL STORE

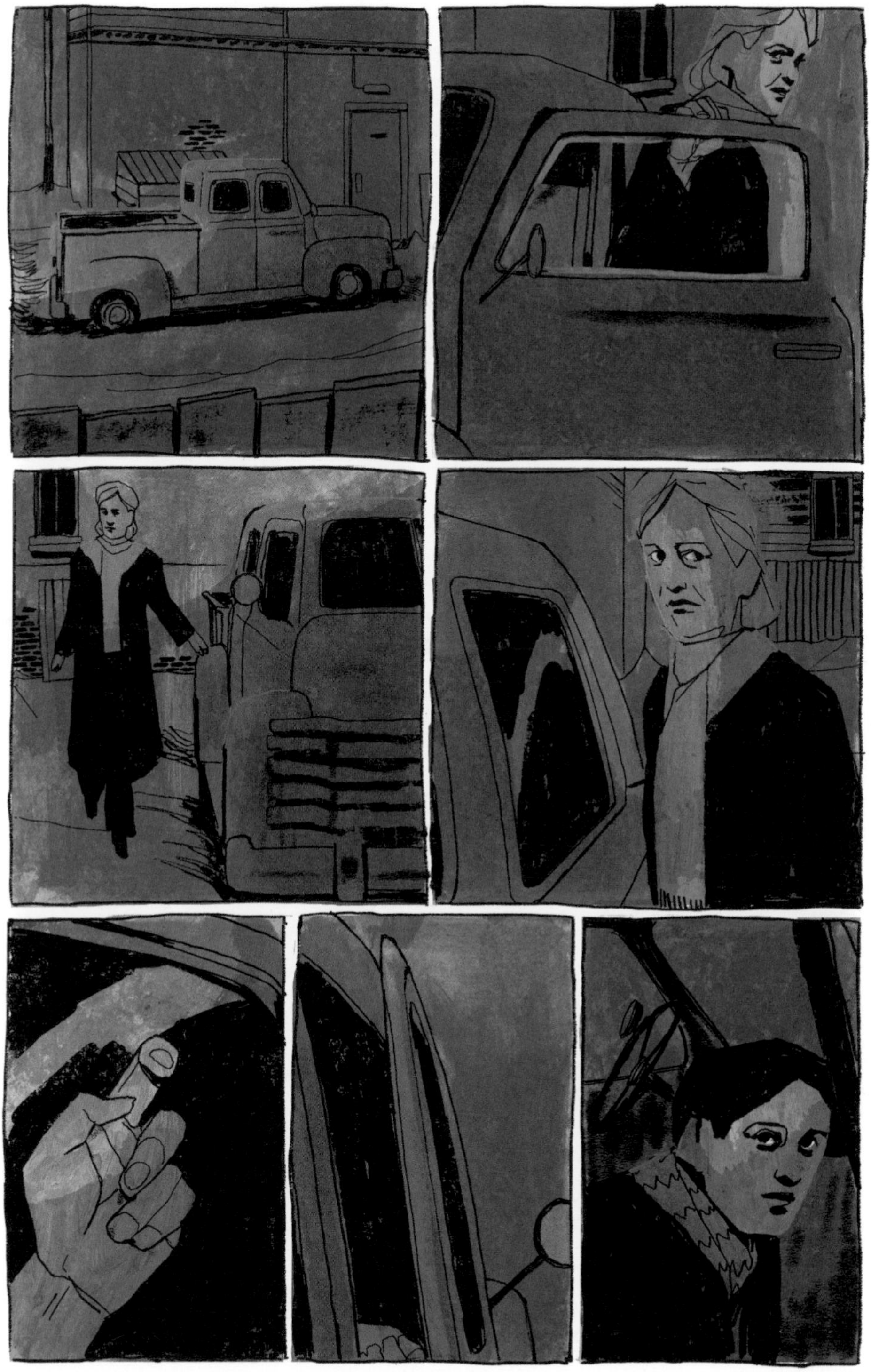

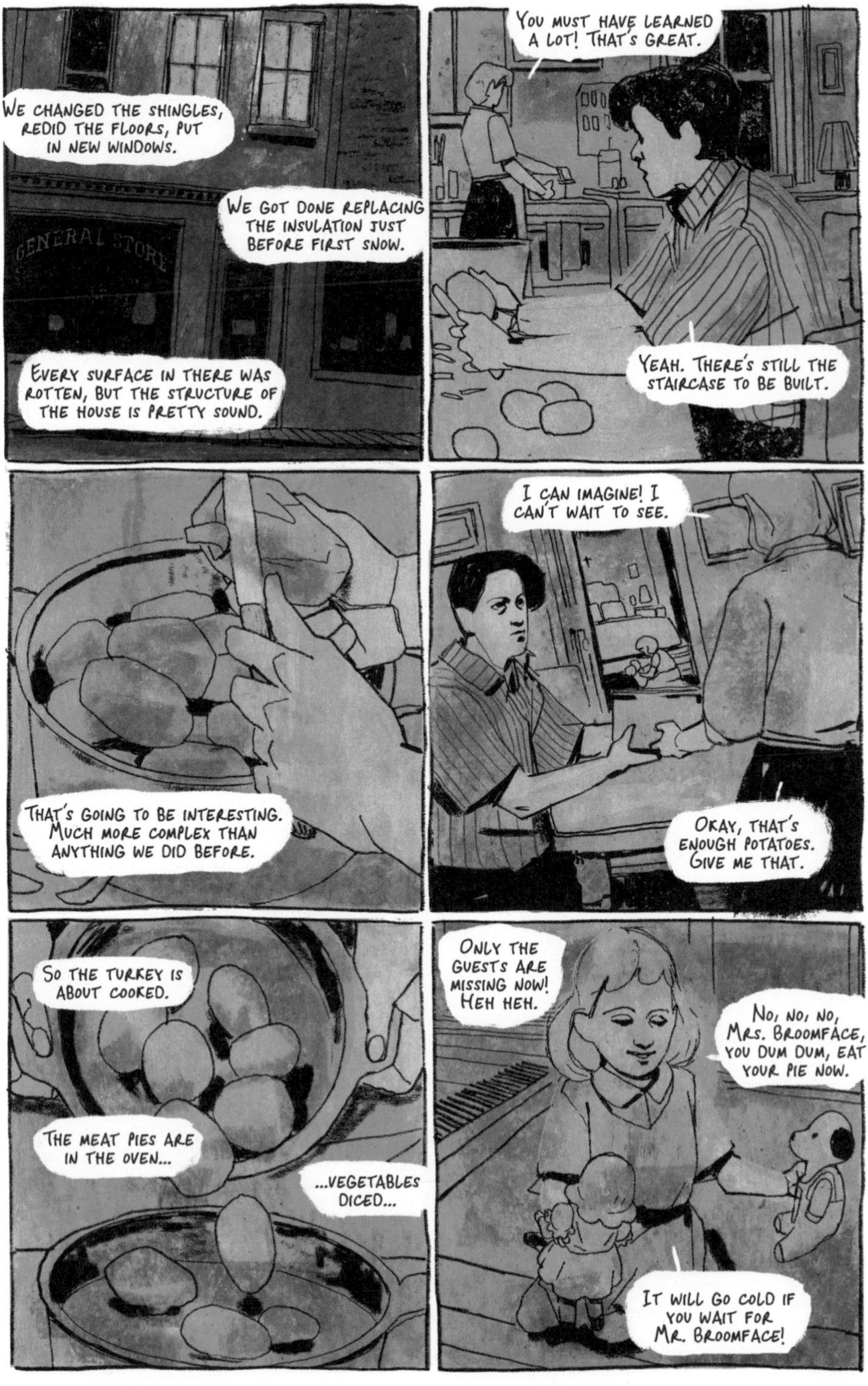

We changed the shingles, redid the floors, put in new windows.
We got done replacing the insulation just before first snow.
Every surface in there was rotten, but the structure of the house is pretty sound.
GENERAL STORE
You must have learned a lot! That's great.
Yeah. There's still the staircase to be built.
That's going to be interesting. Much more complex than anything we did before.
I can imagine! I can't wait to see.
Okay, that's enough potatoes. Give me that.
So the turkey is about cooked.
The meat pies are in the oven...
...vegetables diced...
Only the guests are missing now! Heh heh.
No, no, no, Mrs. Broomface, you dum dum, eat your pie now.
It will go cold if you wait for Mr. Broomface!

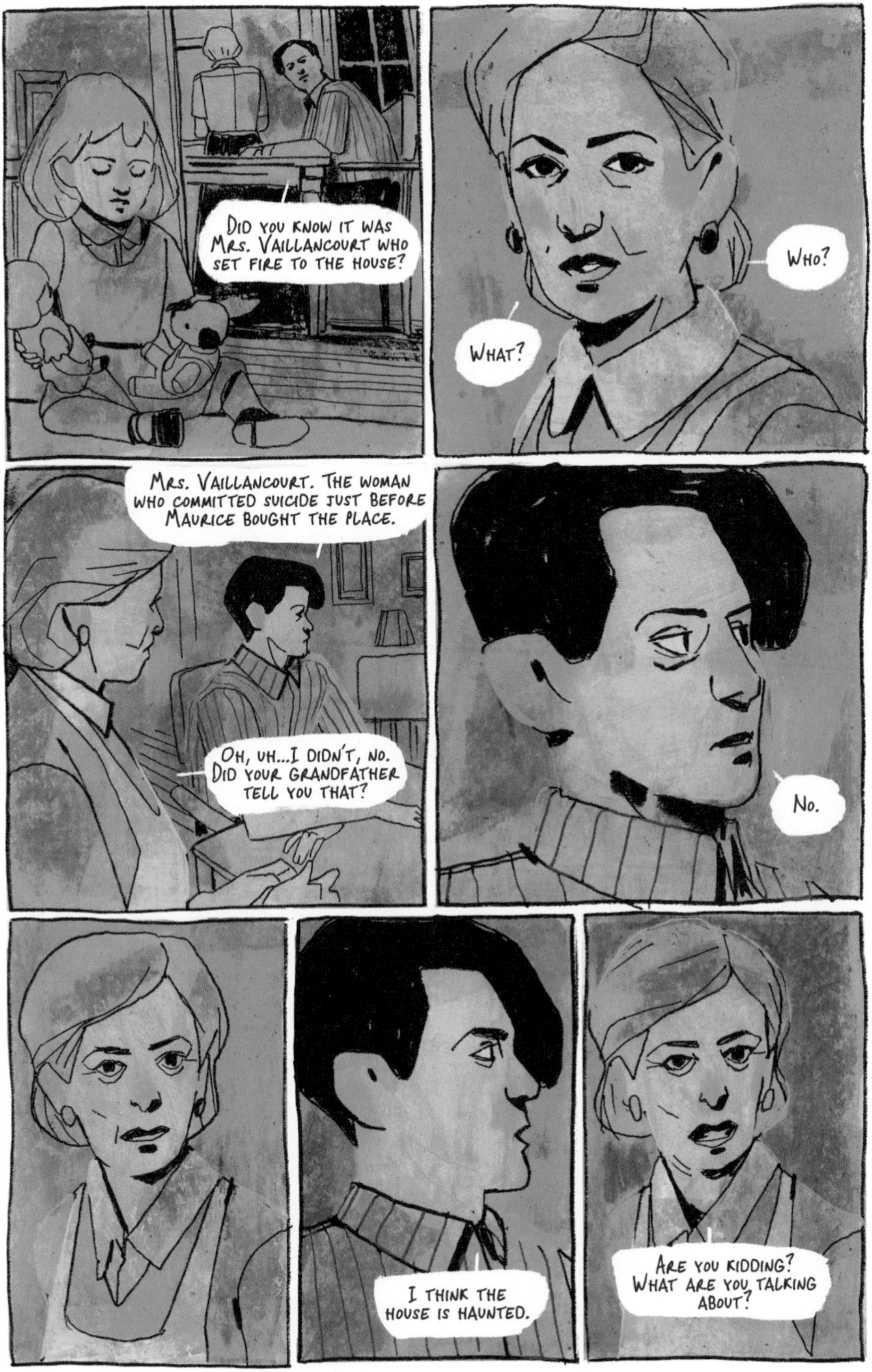
Did you know it was Mrs. Vaillancourt who set fire to the house?
What?
Who?
Mrs. Vaillancourt. The woman who committed suicide just before Maurice bought the place.
Oh, uh...I didn't, no. Did your grandfather tell you that?
No.
I think the house is haunted.
Are you kidding? What are you talking about?

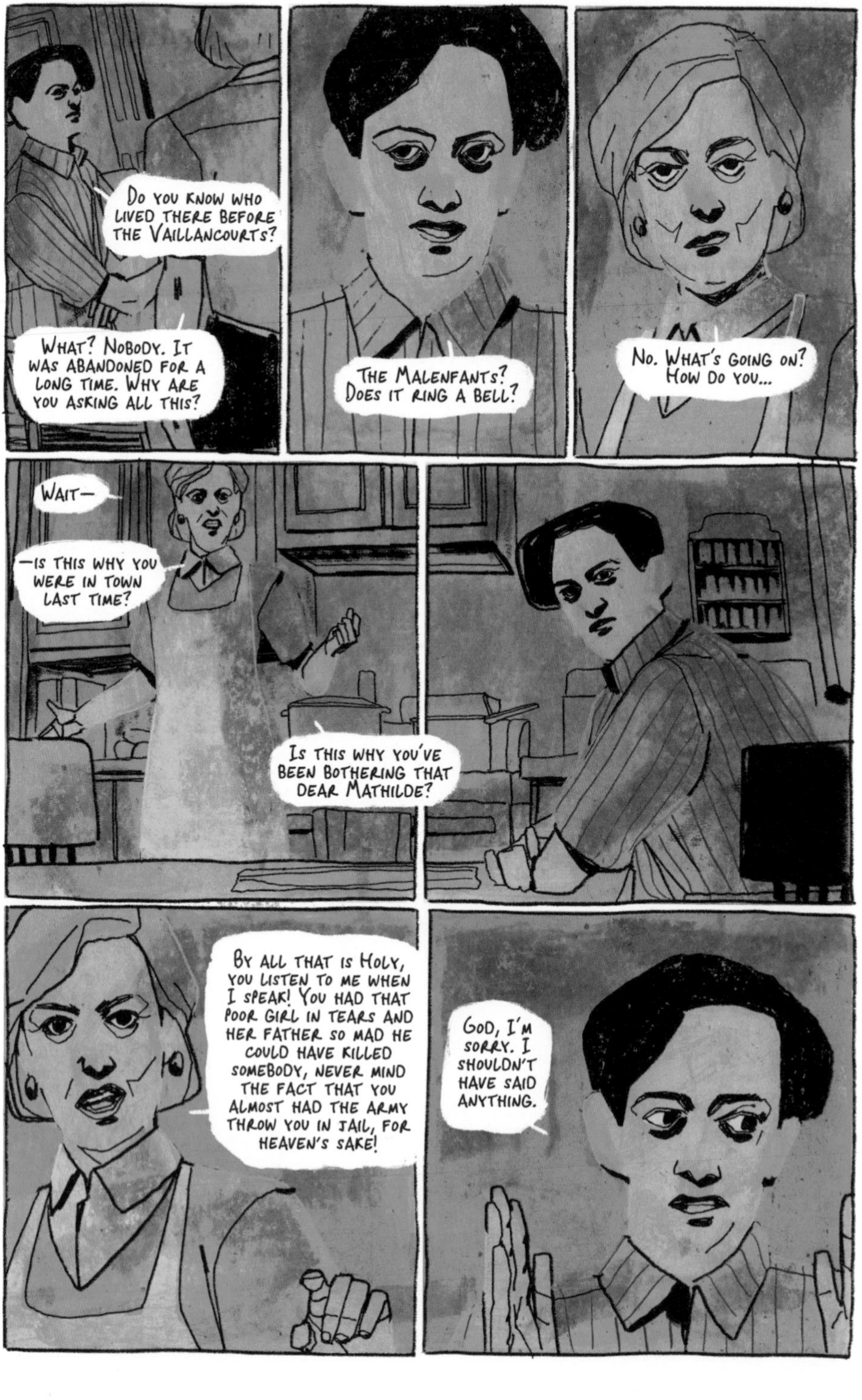

Do you know who lived there before the Vaillancourts?
What? Nobody. It was abandoned for a long time. Why are you asking all this?
The Malenfants? Does it ring a bell?
No. What's going on? How do you...
Wait—
—is this why you were in town last time?
Is this why you've been bothering that dear Mathilde?
By all that is Holy, you listen to me when I speak! You had that poor girl in tears and her father so mad he could have killed somebody, never mind the fact that you almost had the army throw you in jail, for heaven's sake!
God, I'm sorry. I shouldn't have said anything.

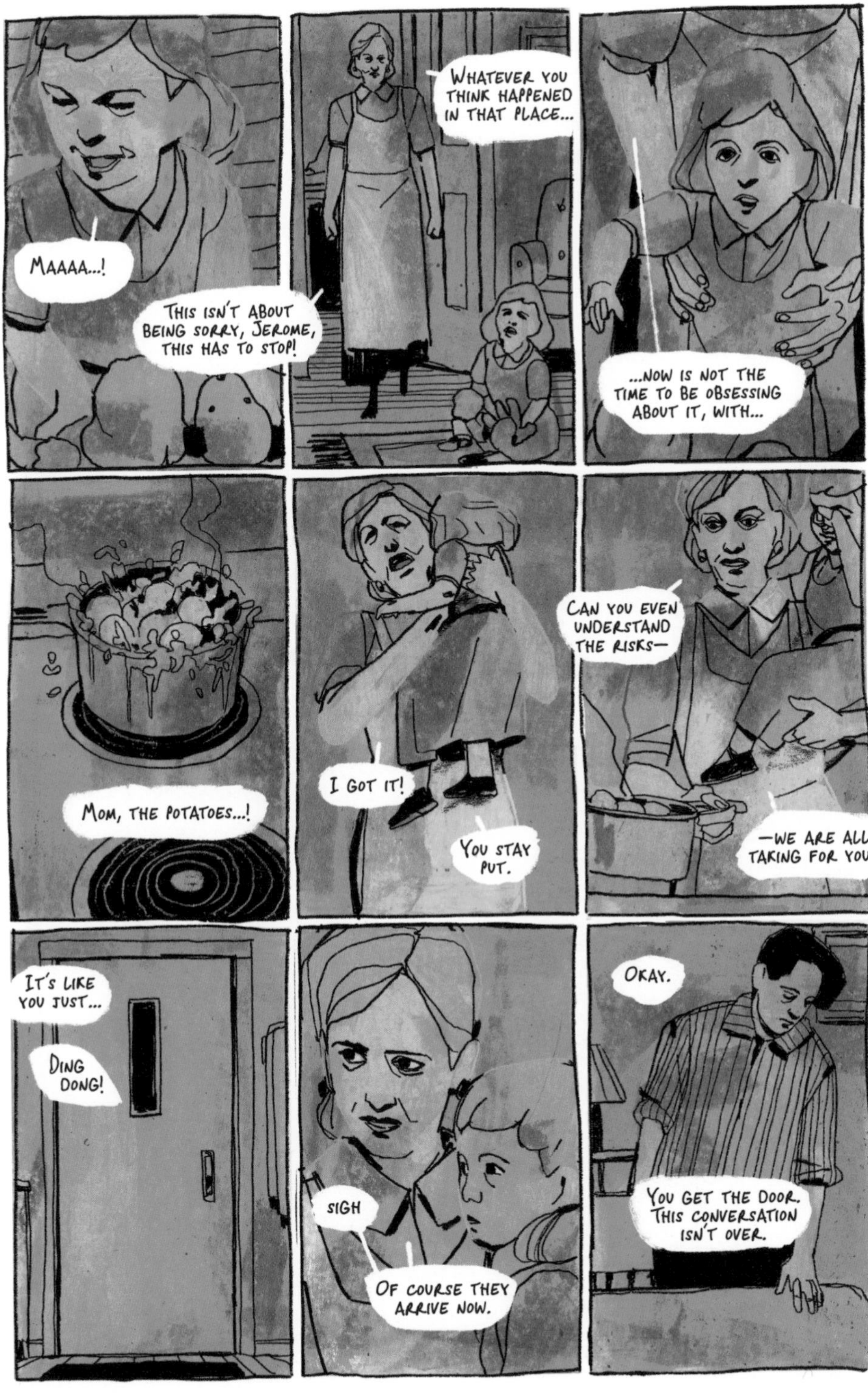
Maaaa...!
This isn't about being sorry, Jerome, this has to stop!
Whatever you think happened in that place...
...now is not the time to be obsessing about it, with...
Mom, the potatoes...!
I got it!
You stay put.
Can you even understand the risks—
—we are all taking for you?
It's like you just...
Ding dong!
sigh
Of course they arrive now.
Okay.
You get the door. This conversation isn't over.

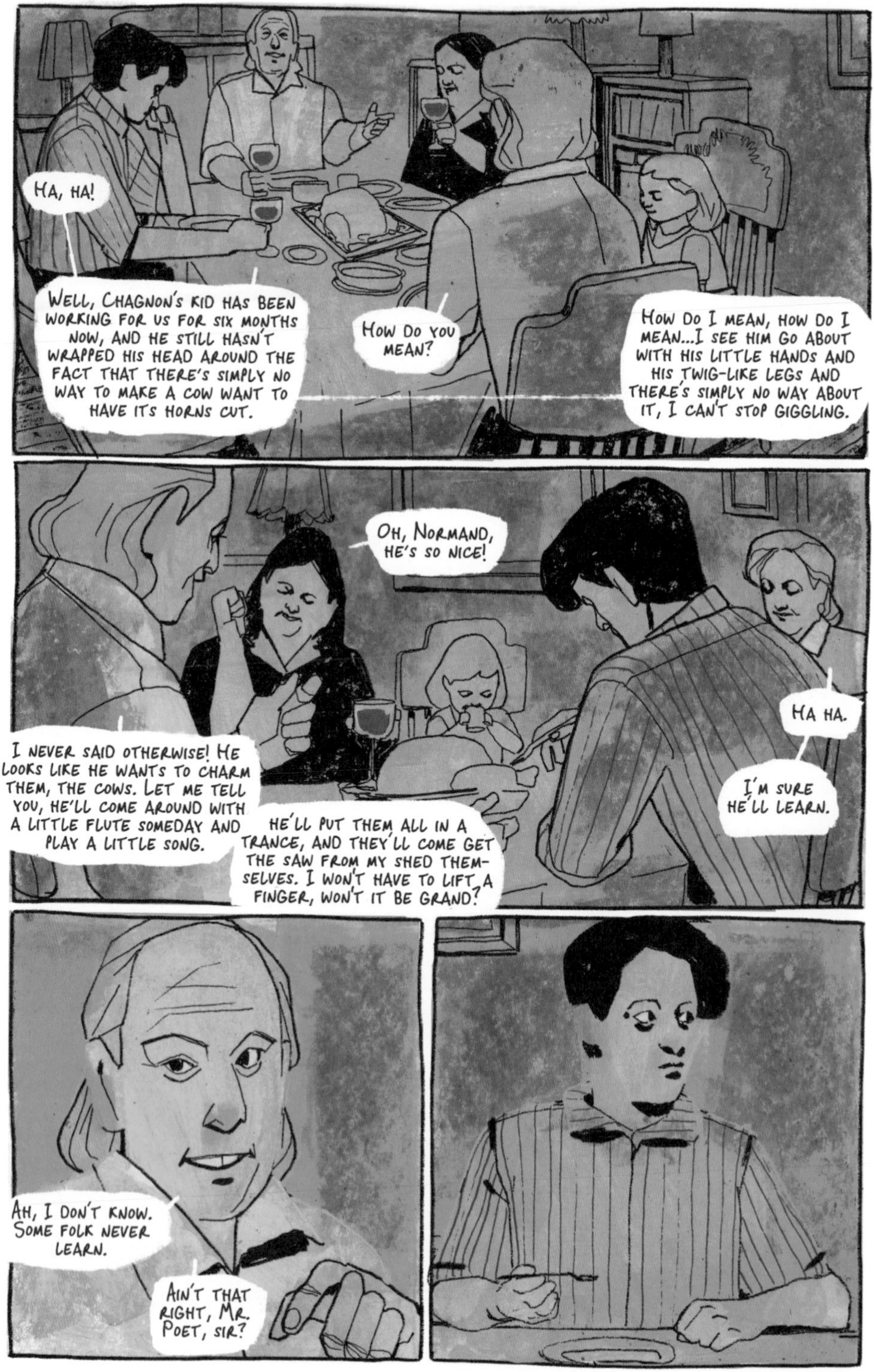
HA, HA!
WELL, CHAGNON'S KID HAS BEEN WORKING FOR US FOR SIX MONTHS NOW, AND HE STILL HASN'T WRAPPED HIS HEAD AROUND THE FACT THAT THERE'S SIMPLY NO WAY TO MAKE A COW WANT TO HAVE ITS HORNS CUT.
HOW DO YOU MEAN?
HOW DO I MEAN, HOW DO I MEAN...I SEE HIM GO ABOUT WITH HIS LITTLE HANDS AND HIS TWIG-LIKE LEGS AND THERE'S SIMPLY NO WAY ABOUT IT, I CAN'T STOP GIGGLING.
OH, NORMAND, HE'S SO NICE!
I NEVER SAID OTHERWISE! HE LOOKS LIKE HE WANTS TO CHARM THEM, THE COWS. LET ME TELL YOU, HE'LL COME AROUND WITH A LITTLE FLUTE SOMEDAY AND PLAY A LITTLE SONG.
HE'LL PUT THEM ALL IN A TRANCE, AND THEY'LL COME GET THE SAW FROM MY SHED THEMSELVES. I WON'T HAVE TO LIFT A FINGER, WON'T IT BE GRAND?
HA HA.
I'M SURE HE'LL LEARN.
AH, I DON'T KNOW. SOME FOLK NEVER LEARN.
AIN'T THAT RIGHT, MR. POET, SIR?

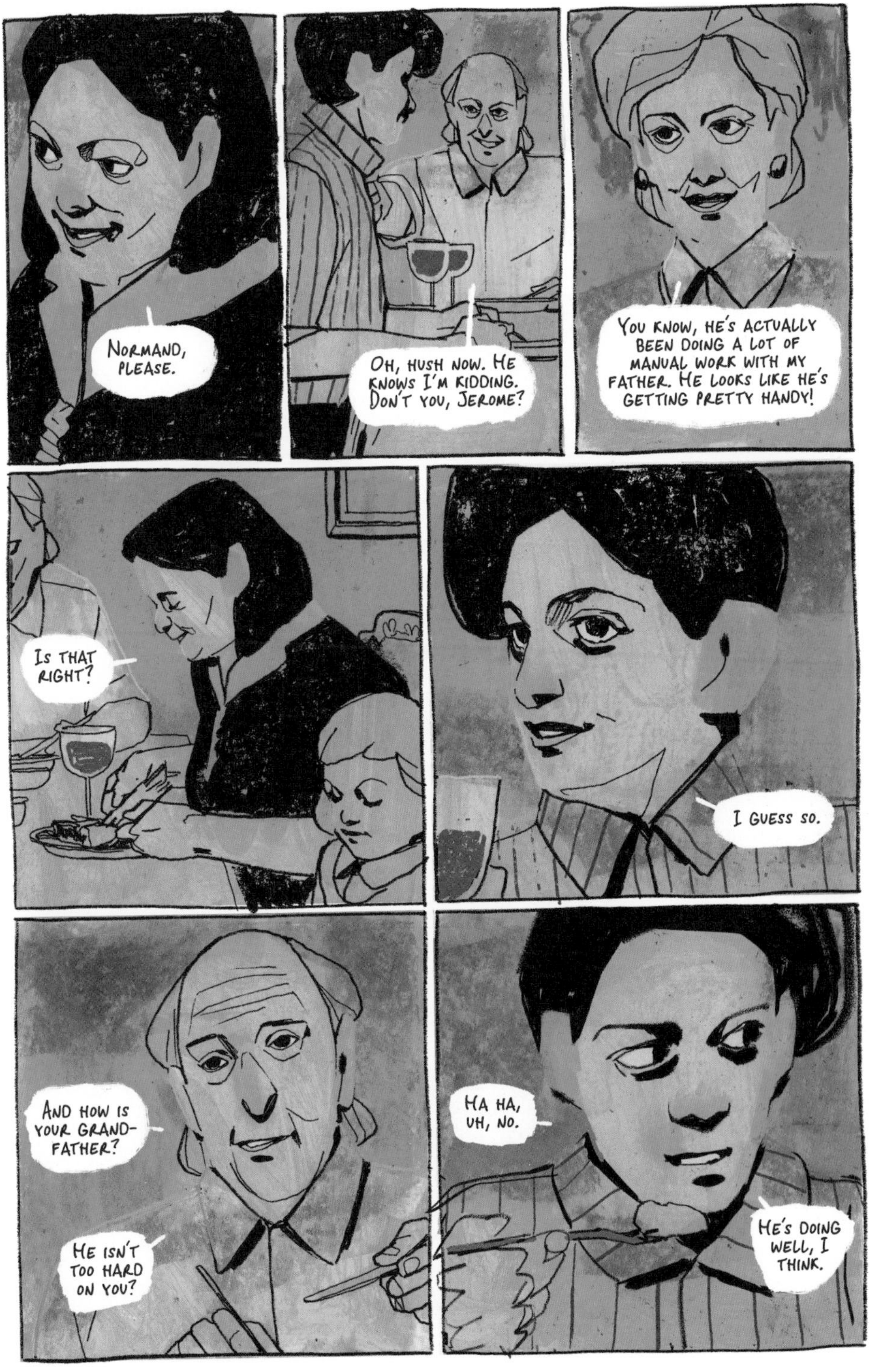
Normand, please.
Oh, hush now. He knows I'm kidding. Don't you, Jerome?
You know, he's actually been doing a lot of manual work with my father. He looks like he's getting pretty handy!
Is that right?
I guess so.
And how is your grand-father?
He isn't too hard on you?
Ha ha, uh, no.
He's doing well, I think.

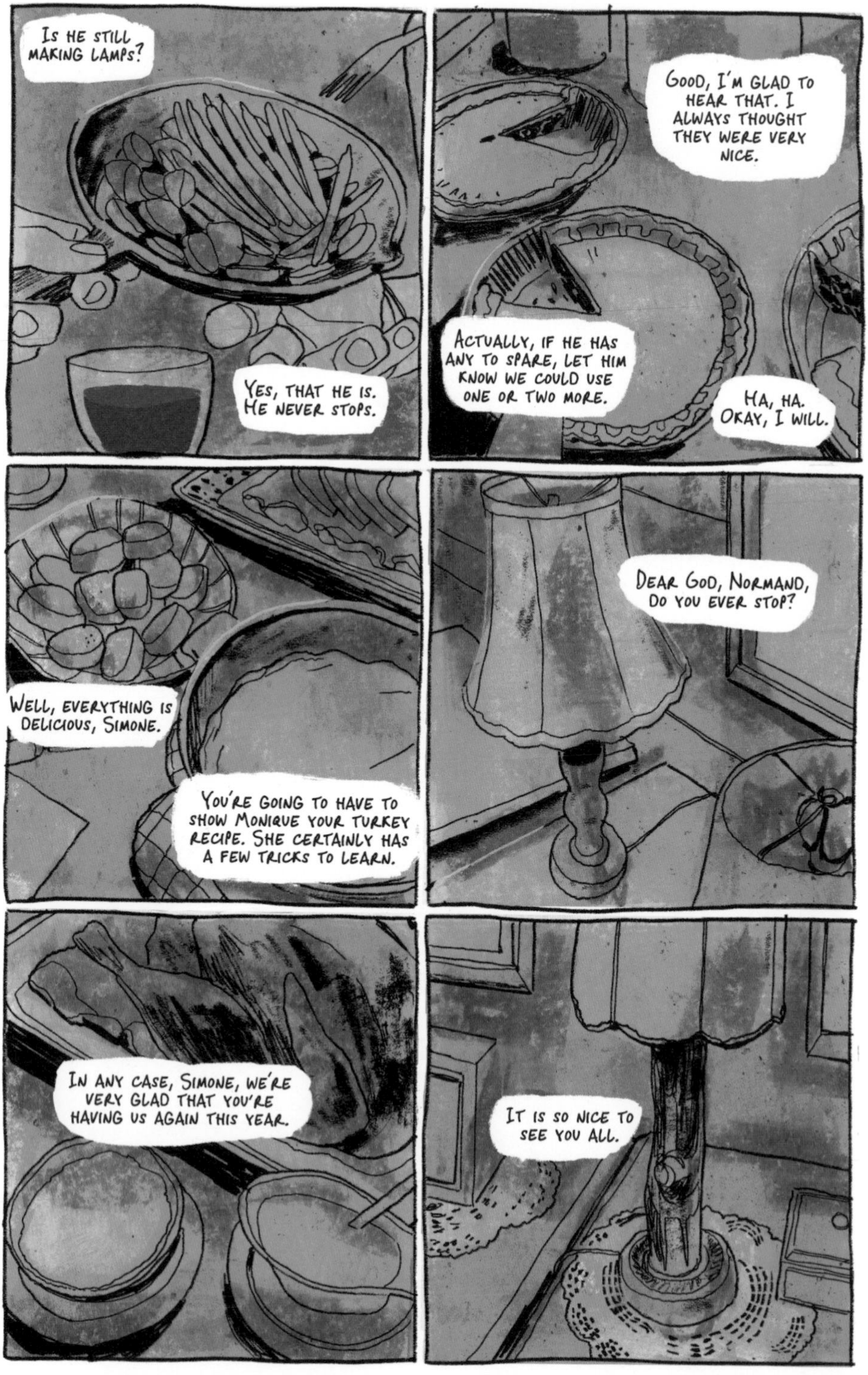

Is he still making lamps?
Yes, that he is. He never stops.
Good, I'm glad to hear that. I always thought they were very nice.
Actually, if he has any to spare, let him know we could use one or two more.
Ha, ha. Okay, I will.
Well, everything is delicious, Simone.
You're going to have to show Monique your turkey recipe. She certainly has a few tricks to learn.
Dear God, Normand, do you ever stop?
In any case, Simone, we're very glad that you're having us again this year.
It is so nice to see you all.

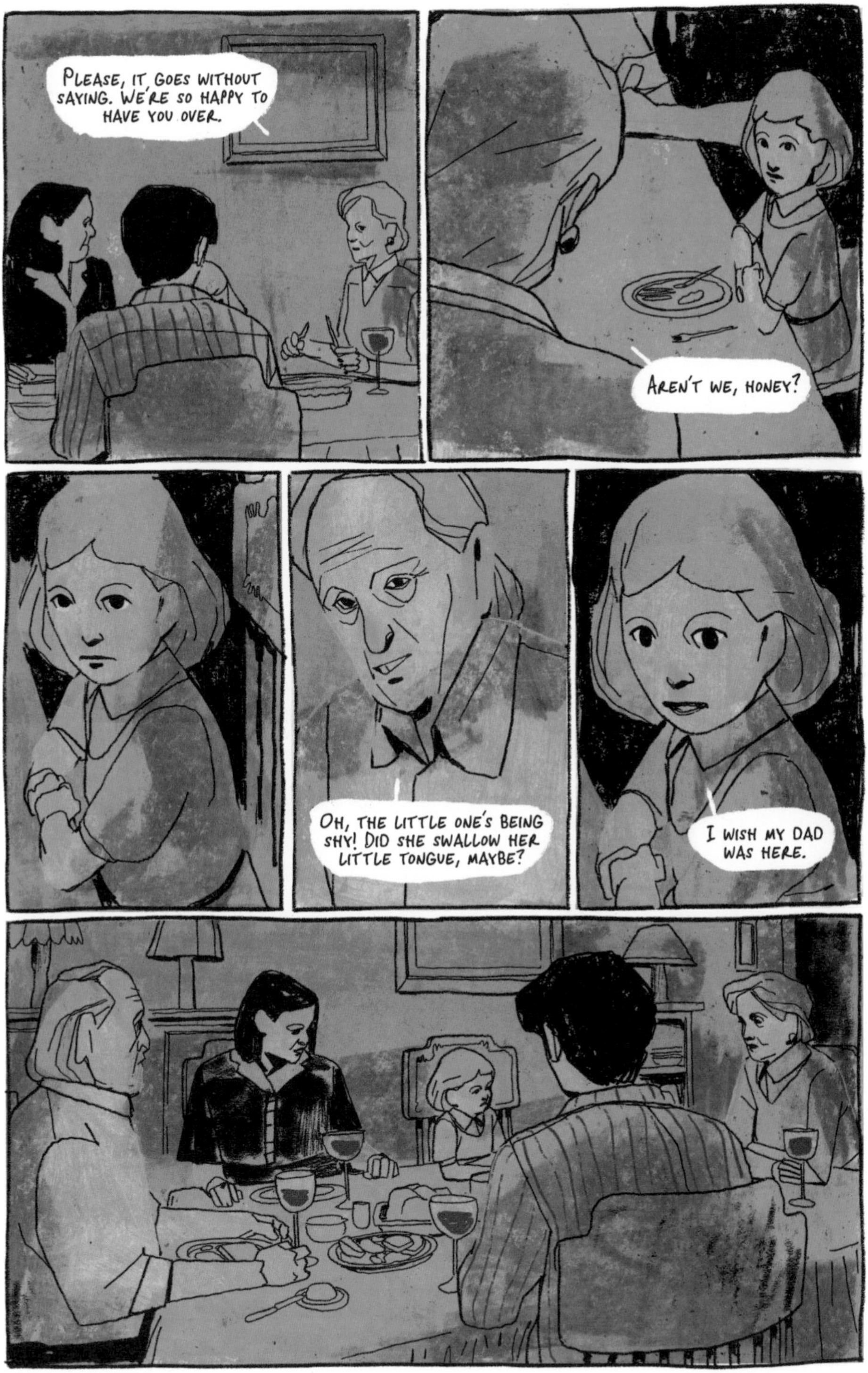
PLEASE, IT GOES WITHOUT SAYING. WE'RE SO HAPPY TO HAVE YOU OVER.
AREN'T WE, HONEY?
OH, THE LITTLE ONE'S BEING SHY! DID SHE SWALLOW HER LITTLE TONGUE, MAYBE?
I WISH MY DAD WAS HERE.

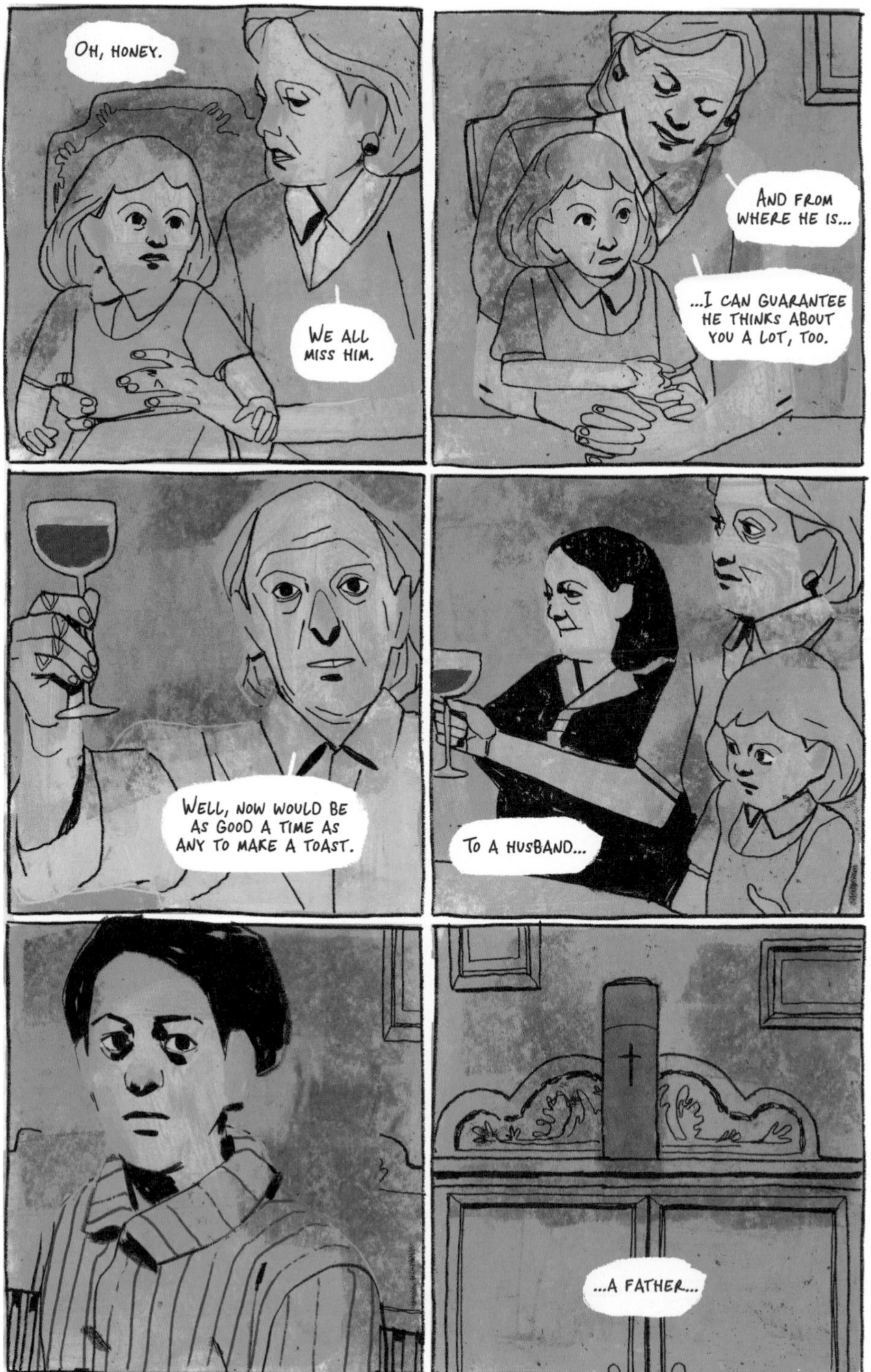
OH, HONEY.
WE ALL MISS HIM.
AND FROM WHERE HE IS...
...I CAN GUARANTEE HE THINKS ABOUT YOU A LOT, TOO.
WELL, NOW WOULD BE AS GOOD A TIME AS ANY TO MAKE A TOAST.
TO A HUSBAND...
...A FATHER...

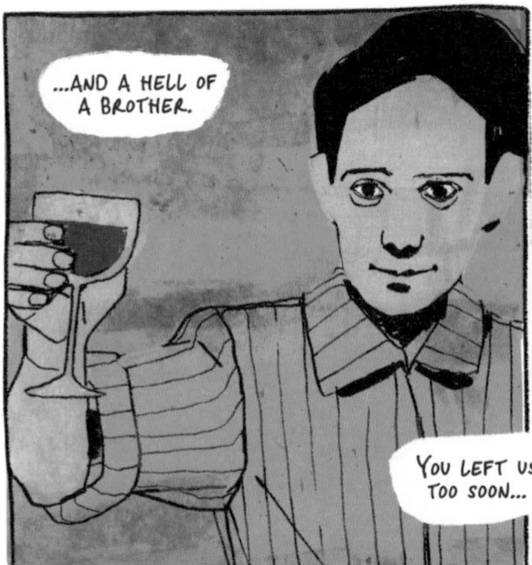
...AND A HELL OF A BROTHER.

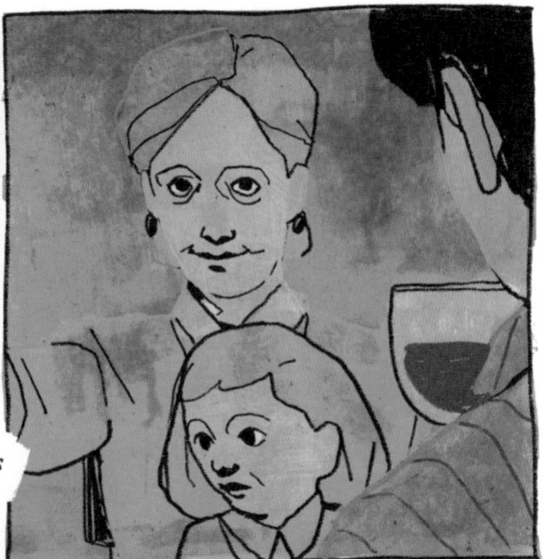
YOU LEFT US TOO SOON...

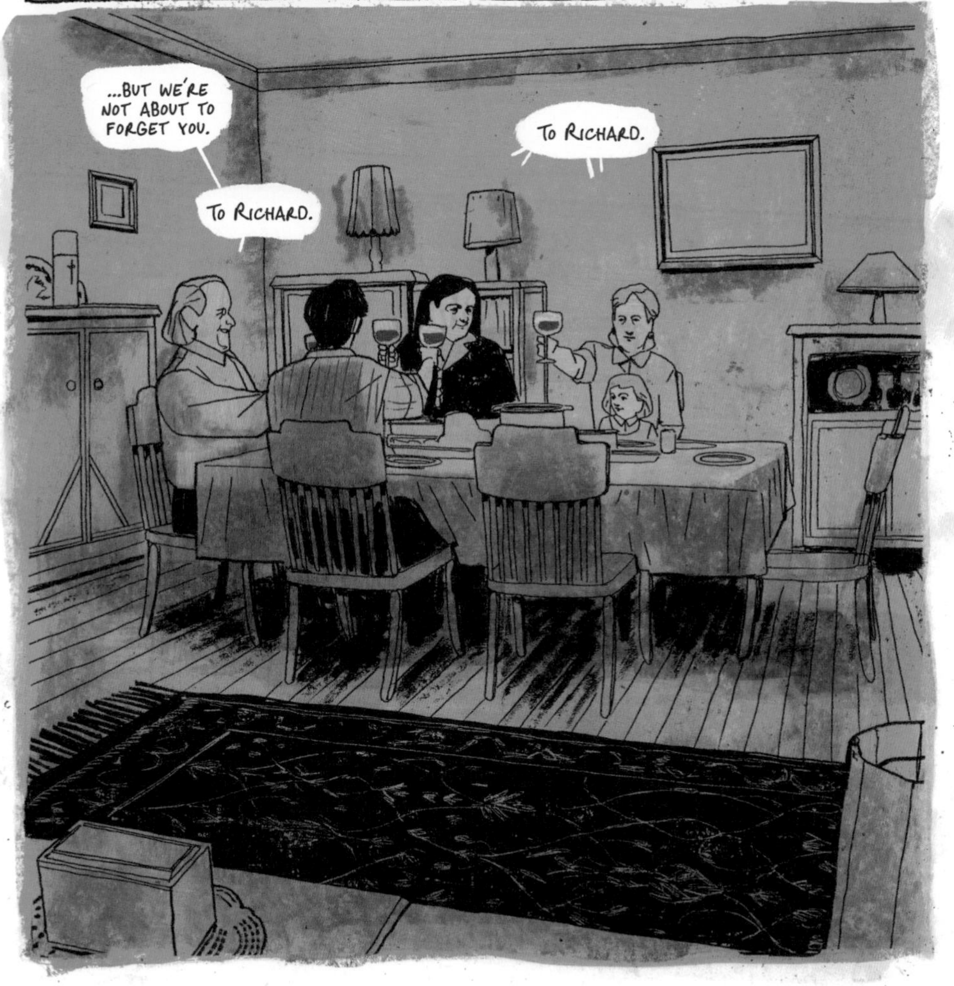
...BUT WE'RE NOT ABOUT TO FORGET YOU.
TO RICHARD.
TO RICHARD.

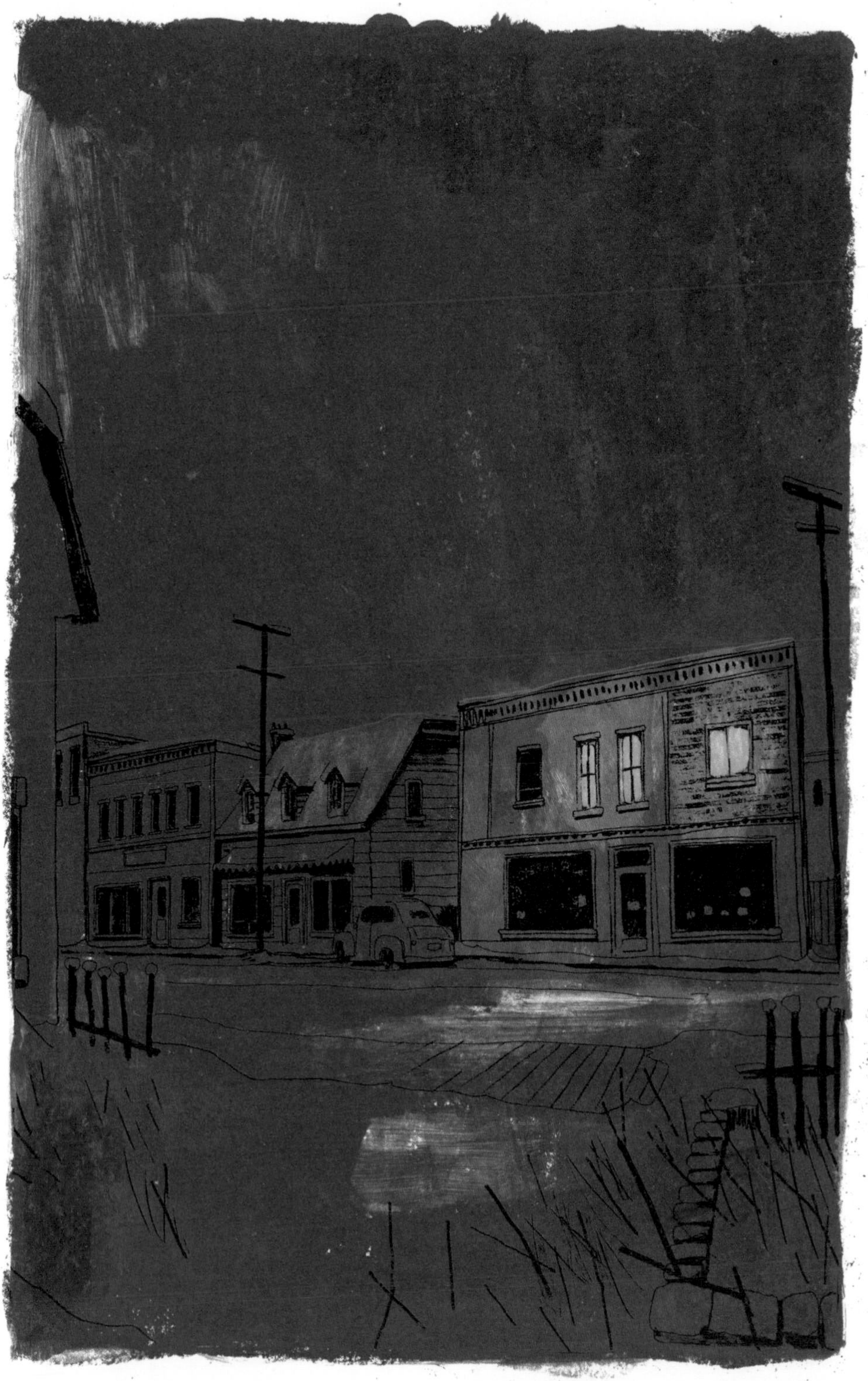

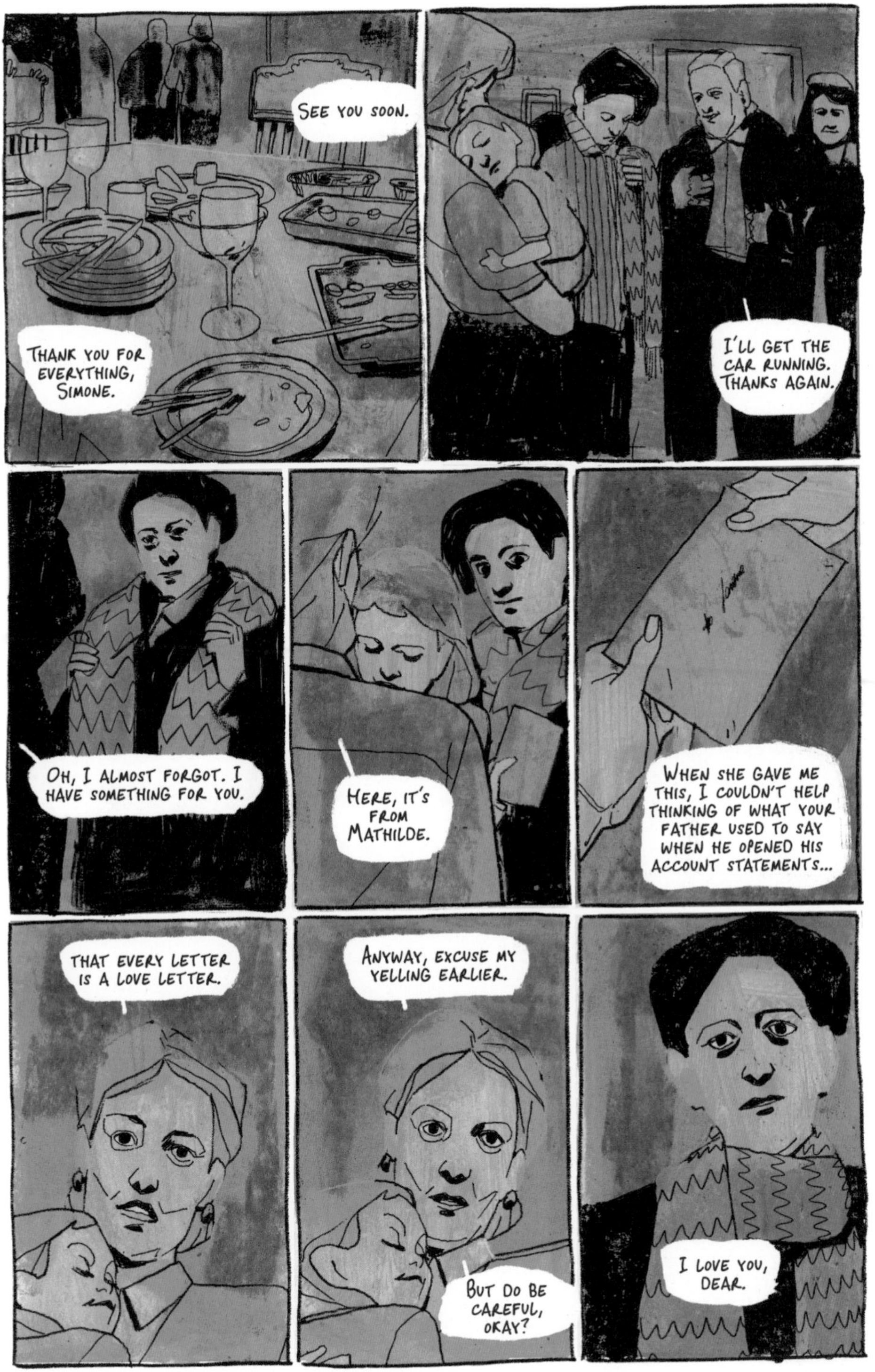
SEE YOU SOON.
THANK YOU FOR EVERYTHING, SIMONE.
I'LL GET THE CAR RUNNING. THANKS AGAIN.
OH, I ALMOST FORGOT. I HAVE SOMETHING FOR YOU.
HERE, IT'S FROM MATHILDE.
WHEN SHE GAVE ME THIS, I COULDN'T HELP THINKING OF WHAT YOUR FATHER USED TO SAY WHEN HE OPENED HIS ACCOUNT STATEMENTS...
THAT EVERY LETTER IS A LOVE LETTER.
ANYWAY, EXCUSE MY YELLING EARLIER.
BUT DO BE CAREFUL, OKAY?
I LOVE YOU, DEAR.

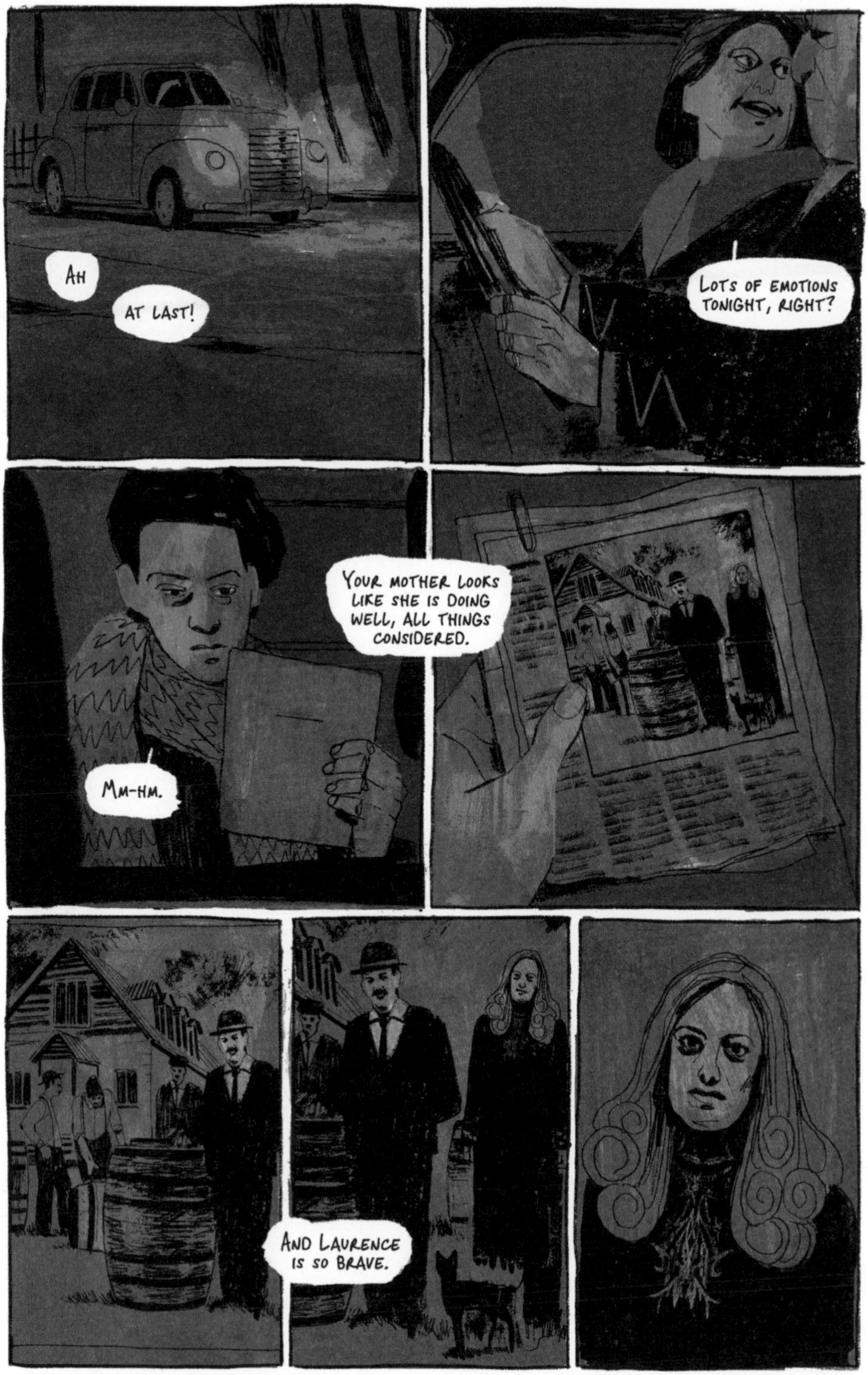
Ah
At last!
Lots of emotions tonight, right?
Your mother looks like she is doing well, all things considered.
Mm-hm.
And Laurence is so brave.

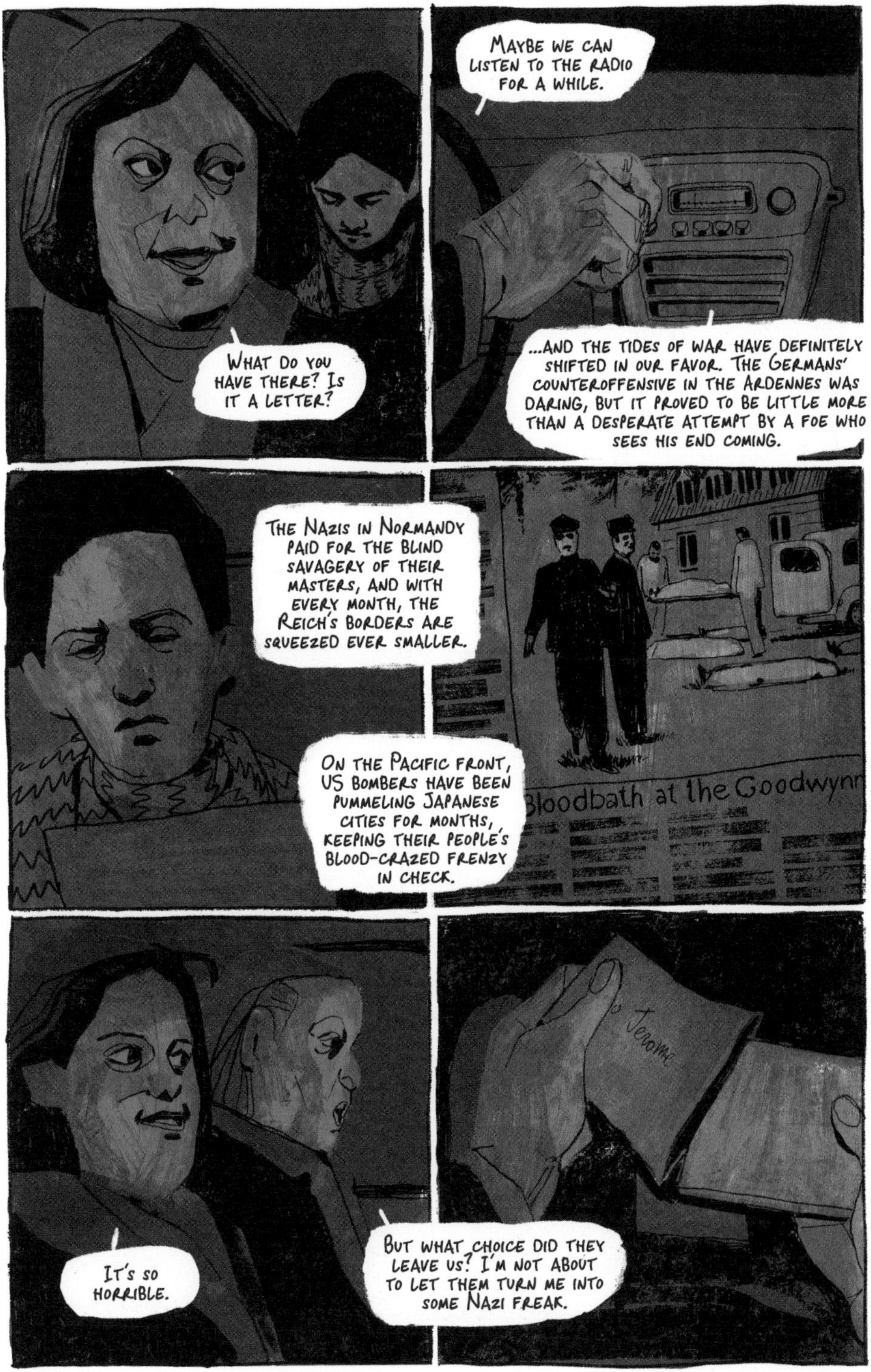
What do you have there? Is it a letter?
Maybe we can listen to the radio for a while.
...and the tides of war have definitely shifted in our favor. The Germans' counteroffensive in the Ardennes was daring, but it proved to be little more than a desperate attempt by a foe who sees his end coming.
The Nazis in Normandy paid for the blind savagery of their masters, and with every month, the Reich's borders are squeezed ever smaller.
On the Pacific front, US bombers have been pummeling Japanese cities for months, keeping their people's blood-crazed frenzy in check.
Bloodbath at the Goodwynn
Jerome
It's so horrible.
But what choice did they leave us? I'm not about to let them turn me into some Nazi freak.

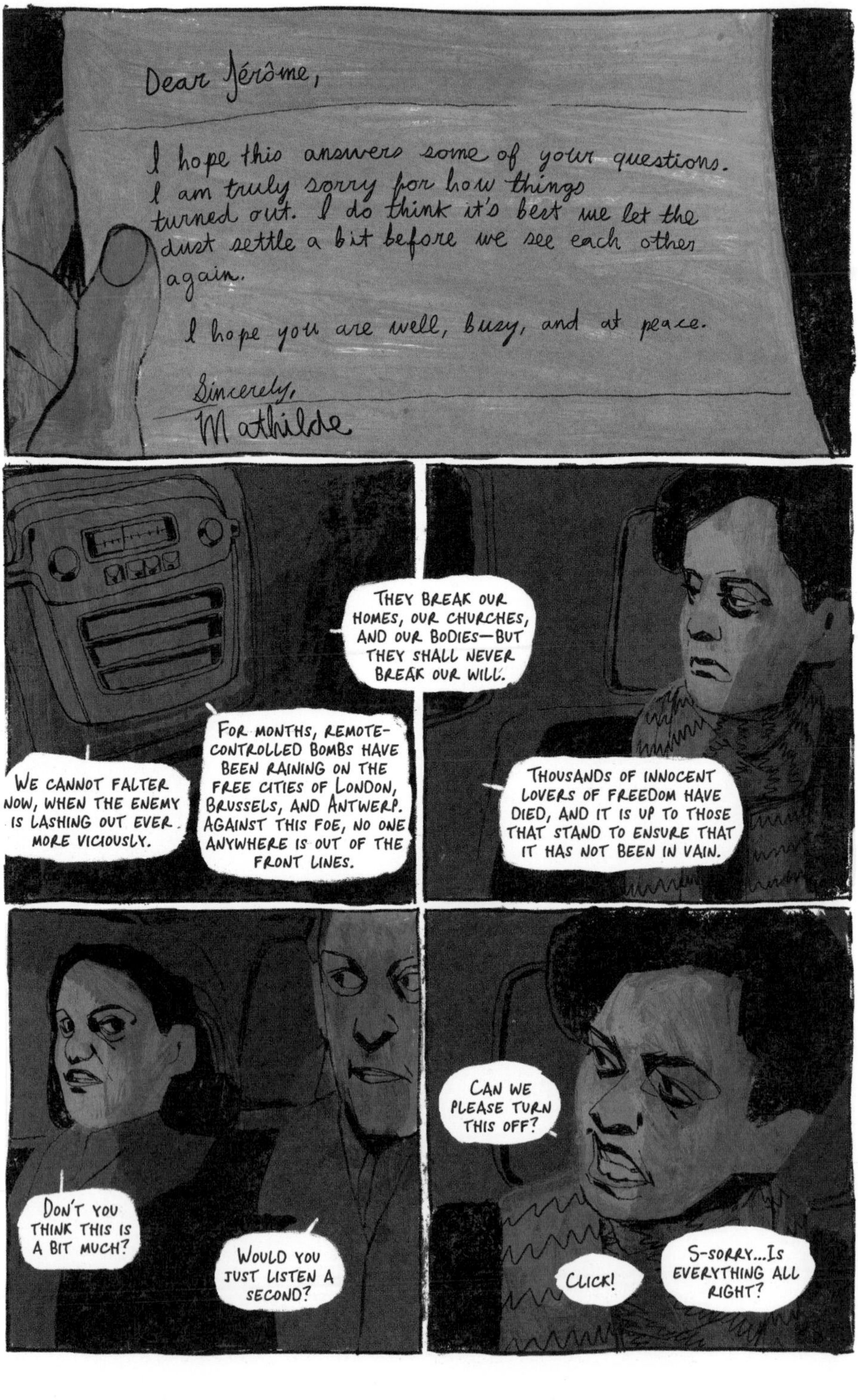
Dear Jérôme,
I hope this answers some of your questions. I am truly sorry for how things turned out. I do think it's best we let the dust settle a bit before we see each other again.
I hope you are well, busy, and at peace.
Sincerely,
Mathilde
THEY BREAK OUR HOMES, OUR CHURCHES, AND OUR BODIES—BUT THEY SHALL NEVER BREAK OUR WILL.
FOR MONTHS, REMOTE-CONTROLLED BOMBS HAVE BEEN RAINING ON THE FREE CITIES OF LONDON, BRUSSELS, AND ANTWERP. AGAINST THIS FOE, NO ONE ANYWHERE IS OUT OF THE FRONT LINES.
WE CANNOT FALTER NOW, WHEN THE ENEMY IS LASHING OUT EVER MORE VICIOUSLY.
THOUSANDS OF INNOCENT LOVERS OF FREEDOM HAVE DIED, AND IT IS UP TO THOSE THAT STAND TO ENSURE THAT IT HAS NOT BEEN IN VAIN.
DON'T YOU THINK THIS IS A BIT MUCH?
WOULD YOU JUST LISTEN A SECOND?
CAN WE PLEASE TURN THIS OFF?
CLICK!
S-SORRY...IS EVERYTHING ALL RIGHT?

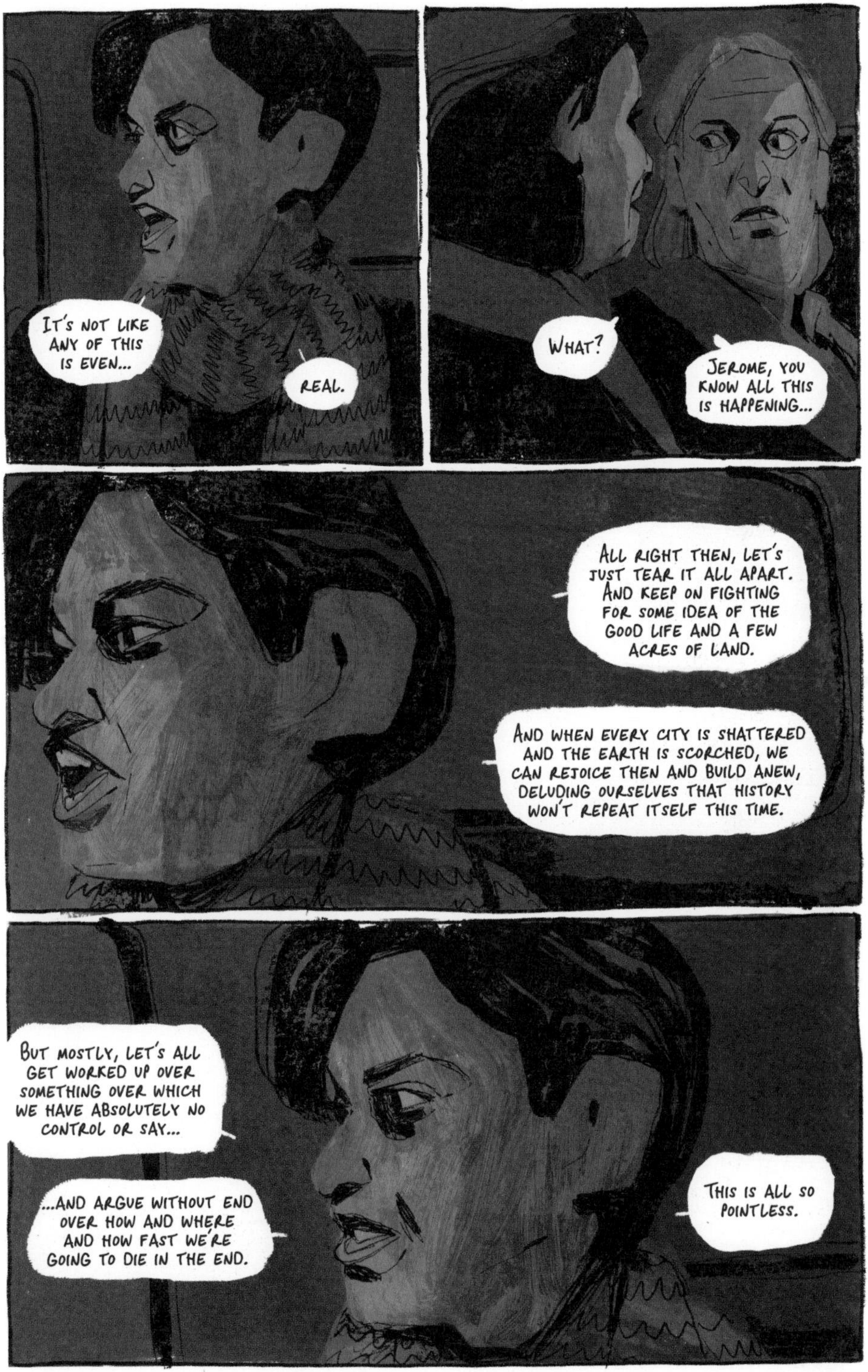
It's not like any of this is even...
real.
What?
Jerome, you know all this is happening...
All right then, let's just tear it all apart. And keep on fighting for some idea of the good life and a few acres of land.
And when every city is shattered and the earth is scorched, we can rejoice then and build anew, deluding ourselves that history won't repeat itself this time.
But mostly, let's all get worked up over something over which we have absolutely no control or say...
...and argue without end over how and where and how fast we're going to die in the end.
This is all so pointless.

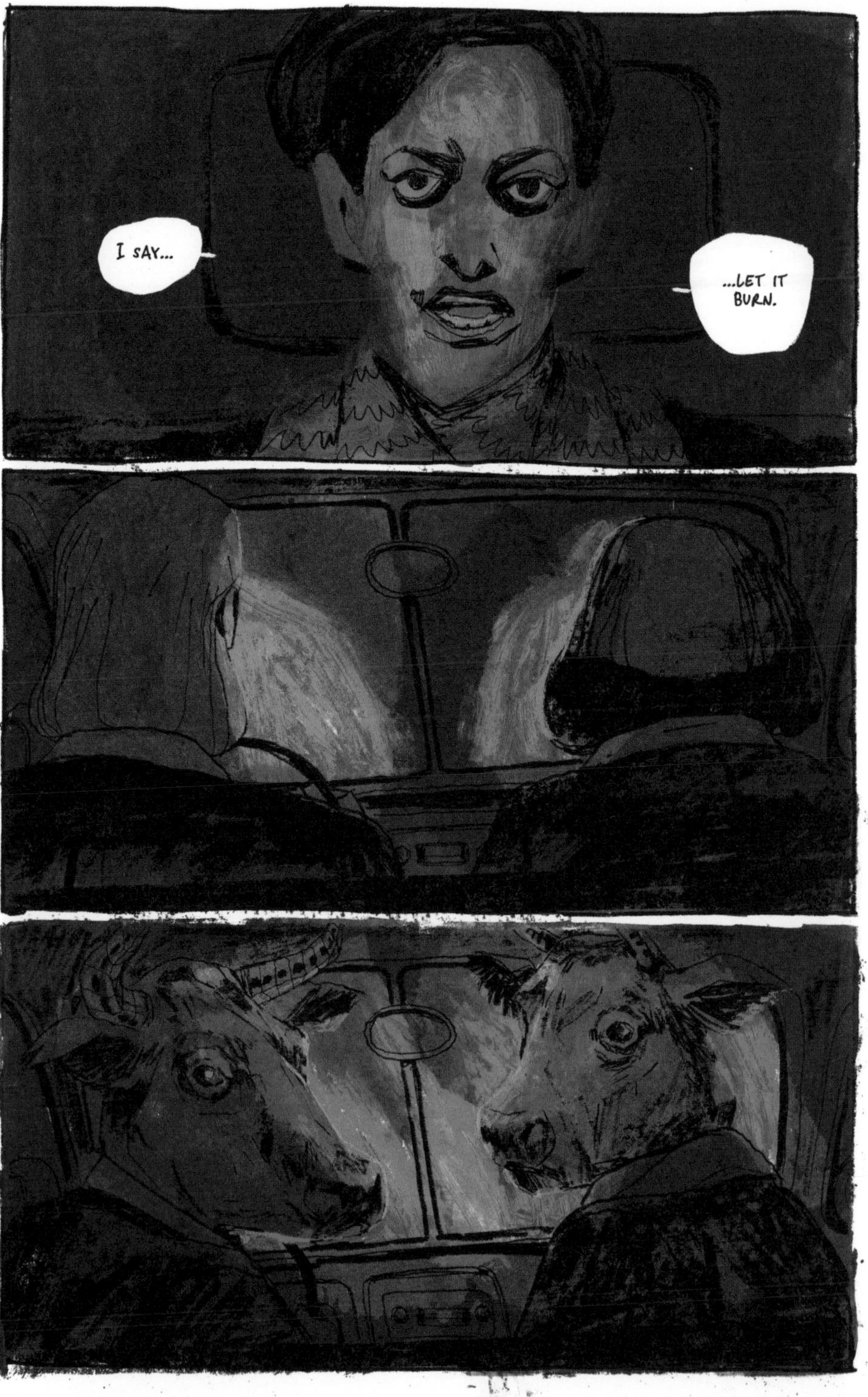
I SAY...
...LET IT BURN.

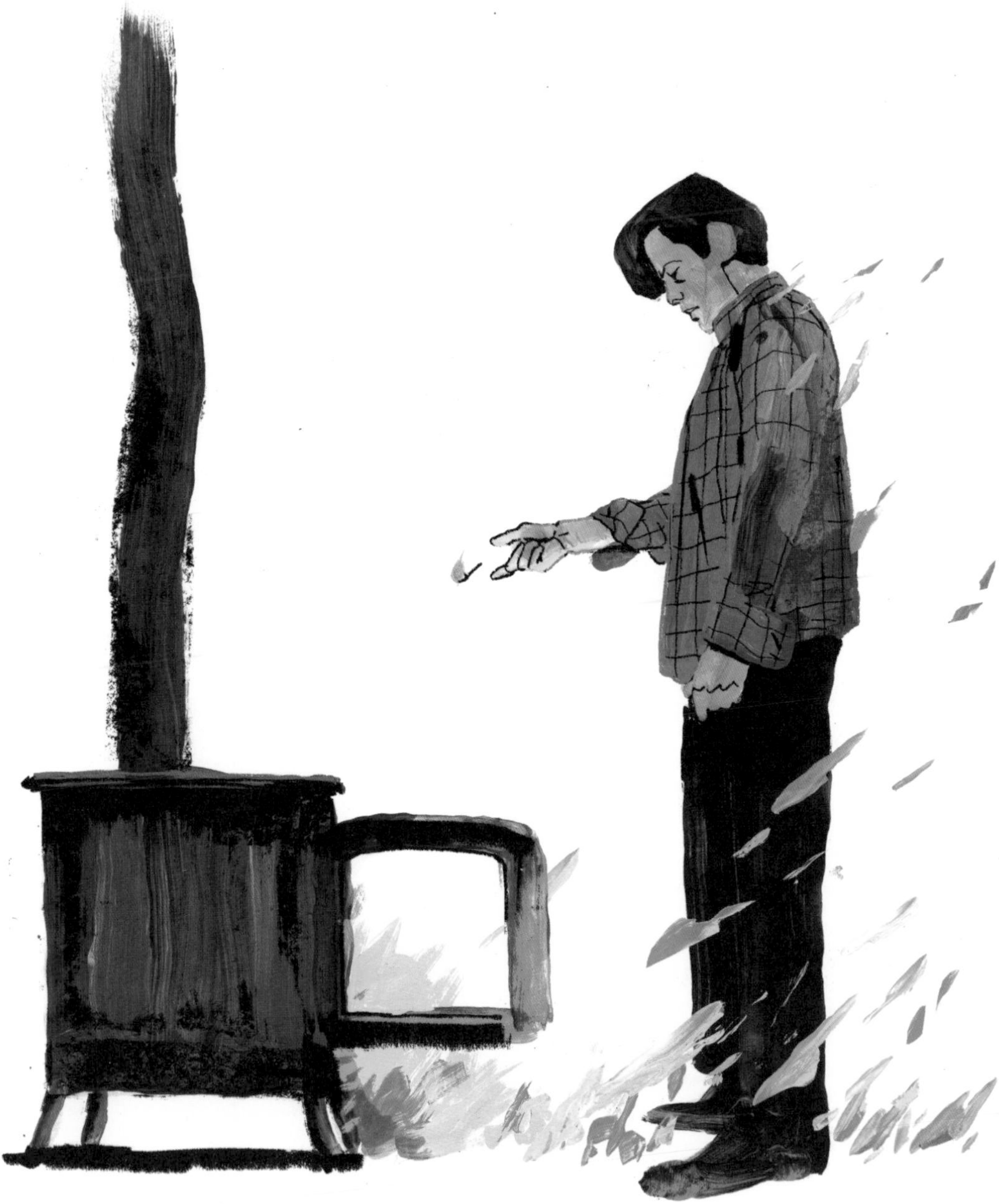

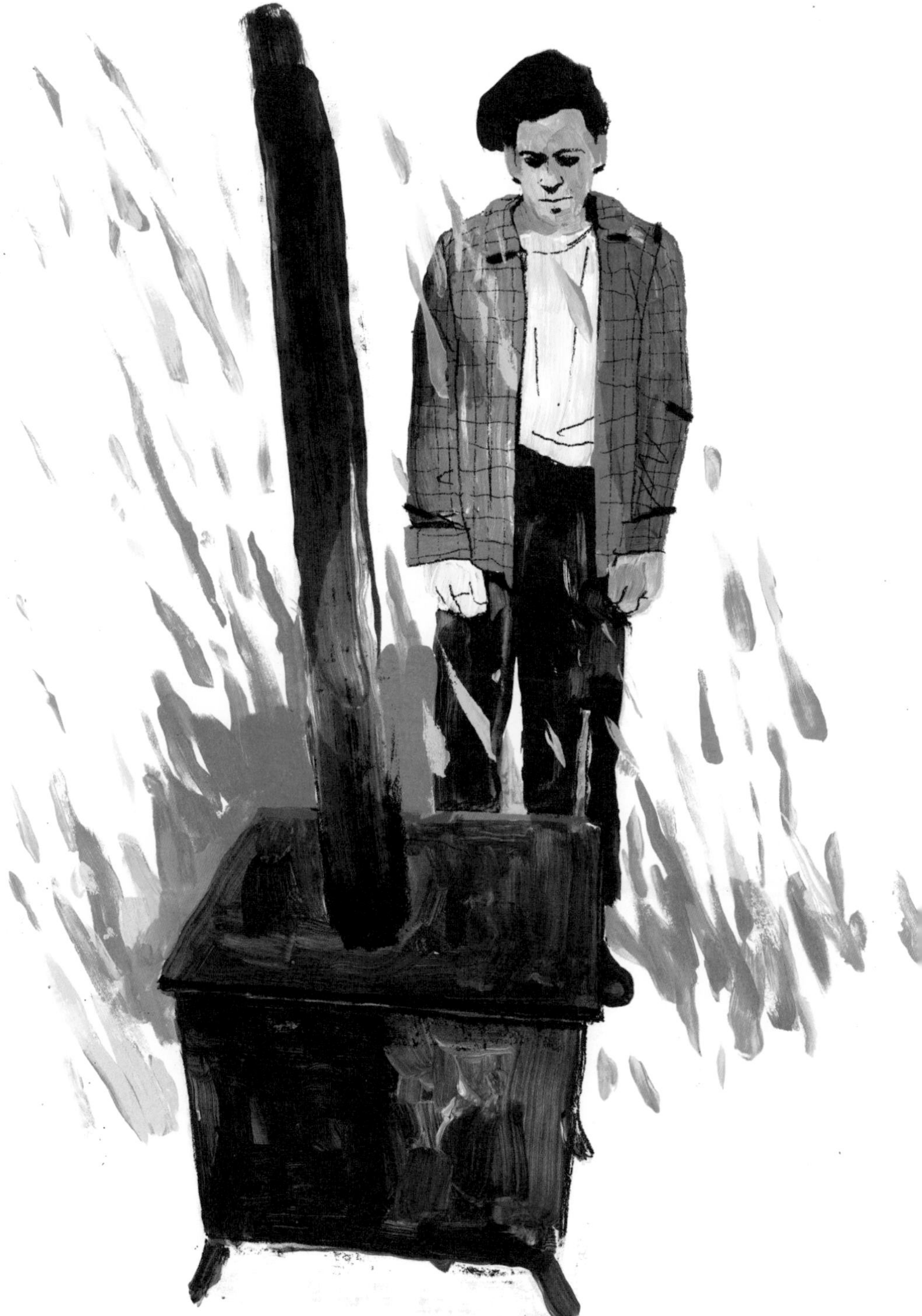

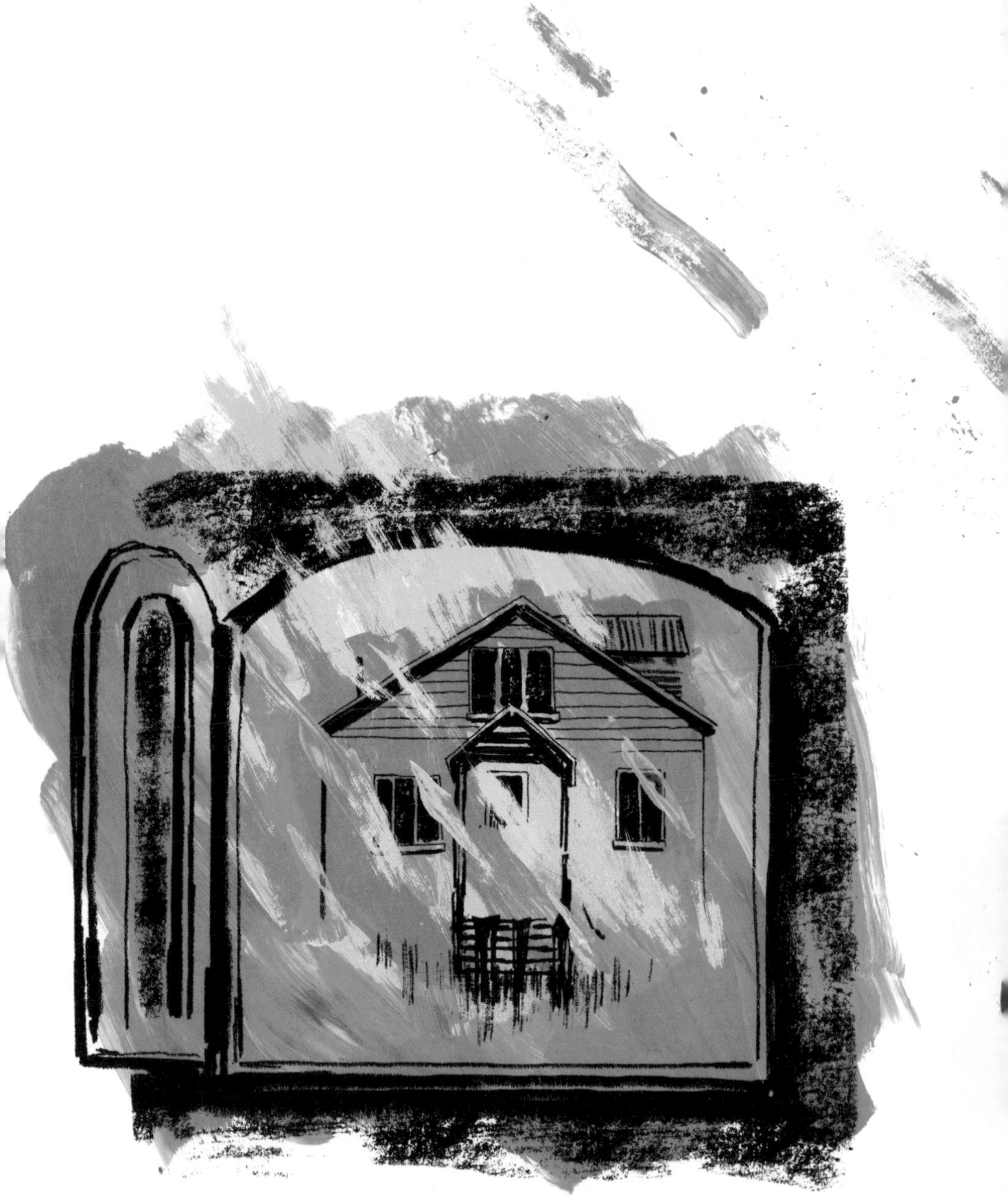

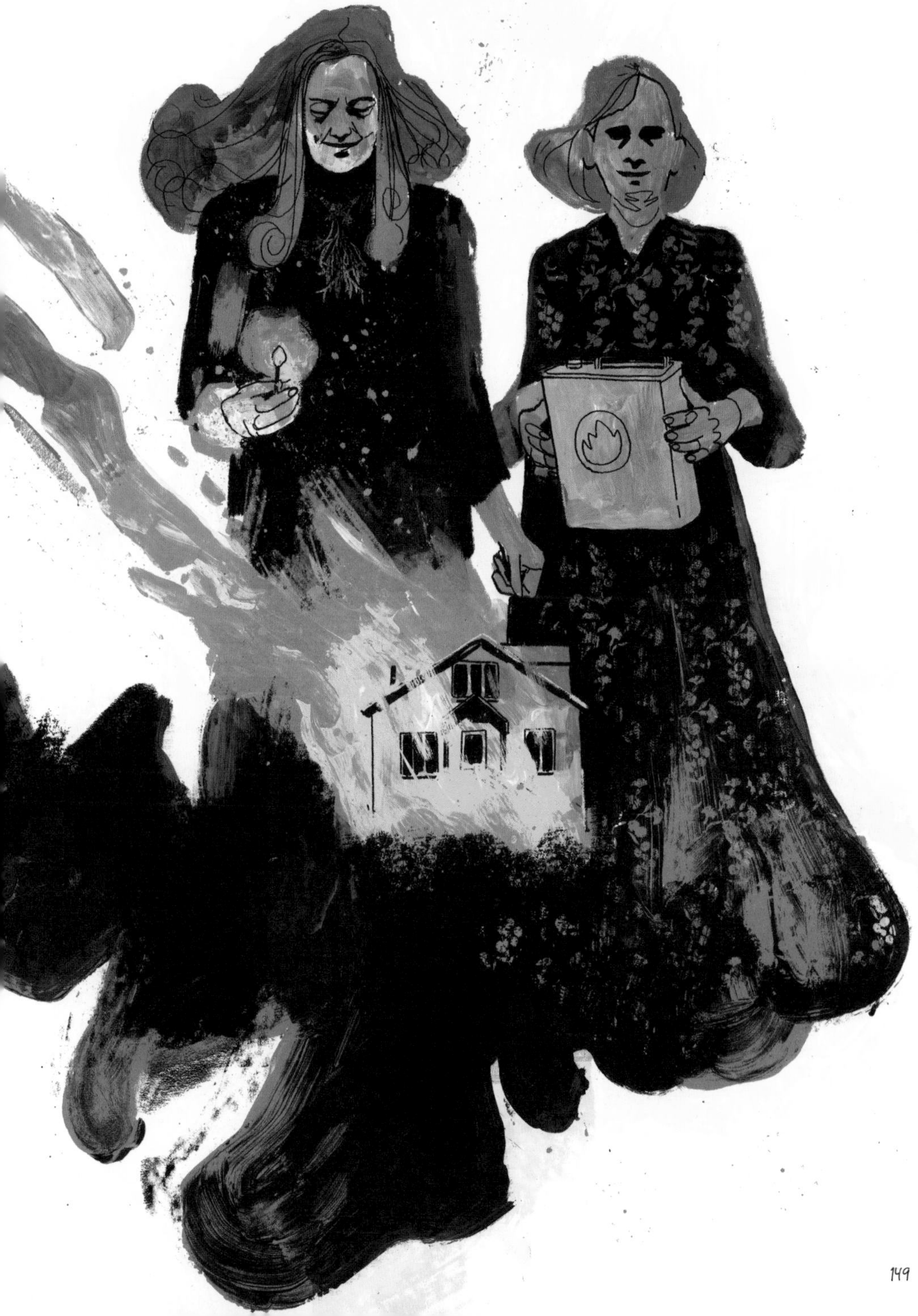

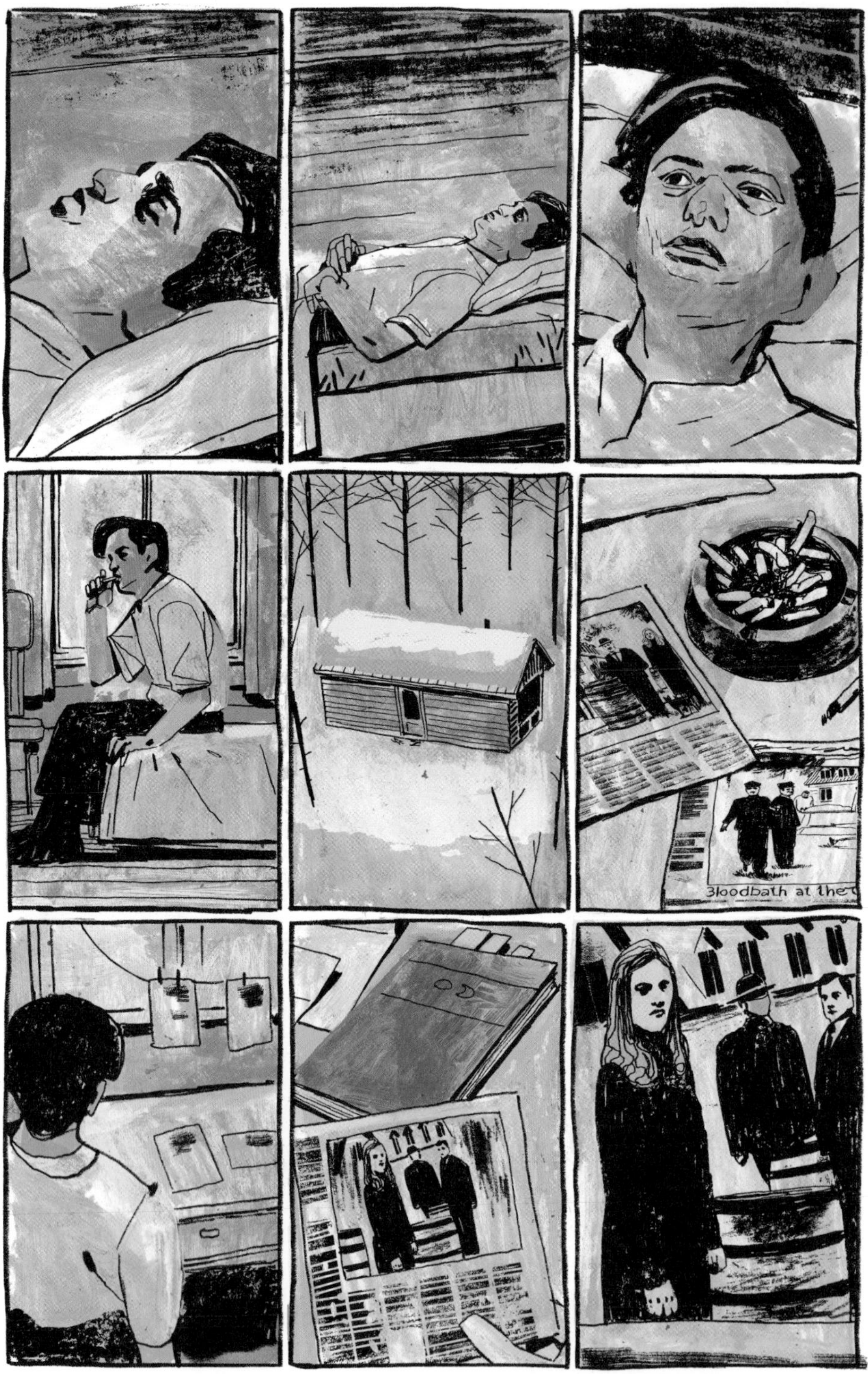
Bloodbath at the

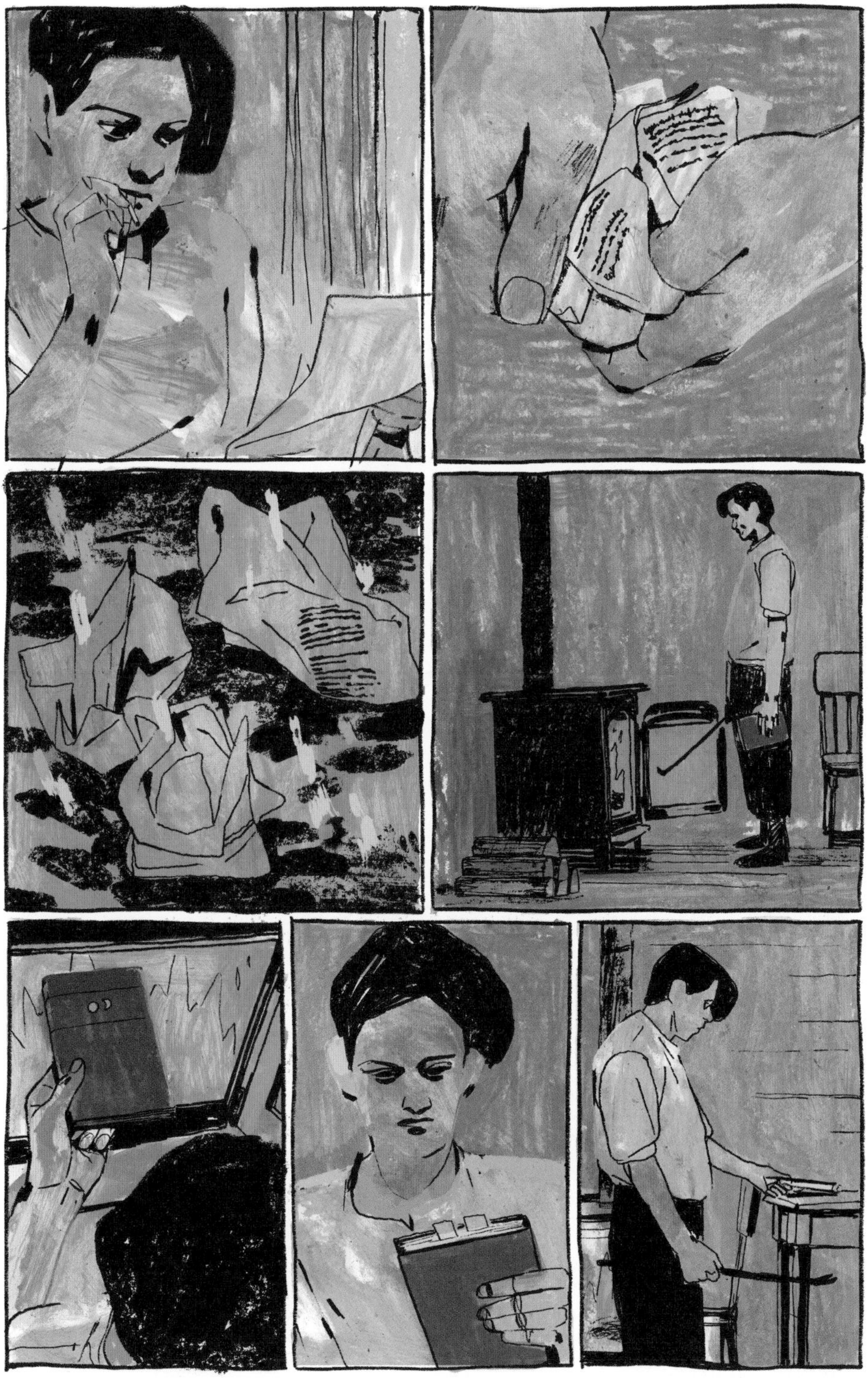

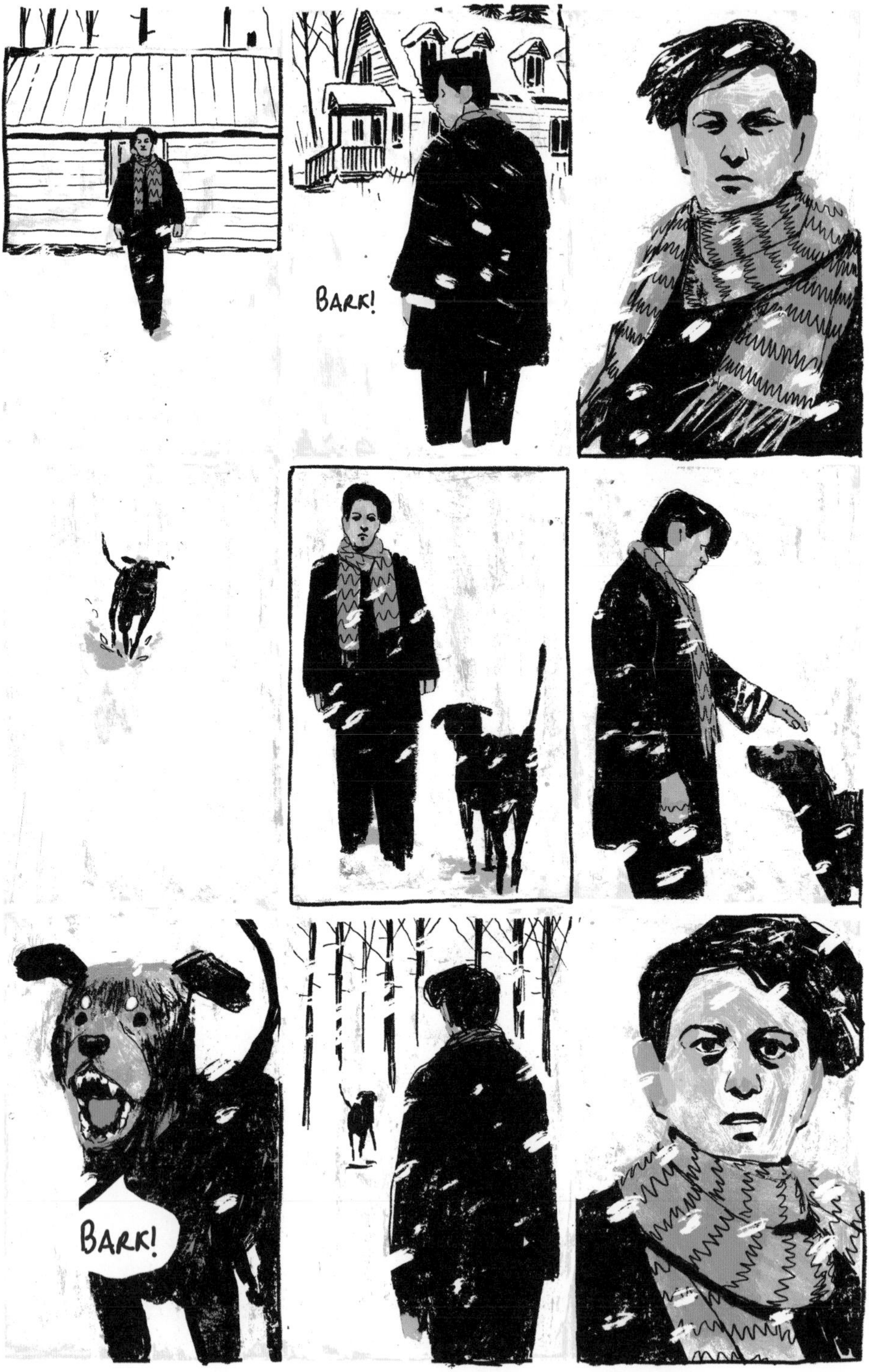
BARK!
BARK!

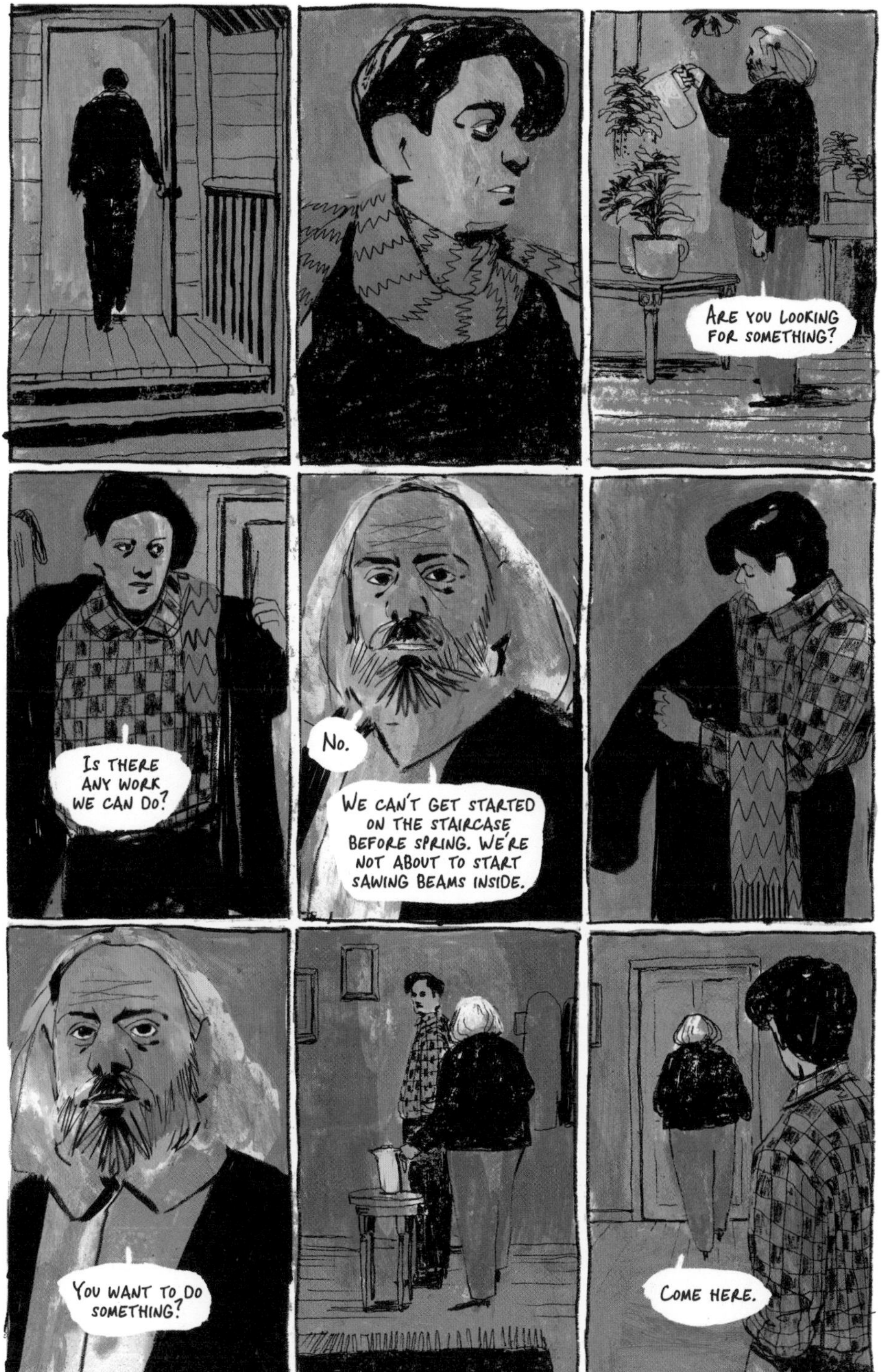
Are you looking for something?
Is there any work we can do?
No.
We can't get started on the staircase before spring. We're not about to start sawing beams inside.
You want to do something?
Come here.

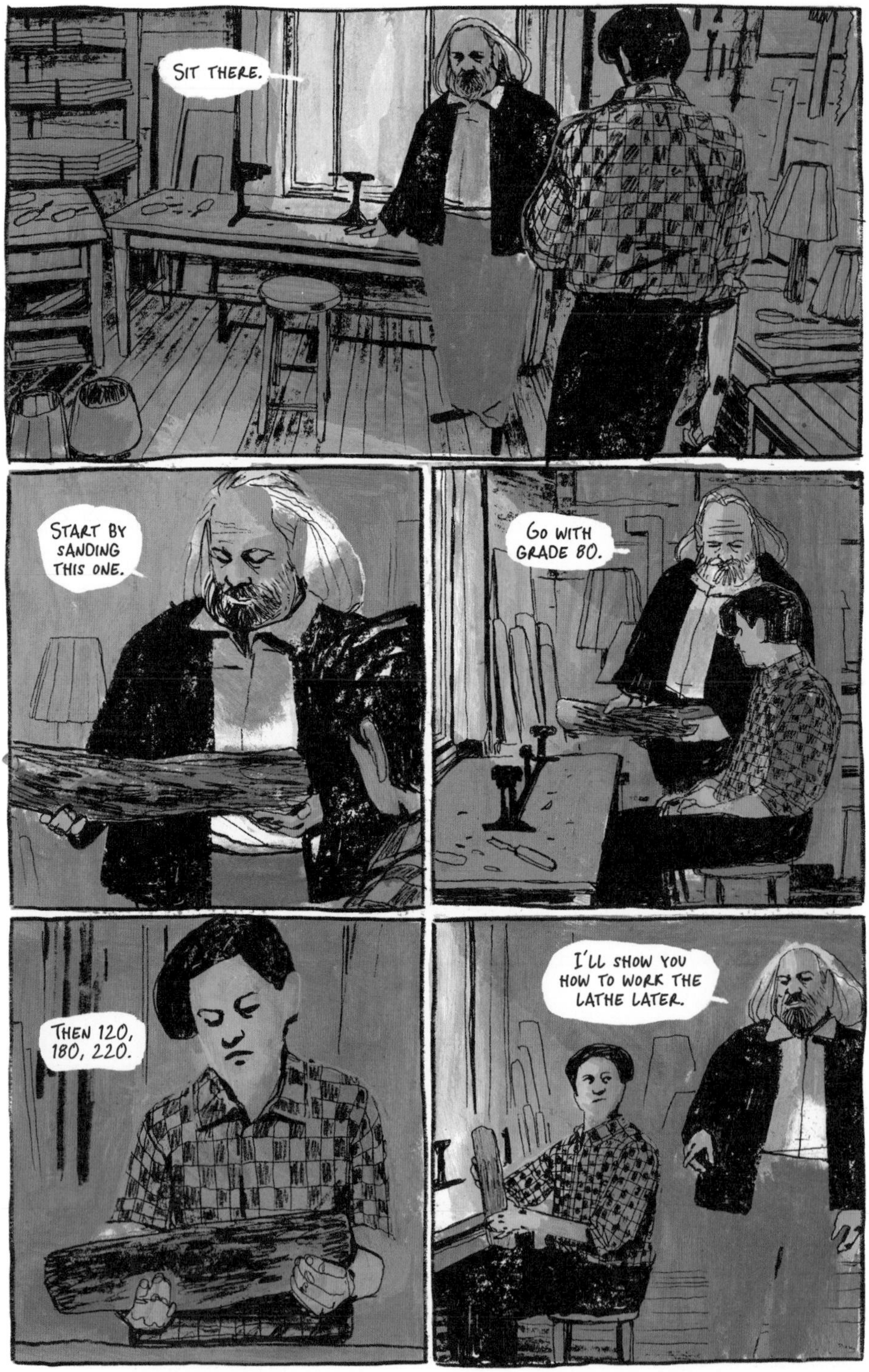
SIT THERE.
START BY SANDING THIS ONE.
GO WITH GRADE 80.
THEN 120, 180, 220.
I'LL SHOW YOU HOW TO WORK THE LATHE LATER.

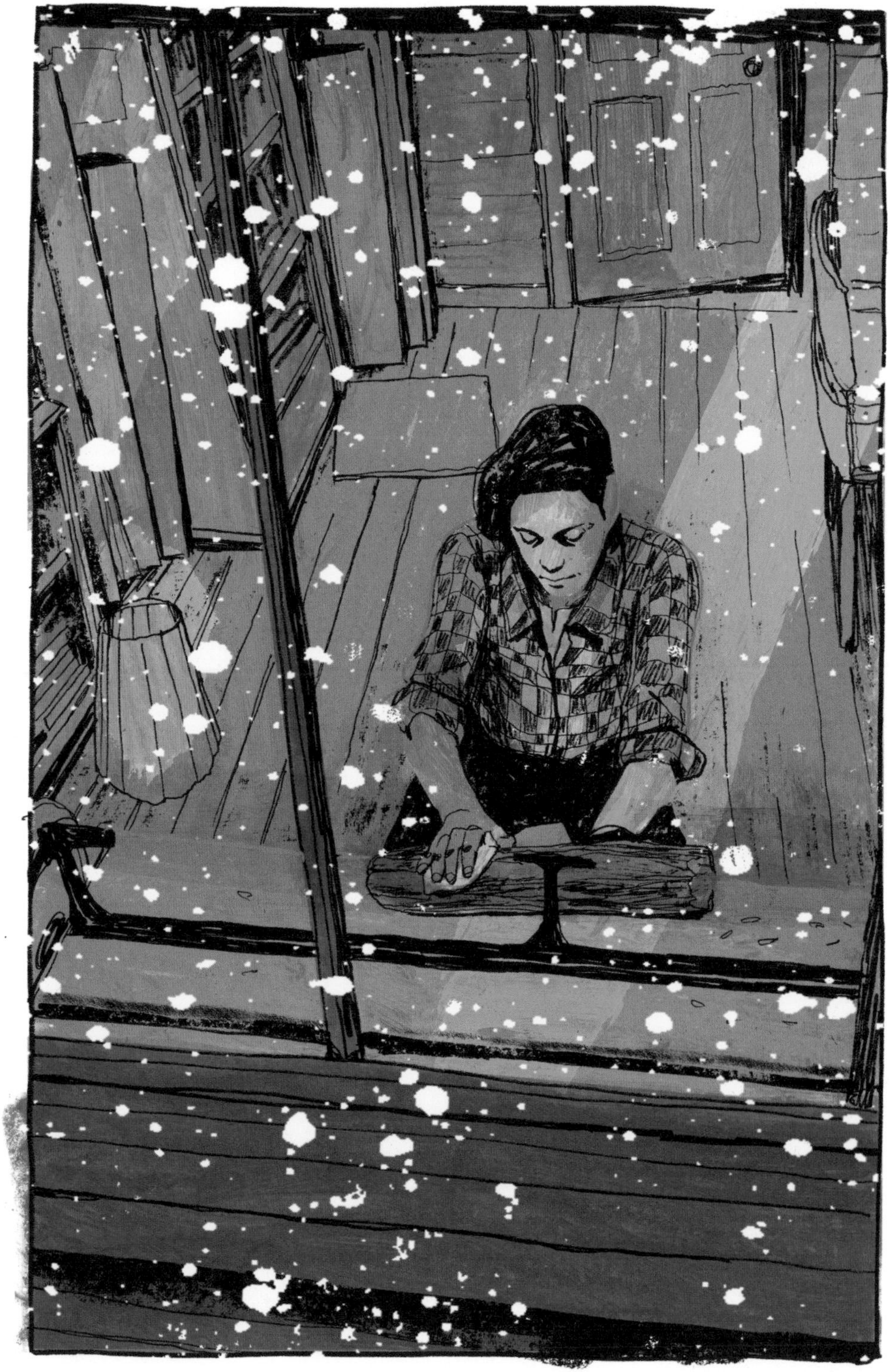

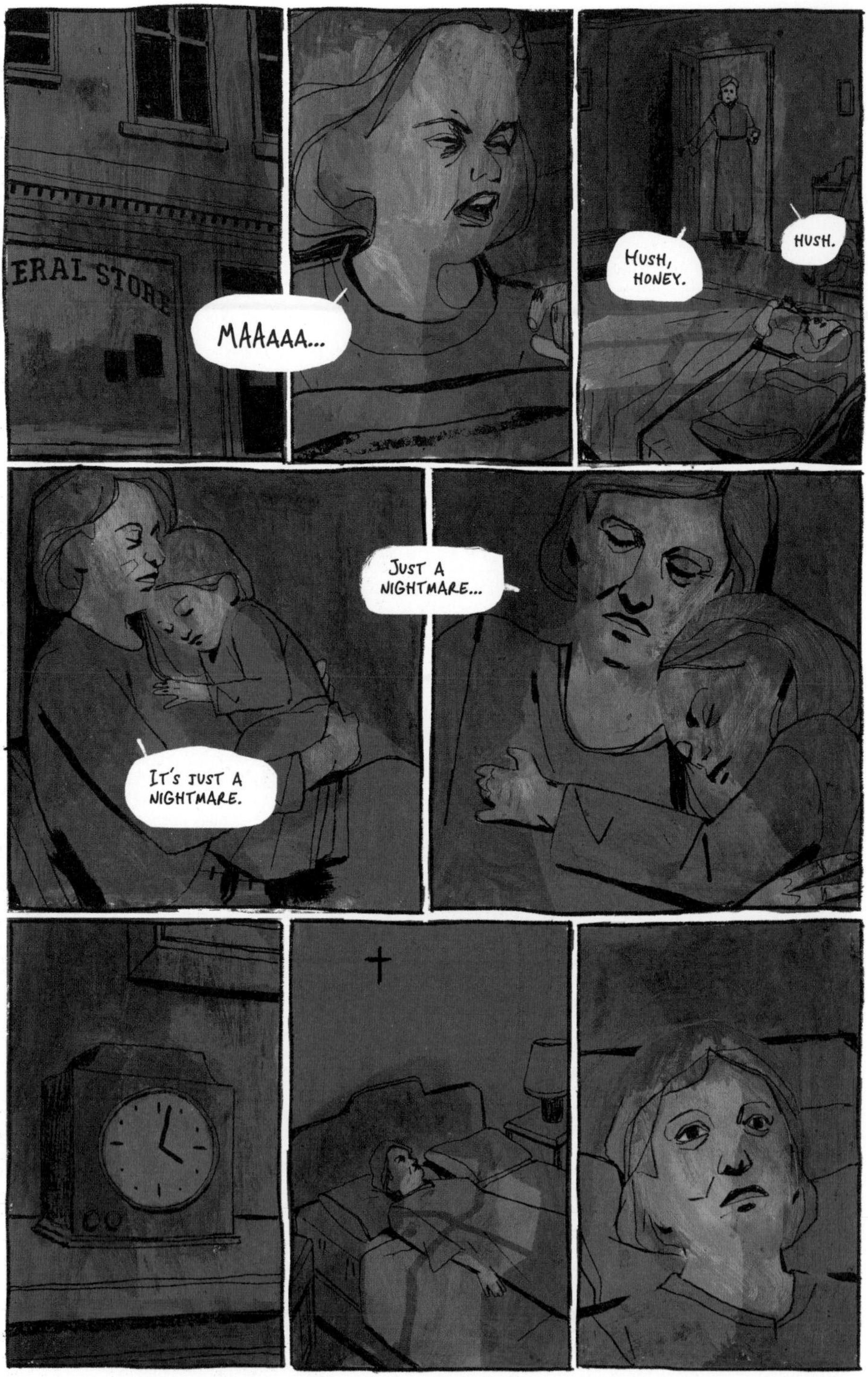
ERAL STORE
MAAAAA...
HUSH, HONEY.
HUSH.
IT'S JUST A NIGHTMARE.
JUST A NIGHTMARE...

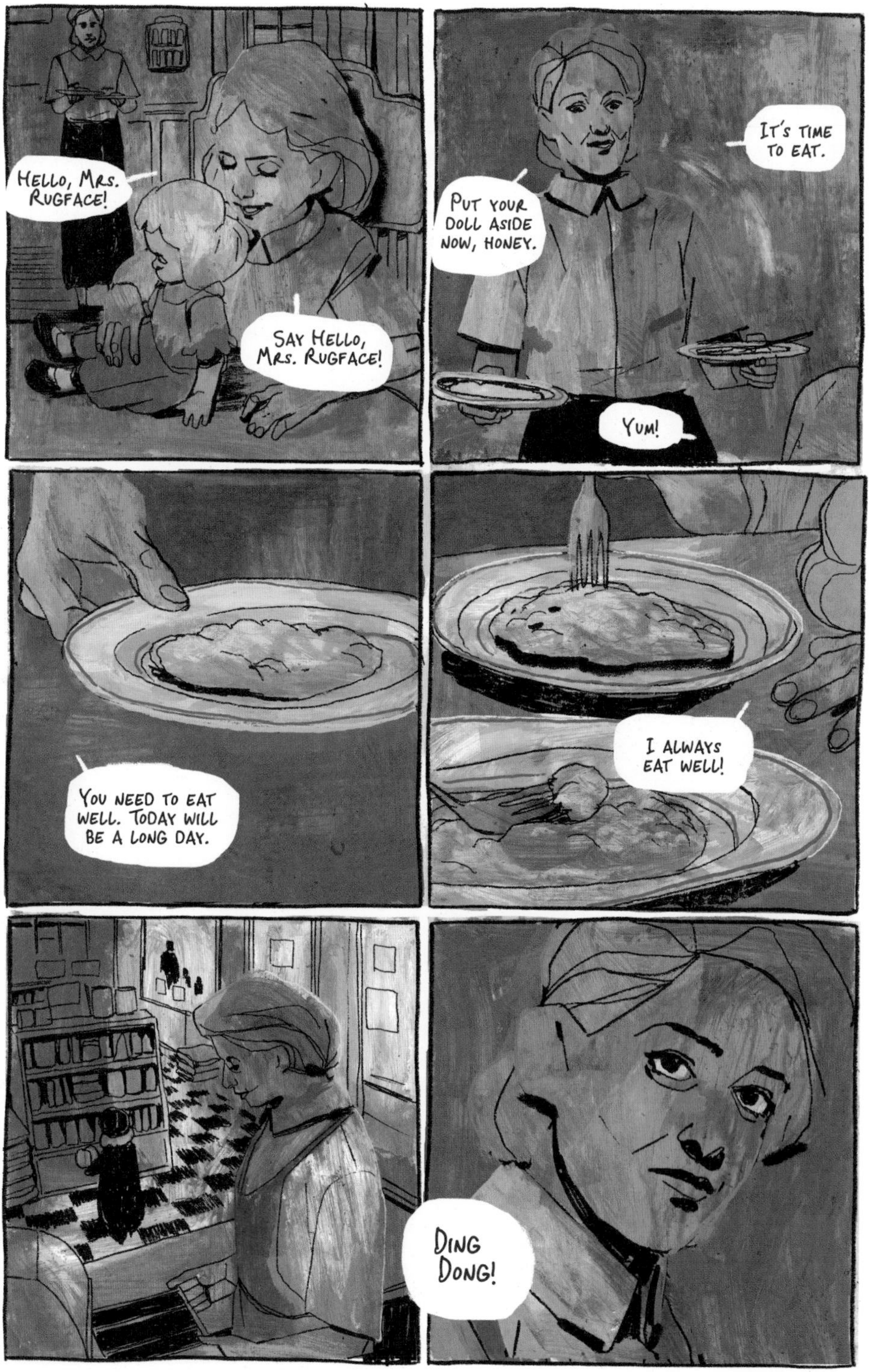
Hello, Mrs. Rugface!
Say Hello, Mrs. Rugface!
It's time to eat.
Put your doll aside now, honey.
Yum!
You need to eat well. Today will be a long day.
I always eat well!
Ding Dong!

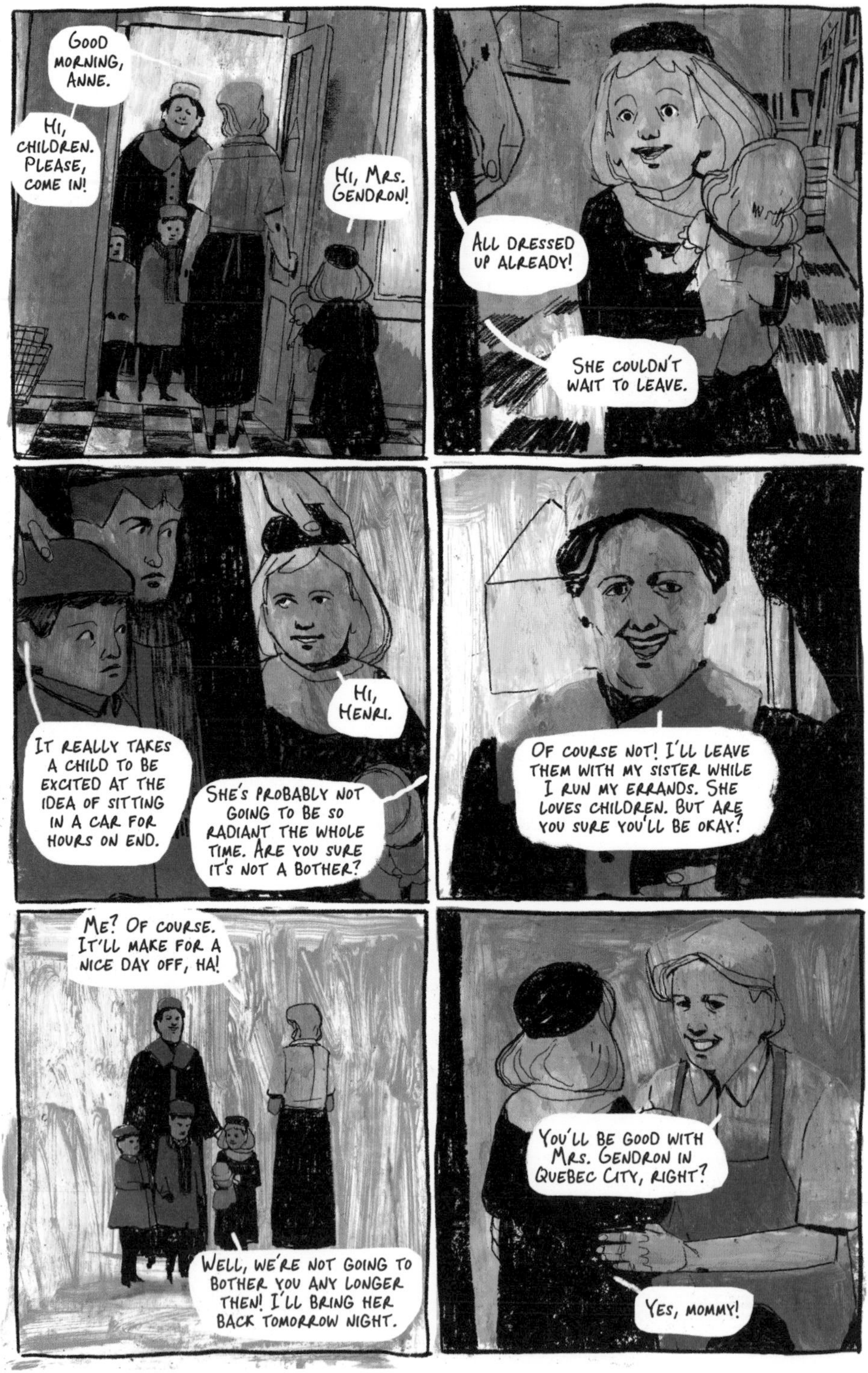
Good morning, Anne.
Hi, children. Please, come in!
Hi, Mrs. Gendron!
All dressed up already!
She couldn't wait to leave.
It really takes a child to be excited at the idea of sitting in a car for hours on end.
Hi, Henri.
She's probably not going to be so radiant the whole time. Are you sure it's not a bother?
Of course not! I'll leave them with my sister while I run my errands. She loves children. But are you sure you'll be okay?
Me? Of course. It'll make for a nice day off, ha!
Well, we're not going to bother you any longer then! I'll bring her back tomorrow night.
You'll be good with Mrs. Gendron in Quebec City, right?
Yes, mommy!

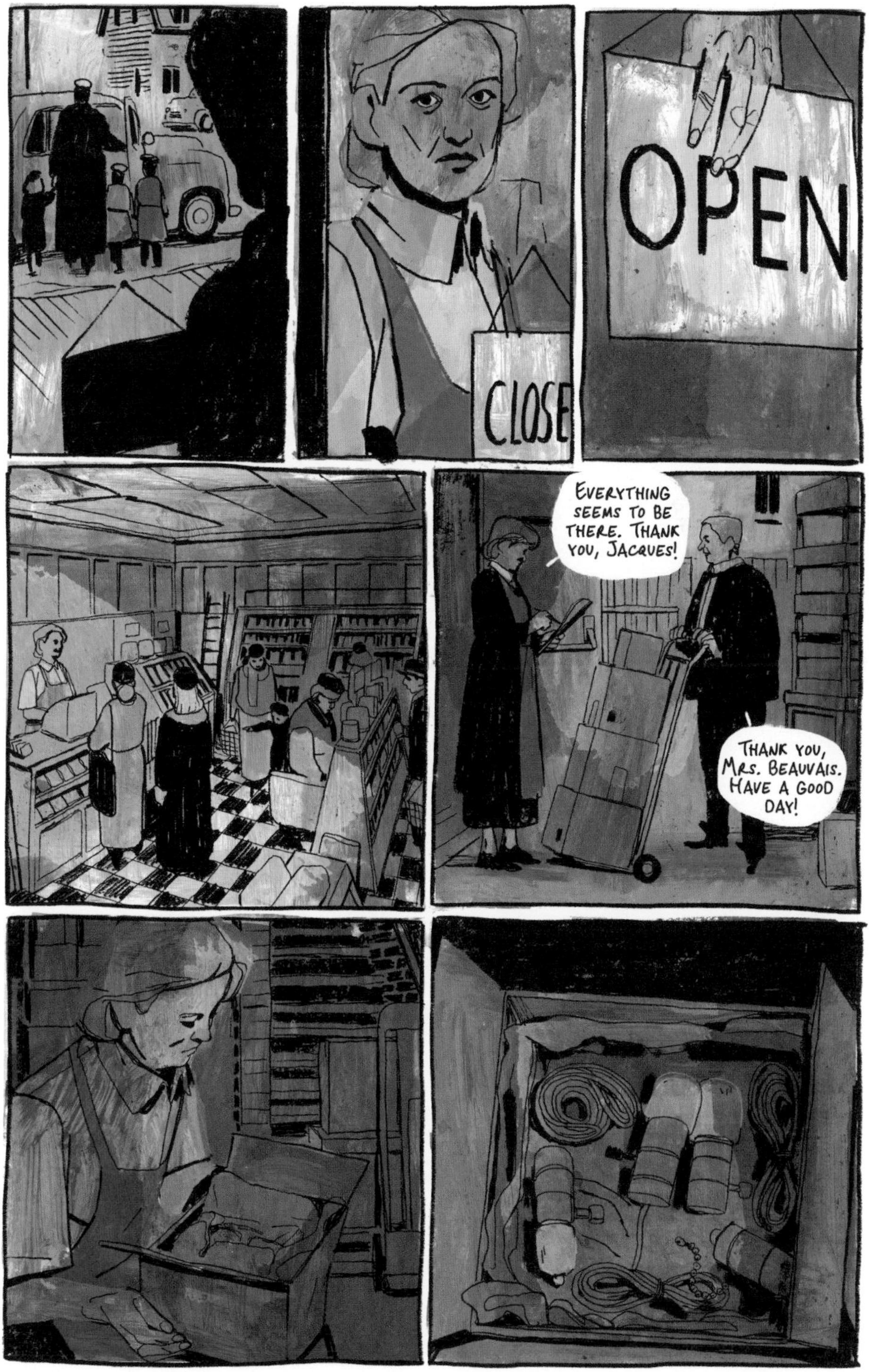
CLOSE
OPEN
EVERYTHING SEEMS TO BE THERE. THANK YOU, JACQUES!
THANK YOU, MRS. BEAUVAIS. HAVE A GOOD DAY!

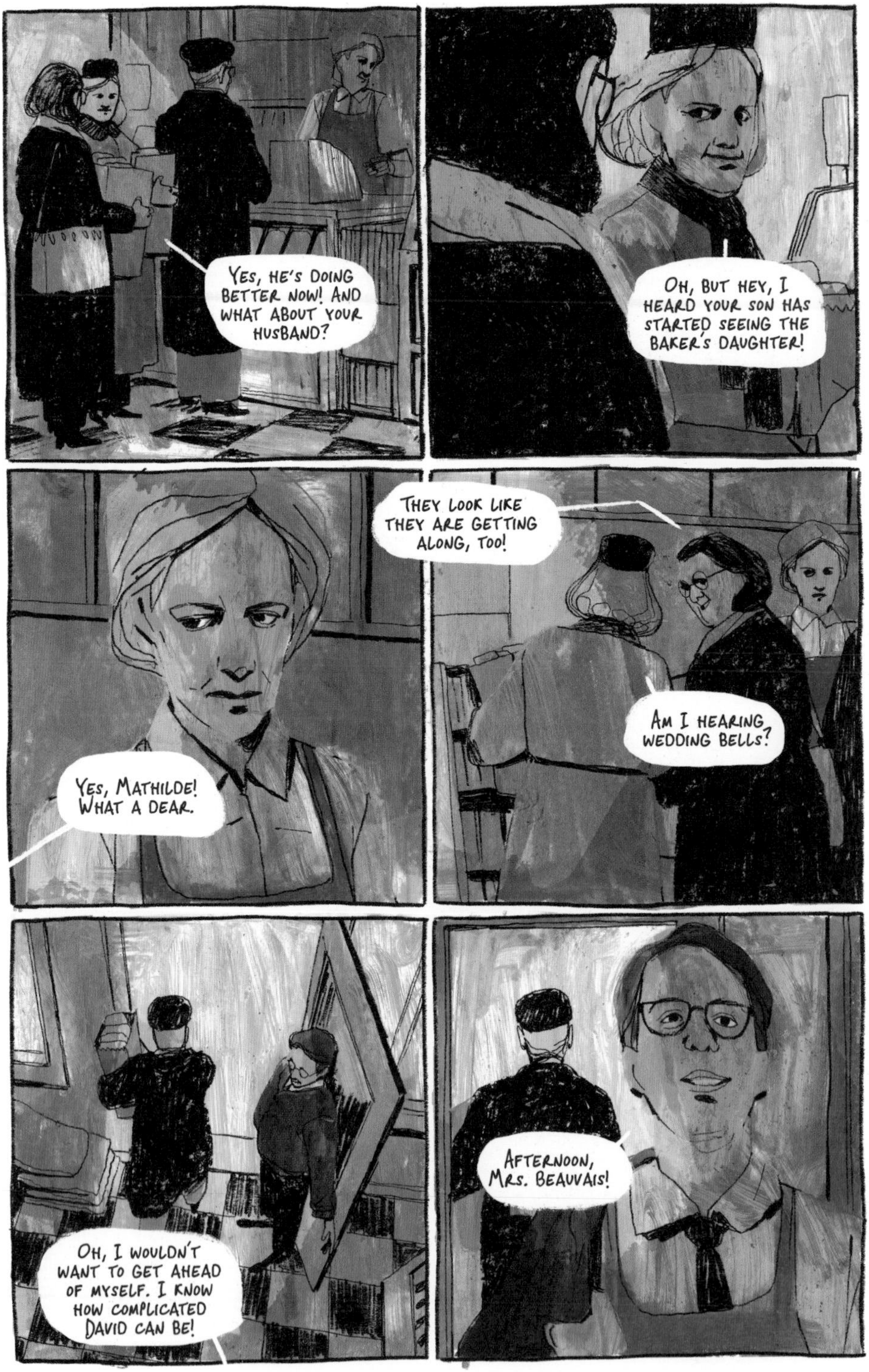
Yes, he's doing better now! And what about your husband?
Oh, but hey, I heard your son has started seeing the baker's daughter!
Yes, Mathilde! What a dear.
They look like they are getting along, too!
Am I hearing wedding bells?
Oh, I wouldn't want to get ahead of myself. I know how complicated David can be!
Afternoon, Mrs. Beauvais!

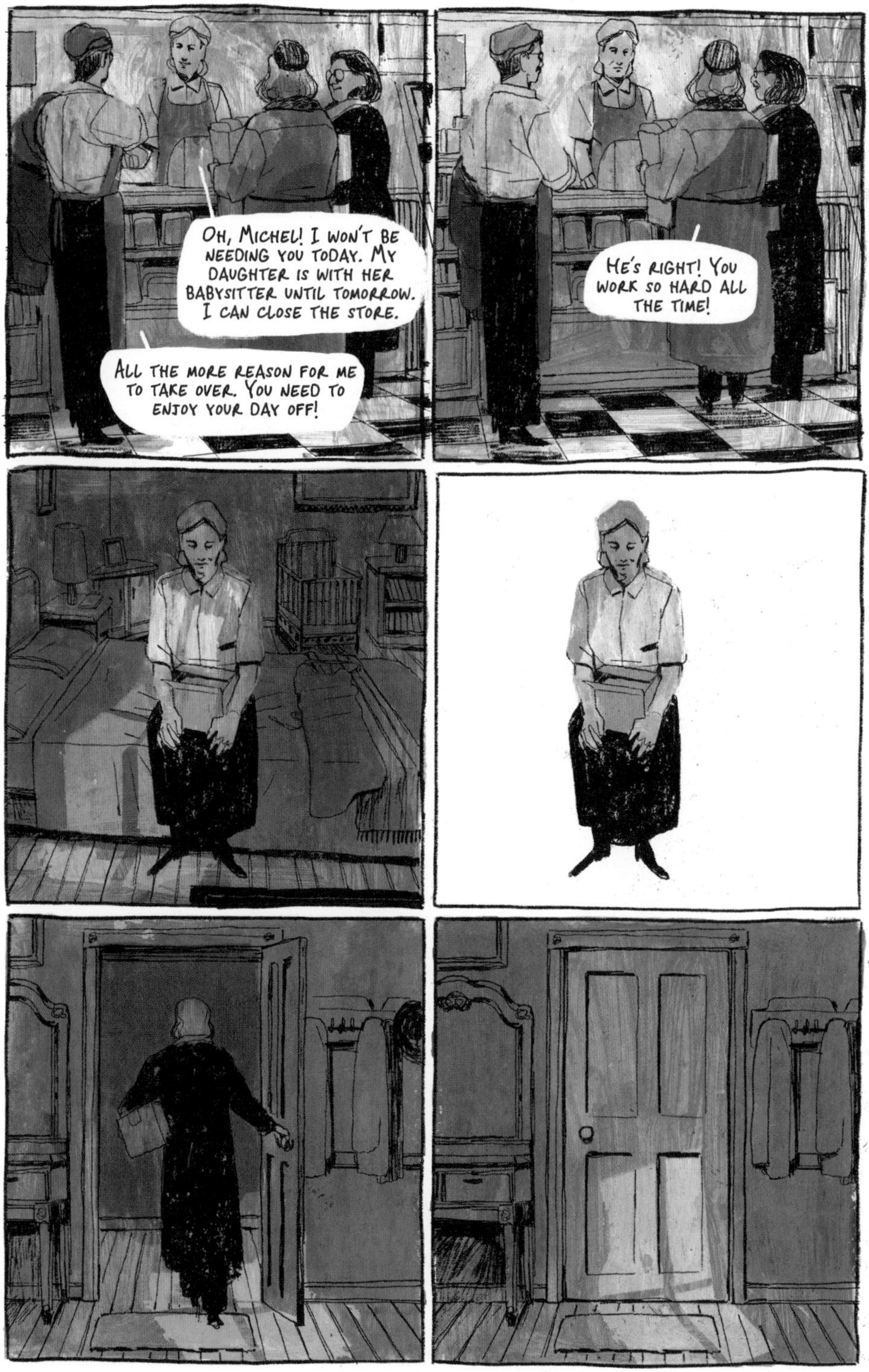
OH, MICHEL! I WON'T BE NEEDING YOU TODAY. MY DAUGHTER IS WITH HER BABYSITTER UNTIL TOMORROW. I CAN CLOSE THE STORE.
ALL THE MORE REASON FOR ME TO TAKE OVER. YOU NEED TO ENJOY YOUR DAY OFF!
HE'S RIGHT! YOU WORK SO HARD ALL THE TIME!

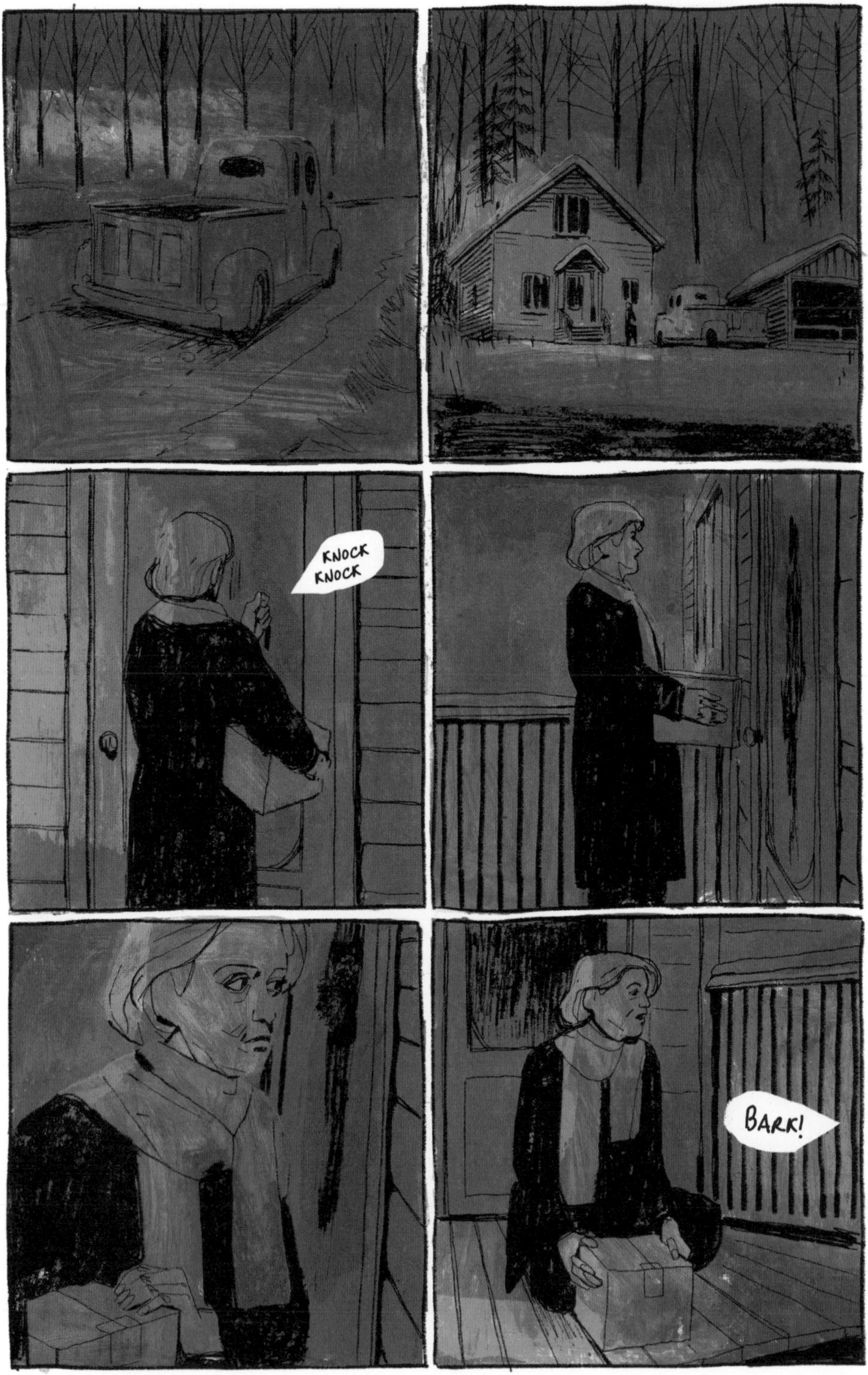
KNOCK
KNOCK
BARK!

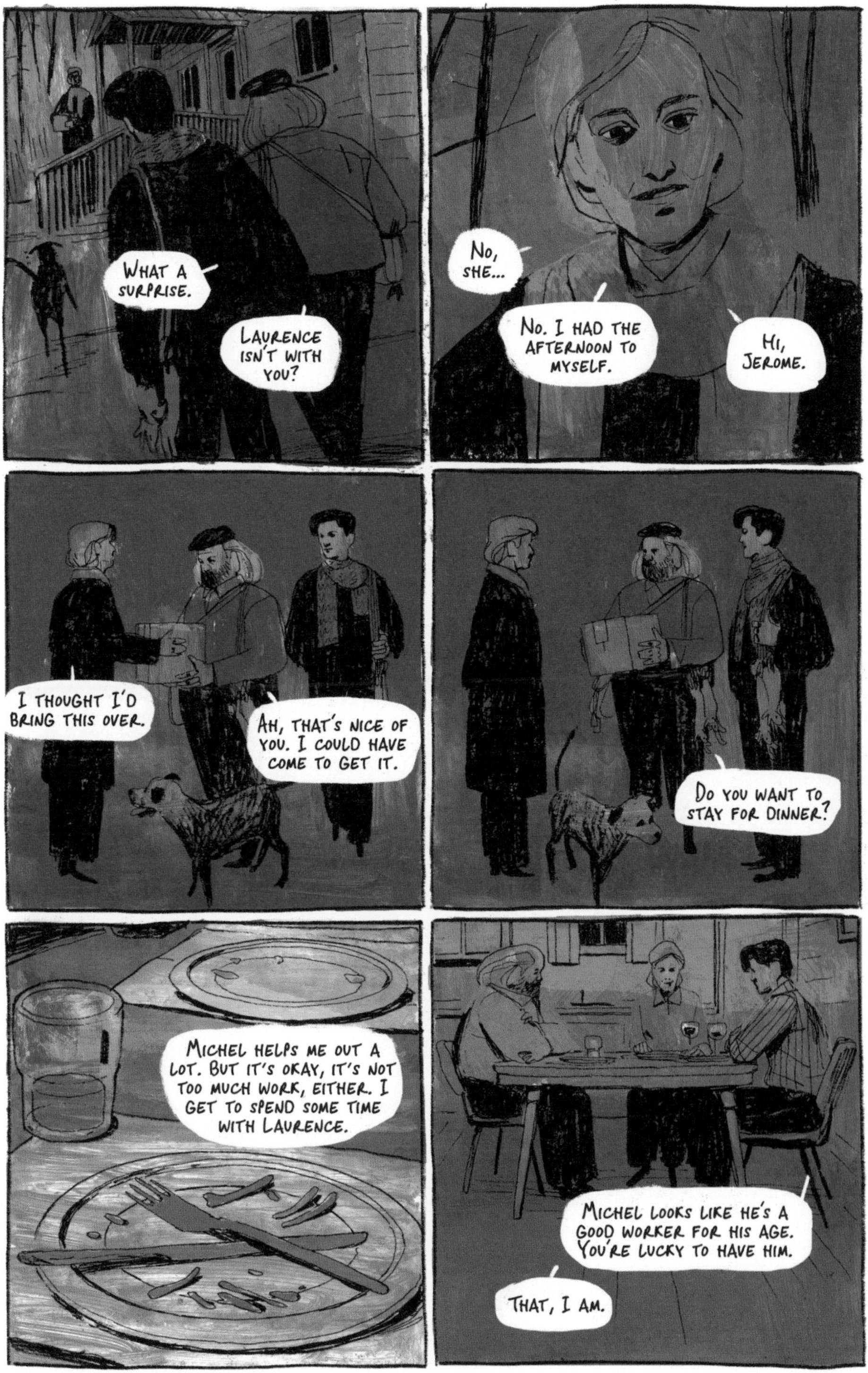
WHAT A SURPRISE.
LAURENCE ISN'T WITH YOU?
NO, SHE...
NO. I HAD THE AFTERNOON TO MYSELF.
HI, JEROME.
I THOUGHT I'D BRING THIS OVER.
AH, THAT'S NICE OF YOU. I COULD HAVE COME TO GET IT.
DO YOU WANT TO STAY FOR DINNER?
MICHEL HELPS ME OUT A LOT. BUT IT'S OKAY, IT'S NOT TOO MUCH WORK, EITHER. I GET TO SPEND SOME TIME WITH LAURENCE.
MICHEL LOOKS LIKE HE'S A GOOD WORKER FOR HIS AGE. YOU'RE LUCKY TO HAVE HIM.
THAT, I AM.

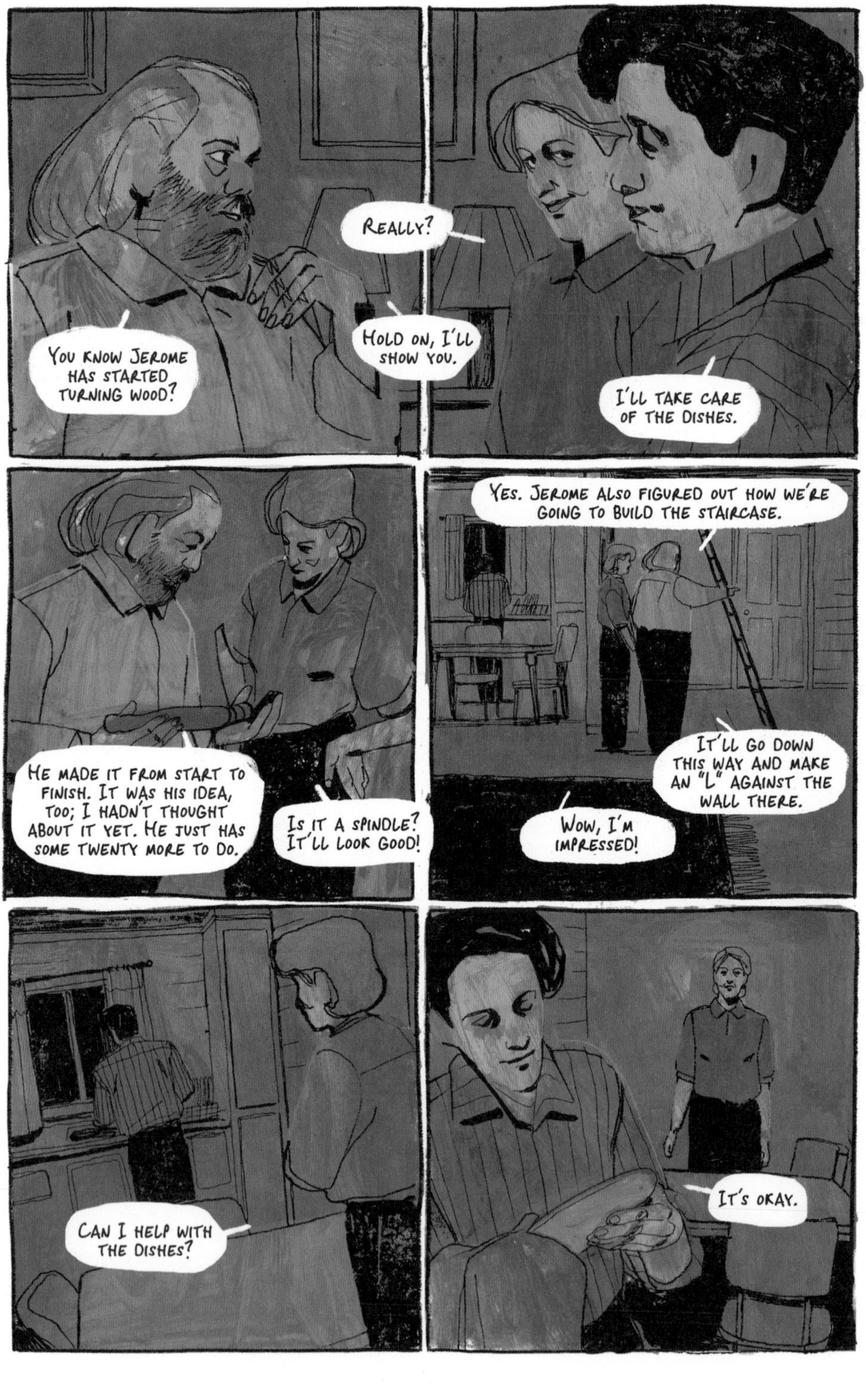
You know Jerome has started turning wood?
Really?
Hold on, I'll show you.
I'll take care of the dishes.
He made it from start to finish. It was his idea, too; I hadn't thought about it yet. He just has some twenty more to do.
Is it a spindle? It'll look good!
Yes. Jerome also figured out how we're going to build the staircase.
It'll go down this way and make an "L" against the wall there.
Wow, I'm impressed!
Can I help with the dishes?
It's okay.

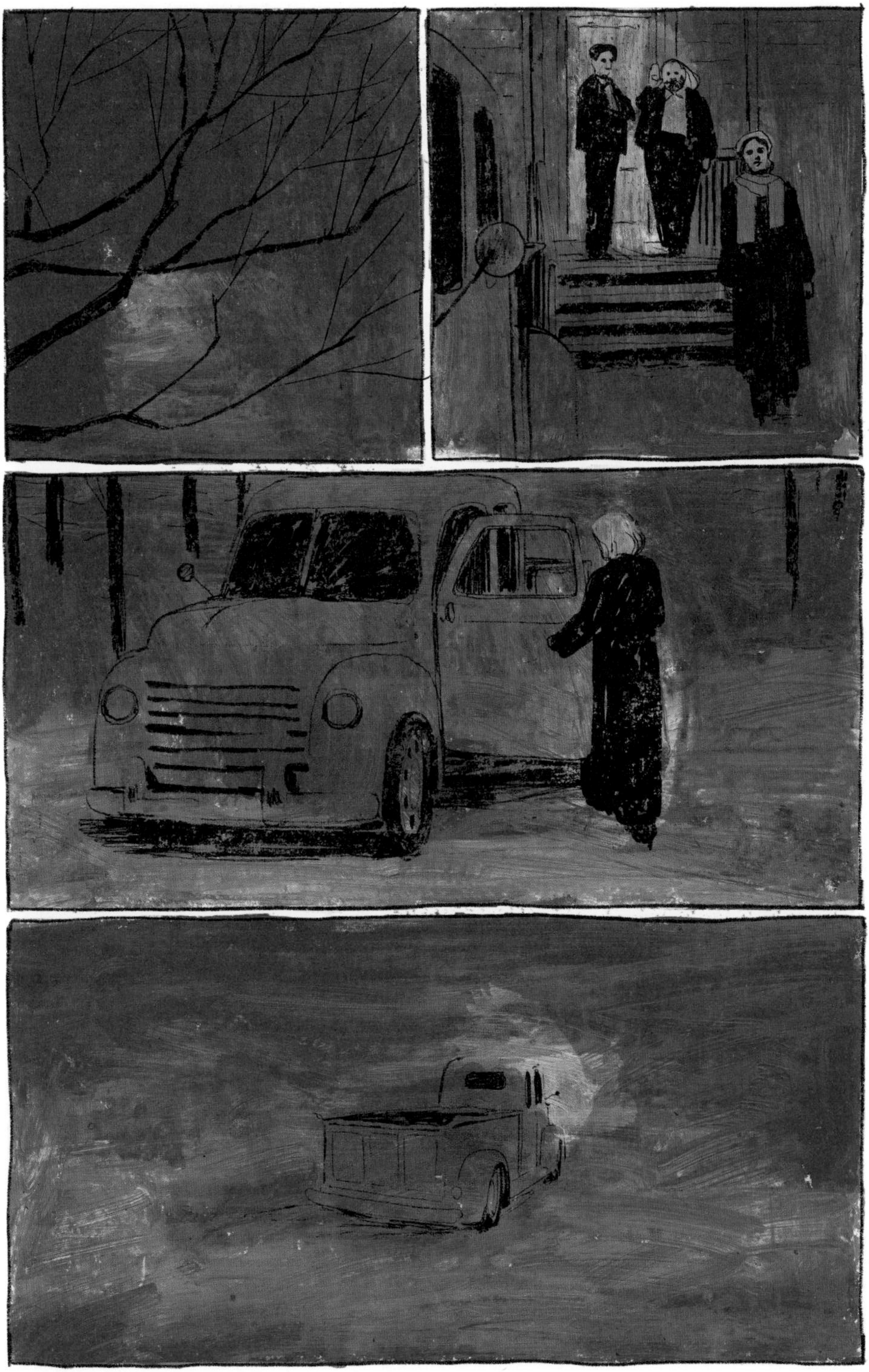

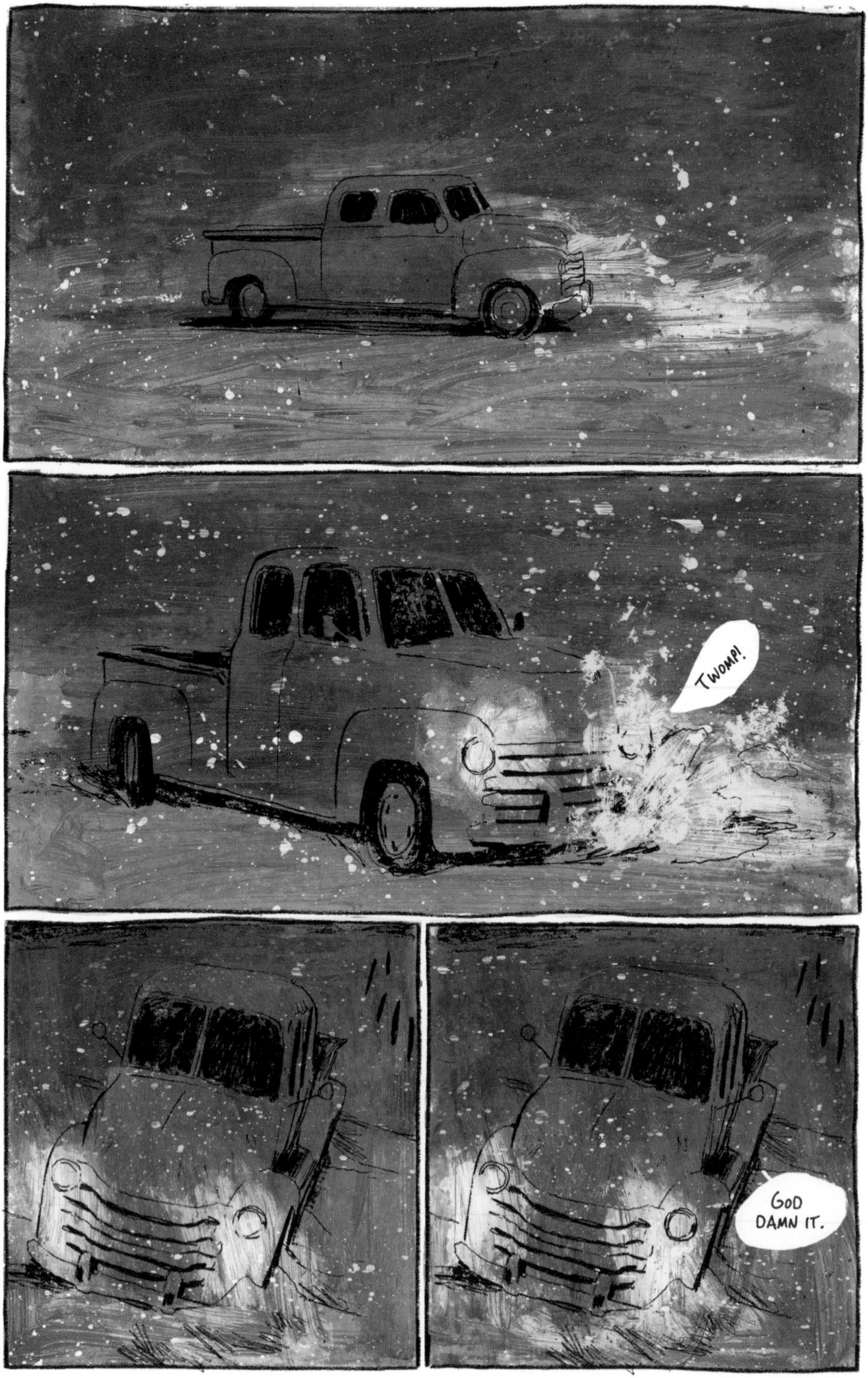
TWOMP!
GOD DAMN IT.

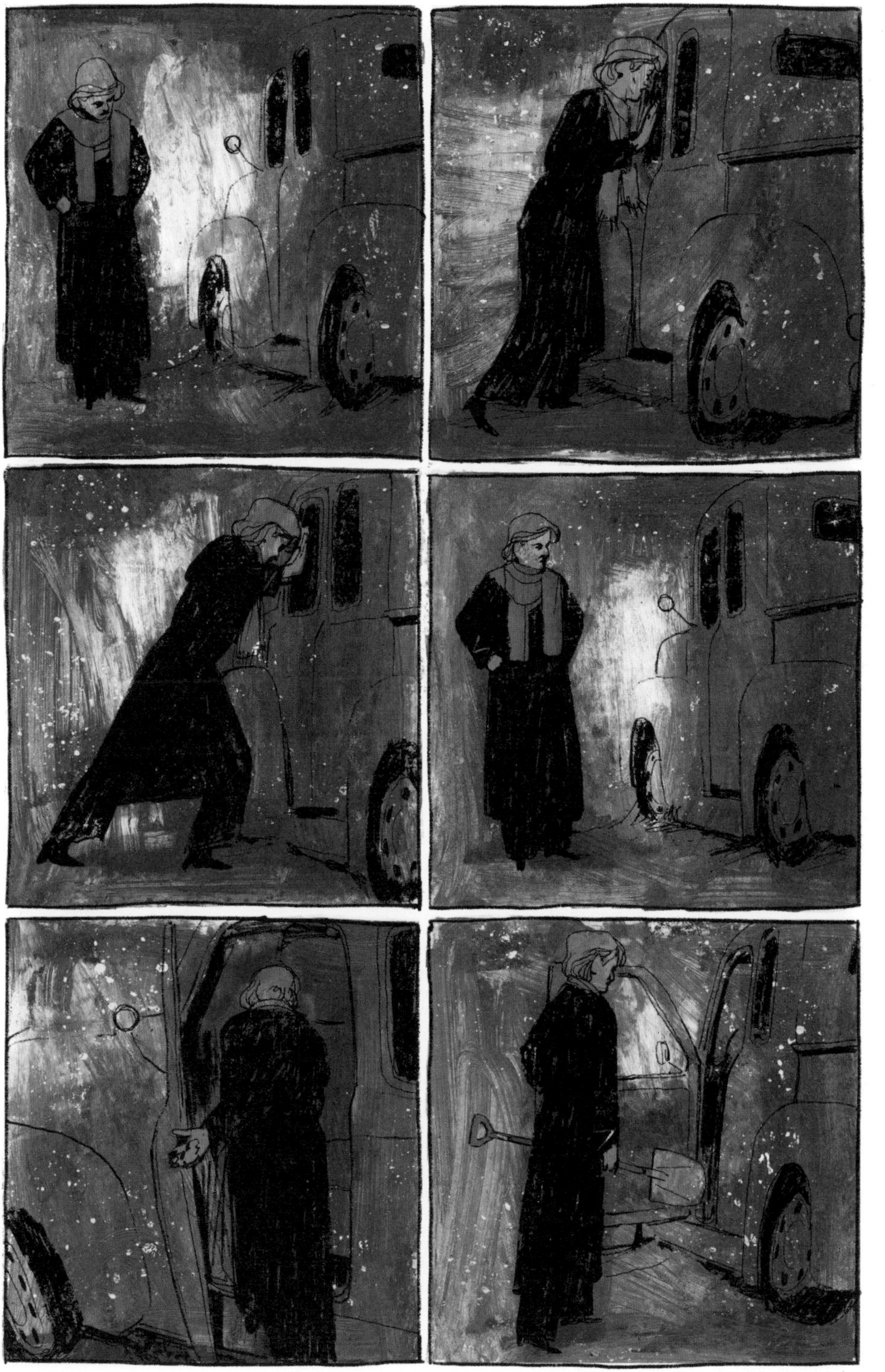

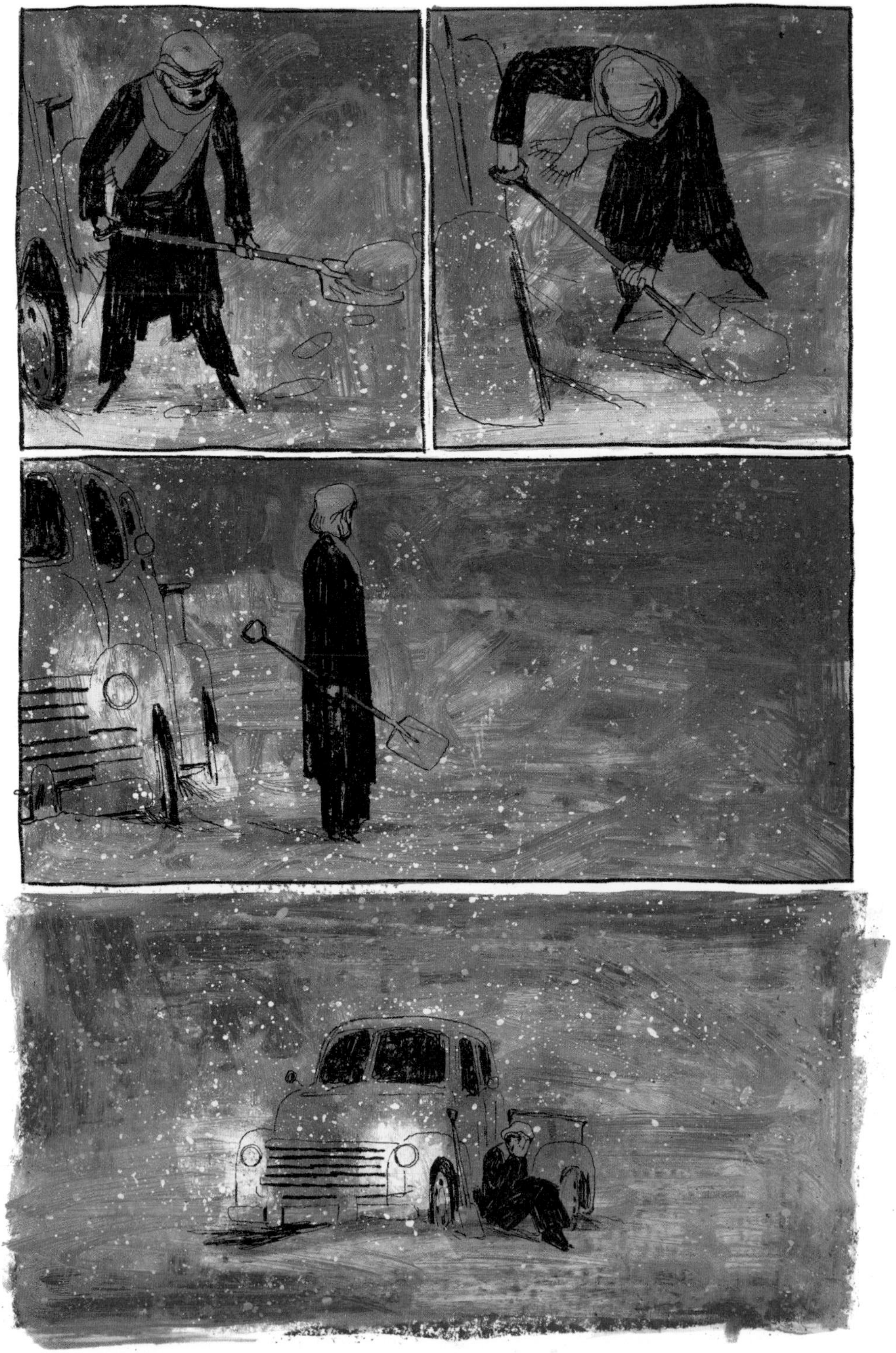

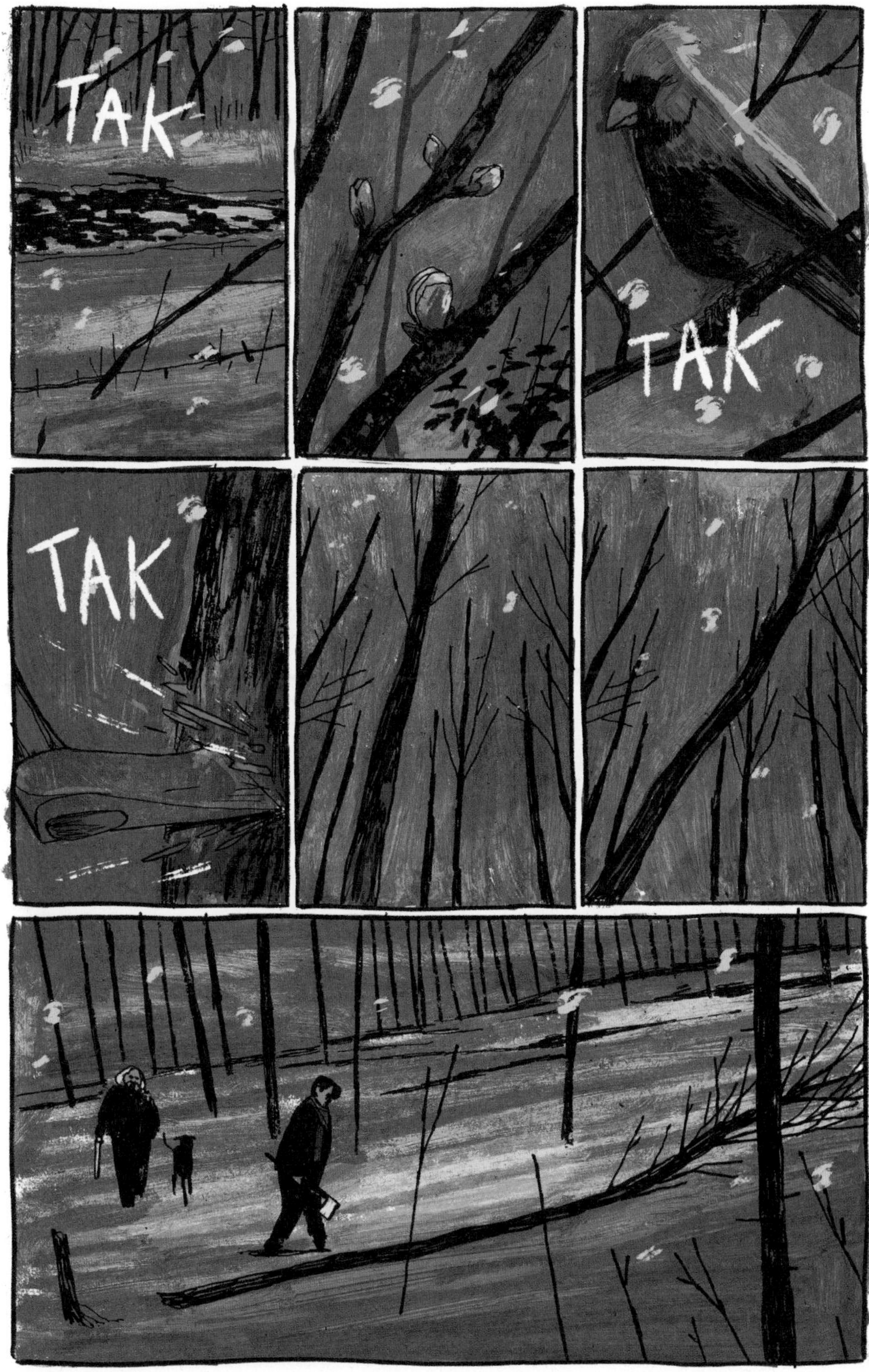
TAK
TAK
TAK

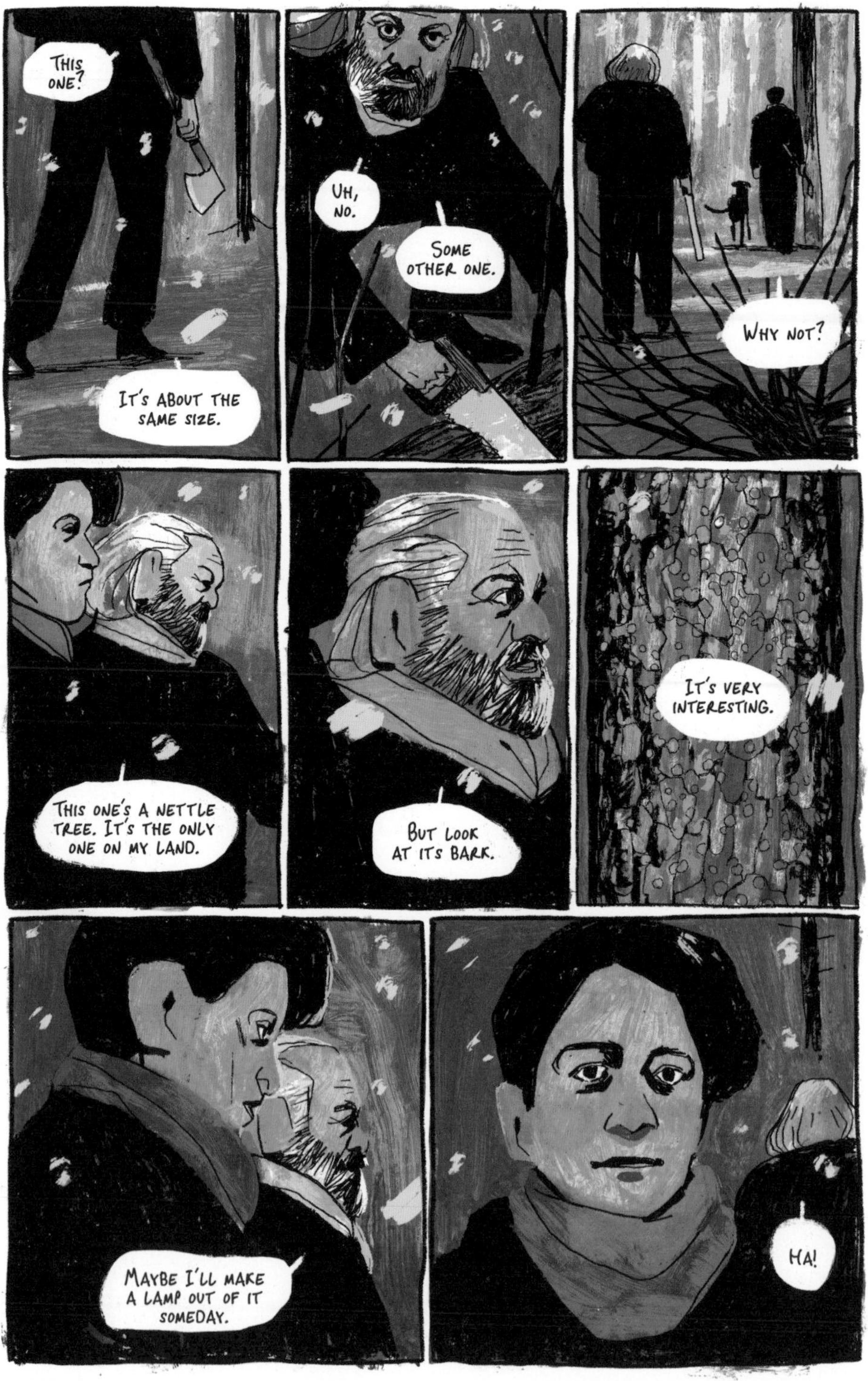
THIS ONE?
IT'S ABOUT THE SAME SIZE.
UH, NO.
SOME OTHER ONE.
WHY NOT?
THIS ONE'S A NETTLE TREE. IT'S THE ONLY ONE ON MY LAND.
BUT LOOK AT ITS BARK.
IT'S VERY INTERESTING.
MAYBE I'LL MAKE A LAMP OUT OF IT SOMEDAY.
HA!

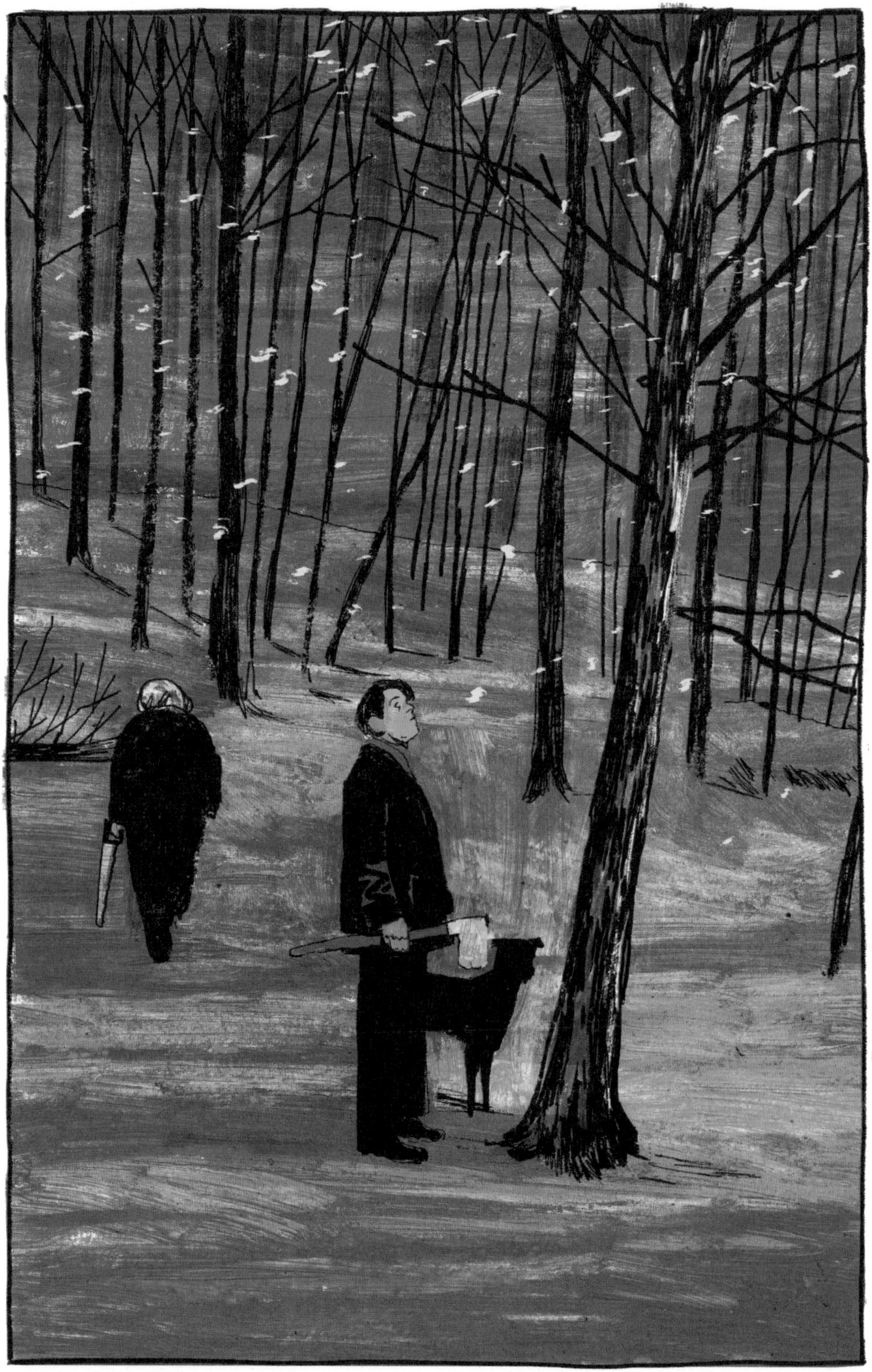

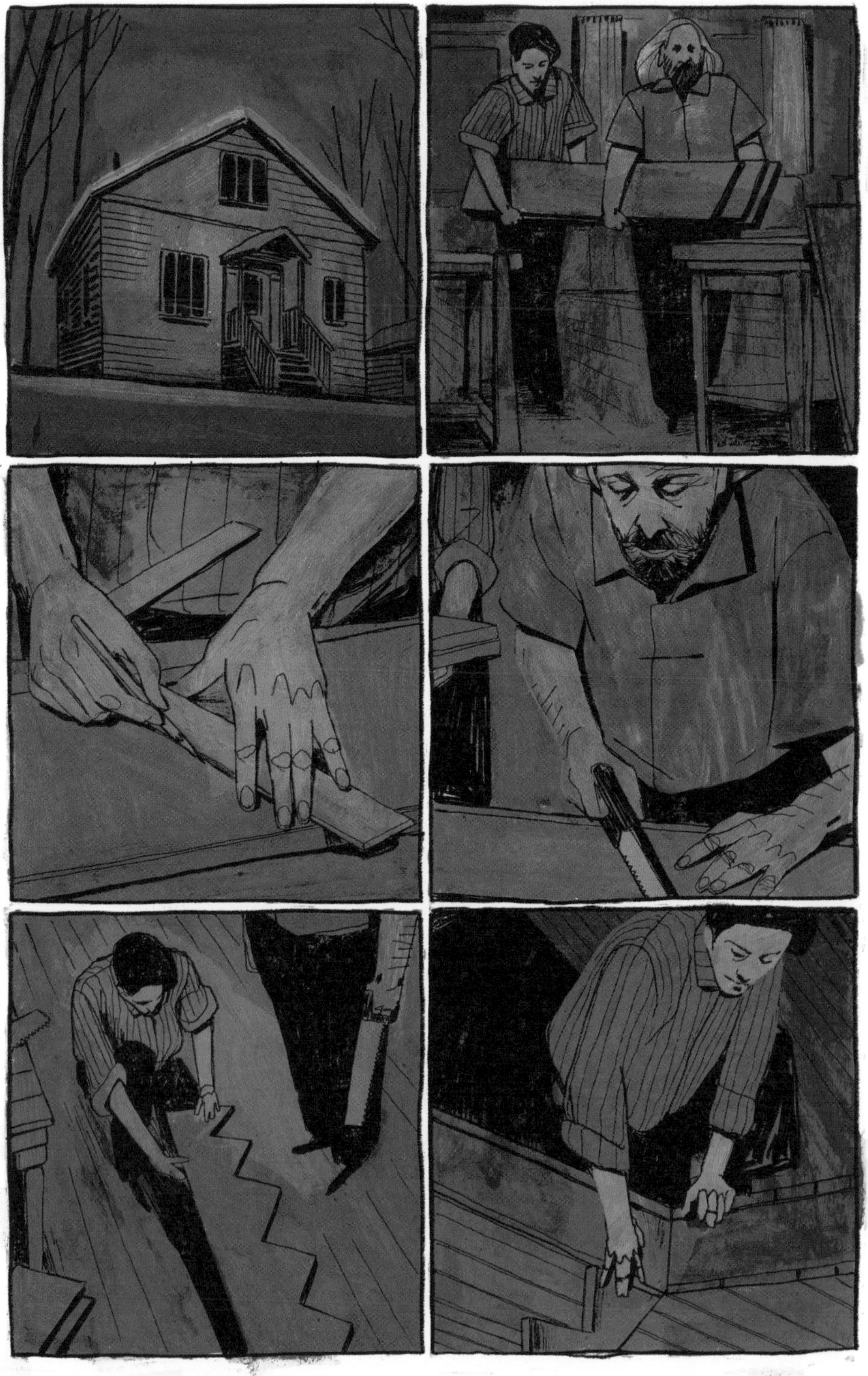

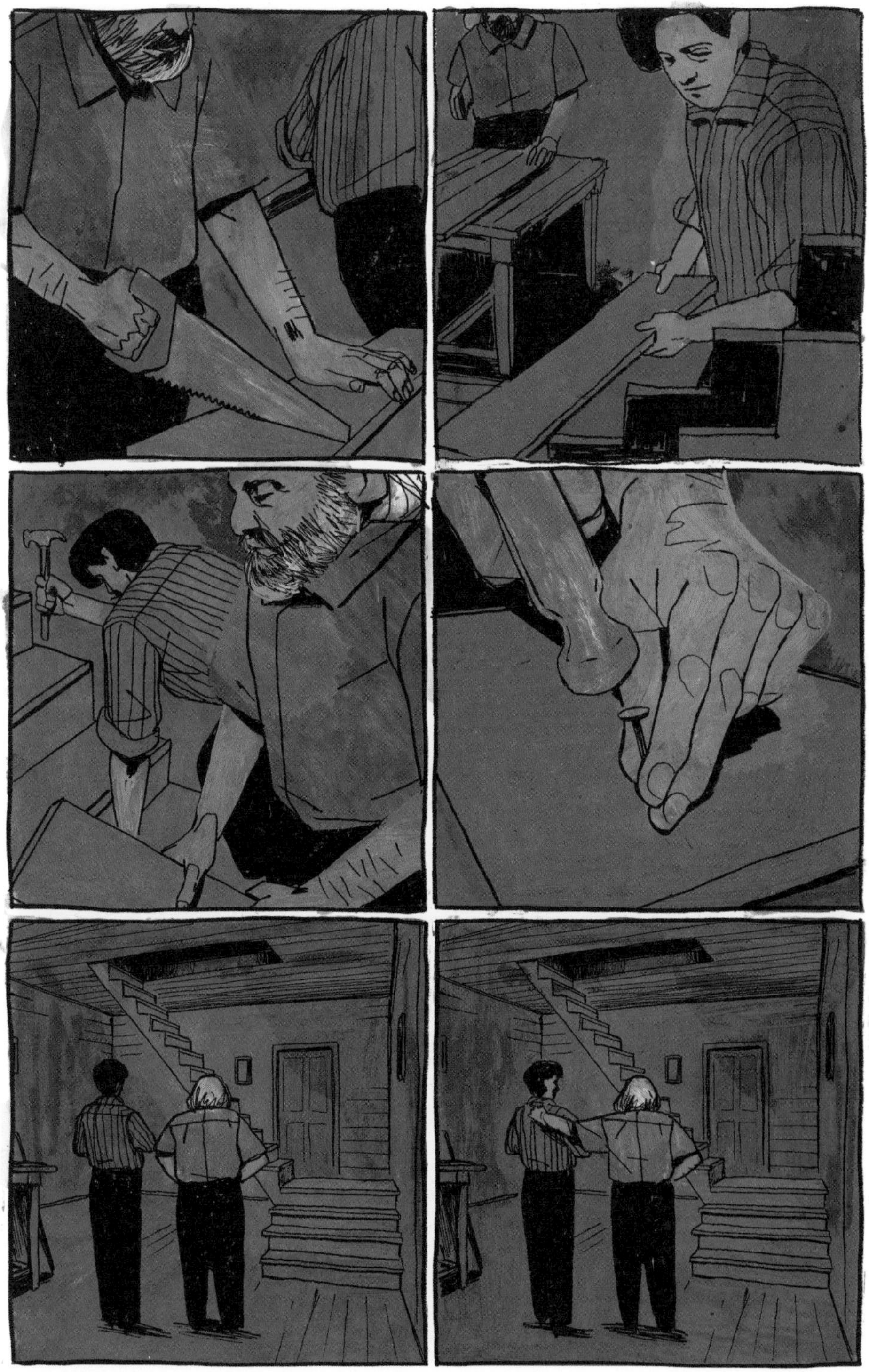

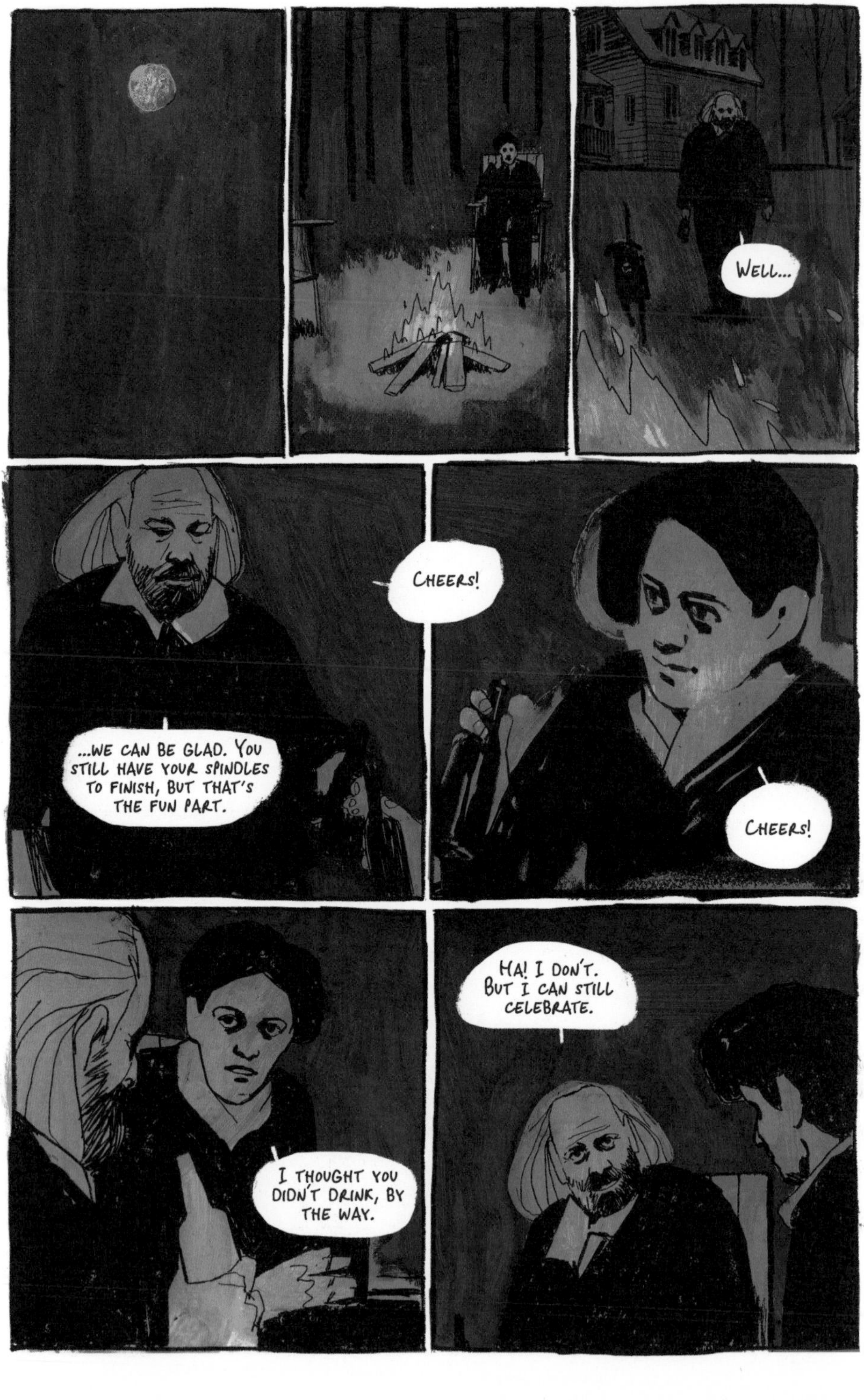
WELL...
...WE CAN BE GLAD. YOU STILL HAVE YOUR SPINDLES TO FINISH, BUT THAT'S THE FUN PART.
CHEERS!
CHEERS!
I THOUGHT YOU DIDN'T DRINK, BY THE WAY.
HA! I DON'T. BUT I CAN STILL CELEBRATE.

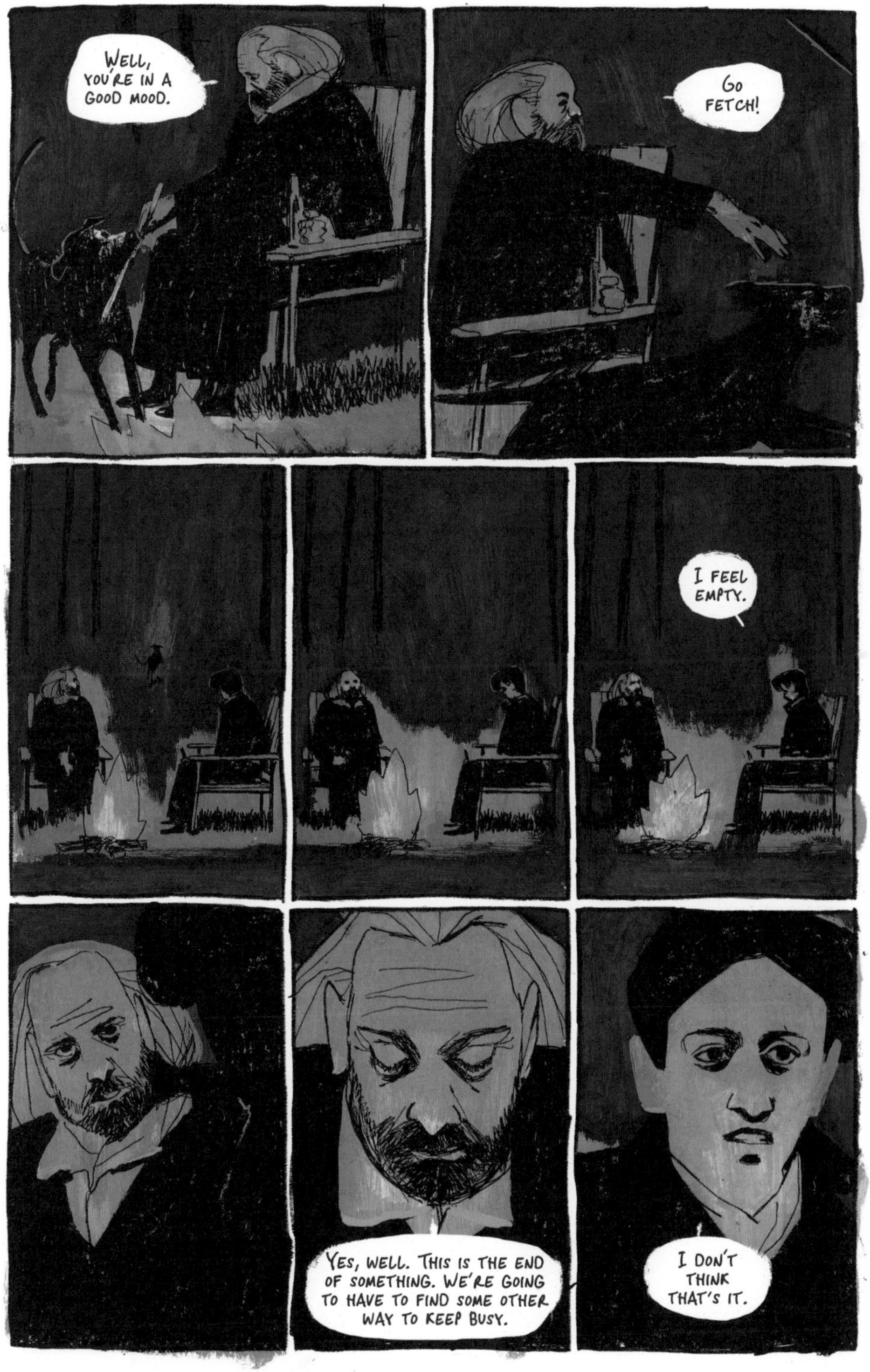
WELL, YOU'RE IN A GOOD MOOD.
GO FETCH!
I FEEL EMPTY.
YES, WELL. THIS IS THE END OF SOMETHING. WE'RE GOING TO HAVE TO FIND SOME OTHER WAY TO KEEP BUSY.
I DON'T THINK THAT'S IT.

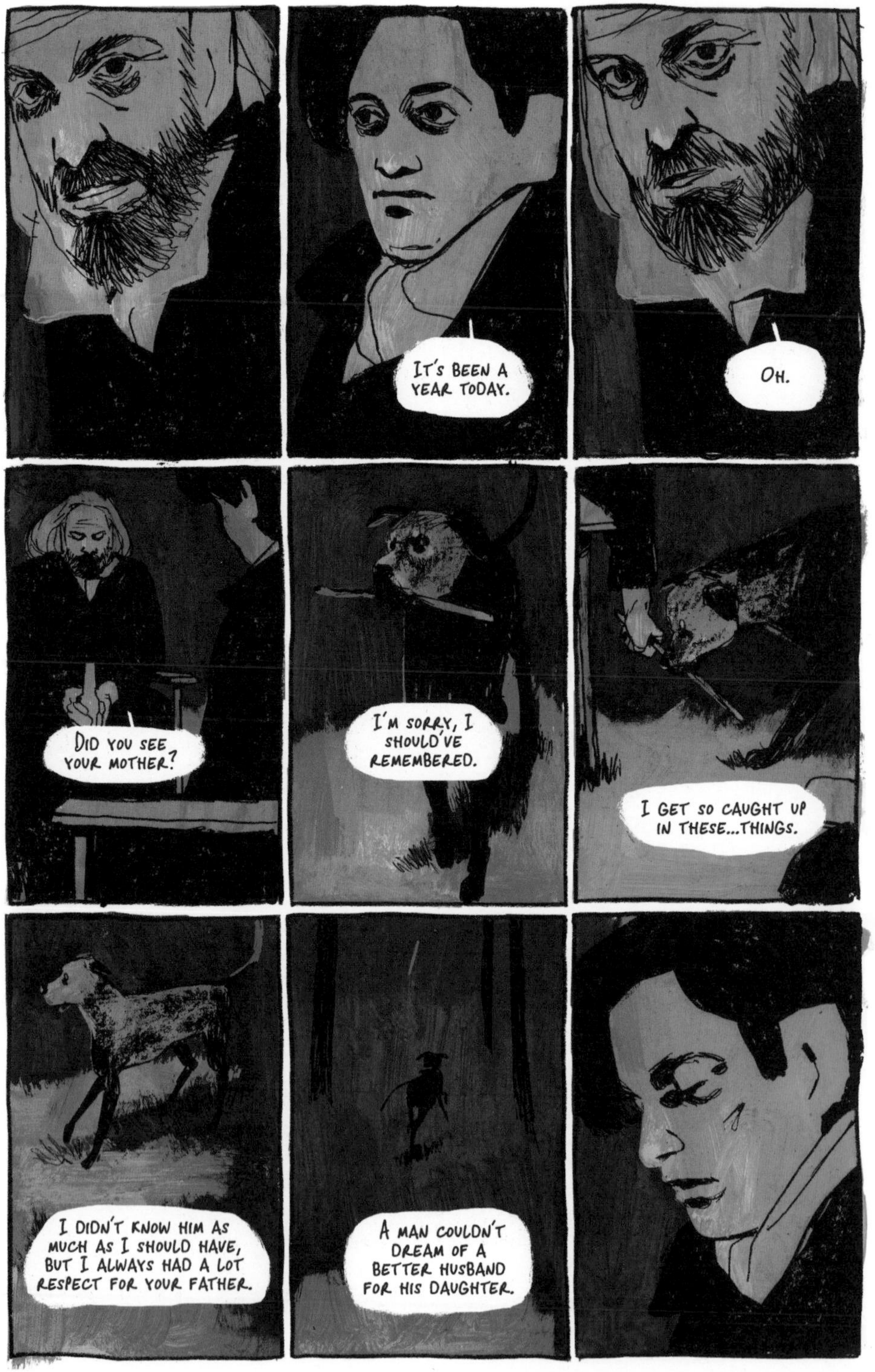

IT'S BEEN A YEAR TODAY.
OH.
DID YOU SEE YOUR MOTHER?
I'M SORRY, I SHOULD'VE REMEMBERED.
I GET SO CAUGHT UP IN THESE...THINGS.
I DIDN'T KNOW HIM AS MUCH AS I SHOULD HAVE, BUT I ALWAYS HAD A LOT RESPECT FOR YOUR FATHER.
A MAN COULDN'T DREAM OF A BETTER HUSBAND FOR HIS DAUGHTER.

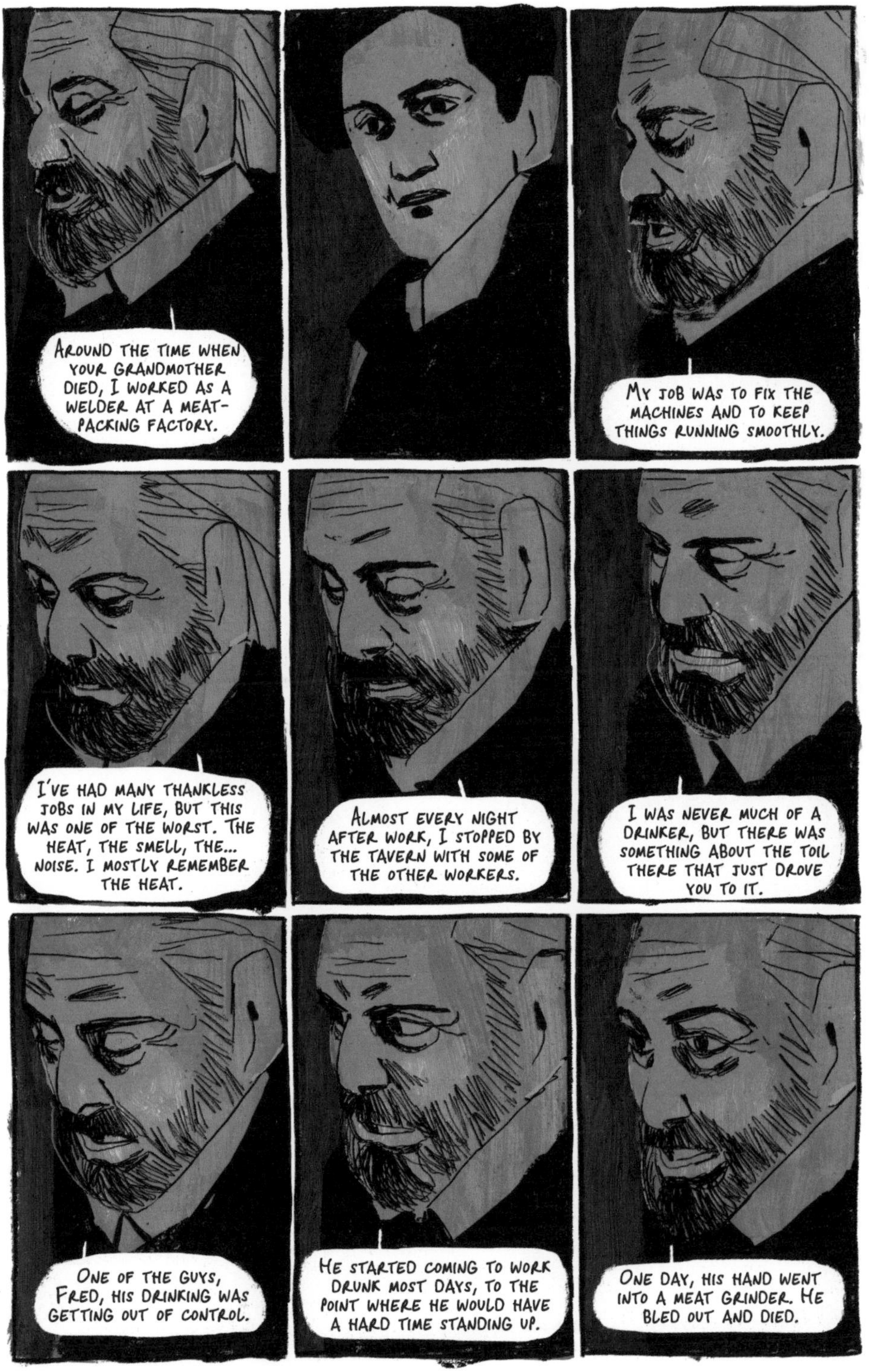
Around the time when your grandmother died, I worked as a welder at a meat-packing factory.
My job was to fix the machines and to keep things running smoothly.
I've had many thankless jobs in my life, but this was one of the worst. The heat, the smell, the... noise. I mostly remember the heat.
Almost every night after work, I stopped by the tavern with some of the other workers.
I was never much of a drinker, but there was something about the toil there that just drove you to it.
One of the guys, Fred, his drinking was getting out of control.
He started coming to work drunk most days, to the point where he would have a hard time standing up.
One day, his hand went into a meat grinder. He bled out and died.

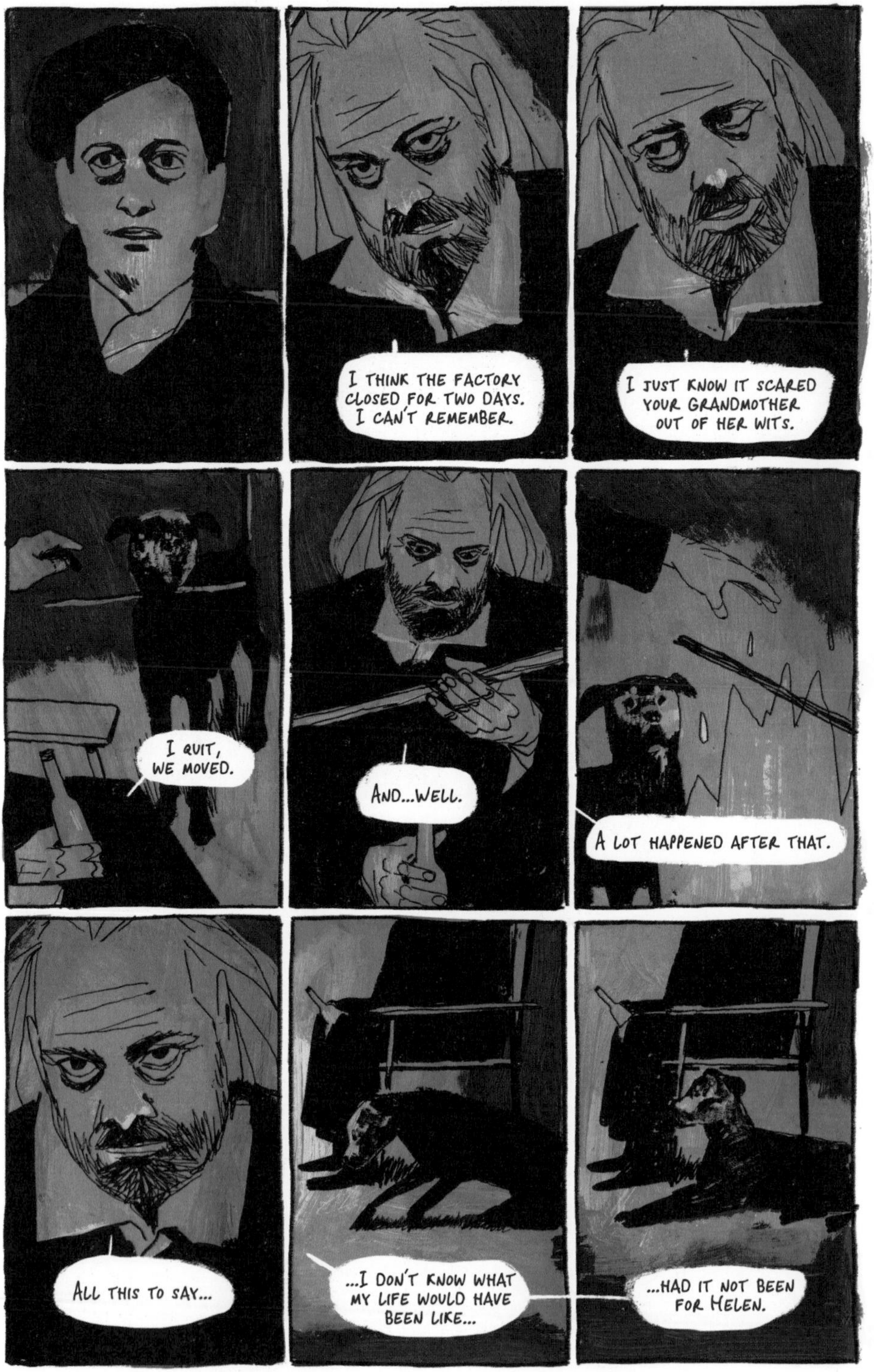
I THINK THE FACTORY CLOSED FOR TWO DAYS. I CAN'T REMEMBER.
I JUST KNOW IT SCARED YOUR GRANDMOTHER OUT OF HER WITS.
I QUIT, WE MOVED.
AND...WELL.
A LOT HAPPENED AFTER THAT.
ALL THIS TO SAY...
...I DON'T KNOW WHAT MY LIFE WOULD HAVE BEEN LIKE...
...HAD IT NOT BEEN FOR HELEN.

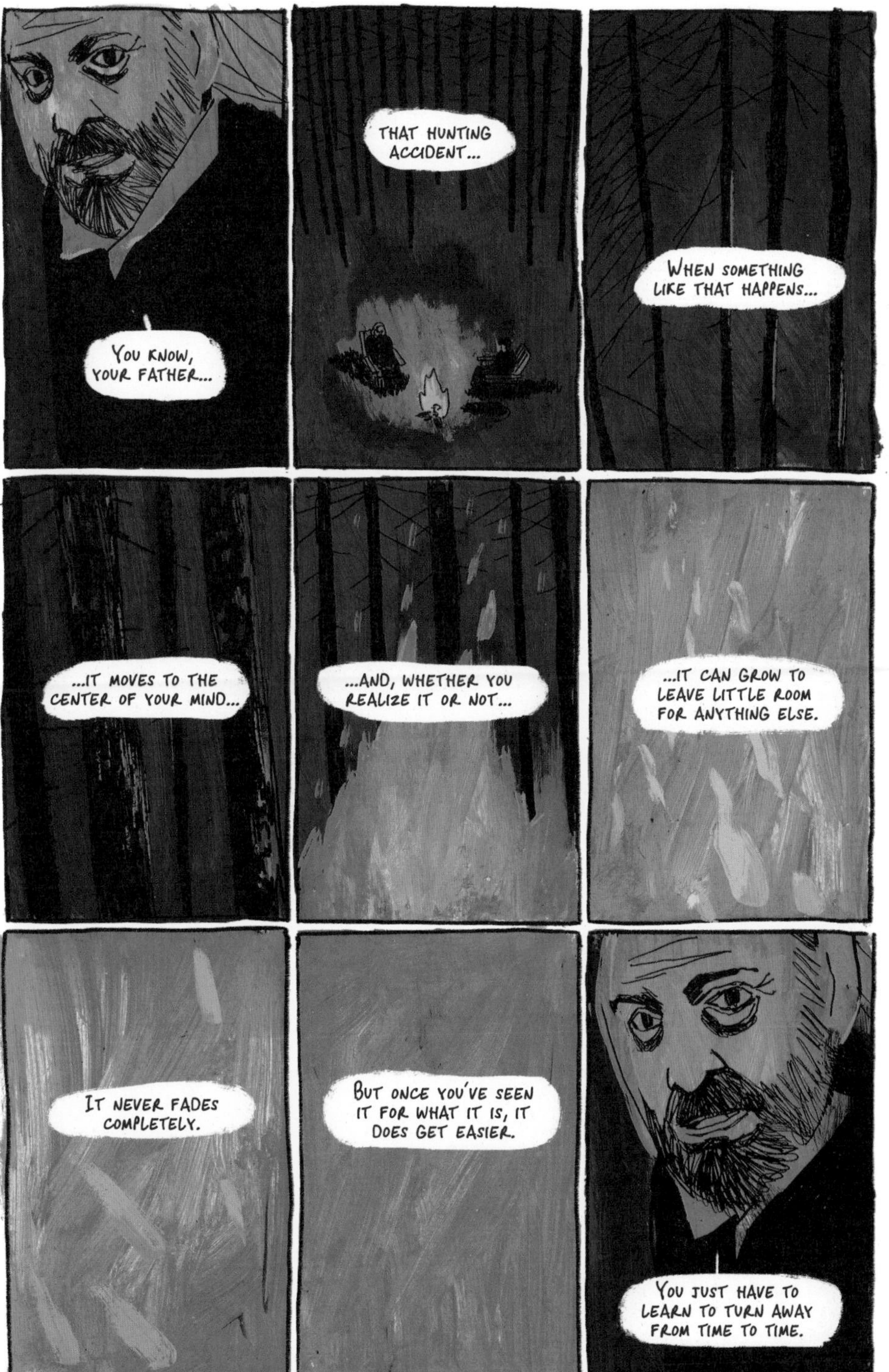
You know, your father...
That hunting accident...
When something like that happens...
...it moves to the center of your mind...
...and, whether you realize it or not...
...it can grow to leave little room for anything else.
It never fades completely.
But once you've seen it for what it is, it does get easier.
You just have to learn to turn away from time to time.

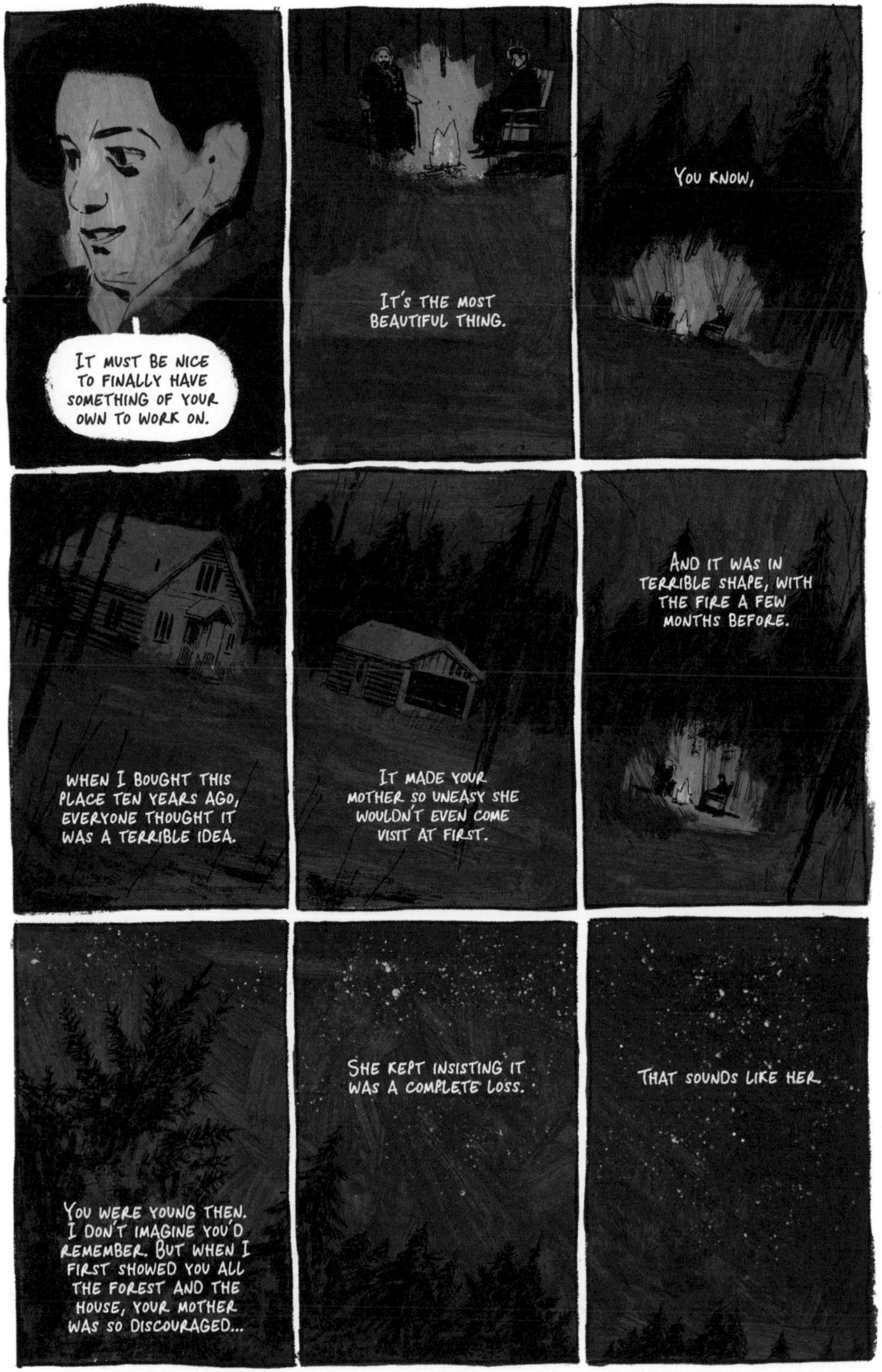

It must be nice to finally have something of your own to work on.
It's the most beautiful thing.
You know,
When I bought this place ten years ago, everyone thought it was a terrible idea.
It made your mother so uneasy she wouldn't even come visit at first.
And it was in terrible shape, with the fire a few months before.
You were young then. I don't imagine you'd remember. But when I first showed you all the forest and the house, your mother was so discouraged...
She kept insisting it was a complete loss.
That sounds like her.

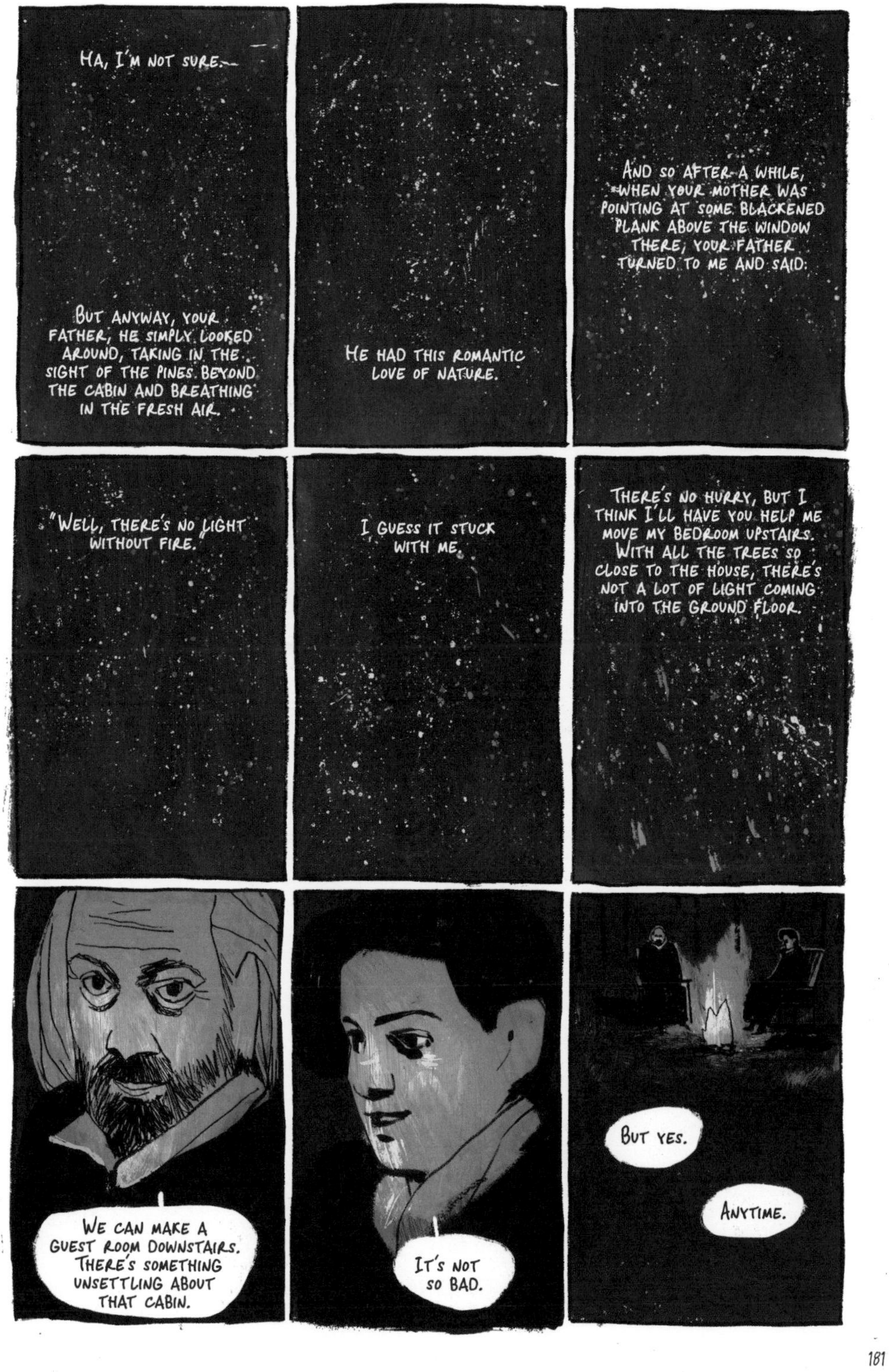

HA, I'M NOT SURE.
BUT ANYWAY, YOUR FATHER, HE SIMPLY LOOKED AROUND, TAKING IN THE SIGHT OF THE PINES BEYOND THE CABIN AND BREATHING IN THE FRESH AIR.
HE HAD THIS ROMANTIC LOVE OF NATURE.
AND SO AFTER A WHILE, WHEN YOUR MOTHER WAS POINTING AT SOME BLACKENED PLANK ABOVE THE WINDOW THERE, YOUR FATHER TURNED TO ME AND SAID:
"WELL, THERE'S NO LIGHT WITHOUT FIRE."
I GUESS IT STUCK WITH ME.
THERE'S NO HURRY, BUT I THINK I'LL HAVE YOU HELP ME MOVE MY BEDROOM UPSTAIRS. WITH ALL THE TREES SO CLOSE TO THE HOUSE, THERE'S NOT A LOT OF LIGHT COMING INTO THE GROUND FLOOR.
WE CAN MAKE A GUEST ROOM DOWNSTAIRS. THERE'S SOMETHING UNSETTLING ABOUT THAT CABIN.
IT'S NOT SO BAD.
BUT YES.
ANYTIME.

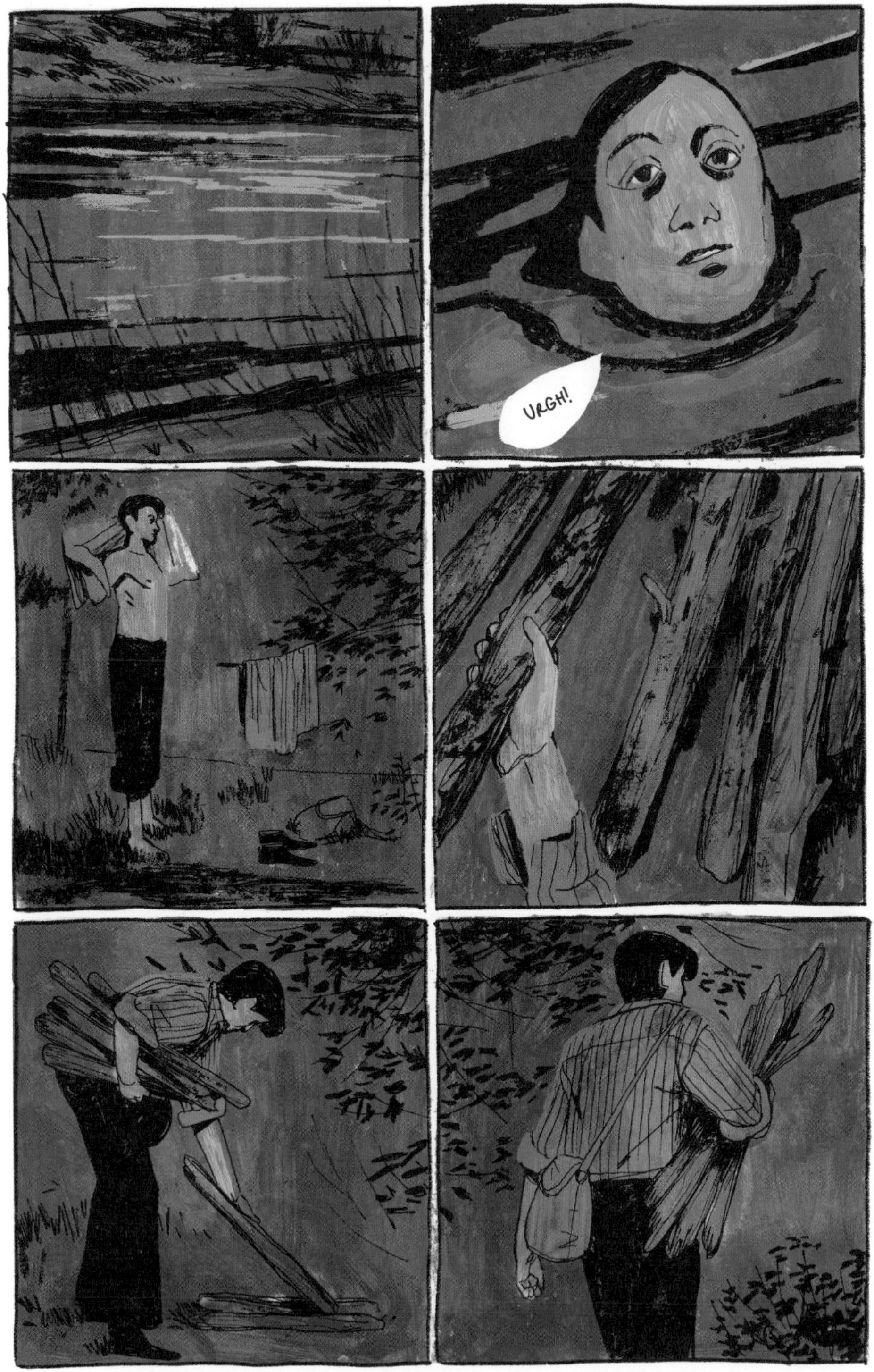
URGH!

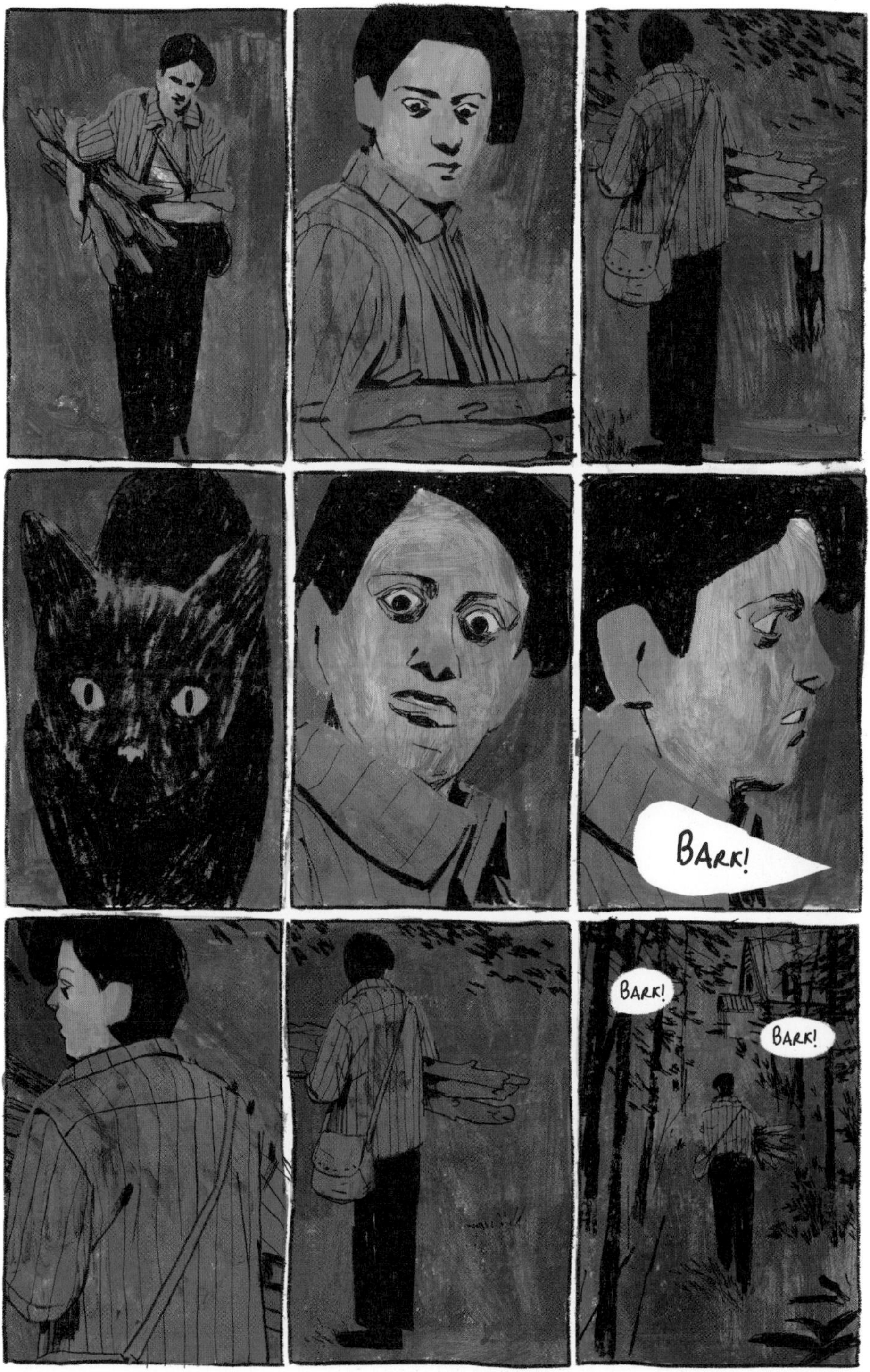
BARK!
BARK!
BARK!

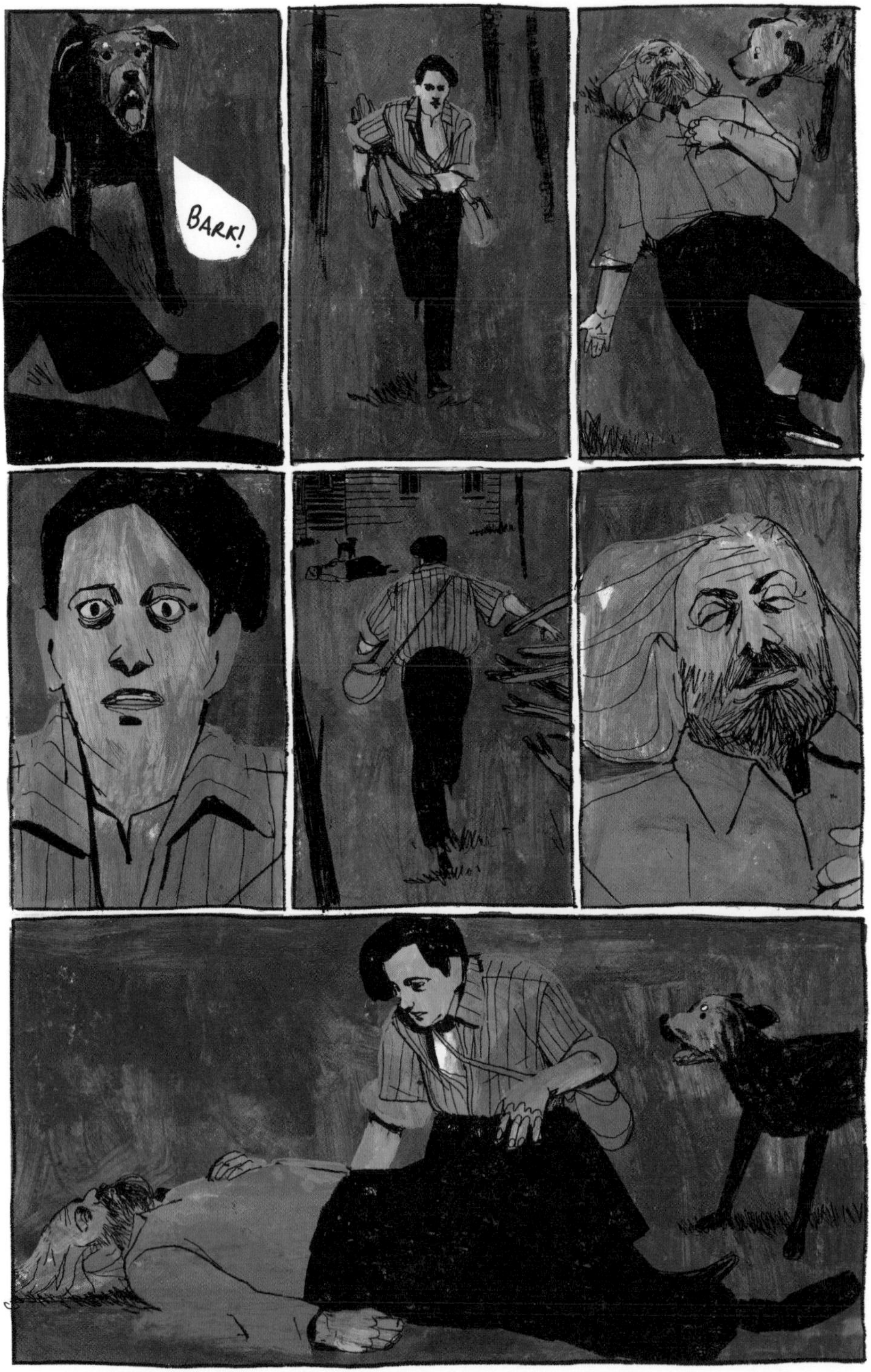
BARK!

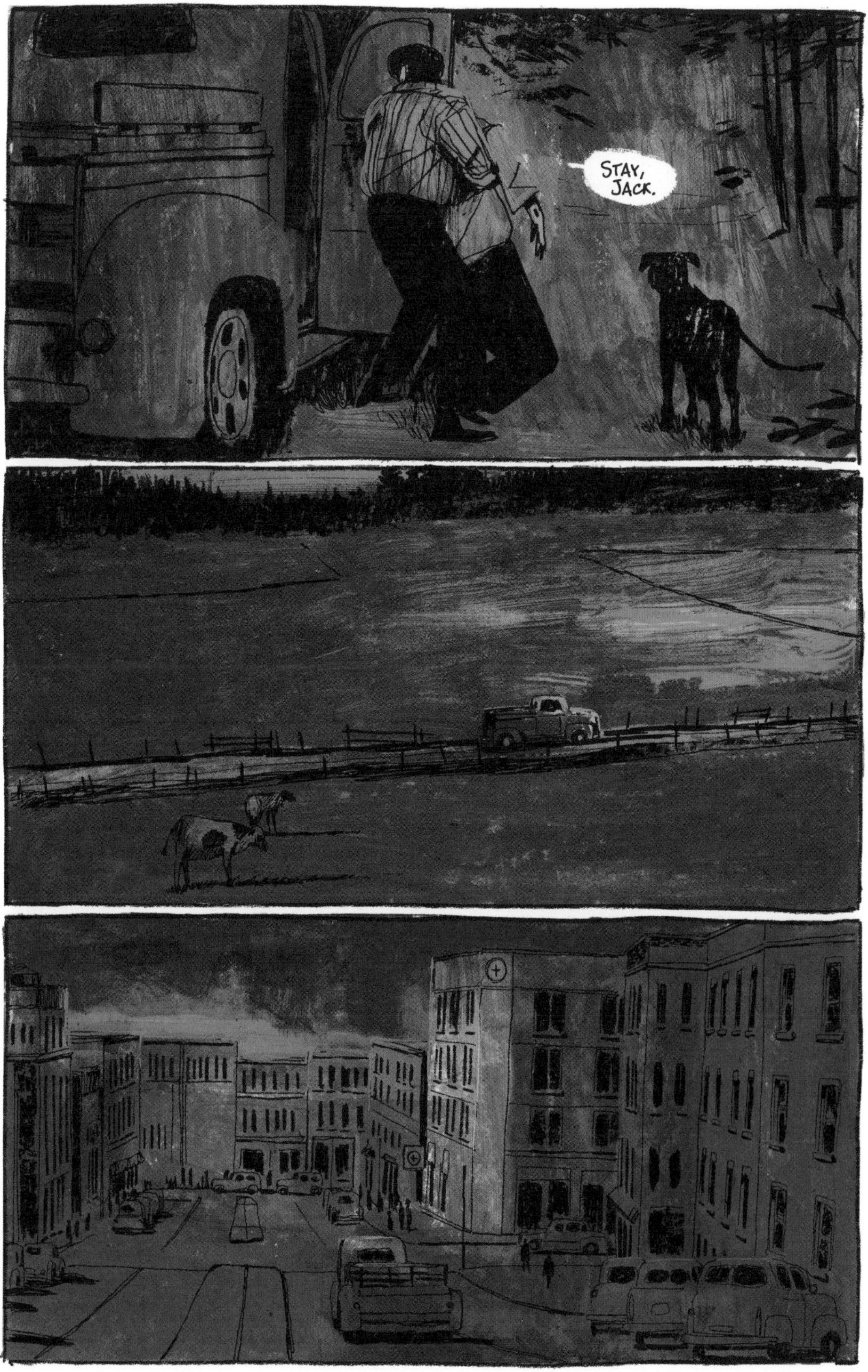
STAY, JACK.

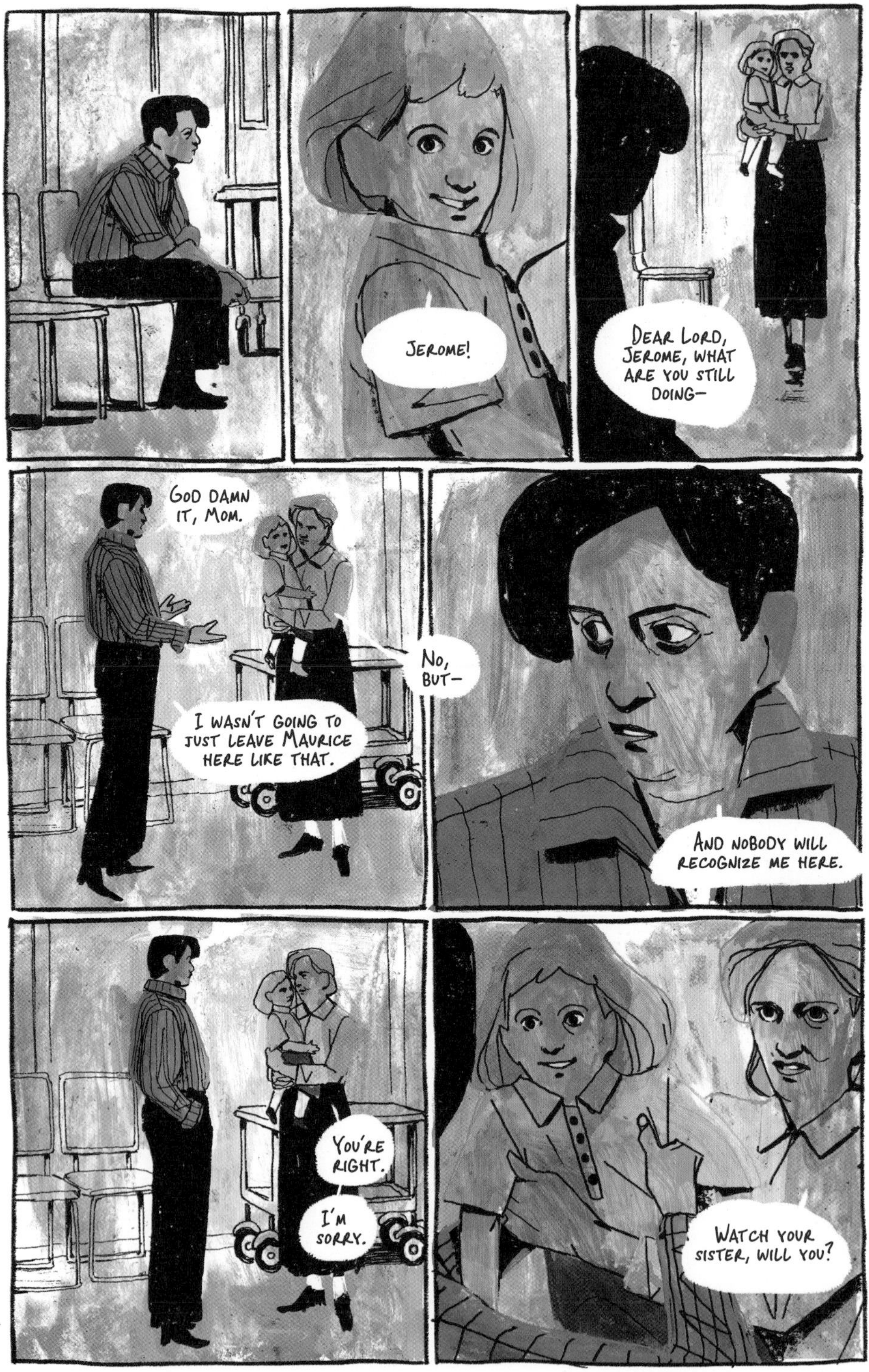
Jerome!
Dear Lord, Jerome, what are you still doing—
God damn it, Mom.
No, but—
I wasn't going to just leave Maurice here like that.
And nobody will recognize me here.
You're right.
I'm sorry.
Watch your sister, will you?

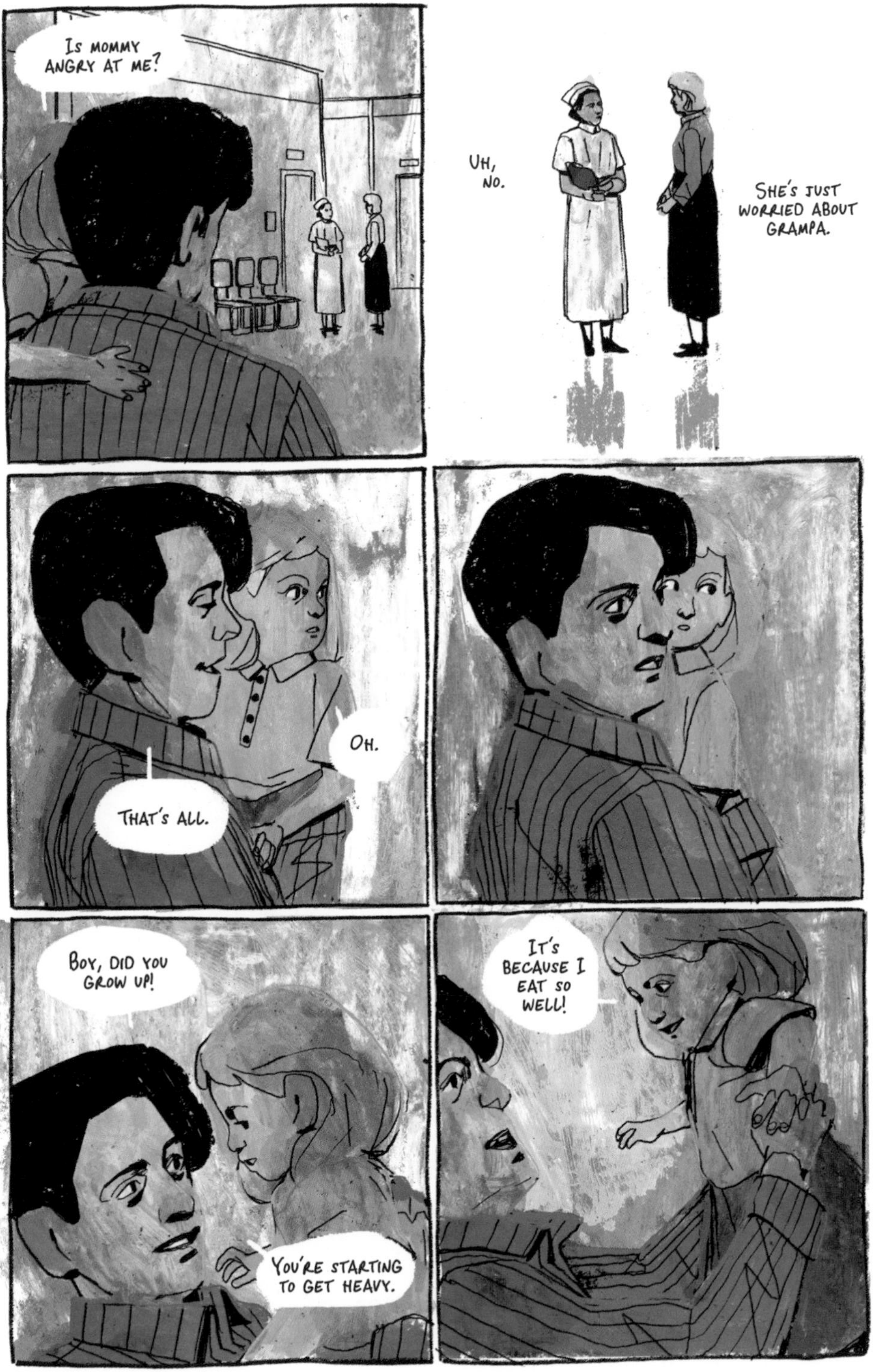
IS MOMMY ANGRY AT ME?
UH, NO.
SHE'S JUST WORRIED ABOUT GRAMPA.
THAT'S ALL.
OH.
BOY, DID YOU GROW UP!
YOU'RE STARTING TO GET HEAVY.
IT'S BECAUSE I EAT SO WELL!

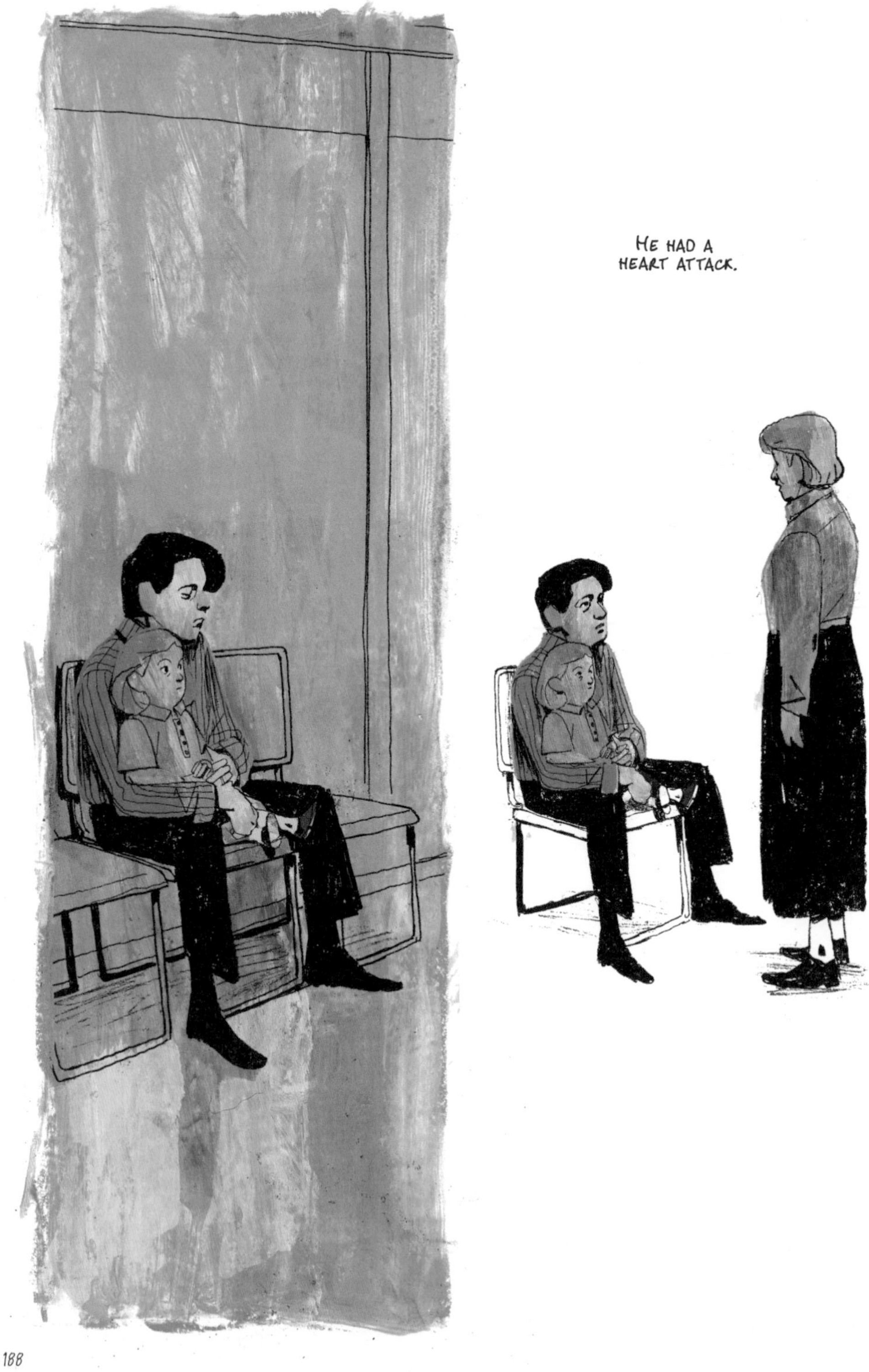
HE HAD A HEART ATTACK.

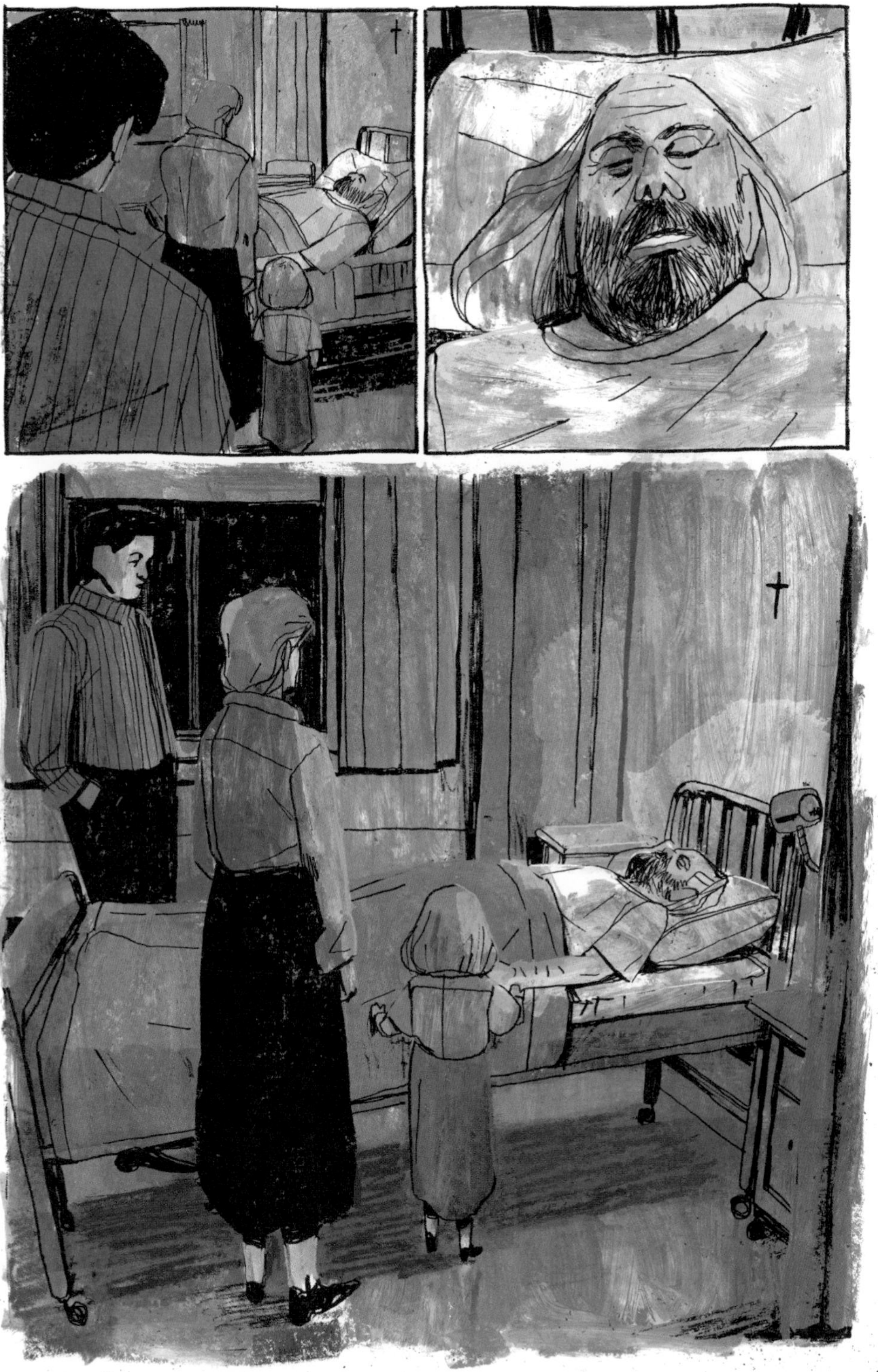

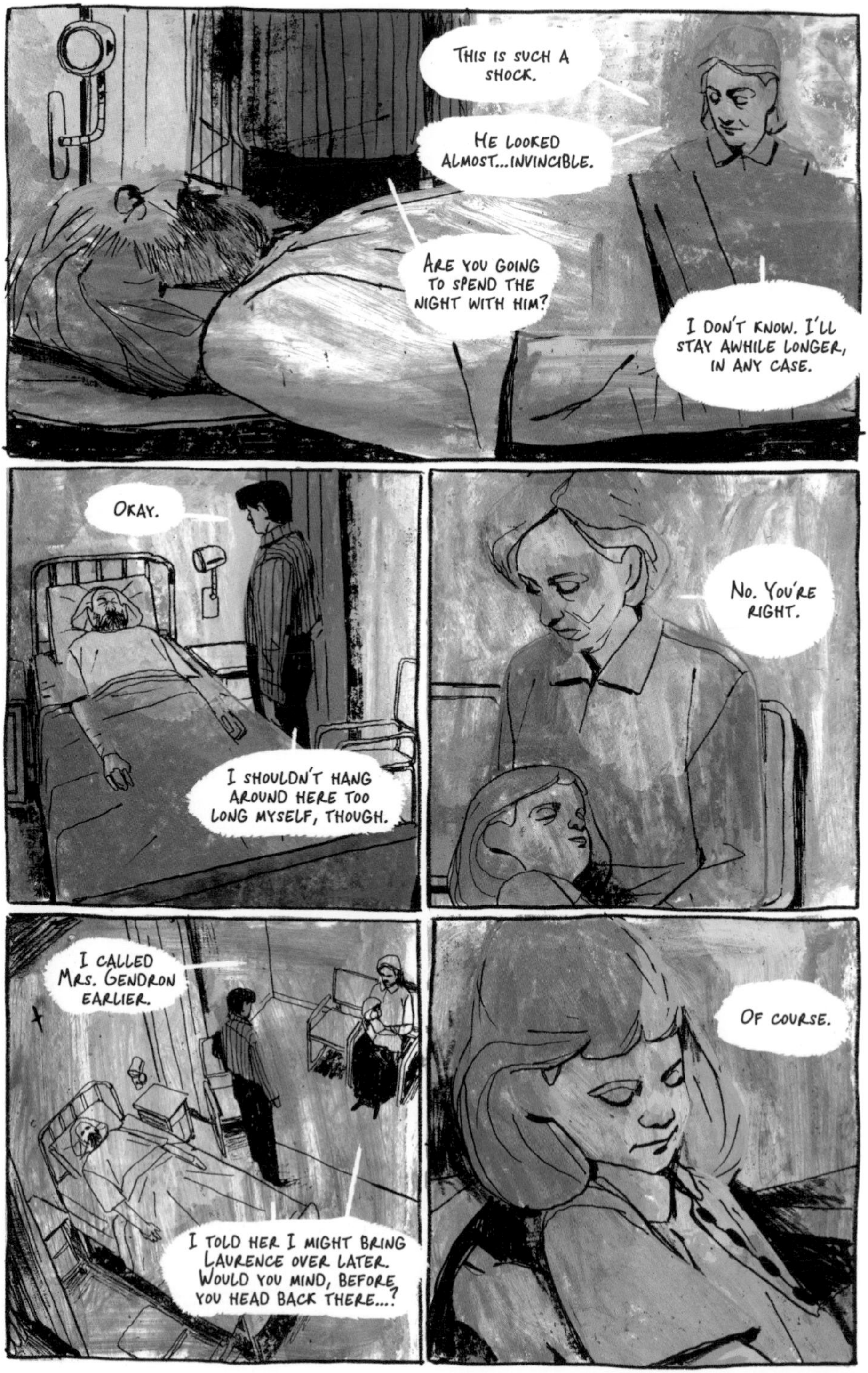
This is such a shock.
He looked almost...invincible.
Are you going to spend the night with him?
I don't know. I'll stay awhile longer, in any case.
Okay.
I shouldn't hang around here too long myself, though.
No. You're right.
I called Mrs. Gendron earlier.
I told her I might bring Laurence over later. Would you mind, before you head back there...?
Of course.

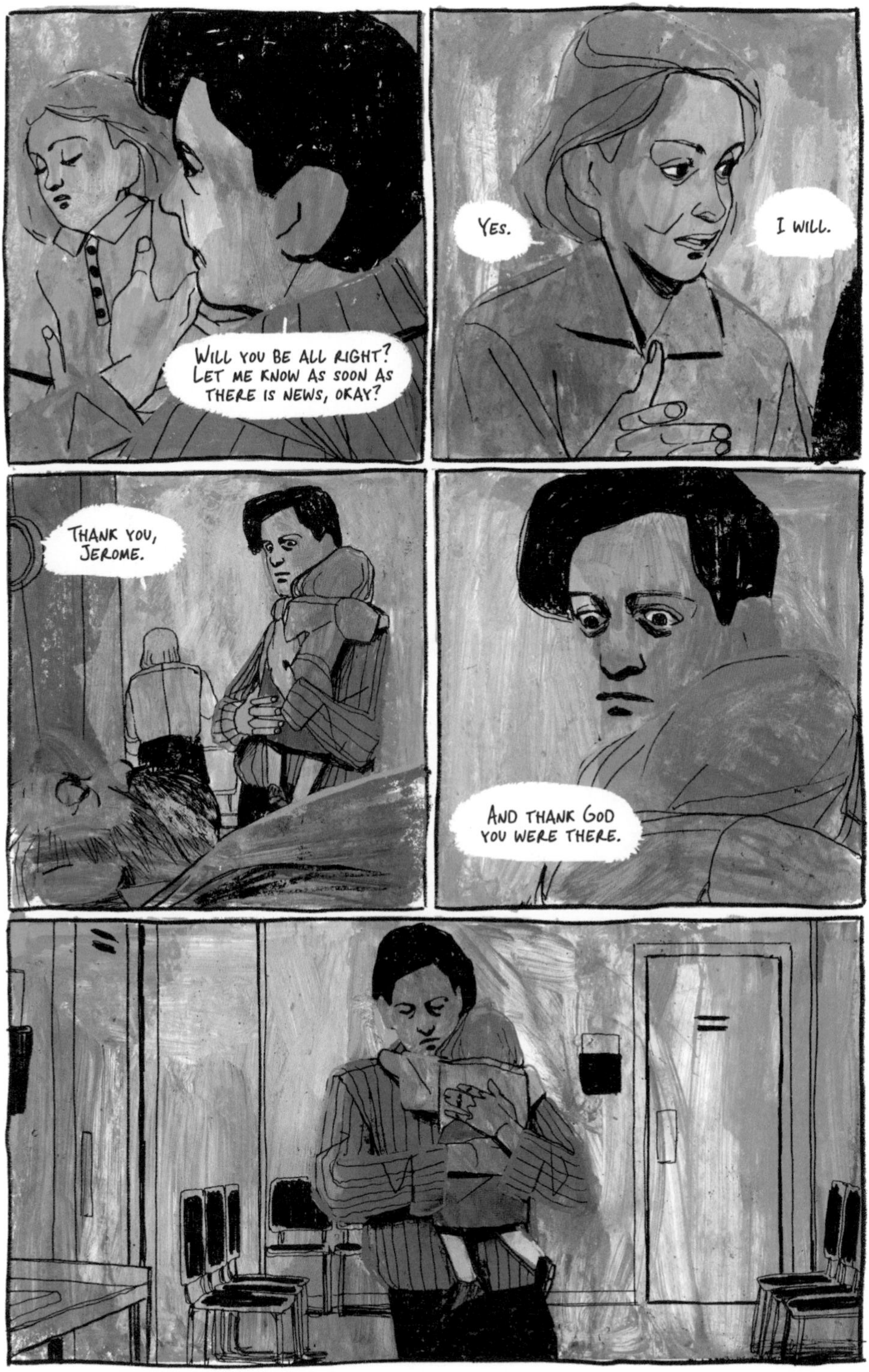
WILL YOU BE ALL RIGHT? LET ME KNOW AS SOON AS THERE IS NEWS, OKAY?
YES.
I WILL.
THANK YOU, JEROME.
AND THANK GOD YOU WERE THERE.

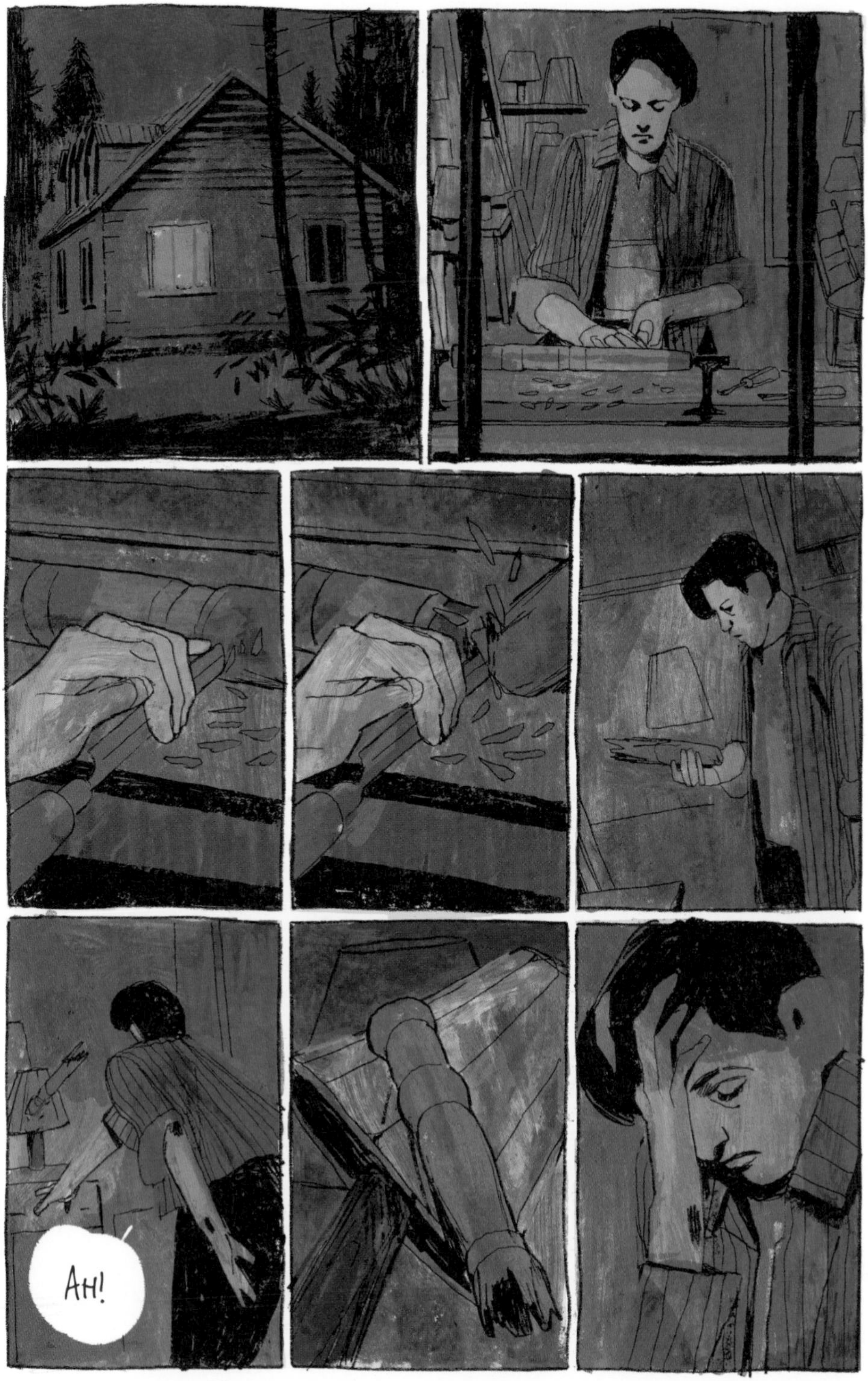
AH!

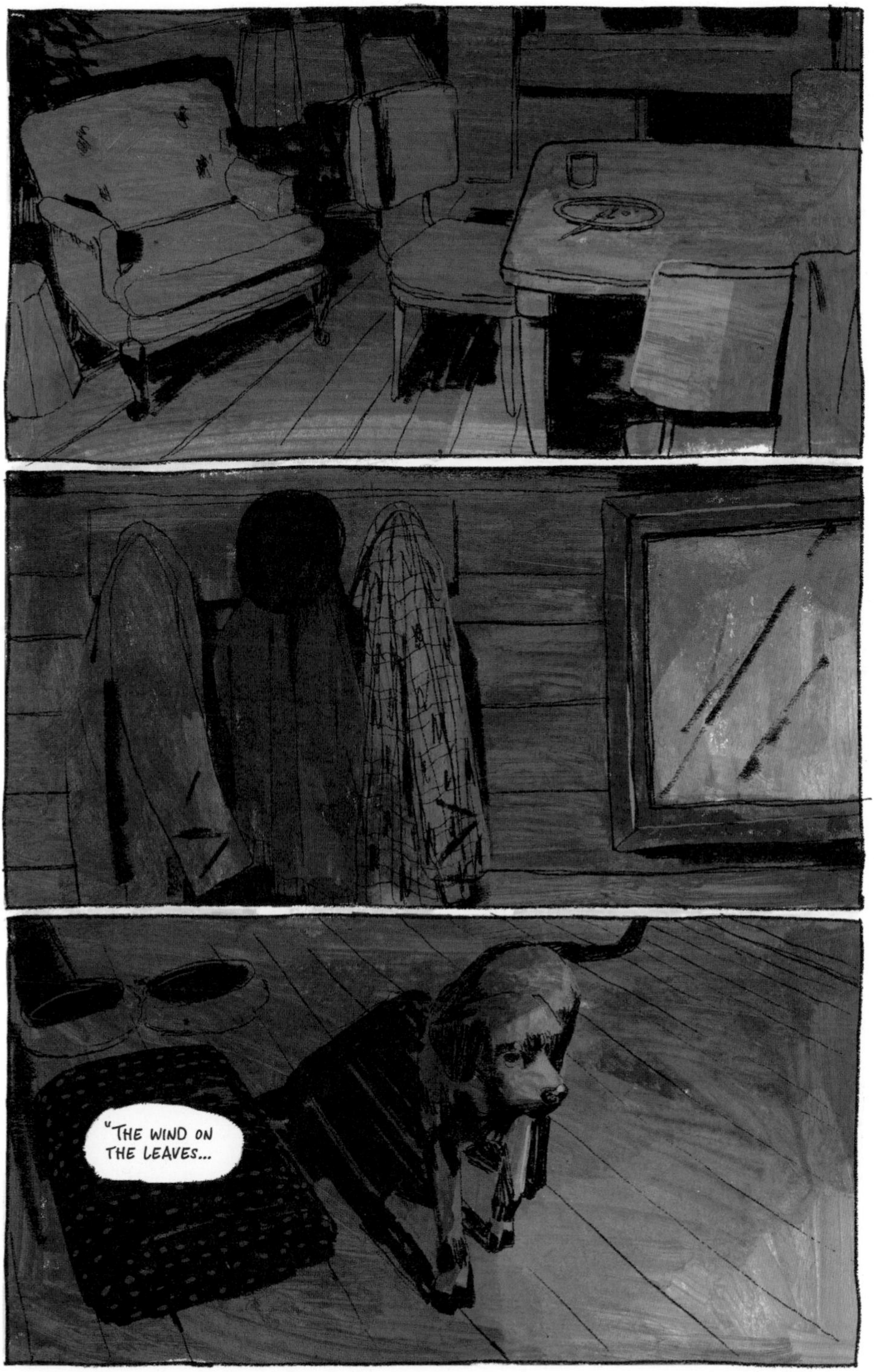
"THE WIND ON THE LEAVES...

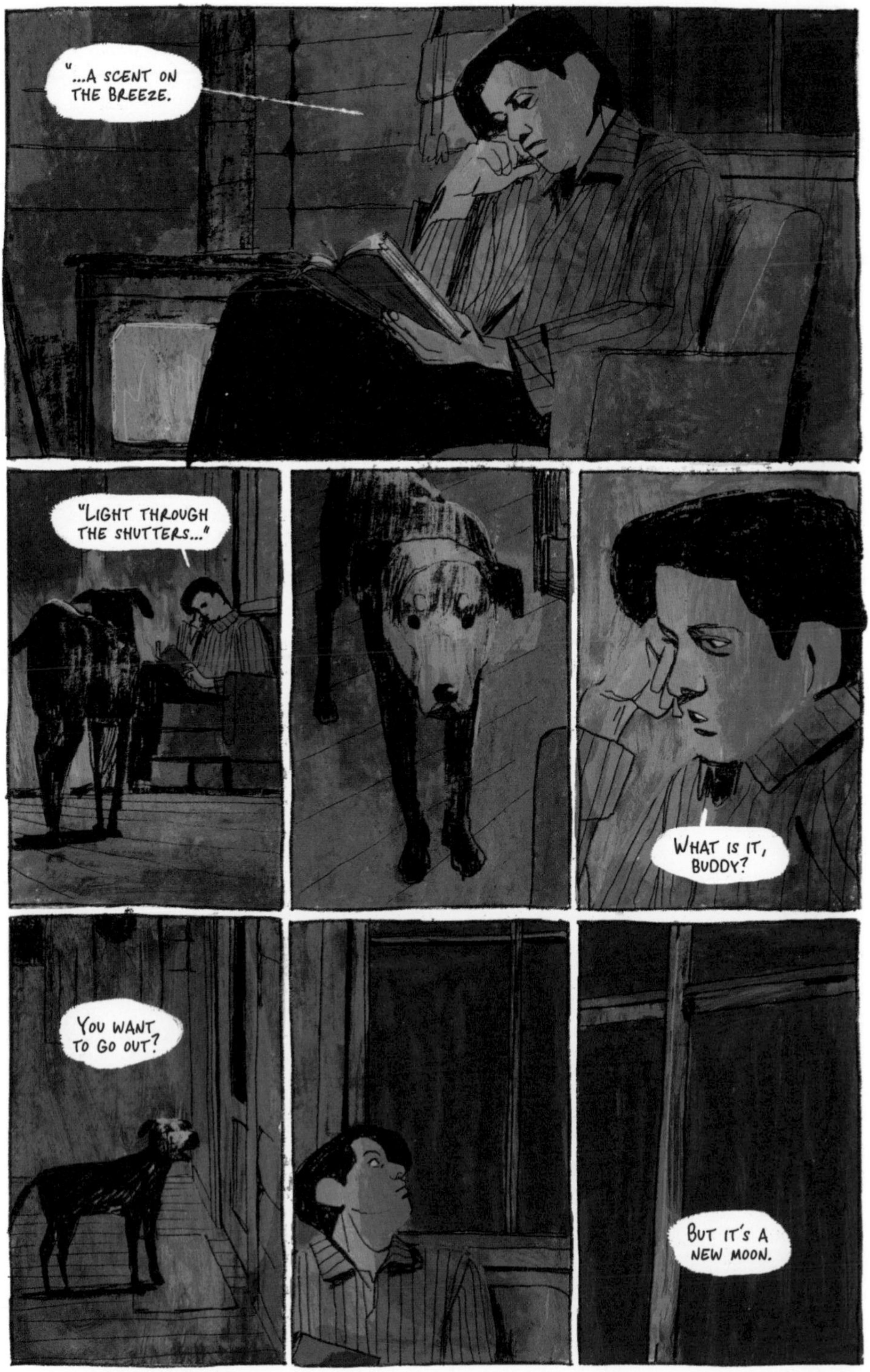
"...A SCENT ON THE BREEZE.
"LIGHT THROUGH THE SHUTTERS..."
WHAT IS IT, BUDDY?
YOU WANT TO GO OUT?
BUT IT'S A NEW MOON.

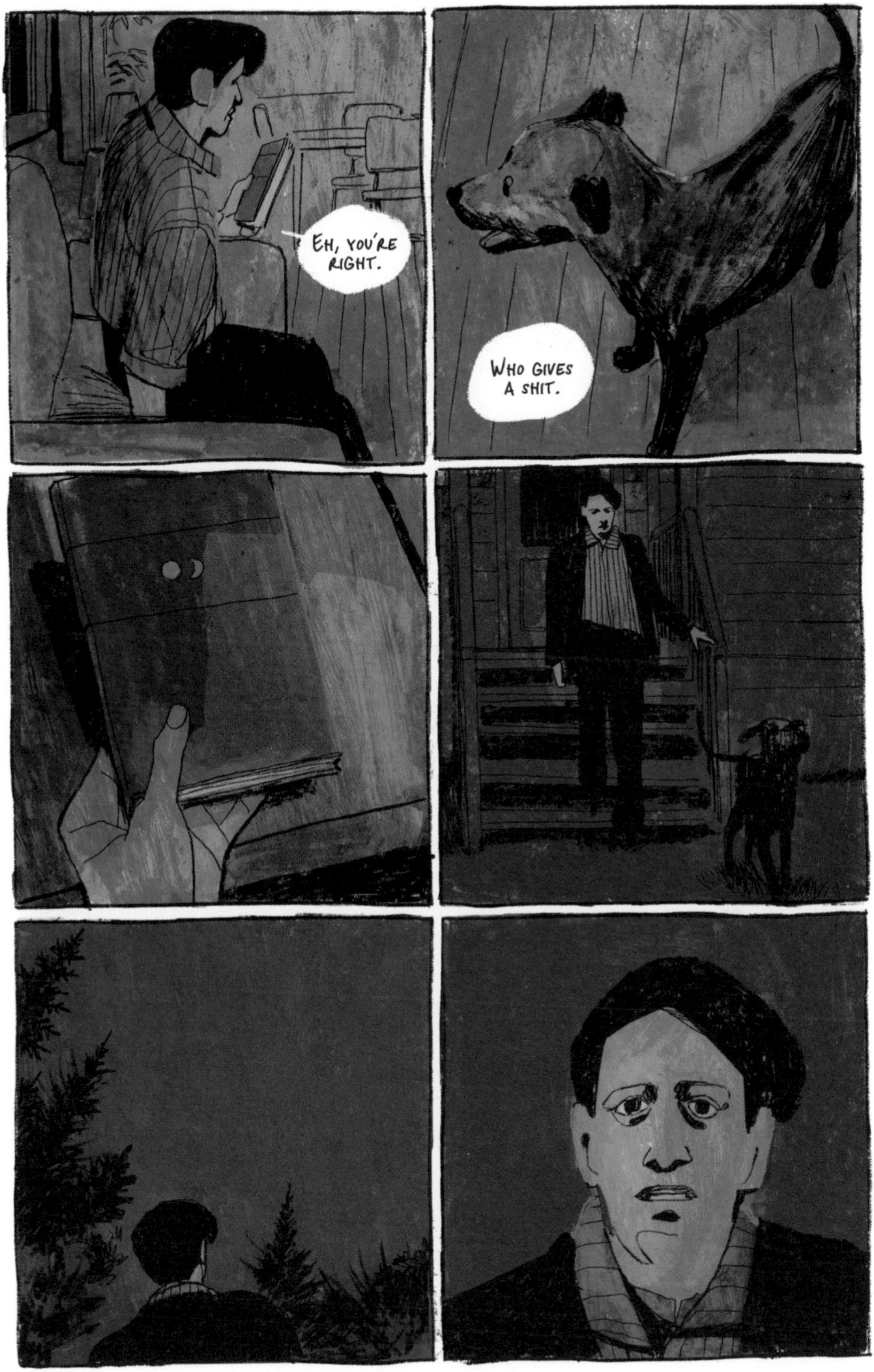
EH, YOU'RE RIGHT.
WHO GIVES A SHIT.

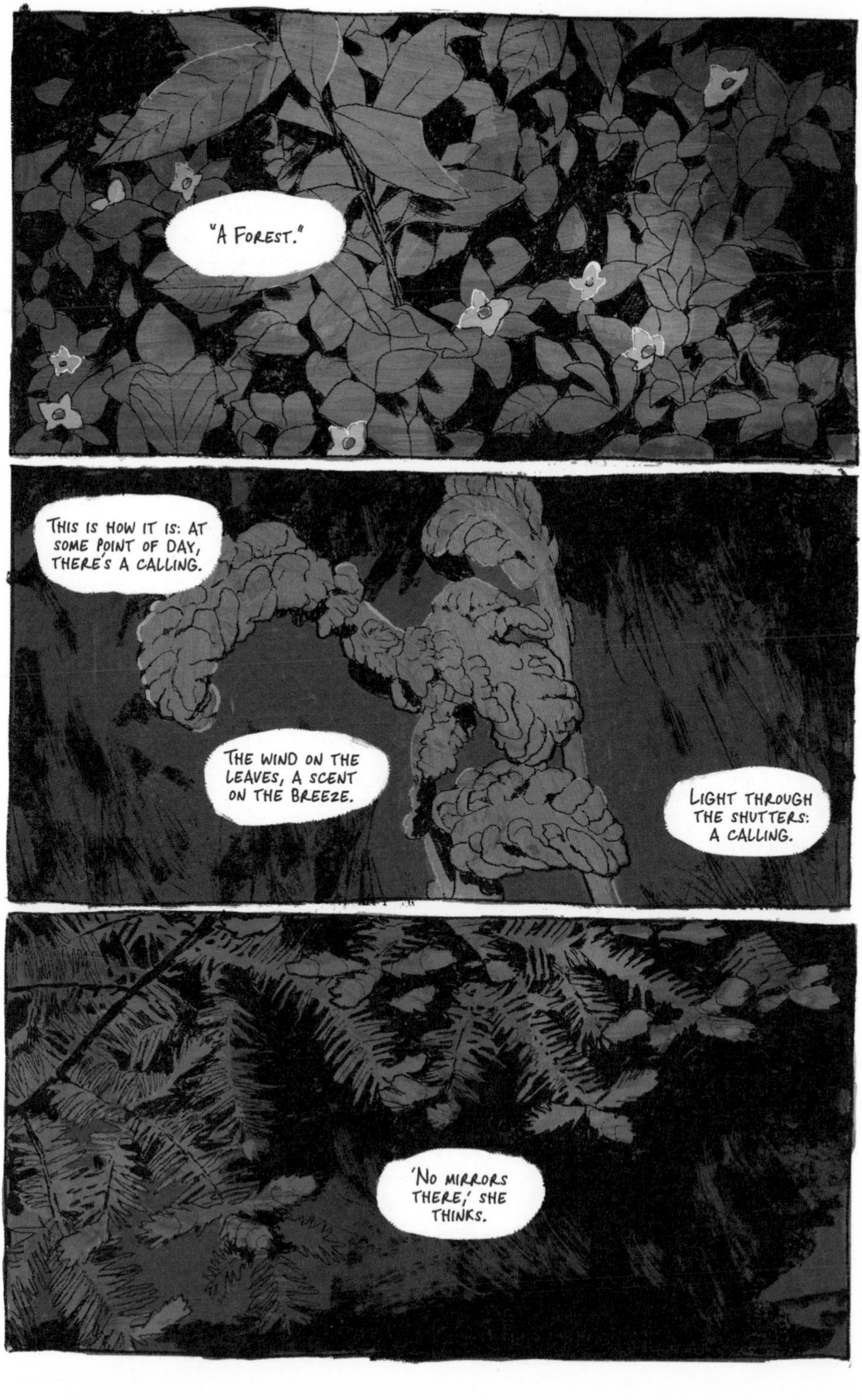
"A Forest."
This is how it is: at some point of day, there's a calling.
The wind on the leaves, a scent on the breeze.
Light through the shutters: a calling.
'No mirrors there,' she thinks.

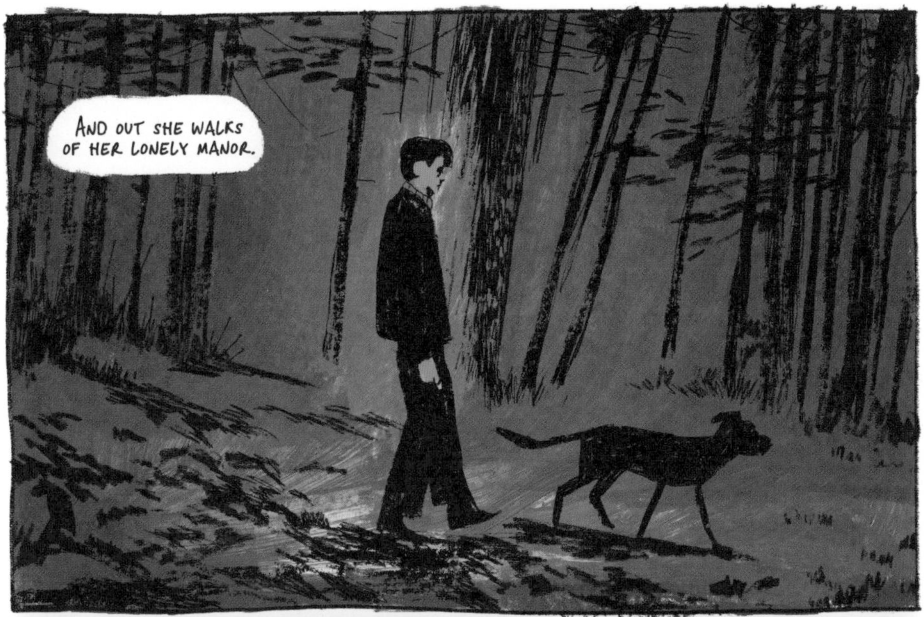
AND OUT SHE WALKS
OF HER LONELY MANOR.

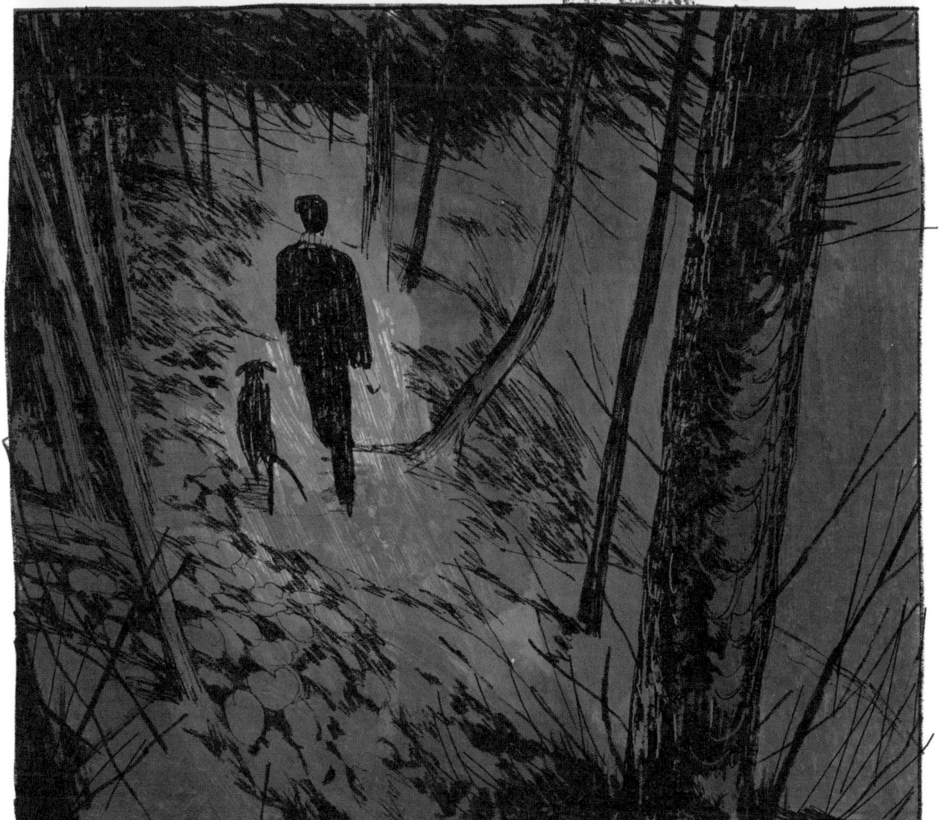

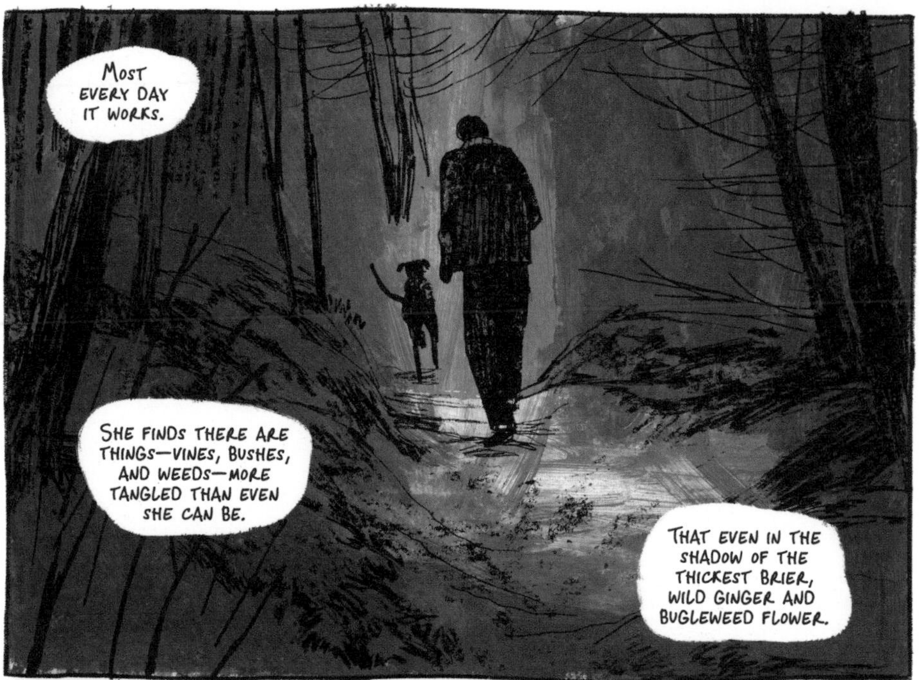

Most every day it works.
She finds there are things—vines, bushes, and weeds—more tangled than even she can be.
That even in the shadow of the thickest brier, wild ginger and bugleweed flower.

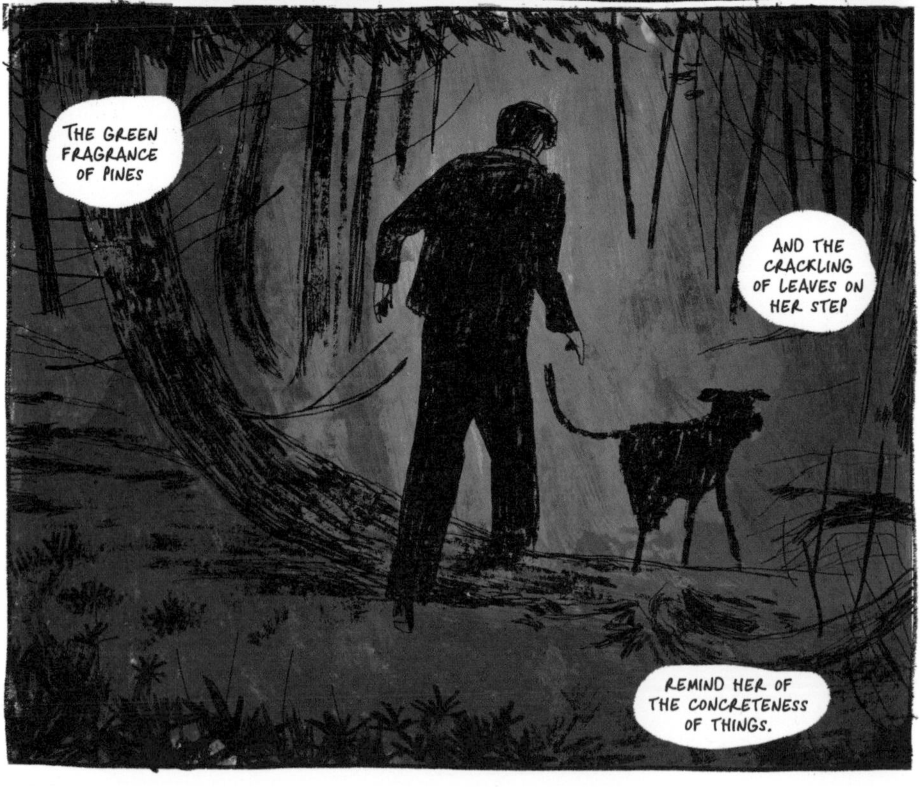

The green fragrance of pines
And the crackling of leaves on her step
Remind her of the concreteness of things.

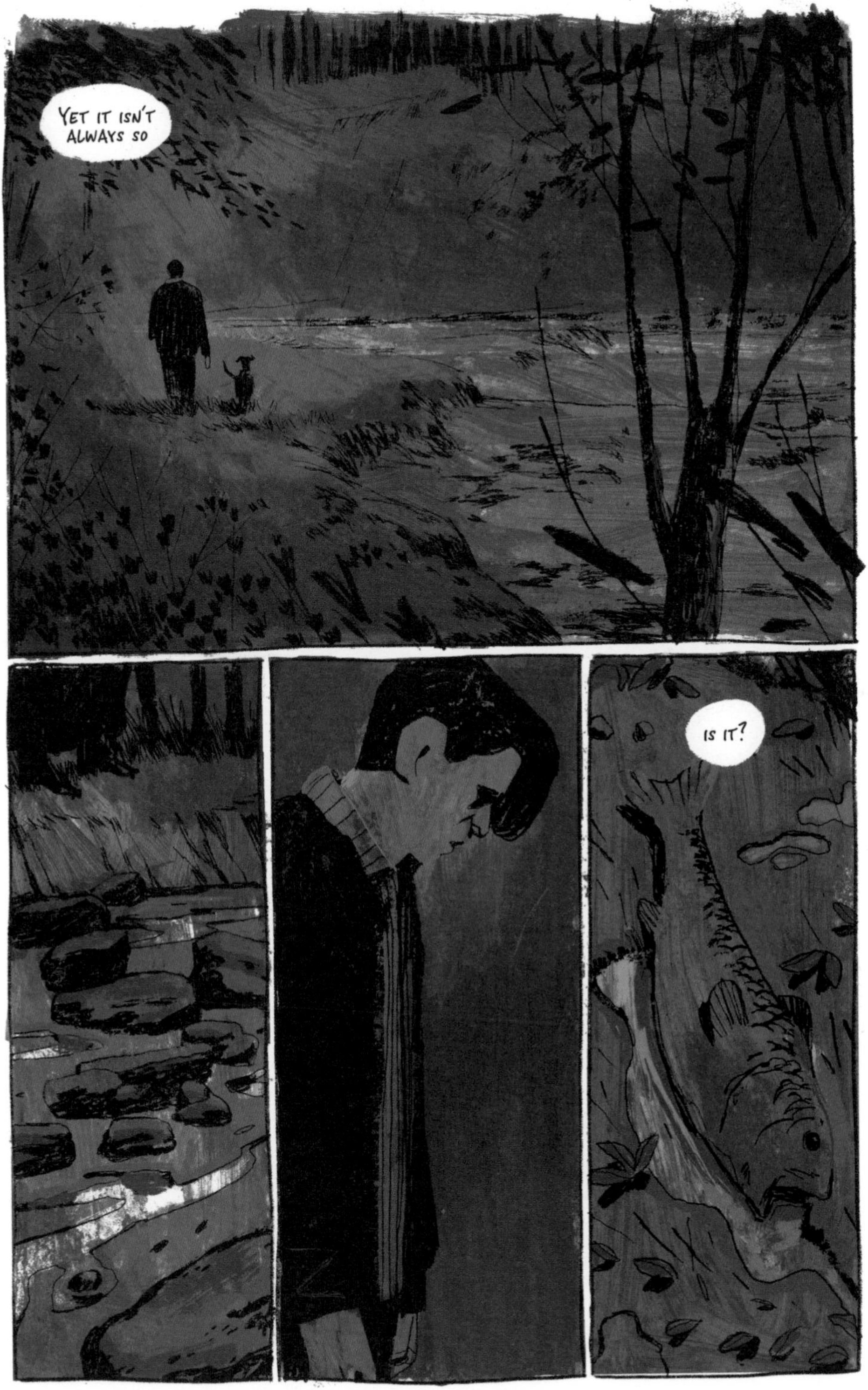
YET IT ISN'T ALWAYS SO
IS IT?

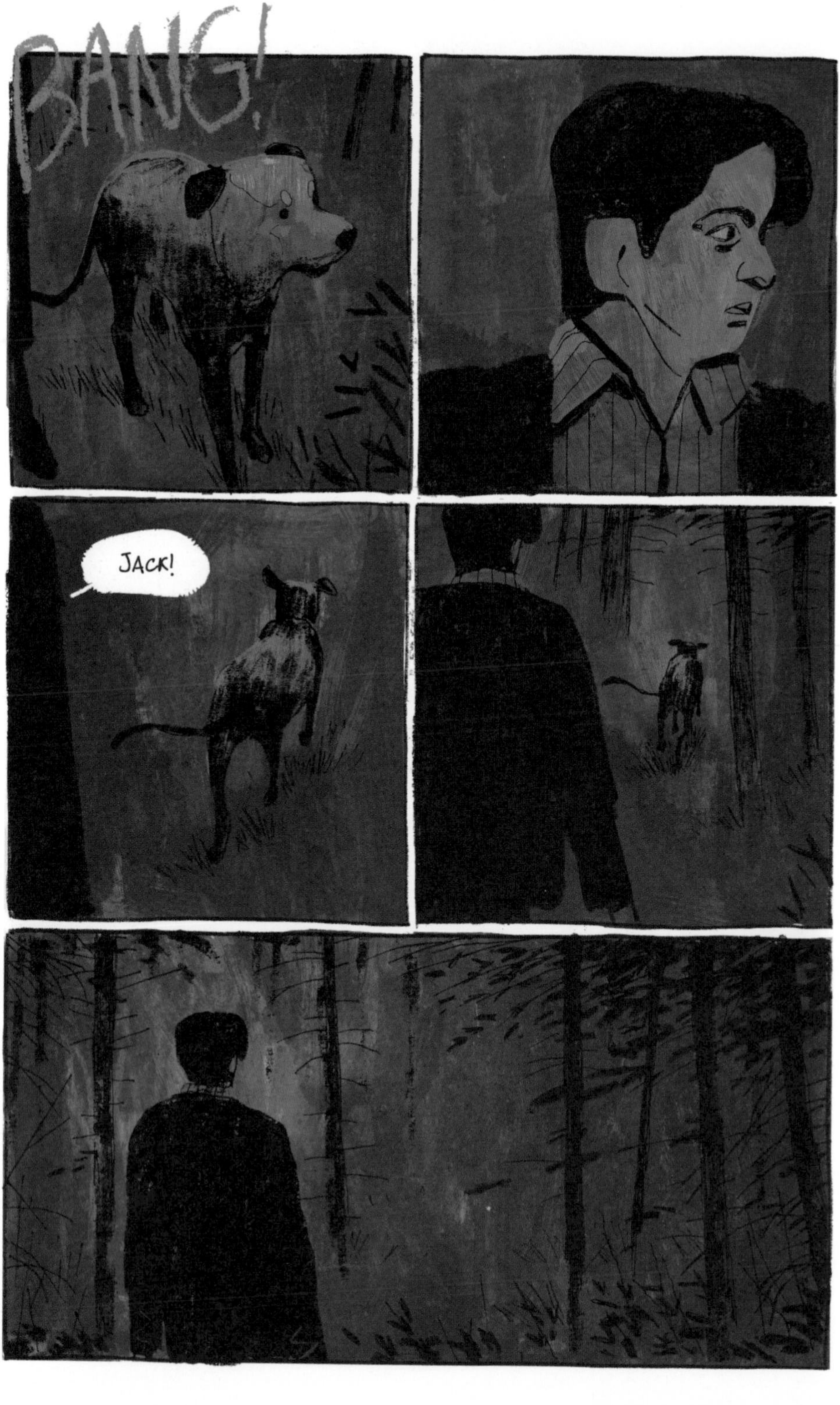
BANG!
JACK!

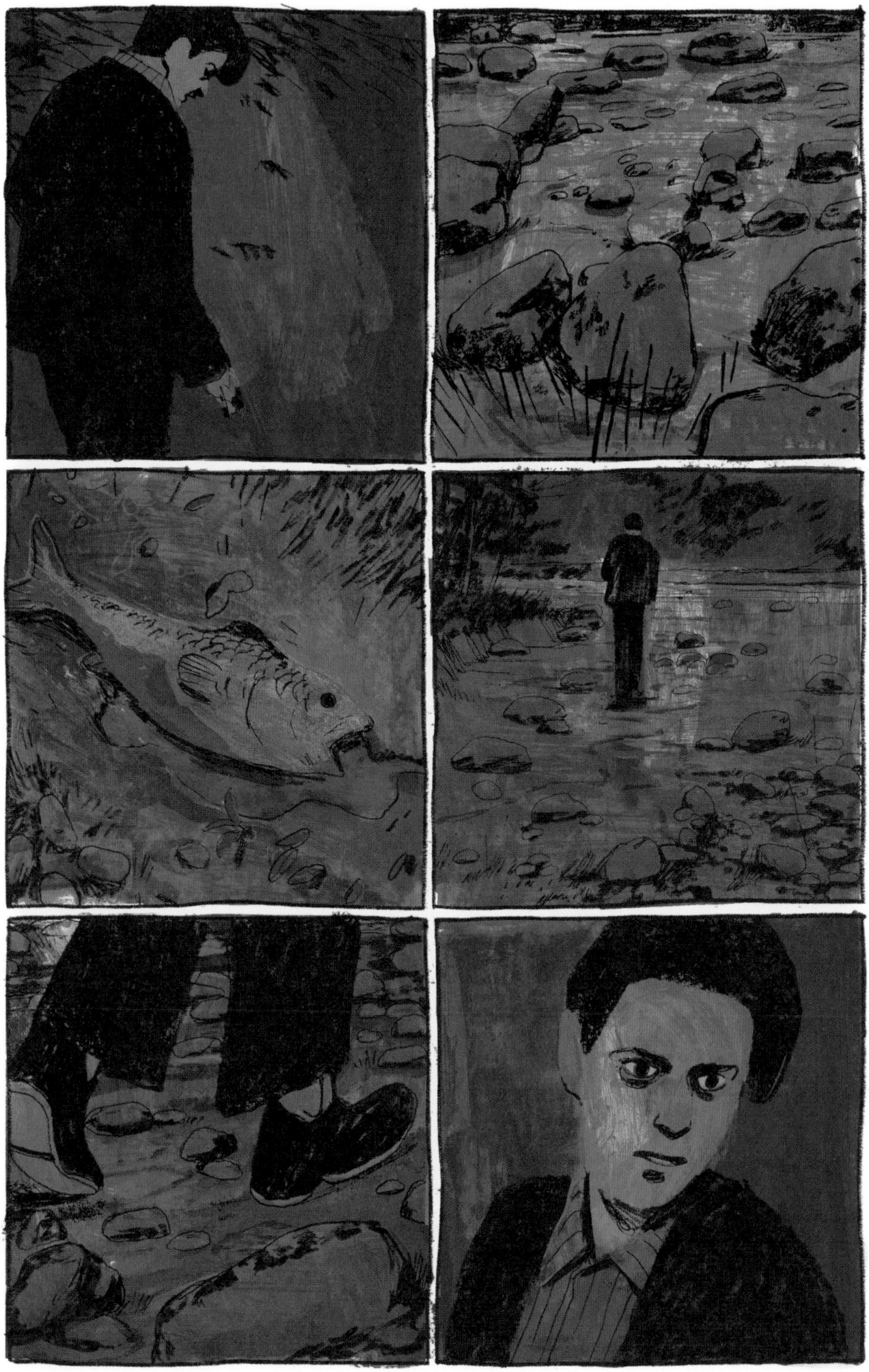

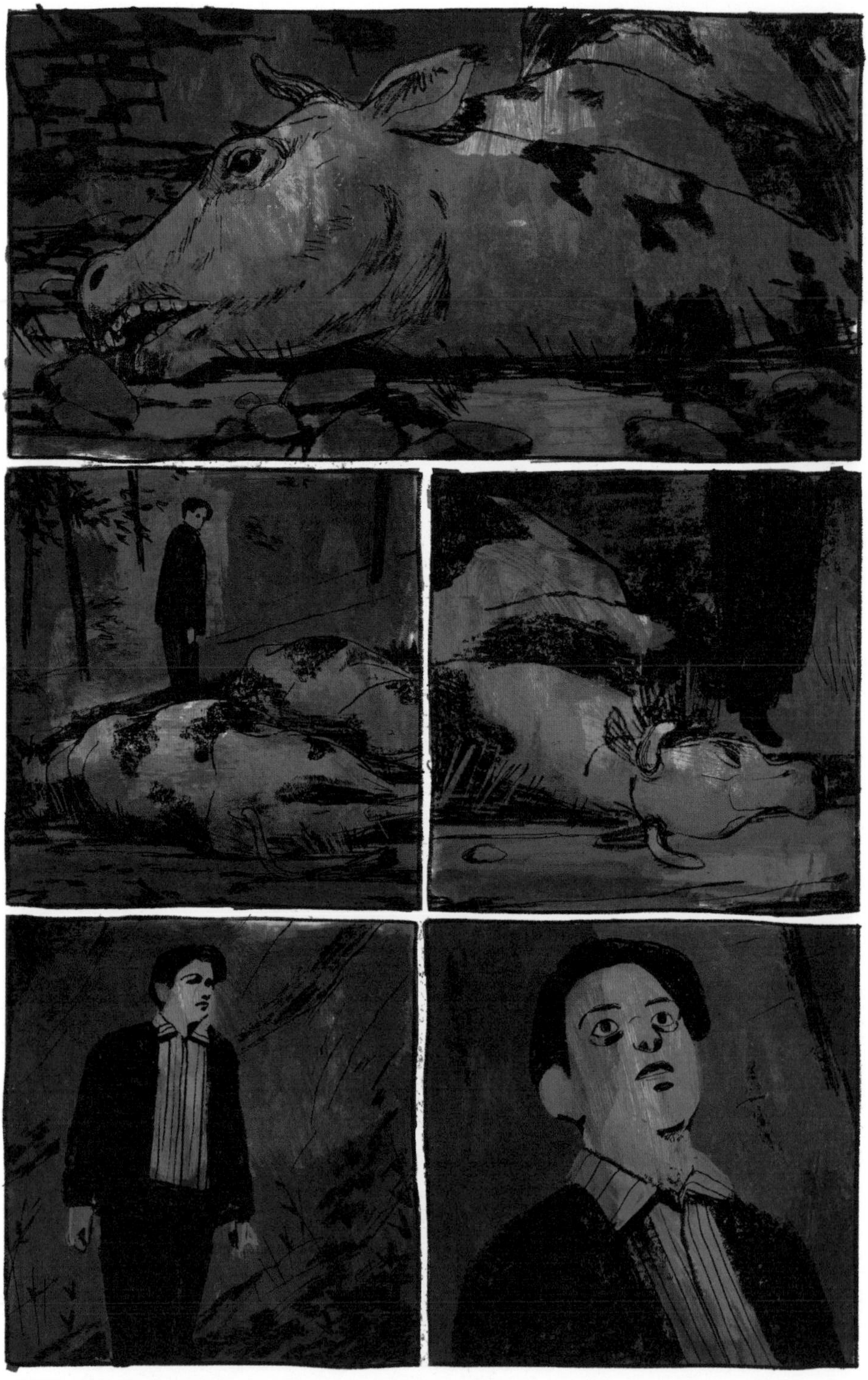

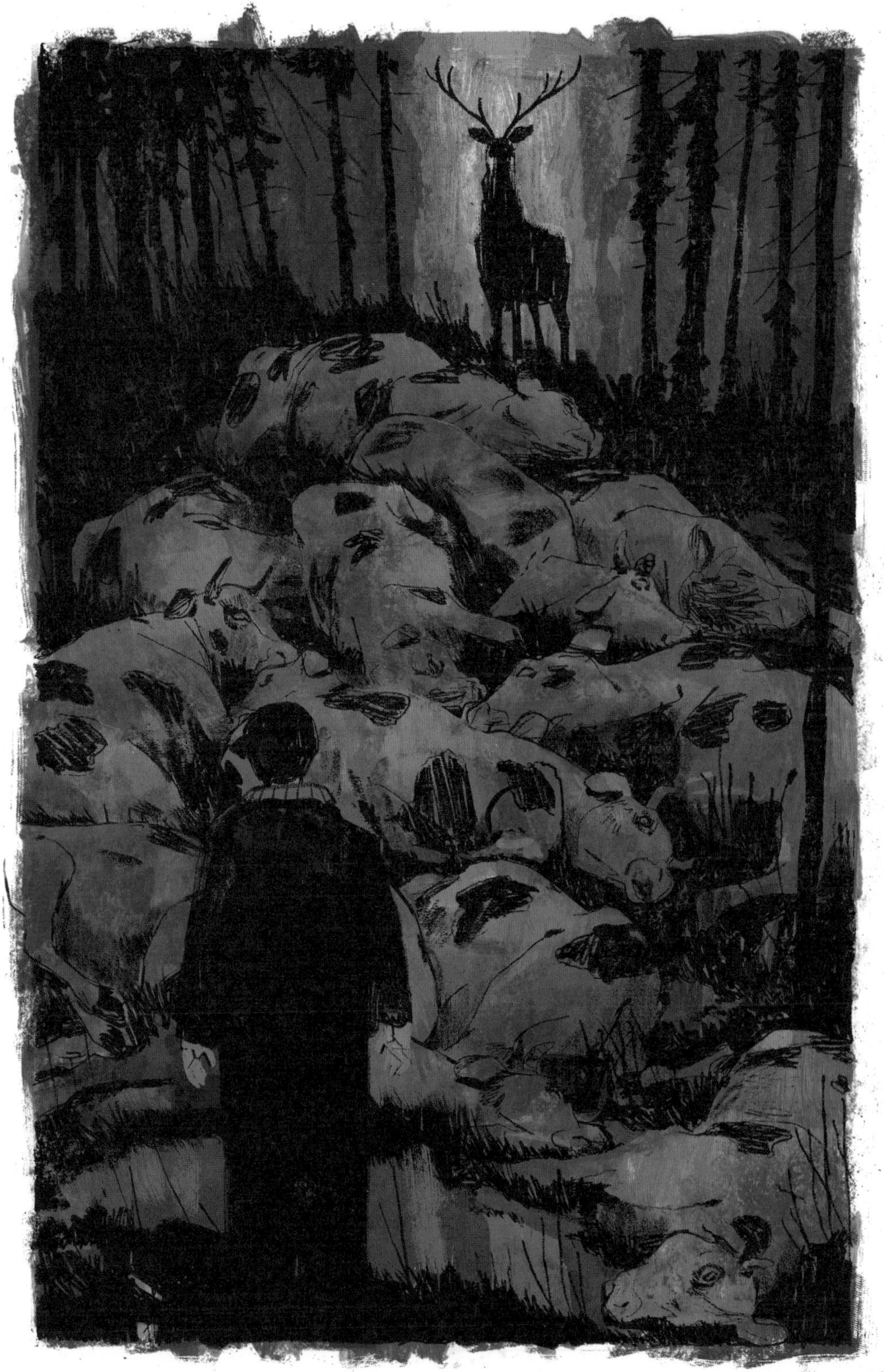

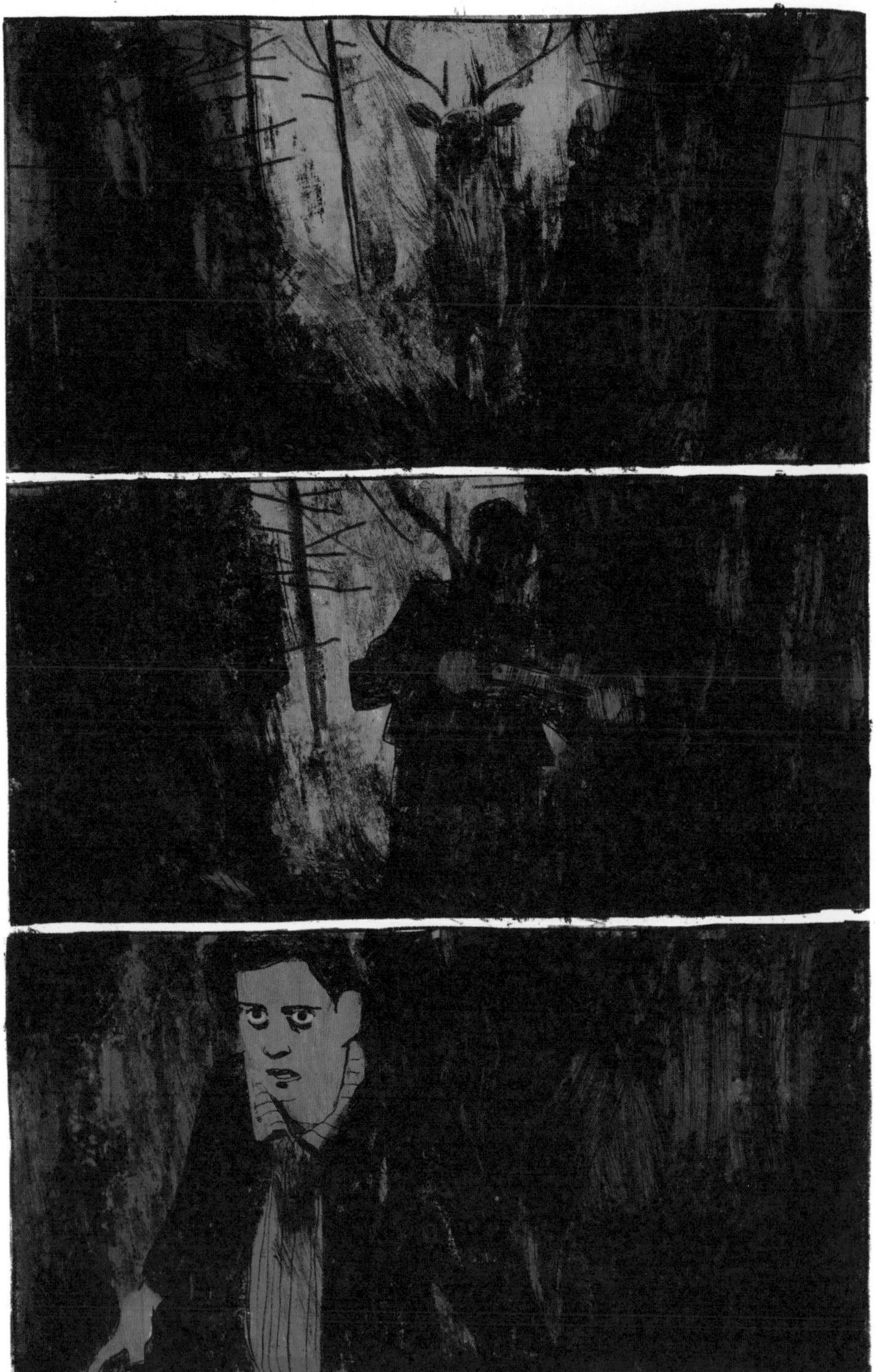

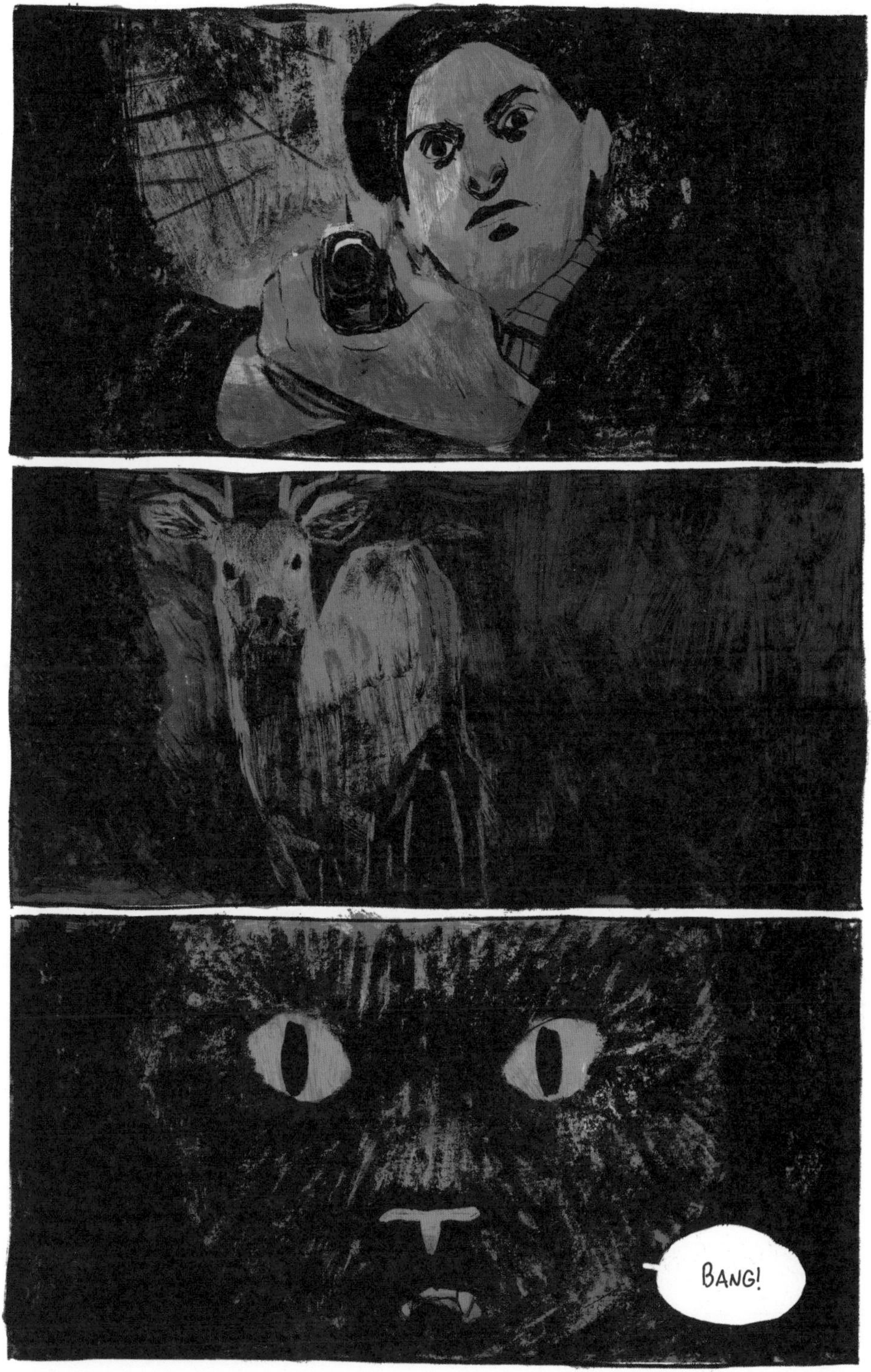
BANG!

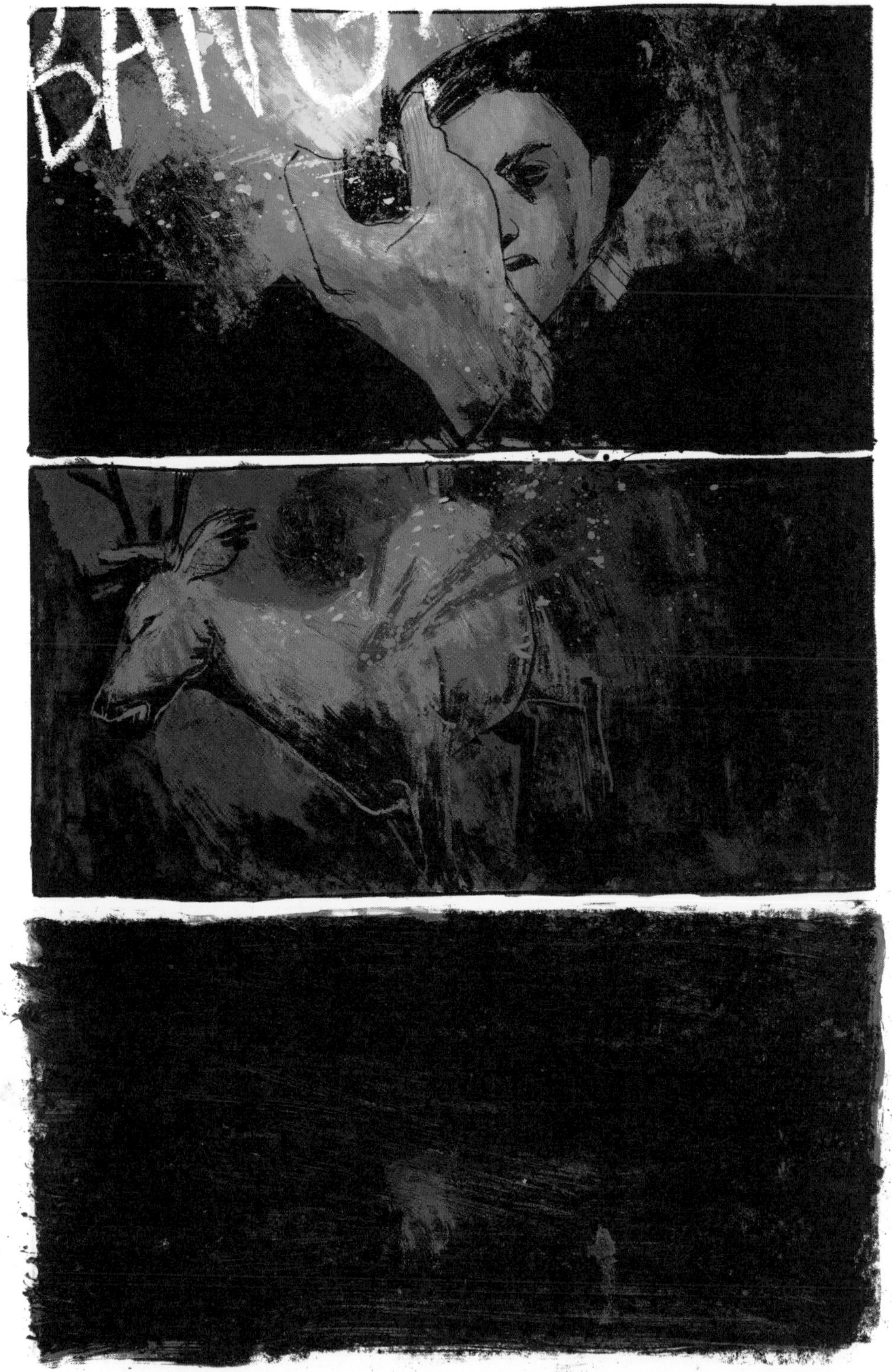
BANG

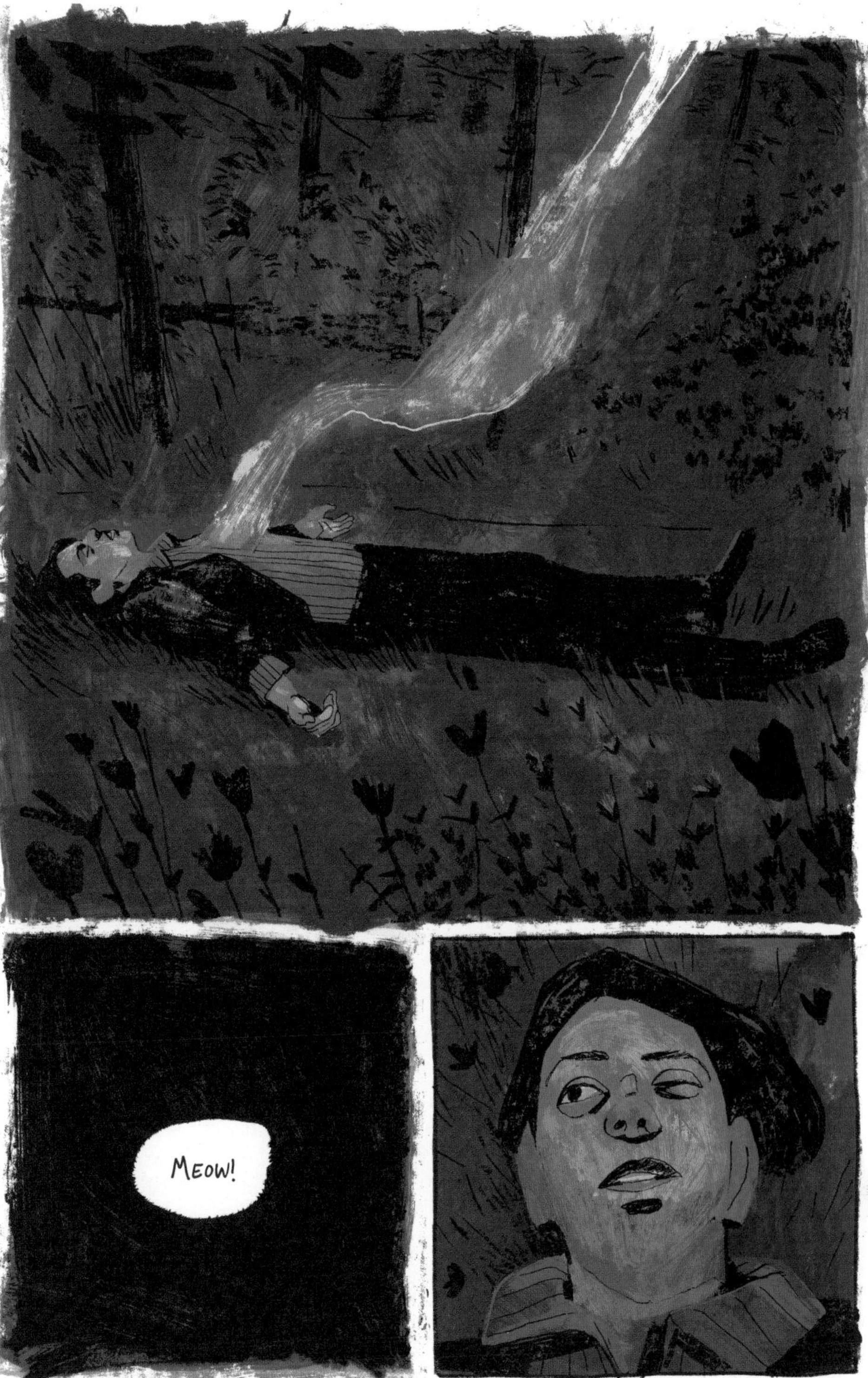
MEOW!

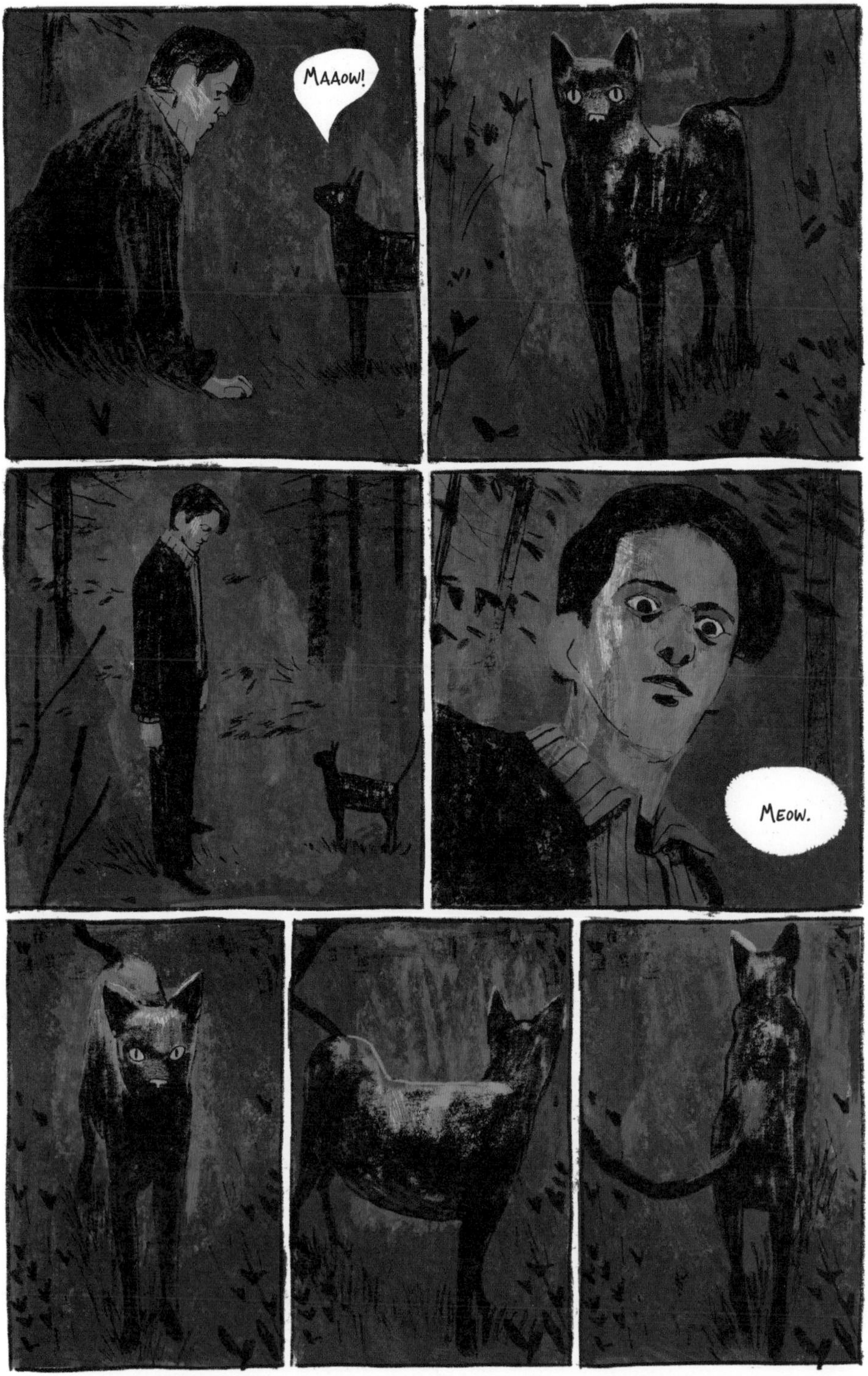
MAAOW!
MEOW.

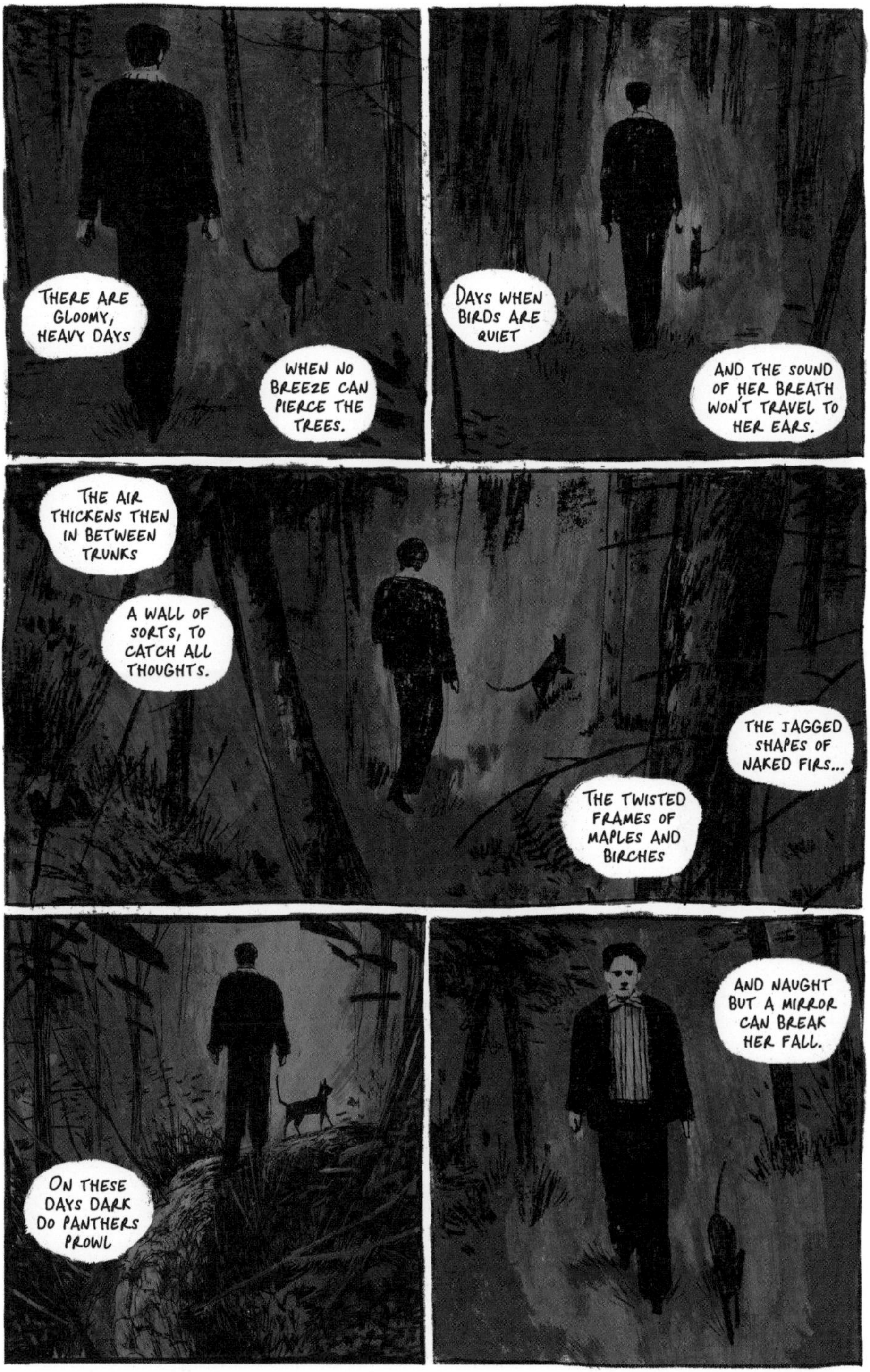
THERE ARE GLOOMY, HEAVY DAYS
WHEN NO BREEZE CAN PIERCE THE TREES.
DAYS WHEN BIRDS ARE QUIET
AND THE SOUND OF HER BREATH WON'T TRAVEL TO HER EARS.
THE AIR THICKENS THEN IN BETWEEN TRUNKS
A WALL OF SORTS, TO CATCH ALL THOUGHTS.
THE JAGGED SHAPES OF NAKED FIRS...
THE TWISTED FRAMES OF MAPLES AND BIRCHES
ON THESE DAYS DARK DO PANTHERS PROWL
AND NAUGHT BUT A MIRROR CAN BREAK HER FALL.

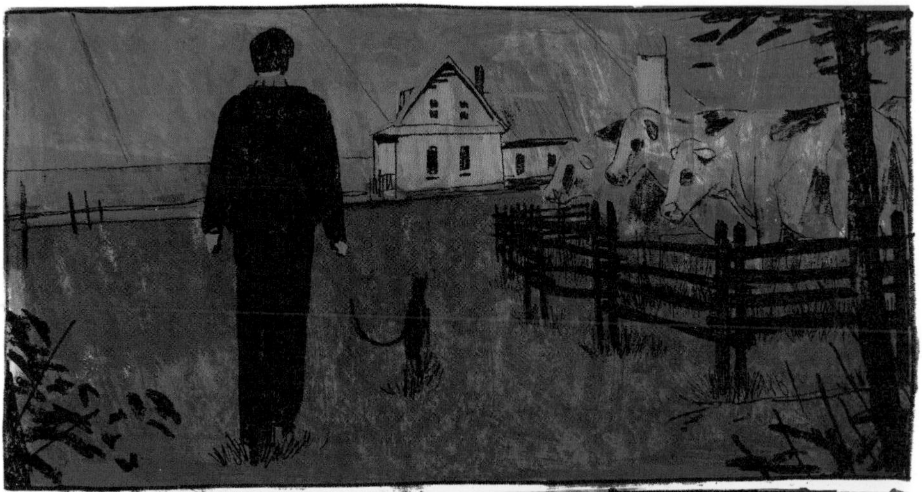
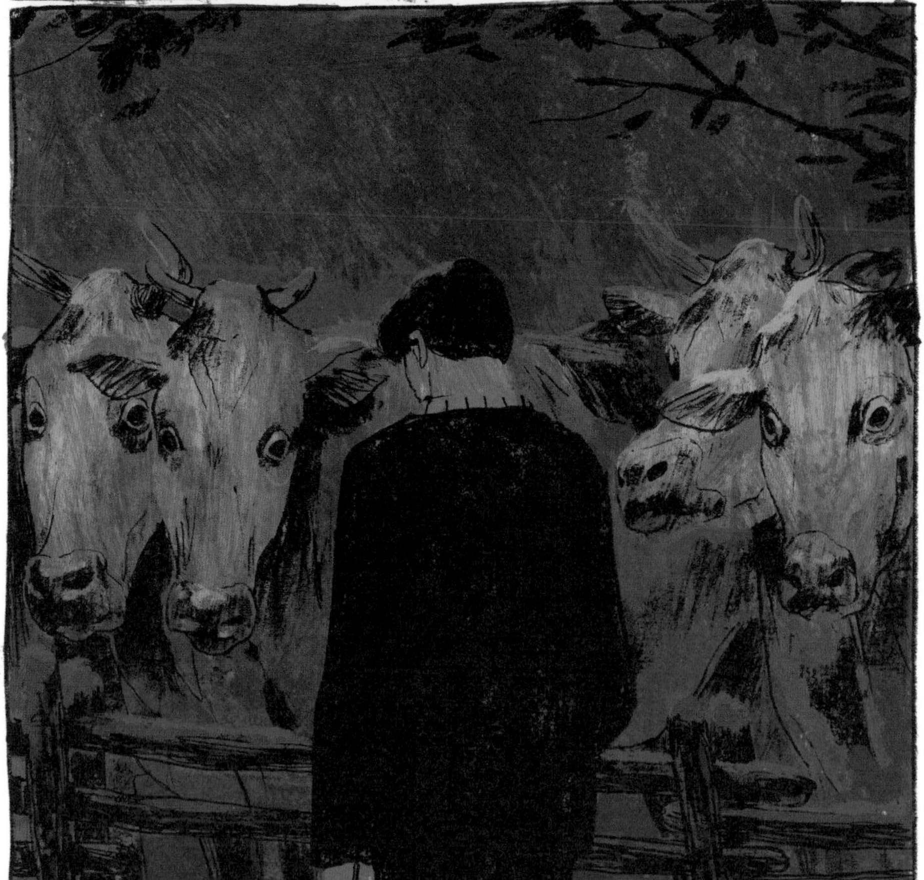

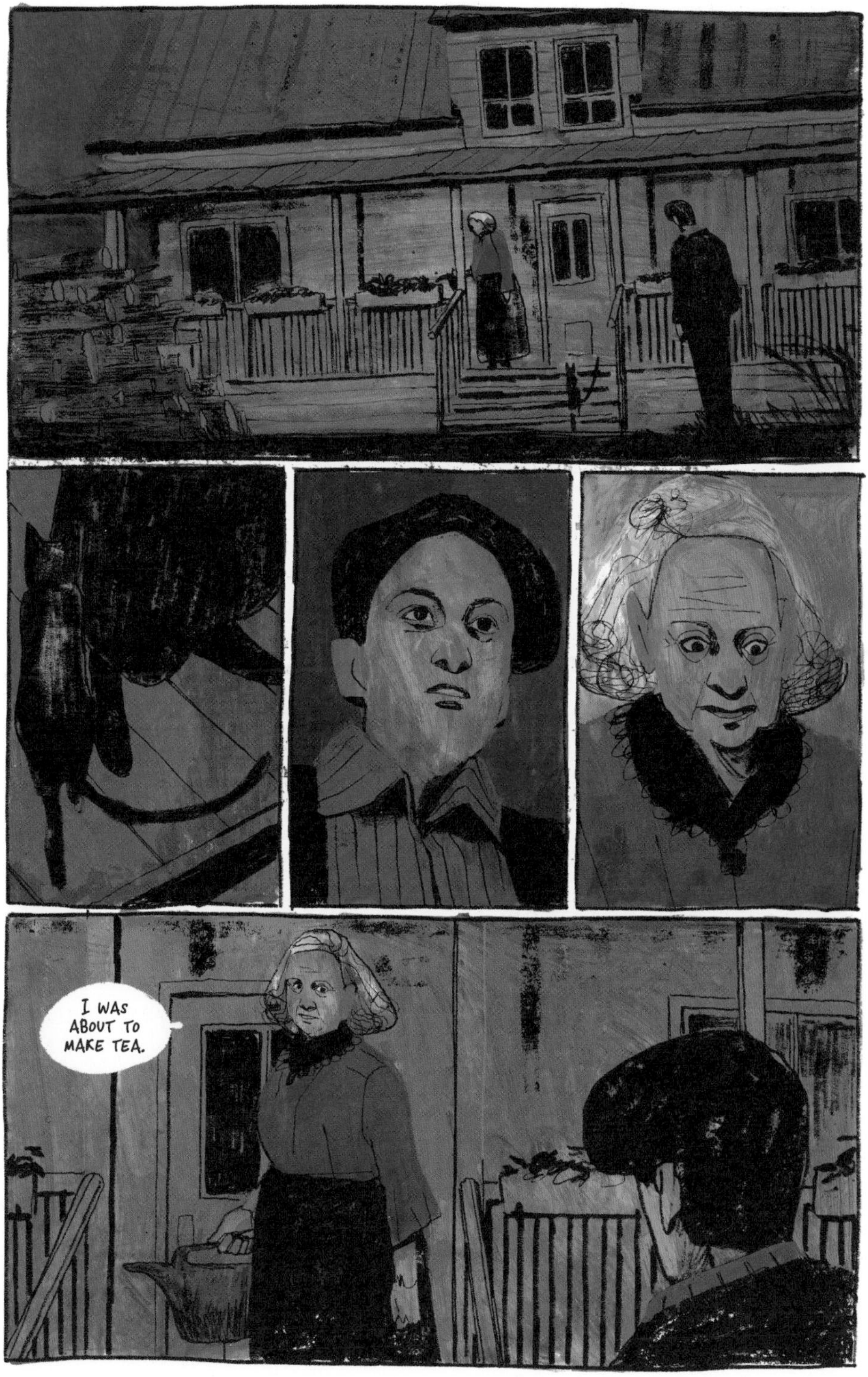
I WAS ABOUT TO MAKE TEA.

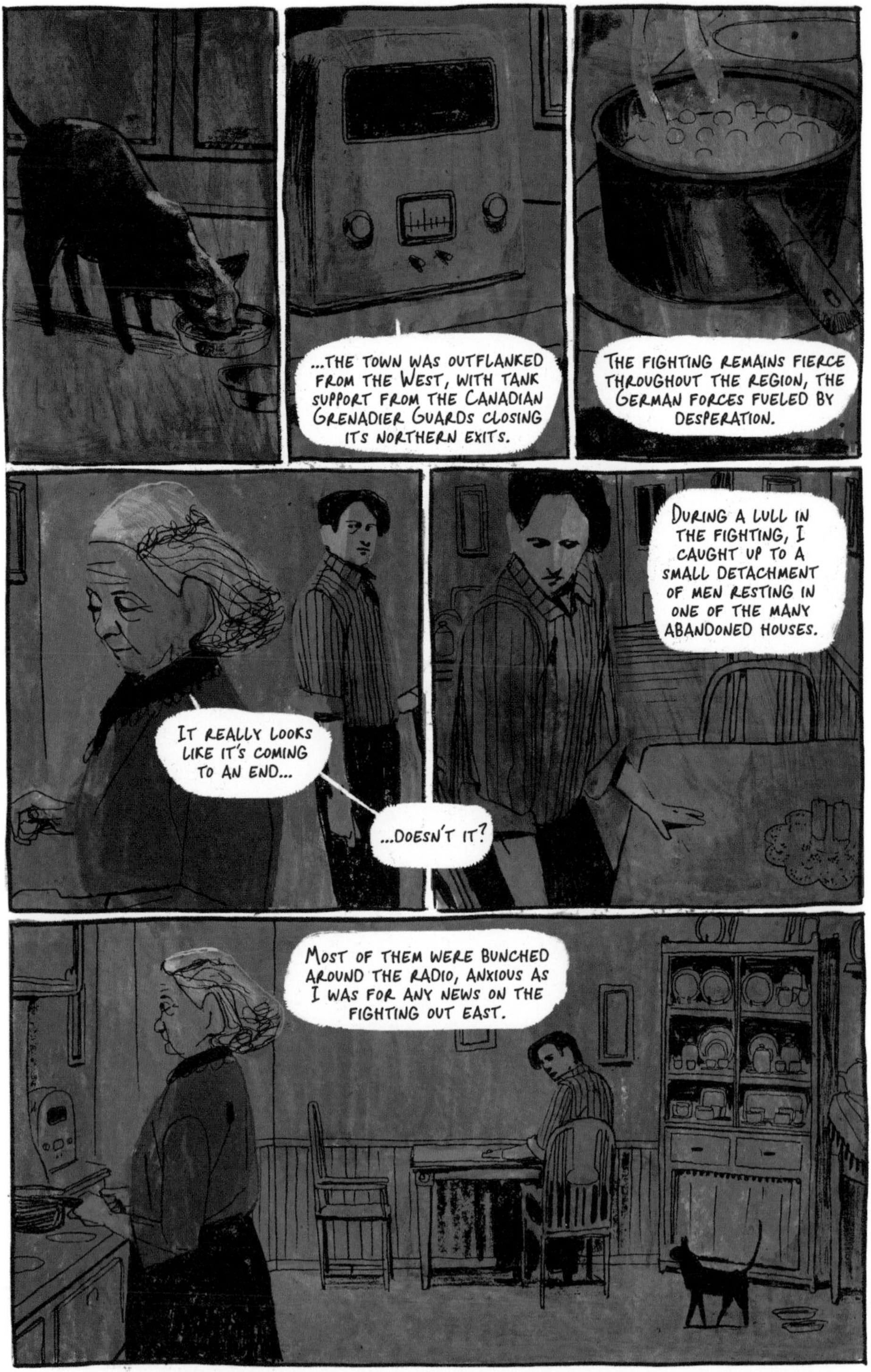
...THE TOWN WAS OUTFLANKED FROM THE WEST, WITH TANK SUPPORT FROM THE CANADIAN GRENADIER GUARDS CLOSING ITS NORTHERN EXITS.
THE FIGHTING REMAINS FIERCE THROUGHOUT THE REGION, THE GERMAN FORCES FUELED BY DESPERATION.
IT REALLY LOOKS LIKE IT'S COMING TO AN END...
...DOESN'T IT?
DURING A LULL IN THE FIGHTING, I CAUGHT UP TO A SMALL DETACHMENT OF MEN RESTING IN ONE OF THE MANY ABANDONED HOUSES.
MOST OF THEM WERE BUNCHED AROUND THE RADIO, ANXIOUS AS I WAS FOR ANY NEWS ON THE FIGHTING OUT EAST.

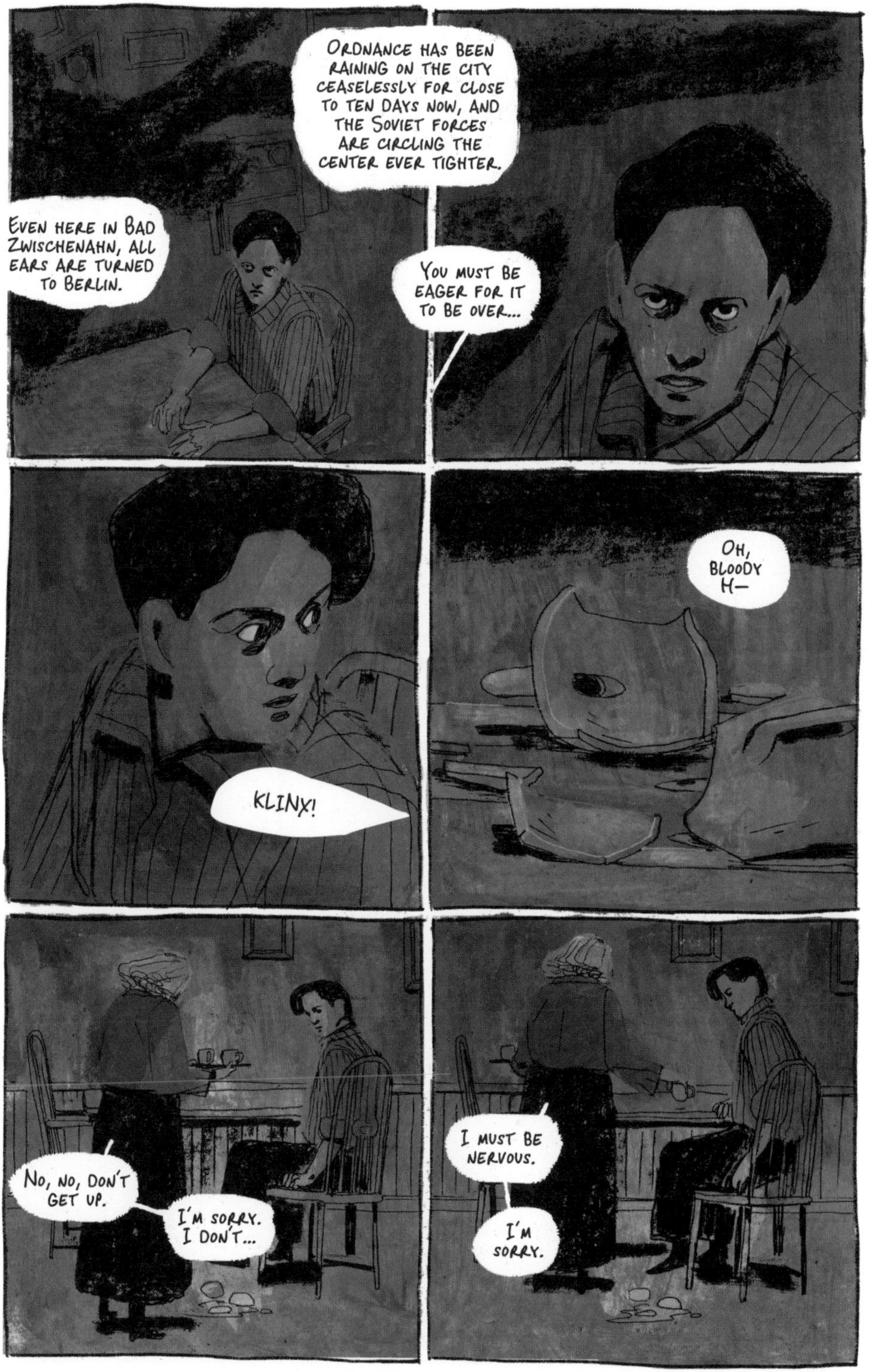
Ordnance has been raining on the city ceaselessly for close to ten days now, and the Soviet forces are circling the center ever tighter.
Even here in Bad Zwischenahn, all ears are turned to Berlin.
You must be eager for it to be over...
KLINX!
Oh, bloody H—
No, no, don't get up.
I'm sorry. I don't...
I must be nervous.
I'm sorry.

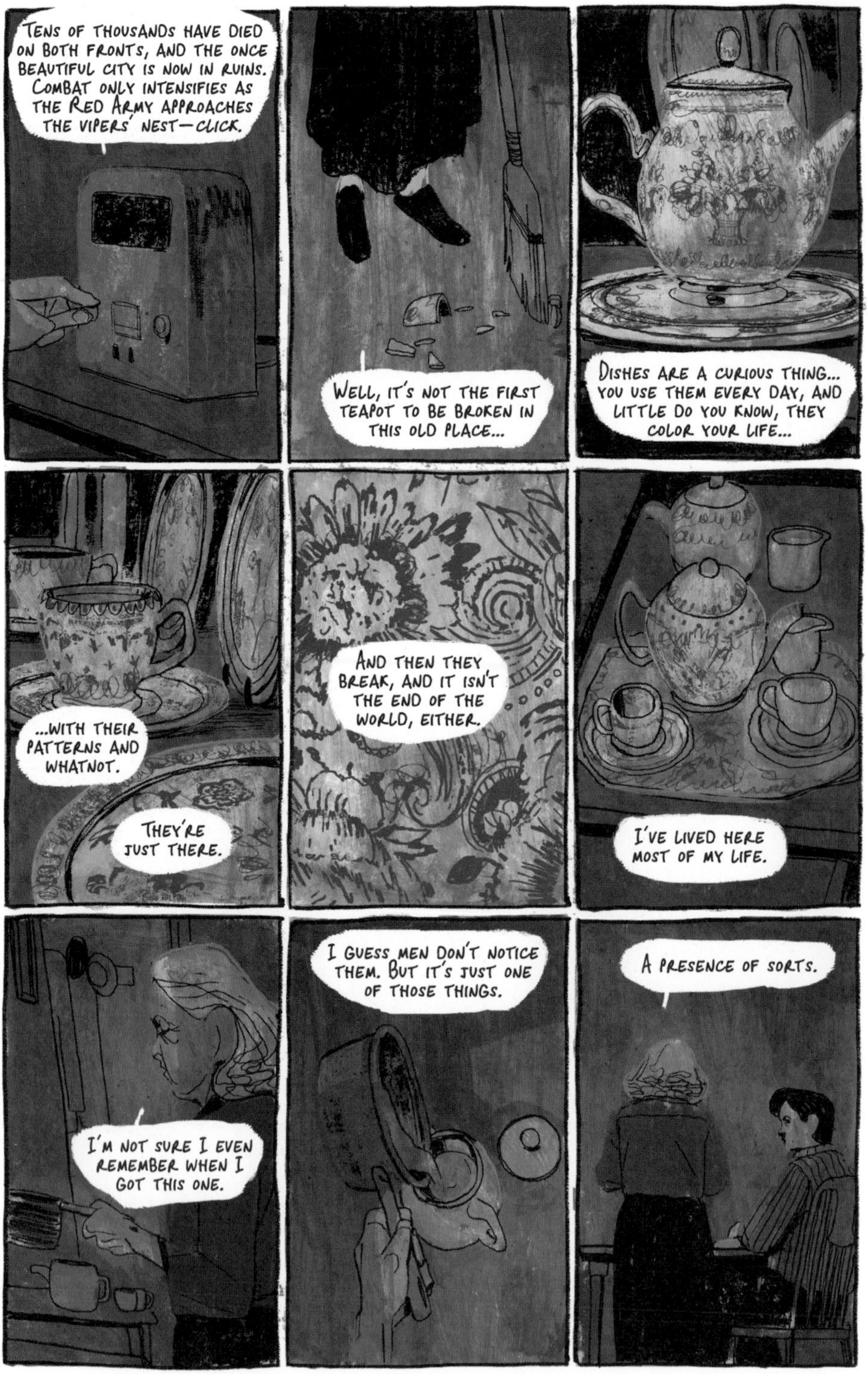
TENS OF THOUSANDS HAVE DIED ON BOTH FRONTS, AND THE ONCE BEAUTIFUL CITY IS NOW IN RUINS. COMBAT ONLY INTENSIFIES AS THE RED ARMY APPROACHES THE VIPERS' NEST—CLICK.
WELL, IT'S NOT THE FIRST TEAPOT TO BE BROKEN IN THIS OLD PLACE...
DISHES ARE A CURIOUS THING... YOU USE THEM EVERY DAY, AND LITTLE DO YOU KNOW, THEY COLOR YOUR LIFE...
...WITH THEIR PATTERNS AND WHATNOT.
THEY'RE JUST THERE.
AND THEN THEY BREAK, AND IT ISN'T THE END OF THE WORLD, EITHER.
I'VE LIVED HERE MOST OF MY LIFE.
I'M NOT SURE I EVEN REMEMBER WHEN I GOT THIS ONE.
I GUESS MEN DON'T NOTICE THEM. BUT IT'S JUST ONE OF THOSE THINGS.
A PRESENCE OF SORTS.

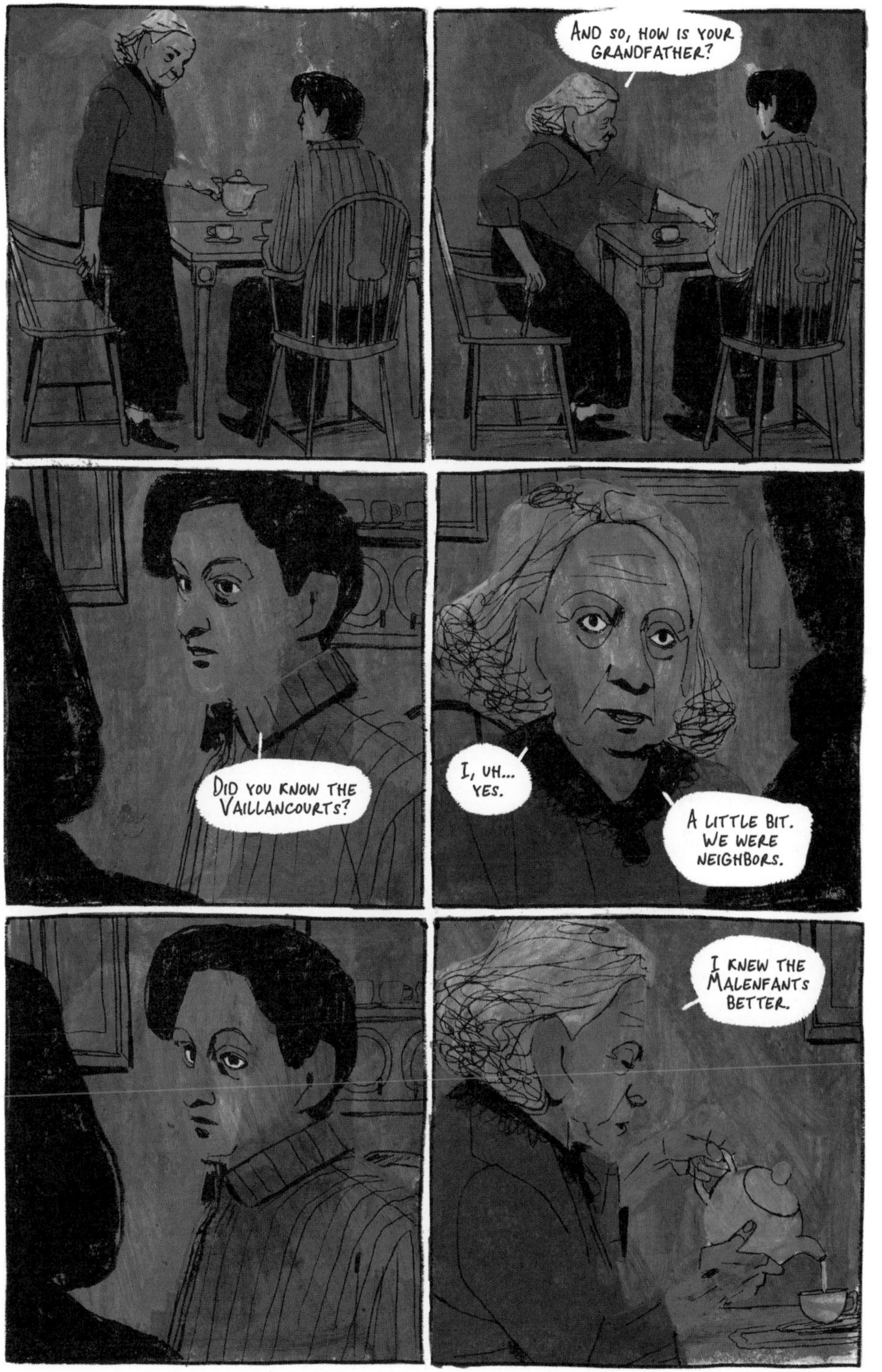
AND SO, HOW IS YOUR GRANDFATHER?
DID YOU KNOW THE VAILLANCOURTS?
I, UH... YES.
A LITTLE BIT. WE WERE NEIGHBORS.
I KNEW THE MALENFANTS BETTER.

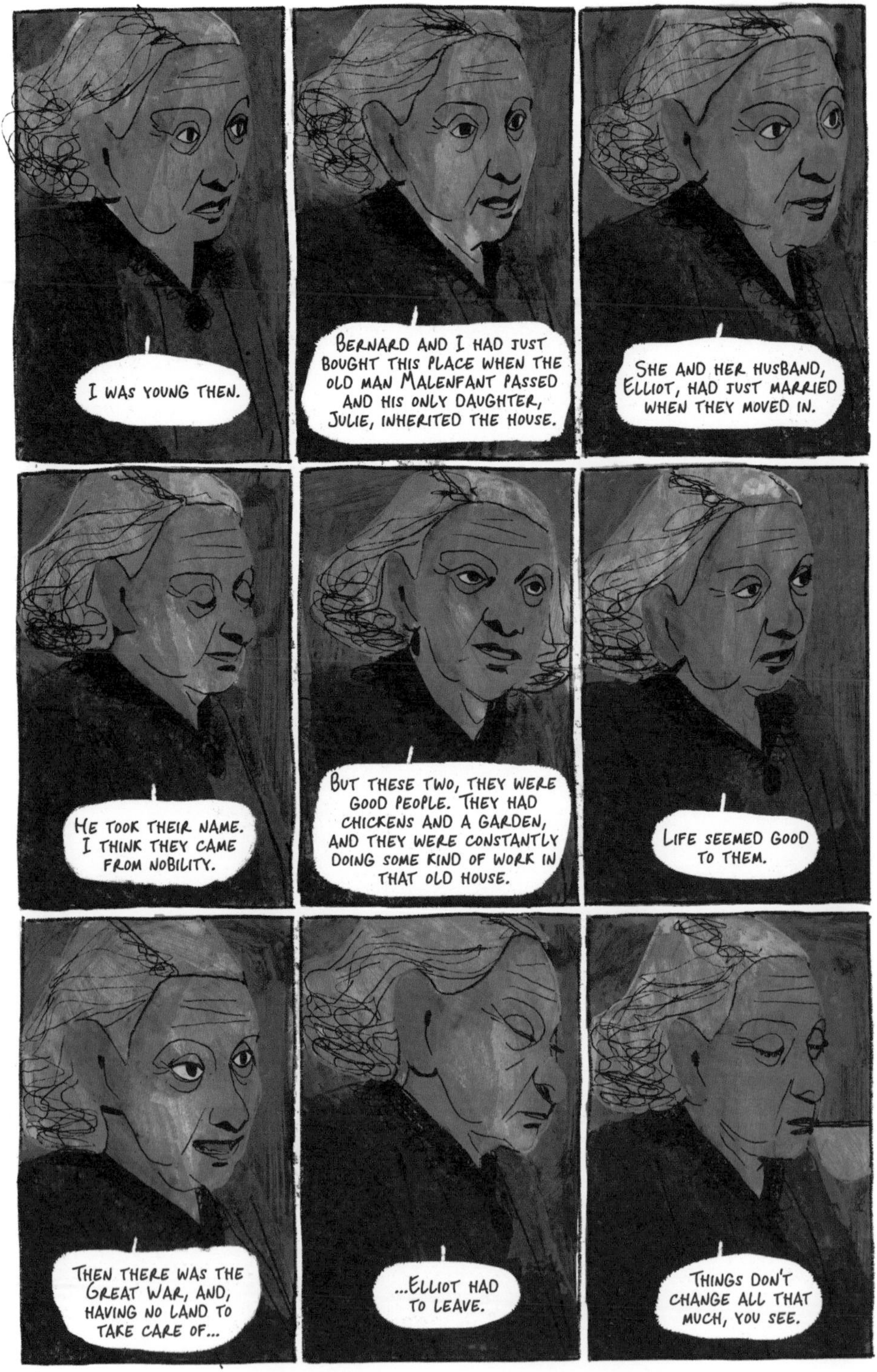
I WAS YOUNG THEN.
BERNARD AND I HAD JUST BOUGHT THIS PLACE WHEN THE OLD MAN MALENFANT PASSED AND HIS ONLY DAUGHTER, JULIE, INHERITED THE HOUSE.
SHE AND HER HUSBAND, ELLIOT, HAD JUST MARRIED WHEN THEY MOVED IN.
HE TOOK THEIR NAME. I THINK THEY CAME FROM NOBILITY.
BUT THESE TWO, THEY WERE GOOD PEOPLE. THEY HAD CHICKENS AND A GARDEN, AND THEY WERE CONSTANTLY DOING SOME KIND OF WORK IN THAT OLD HOUSE.
LIFE SEEMED GOOD TO THEM.
THEN THERE WAS THE GREAT WAR, AND, HAVING NO LAND TO TAKE CARE OF...
...ELLIOT HAD TO LEAVE.
THINGS DON'T CHANGE ALL THAT MUCH, YOU SEE.

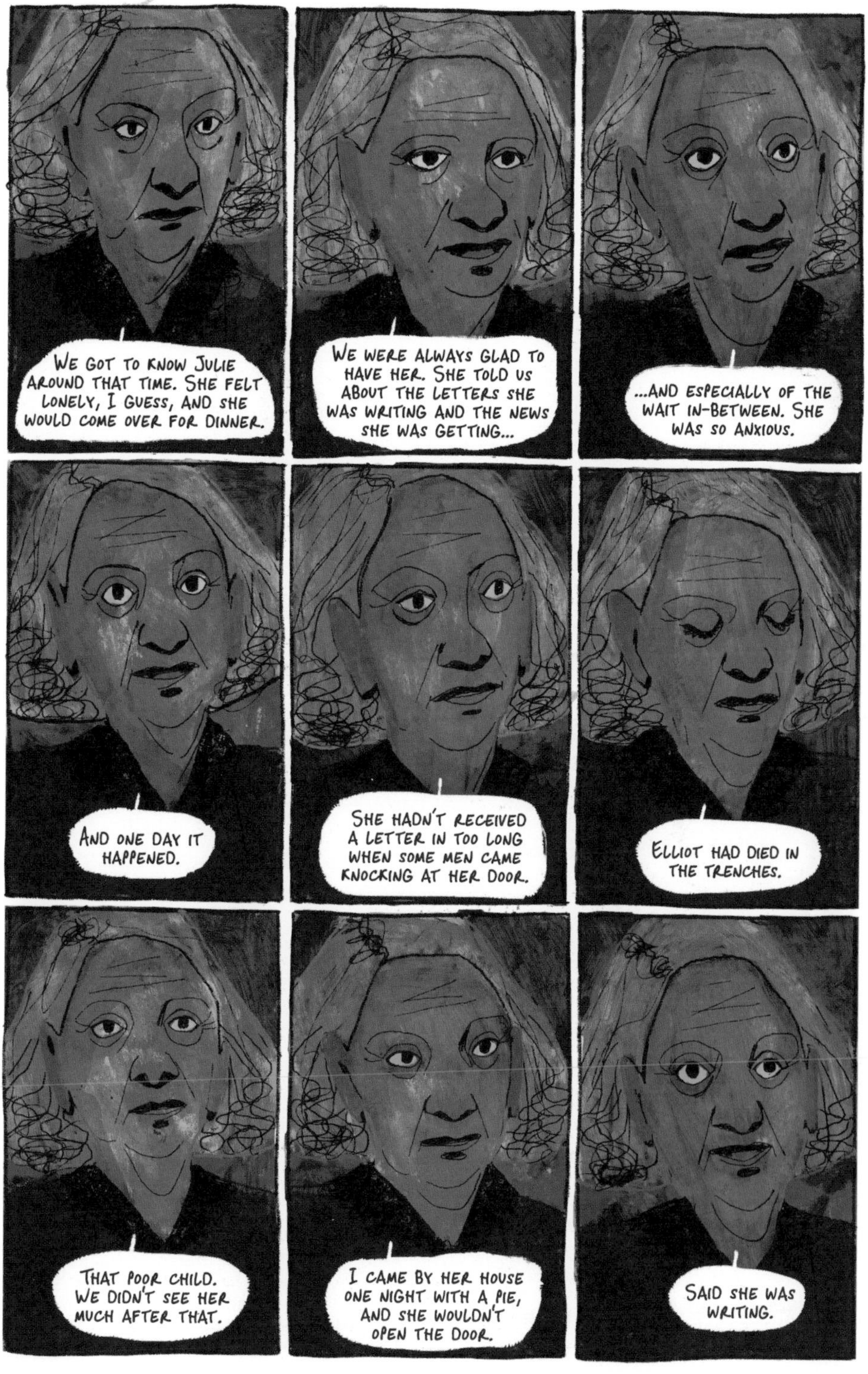
WE GOT TO KNOW JULIE AROUND THAT TIME. SHE FELT LONELY, I GUESS, AND SHE WOULD COME OVER FOR DINNER.
WE WERE ALWAYS GLAD TO HAVE HER. SHE TOLD US ABOUT THE LETTERS SHE WAS WRITING AND THE NEWS SHE WAS GETTING...
...AND ESPECIALLY OF THE WAIT IN-BETWEEN. SHE WAS SO ANXIOUS.
AND ONE DAY IT HAPPENED.
SHE HADN'T RECEIVED A LETTER IN TOO LONG WHEN SOME MEN CAME KNOCKING AT HER DOOR.
ELLIOT HAD DIED IN THE TRENCHES.
THAT POOR CHILD. WE DIDN'T SEE HER MUCH AFTER THAT.
I CAME BY HER HOUSE ONE NIGHT WITH A PIE, AND SHE WOULDN'T OPEN THE DOOR.
SAID SHE WAS WRITING.

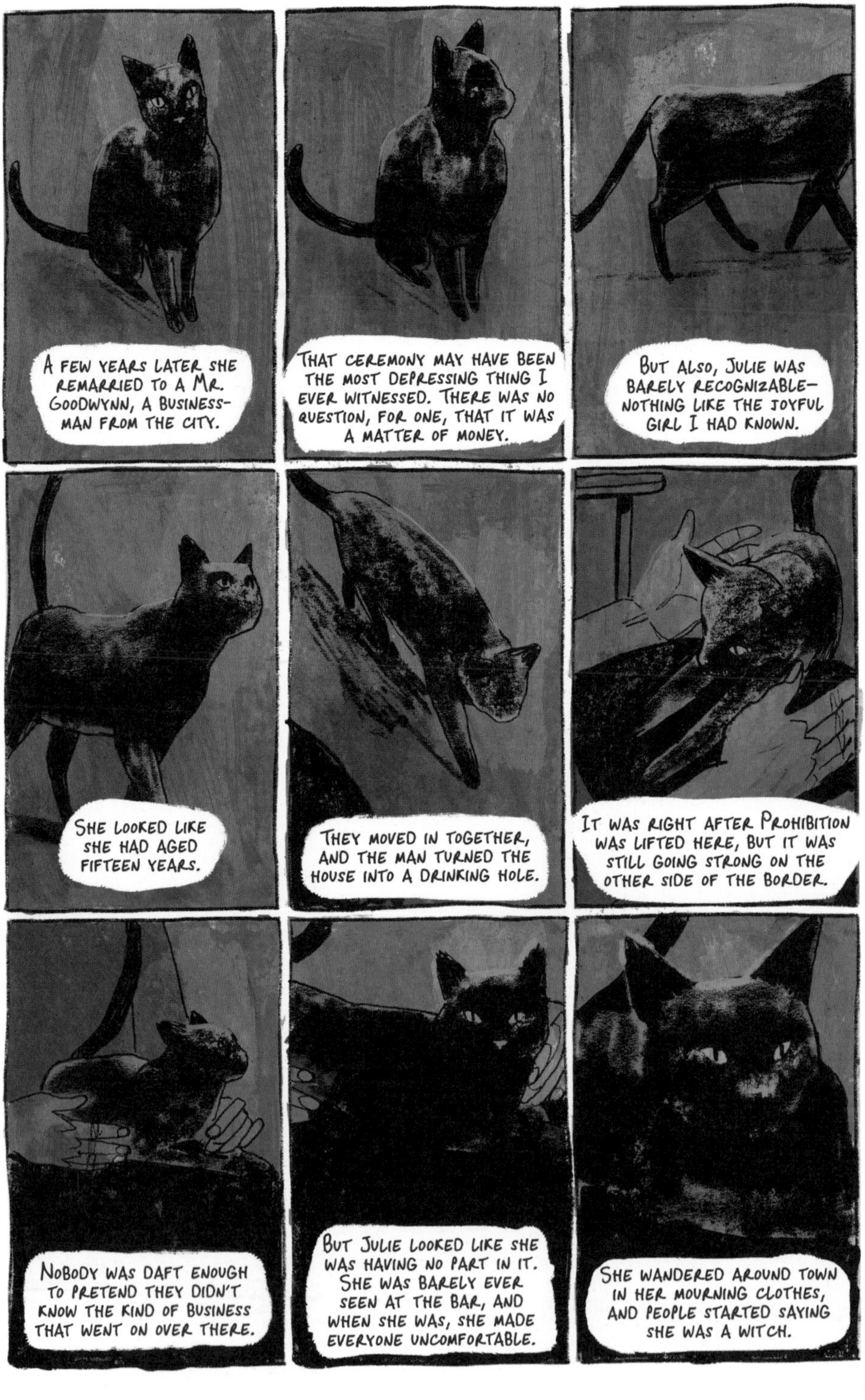
A FEW YEARS LATER SHE REMARRIED TO A MR. GOODWYNN, A BUSINESSMAN FROM THE CITY.
THAT CEREMONY MAY HAVE BEEN THE MOST DEPRESSING THING I EVER WITNESSED. THERE WAS NO QUESTION, FOR ONE, THAT IT WAS A MATTER OF MONEY.
BUT ALSO, JULIE WAS BARELY RECOGNIZABLE—NOTHING LIKE THE JOYFUL GIRL I HAD KNOWN.
SHE LOOKED LIKE SHE HAD AGED FIFTEEN YEARS.
THEY MOVED IN TOGETHER, AND THE MAN TURNED THE HOUSE INTO A DRINKING HOLE.
IT WAS RIGHT AFTER PROHIBITION WAS LIFTED HERE, BUT IT WAS STILL GOING STRONG ON THE OTHER SIDE OF THE BORDER.
NOBODY WAS DAFT ENOUGH TO PRETEND THEY DIDN'T KNOW THE KIND OF BUSINESS THAT WENT ON OVER THERE.
BUT JULIE LOOKED LIKE SHE WAS HAVING NO PART IN IT. SHE WAS BARELY EVER SEEN AT THE BAR, AND WHEN SHE WAS, SHE MADE EVERYONE UNCOMFORTABLE.
SHE WANDERED AROUND TOWN IN HER MOURNING CLOTHES, AND PEOPLE STARTED SAYING SHE WAS A WITCH.

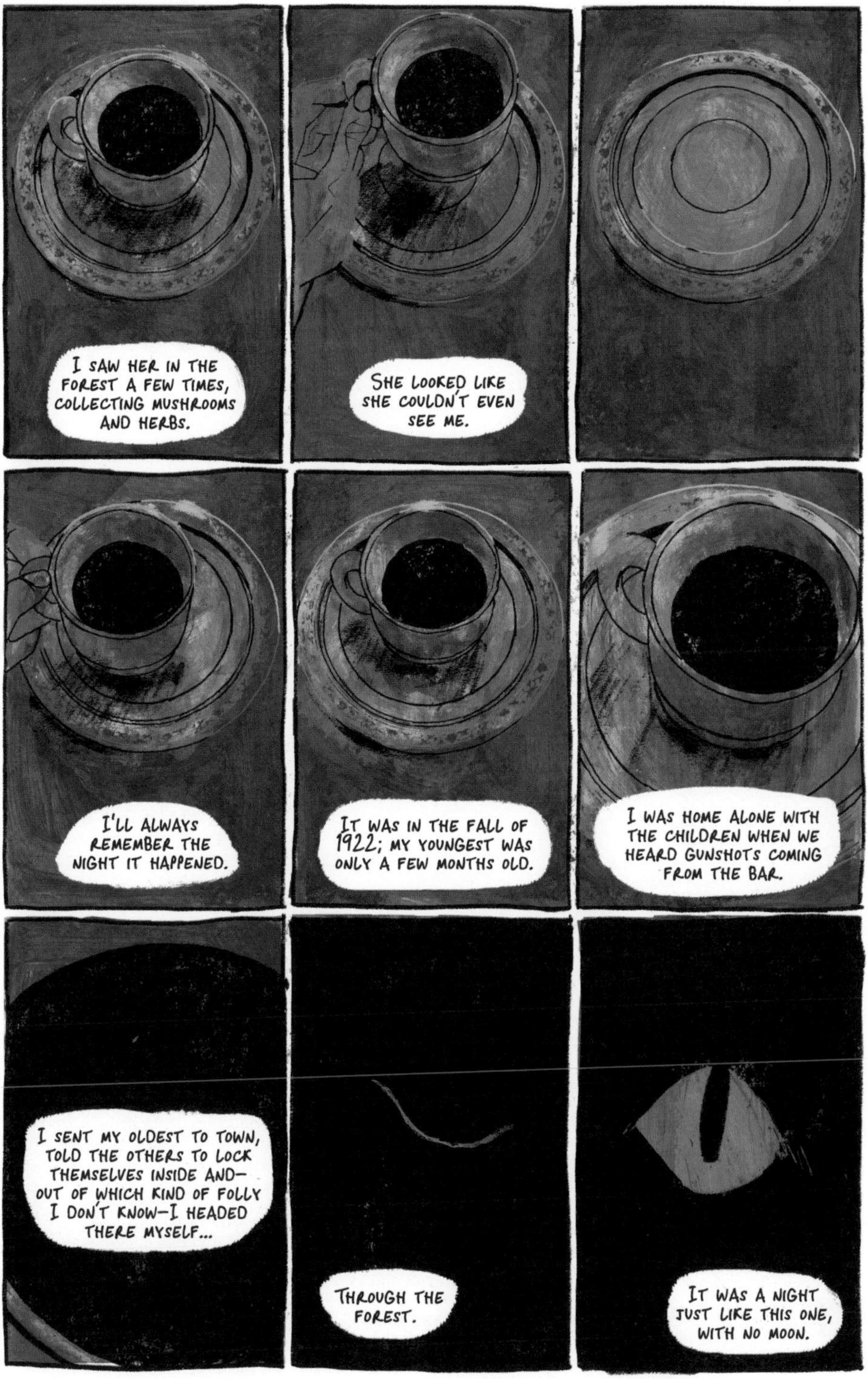
I SAW HER IN THE FOREST A FEW TIMES, COLLECTING MUSHROOMS AND HERBS.
SHE LOOKED LIKE SHE COULDN'T EVEN SEE ME.
I'LL ALWAYS REMEMBER THE NIGHT IT HAPPENED.
IT WAS IN THE FALL OF 1922; MY YOUNGEST WAS ONLY A FEW MONTHS OLD.
I WAS HOME ALONE WITH THE CHILDREN WHEN WE HEARD GUNSHOTS COMING FROM THE BAR.
I SENT MY OLDEST TO TOWN, TOLD THE OTHERS TO LOCK THEMSELVES INSIDE AND—OUT OF WHICH KIND OF FOLLY I DON'T KNOW—I HEADED THERE MYSELF...
THROUGH THE FOREST.
IT WAS A NIGHT JUST LIKE THIS ONE, WITH NO MOON.

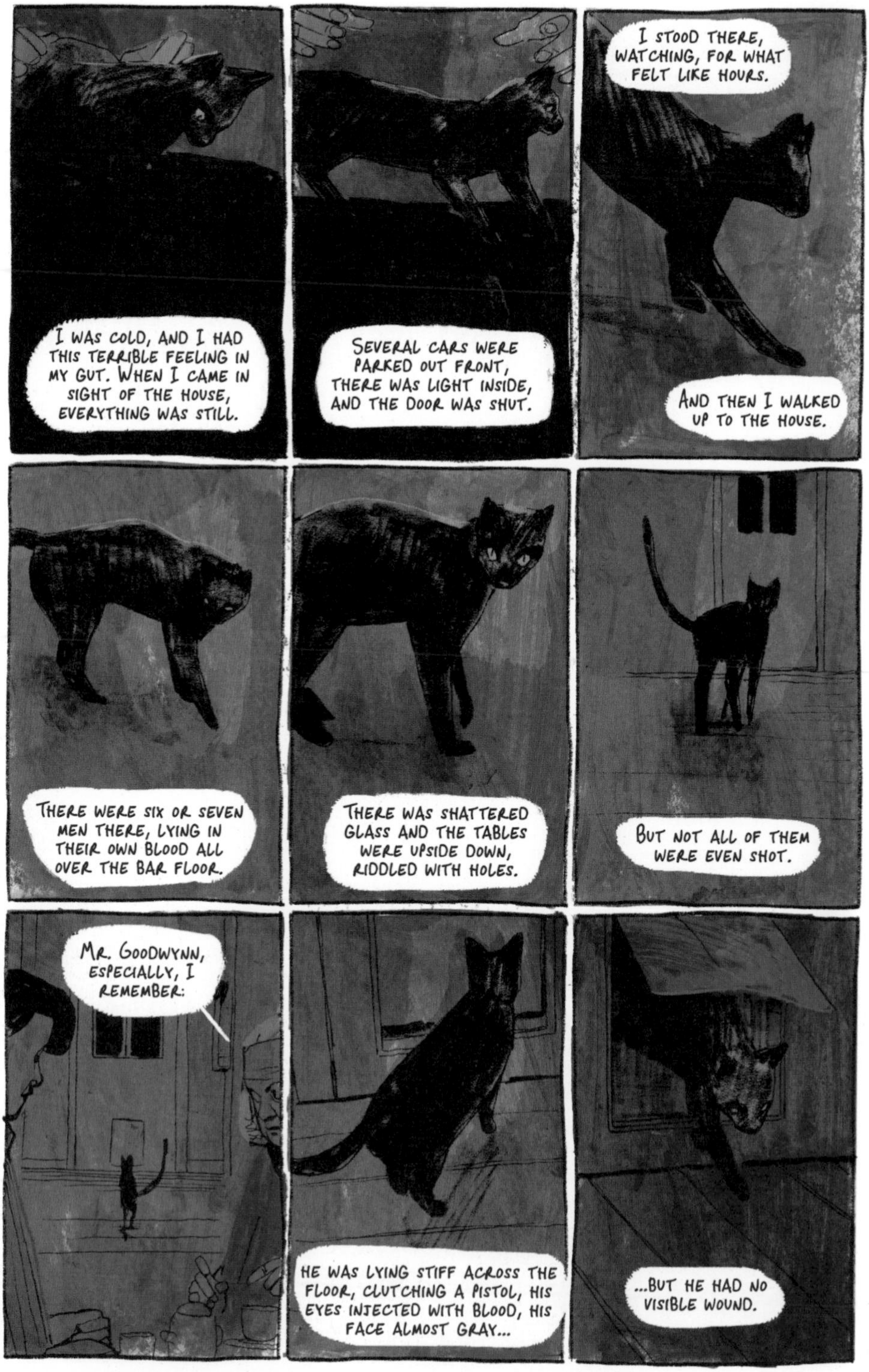
I WAS COLD, AND I HAD THIS TERRIBLE FEELING IN MY GUT. WHEN I CAME IN SIGHT OF THE HOUSE, EVERYTHING WAS STILL.
SEVERAL CARS WERE PARKED OUT FRONT, THERE WAS LIGHT INSIDE, AND THE DOOR WAS SHUT.
I STOOD THERE, WATCHING, FOR WHAT FELT LIKE HOURS.
AND THEN I WALKED UP TO THE HOUSE.
THERE WERE SIX OR SEVEN MEN THERE, LYING IN THEIR OWN BLOOD ALL OVER THE BAR FLOOR.
THERE WAS SHATTERED GLASS AND THE TABLES WERE UPSIDE DOWN, RIDDLED WITH HOLES.
BUT NOT ALL OF THEM WERE EVEN SHOT.
MR. GOODWYNN, ESPECIALLY, I REMEMBER:
HE WAS LYING STIFF ACROSS THE FLOOR, CLUTCHING A PISTOL, HIS EYES INJECTED WITH BLOOD, HIS FACE ALMOST GRAY...
...BUT HE HAD NO VISIBLE WOUND.

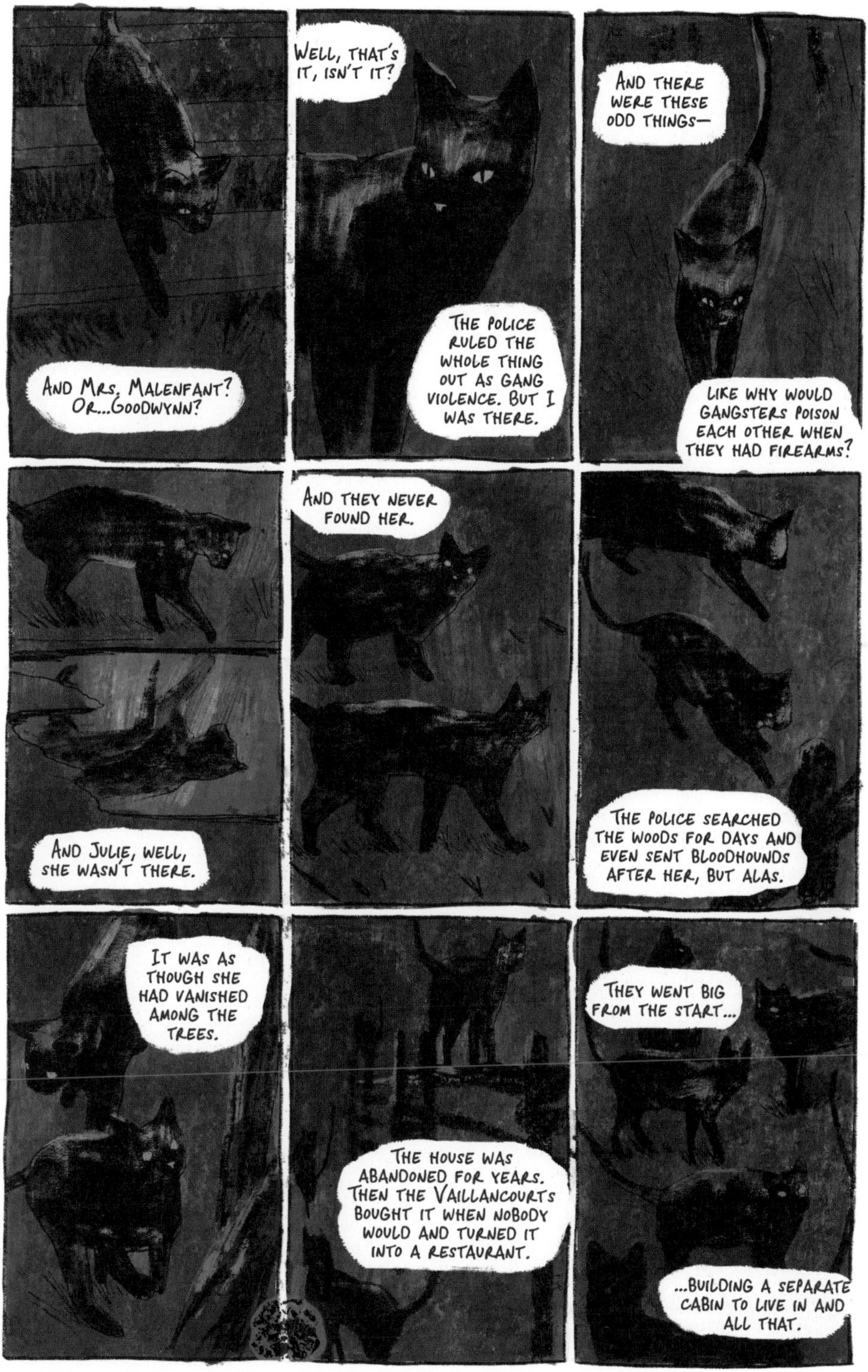
And Mrs. Malenfant? Or...Goodwynn?
Well, that's it, isn't it?
The police ruled the whole thing out as gang violence. But I was there.
And there were these odd things—
Like why would gangsters poison each other when they had firearms?
And Julie, well, she wasn't there.
And they never found her.
The police searched the woods for days and even sent bloodhounds after her, but alas.
It was as though she had vanished among the trees.
The house was abandoned for years. Then the Vaillancourts bought it when nobody would and turned it into a restaurant.
They went big from the start...
...building a separate cabin to live in and all that.

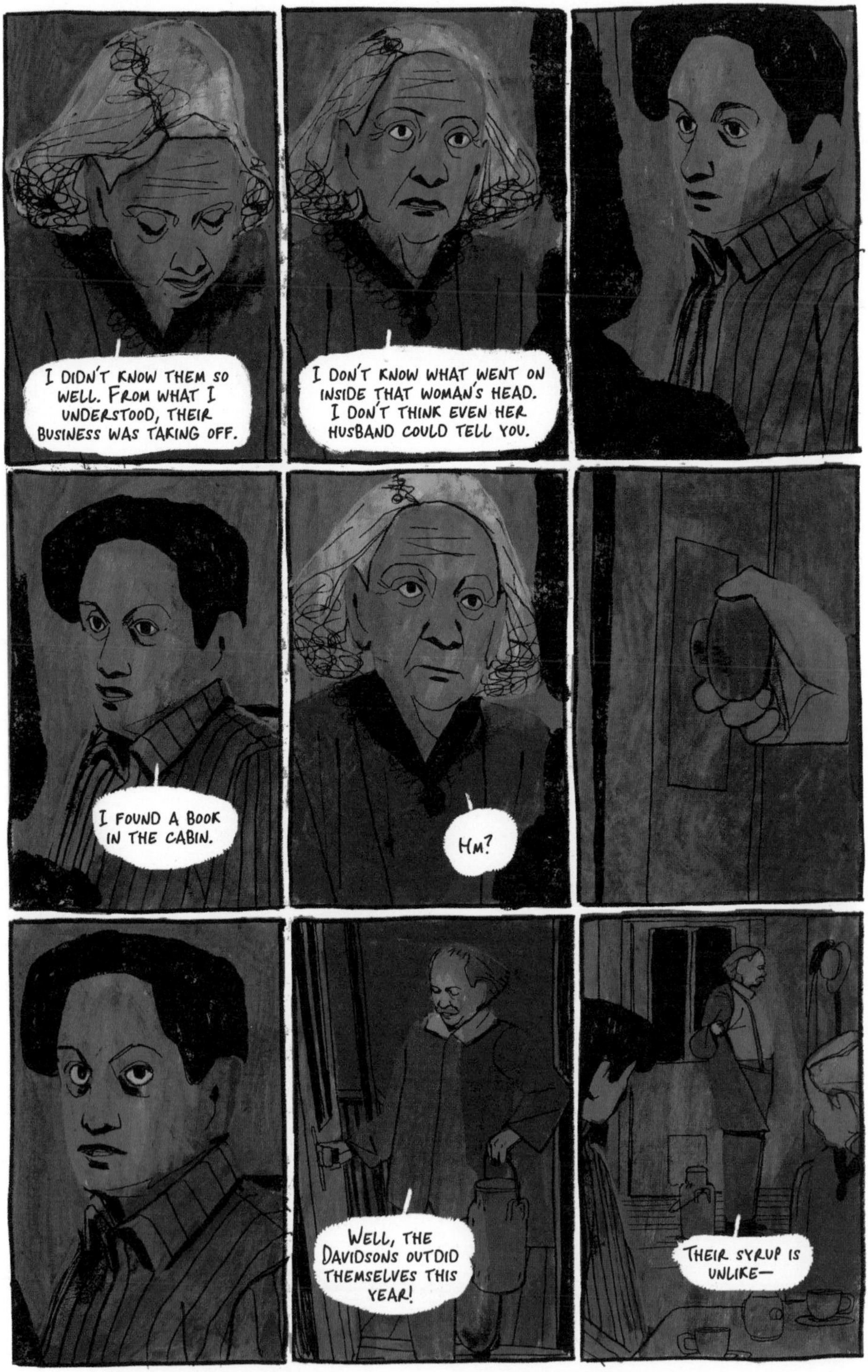
I DIDN'T KNOW THEM SO WELL. FROM WHAT I UNDERSTOOD, THEIR BUSINESS WAS TAKING OFF.
I DON'T KNOW WHAT WENT ON INSIDE THAT WOMAN'S HEAD. I DON'T THINK EVEN HER HUSBAND COULD TELL YOU.
I FOUND A BOOK IN THE CABIN.
HM?
WELL, THE DAVIDSONS OUTDID THEMSELVES THIS YEAR!
THEIR SYRUP IS UNLIKE—

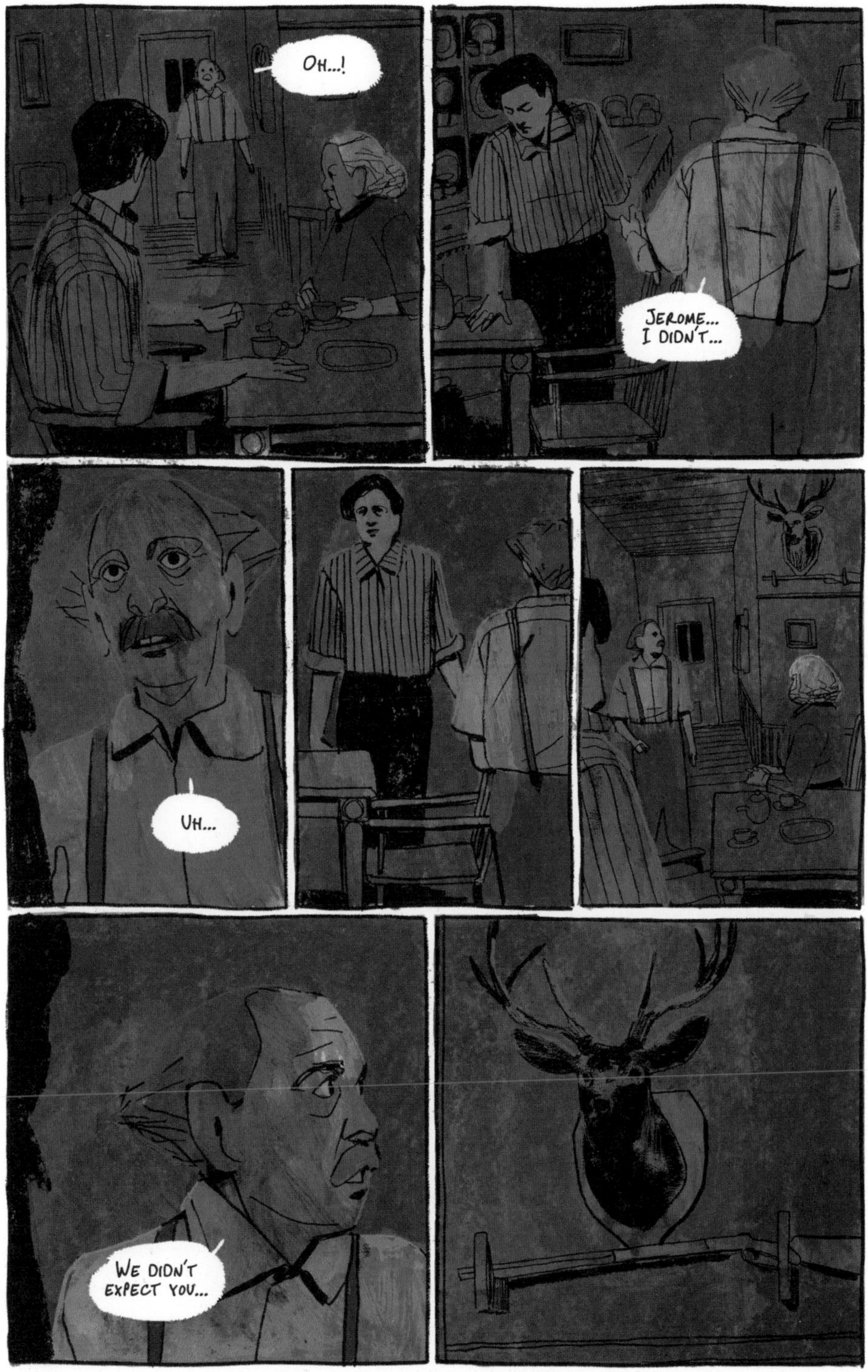
OH...!
JEROME... I DIDN'T...
UH...
WE DIDN'T EXPECT YOU...

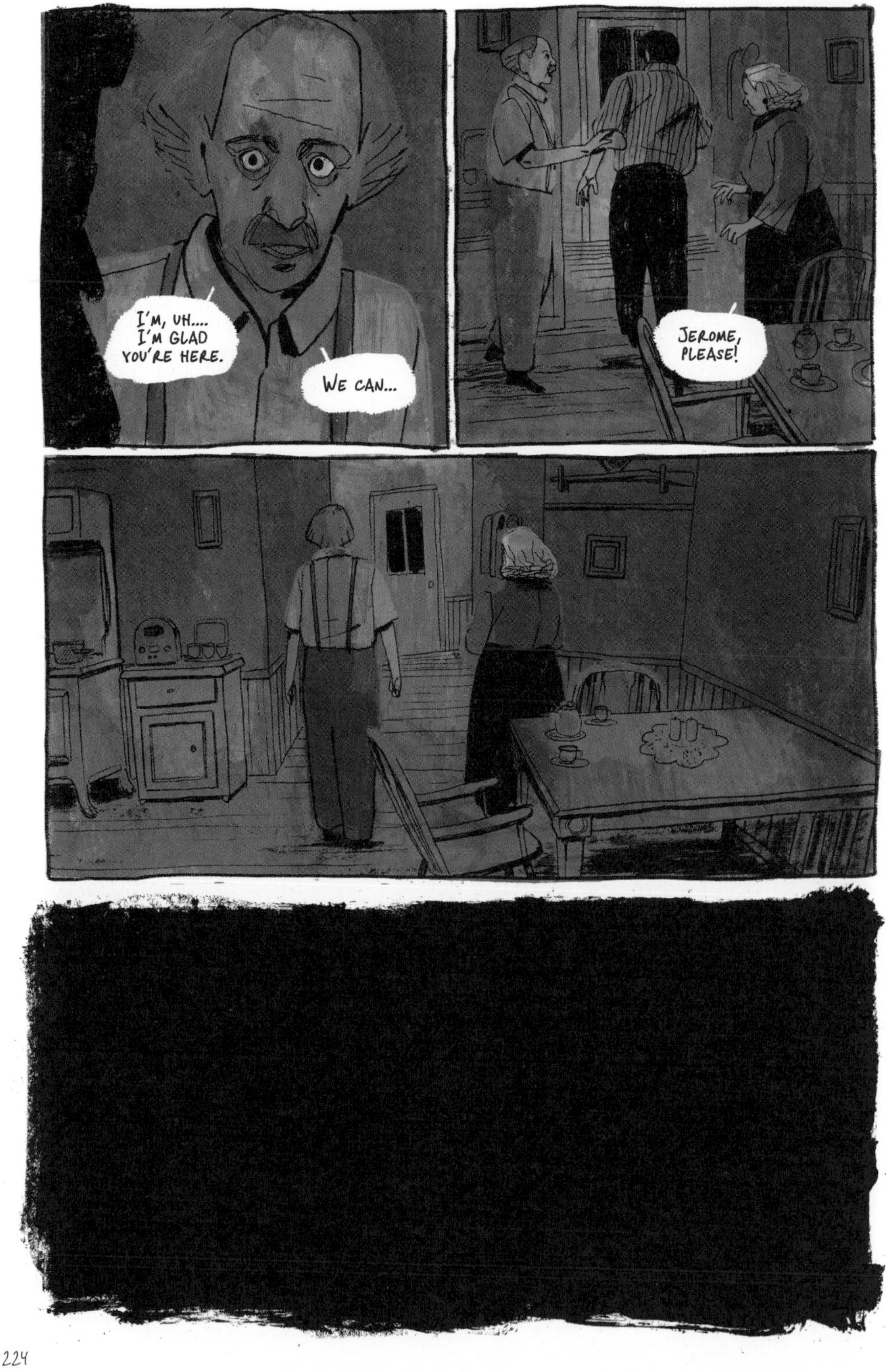
I'M, UH....
I'M GLAD
YOU'RE HERE.
WE CAN...
JEROME,
PLEASE!

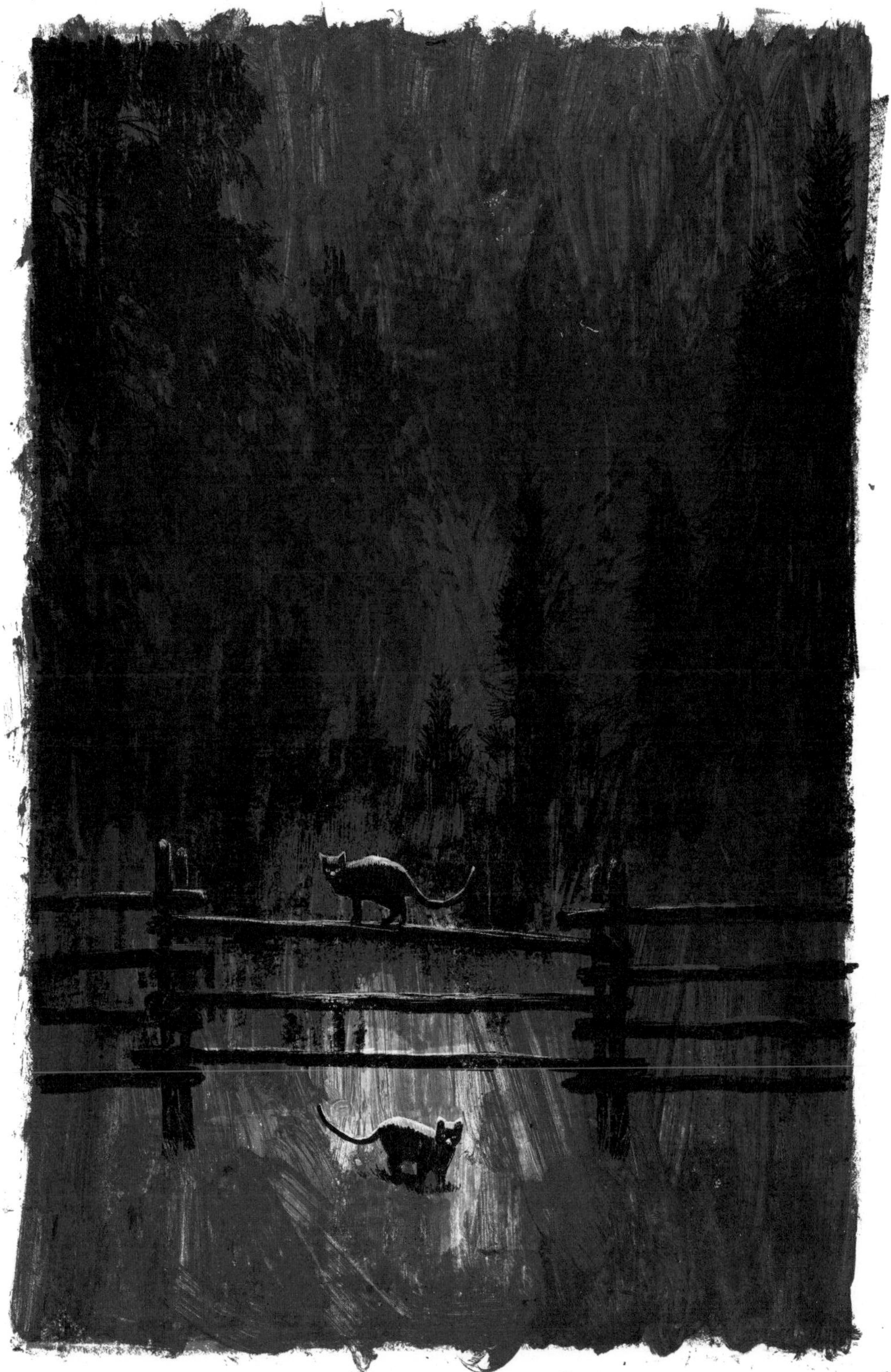

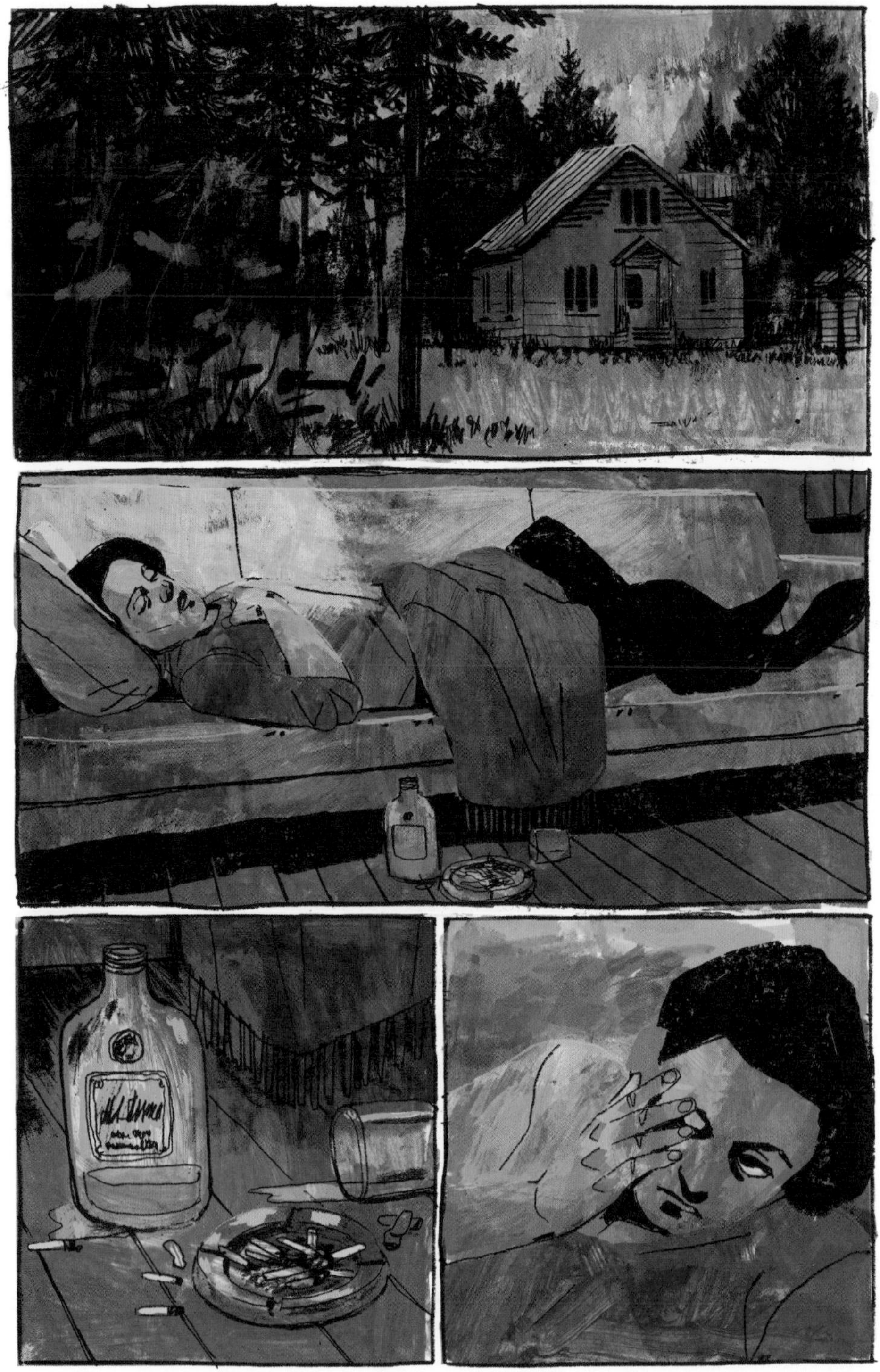

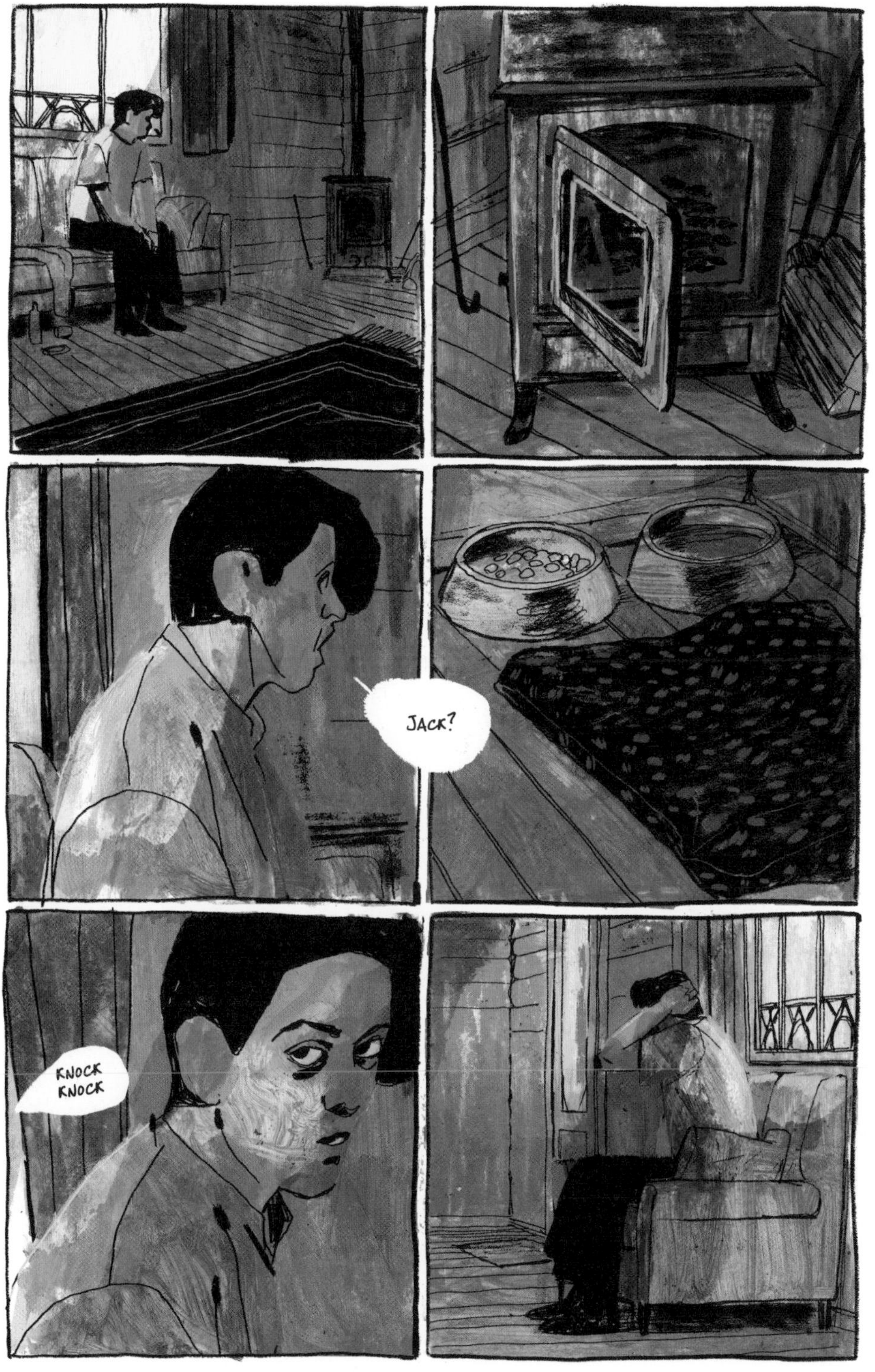
JACK?
KNOCK
KNOCK

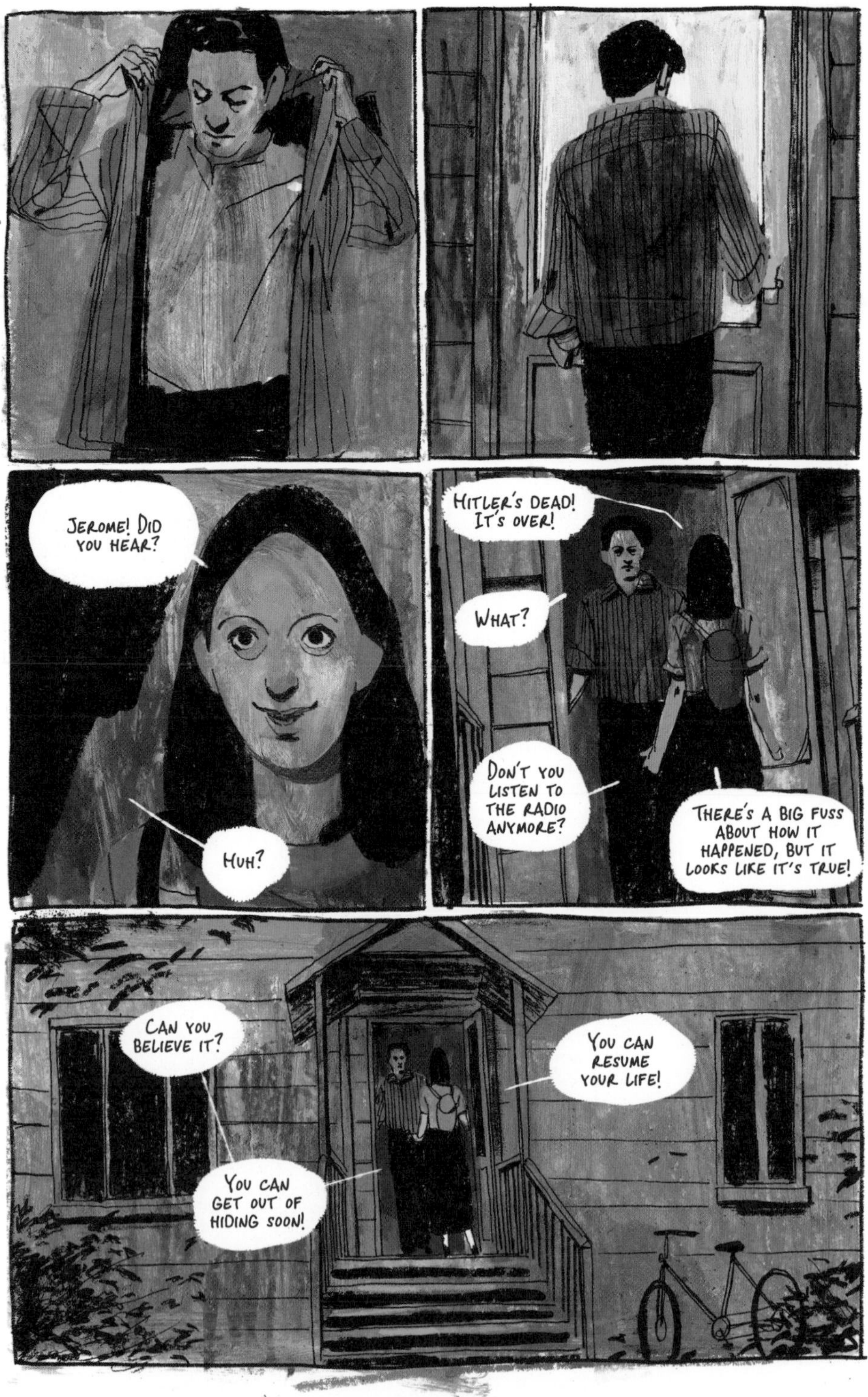

JEROME! DID YOU HEAR?
HUH?
HITLER'S DEAD! IT'S OVER!
WHAT?
DON'T YOU LISTEN TO THE RADIO ANYMORE?
THERE'S A BIG FUSS ABOUT HOW IT HAPPENED, BUT IT LOOKS LIKE IT'S TRUE!
CAN YOU BELIEVE IT?
YOU CAN RESUME YOUR LIFE!
YOU CAN GET OUT OF HIDING SOON!

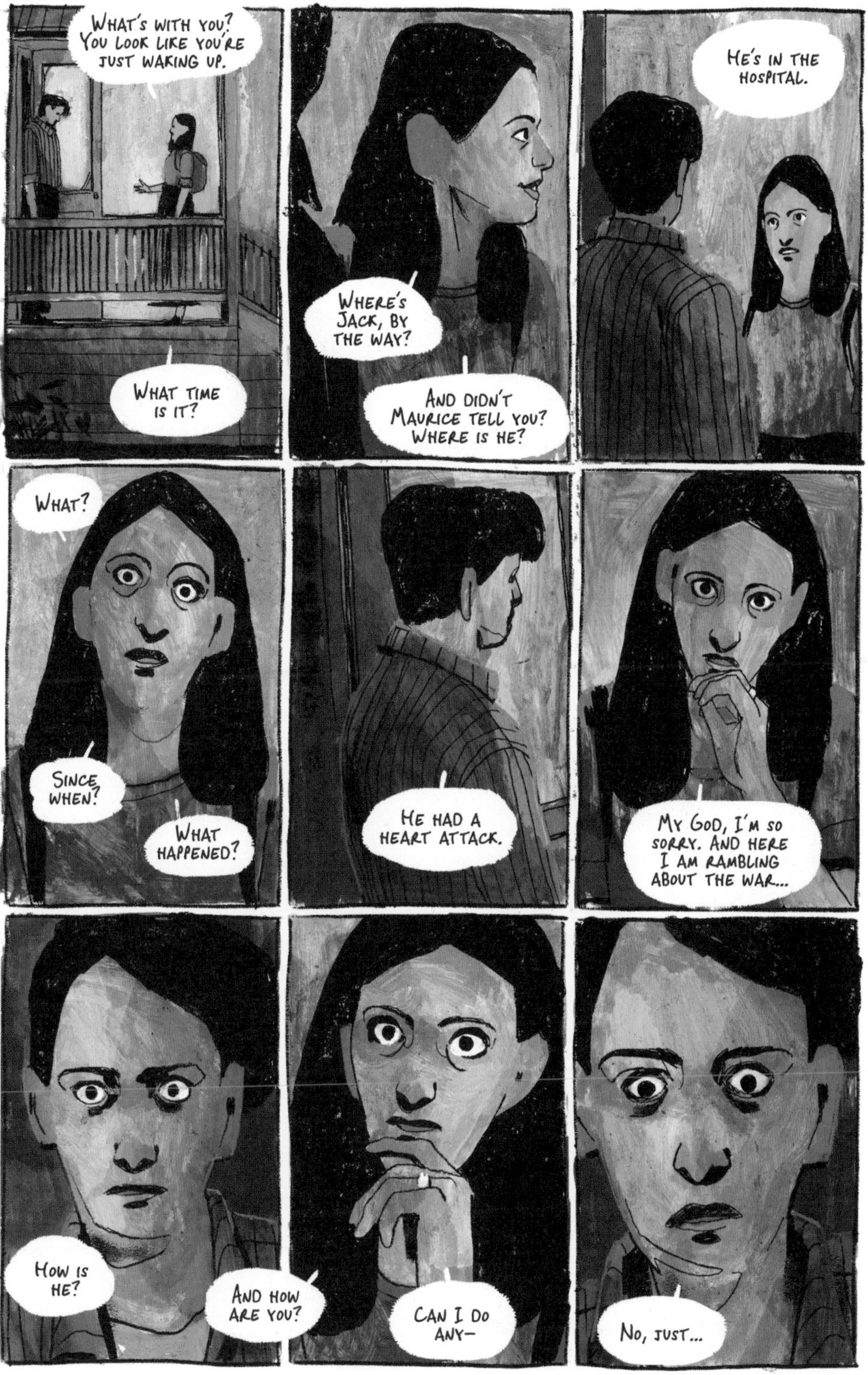
WHAT'S WITH YOU? YOU LOOK LIKE YOU'RE JUST WAKING UP.
WHAT TIME IS IT?
WHERE'S JACK, BY THE WAY?
AND DIDN'T MAURICE TELL YOU? WHERE IS HE?
HE'S IN THE HOSPITAL.
WHAT?
SINCE WHEN?
WHAT HAPPENED?
HE HAD A HEART ATTACK.
MY GOD, I'M SO SORRY. AND HERE I AM RAMBLING ABOUT THE WAR...
HOW IS HE?
AND HOW ARE YOU?
CAN I DO ANY–
NO, JUST...

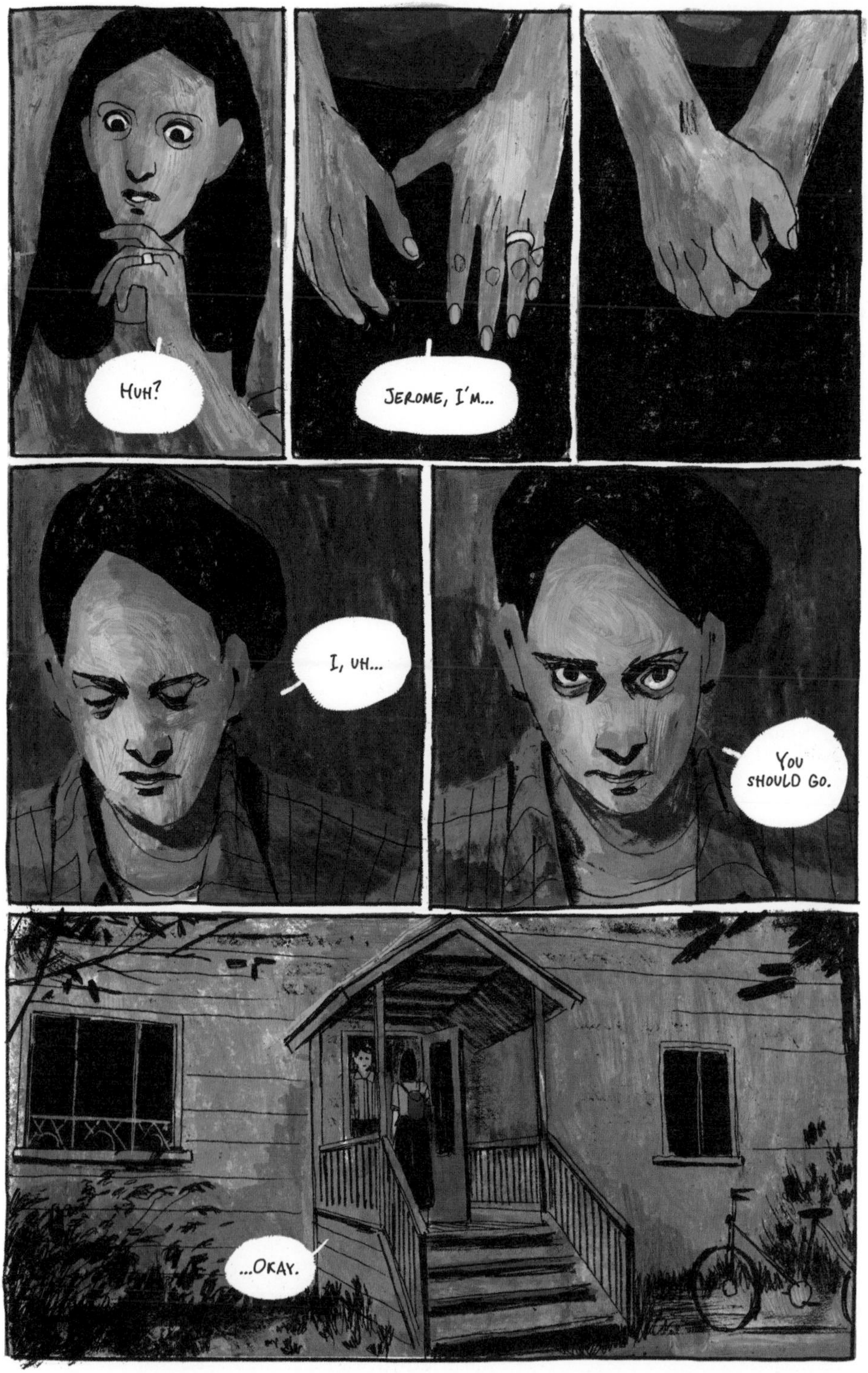
HUH?
JEROME, I'M...
I, UH...
YOU SHOULD GO.
...OKAY.

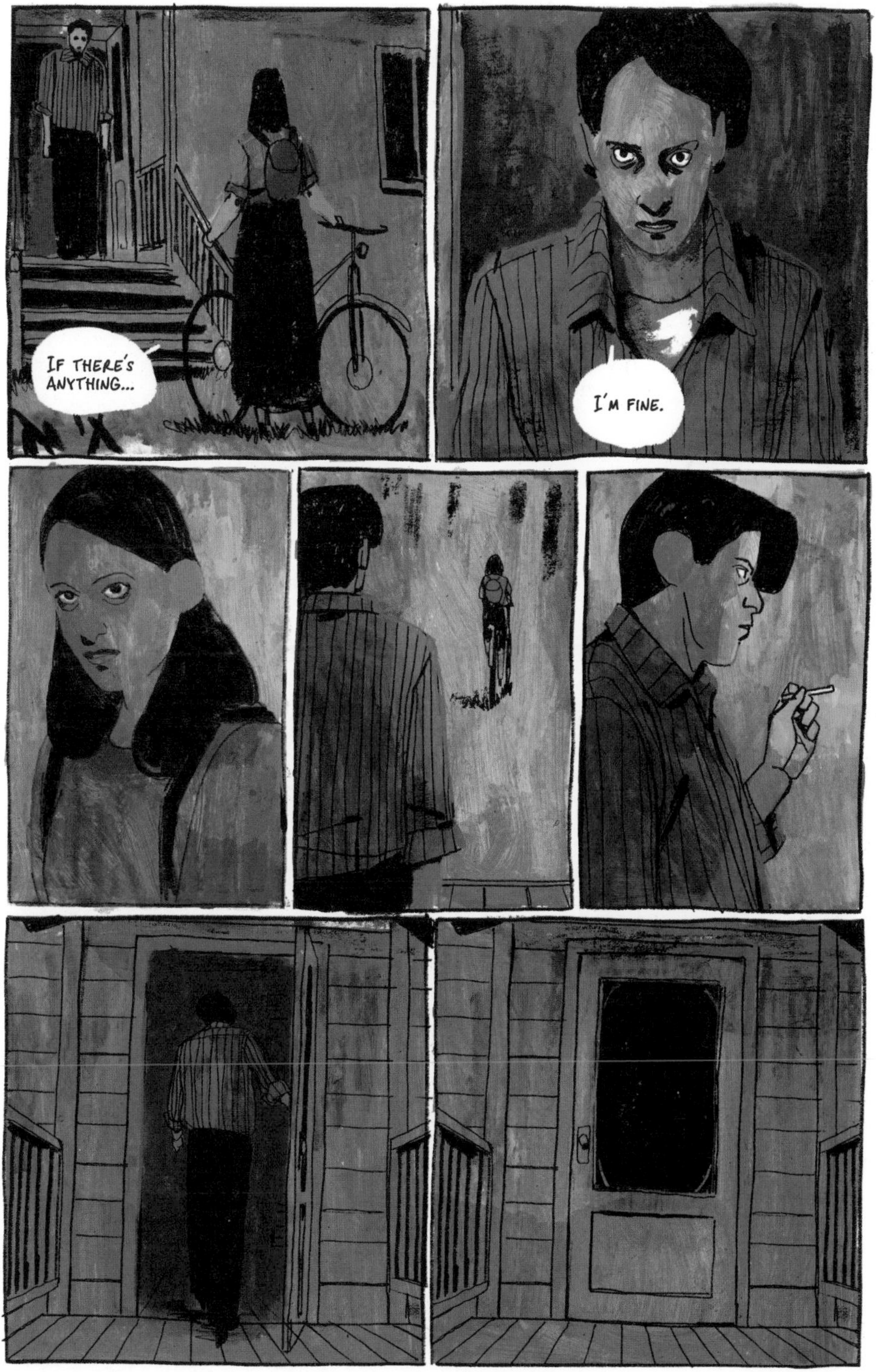
If there's anything...
I'm fine.

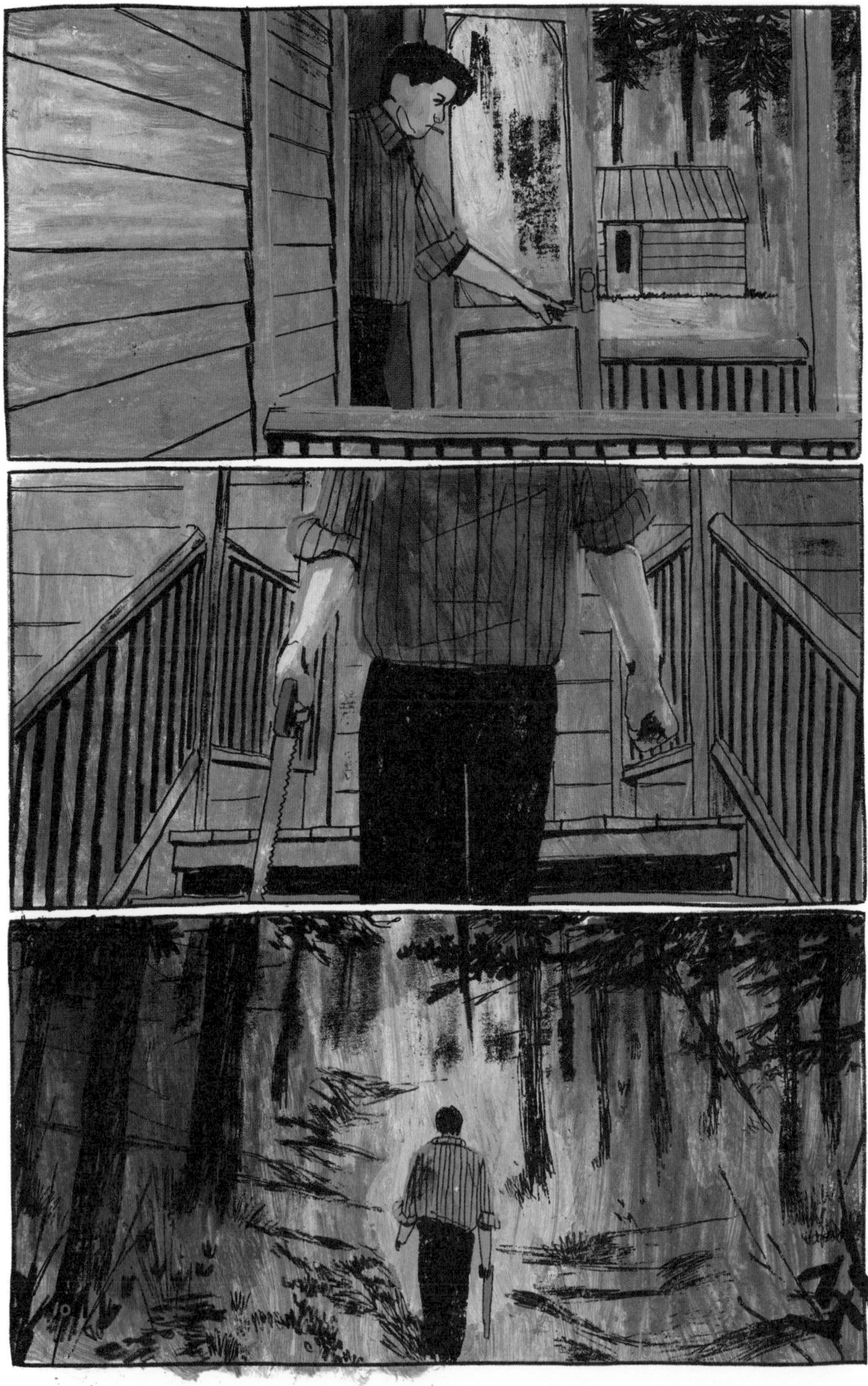

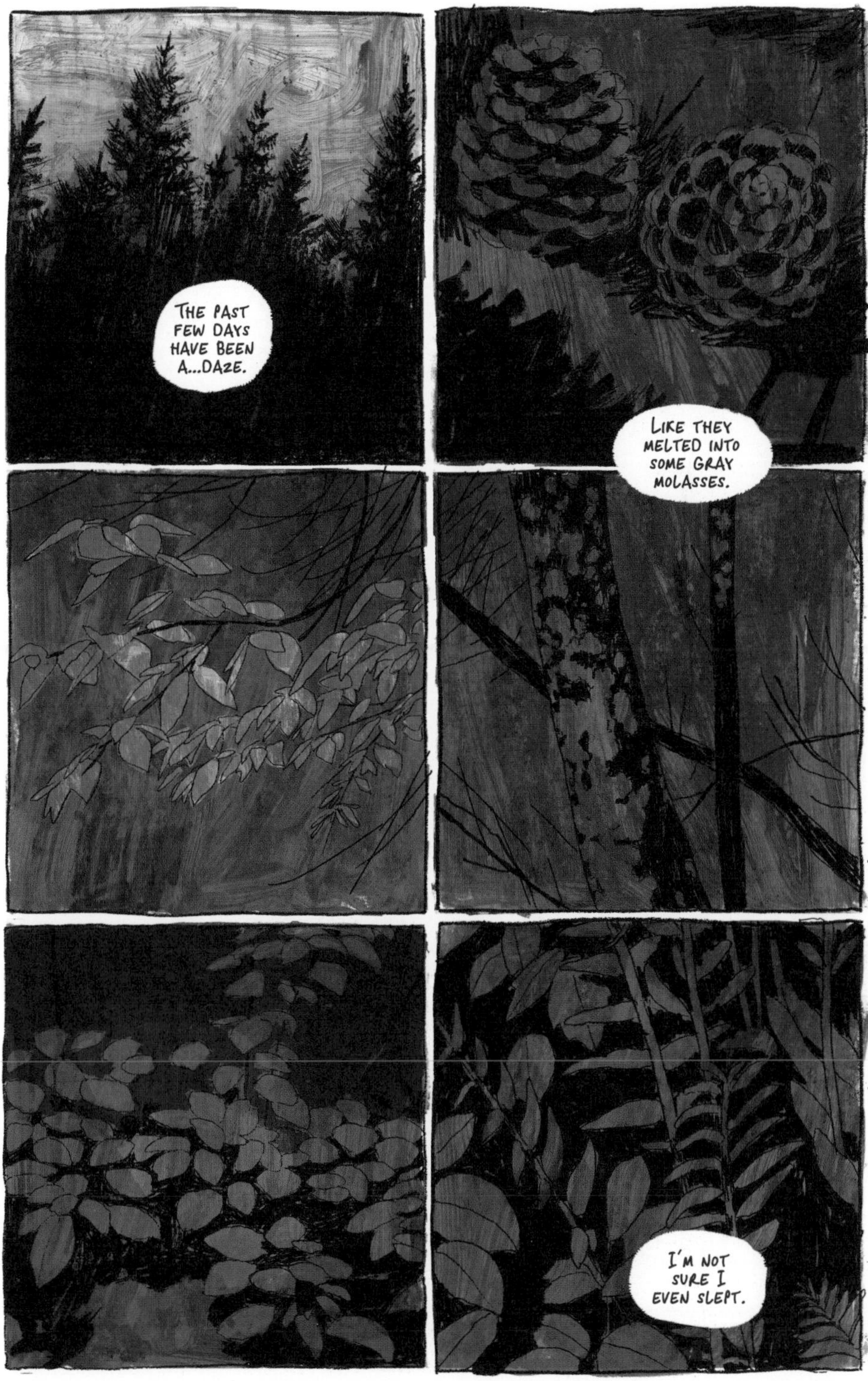
THE PAST FEW DAYS HAVE BEEN A...DAZE.
LIKE THEY MELTED INTO SOME GRAY MOLASSES.
I'M NOT SURE I EVEN SLEPT.

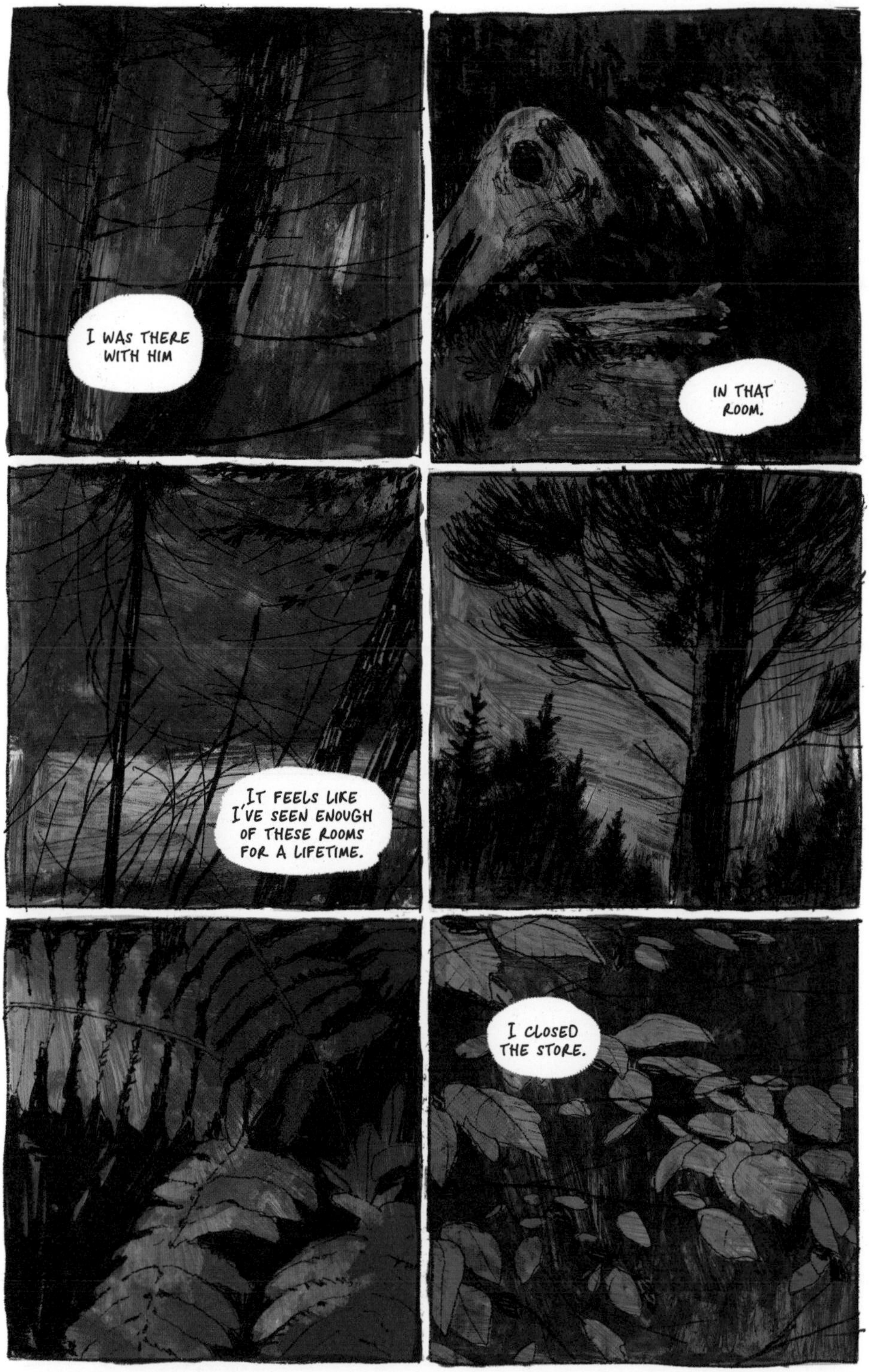
I WAS THERE WITH HIM
IN THAT ROOM.
IT FEELS LIKE I'VE SEEN ENOUGH OF THESE ROOMS FOR A LIFETIME.
I CLOSED THE STORE.

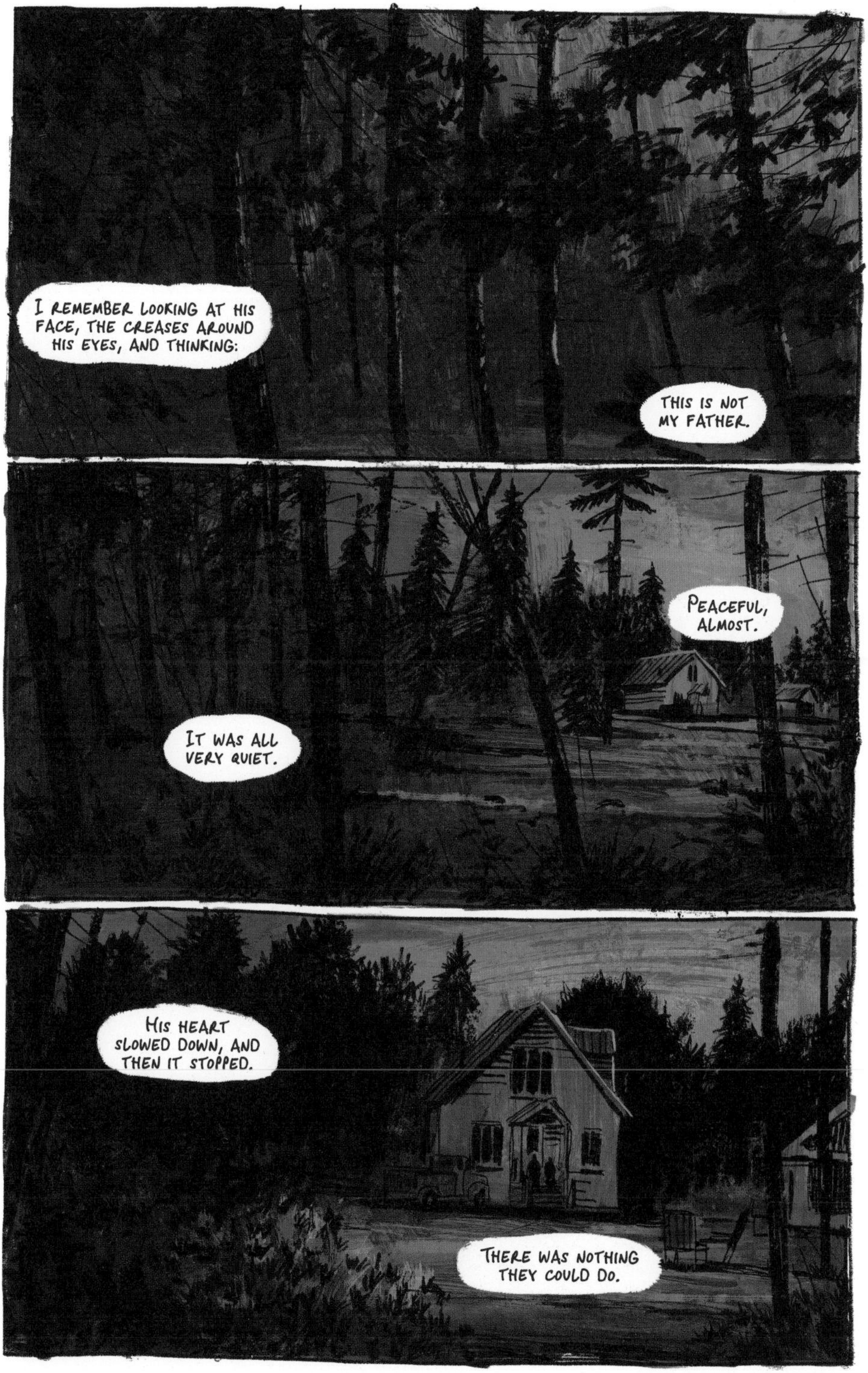
I REMEMBER LOOKING AT HIS FACE, THE CREASES AROUND HIS EYES, AND THINKING:
THIS IS NOT MY FATHER.
PEACEFUL, ALMOST.
IT WAS ALL VERY QUIET.
HIS HEART SLOWED DOWN, AND THEN IT STOPPED.
THERE WAS NOTHING THEY COULD DO.

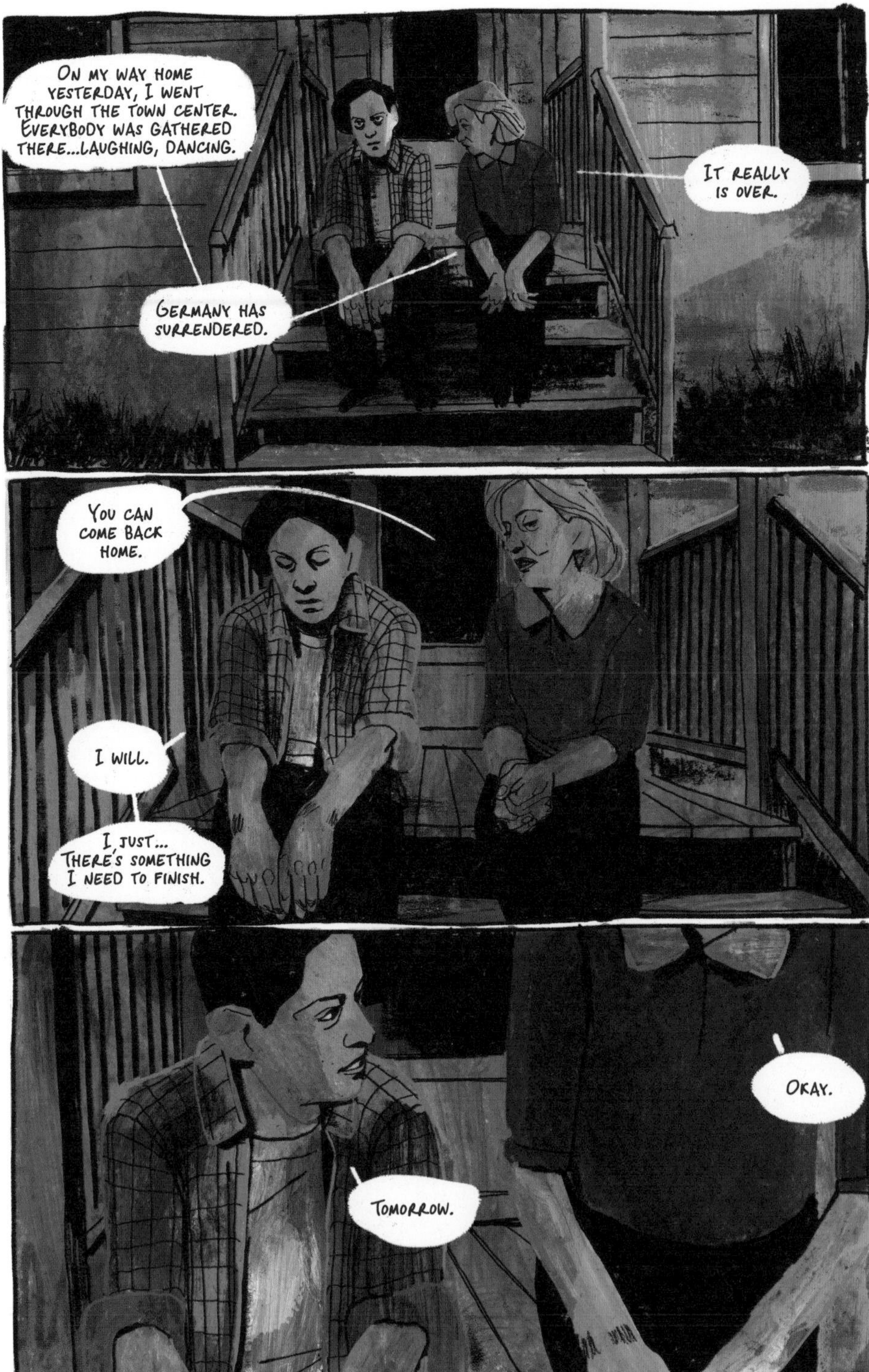
On my way home yesterday, I went through the town center. Everybody was gathered there...laughing, dancing.
It really is over.
Germany has surrendered.
You can come back home.
I will.
I just... There's something I need to finish.
Okay.
Tomorrow.

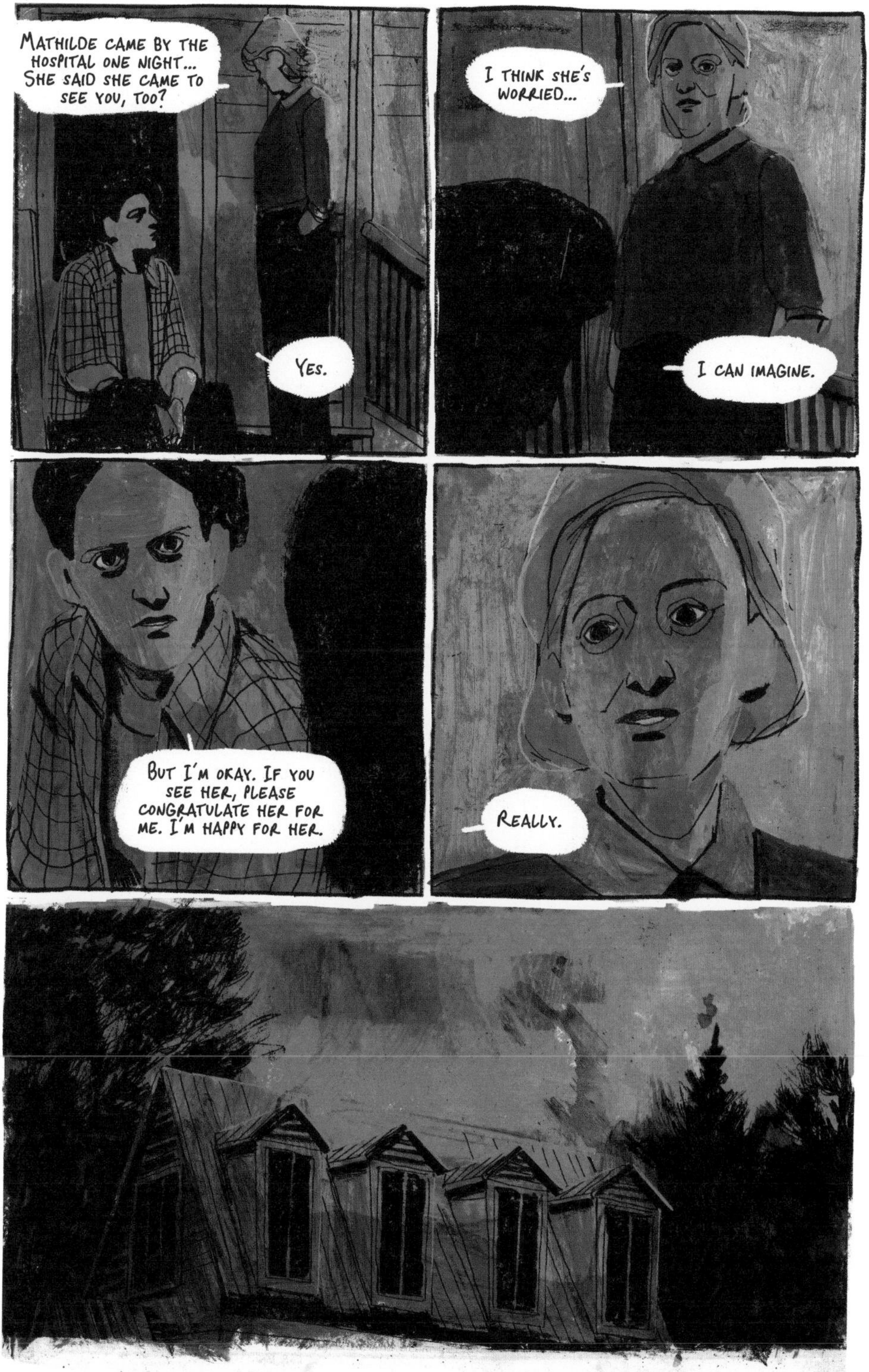
MATHILDE CAME BY THE HOSPITAL ONE NIGHT... SHE SAID SHE CAME TO SEE YOU, TOO?
YES.
I THINK SHE'S WORRIED...
I CAN IMAGINE.
BUT I'M OKAY. IF YOU SEE HER, PLEASE CONGRATULATE HER FOR ME. I'M HAPPY FOR HER.
REALLY.

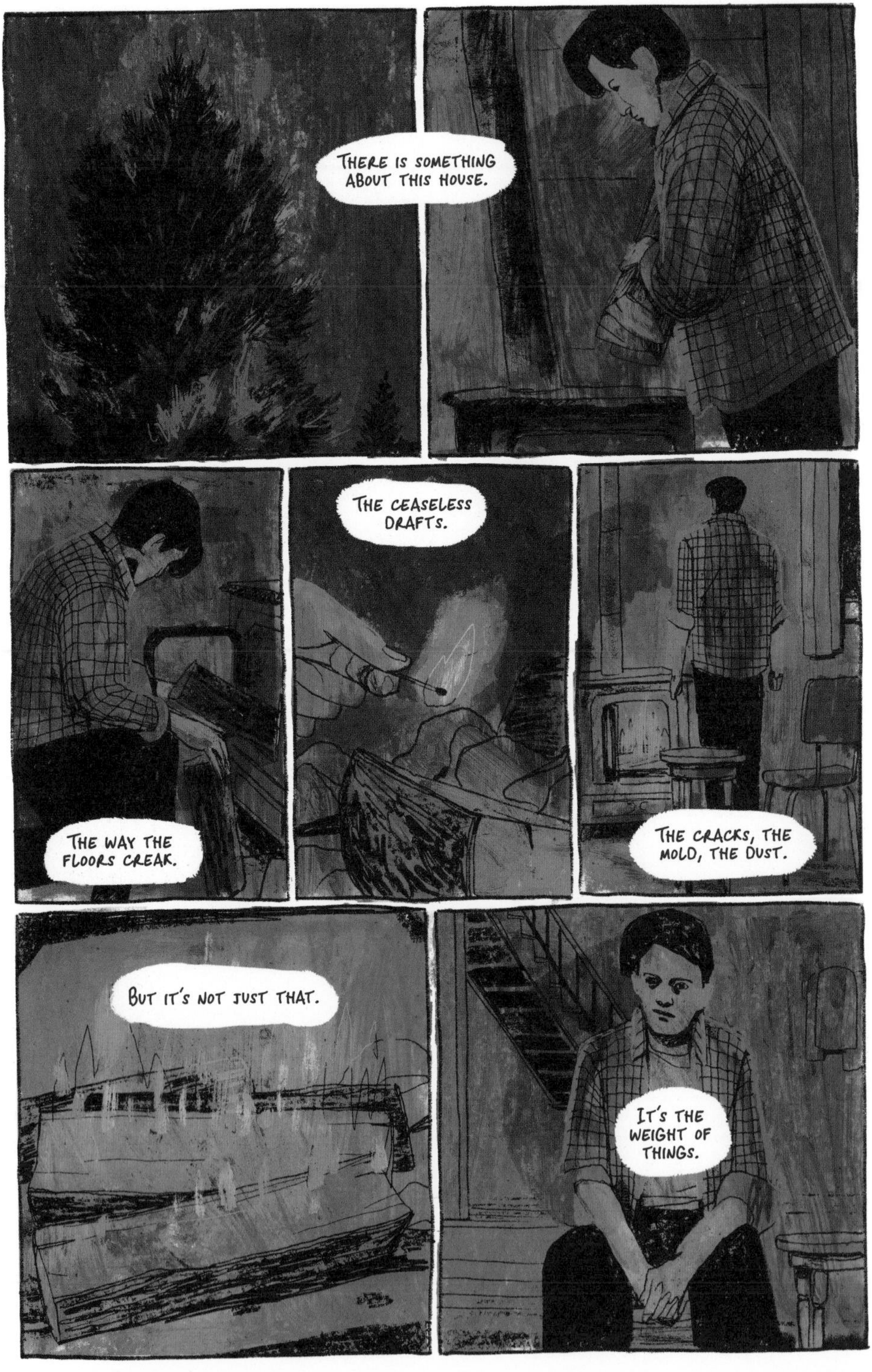
THERE IS SOMETHING ABOUT THIS HOUSE.
THE WAY THE FLOORS CREAK.
THE CEASELESS DRAFTS.
THE CRACKS, THE MOLD, THE DUST.
BUT IT'S NOT JUST THAT.
IT'S THE WEIGHT OF THINGS.

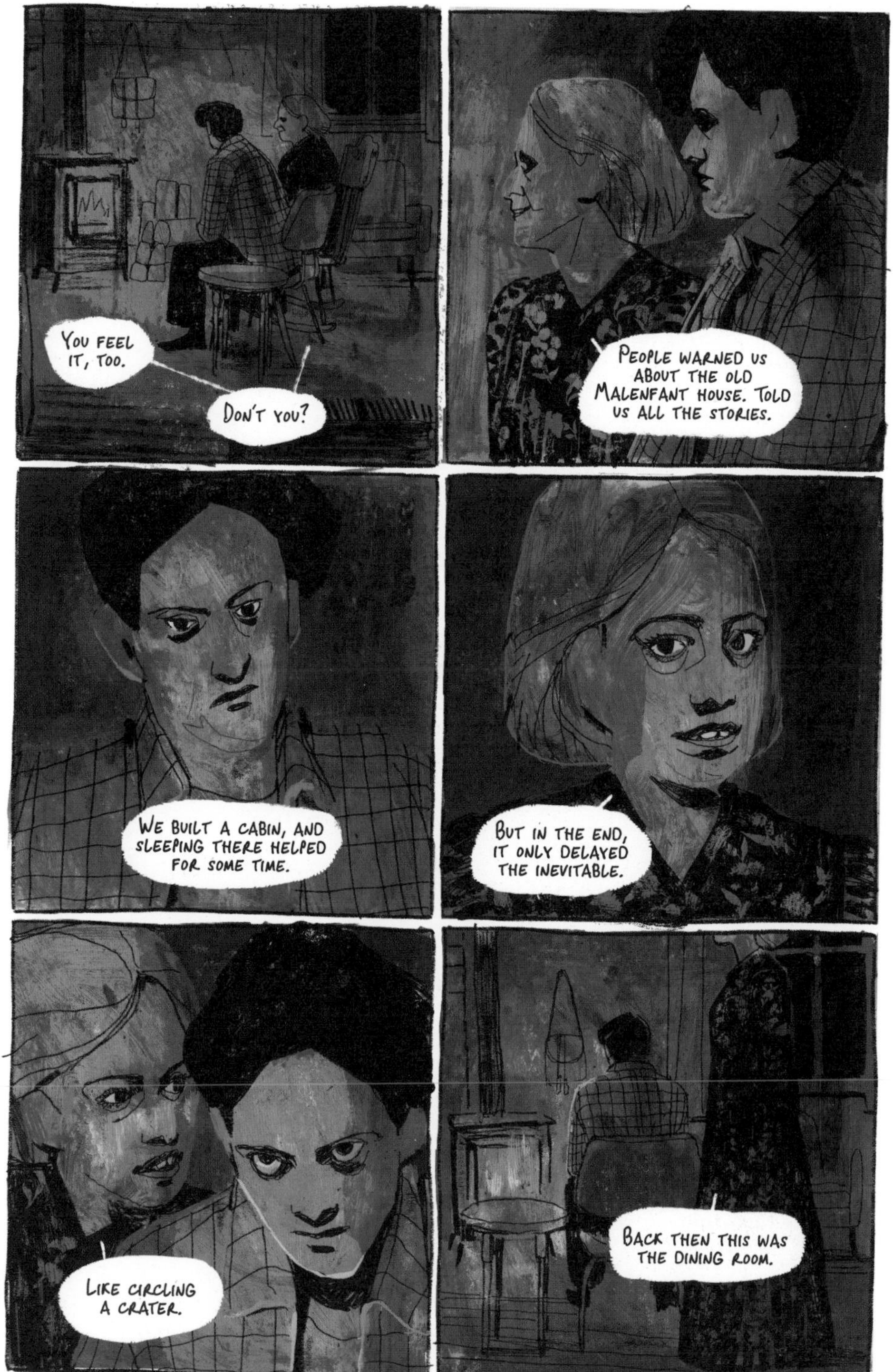
You feel it, too.
Don't you?
People warned us about the old Malenfant house. Told us all the stories.
We built a cabin, and sleeping there helped for some time.
But in the end, it only delayed the inevitable.
Like circling a crater.
Back then this was the dining room.

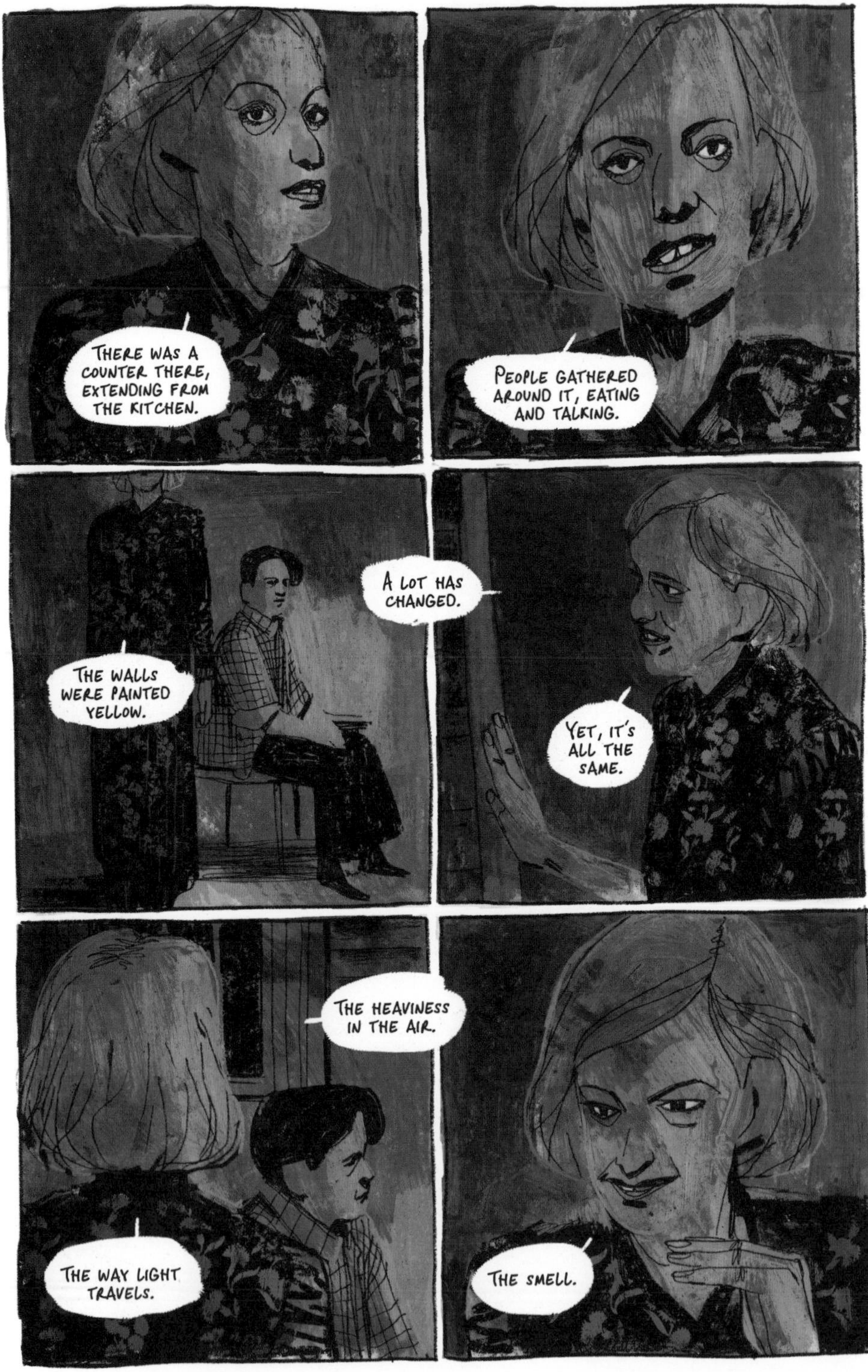
THERE WAS A COUNTER THERE, EXTENDING FROM THE KITCHEN.
PEOPLE GATHERED AROUND IT, EATING AND TALKING.
THE WALLS WERE PAINTED YELLOW.
A LOT HAS CHANGED.
YET, IT'S ALL THE SAME.
THE HEAVINESS IN THE AIR.
THE WAY LIGHT TRAVELS.
THE SMELL.

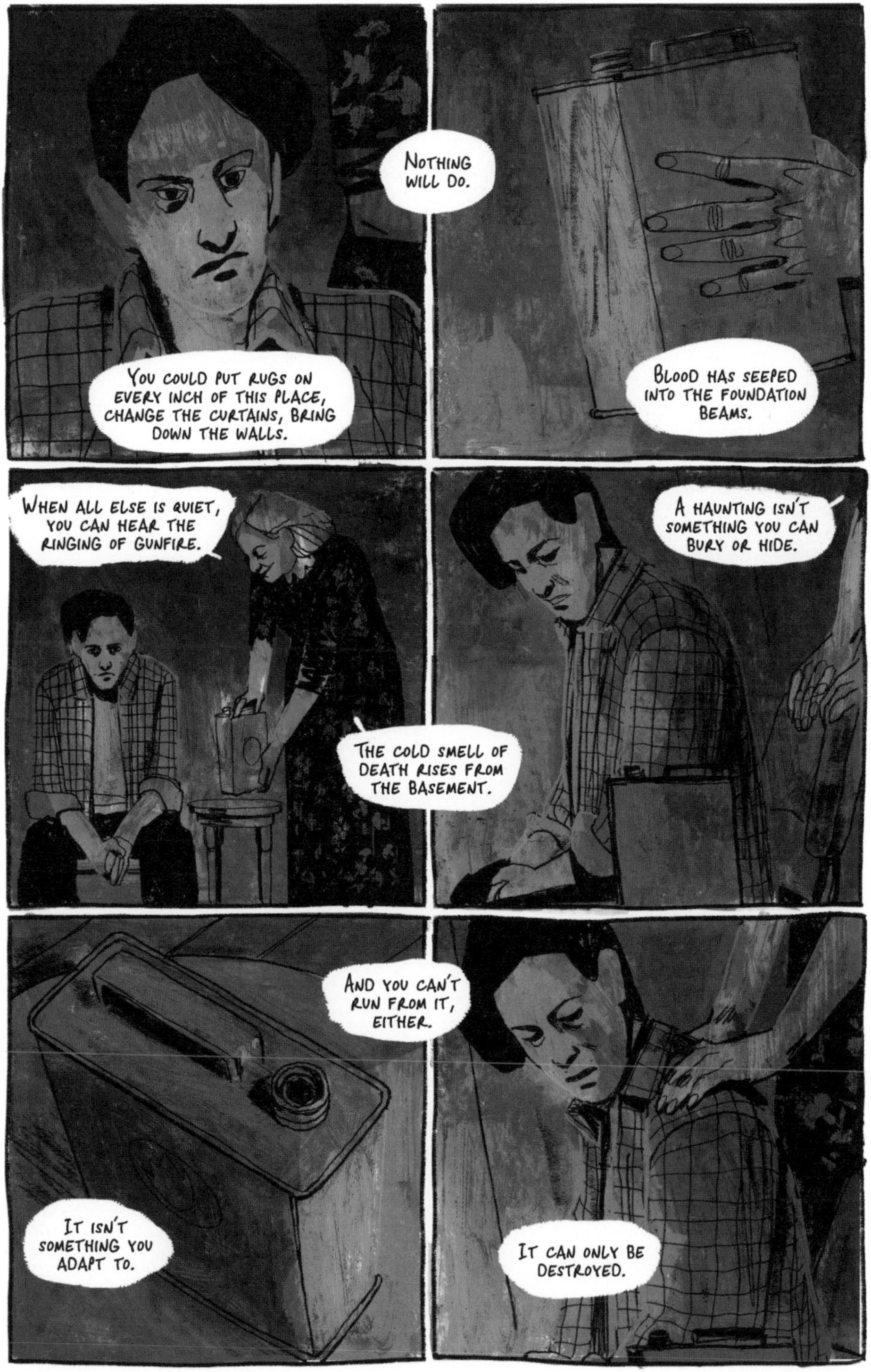
Nothing will do.
You could put rugs on every inch of this place, change the curtains, bring down the walls.
Blood has seeped into the foundation beams.
When all else is quiet, you can hear the ringing of gunfire.
The cold smell of death rises from the basement.
A haunting isn't something you can bury or hide.
And you can't run from it, either.
It isn't something you adapt to.
It can only be destroyed.

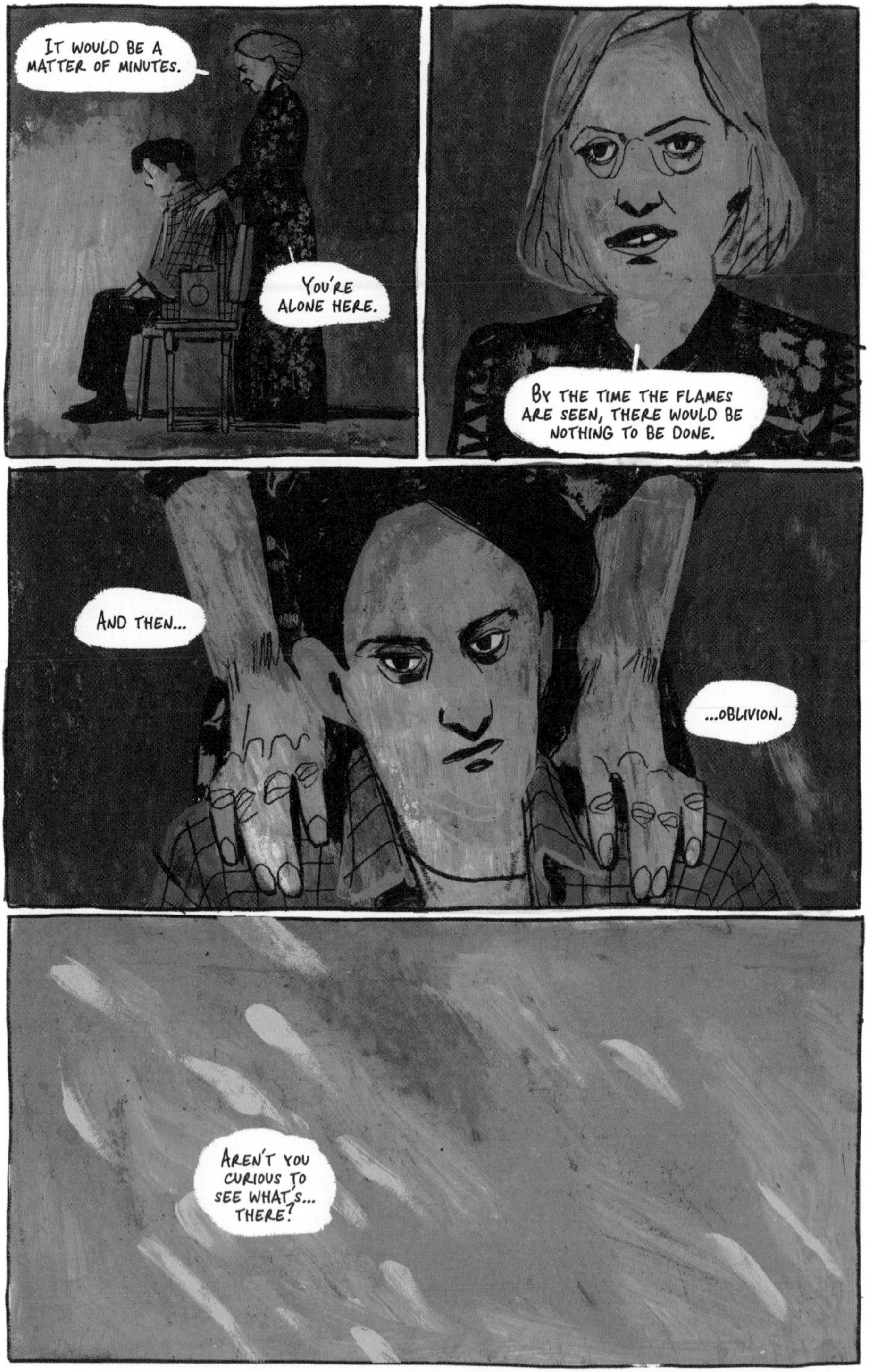
It would be a matter of minutes.
You're alone here.
By the time the flames are seen, there would be nothing to be done.
And then...
...oblivion.
Aren't you curious to see what's... there?

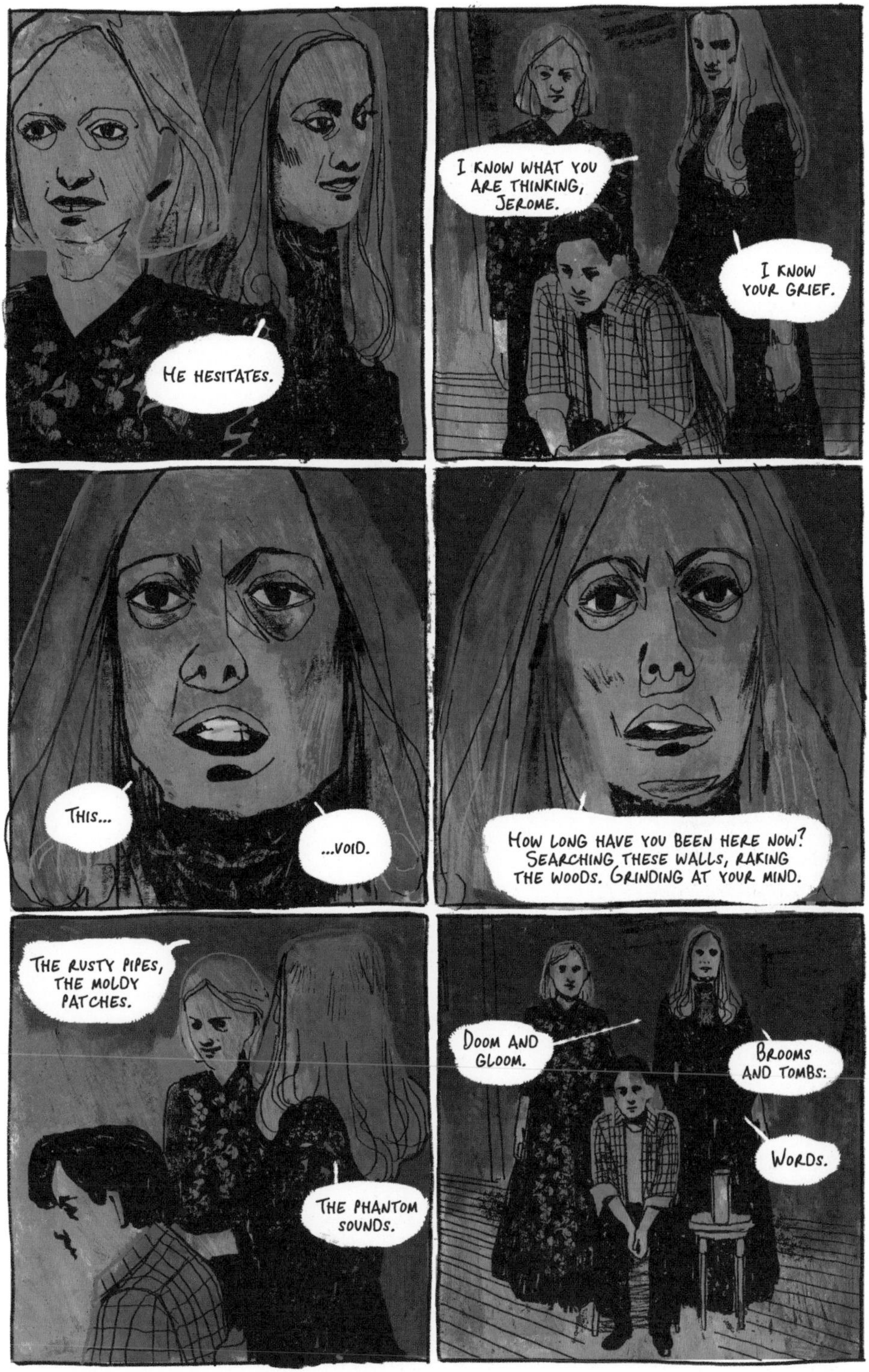
He hesitates.
I know what you are thinking, Jerome.
I know your grief.
This...
...void.
How long have you been here now? Searching these walls, raking the woods. Grinding at your mind.
The rusty pipes, the moldy patches.
The phantom sounds.
Doom and gloom.
Brooms and tombs:
Words.

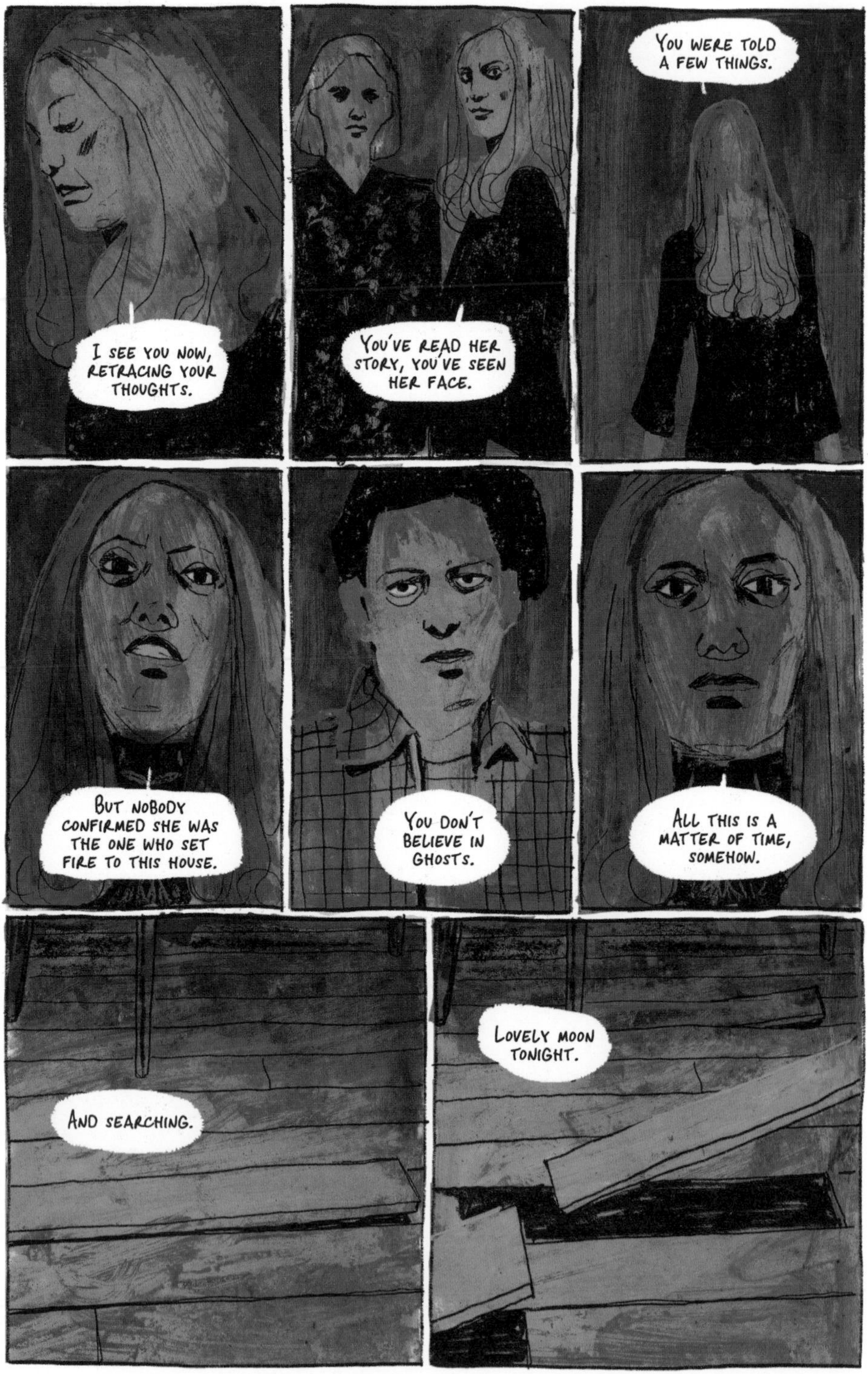
I see you now, retracing your thoughts.
You've read her story, you've seen her face.
You were told a few things.
But nobody confirmed she was the one who set fire to this house.
You don't believe in ghosts.
All this is a matter of time, somehow.
And searching.
Lovely moon tonight.

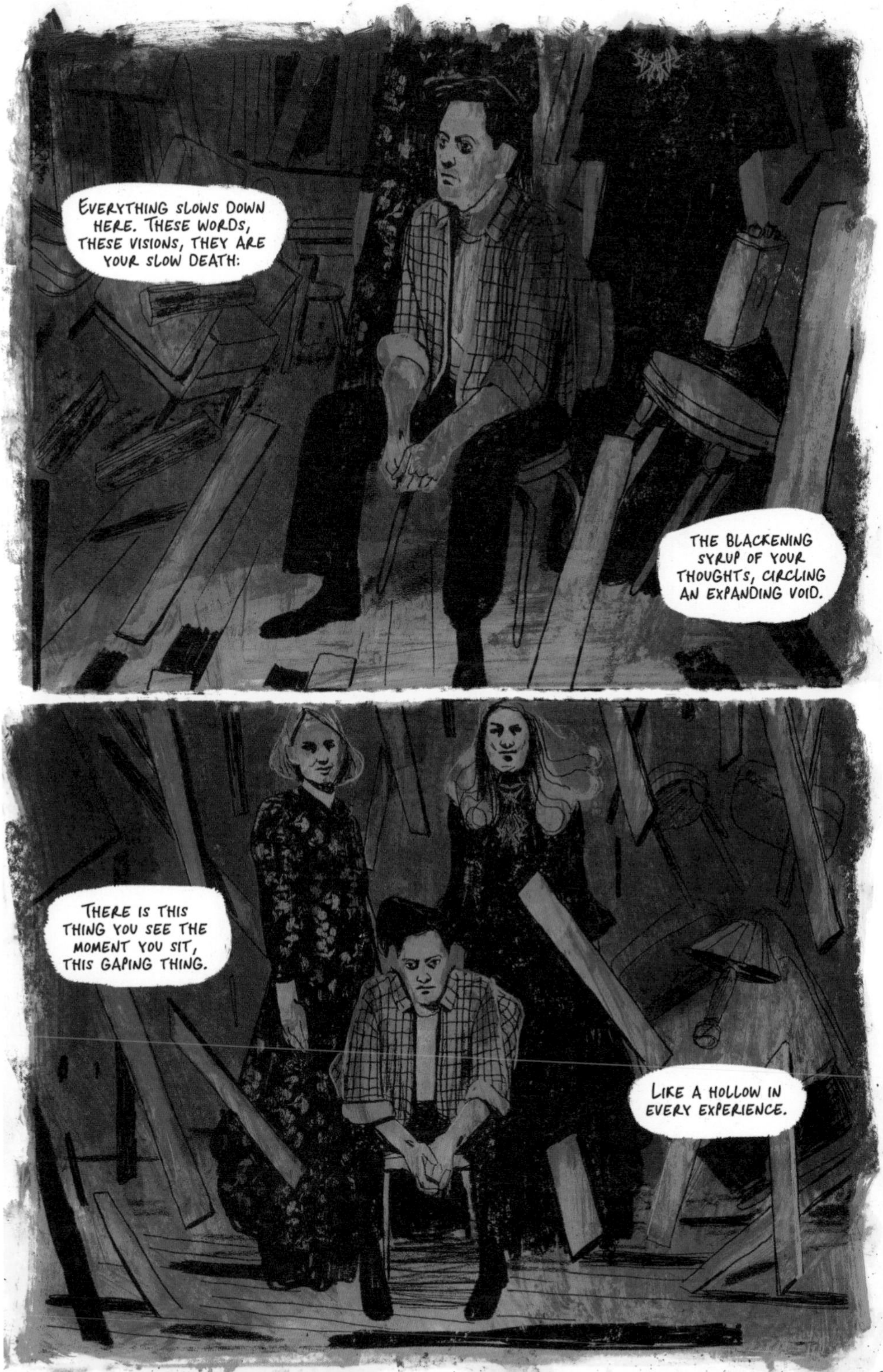
EVERYTHING SLOWS DOWN HERE. THESE WORDS, THESE VISIONS, THEY ARE YOUR SLOW DEATH:
THE BLACKENING SYRUP OF YOUR THOUGHTS, CIRCLING AN EXPANDING VOID.
THERE IS THIS THING YOU SEE THE MOMENT YOU SIT, THIS GAPING THING.
LIKE A HOLLOW IN EVERY EXPERIENCE.

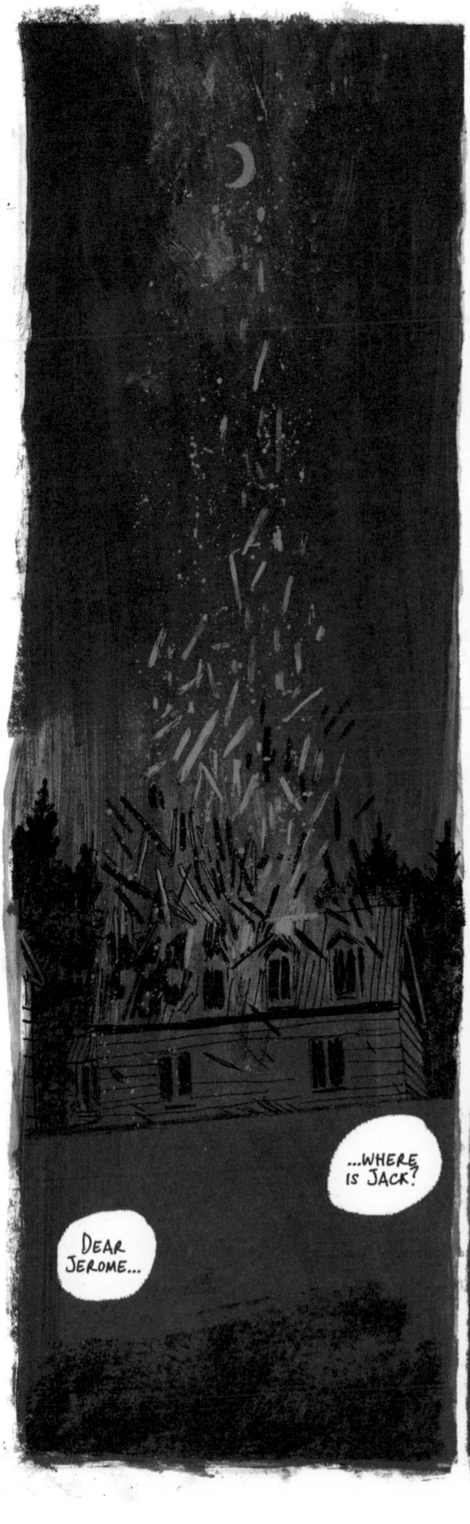
...WHERE IS JACK?
DEAR JEROME...
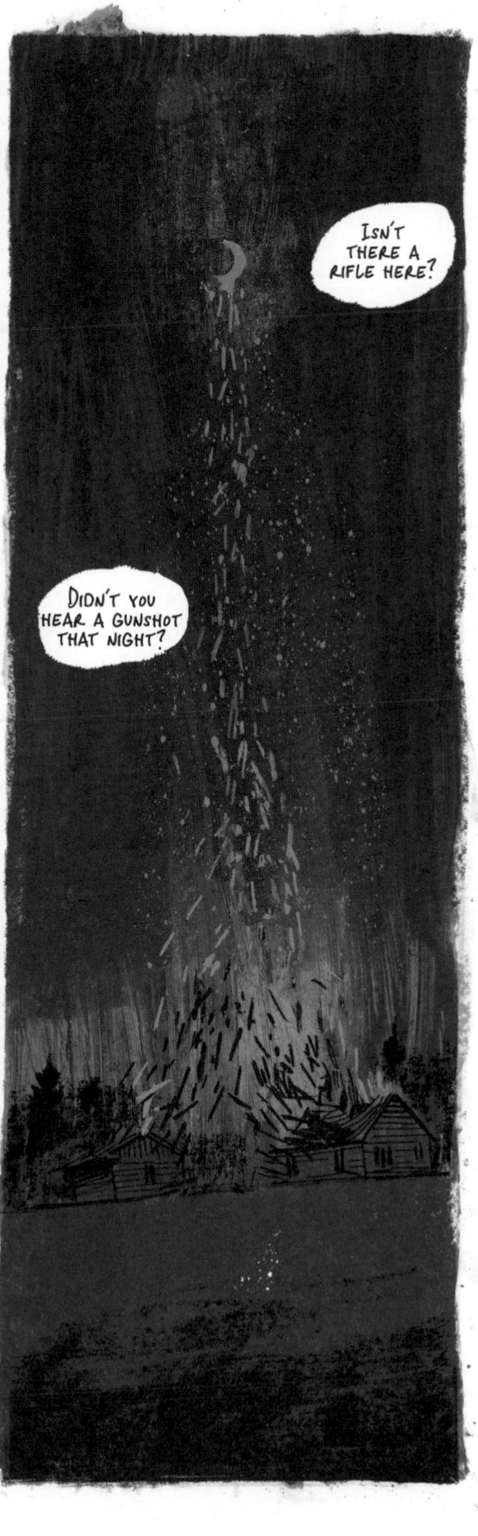
ISN'T THERE A RIFLE HERE?
DIDN'T YOU HEAR A GUNSHOT THAT NIGHT?

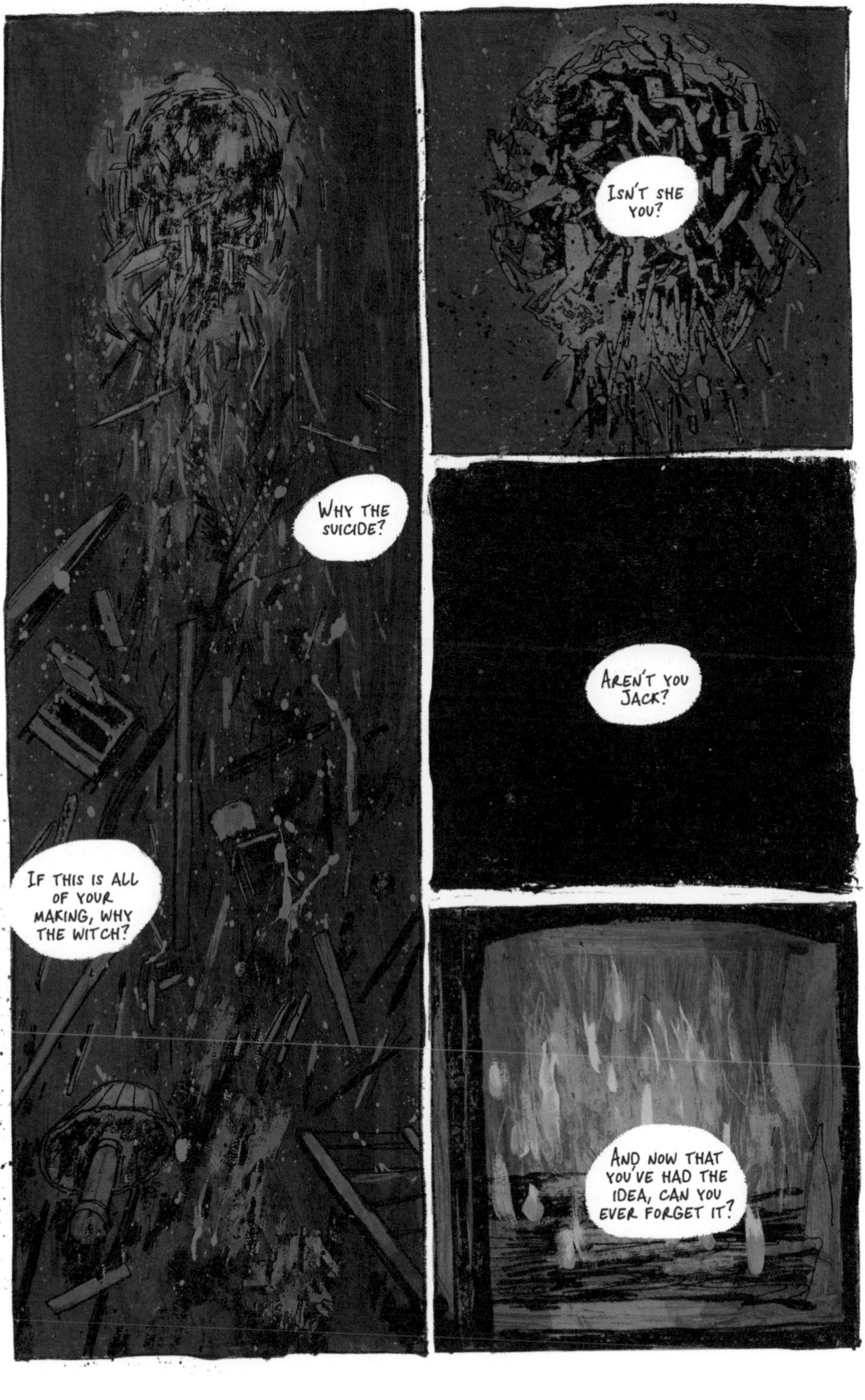
Why the suicide?
If this is all of your making, why the witch?
Isn't she you?
Aren't you Jack?
And now that you've had the idea, can you ever forget it?

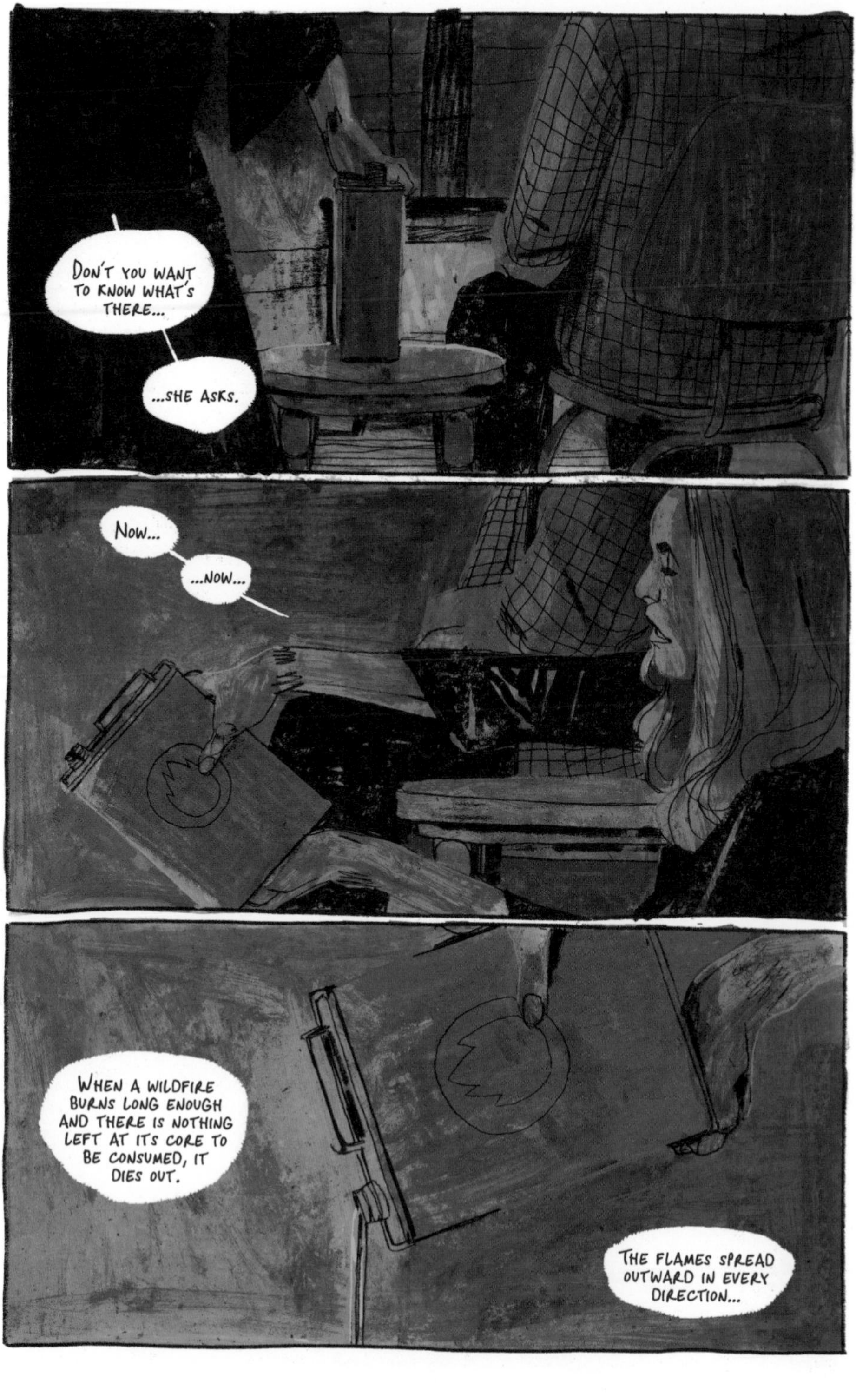
DON'T YOU WANT TO KNOW WHAT'S THERE...
...SHE ASKS.
NOW...
...NOW...
WHEN A WILDFIRE BURNS LONG ENOUGH AND THERE IS NOTHING LEFT AT ITS CORE TO BE CONSUMED, IT DIES OUT.
THE FLAMES SPREAD OUTWARD IN EVERY DIRECTION...

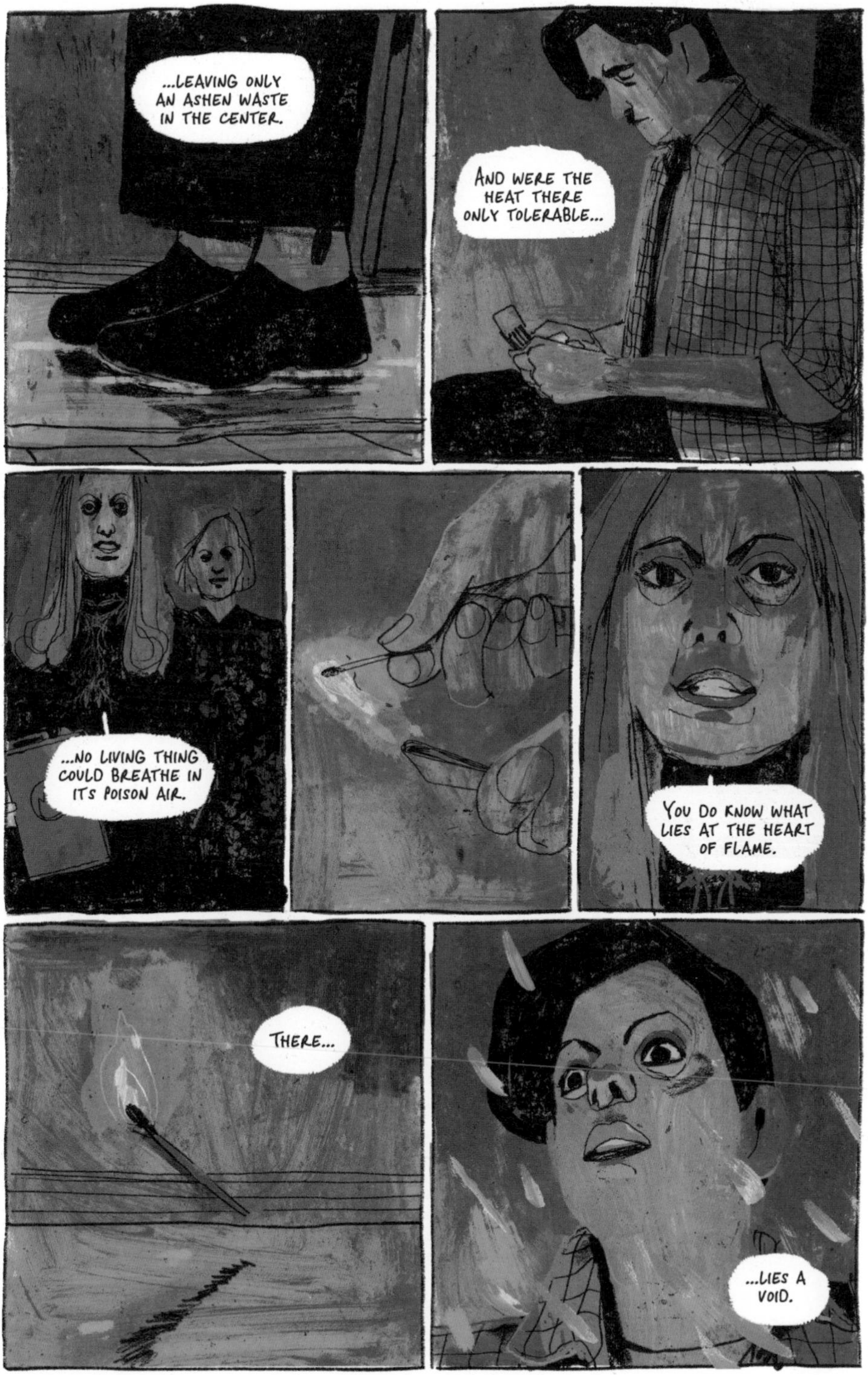
...LEAVING ONLY AN ASHEN WASTE IN THE CENTER.
AND WERE THE HEAT THERE ONLY TOLERABLE...
...NO LIVING THING COULD BREATHE IN ITS POISON AIR.
YOU DO KNOW WHAT LIES AT THE HEART OF FLAME.
THERE...
...LIES A VOID.

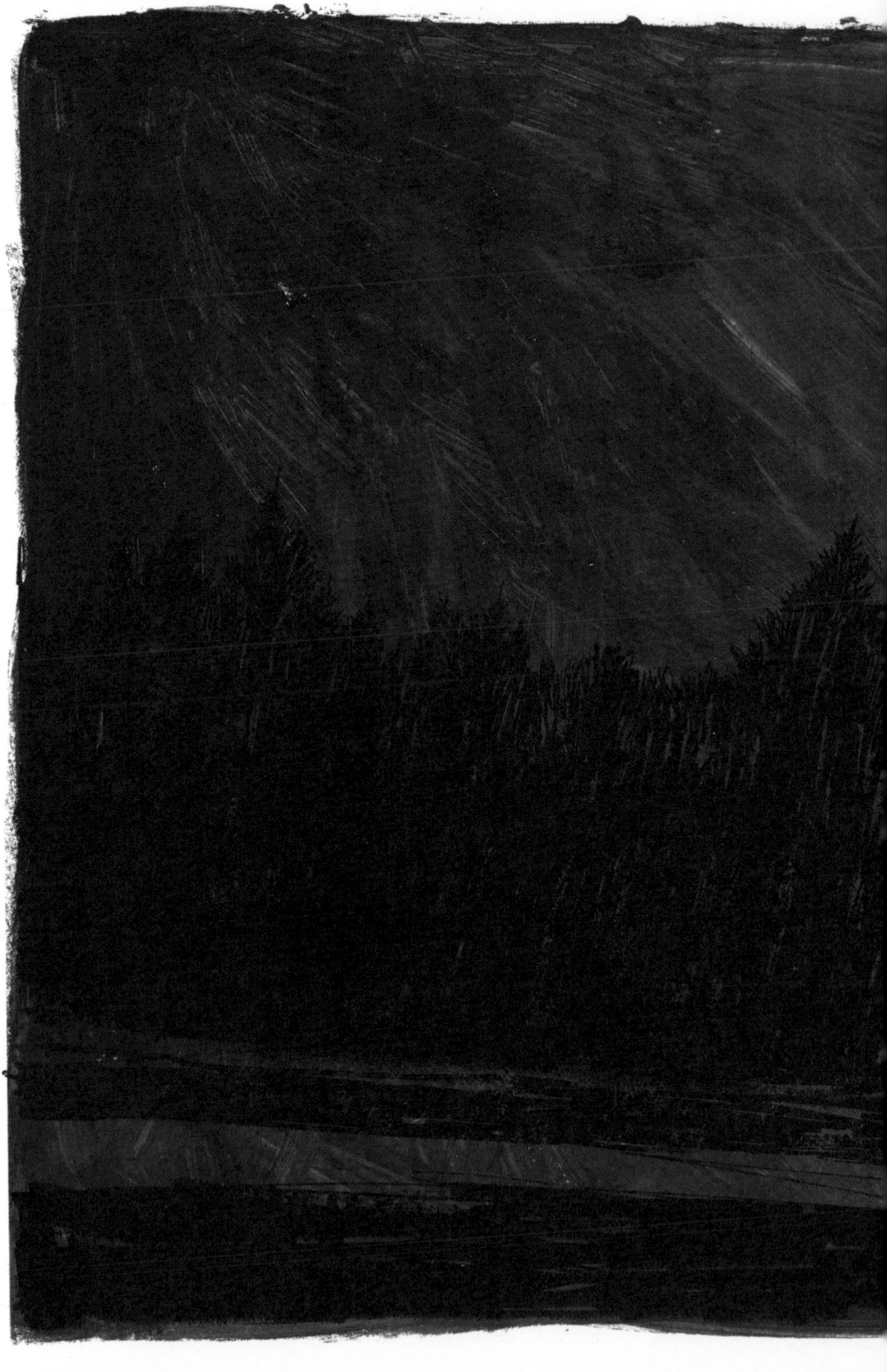

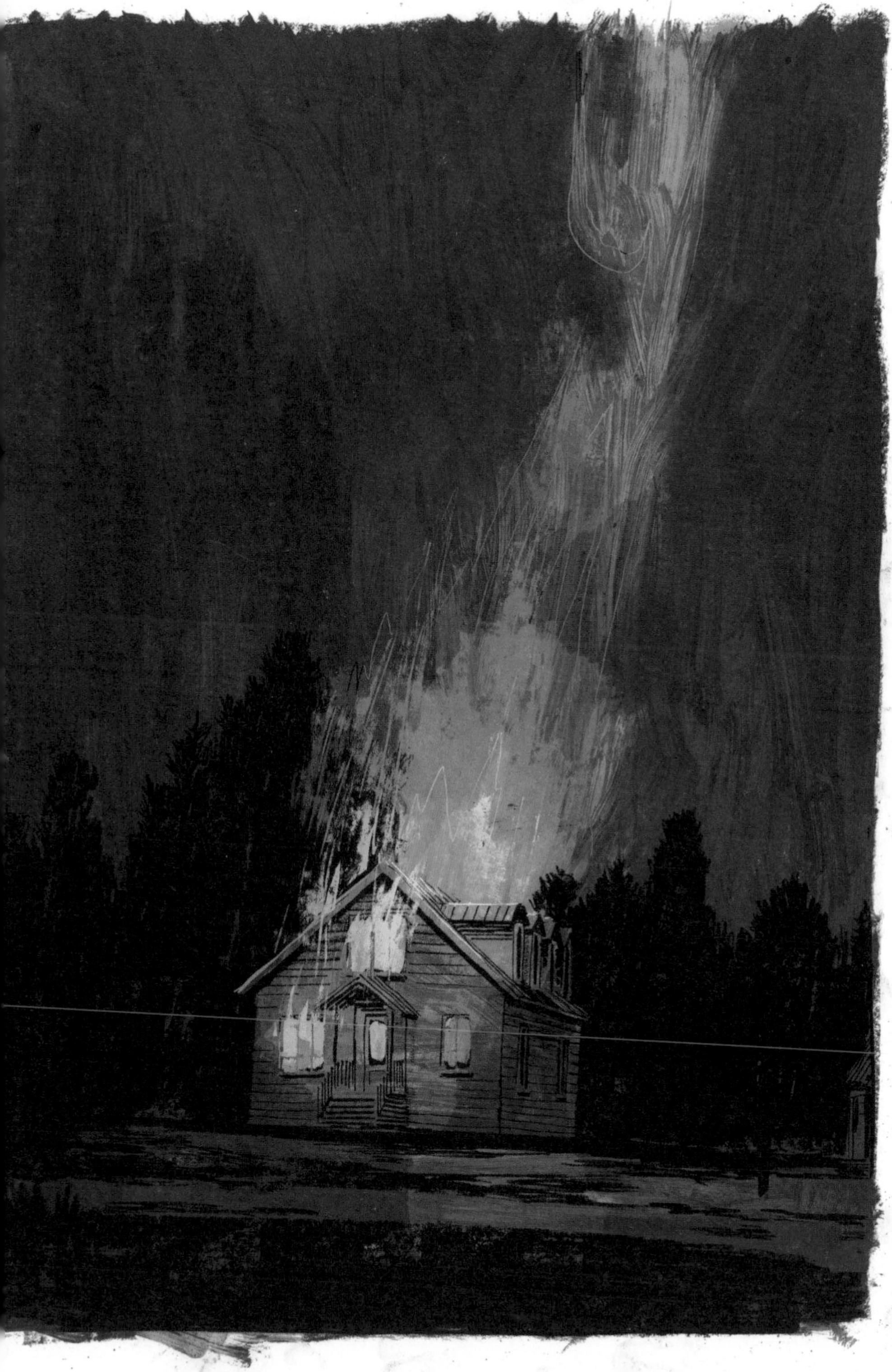

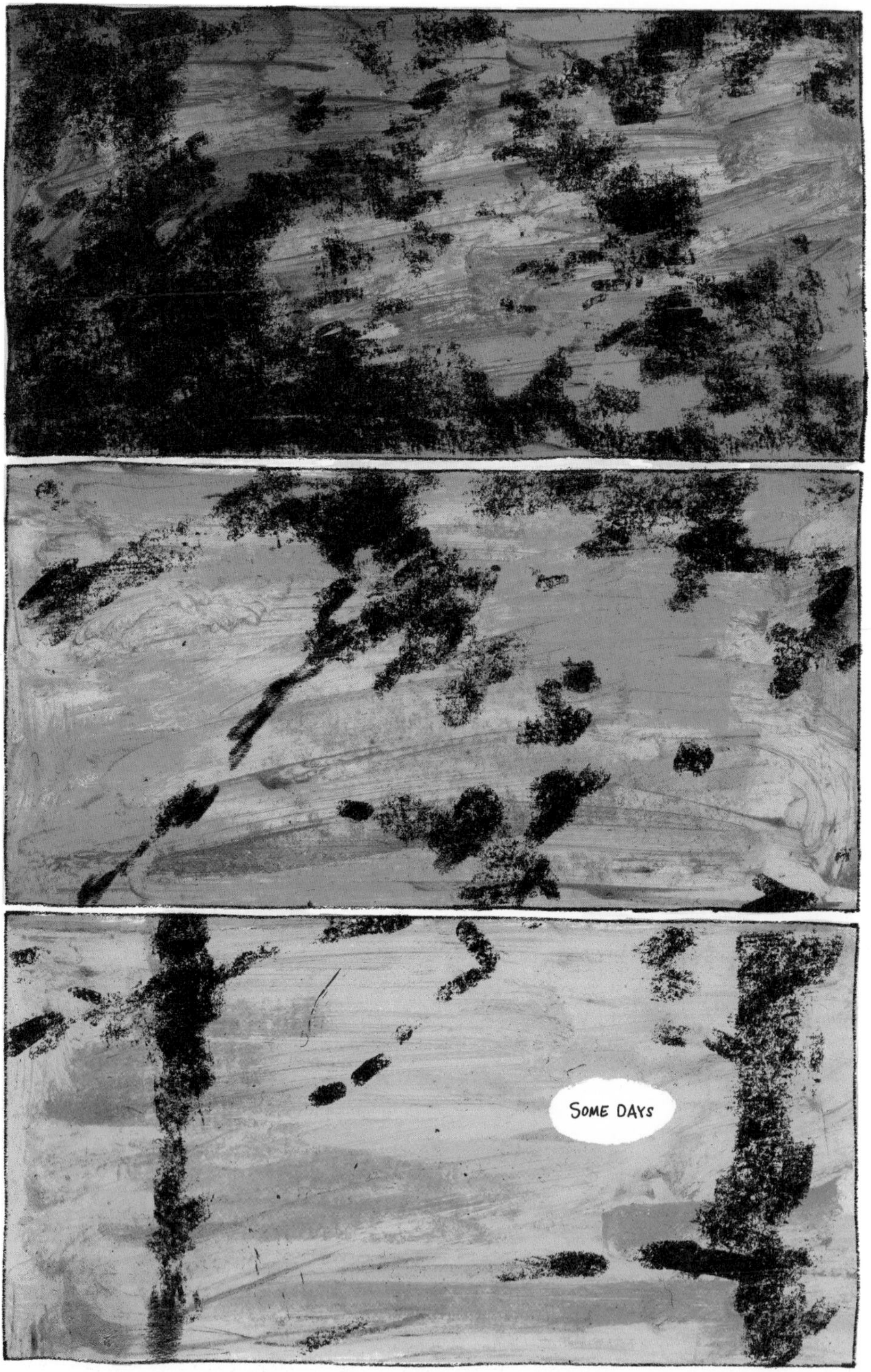
SOME DAYS

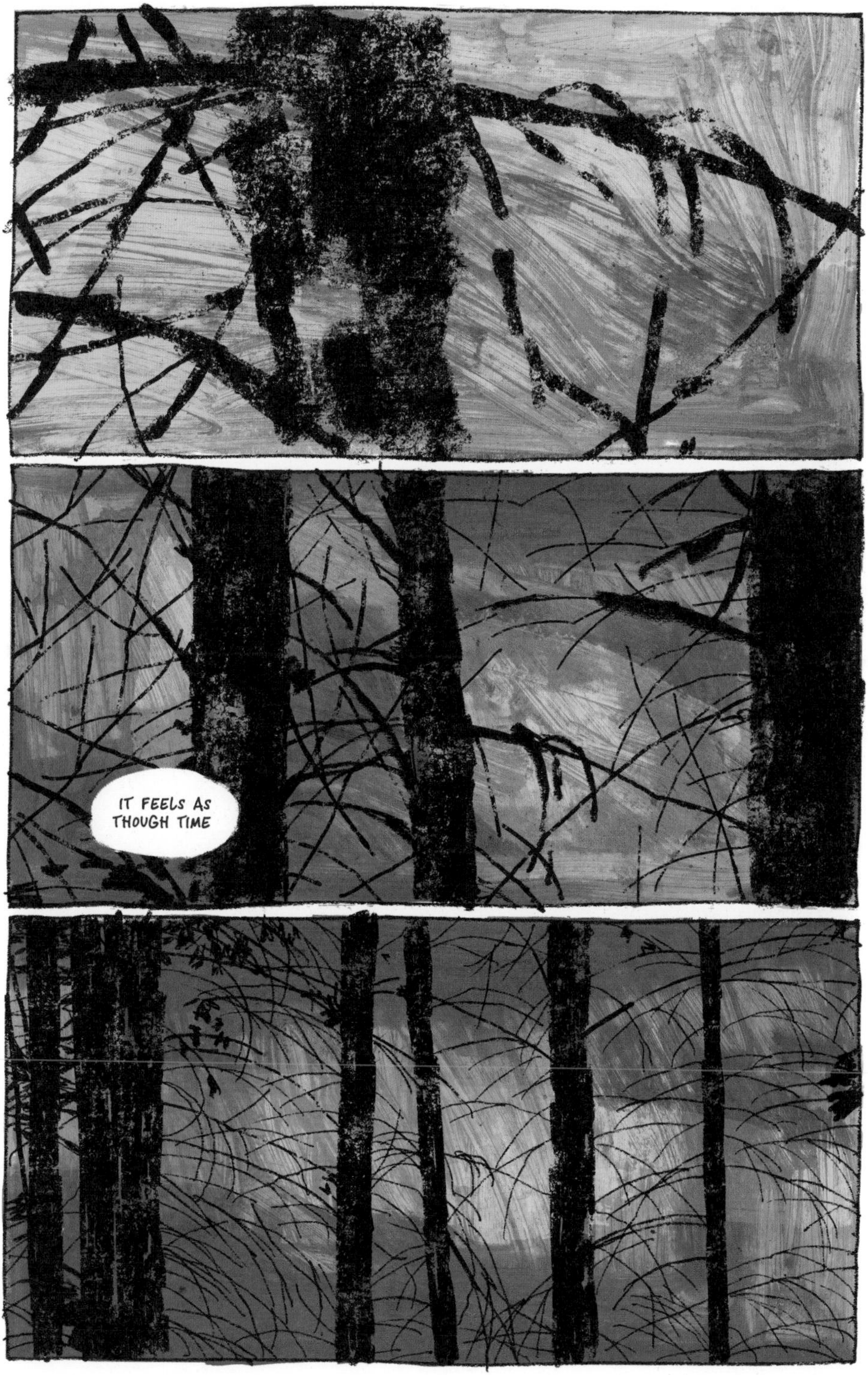
IT FEELS AS THOUGH TIME

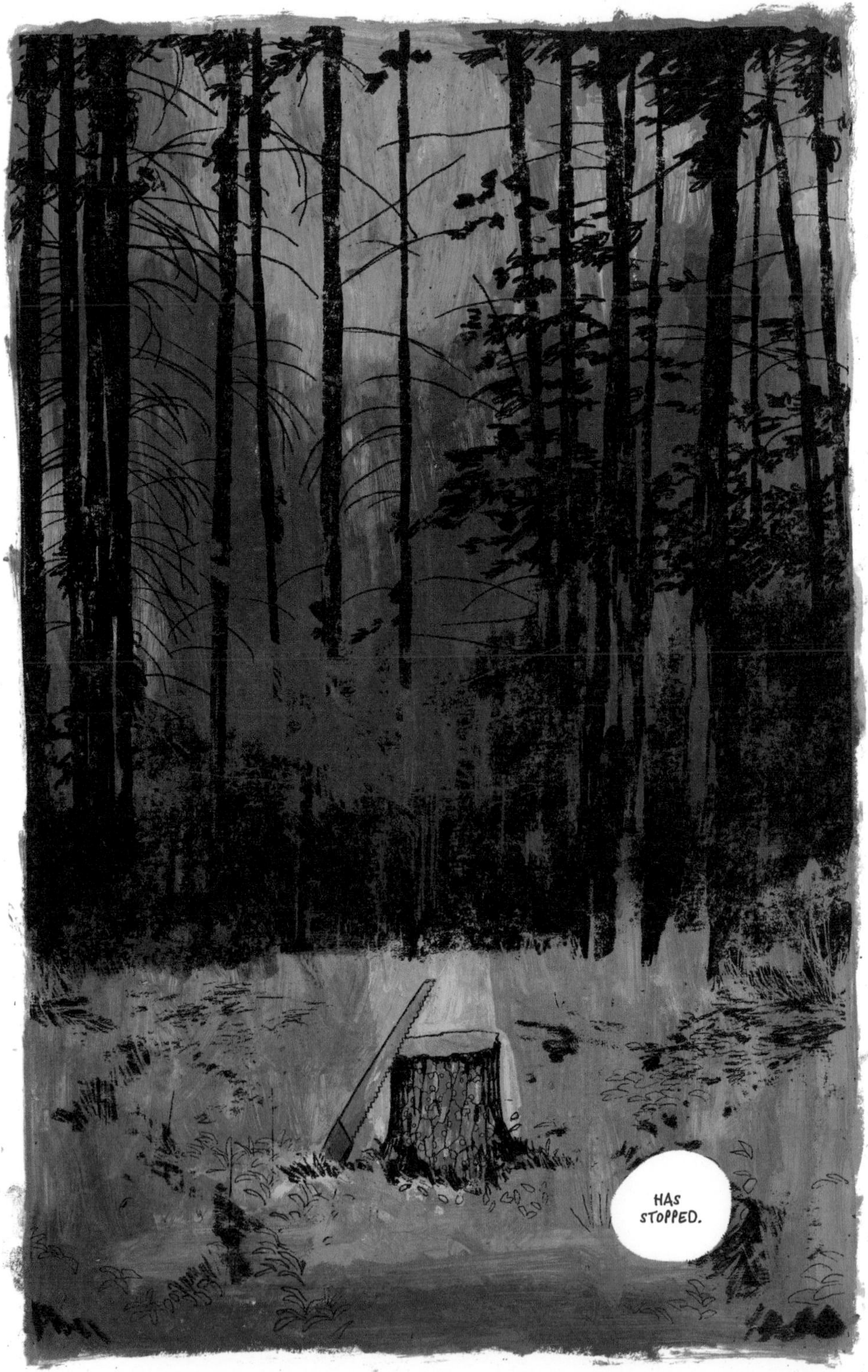
HAS
STOPPED.

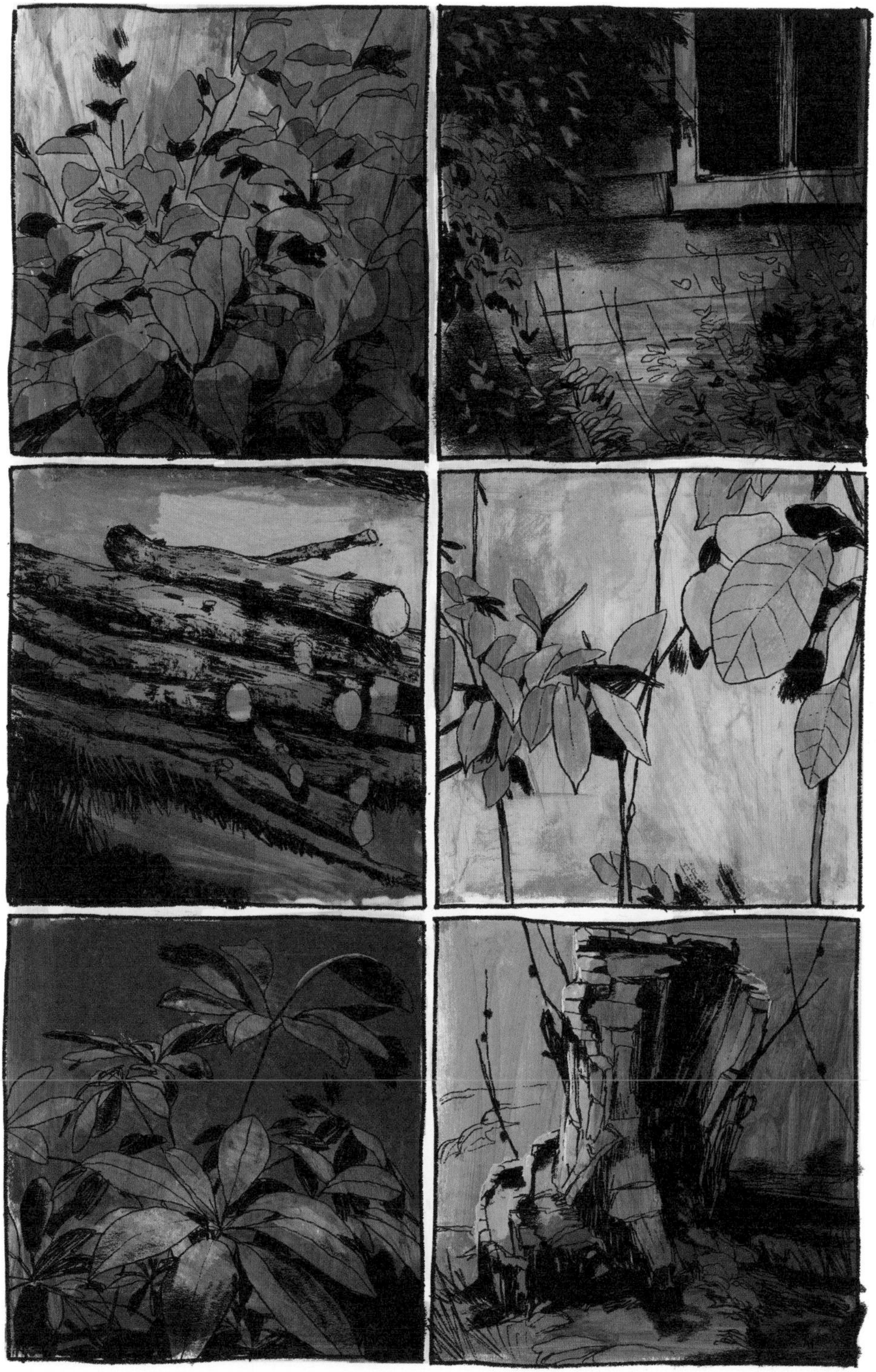

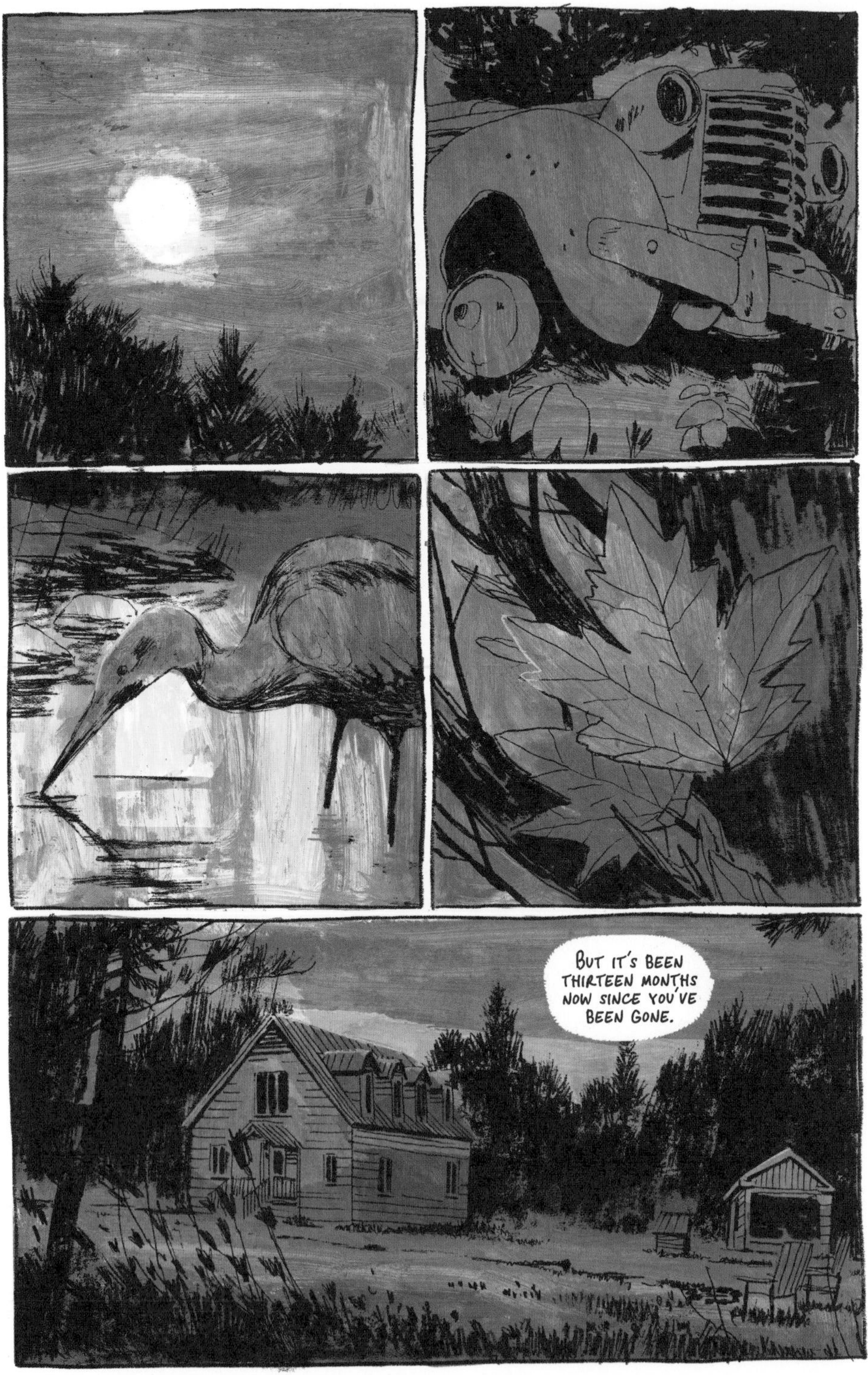
But it's been thirteen months now since you've been gone.

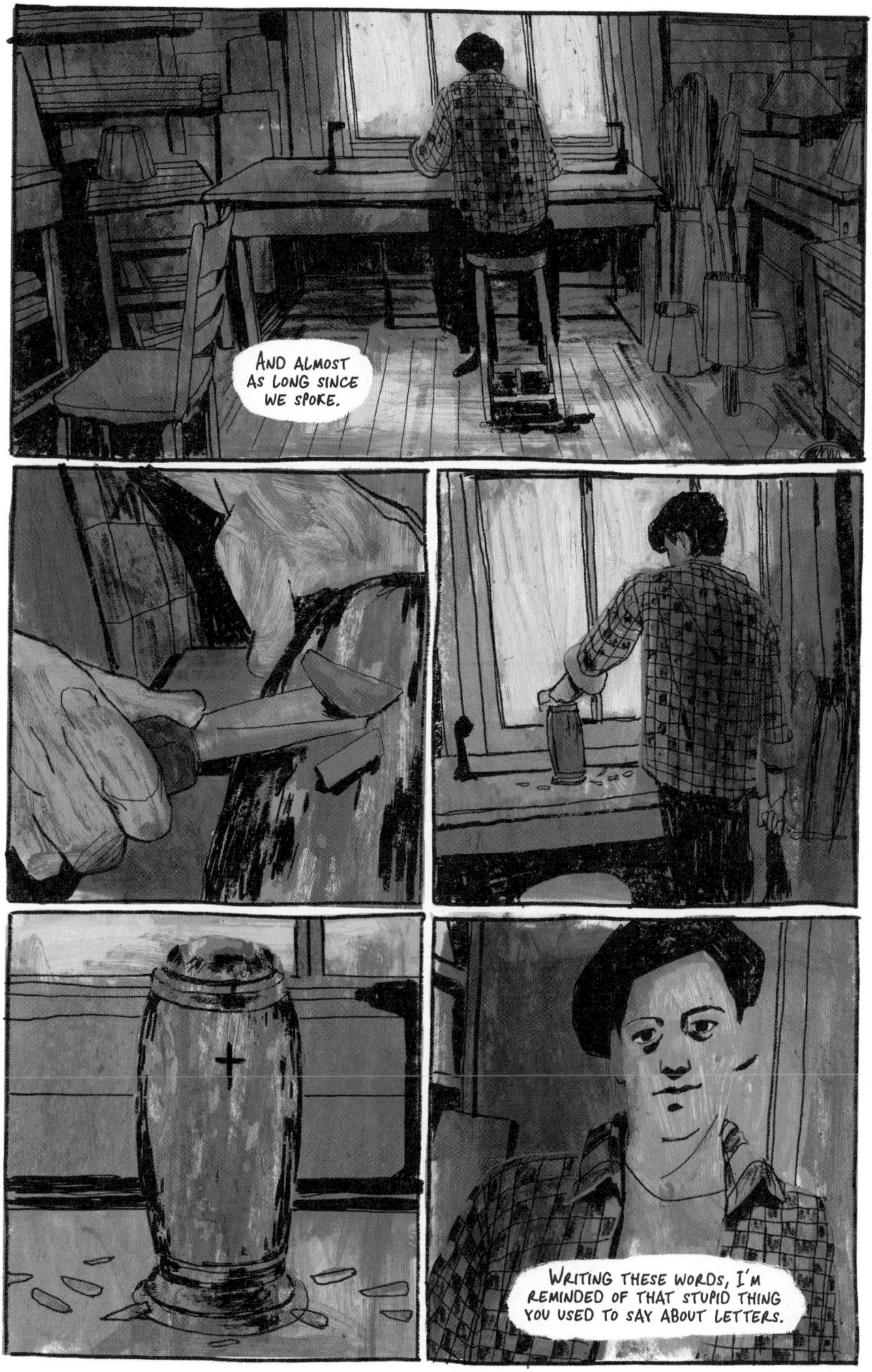
AND ALMOST AS LONG SINCE WE SPOKE.
WRITING THESE WORDS, I'M REMINDED OF THAT STUPID THING YOU USED TO SAY ABOUT LETTERS.

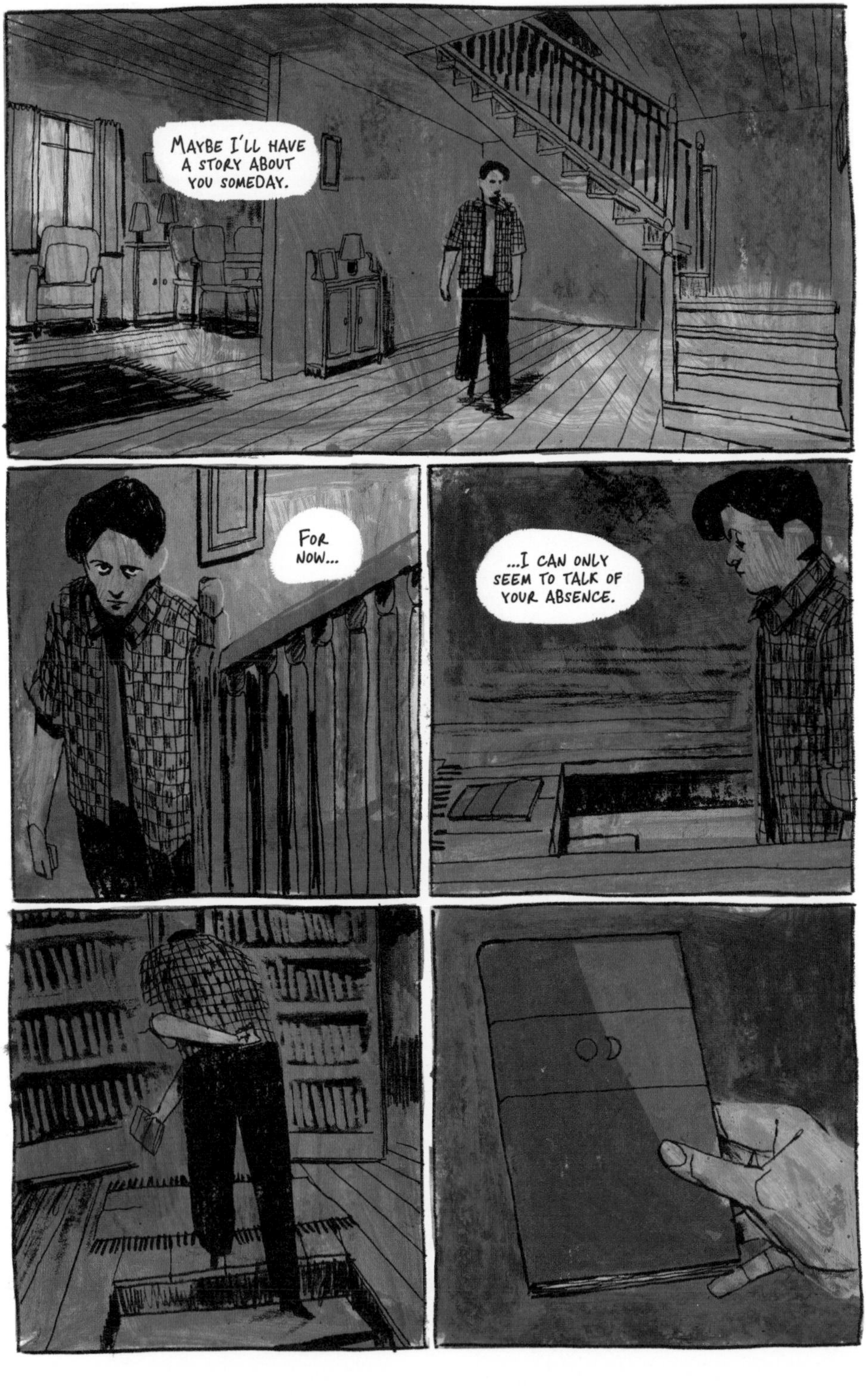
MAYBE I'LL HAVE A STORY ABOUT YOU SOMEDAY.
FOR NOW...
...I CAN ONLY SEEM TO TALK OF YOUR ABSENCE.

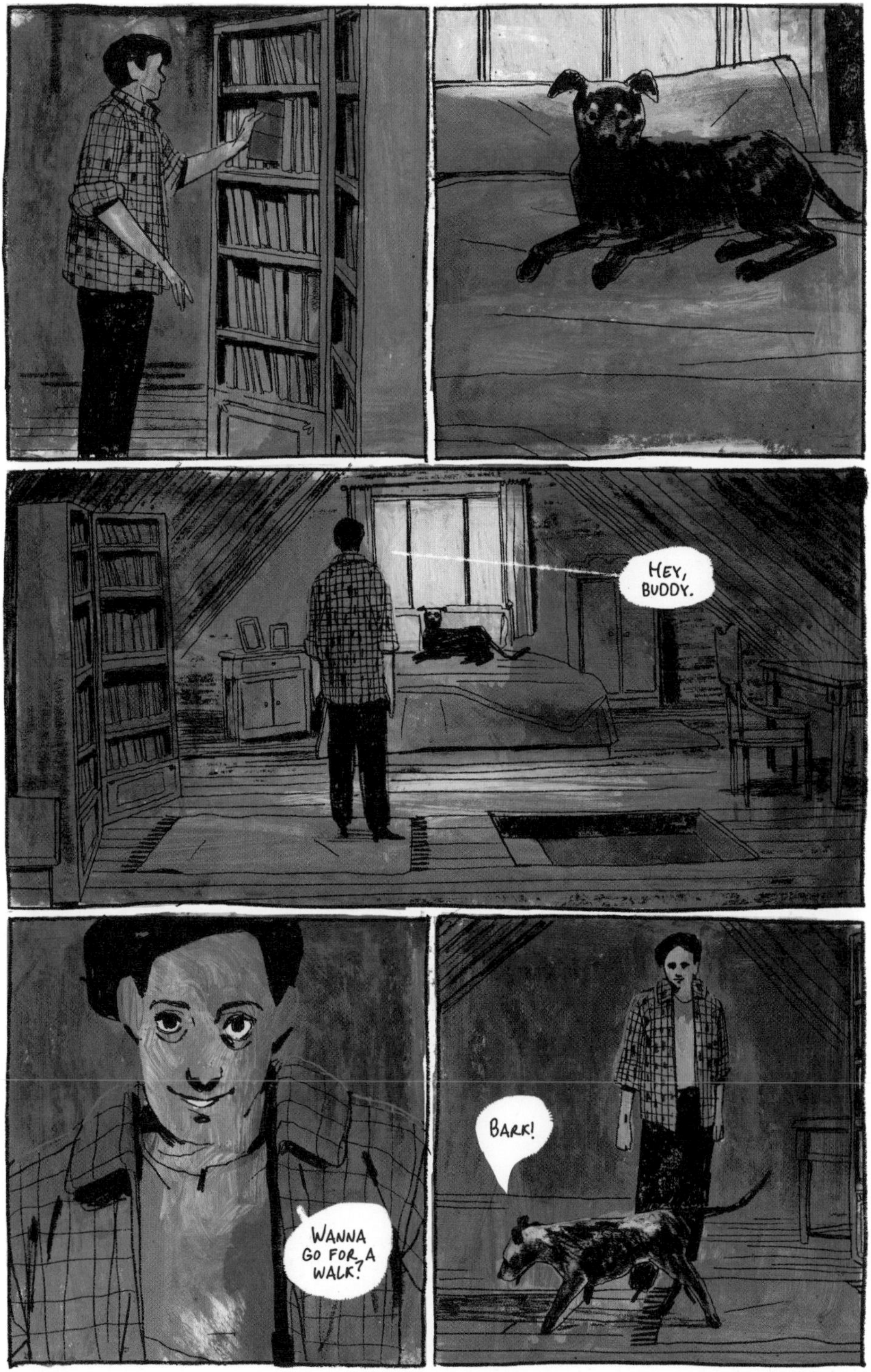
HEY, BUDDY.
WANNA GO FOR A WALK?
BARK!

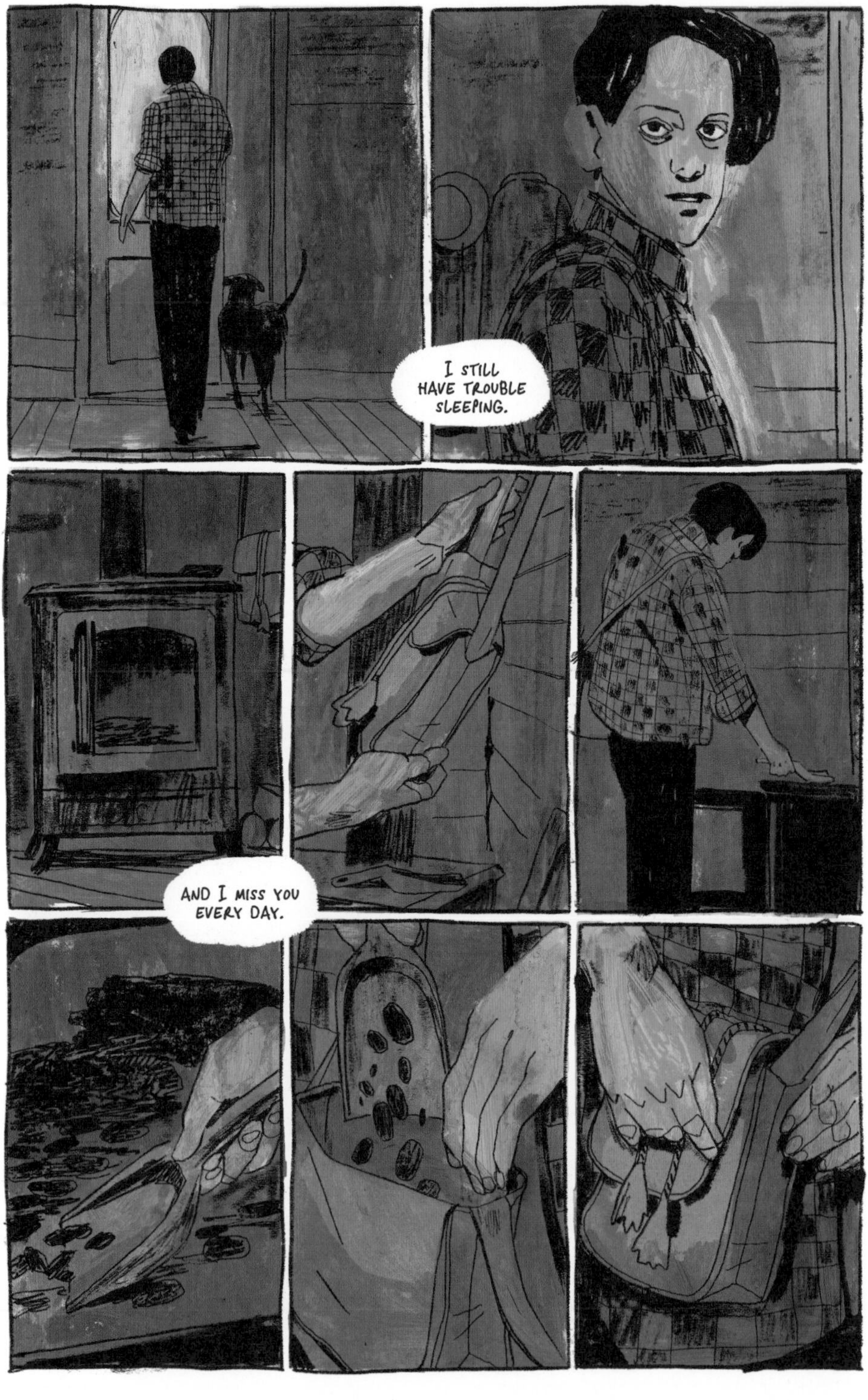
I STILL HAVE TROUBLE SLEEPING.
AND I MISS YOU EVERY DAY.

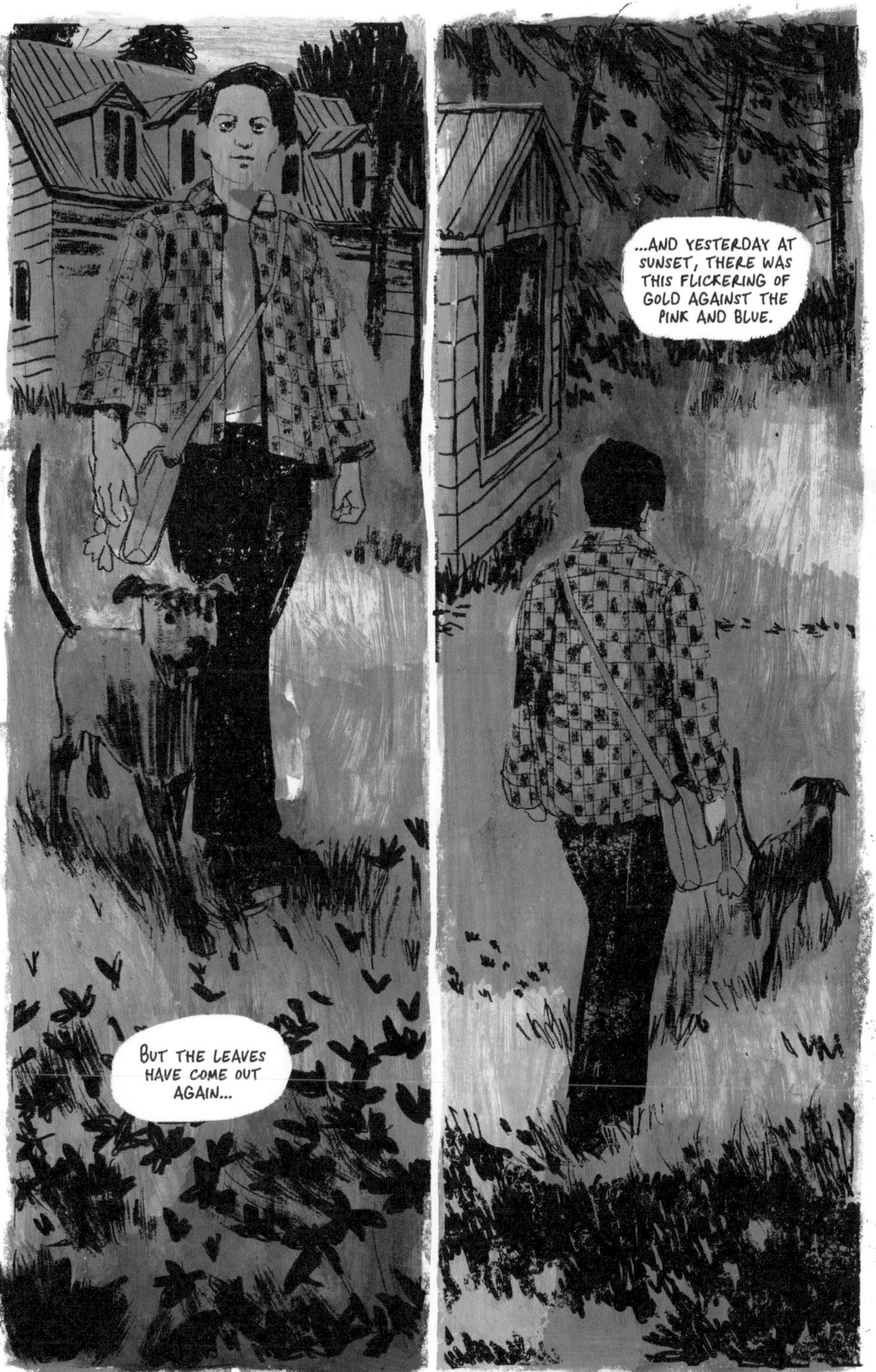
BUT THE LEAVES HAVE COME OUT AGAIN...
...AND YESTERDAY AT SUNSET, THERE WAS THIS FLICKERING OF GOLD AGAINST THE PINK AND BLUE.

I GUESS IT'S
SOMETHING.